A

GRAMMAR

OF THE

NEW TESTAMENT DIALECT

BY M. STUART

PROF. OF SACRED LITERATURE IN THE THEOL. SEMINARY AT ANDOVER.

Second Edition, corrected and mostly written anew.

Wipf & Stock
PUBLISHERS
Eugene, Oregon

Wipf and Stock Publishers
199 W 8th Ave, Suite 3
Eugene, OR 97401

Grammar of the New Testament Dialect, Second Edition
By Stuart, Moses
ISBN: 1-59244-775-9
Publication date 7/28/2004
Previously published by Allen and Morrill, 1841

PREFACE.

The first edition of this Grammar having been for some time exhausted, I have come, not without reluctance, to the preparation of a second. Since the publication of the first, the science of Greek Grammar has been greatly enlarged; and whoever will keep pace with it, has no small labour to perform, in case he means to lay the result of his labours before the public.

My engagements and my feeble state of health, for a while, forbade an attempt to make any considerable alterations in the present publication. But when I had once commenced the work of preparing it anew for the press, I found much more to do than I had anticipated. The recent publication of Essays on all the leading parts of Greek Grammar, by distinguished philologists in Germany, has rendered much reading and study necessary, in order even to know what has been accomplished for the improvement of this science. The mention of a few of these may aid the reader, in forming some proper judgment of the zeal with which this object is pursued abroad. Among the most distinguished Essays may be named Krüger's *Grammatical Investigations*; F. Franke, *On the negative Particles of the Greek*; Richter's *Specimens of Greek Anacolutha*; Reimnitz's *System of Greek Declensions*; Max Schmidt, *On Greek and Latin Pronouns*; Götting's *Doctrine of Greek Accents*; Spitzner's *Guide to Greek Prosody*; Liscovius' *Pronunciation of the Greek*; Landvoight's *Essay on the forms of Tenses and Persons in the Greek Verb*; Merleker's *Greek Accentuation*; Eichhoff, *On the Inf. Mode*; Hartung, *On the Greek Particles*; the same, *On the Formation of Cases*; and, above all, the masterly *Greek Grammar* of G. Kühner, in two large octavo volumes, containing, in a condensed and scientific form, the results of all these Essays and many more of a similar nature. Buttmann and Hermann laid the foundation for recent improvements; Kühner has shown to what an extent they have been carried. The science of grammar has been simplified, and *principle* is now substituted in a multitude of cases, for what had before been little better than a chaotic mass of facts. It would seem that not much further room is left for any important improvements; yet the history of the past may well admonish us, not to exclude the hope of still further accessions to grammatical science.

In this state of things, nothing remained for me but to apply myself in earnest to the study of these new developments, or else to remain behind the progress of the times in which we live. The reader will not wonder, therefore, that a great portion of the following work has been written entirely anew. It would ill become one to whom the public has shown so much indulgence, to requite this with neglect so as to any improvements which the present time demands. I have not scrupled, therefore, to alter and write anew, just as often as I have thought my book might be improved.

PREFACE.

Since the first edition was published, the great work of Winer on the New Testament Idiom has appeared in our own language, translated by Messrs. J. H. Agnew and O. G. Ebbeke. It is cheering to the cause of sacred literature in this country, that this important work is thus made accessible to those who cannot read the German language. But still I have not thought that the present work is superseded by this *Critical Commentary* of Winer; for so it may be justly named. Winer every where *presupposes* a thorough knowledge of Greek Grammar on the part of his readers, and of this as it is taught in his own country; a thing which cannot be taken for granted here. In fact, so far is this from being true, that scarcely any two colleges are agreed as to the Greek Grammar which they use; and few indeed have adopted any of the German Grammars. In such a state of things, I have thought that the proper path to usefulness in our country, so far as this subject is concerned, was opened only in the direction that I have chosen, viz. by making a Grammar which in itself would serve to introduce any student to a knowledge of the κοινὴ διάλεκτος of the Greek, with appropriate notices of departures from this by the writers of the New Testament.

Whoever will compare the present with the former edition of this work, will find the changes to be more numerous than could be well recounted. I would hope that they are for the better; but of this others must judge.

A meagre *skeleton* of New Testament Grammar would not correspond with my views of utility, although I am aware that there is a class of readers who desire such a work. But the demands of sacred philology cannot be answered in this way, whoever may attempt so to satisfy them. Beginners and hasty readers may complain, perhaps, of the *copiousness* of the present work; but those who are seriously bent upon the acquisition of a more enlarged knowledge of the New Testament idiom, will be the last to complain of its copiousness. Winer has occupied much more room with Syntax alone, than I have taken up with the whole compass of grammar. I do not complain of this in him; but I may repel criticism in respect to this subject which is not well grounded, by appeal to distinguished examples of much greater copiousness than my own.

Of the *importance* of a New Testament Grammar for the purposes of sacred criticism, it does not seem necessary to say any thing, at the present time. It is an encouraging circumstance, that our country is beginning to appreciate this subject in some degree as it deserves to be appreciated.

The present edition is furnished with some important apparatus for the convenience of the student, which was wanting in the first. I refer to the copious English and Greek Indexes at the close of the book, which will enable the reader very readily to find whatever he wishes, which is contained in the work.

M. STUART.

Theol. Seminary, Andover,
  June, 1841.

INTRODUCTION.

§ 1. *Definitions.*

(1) LANGUAGE consists of the external signs of ideas and feelings. It may be spoken or written. In the first case, it consists of *articulate sounds* uttered by the human voice; in the second, of conventional signs called *letters* and *words*, which are representatives of articulate sounds.

(2) Grammar is that science which teaches the manner of forming and declining words, and also the manner in which they are joined together in order to construct sentences or parts of sentences. It may be divided, therefore, into two parts, viz. *formal*, i. e. that which respects forms of words, and *syntactic*, i. e. that which respects the manner of arranging words together in order to express our ideas.

(3) Every language is exposed to changes, and actually suffers more or less of them, through all the periods of time in which it is spoken. Any noticeable departure from what has once been a general custom, or the most approved usage, of speaking or writing a language, is called a *dialect* (διάλεκτος). Among a nation widely extended, or consisting of various smaller tribes, dialects nearly always exist. In such a case, *the differences in the forms of words*, or *in their syntax*, are the things taken into the account in order to make out the notion of what is strictly called *dialect*; which word is, and always must be, used in a *comparative* sense, when it is properly used. Departure, in more or less particulars, from some *supposed standard* or *predominant usage* among the more cultivated part of a nation, is that which general custom names *dialect*.

§ 2. *Of the dialects of Greece.*

(1) The most ancient Greek language, if it were *universal*, could not properly be named *dialect*. In comparison, however, with most of the Greek which has come down to us, it may be so called. The most ancient Greek is, with good reason, supposed to be for substance exhibited to us, in the poetry of Ho-

mer and Hesiod; who, as we may with much probability believe, wrote the dialect which they spoke in common with the people around them. This *ancient* dialect, (called also the *epic* dialect because it is exhibited in the poems of Homer and Hesiod), appears to have been the common mother of all the later dialects of Greece; and probably it differs from the spoken language, only as the language of elevated poetry commonly differs from that which is spoken by the mass of the people. New words, new forms of old words, and new modes of expression, are almost of course exhibited in the higher kinds of poetry.

NOTE. The supposition that Homer was acquainted with all the later and different dialects of Greece, and *designedly* introduced them into his poem, seems very improbable. Much more probable is it, that the language which he employed was the common mother of all the dialects. In this way we may easily and naturally account for all of his alleged dialectic peculiarities.

(2) The Hellenians or Greeks, who immigrated through Thrace into Hellas (so called), consisted of several tribes, of which the two principal ones were Dorians and Ionians. The *original* seat of the Dorians in Greece, was the Peloponnesus; of the Ionians, Attica. From these sprung the *Doric* and *Ionic* dialects, which constituted the two principal dialects of Greece, from the time that the Greek nation came to be much known in authentic history.

(3) The DORIC DIALECT, which was the most extensively spoken, prevailed in Hellas proper, viz. in Sparta, Argos, and Messenia; also in Crete, Sicily, Magna Graecia or Lower Italy, and in the Dorian colonies of Asia Minor. In the course of time, it became the appropriate dialect of *lyric* and *bucolic* poetry. It is exhibited in the fragments of Epicharmus and Sophron, and in the works of Pindar, Alcaeus, Sappho, Corinna, Theocritus, Bion, and Moschus. The *lyric* parts of the Attic tragedy, i. e. the chorus, also exhibit it. The peculiar characteristics of this dialect are, a certain harshness or roughness in the construction of words, and a kind of indistinctness of sound occasioned by the frequent use of the close vowel A; which the Greeks called πλατειασμός.

NOTE. Branches or subdivisions of this dialect were the Laconic, Boeotian, Thessalian, and Sicilian dialects; no specimens of which are preserved, excepting a few fragments. The Aeolic was also a branch or variety of the Doric. It became at length a cultivated language, and was spoken in Middle Greece, with the exception of Attica, Megaris, and Doris. Sappho and Alcaeus afford specimens of this species of the Doric.

(4) The IONIC DIALECT was spoken originally in Attica. Nu-

INTRODUCTION: § 2. DIALECTS.

merous colonies emigrated, however, from this country to Asia Minor, which gradually became the principal, and at last the only seat of the dialect, if we include the islands which lie along its coasts in the Aegean sea. This dialect is characterized by softness of sound, and the resolution of the harsher sounds by the insertion of letters that mitigated them. The works of Herodotus, Hippocrates, and Anacreon, are composed in the Ionic.

NOTE. This dialect approaches nearer to the epic or old Greek than any other; so that the epic is sometimes called the *old* Ionic, and the proper Ionic the *new* Ionic.

(5) The Attic dialect was formed out of the Ionian, by the remnant of the Ionian people which remained in Attica, after its colonies were sent out to Asia Minor. It holds a middle course between the harshness of the Doric, and the softness of the Ionic dialect. The political importance of Attica, the high culture of its citizens, and the great number of excellent writers which it produced, caused this dialect to become far more renowned and more an object of study than any of the others. The works of Thucydides, Xenophon, Plato, Demosthenes, Lysias, Isocrates, Aeschines, etc., and also of Aeschylus, Euripides, Sophocles, Aristophanes, and others, being in the Attic, have immortalized the dialect in which they were written.

(6) After the freedom of Greece was destroyed by Philip, the Attic language began to be adopted by degrees among all its different tribes, now united together under Alexander and his successors. Yet every tribe that had once been distinct, in adopting it, would naturally give to it a great many turns and modifications; and these of course would constitute departures from its original form. It was this general dialect, as spoken and modified by Greece at large and particularly by those who were not natives of Attica, that came at last to be called the *common* or *Hellenic* dialect. Of course the *basis* of the κοινὴ διάλεκτος is Attic; but still, the Attic as contained in the κοινὴ is modified, in some respects, both as to form and syntax. Thus modified it is the usual standard of our grammars and lexicons; and departures from this are particularly specified by the names of particular dialects.

NOTE. Writers of this kind of Greek, i. e. of the κοινή, are Aristotle, Theophrastus, Pausanias, Apollodorus, Polybius, Diodorus, Plutarch, Strabo, Dionysius Halicarnassensis, Lucian, Aelian, Arrian, etc.

(7) In Macedonia the Attic dialect received many and peculiar modifications. Moreover, the successors of Alexander in Egypt cultivated literature with greater ardour than any other of the Gre-

cian princes. Hence Alexandria became the place where this peculiar dialect, (sometimes called *Macedonian* and sometimes *Alexandrine*), particularly developed itself. A great number of the later Greek works proceeded from this source, and they exhibit the dialect in question.

(8) The Jews, who left Palestine and settled at Alexandria during the reign of the Ptolemies, learned this dialect; and when the O. Test. was translated by them into Greek, for the use of their synagogues, this version exhibited a specimen of the Alexandrine Greek, modified of course by the Hebrew. For substance this same dialect, thus modified, appears in the N. Test., and in the early Christian fathers; yet not without many variations. Rost (the grammarian) calls this *ecclesiastical* Greek; it has usually been called the *Hellenistic* language; but it might more appropriately and significantly be called *Hebrew-Greek* ; which appellation would designate both the cause and manner of its modifications.

§ 3. *Character of the N. Test. Greek.*

(1) Soon after the commencement of the 17th century, a contest began among the learned in Europe respecting the character of the N. Test. diction. One class of writers claimed for it all the purity and elegance of the old Greek ; while others not only acknowledged a Hebrew colouring in it, but strove to show that it every where abounded in this. About the end of the 17th century this last party became the predominant one ; but the contest did not entirely cease until about the middle of the 18th century, when the *Hebraists* became almost universally triumphant. The *Purists* (as the former party were called) have now become wholly extinct, at least among all well informed linguists and critics ; but a new party (if it may be so named) has arisen, who have chosen a kind of middle way between the two older parties, avoiding the extremes of both, and occupying a ground which seems to be so well established as to afford no apprehension that it can be shaken. This third party bids fair speedily to become universal.

NOTE. So early as the latter part of the 16th century, Beza (*De dono Linguae*, etc., on Acts 10: 46) acknowledged the Hebraisms of the N. Test., but extolled them as being "of such a nature that in no other idiom could expressions be so happily formed ; nay, in some cases not even formed at all" in an adequate manner. He considered them as "gems with which [the apostles] had adorned their writings." The famous Robert Stephens (Pref. to his N. Test. 1576) declared strongly against those, "qui in his scriptis [sacris] inculta omnia et horrida esse putant;" and he laboured not only to show that the N. Test. contains many of the elegancies of the true Grecian style, but that even its Hebraisms give inimitable strength and energy to its diction. Thus far, then, Hebraism was not denied but vindicated; and it was only against allowing an excess of it, and against alleged incorrectnesses and barbarisms, that Beza and Stephens contended.

Sebastian Pfochen (*Diatribe de Ling. Graec. N. Test. puritate*, 1629) first laboured in earnest, to show that all the expressions employed in the N. Test. are found in good classic Greek authors. In 1658, Erasmus Schmidt vindicated the same ground. But before this, J. Junge, rector at Hamburgh, published (in 1637, 1639) his opinion in favour of the *purity* (not the classic elegance) of the N. Test. diction; which opinion was vindicated by Jac. Grosse, pastor in the same city, in a series of five essays published in 1640 and several successive years. The last four of these were directed against the attacks of opponents, i. e. of advocates for the *Hellenistic* diction of the N. Test.; viz. against Dan. Wulfer's *Innocentia Hellenist. vindicata* (1640), and an essay of the like nature by J. Musaeus of Jena (1641—42).

Independently of this particular contest, D. Heinsius (in 1643) declared himself in favour of *Hellenism*; as also Thos. Gataker (1648), who avowedly wrote in opposition to Pfochen, with much learning, but rather an excessive leaning to Hebraism. Joh. Vorstius (1658, 1665) wrote a book on Hebraisms, which is still common. On some excesses in this book, Horace Vitringa made some brief but pithy remarks. Somewhat earlier than these last writings, J. H. Boecler (1641) published remarks, in which he took a kind of middle way between the two parties; as did J. Olearius (1668), and J. Leusden about the same time. It was about this time also, that the majority of critical writers began to acknowledge a Hebrew element in the N. Test. diction, which, however, they did not regard as constituting *barbarism*, but only as giving an oriental hue to the diction. M. Solanus, in an able essay directed against the tract of Pfochen, vindicated this position. J. H. Michaelis (1707), and A. Blackwall (*Sacred Classics*, 1727), did not venture to deny the Hebraisms of the N. Test., but aimed principally to show, that these did not detract from the qualities of a good and elegant style; so that, in this respect, the N. Test. writers were not inferior to the classical ones. The work of the latter abounds with so many excellent remarks, that it is worthy of attention from every critical reader even of the present time.

In 1722, Siegm. Georgi, in his *Vindiciae*, etc., and in 1733 in his *Hierocriticus Sacer*, vindicated anew the old opinion of the Purists; but without changing the tide of opinion. The same design J. C. Schwarz had in view, in his *Comm. crit. et philol. in Ling. Graec.* (1636); who was followed, in 1752, by E. Palairet (*Observ. philol. crit. in N. Test.*), the last, I believe, of all the Purists.

Most of the earlier dissertations above named, with some others, were published together in a volume by J. Rhenferd, entitled *Dissertationum philol. theol. de Stylo N. Test. Syntagma*, 1702; and the later ones by T. H. Van den Honert, in his *Syntagma Dissertatt. de Stylo N. Test. Graeco*, 1703.

2. The Purists in general committed several errors in their efforts to establish the *Graecism* or *classic purity* of the New Testament. (*a*) They not unfrequently named that *Graecism*, which is the common property of all cultivated languages, and so is properly neither Graecism nor Hebraism.

10 INTRODUCTION: § 3. N. T. DIALECT.

E. g. in respect to διψῶντες τὴν δικαιοσύνην, Matt. 5: 6, examples are adduced from various Greek writers, to show that the verb διψάω is tropically employed by them to signify *strong desire*. But so the corresponding verb in Latin is used; and in most other languages; and, consequently, such a usage is properly neither *Graecism* nor *Hebraism*. The like may be said of ἐσθίειν used to signify *devouring, consuming*, etc.; of γενεά for a *particular generation of men*; of χείρ as designating *power*; and so of many like words. When Pfochen converted all such expressions into evidences of the *classical* elegance of the N. Test., he made claims which cannot properly be allowed.

As a specimen of the excess to which he carried his *classical* illustrations, we may refer to Matt. 10: 27, κηρύξατε ἐπὶ τῶν δωμάτων. To vindicate this he brings from Aesop the following sentence: ἔριφος ἐπί τινος δώματος ἑστώς, *a kid was standing on a certain house*!

(*b*) They did not make sufficient distinction between mere prosaic and poetic diction; nor between those tropes which are occasionally used and for special purposes, and those which have become the common property of the language.

E. g. to prove from the Greek *poets*, that κοιμάομαι sometimes means *to be dead*; that σπέρμα means *offspring*; ποιμάνειν, *to rule*; ἰδεῖν θάνατον, *to die*; ποτήριον πίνειν, *to participate of suffering*; and πίπτειν, *to fail, to be frustrated*; would not be to show that the diction of the N. Test. is the classic Greek of *prose*; although Georgi, Schwarz, and others have resorted to such proof.

(*c*) They did not make proper allowance for Hebraism, when an expression is common indeed to the Hebrew and Greek languages, but still the natural probability is, that the N. Test. writers chose it from their feelings as Hebrews.

E. g. γινώσκειν ἄνδρα probably came from the Heb. אִישׁ יָדַע. So σπλάγχνα as meaning *compassion*, ξηρά *dry land* in distinction from water, χεῖλος *shore*, στόμα *edge* of the sword, παχύνειν, *to be stupid*, κύριος κυρίων, εἰσέρχεσθαι εἰς τὸν κόσμον, etc., were all introduced, as we may well suppose, from the Hebrew, and they need not be accounted for by any parallels from Herodotus, Aelian, Xenophon, etc.

(*d*) The same word, if not employed in the same sense, can prove nothing to the purpose of the Purists.

E. g. Pfochen cites ἦλθε . . . ἐν νηΐ μελαίνῃ to show that ἐν is classically used in the N. Test. before the Dat. of *instrument*; whereas in the passage cited it means *in*, not *by*. So χορτάζειν, *to feed men*, is illustrated from Plato, Rep. II., where it is used for *feeding swine*; and many other things of the like nature.

(*e*) *Similar* meanings of words, but yet not fully the same, will not constitute good proof of classic purity.

E. g. εὑρίσκειν χάριν παρά τινα is not properly confirmed by εὑρίσκειν τὴν εἰρήνην—τὴν δωρεάν, which Georgi brings from Demosthenes; ποτήριον, *lot, destiny*, is not confirmed by κρατὴρ αἵματος from Aristophanes;

INTRODUCTION: § 3. N. T. DIALECT. 11

nor πίπτειν, to be frustrated, by οὐ χαμαὶ πεσεῖται ὅ τι ἂν εἴποις from Plato; nor ἀπὸ μικροῦ ἕως μεγάλου, by οὔτε μέγα οὔτε σμικρόν; nor δύο δύο by πλέον πλέον, etc.

(*f*) The Byzantine historians cannot be safely appealed to as examples of pure Greek, because the lateness of their productions, and the plain fact that their style was affected by the N. Test., render them unsafe authorities in such a case.

E. g. to confirm the classical authority of στηρίζειν τὸ πρόσωπον and ἐνωτίζεσθαι, as Schwarz has endeavoured to do, by examples out of Nicetas; or of ἡ ξηρά *dry land* by appealing to Cinnam. Hist., as Georgi has done; is little to the purpose.

(*g*) It should now be added, that many phrases of the N. Test., of which the Purists could find no parallel in Greek classic authors, are passed over in silence by them, and kept entirely out of view. No wonder, therefore, that their opponents, the Hebraists, gained a victory in the end which seemed to be complete. All, however, that was contended for, and that was supposed to be won by the Hebraists, could not afterwards be retained.

NOTE. The best works on the true dialect of the N. Test. are Salmasius, *De Lingua Hellenistica*; Sturtz, *De Dialecto Alexandrina* (1809); and Planck, *De vera Natura et Indole Orat. Graec. N. Test.*, translated and printed in the Bib. Repository, Vol. I. pp. 650 seq., Andover, 1831. Almost all the *Introductions* to the N. Test. contain more or less in relation to this subject; but none can be fully confided in, which were written before the above mentioned essay of Planck made its appearance.

(2) *Ground-element of the N. Test. Greek.* When all Greece were united under one dominion, during the time of Alexander the Great and his successors, both the *written* and *spoken* language underwent some change. The first, taking the Attic for its stock, grafted upon it many words that were common and general Greek, and even some provincialisms; this is ἡ κοινὴ διάλεκτος. The second, i. e. the language of intercourse, taking the same basis, adopted and intermixed more or less words from all the different dialects; among which the Macedonian dialect was especially the predominant one. It was by the *speaking* of Greek, that the Hebrews in Alexandria and elsewhere became acquainted with this language; and of course the Greek which they wrote, would partake of the character of the Greek *spoken* in the times succeeding those of Alexander.

NOTE. That the Jews of Alexandria learned Greek by intercourse with those who spoke it there, is manifest from the nature of the case, and from the fact that the Jews, almost without exception, were averse to the *learned* study of the Greek language. Philo and Josephus are among the exceptions. The style of the latter, when compared with that of the Seventy, in those parts of his works (for example) which relate to the O. Test. history, shows that he had cultivated the *classical* Greek of the times; while the Sept. exhibits a kind of Greek quite discrepant from that of Philo or of Josephus. Subsequently to the period when the Sept. version was made, the Greek style of the Jews was of course affected more or less by it. Hence the apocryphal Greek writings of the Jews, and the N. Test., partake more or less of the style of the Septuagint. Still, as the Sept. is a *translation* of the Hebrew Scriptures, we might naturally expect it would abound more in Hebraisms than the writings last named, which were *original* productions; and such is the fact. The N. Test. writings are more free from peculiarities as to words or phrases, than the Alexandrine version or Septuagint.

The ground-element, then, of the N. Test. diction, is the later Greek as modified at Alexandria; i. e. the Attic dialect, as modified by the intermixture of words used in other dialects, especially in the dialect of the Macedonians, and as employed in the language of intercourse. In other words, *its predominant ingredient is the Attic dialect;* while its subordinate constituents are principally the Macedonian dialect, mixed with the peculiarities of those to whom Hebrew was vernacular.

NOTE 2. The κοινὴ διάλεκτος, then, i. e. the later Greek as modified by the times which succeeded the period of Alexander's reign, is nearest of all the profane Greek writings to the diction of the N. Test. Hence the study and comparison of the *later* Greek authors is peculiarly important to the interpreter of the N. Testament. The difference between their diction and that of the N. Test., arises principally from two sources; viz. first, the Hebrews wrote from their acquaintance with the *conversation-Greek,* which naturally allowed more latitude than the written Greek to departures from the Attic style, and more frequently indulged in the use of words not classical, in constructions not agreeable to the strict rules of syntax, and in assigning to words new meanings; and secondly, every Jew, in speaking or writing a foreign language, would necessarily introduce many of the idioms of his own vernacular language.

(3) The peculiarities of the N. Test. diction may be classed under two heads, viz. *lexical* and *grammatical*.

1. The lexical relates to the choice of words; to new forms of them; to the frequency with which they were employed; to the new and different meanings assigned to them; and to the coining of words anew.

(a) Words were chosen from all the dialects; (1) The Attic; e. g. ὕαλος, ὁ σκότος (masc.), ἀετός, φιάλη, ἀλήθειν, πρύμνα, ἱλεώς. (2) The Doric; e. g. τιάζω, κλίβανος, ἡ λιμός, ποία. (3) Ionic; e. g. γογγύζω, ῥήσσω, πρηνής, βαθμός, σκορπίζειν, φύω (intrans.) (4) Macedonic; e. g. παρεμβολή *camp,* ῥύμη *street.* (5) Cyrenaic; e. g. βουνός *hill.* (6) Syracusan; e. g. εἰπόν (Imper.).

(b) New forms (mostly prolonged ones) were given to words; e. g. ἀνάθεμα (ἀνάθημα), ἔκπαλαι (πάλαι), ἐξάπινα (ἐξαπίνης), καύχησις (καύχημα),

INTRODUCTION: § 3. N. T. DIALECT. 13

ἀποστασία (ἀπόστασις), πετάομαι (πέτομαι), βιβλαρίδιον (βιβλίδιον), ὀμνύω (ὄμνυμι), μοιχαλίς (μοιχάς), etc. etc.

(c) Uncommon or poetic words are used in common style; e. g. αὐθεντεῖν, μεσονύκτιον, ἀλάλητος, ἔσθησις, ἀλέκτωρ, βρέχειν to irrigate, etc.

(d) New and different meanings; e. g. παρακαλεῖν to beg, παιδεύειν to chastise, ἀνακλίνειν to recline at table, ἀποκριθῆναι to answer, ξύλον living tree, νέκρωσις in a passive sense, ὀψώνιον wages, πτῶμα corpse, etc. etc. The N. Test. has many such words.

(e) Words were formed de novo; e. g. by composition, as ἀλλοτριοεπίσκοπος, ἀνθρωπάρεσκος, μονόφθαλμος, ἀγαθουργεῖν, οἰκοδεσποτεῖν, etc. Nouns in -μα are frequent; as κατάλυμα, γέννημα, βάπτισμα; so nouns with συν, as συμμαθητής, συμπολίτης; adjectives, in -ινος, as ὄρθρινος, ὄψινος, πρωϊνος; verbs in -όω, as ἀνακαινόω, δολιόω, σθενόω; also in -ίζω, as δειγματίζω, ὀρθρίζω; also new forms of adverbs, as πάντοτε, παιδιόθεν, πανοικί, etc. etc.

2. The *grammatical* peculiarities are limited mostly to the forms of nouns and verbs. Some of these in the Hebrew-Greek are new; some not classically used; and some are foreign to the Attic book-language. The use of the *dual* is superseded. In a proper *syntactical* respect, the Hellenistic dialect has little that is peculiar. There are indeed a few examples of *verbs* constructed with such cases as are not usual in classic Greek; and of *conjunctions*, elsewhere joined with the Optative and Subjunctive modes, but here sometimes connected with the Indicative. The Optative, moreover, is seldom employed here in oblique speech, etc.

NOTE. That each country and province even, where Hebrew-Greek was spoken, had some peculiarities of its own, is almost certain from the nature of the case. But it is difficult for us, at present, to ascertain the limits of these peculiarities. We only know, that in the Hebrew-Greek there are a number of words which are not found in any of the later Greek authors.

(4) Any nation which continues the use of its own language, and also learns to speak a foreign one, will intermix that foreign one with many idioms of its own. Such was the case, as has already been hinted, with the Jews at Alexandria and in Palestine. The general tone of style, in the writings of these Hebrews, naturally inclined to the Hebrew. Many turns of expression would naturally be mere Hebrew, translated into the corresponding Greek words; and these were altogether intelligible to a Jew, although scarcely so to a native Greek. In a *lexical* respect, also, the native language of a Jew would have much influence. He would naturally extend the meaning of a Greek word, that in a single respect corresponded well to one meaning of a Hebrew word, so as to make its significations correspond in all respects with those of the Hebrew one. In some cases, the difficulty of

fully expressing the Hebrew in Greek words already extant, would lead him to coin new ones which might better correspond with his own vernacular tongue. In a word, the manner of thinking and feeling, which was peculiar to the Hebrew, would still remain when he spoke or wrote Greek. His style, then, would consist of *Hebrew thoughts clothed in a Greek dress.* But as the native language of Greece was not, and from the nature of the case could not be, so formed as to convey all the conceptions and feelings of Hebrews, no way could be devised of conveying them in Greek, except by some such modifications of this language, i. e. either by assigning a new sense to words already extant, or by coining new words. The Hellenists, therefore, have done no more, in general, than the nature of the case compelled them to do, in order to express their ideas in Greek. What they have thus done, constitutes the Hebraism of the Hellenistic dialect.

NOTE. By *Hebrew*, in this case, is meant the *later* Hebrew, made up in a great measure of Chaldee and Syriac, and often called the *Syro-Chaldaic*. The idioms of this, however, are for the most part so like to those of the proper Hebrew, that no important error will arise from calling them *Hebrew*, and treating them as such.

(5) The reason why the Greek of the Sept. and the N. Test. is called *Hellenistic*, seems to be derived from the usage of the N. Test. in naming Jews *Hellenists*, who spoke the Greek language; see Acts 6: 1. It is a matter of little consequence, however, as to the name which we give to this dialect. We may call it indifferently, the *Hebrew-Greek*, or the *Hellenistic dialect*. Joseph Scaliger (in Euseb. p. 134) was the first who gave it this latter name; which has been very generally adopted.

NOTE. The principal books which exhibit collectively the so called *Hebraisms* of the N. Test., are Vorstius, *De Hebraismis*; Leusden, *Philologus Hebraeus*; and Olearius, *De Stylo Nov. Test.* In these and other similar works, however, several errors have been committed. (*a*) The authors have not paid due attention to the idiom of the Aramaean or Syro-Chaldaic language, which was the vernacular tongue of the N. Test writers. (*b*) They have not accurately observed the difference as to Hebraizing, between the different authors of the N. Test.; which, in some cases, is very considerable. (*c*) They have not shewn the relation of the N. Test. to the Sept. Greek; which, with all its points of similitude, is still considerably discrepant. (*d*) They have put much to the account of *Hebraism*, which is the common property of both Greek and Hebrew, yea, of language in general; e. g. φυλάσσειν νόμον, αἷμα *slaughter*, ἀνήρ with an appellative (as ἀνὴρ φονεύς), παῖς *servant*, μεγαλύνειν *to praise*, etc. (*e*) They have made some things into Hebraisms, by putting a forced construction upon them; e. g. Eph. 5:26, ἐν ῥήματι ἵνα, construed as an equivalent to עַל־דְּבַר אֲשֶׁר, *in order that*; Matt. 25: 23, χαρά *feast*, like the Arabic חֶדְוָה; Matt. 6:1, δικαιοσύνη *alms*, like the Chaldee צִדְקָא, etc.

INTRODUCTION: § 3. N. T. DIALECT. 15

(6) Hebraism, properly so called, may be divided into two kinds, viz. *perfect* and *imperfect*. (*a*) PERFECT HEBRAISM is that which has no parallel in the native Greek, and which is modelled altogether after the Hebrew.

E. g. σπλαγχνίζεσθαι, ὀφειλήματα ἀφιέναι, πρόσωπον λαμβάνειν, οἰκοδο– μεῖν to *edify*, πλατύνειν τὴν καρδίαν, πορεύεσθαι ὀπίσω, οὐ πᾶς (for οὐδείς), ἐξομολογεῖσθαι ἔν τινι, etc.

(*b*) IMPERFECT HEBRAISM is that which has some parallel in the Greek, but which having a more perfect one in the Hebrew, was probably derived from the Hebrew idiom.

E. g. σπέρμα *offspring*, from זֶרַע; ἀνάγκη *trouble*, from מָצוֹק, צַר; εἰς ἀπάντησιν, לִקְרַאת; πέρατα τῆς γῆς, אַפְסֵי הָאָרֶץ; χεῖλος *shore*, שָׂפָה, etc. Now although Greek parallels may be found to these expressions, and to others of the like kind, yet they are not of common occurrence, and therefore the probability is, that the N. Test. writers derived them from the Hebrew.

NOTE. The reason of employing both these kinds of Hebraism has been already stated. No Hebrew would divest himself, without much learned training, of the native element of his own peculiar style. When he wrote Greek, he would of course clothe Hebrew conceptions in Greek words. Hence his departures from the native Greek, in cases of perfect Hebraism. Hence too the probability, that he drew the imperfect Hebraisms from his own native tongue.

(7) The simple historical style of the Gospels, of the Acts, and of the Apocrypha, exhibits this influence of Hebrew in its most complete state; because here religious technics (which a Hebrew must employ in speaking of religious matters) are less frequent. And here the use of prepositions is more frequent than in native Greek; minute circumstances (like ἐγράφη διὰ χειρός, πάντος ἀπὸ μικροῦ ἕως μεγάλου, etc.) are more commonly inserted; and besides this, the accumulation of pronouns, especially after the relative; the formula καὶ ἐγένετο in the transitions of narrative; the simple construction of sentences, in which the parts of a complex one are rather *coordinate* than subordinate; the unfrequency of conjunctions and of accumulated connective particles; much uniformity in the use of the tenses; a want of periodic rounding, and of the union of subordinate propositions with the main one; the unfrequent use of participial constructions in the widely extended latitude of the native Greek; the *direct* citation of another's words in narration, where the Greek commonly employ the *indirect* one; the neglect of the Optative mood—all these things characterize the Hellenistic Greek, and separate it from that which is common among classic authors.

NOTE. The Hebraisms of the N. Test., as has been stated above, are

16   INTRODUCTION: § 3. N. T. DIALECT.

divisible into perfect and imperfect. This division has reference to their internal nature. But if we look at the sources whence they are derived, or the causes which operated to produce them, we may class them under four distinct heads, each of which deserves particular notice.

(a) Where the original and fundamental meaning of a Greek and Hebrew word was the same, a Hebrew very naturally attached the same secondary or derived meanings to the Greek word as belonged to the Hebrew one; e. g. δικαιοσύνη and צְדָקָה agree in their original meaning, and so it was natural for the Hebrew to attach to δικαιοσύνη the secondary sense of *liberality, kindness*, because צְדָקָה sometimes bore this meaning. So ὀφείλημα, not only *debt* but *sin*, like the Aramaean חוֹב; so νύμφη, *bride* and also *daughter in law*, like כַּלָּה; εἷς, *one* and *first*, like אֶחָד; ἐξομολογεῖσθαί τινι, *to praise one*, like הוֹדָה לְ; ἐρωτᾶν, *to ask* and also *to beg*, like שָׁאַל. Very frequent is this usage in regard to a secondary sense which is *tropical* ; e. g. ποτήριον, *cup* and *lot*, like כּוֹס; σκάνδαλον, *offence* in a moral sense, like מִכְשׁוֹל; γλῶσσα, *tongue* and *nation*, like לָשׁוֹן; ἐνώπιον τοῦ θεοῦ *in the view* or *judgment of God*, like לִפְנֵי יְהוָֹה; ἀνάθεμα, *that which is devoted to destruction*, like the Hebrew חֵרֶם, etc. etc.

(b) Peculiar Hebrew phrases were literally translated by corresponding Greek words, which when put together, constitute an idiom altogether foreign to native Greek; e. g. πρόσωπον λαμβάνειν for נָשָׂא פָנִים; ζητεῖν ψυχήν for בִּקֵּשׁ נֶפֶשׁ; ποιεῖν ἔλεος (or χάριν) μετά τινος for עָשָׂה חֶסֶד עִם; ἄρτον φαγεῖν (*to sup*) from אָכַל לֶחֶם; υἱὸς θανάτου for בֶּן־מָוֶת; ὀφείλημα ἀφιέναι for שְׁבַק חוֹבָא (Talmudic); πᾶσα σάρξ for כָּל־בָּשָׂר; etc. etc.

(c) Derivate Greek verbs were formed so as to correspond with derivate Hebrew ones; e. g. σπλαγχνίζεσθαι from σπλάγχνα, like רִחַם from רַחֲמִים; ἐγκαινίζειν from ἐγκαίνια, like חָנַךְ and חֲנֻכָּה; ἀναθηματίζειν from ἀνάθεμα, like הֶחֱרִים from חֵרֶם, etc. etc.

(d) The religious views and feelings of the writers of the N. Test. occasioned a kind of *technological* use of many Greek words, in a sense quite different from that of classical usage; e. g. such words as ἔργα, πίστις, πιστεύειν εἰς Χριστόν, δικαιοῦσθαι, ἐκλέγεσθαι, οἱ ἅγιοι, ἀπόστολος, βάπτισμα, δικαιοσύνη, and many others, used particularly by Paul in his epistles. This was altogether unavoidable; inasmuch as the classic Greek could furnish no words, which according to the *usus loquendi* of the Greek would convey the ideas of a Hebrew in relation to these subjects. So it is, also, with such words as θεός, ἄγγελος, οὐρανός, πνεῦμα, etc.

(8) As to the *grammatical* character of the N. Test. diction, in general this does not differ from that of the later Greek. The common laws of syntax are applicable almost throughout; at least, there is seldom any departure from them. Even some of the nicer peculiarities of the Greek language, such as the attraction of the relative pronoun, and the distinction between οὐ and μή in negations and questions, (which is quite remote from the Hebrew idiom), are somewhat strictly observed. The peculiarities of the later Greek itself (which also belong to the N. Test.) consist more in the forms of words, and the use of pecu-

liar tenses, than in any diverse *principles* of syntax. In all parts of the N. Test., indeed, Hebrew modes of thinking and feeling of course develope themselves. In the *grammatical* mode of expressing these, however, the most important variation from the native Greek is, that prepositions are more commonly employed in the government of nouns, etc., than was usual among Greek authors.

NOTE 1. The meaning of words changes much easier than the forms; the forms much easier than the syntax; so that while the later Greek (and consequently the N. Test. Greek) admitted many variations in the meaning and even in the forms of words, it still retained the common syntax, with some little enlargement. Accordingly we find, in the N. Test., several forms which were not current at an early period, or else belong to some of the dialects. Of the latter are, (*a*) *Attic* forms; such as ἠβουλή-θην (η for the augment), ἤμελλε, βούλει (2nd pers. for βούλῃ), ὄψει. (*b*) *Doric*; as ἤτω (for ἔστω), ἀφέωνται (for ἀφεῖνται). (*c*) *Aeolic*; such as the Opt. in -εια of Aor. 1st. (*d*) *Ionic*; as γήρει, εἶπα (Aor. 1). Of the forms not used in the more ancient language, we may cite the Dative νοΐ, Imp. κάθου, Perf. ἔγνωκαν (for ἐγνώκασι), Aor. 2 κατελίποσαν, Imperf. ἐδολιοῦσαν, Aor. 2 εἴδαμεν, ἔφυγαν. The regular forms of tenses in certain verbs, not employed more anciently, are employed in the N. Test.; e. g. ἡμάρτησα (for ἥμαρτον), αὔξω (for αὐξάνω), ἥξα (for ἥκω), φάγομαι (for ἔδομαι) etc., In consequence of this, there is an increase of the forms of verbs and of the tenses actually employed, in the later Greek. To all this must be added, that a new gender is assigned to some nouns; e. g. ὁ (instead of ἡ) βάτος; τὸ ἔλεος, τὸ πλοῦτος (neut. instead of masc.), which casts them into the 3d instead of the 2nd declension.

NOTE 2. As to *Syntax*, the peculiarities consist mostly in using ὅταν, in a few cases with the Ind. Praeter; εἰ with the Subj.; ἵνα with the Ind. Pres.; the construction of such verbs as γενέσθαι with the Acc., προσκύνειν with the Dat.; such formulas as θέλω ἵνα, ἄξιος ἵνα (instead of the Inf.); the employment of the Subj. instead of the Opt. in historical diction and after the Praeter; and in general the rare employment of the Opt., (which has entirely disappeared in modern Greek). Moreover the Inf. Aor. is oftener used after μέλλειν, θέλειν, etc.; and a disregard to declension (so conspicuous in modern Greek) appears just in its inceptive state; e. g. εἰς καθείς, καθείς, ἀνὰ εἶς, εἷς παρ' εἷς. A similar disregard to case and tense also appears in a few cases. The Dual is altogether neglected.

Even the Seventy, in their version, have in general conformed to the Greek Syntax. Some departures from a diction purely Greek would of course be expected. Instead of the Opt., they say (with the Heb.), τίς με καταστήσεται κριτήν; They also say: θανάτῳ ἀποθανεῖσθε, מוֹת תָּמוּתוּן; μισῶν ἐμίσησας, שָׂנֹא שָׂנֵאתָ. They also imitate, in some cases, the Hebrew composite verbs, (which are made by a preposition following them); as φείδεσθαι ἐπί τινι, οἰκοδομεῖν ἔν τινι, ἐπερωτᾶν ἐν κυρίῳ, etc. The N. Test., however, which is not a *translation* of the Hebrew, but an *original* work, is more free from these peculiarities. Yet in general, even here, the use of prepositions is more frequent than with the Greeks, viz., in such cases as ἀποκρύπτειν τι ἀπό τινος, ἐσθίειν ἀπό τῶν ψιχίων, ἀθῶος ἀπο τοῦ αἵματος, κοινωνὸς ἔν τινι, etc.; the like to which may indeed be found in the ancient Greek. But in some cases the imitation of the Hebrew has led the writers of the N. Test. to adopt expressions which would sound in a singular manner to a native Greek; e. g. (*a*) Such as ὁμολογεῖν ἔν τινι, βλέπειν ἀπό to beware of, προσέθετο πέμψαι to send again, and the form of the oath in the *negative* sense, εἰ δοθήσεται. (*b*) The repetition of the same word, in order to signify distribution; as δύο δύο two by two (instead of ἀνὰ δύο). (*c*) The frequent and varied use of the Inf. with τοῦ before it. (*d*) The imitation of the Inf. abs. in Hebrew joined with a definite mood and tense; as in μισῶν ἐμίσησας above. (*e*) The frequency of nouns in the Gen., which stand in the place of adjectives. (*f*) The often repeated use of the Inf. with a preposition, in historical narration. Nos. *a*, *b*, may be classed among the *pure* Hebraisms. The rest are to be found in native Greek, although not with the like frequency.

(9) On the whole, when we consider that many of even the niceties of Greek syntax are observed in the N. Test., e. g. the distinctions in the use of the Praeter tenses, the construction of verbs with ἄν, the attraction of the relative pronoun, the singular number of the verb with *neuter* plurals, such idioms also as οἰκονομίαν πεπίστευμαι, etc.; moreover, that the periphrasis for the Opt. which the Seventy use, is here not employed; there is, in fact, very little reason for the charge of *ungrammatical* composition against the writers of the N. Test. Much has been said on this subject, by writers for and against the *purity* of the N. Test., which is very inapposite, or has little foundation. Patient, protracted, and widely extended examination has at last corrected the errors of both the parties of former days, and brought the whole matter very near to that middle ground, which those consummate Greek scholars, Robert Stephens and Theodore Beza, seem first to have occupied.

PART I.

LETTERS AND THEIR CHANGES.

§ 4. *Greek Alphabet.*

		Pronounced.	Name.		Numeral Value.	
A	α	*a* in *father*	Ἄλφα	alpha	1	
B	β, ϐ	*b*	Βῆτα	beta	2	
Γ	γ, Γ	*g* hard	Γάμμα	gamma	3	
Δ	δ	*d*	Δέλτα	delta	4	
E	ε	*e* in *met*	Ἐψιλόν	epsilon, i. e. ε simple	5	ϛ 6
Z	ζ	*sd*	Ζῆτα	zeta	7	(στίγμα)
H	η	*e* long	Ἦτα	eta	8	
Θ	ϑ, θ	*th* sharp	Θῆτα	theta	9	
I	ι	*i*	Ἰῶτα	iota	10	
K	κ	*k*	Κάππα	kappa	20	
Λ	λ	*l*	Λάμβδα	lambda	30	
M	μ	*m*	Μῦ	mu	40	
N	ν	*n*	Νῦ	nu	50	
Ξ	ξ	*x*	Ξῖ	xi	60	
O	ο	*o* short	Ὀμικρόν	omicron, i. e. short *o*.	70	
Π	π, ϖ	*p*	Πῖ	pi	80	ϙ 90
P	ρ	*r*	Ῥῶ	rho	100	(κόππα)
Σ, C	σ, ς	*s* sharp	Σίγμα	sigma	200	
T	τ, 7	*t*	Ταῦ	tau	300	
Υ	υ	*u*	Ὑψιλόν	upsilon, i. e. υ simple	400	
Φ	φ	*f*	Φῖ	phi	500	
X	χ	*ch* guttural	Χῖ	chi	600	
Ψ	ψ	*ps*	Ψῖ	psi	700	(σαμπῖ)
Ω	ω	*o* long	Ὦ μέγα	omĕga, i. e. long *o*.	800, ϡ 900.	

§ 4. ALPHABET.

NOTE 1. About the pronunciation of these letters there is still a discrepancy of opinion and of practice among the learned. Reuchlin, the father of Greek literature in western Europe, introduced the pronunciation of the modern Greeks, which sounds ι, η, ει, οι, υ, υι, all as *i* in *machine* (hence called *Itacism*); αι like *a* in *hate*; υ after α, ε, η, ω, as *f* or *v*, e. g. αὐτός=*aftos*, Ζεὺς=*zefs*, (the Romaic sounding *v*, now softer, now harder); and β as *v*. By the same usage, γ before the sounds *E*, *I*, is pronounced nearly as our *y*, in other cases *gutturally*; δ=*th*; ου=*oo*; χ=*h* or *hk*. Erasmus, on the other hand, commended the usual (continental) sound of the vowels; and the diphthongs he directed to be sounded so that both vowels should be distinctly touched in one prolonged sound. It is utterly impossible, at the present time, to arrive with certainty at any well established conclusions in regard to many of the letters, and especially of the diphthongs. The easiest and best course therefore is, (since it is a matter of very inferior moment), to follow in general the analogy of our own language in the pronunciation of the letters of the Greek alphabet. Our time is wasted to little purpose in striving to build up any particular system of orthoepy, since we can never ascertain whether we are in the right. It is proper to remark, however, that γ before the cognate letters, κ, γ, χ, ξ, is sounded like *n* or *ng* nasal.

NOTE 2. Ancient tradition attributes the introduction of the alphabet into Greece, to Cadmus (קדמון *orientalis* ?) of Phenicia. Sixteen letters only are said to have been introduced by him; while Palamedes, at the siege of Troy, is vaguely reported to have added four more, viz. ϑ, ξ, φ, χ; and Simonides, during the Persian war, ζ, η, ψ, ω. But tradition is not uniform, and evidently the story is in some degree fictitious; for the Greek alphabet, beyond all question, sprung from the Hebrew or Phenician one, which contains twenty-two letters. The probability is, that such letters in this latter alphabet as coincided in sound with the Greek sounds, were retained; that of the *four* sibilants in Hebrew, some two were laid aside; and that *Baῦ* or *Vaῦ* and *Koppa* were also dismissed as not correspondent with Greek sounds, or as superfluous. The ξ is only an abridged method of writing κσ, ψ of πσ, and ζ of σδ; while η and ω are only a convenient method of designating εε and οο, etc. In this way, and by recurring to the fact that a difference must have existed between some of the elementary sounds in Greek and Hebrew, we may account for it that the Cadmaean Greek alphabet did not exhibit all the Hebrew one, although derived from it. We may also see the reason why subsequent additions were made by learned Greeks; some from necessity, in order to make a full designation of sounds; and some from convenience, as being a kind of short-hand mode of writing the letters. Thus the Greeks came to have *twenty-four* letters, most of them (but not all) corresponding to the Hebrew alphabet; while some of the latter alphabet are dismissed from their *phonetic* use and made only the representatives of numbers (viz. *Baῦ*, *Κόππα*, *Σαμπῖ*), and new letters are added, either from necessity or for the sake of convenience.

NOTE 3. The letters ζ, ϑ, φ, χ, occur in the oldest Greek monuments, so that the use of them must have been very early; while in almost all ancient Attic inscriptions, nothing is more common than ε for η, ει for η, ο for ω, οι for ω, χσ for ξ, φσ for ψ, and even ο for ου, showing that the long vowels, and also ξ and ψ were of *later* date than the other letters. But, on the other

§ 5. DIVISION OF LETTERS.   21

hand, the letters ζ, ϑ, φ, χ, appear to have been coeval with the alphabet in general, so far as we can now judge from ancient inscriptions. The whole alphabet, in the full form in which it appears at present, seems to have first come from Ionia to Athens in the time of the archon Euclides, in the year 403 A. C., when it was employed in public writings.

That the reader may judge for himself respecting a matter so curious and interesting as the origin of the Greek letters, I subjoin the Greek and Hebrew alphabets in such a way as will make the comparison easy; premising only, that the Hebrew letters here employed are not the most *ancient* ones, and that those ancient ones (the Samaritan) bear a nearer resemblance to the old Greek alphabet, than the present Hebrew square characters which are here employed.

א	ב	ג	ד	ה	ו	ז	ח	ט	י	כ	ל	מ	נ	ס	ע	פ	צ	ק	ר	ש	ת
A	B	Γ	Δ	E	F	Z	H	Θ	I	K	Λ	M	N	Ξ	O	Π		Ϙ	P	Σ	T
α	β	γ	δ	ε		ζ	η	ϑ	ι	κ	λ	μ	ν	ξ(σ)	ο	π			ρ	σ	τ

NOTE 4. An inspection of the alphabet, on p. 19, will render plain the Greek method of notation. The original letter, in the *sixth* place of the alphabet, appears to have been F, i. e. *Baũ* or *Faũ*, corresponding to the Heb. ו; but Kuhner places F at the end of the old alphabet. Inasmuch as F was used both for the Digamma (= our F) and also for the vowel v, the notation of it in the alphabet was dropped in respect to its digamma sound, and retained only in the v sound, which was placed at the end of the original alphabet. Instead of F, as designating 6, was introduced the somewhat similar ς *Stigma* or στ, as it appears on the right-hand margin of the Alphabet, p.19; *Koppa* = 90 (from the Heb. ק), not being needed as a phonetic letter, merely retained its *numeral* significancy. It has three different shapes, viz. Ϙ, 4, Ϟ. The last is the usual one. Sampi = 900 was evidently the Heb. ש = *sh*, and was retained only as a *numeral*, because the Greek alphabet had no corresponding sound. The abridged methods of notation, and the way of making out composite numbers, etc., may be found in Buttm. Gramm. § 2. Notes 3, 4.

§ 5. *Division of the Letters.*

(1) The natural division is into *vowels* and *consonants*. Of the former there are *seven*; of the latter there are properly only *fourteen*, because ζ stands for σδ, ξ for κσ, and ψ for πσ, and these three *double* letters, to which we may add ς (Sti or Stigma) = στ, are not properly to be reckoned as *component* parts of the alphabet, because their simple elements are contained and counted in the others.

(2) The fourteen consonants may be named, (*a*) From the *organ* with which they are enounced; and so β, π, φ, μ, are LABIALS; τ, δ, ϑ, λ, ν, ρ, σ, are LINGUALS; and κ, γ, χ PALATALS. A much more important classification is,

(*b*) According to their *power*; by which they are distributed into SEMI-VOWELS and MUTES. Semi-vowels are the liquids λ, μ, ν, ρ, and the sibilant σ; Mutes are

§ 5. Division of Letters.

1	2	3	
π	κ	τ	smooth.
β	γ	δ	middle.
φ	χ	θ	rough.

Note 1. The first perpendicular column consists of *labials*, the second of *palatals*, and the third of *linguals*; and, in the same order, the same columns are said to be of the *P* sound, of the *K* sound, and of the *T* sound, because of the leading letter in each.

Note 2. The importance of the semi-vowels, ν, ρ, σ, may be recognized from the singular fact, that *no genuine Greek word can end in any other* consonant; ἐκ and οὐκ excepted, and these only in the middle of a phrase, being elsewhere ἐξ=ἐκς, and οὐ.

(3) The seven vowels are divided into *short*, *long*, and *double-timed*.

Note. Short, ε, ο; long, η, ω; double-timed, α, ι, υ. The three last are sometimes long, and at other times short, i. e. the same letter stands for a long sound at one time, and a short one at another; but they are never short and long at the same time and place.

(4) Diphthongs are a coalescence of two vowel sounds. The second of these vowels is always an ι or υ.

Note 1. Diphthongs are formed by suffixing ι or υ to α, ε, ο, υ, either short or long. When the first letter is *short*, the diphthong is called proper; when it is *long*, it is called improper. Υ of course can admit only ι after it; the other vowels named admit both ι and υ after them; but when ι follows ᾱ, η, ω, it is *subscribed*.

Proper Dipht.		Improper Dipht.	
αι	αυ	ᾳ	ᾱυ
ει	ευ	ῃ	ηυ
οι	ου	ῳ	ωυ (Ion.)
υι		ῡι	

But *ιι* combined make merely ῑ long; and *ιυ* do not form a diphthongal sound, e. g. ἰύζω is trisyllabic.

Note 2. The pronunciation of the diphthongs (see Note 1. § 4) is not, and cannot now be, accurately determined. It is however agreed, that where Iota is *subscript*, it is practically to be regarded as quiescent, although it was probably sounded slightly by the Greeks. To distinguish in *pronunciation* the proper and improper diphthongs, would be difficult indeed at the present time. It might perhaps be said with a good degree of assurance, that the Greeks sounded ου as our *oo*, ει = our proper *i*; οι = *oi*; and perhaps αι = our *a* in hate. Beyond this is uncertain ground. The Iota *subscript* was not introduced until about the 13th century. Anciently it was written *in the line*; as it now is, when capital letters are employed, e. g. "ΑΙΔΗΣ or "Αιδης = ᾅδης.

Note 3. When vowels come together which usually make a diphthong, but which must in pronunciation be actually separated, two points (called *di-*

§ 6. BREATHINGS. 23

aeresis) are placed over the second vowel; e. g. ὄϊς, πραΰς, each being dissyllabic.

§ 6. *Breathings* (*Spiritus*.)

(1) These are the smooth (᾿), and the rough (῾); the last is sounded as a slight *H*; the first, in most cases, is capable of no distinct enunciation which is perceptible by the ear.

NOTE 1. One of these breathings stands on all words beginning with a vowel; and when they begin with a *proper* diphthong, the *spiritus* is placed over the second vowel, as in εὐθύς; but it remains on the first, in the diphthongs ᾳ, ῃ, ῳ, even when the Iota is written in the line, as Ἅιδης.

NOTE 2. All words beginning with υ, have (in all the dialects except the Aeolic) the *rough* breathing, as ὑμεῖς; and so, also, all words beginning with ρ; and when double ρ occurs in the middle of a word, the first takes the smooth breathing, the second the rough one, as πύῤῥος.

NOTE 3. Originally, only the rough breathing was noted; and this by the letter *H* inserted in the line like the other letters, and formerly sounded as our *H*. When this sign (*H*) came to be used for η, the letter was divided, and the right-hand half used for marking the *smooth* breathing, and the other half to designate the *rough* ; then came Γ and ꓶ, and finally the present *Spiritus*. Aristophanes of Byzantium (about 200 A. C.) is said to have made this arrangement. Before this the smooth breathing appears not to have been marked; and the marking of it seems indeed to be of little or no significancy to us; yet as the ancients wrote originally without any marked division of words, this sign placed upon words *beginning* with a vowel would often aid the reader.

NOTE 4. Besides these two breathings, (which correspond to alphabetic letters, e. g. the smooth one (᾿) to the א of the oriental alphabet, and the rough one (῾) to the ה of the same alphabet and the *h* of the western nations), the most ancient Greek alphabet had a third aspirate (*Fau* or *Bau*, *F*), which corresponded very nearly or altogether with the Hebrew ו *Vav*; as both the name and sound indicate. This, from its shape, is called *Digamma*, i. e. double Gamma; also the *Aeolic* Digamma, because the Aeolians longest retained it; and although even in ancient times it was dropped in writing, yet it is supposed, without any doubt, to belong to many words in the poems of Homer. Words which once exhibited it, have in some cases substituted for it a β, in others a γ, or υ, or the smooth or rough *spiritus*. The substitute υ remains at the end of a word (as βοῦ for βόF); and in the middle of a word before a consonant, (as βουσί for βοFσί). But the Digamma has entirely vanished, (1) At the beginning of a word, before vowels and ρ; as οἶνος (Fοῖνος), ῥόδον (Fρόδον). (2) Between two vowels in the middle of a word; as ὠόν (ὠFόν, ovum). See Kühner, § 14.

NOTE 5. Kühner makes two more *Aspirates* still, viz. X and Σ. The X, it would seem, was originally a mere aspirate; but gradually it came to be sometimes used as a guttural (*hh*, or *ch* German); partly however as a *K*, and partly as a *Spiritus asper*. This letter (X) he calls a *palatal* aspirate. The Σ he calls the *lingual* aspirate; and he shows that it easily went over into the proper rough aspirate (e. g. σῦς, ὗς); or, like the Digamma, it fell away between vowels in the middle of a word, e. g. τύπτεσαι, τύπτεαι, which (being contracted) makes the usual τύπτῃ, the 2d pers. sing. of the Pres. passive.

§ 7. Accents.

(1) By these are meant *the grammatical notations of the tone,* i. e. of the stress of voice which is to be laid on each word.

NOTE 1. All languages, whether written or not, must of course have *tone-syllables,* as pronounced with the voice; but it appears that the grammatical *notation* of the accents in books was begun by Aristophanes of Byzantium, about 200 years A. C. Most probably it was first designed, like the notation of the tone-syllable in some of our English reading books, merely to facilitate the proper reading of the Greek by learners. But this notation never became general in Mss., until six or seven centuries after the commencement of the Christian era.

NOTE 2. See Villoison, Epist. Vinar. p. 115 seq., for the proof of the above position. Hermann (de Emend. Gramm. Graec. p. 60) expresses very confidently the opinion, that the notation of the accents is as old as the times of Homer; which he has endeavored to prove in his book *De Metris,* I. c. 22. 23. The general opinion, however, is as stated above.

(2) Every Greek word has regularly, in and of itself, an accent of some kind. To the few words called *enclitics,* the accent belongs when they stand unconnected with other words.

NOTE. Even the so-called *toneless* words (*atona*) or *proclitics,* viz. οὐ, οὐκ, οὐχ, ὡς, εἰ, ἐν, εἰς, ἐς, ἐκ, ἐξ, ὁ, ἡ, οἱ, αἱ, whenever they stand *unconnected* with, or are placed *after,* the words on which they depend, take an accent. All words, therefore, without an accent, are so merely because they are regarded as conjoined with some other word which has an accent.

(3) Strictly speaking, and in reference to real pronunciation in one respect, there is only one kind of accent, i. e. every accent marks a stress of voice. But in reference to actual *designations* or *written signs,* we may say that there are now three kinds of accents; viz., (*a*) The *acute* (´), the sign of elevating the tone. (*b*) The *grave* (`), the sign of the falling slide of the voice. (*c*) The *circumflex* (˜), the sign of compound and prolonged tone on the accented syllable.

The Greeks named the accents προσῳδία. The acute (´) they called ὀξεῖα; the grave (`) βαρεῖα; the circumflex (˜) περισπωμένη, i. e. *drawn out, protracted.* Hence words were named with a reference to accentuation, i. e. in accordance with the name and place of the accent; e. g. with the acute (either ascending ´ or descending `) on the last syllable, *oxytone;* on the penult, *paroxytone;* on the antepenult, *proparoxytone.* On the other hand, words with the circumflex on the last syllable are called *perispome;* on the penult, *properispome.* Properly speaking, *barytone* words are all those, which, according to the *original* accentuation of the Greeks, had a *grave* accent on the ultimate; but, in other words and speaking according to present usage, all words whose ultimate is *unaccented* or *toneless* are barytone. All words, then, except *oxytones* and *perispomes*, belong to the barytones.

Note 1. The ancients used the *grave* accent (`` ` ``) to mark all *toneless* syllables. But as this was superfluous, it came at length, and is now exclusively employed, to denote the *acute descending*, i. e. the falling slide of the voice. But *oxytones* at the end of a sentence, before a colon, and even before a comma which makes a plain break or pause in the sense, preserve the acute *ascending* ; but in continuous discourse closely connected, the accent is written with the sliding fall. Kühn. § 71. I.

Note 2. The circumflex (`` ˜ ``) is used to denote a *prolonged* accent, made up of the acute and the grave (´`), with some change of form for the sake of convenience in writing; of course the circumflex can stand only on long vowels which have been made by contracting two vowels into one sound; and in this case *only where the acute was to be placed on the first of these vowels*; e. g. ὅο=ὦ. But ὀό contracted = ώ (not ῶ); plainly because the circumflex accent represents only ´`, and not `´. In all cases, therefore, where the circumflex is employed, we may take it for granted that originally there were two vowels with separate sounds, the first of which had the acute accent; so that δῆλος=δέελος, σῶμα=σόομα, φῶς=φάος, ὁμοῖος=ὁμόϊος, τιμῶ=τιμάω, φιλῶ=φιλέω, etc.

(4) The accent may be placed on either of the three last syllables of any word, just as the tone of the word and the nature of the quantity in one or more of these syllables require or permit ; but never farther back than the *antepenult* syllable.

Note. The *acute* accent may stand, as the nature of each case shall require, on either of the three ultimate syllables ; the *grave*, only on the last; the *circumflex*, on the last, or on the penult. The reason why the *circumflex* can go no farther back, is evident from Note 2 above; since, when it stands apparently on the penult, it stands really on the antepenult. The *grave* is only a peculiar form of the acute, when it falls on the ultimate in case of some pause.

(5) Place of the accent. (*a*) The acute and the grave may stand on any vowel, long or short ; but the acute can never stand on the antepenult syllable, unless the final syllable of the word be short. (*b*) The circumflex can stand only on a vowel that is *long by nature*, (not by position merely). When the penult is long by nature, and the ultimate is either short or long merely by position, a word must necessarily take the *circumflex ;* but this last rule does not include words compounded with an enclitic, e. g. οὔτε, ἥτις, etc. (*c*) When the ultimate is accented, it is more usually *oxytone ;* but adverbs, and some other words, frequently take a *circumflex* on the ultimate.

Note 1. Accents of all kinds are written only over a vowel ; and in case of a *proper* diphthong, only over its second letter. When the *improper*

§ 7. Accents.

diphthongs which usually have Iota subscript, are written with this Iota in the line, the accent is still placed over the first letter; e. g. Ἅιδης.'

NOTE 2. There is not a little which seems arbitrary to us, in estimating the quantity of vowels with reference to accentuation. E. g. (1) The diphthongs αι and οι at the *end* of words, are treated as *short*; as in χῶροι, γλῶσσαι, ἄνθρωποι, τράπεζαι. The exceptions to this are, (*a*) Verbs ending in -οι -αι, in the Opt. mode, as λείποι, τιμήσαι. (*b*) The adverb οἴκοι, and some compounds with enclitics, as ἤτοι, etc. (2) The endings -ως -ων of the Attic forms of Dec. II. and III., also the Ionic Gen. -ω of Dec. I., are treated as short; e. g. ἀνώγεων, ἴλεως—πόλεως, πόλεων—δεσπότεω. (3) Before ξ and ψ, in a final syllable, ῑ and ῡ are treated as *short* in assigning the accent; e. g. φοῖνιξ, κῆρυξ, etc. Kühner, § 66. 5.

NOTE 3. The *ultimate* syllable is excepted from the common rule (*c*) above, and receives a *circumflex*, (*a*) In case of appropriate contraction, as αἰδόα, contr. αἰδῶ. (*b*) In adverbial endings in -ως, *when derived from oxytone adjectives*; e. g. καλῶς, σοφῶς. So in local adverbs in -οι, e. g. Ἰσθμοῖ. (3) Generally, the Gen. and Dat. endings of all oxytones of Dec. I. and II. have the circumflex; also the Gen. and Dat. dual and plural of Dec. III., in all words with monosyllabic ground-forms; see the paradigms, and the exceptions in the notes. (4) So also the Voc. endings in Dec. III.; of nouns in -εύς and fem. -ώ -ώς; e. g. βασιλεῦ, ἠχοῖ, αἰδοῖ. (5) Oftentimes in monosyllabic words; e. g. πᾶς, νῦν, etc.

NOTE 4. A slight attention to the forms of DECLENSION, in respect to all the parts of speech which are capable of it, will lead any one to see readily, that the continual variations of the ending of words must vary the *quantity* of end-syllables, and of course demand corresponding changes in the accentuation of the words thus varied. Taking the above rules with their exceptions into view, however, it is for the most part easy to account for all these, when we once know the accentuation of the ground-form, and the general rules respecting the tone which belongs to it.

ADDITIONS to words by compounding them with others, or made in the course of conjugation or declension; CONTRACTION of words; PECULIARITIES of dialects or of meanings; ANOMALIES by usage; and SPECIALITIES of declension, mode, tense, etc.; all have an influence on accentuation. These must be sought for under the respective heads where they are treated of. See an admirable summary of the general principles of accentuation, in Kühner I. §§ 64—79.

NOTE 5. Besides the special causes already named, which occasion changes of accentuation, there are several others; viz. (*a*) *Krasis*, i. e. the coalescence of two words in one; e. g. τοὔργον=τὸ ἔργον. (*b*) *Elision*, i. e. the striking out of a vowel at the end of a word; e. g. πολλ' ἔπαθον=πολλὰ ἔπαθον· ἀλλ' ἐγώ=ἀλλὰ ἐγώ. See § 8. 4. (*c*) *Anastrophe*, i. e. a transfer of a preposition to a place behind the noun which it governs; in which case the accent (if the nature of the preposition allows it) reverts towards the noun, as καλῶν πέρι instead of περὶ καλῶν. (*d*) *Proclitics* (see § 7. 2 Note), when in any way separated from connection and dependence on the discourse, receive an accent; e. g. πῶς γὺρ οὔ; κακῶν ἒξ instead of ἐκ κακῶν. (*e*) *Enclitics*, i. e. words which usually throw off their accent and attach themselves to the preceding word, in many circumstances become accented.

§ 7. ACCENTS. 27

REMARK I. It would be out of place to pursue the details of accentuation, in a work like the present. For a minute account of all the topics to which I have merely adverted in the above notes, I must refer the reader to Buttmann, Rost, Matthiae, and specially to the recent and noble work of Kühner (Ausführliche Grammatik), I. §§ 64—79.

REMARK II. Buttmann, Kühner, and other distinguished grammarians, insist much on regard to the accent in reading Greek, even where apparent quantity must be sacrificed in order to accomplish this. The later Greek poets and the modern Greeks have in fact made the *quantity* altogether subordinate to the accent. It is obvious, however, that no great advantage to the critic, as such, can accrue from scrupulous attention to rules of this kind; although the knowledge of them, as an accomplishment of a rhetorical nature, may properly claim some attention. However the reader may estimate this, let him not suppose, for a moment, that attention to the subject of accentuation is altogether needless or superfluous. Many words are distinguished from each other solely by the accent; e. g. εἰμί *I am*, εἶμι *I go*; τίς *who*? τις or τις *some one*; ὁ *the* (article), ὅ *which*; πότε *when*, ποτέ *at some time*, etc. etc. And if such indications of distinction are not important for the adept in Greek, still they are very convenient for the learner.

REMARK III. The written accentuation of the N. Test. is designed to be conformed to the common laws of Greek accentuation. The age of this written accentuation, in some of the Mss. of the N. Test., cannot be ascertained with certainty. It is certain, however, that it is older than the *interpunction* of the same book. The writings of profane Greek authors were, as we have seen, accented to some extent before the Christian era. In the 4th century, Epiphanius speaks of the Sept. as furnished with various kinds of accents; the doing of which he names στίζειν κατὰ προσῳδίαν.* Possibly the N. Test. may, even at this period, have been written in like manner. But we have no certain account of its accentuation until Euthalius, a deacon of the church at Alexandria, about A. D. 464, published the first edition of the Pauline epistles κατὰ στίχους. In his preface, still extant,† he speaks of *making marks of distinction (ἀνάγνωσιν)*, and these κατὰ προσῳδίαν, i. e. accentuation. This work of Euthalius, which he extended afterwards to the Acts and the Catholic Epistles, (probably to the whole of the N. T. also), whose στίχοι answered in general to our modern interpunction and were therefore valuable to readers, came soon into very extensive use; so that, at least in the latter half of the *fifth* century, there must have been a great number of Mss. in circulation that were *accented*.

REMARK IV. As the laws of accentuation never have been universally agreed upon in all their minutiae, (which is no more strange than the case of our own English accentuation), so, notwithstanding all that prosodists and grammarians have written, not a few points, and even the notation in respect to many particular words, remain under dispute down to the present hour; e. g. ἰδέ and ἴδε, numerals ending in -ετης which are written -έτης and -ετής, κῆρυξ and κήρυξ, φοῖνιξ and φοίνιξ, ποῦς and πούς, λαῖλιψ and λαῖλαψ, θλῖψις and θλίψις, ἐριθεια and ἐριθείη, μύλων and μυλών, εἶπον (Imper.) and εἶπόν, λάβε and λαβέ, etc. It can be of but little importance to the sacred interpreter to settle these questions; but the question whether

---

* Hug, Einleit. in N. Test. I. § 43.   † In Gallandi Biblioth. Pat. X. p. 201.

μενεῖ or μένει (1 Cor. 3:14), τῳ=τινι or τῷ the article (1 Cor. 15:8), εἶμι *I go* or εἰμί *I am* (John 7: 34, 36), τρόχος *course* or τροχός *wheel* (James 3: 6), and the like, be the true reading, of course has a connection with exegesis of some importance, and the accentuation must therefore depend on this, and cannot be settled in any other way. It is still disputed, also, whether the personal pronouns that are enclitic, should be so written after prepositions in all cases; and we find high authorities for writing παρά σου and παρὰ σοῦ, ἔν μοι and ἐν ἐμοί, πρός με and πρὸς ἐμέ, etc. This question, however, is scarcely worth a serious investigation. Either usage is good; at least, if authority can make it so. Even Kuhner, with his masterly talent at exhibition, has not steered clear of some perplexities, not to say contradictions, in his rules respecting accents. E. g. in § 63. 4, he represents 'the circumflex as arising only from the combination of two *short* vowels the *first* of which has the acute accent.' But what is the circumflex in τιμῶ=τιμάω, in φιλῶ=φιλέω, etc.? Is not the ω here of and by itself *long*? Again, we have ἑσταώς, contr. ἑστώς, according to rule; but Gen. ἑσταότος contr. ἑστῶτος, although the full form (-αό-) has the accent on the *latter* of the two vowels. The truth seems to be here, that the law arising from the last syllable being short and the penult long, renders the circumflex necessary in spite of the other principle which respects the *order* of the accents. Other perplexities, also, the attentive reader will find, after all that has been done to elucidate the subject; but this is not the place to discuss them.

§ 8. *Signs or characters to aid the reader.*

(1) INTERPUNCTION. This consists of the comma and period, like our own; and of the colon, which is a point just *above* the line (e. g. λέγει·) and answers to our colon and semicolon.

NOTE 1. In many editions of Greek books, a point of the same shape and position as the *period*, is used in the room of a colon or semicolon, (e. g. in the Leipsic edition of Plato, in Bloomfield's N. Test., and many other books), in which case the following word has a *small* and not a capital letter, in order to show that a new sentence does not begin with it. This practice is to be regretted, as it tends to create confusion in the reader. The interrogation point is our semicolon (;)—and in recent editions of several authors the note of exclamation (!) is also introduced.

NOTE 2. The history of the rise of interpunction is interesting to the critic, and may be satisfactorily traced, as it respects the N. Testament. The στίχοι of Euthalius (see Rem. III. above) consisted of short parts of sentences that were closely connected in sense, or of single words (as the case might be) that made sense by themselves, each of which was written in a line by itself (which was then called στίχος), so that the reader might never doubt where he should make his pauses; e. g. Tit. 2: 2.

ΠΡΕΣΒΥΤΑΣ ΝΗΦΑΛΙΟΥΣ ΕΙΝΑΙ
ΣΕΜΝΟΥΣ
ΣΩΦΡΟΝΑΣ
ΥΓΙΑΙΝΟΝΤΑΣ ΤΗ ΠΙΣΤΕΙ
ΤΗ ΑΓΑΠΗ

§ 8. READING-SIGNS.

ΠΡΕΣΒΥΤΙΔΑΣ ΩΣΑΥΤΩΣ
ΕΝ ΚΑΤΑΣΤΗΜΑΤΙ ΙΕΡΟΠΡΕΠΕΙΣ
ΜΗ ΔΙΑΒΟΛΟΥΣ
ΜΗ ΟΙΝΩ ΠΟΛΛΩ ΔΕΔΩΛΟΥΜΕΝΑΣ
ΚΑΛΟΔΙΔΑΣΚΑΛΟΥΣ

In this way was the N. Test. published by Euthalius; and the work soon obtained great celebrity and a wide circulation, for this obviously answered nearly all the purposes of our modern system of interpunction. Moreover, that from the στίχοι thus arranged the interpunction of modern times came, can hardly be doubted. Parchment was too costly, in ancient times, to permit book makers to leave for any great length of time more than one half of the page blank, as the method of writing ἐν στίχοις obliged them to do; and so the copyists or editors fell upon the simple and obvious device of writing the page nearly full, but of making a point (a cross, or some other sign), after each word that had stood, in older editions, at the end of a στίχος. So the *Codex Cyprius* is written throughout. But intelligent readers soon saw, that some of these points or signs ought to mark greater breaks in the sense than others; and therefore they began to note them by appropriate and distinctive signs. Thus arose gradually the *interpunction-system*. The exact time of its first rise cannot be definitely traced; but we know thus much, viz., that in the 10th century a regular interpunction of the N. Test. was already in existence, and that it is to be met with occasionally in Mss. of the century preceding this, and perhaps even earlier.

(2) DIASTOLE or HYPODIASTOLE. This is of the same form with the comma, and has the same place in the line; but still it is used merely to mark certain words in order to distinguish them from others.

E. g. ὅ, τι (neut. of ὅστις) with a comma *(diastole)* between the two words, in order to distinguish them from ὅτι *because;* so ὅ, τε (from ὅς and τε), not ὅτε *when.* Recent editions generally neglect the *diastole,* and print the words, formerly written with it, thus: ὅ τι, ὅ τε; which seems to be much preferable, as no one can hesitate or be misled on account of this.

(3) APOSTROPHE. All the *short* vowels (ὐ excepted), when standing at the end of many words which frequently occur, and before another word beginning with a vowel, may suffer *elision,* i. e. may be dropped; and their absence is then marked by a comma *above* the line (as τουτ' for τοῦτο), which in such a case is called *apostrophe.*

NOTE 1. When a *smooth mute* comes by elision to be the last letter of a word with an apostrophe, and the next word has the rough breathing, that smooth mute becomes rough; e. g. ἀπὸ οὗ, with apostrophe ἀφ' οὗ.

NOTE 2. No uniformity or *settled* rule exists as to elision, and consequently as to the use of apostrophe. Mss., dialects, and editors differ; so do poetry and prose, the former taking far the greater liberty, and

§ 8. READING-SIGNS.

sometimes eliding even the diphthong—*αι*. In the N. Test., by the usage of Mss., ἄρα, ἵνα, εἶτα, ἔτι, never suffer *elision;* although they often do this in other writings. As a general rule of the Greek language, words ending in *υ*, monosyllables in *α, ι, ο* (ῥά excepted), and the prepositions πρό and περί, never suffer elision.

NOTE 3. The object of elision, in all cases of apostrophe, is to get rid of the *hiatus* in sound which occurs where two vowels immediately succeed each other, and one of them has a breathing either rough or smooth.

(4) CORONIS. The point called *coronis* is of the same form as the comma or apostrophe, and marks the *union* or *mixture* (κρᾶσις it is called) of two vowels in one sound, where one word ends and the next begins with a vowel usually short.

NOTE 1. In this case, *the two vowels follow the usual laws of contraction;* both words are then written in one, and furnished with a *coronis*, in order to designate a contraction and union; e. g. τἀμά for τὰ ἐμά, τἆλλα for τὰ ἄλλα, ἐγᾦδα for ἐγὼ οἶδα, κἀγώ for καὶ ἐγώ, etc. In the N. Test. this practice is quite unfrequent.

NOTE 2. The object of *Crasis*, (which is marked by the *Coronis*), is the same in general as that of elision and apostrophe, viz., to get rid of *hiatus* between two vowels at the end of one word and the beginning of another. The coronis, however, stands over the *middle* of a composite word, (not at the *end* of a word, like apostrophe), and denotes *contraction*, not properly elision.

NOTE 3. In classic Greek, particularly in epic poetry, *crasis* in reading (not in writing) is exceedingly common. It is then called *synizesis* (συνίζησις, connecting together, i. e. σύν—ἵζω). In every page and almost every line of Homer something of this is necessary; but in what way these contractions are to be made, so far as *pronunciation* is concerned, oftentimes cannot well be determined.

(5) PARAGOGIC NUN. The Greeks called it ν ἐφελκυστικόν, i. e. *Nun appended;* which sufficiently defines it. The object of it is the same as that of elision and crasis, i. e. to prevent hiatus.

NOTE. In order to effect this, it is appended to the *third* persons of verbs ending in ε or ι, and to the Dat. plur. ending in σι. Hiatus, therefore, must have been very disagreeable to a refined Grecian ear; for no less than three expedients are practised in order to get rid of it.

(6) IOTA SUBSCRIPT. This is used only in three of the improper diphthongs; see § 5. 4. Anciently it seems to have been *pronounced*, but afterwards to have become *mute* by usage; and therefore it is *subscribed*, that the reader may be aware of this.

Peculiarities.

(1) Οὕτω before a word beginning with a vowel, is commonly written οὕτως. But here Mss. and editions differ, οὕτως being sometimes written

§ 10. MUTATIONS OF THE CONSONANTS. 31

before consonants. The like principle applies to the writing of ἄχρι and ἄχρις, of μέχρι and μέχρις; but still, the like variations also exist.

(2) Several recent editors write the *Sigma* at the end of the first part of a composite word in the shape of ς final; e. g. ὡςπερ, εἰςφέρω, etc. But where can this practice end? Must we write θεόςδοτος, δυςσεβής, λαοςσόος, etc.? The practice has not the authority of Mss. or ancient grammarians; and it is condemned by Matthiae, Buttmann, Winer, Kühner, and others, although Winer himself follows it.

(3) Practice is different among different editors, as to writing various small words that come together as one, or separating them; e. g. διάτι and διὰ τί, εἴπερ and εἴ περ, οὐκ ἔτι and οὐκέτι, etc. It is of little or no consequence which method is adopted, provided an editor is consistent with himself.

§ 10. *Mutations of the Consonants.*

The delicate ear of the Greeks could not bear the harshness, which (as they estimated it) arose from the juxta-position of certain consonants. From this source come nearly all the numerous changes, which consonants undergo in the Greek language. The *mutes* are the principal letters which undergo these changes.

The subject itself of these changes is so deeply concerned with the forms that words assume in the course of declension, and even of composition, that MINUTE AND THOROUGH ATTENTION TO IT IS ABSOLUTELY INDISPENSABLE, on the part of every one who intends to be able well and thoroughly to understand the laws and usages of Greek declensions and forms.

I. *Changes of Mutes before each other.*

The mutes are here subjoined for the aid of the reader, and classified for convenience' sake.

1	2	3	
π	κ	τ	smooth.
β	γ	δ	middle.
φ	χ	θ	rough, (also called *aspirates*).

To avoid any misunderstanding it should be stated, that the perpendicular line of letters under No. 1, is called the *P* class of mutes or the *first* class, which are LABIALS; under No. 2, the *K* or *second* class, which are PALATALS; under No. 3, the *T* or *third* class, which are LINGUALS. The *quality* of mutes refers to their being *smooth*, *middle*, or *rough*. Those of the same *quality*, therefore, are all such as are smooth, or middle, or rough, although they may be of different *classes*; e. g. π, κ, τ are all of the same *quality*, i. e. all smooth, but they are, at the same time, of three different classes; and so of the others.

RULE I. It is a general principle (with very few exceptions), that mutes of the first and second class are not doubled; nor do they immediately follow each other; but when mutes come together, the second of them must be of the *T* or third class.

§ 10. Changes of the Mutes.

Note. The mute τ is the only one of all which it is very common to double; e. g. as in τάττω. The *aspirates* are sometimes thrown together; but in such cases, the first of them is changed, as will be presently seen. A few cases exist like ἵππος, κόκκος; but such examples are against the general analogy.

Rule 2. Mutes, in order to come together, must be of the same *quality*, i. e. smooth must be joined to smooth, middle to middle, and rough to rough; and here the *quality* of the first mute is made to conform to that of the second.

E. g. ἑπτά, νυκτός, ῥάβδος, ὄγδοος, ἄχθος, ἐτύφθην.

Note 1. To express the rule in another way; τ admits before it only π, κ, smooth mutes of the other classes; δ, only β, γ; θ, only φ, χ. If by any cause in composition or declension, the second mute thus harmonized becomes changed as to *quality*, the other must also of course change its quality in like manner; e. g. ἑπτά becomes ἕβδομος in the adjective form, the π going into β (middle mute) in order to conform to the quality of the following δ which constitutes the *adjective* form of the word; so ὀκτώ makes ὄγδοος, etc. The κ in ἐκ, however, is in all cases of composition immutable. To Rule 2, however, there are exceptions; viz.

Rule 3. The *rough* mutes will not bear to be repeated, but require a smooth mute of the same class before them.

E. g. Σαπφώ, not Σαφφώ; Βάκχος, not Βάχχος; Ἀτθίς, not Ἀθθίς.

Rule 4. The same principle is generally applied even to the syllable that immediately *precedes* a rough mute; for such syllable must regularly (in case it has a mute) take a *smooth* one. Even the *spiritus asper* in this syllable becomes *lenis*.

E. g. πεφίληκα, not φεφίληκα; κεχώρηκα, not χεχώρηκα; τάφος, not θάφος, etc. So also ἔχω for ἕχω (comp. Fut. ἕξω), where the *smooth* breathing is adopted because of the χ in the next following syllable.

Note 2. The principle here laid down, however, is limited mostly to the syllables belonging to the mere *root* of a word, or to that and a preceding syllable made by *reduplication*; e. g. τρέφω (from θρεφ-ω), κέχυται (from χύ-ω). But additions at the *close* of words, whether occasioned by *flexion* or *derivation*, do not produce such an effect on preceding aspirates; e. g. ἐθάφ-θην, θαφ-θείς, ἐχύ-θην. So in the Imper. ending -θι, as φά-θι; in the adverbial endings -θεν -θι; in derivative words with a formative syllable commencing with θ, as φθί-θω, root ΦΘΙ; and in the aspir. Perf. ending -α, when this letter is preceded by a P or K mute, as τέθαφα.—The anomalies are a few; e. g. θύω and τίθημι follow the general rule, even when they receive flexion endings beginning with θ, as ἐτύθην, ἐτέθην. Moreover the Aor. 1 Pass. Imper., which would regularly be -θηθι, makes -θητι, preserving the first θ as the characteristic of the tense.

Note 3. *Composite* words are not subject to the general law, in regard to the preceding aspirate; e. g. ἀχθο-φόρος, ἐφύφη.

§ 10. CHANGES OF THE MUTES. 33

RULE 5. A *smooth* mute before the rough breathing becomes aspirated; e. g. ἀφ' οὖ, not ἀπ' οὖ, etc.

In the flexion of verbs, *middle* mutes may become aspirated; but not elsewhere; e. g. εἴλοχα instead of εἴλογ-α.

II. *Changes of Mutes before σ.*

RULE 6. Of the first class, σ admits before it only the smooth π sound; of the second, only the smooth κ sound; and the third is rejected before the σ, which also rejects ζ=σδ, because of the δ in it.

NOTE 4. The meaning is, that before σ, the letters β, φ, become π; the letters γ, χ, become κ; and the third class (also ζ) are dropped. In the first case, when π precedes σ (=πσ), the two letters are of course written ψ, as τύψω=τυπσω; in the second, κς is written ξ, as in λέξω=λέκσω.

NOTE 5. Examples of the rule are λείπω, λείψω; τρίβω, τρίψω; γράφω, γρίψω; πλέκω, πλέξω; λέγω, λέξω; στείχω, στείξω. Examples of dropping class third, are σώμασι (not σώμασι); ἄδω, ἄσω (not ἄδσω); πείθω, πείσω (not πείθσω); φράζω, φράσω (not φράζσω).

NOTE 6. If ν precedes any letter of the third class of mutes, in such cases, it is also dropped with them; and when a short vowel precedes the two letters thus dropped, that vowel becomes prolonged; i. e. ε goes into ει; ο into ου; and short α, ι, υ, become long; e. g. σπένδω, σπείσω; λέουσι for λέοντσι; πᾶσι for πάντσι; δεικνῦσι for δείκνυντσι, etc. See below, under Note 8.

III. *Changes of mutes before μ.*

RULE 7. Before μ, the first class of mutes assimilate.

E. g. λείπω, λέλειμ-μαι; τρίβω, τέτριμ-μαι; γράφω, γέγραμ-μαι.

RULE 8. Before μ, the second class of mutes become γ.

E. g. πλέκω, πέπλεγ-μαι; τεύχω, τέτευγ-μαι; and so λέγω, λέξω, λέλεγμαι. Some exceptions exist in the formation of nouns, as ἀκμή, ἔχμα, etc.

RULE 9. Before μ the third class of mutes go into σ; as also does ζ=σδ.

E. g. ἀνύτω, ἤνυσ-μαι; ἐρείδω, ἤρεισ-μαι; πείθω, πέπεισ-μαι; ψηφίζω, ψήφισ-μαι. There are frequent departures from this in the epic and Ionic dialect, as ὀδμή, ἴδμεν, etc.

IV. *Peculiar changes in the third or T class of Mutes.*

RULE 10. When the third class come together, the first letter often goes into σ.

E. g. ἥδω, ἥσ-θην; πείθω, ἐπείσ-θην, πεισ-τέον. But forms of mere reduplication, like πράττω, Ἀτθίς, etc., are common in respect to the letter τ.

5

V. *Changes of N.*

RULE 11. Before the P class of mutes, and also before ψ=πσ, ν goes into μ.

E. g. in composite words, such as συμπάσχω, ἐμβάλλω, συμφέρω, ἐμψύχω, where σύν and ἐν are prefixed.

NOTE 7. By the usual laws respecting ν, the Greeks must have read τόν πατέρα καὶ τὴν μητέρα as if written τόμ πατέρα καὶ τὴμ μητέρα; and so grammarians direct us to read. This usage, however, for those who are not to speak the language, is hardly worth the trouble that it costs.

RULE 12. Before the K class of mutes, and also before ξ=κσ, the ν becomes a γ in the *written* language; but it is read as ν, or *ng* nasal.

E. g. ἐγκαλῶ, συγγενής, συγχαίρω, συγξαίνω.

RULE 13. Before the liquids λ, μ, ρ, the ν is usually assimilated.

E. g. συλλέγω, ἐμμένω, συρρίπτω; but also ἐνρίπτω.

RULE 14. Before ζ the ν is always dropped.

E. g. συζυγία for συνζυγία.

RULE 15. Before σ the ν is dropped in the course of declension; and in the composition of words, where σ is followed by another consonant.

E. g. αἰῶσι (not αἰῶνσι); σύστημα (not σύνστημα). Some exceptions occur, as πέφανσαι, ἕλμινς, etc.; but these are few. The preposition ἐν, moreover retains the ν; as ἔνσοφος. The ν in σύν assimilates before σ; as συσσώζω.

RULE 16. Final ν in verbs and Dat. plurals may be omitted or inserted, as the case may require, i. e. according as a consonant or a vowel immediately follows.

VI. *Changes to avoid the concurrence of too many consonants.*

RULE 17. As a general rule, three consonants, or (which is the same thing) one consonant and a double letter, cannot come together, unless either the first or the last of them, or each of these, is a liquid, or σ.

NOTE 8. The letter most commonly dropped, in such cases, is σ followed by θ in the flexion-syllables of verbs; e. g. τέτυφθε instead of τέτυφσθε, πεπλέχθαι instead of πεπλέχσθαι, etc. In like manner ν is sometimes dropped before τ; e. g. τετύφαται instead of τετύφανται, etc. See above, under Note 6.

NOTE 9. Examples of three consonants together, when the first or the

§ 12. CHANGES OF THE VOWELS. 35

last of them is a *liquid*, are πεμφθείς, σκληρός, αἰσχρός, etc. In like manner γ may stand before a K-sound; e. g. τέγξω=τέγκσω, and sounded as τένκσω.

NOTE 10. In compounding words this rule is not observed, in cases where the observation of it would obscure the etymology; e. g. ἐκπτύω, ἐκσπένδω, etc.

GENERAL REMARK. Letters of the same organ, or of the same power, are the ones which are usually exchanged for each other. Thus in the different dialects, all classes of the mutes are sometimes exchanged for each other; and so are the liquids with each other; the double letters with the kindred single ones; σ with the *linguals* (particularly σσ with ττ); so ρσ with ῤῥ, etc. Beyond these general principles the changes do not ordinarily extend; and even here, the law of exchange is far from being universal. Grammars which treat of the dialectical forms, will give particulars.

§ 11. *Doubling and transposition of the Consonants.*

(1) The liquids are most frequently doubled, especially in epic poetry; and, next to these, the mute τ, and the sibilant σ. In the common language, moreover, words beginning with ρ always double this letter, when they receive an accession at the beginning.

E. g. ῥίπτω, ἔῤῥιπτον; ἀπόῤῥητος, from ἀπό and ῥέω. Yet in the N. Test. this is not unfrequently omitted; e. g. ἐραβδίσθην, ἐράντισε, etc.

(2) Transposition sometimes takes place, when a mute, originally separated from a liquid by a vowel, brings that liquid into immediate conjunction with it.

E. g. κραδίη for καρδία; τέθηκα (root θαν), transposed θνα; ἔπραθον root περθ, transposed πραθ. In such cases the vowel of the transposed syllable is not unfrequently changed, as in the last example.

§ 12. *Changes of the Vowels.*

(1) EXCHANGE OF VOWELS. The cases in which vowels are *exchanged* for each other, are very numerous; and they are so various that no general laws regulating them all can well be made out. The student can fully learn them only from usage.

He may easily find that πέρθω, in its derivatives, goes into ἔπραθον and πέπορθα; and so of many others, more or less irregular; but *why* these changes were originally made, lies at present beyond our knowledge, excepting that analogies of other languages afford the like examples, e. g. *do, did; give, gave;* Germ. *geben, gab,* etc.

(2) CHANGE OF QUANTITY. A second change of vowels is that which arises from *lengthening* or *shortening* them into the corresponding long or short vowels or diphthongs. In this case ε commonly goes into ει (rarely η), and ο into ου (rarely ω).

(3) A great part of the differences between the several dia-

lects of Greece, consists in the different vowels which they employ to write and speak the same word.

A minute account of these belongs only to lexicons and grammars designed for the classics.

§ 13. *Elision and Contraction of the Vowels.*

(1) We have seen, in § 10, what changes the Greeks introduced among their consonants, and how frequently they omitted some of them, in order to avoid sounds disagreeable to their ears. From the like source originated the elision and contraction of their vowels, when there was a concurrence of so many, or of such, as made a sound unpleasant to them.

The laws of these contractions, given in the sequel, are very general: but they do not reach every case. The lexicons give the necessary information as to anomalous particulars.

(2) ELISION of vowels is very common in Greek, and has already been treated of in § 8. 3.

(3) CONTRACTION OF VOWELS. This is divided into two kinds, viz. *proper* and *improper*.

I. *Proper contraction* is the union of two vowels into one sound which preserves them both.

E. g. ε ι in ει   η ι in η   ᾰ ᾰ in ᾱ
       ο ι — οι   ω ι — ῳ   ῐ ῐ — ῑ
       α ι — ᾳ   υ ι — υι   (ῠ ῠ does not contract.)

II. *Improper contraction* is of various kinds. It takes place:
(1) When two vowels are combined in one *long kindred* vowel.

1. ᾰ ο ⎫
2. ο ᾰ ⎬ in ω (ου)
3. ο η ⎭

4. ε α in η
5. ε α — ᾱ
6. ε ε — ει

7. ο ο ⎫
8. ο ε ⎬ in ου.
9. ε ο ⎭

E. g. (1) τιμάομεν—τιμῶμεν. (2) αἰδόα—αἰδῶ; μείζονας, μείζους. (3) μισθόητε—μισθῶτε. (4) τείχεα—τείχη. But (5) when a vowel precedes -εα it contracts into ᾱ, as in κλέεα—κλέα, ὑγιέα—ὑγιᾱ. (6) ποίεε—ποίει. (7) μισθόομεν—μισθοῦμεν. (8) μίσθοε—μίσθου. (9) ποιέομεν—ποιοῦμεν.

(2) Improper contraction takes place, when a long vowel or diphthong *ejects* a short vowel, which either precedes or follows it.

E. g. τιμάω—τιμᾷ, φιλέω—φιλῶ, χρυσόω—χρυσῶ, ὑλήεσσα—ὑλῆσσα, λάας —λᾶς; and so before the diphthongs, as φιλέῃς—φιλῇς, φιλέου—φιλοῦ, φιλέοιμι—φιλοῖμι, ἁπλόαι—ἁπλαῖ, etc. But let the reader note, that the rule is not without exceptions, e. g. μισθόητε—μισθῶτε, where the contraction is brought about in another way, i. e. according to No. 1. (3) above. The particular diversities in the mode of contraction must be learned by prac-

§ 13. Contraction of the Vowels. 37

tice. In respect to ω, the short vowel must *precede* it in order to apply the rule; except in the Acc. of some nouns in Dec. III., as ἥρωα—ἥρω.

(3) Also, when the short vowels ἄ, ῐ, ῠ, placed before another vowel, eject it and become long.

1. ἄ ε } into ᾱ
2. ἄ η
3. ῐ α } into ῑ
4. ῐ ε
5. υ ε
6. υ α } into ῡ.
7. υ ι
8. υ η

E. g. (1) τίμαε—τίμᾱ. (2) τιμάητε—τιμᾶτε. (3) πόλιας—πόλῑς. (4) ὄϊες—οἷς. (5) ἰχθύες—ἰχθῦς. (6) ἰχθύας—ἰχθῦς. (7) λελύϊτο—λέλῦτο. (8) δεικνύηται—δεικνῦται, and so in verbs in -υμι.

(4) Another mode of improper contraction is, when a simple vowel precedes a diphthong, and unites with the first letter of it according to the rules already given; and then, if the last letter of the diphthong be ι, it is *subscribed* in case the preceding vowel admits of it, otherwise the last letter of the original diphthong is rejected.

1. α η } into ᾳ
2. α ει
3. α οι into ῳ
4. α ου — ω
5. ε αι — η
6. ε ου } into ου.
7. ο ου

E. g. (1) τιμάῃς—τιμᾷς. (2) τιμάει—τιμᾷ. (3) τιμάοιμι—τιμῷμι. (4) τιμάου—τιμῶ. (5) τύπτεαι—τύπτῃ. (6) ποιέουσι—ποιοῦσι. (7) μισθόουσι—μισθοῦσι. In contracted verbs more vowels than the above rule contemplates would sometimes come together in the full forms, and then a *double* contraction takes place, first of the flection ending, and then of this with the vowel of the root; e. g. ποιέ-εαι, ποιέ-ῃ, ποιῇ · ἐποιέ-εο, ἐποιέ-ου, ἐποιοῦ. The longer forms are the ancient ones; and even they themselves are abridged by omitting the σ in the primitive 2 pers. sing. passive; e. g. the oldest forms were as ποιε-εσαι, ἐποιε-εσο, etc. See § 6, Note 5 for the omission of the σ; also § 10. Note 8.

(5) Peculiar and anomalous are a few contractions, viz.

(1) ο η into οι.   (2) ο ει into οι.   (3) οι into ου.

E. g. (1) μισθόῃ—μισθοῖ. (2) μισθόει—μισθοῖ. (3) μισθόειν—μισθοῦν; but this last comes from the old form μίσθοεν.

Note 1. The attentive reader will of course perceive, that some of the above rules or principles of contraction are seemingly at direct variance with each other; e. g. in No. 2 we have a rule, that *long* vowels or *diphthongs* eject short vowels both before and after them, (and the *extent* of this grammarians do not even attempt to define), while in No. 3 we find short vowels ejecting long ones in some cases. Again, in No. 4 we find that short vowels coming before a diphthong, coalesce with its first letter and frequently subscribe or reject its second, while the diphthongs are said in No. 2 to *throw out* the short vowel. Moreover, the contractions in No. 5 are manifestly discrepant from those in both Nos. 2, 4. The amount of the whole is, that all the different methods of contraction are practised, these on one set of words (e. g. contract verbs), those on another (e. g. nouns, etc. of Dec. I., II., or III.) Usage only can familiarize the learner with the different cases. Still, it should be noted, that ONLY IN VERY FEW CASES DOES THE SAME CONCOURSE OF VOWELS CONTRACT IN DIFFERENT WAYS; viz. ε α into η and ᾱ, and ο ει into οι and ου. The indefinite rule in No. 2 may be rendered somewhat more definite by the remark, that the contractions there designated belong mainly to contract *verbs*; as do those also in Nos. 4, 5.

NOTE 2. The accent is not to be placed on a contracted syllable, unless one of the syllables contracted possessed it before contraction; e. g. ἀοιδή, ᾠδή (still oxytone). But if one of the contracted syllables had the accent, then it is retained and written as circumflex, i. e. if the first syllable was accented and quantity permits, as πλόος, πλοῦς; or, in case the second syllable is accented, as acute, e. g. ἑσταός, ἑστώς.

REMARKS. The Attic very generally (but not always even where it was practicable) made use of the *contracted* forms, in cases such as the above; the Ionic of the *uncontracted* ones. Moreover, the student must understand, that these rules do not reach every individual case of contraction in the Greek language. Particulars are given in good lexicons; the most important of them, however, will be mentioned hereafter under declensions, etc., where they occur.

In Greek poetry, contraction (by synizesis) is to be made by the reader, in very numerous cases, where none is made in writing; see § 8. 4. Note 3.

In a very few cases, contraction causes the accent to be shifted, as ἄεργος, ἀργός; and in some others, the long quantity of contracted syllables is by *usage* short. The lexicons give the necessary information.

§ 14. *Syllabication.*

(1) The general rule is, that a syllable ends with a vowel; but the *final* syllable may end with either a vowel, or with ν, ρ, or σ.

(2) But syllables in the midst of a word often end with a consonant. E. g.

(a) Where the same letter is doubled; as ἄλ-λος, ἄμ-μος, etc. (b) Where a consonant comes after a liquid; as ἕλ-κω. ἀμ-φί, καρ-πός, etc. (c) Where a smooth mute precedes a rough one; as Σαπ-φώ, Βάκ-χος, etc.

NOTE. Recent grammarians prescribe a division of syllables to be made in such a way, that to the succeeding syllable must be attached all concurring consonants which can begin a word in Greek. Consequently, in printing books, we must divide words at the end of a line thus: ὄ-γδοος, ἴ-δμεν, τυ-φθείς, γα-μβρός, etc. But the *ancient* inscriptions follow no such rule; and Kuhner says, it has no internal grounds of support and is contrary to reason. The whole matter is plainly one of mere convenience; and very little if any regard is due to such prescriptions. The best way in printing or writing Greek, is to divide it in such a way as that we can pronounce the syllables in the easiest manner.

PART II.

GRAMMATICAL FORMS AND FLEXIONS.

§ 15. *Parts of speech.*

Logically considered we may divide speech into subject or object, i. e. nouns; predicate, i. e. verbs; and circumstances and relations, i. e. particles. But a much more convenient division, for grammatical purposes, is into *noun, pronoun, article; verb, participle, adjective; adverb, preposition, conjunction, and interjection.*

NOUNS.

§ 16. *Gender of Nouns.*

(1) This is divided into *masculine, feminine,* and *neuter;* which are designated by the prepositive article ὁ, ἡ, τό.

(2) No universal rules can be given respecting gender, which will be of much real use to the student. Of course the names of males, rational and irrational, are generally *masculine;* of females, and also of trees, plants, cities, towns, and countries, *feminine.*

NOTE. Even these laws are far from being universal; e. g. τὸ γύναιον *woman,* τὸ μειράκιον *youth,* τὸ τέκος *child,* τὸ ἀνδράποδον *slave,* all of the neuter gender. So also the names of many places, trees, plants, etc., are *masculine;* e. g. οἱ Φίλιπποι *Philippi,* ὁ φοῖνιξ *the palm-tree,* etc.

(3) A large class of nouns are ἐπίκοινοι (*epicoene*), i. e. common both to the masc. and fem. gender, because they are designations of a *generic* nature, and include both species under them.

E. g. ὁ and ἡ Θεός, ὁ and ἡ ἄγγελος, ὁ and ἡ βοῦς, etc.

§ 17. *Number.*

(1) The Greeks have three numbers, *singular, dual,* and *plural,* in the declension of nouns, pronouns, the article, adjectives, participles, and verbs.

But the dual number is not employed at all in the N. Test.; was not used in the Aeolic dialect; is rare inthe later Greek writers; and is dropped altogether in modern Greek. It appears never to have been much in popular usage; for it is but imperfectly developed, having only two appropriate forms in nouns, etc.; and only so many, or even less, in most of the tenses of verbs.

§ 18. *Declension and Case.*

(1) *Declension* of nouns means a change in their form, in order to designate the different relations in which they stand to other words. The different changes made for this purpose, are called Cases.

(2) There are usually reckoned, at present, *three* declensions in Greek; the first and second are *parisyllabic*, i. e. none of the forms exceed the number of syllables in the ground-form,* the third is *imparisyllabic*.

Originally, as we shall see in the sequel, there appears to have been but *one* declension in Greek. In process of time, however, such changes took place in regard to certain classes of nouns, that they were arranged under different and distinct declensions. The leading ground of distinction or division is *the forms of the dual and plural*. When these are the *same*, however diverse the singular forms may be (e. g. as in Dec. I.), they are ranged under one category.

(3) The Cases are usually reckoned to be *five*. The place of an Ablative is supplied by the Gen., and sometimes by the Dative.

Properly speaking, and in accordance with the definition given above, there are generally but *three* cases in Greek, viz. Gen. Dat. and Acc.; occasionally the Vocative assumes a *varied* form. The Nom. and Voc. are called *independent* cases (casus recti); the Gen. Dat. and Acc., are named *oblique* cases (casus obliqui).

(4) The declensions are distinguished from each other, partly by their endings in the *ground-forms*, partly by the endings of their *oblique* cases in the singular; but principally by the different forms of the dual and plural.

Table of declension endings.

Sing.	Dec. I.		Dec. II.	Dec. III.	
Nom.	η, ᾱ, ᾰ	ης, ᾱς	ος Neut. ον	ς	
Gen.	ης—ᾱς	ου	ου	ος (ως)	
Dat.	η—ᾳ		ῳ	ι	
Acc.	ην—αν		ον	α or ν.	Neut. like the Nom.
Voc.	η—α		ε Neut. ον	—	
Dual.					
N. A. V.	ᾱ		ω	ε	
G. D.	αιν		οιν	οιν	
Plur.					
Nom.	αι		οι Neut. α	ες Neut. ᾰ	
Gen.	ῶν		ων	ων	
Dat.	αις		οις	σιν (σι)	
Acc.	ᾱς		ους α	ᾱς	ᾰ
Voc.	αι		οι α	ες	ᾰ

* The ground-form is the Nom. singular.

§ 19. *General principles of declension.*

(1) The Gen. plural throughout ends in -ων.
(2) The Dat. singular has an Iota, subscript in the two first declensions, and written in the line in the third.
(3) The Voc. is mostly like the Nominative.
(4) All neuters have the Nom., Acc., and Voc. alike; and in the plural these cases always end regularly in -α.

NOTE 1. GROUND OF THESE SIMILARITIES. (a) The present Dec. III. appears to have been formed out of nouns originally ending in a consonant, or in ῐ or ῠ; Dec. II., of those which ended in ο; and Dec. I., out of those which ended in ᾱ. (b) The original mark of the Gen. SINGULAR was ς preceded by ο=ος. (c) The characteristic of the Dat. was ῐ. (d) The Acc. was marked by ν; which, when preceded by α, was frequently dropped. (e) The Voc. was either the same as the Nom., or else the simple root; as euphony might decide.

PLURAL. (f) Nom. character -ες; in Dec. I. II. the ς has fallen out, and the ε is changed into ι, in order to unite with the preceding α and ο—thus making -αι -οι. (g) The original Gen. plur. was -ων added to the Nom. -ες =εσων. Omitting the σ (§ 6. Note 5), we have in Dec. III. -εων, which is contracted into -ων, as κοραξ-έσων, κηραx-έων, κοράκ-ων; and so in Dec. I., the -ων being joined with the vowel α, the latter coalesces, as μουσάων, -μουσῶν; in Dec. II., for λογό-ων we have λόγων. (h) The Dat. plural adds ι or -ιν to the Nom. -ες; as κύν-ες, κύν-εσι (ν). In Dec. I. II. the old Dat. plur. was μούσαισι(ν), λόγοισι(ν)—often this form occurs in Homer, in the Doric, etc.—where the ε in -ες (the common plur. ending) becomes ι, so as to unite in a diphthong with the α of Dec. I. and the ο of Dec. II. (i) The Acc. plur. adds ς to the endings (α or ν) of the Sing., and so makes -ας -νς. But ν before σ falls out of course (§ 10. R. 6), and -ας is adopted in its room. In Dec. I. II. the falling out of the ν is compensated by *prolonging* the preceding vowels; as μούσανς -μούσᾱς, λόγονς -λογούς.

DUAL. (j) The Nom. Acc. and Voc. had originally the end-character -ε. In Dec. I. II. this combines with the preceding vowel; thus μούσαε -μούσᾱ (§ 13. 3. 1), λόγοε -λόγω, (§ 13. 1. 8). (k) The Gen. and Dat. add -ιν to the root; e. g. μούσα-ιν, λόγο-ιν. In Dec. III. the ο in -οιν seems to be a mere union-vowel for the sake of euphony.

These hints respecting the old forms in the declension of nouns, (my limits forbid any more than hints), may help the student to explain the analogies in the declensions, as stated above. The older the Greek, the more traces of these forms are to be found. They will serve to explain many things, moreover, in relation both to the *quantity* of syllables, and the *accentuation* of them; as will be seen in the sequel. It needs but little investigation, in view of the statements just made, in order to see that originally all the declensions were substantially but one. Further developments of this principle will be made in the remarks on each declension.

NOTE 2. To nouns of all declensions the ARTICLE is often attached. As the phases of this are uniform; as they belong alike to all the declensions;

and as it is often convenient to decline by employing the article; it is here inserted for the convenience of the learner.

	Sing.			*Plural.*				*Dual.*		
Nom.	ὁ	ἡ	τό	οἱ	αἱ	τά				
Gen.	τοῦ	τῆς	τοῦ	τῶν	—	—	N. A.	τώ	τά	τώ
Dat.	τῷ	τῇ	τῷ	τοῖς	ταῖς	τοῖς	G. D.	τοῖν	ταῖν	τοῖν
Acc.	τόν	τήν	τό	τούς	τάς	τά				

§ 20. *First Declension.*

(1) Nouns fem. ending in -α -η, and nouns masc. ending in -ᾱς -ης, belong to Dec. I.

Probably the original ending of this Dec. was ᾰς; the ς being a mark of gender, and the α a vowel of the root. In process of time the fem. nouns threw off the ς, while the masc. ones retained it. — The α and η endings seem to be variations by reason of dialects, euphony, etc.; and so in respect to -ᾱς -ης.

(2) PRINCIPLES OF DECLENSION. (*a*) In the *dual* and *plural*, all nouns are declined in the same way.

(*b*) In the *singular*, all nouns ending in -η preserve it uniformly; and the like do all in -α, when a vowel or ρ precedes this -α. In other cases with the -α ending, the Gen. and Dat. take η; but the Acc. and Voc. retain the α.

Exceptions. A few nouns in -ᾱ, of Doric origin, preserve the -ᾱ unchanged, even when it is not preceded by the letters just mentioned; e. g. ἀλαλά -ᾱς, Λήδα -ας, and so of a few other proper names.

(*c*) All masc. nouns in -ας -ης make the regular Gen. in ου (like Dec. II.)

Exceptions. A few common nouns and a considerable number of proper names in -ᾱς, specially contracts in -ᾱς, make the Doric Gen. in -ᾱ; e. g. πατραλοίας, Gen. -ᾱ, Βορρᾶς -ᾱ, Σατανᾶς -ᾱ, etc. This form of proper names is frequent in the N. Testament.

(*d*) The dual and plural of all masc. nouns here, as already noted, are the same as those of the fem. ones. In the *singular*, all nouns in -ας preserve the α throughout, the Gen. sing. and plur. excepted. But nouns in -ης preserve the η only in the Dat. and Accusative singular, elsewhere conforming to the model in -ας, excepting in some Vocatives.

NOTE. The Voc. of nouns in -ης is made by -ᾰ, (1) When the Nom. ends in -της, as μαθέτης, μαθέτα. (2) In the case of *verbals* and *patronymics* ending in -ης; e. g. γεωμέτρης (from γεωμετρέω), γεωμέτρα. Πέρσης, Πέρσα, *a Persian.* With these exceptions, the Voc. preserves the η of the Nom. ending throughout; as Ἀτρείδης, Ἀτρείδη.

§ 20. Nouns: Dec. I. 43

(e) When the ending -α (η) is immediately preceded by ε or α, the usual contraction takes place in a few cases, and the end-syllable then takes a circumflex throughout.

E. g. γαλέη (α), γαλῆ -ῆς, etc.; μνάα, μνᾶ -ᾶς, etc.; Ἑρμέας, Ἑρμῆς -οῦ, etc.; Βορέας, Βορρᾶς -ᾶ (Doric), etc. For this last contraction, see § 13. II. 1. No. 5. But the number of such contracted forms is very small.

(3) The following Paradigms will exhibit the varieties of the first declension.

Sing.	No.1 ή,	No.2. ή,	No.3 ή,	No. 4. ή,	No. 5. ό,	No. 6. ό,	No. 7. ό,
Nom.	τιμή	φιλία	πεῖρα	μοῦσα	νεανίας	προφήτης	γεωμέτρης
Gen.	τιμῆς	φιλίας	πείρας	μούσης	νεανίου	προφήτου	γεωμέτρου
Dat.	τιμῇ	φιλίᾳ	πείρᾳ	μούσῃ	νεανίᾳ	προφήτῃ	γεωμέτρῃ
Acc.	τιμήν	φιλίαν	πεῖραν	μοῦσαν	νεανίαν	προφήτην	γεωμέτρην
Voc.	τιμή	φιλία	πεῖρα	μοῦσα	νεανία	προφῆτα	γεωμέτρα
Dual.							
N.A.V.	τιμά	φιλία	πείρα	μούσα	νεανία	προφήτα	γεωμέτρα
G. D.	τιμαῖν	φιλίαιν	πείραιν	μούσαιν	νεανίαιν	προφήταιν	γεωμέτραιν
Plur.							
Nom.	τιμαί	φιλίαι	πεῖραι	μοῦσαι	νεανίαι	προφῆται	γεωμέτραι
Gen.	τιμῶν	φιλιῶν	πειρῶν	μουσῶν	νεανιῶν	προφητῶν	γεωμετρῶν
Dat.	τιμαῖς	φιλίαις	πείραις	μούσαις	νεανίαις	προφήταις	γεωμέτραις
Acc.	τιμάς	φιλίας	πείρας	μούσας	νεανίας	προφήτας	γεωμέτρας
Voc.	τιμαί	φιλίαι	πεῖραι	μοῦσαι	νεανίαι	προφῆται	γεωμέτραι

Sing.	No. 8. ό,	No. 9. ό,	No. 10, ό,	No 11 ή,	No. 12. ή,	No 13 ό,
Nom.	Ἀτρείδης	Βορρᾶς	Ἀρέτας	γαλ(έη)-ῆ	μν(άα)-ᾶ	Ἑρμ(έας)-ῆς
Gen.	Ἀτρείδου	Βορρᾶ	Ἀρέτα	γαλῆς	μνᾶς	Ἑρμοῦ
Dat.	Ἀτρείδῃ	Βορρᾷ	Ἀρέτᾳ	γαλῇ	μνᾷ	Ἑρμῇ
Acc.	Ἀτρείδην	Βορρᾶν	Ἀρέταν	γαλῆν	μνᾶν	Ἑρμῆν
Voc.	Ἀτρείδη	Βορρᾶ	Ἀρέτα	γαλῆ	μνᾶ	Ἑρμῆ

NOTE 1. *Remarks on the Paradigms.* (1) Nos. 1—4 exhibit the principles of declension as stated in text 2. *b* above. (2) Nos. 5—8 exemplify the principles in text 2. *c. d* and Note, by turning to which the reader will see why Nos. 6, 7, make the Voc. in -ᾰ, while in No. 8 the Voc. preserves the η of the Nominative. (3) Nos. 9, 10, exhibit the Doric Gen. sing., as shown in text 2. *c. Exc.* (4) Nos. 11—13 exhibit the method of declining the few contracts which belong to Dec. I. text 2. *e.* The *full* form is so plain that it needs not to be exhibited. The dual and plural *contracted* are regular, and are circumflexed throughout on the ultimate; e. g. μνᾶ, μναῖν —μναῖ, μνῶν, μναῖς, μνᾶς, μναῖ.

NOTE 2. By turning back to § 19. Note 1, the reader will find, under the account of the formation of the different cases, the ancient forms of words, which solve at once most of the apparent anomalies in quantity and accentuation. E. g. the universally circumflexed Gen. plural comes from the old Gen. -άων, contracted -ῶν; the Gen. and Dat. of *oxytones*, with a circumflex, are accounted for by a reference to the old forms which have been abridged, viz. -άος, -άϊ, and -ήος, -ήϊ, which, when contracted, make

-ᾰς, -ᾰ, and -ῆς, -ῆ. The *long* quantity of -α in the dual, and in the endings -ας, etc., is accounted for in the like way, i. e. by a contraction. For full information, I must remit the reader to Kühner's Grammatik, I. § 256 seq.

NOTE 3. ACCENTUATION. The apparent anomalies have already been mentioned, viz. the Gen. plural always with a circumflex, on the ultimate, and the Gen. and Dat. of all numbers marked in the same way when the noun is *oxytone*. For the rest, the general rule is : *The accent remains on the syllable where it rests in the ground form, so long as the general principles of accentuation allow it.* The meaning is, that the mere change of *quantity* in an end-syllable will not shift the *place* of the accent ; e. g. πολίτης, Voc. πολῖτᾰ, (not πόλιτα because the final -α here is short, although, if mere *quantity* were regarded, this last accentuation would be allowable).

N. B. The particulars of dialectic variations, and the special laws of quantity and accentuation, must be sought for in the larger grammars, as a full exhibition of them would be foreign to the appropriate design of the present work.

§ 21. *Second Declension.*

(1) In common Greek this ends in -ος masc. and feminine, and -ον neuter.

Besides these simple forms, there are some *contracted* ones which are ranged under this Dec.; also some nouns in -ως and -ων, which constitute the so called *Attic* Dec. II.; as will be seen below.

Sing.	N 1. ὁ,	No. 2. ἡ,	No. 3 τό,
Nom.	λόγος	νῆσος	σῦκον
Gen.	λόγου	νήσου	σύκου
Dat.	λόγῳ	νήσῳ	σύκῳ
Acc.	λόγον	νῆσον	σῦκον
Voc.	λόγε (-ος)	νῆσε (-ος)	σῦκον
Dual.			
N. A. V.	λόγω	νήσω	σύκω
G. D.	λόγοιν	νήσοιν	σύκοιν
Plur.			
Nom.	λόγοι	νῆσοι	σῦκα
Gen.	λόγων	νήσων	σύκων
Dat.	λόγοις	νήσοις	σύκοις
Acc.	λόγους	νήσους	σῦκα
Voc.	λόγοι	νῆσοι	σῦκα

NOTE 1. The old Gen. seems to have been, first of all -οος, then (dropping the σ) -οο, and thence -ου comes by *contraction*. The Epic has -οιο ; the Doric, ω ; both derived in like manner.

NOTE 2. The original Dat. plural was -οισι ; which is still common in Epic and Ionic.

NOTE 3. The Voc. in this declension is often like the Nom.; in some words it is *always* so, specially among the Attics. Voc. θεέ occurs in Matt. 27: 46, but θεός is nearly universal in all writers.

§ 22. NOUNS: DEC. II.   45

NOTE 4. A few neuters of this Dec. are *oxytone*; e. g. ζυγόν, πτερόν, etc.

§ 22. Contracts of Dec. II.

(1) Only a small number of words in -ος -ον pure, i. e. preceded by ε or ο, have a form contracted according to the usual rules (see § 13), and then regularly declined.

Sing.	No. 1. ὁ,		No. 2. τό,	
Nom.	πλόος	πλοῦς	ὀστέον	ὀστοῦν
Gen.	πλόου	πλοῦ	ὀστέου	ὀστοῦ
Dat.	πλόῳ	πλῷ	ὀστέῳ	ὀστῷ
Acc.	πλόον	πλοῦν	ὀστέον	ὀστοῦν
Voc.	πλόε	πλοῦ	ὀστέον	ὀστοῦν
Dual.				
N. A. V.	πλόω	πλώ	ὀστέω	ὀστώ
G. D.	πλόοιν	πλοῖν	ὀστέοιν	ὀστοῖν
Plur.				
Nom.	πλόοι	πλοῖ	ὀστέα	ὀστᾶ
Gen.	πλόων	πλῶν	ὀστέων	ὀστῶν
Dat.	πλόοις	πλοῖς	ὀστέοις	ὀστοῖς
Acc.	πλόους	πλοῦς	ὀστέα	ὀστᾶ
Voc.	πλόοι	πλοῖ	ὀστέα	ὀστᾶ

NOTE 1. Anomalies here occur in accentuation; (*a*) The contracted dual Nom. etc. is πλώ, ὀστώ, i. e. it takes only the *acute*, although we should of course expect the circumflex πλῶ, ὀστῶ. (*b*) Compounds with πλοῦς and νοῦς accent the *penult* throughout. (*c*) Some adjectives in -εος -οῦς, although pro-paroxytone, take a circumflex on the ultimate of the contracted forms; e. g. χρύσεος, χρυσοῦς. But it is a *general* law in respect to these endings, when they are contracted either in nouns or adjectives, that *they take a circumflex on the contracted syllable.*

NOTE 2. In the N. Test. νόος is declined as being of Dec. III. throughout; viz. νοῦς, νοός, νοΐ, etc. So in some of the later Greek writers and ecclesiastical fathers. The same is the case with πλοῦς, Gen. πλοός, etc.

§ 23. Attic forms of Dec. II.

(1) These are made by substituting ω for ο or ου, in all cases where the latter would occur in the usual form of declension in -ος -ον; ω is also put for the usual neuter plural ending -α; and Iota in the end-syllable is *subscribed*, whenever it would occur in the usual mode of declension. The rest remains unchanged. As examples we may take λεώς = λαός, and ἀνώγεων = ἀνώγεον.

Sing.	No. 1. ὁ,	No. 1 τό,
Nom.	λεώς	ἀνώγεων
Gen.	λεώ	ἀνώγεω
Dat.	λεῷ	ἀνώγεῳ
Acc.	λεών (-ω)	ἀνώγεων
Voc.	λεώς	ἀνώγεων
Dual.		
N. A. V.	λεώ	ἀνώγεω
G. D.	λεῷν	ἀνώγεῳν
Plur.		
Nom.	λεῴ	ἀνώγεω
Gen.	λεών	ἀνώγεων
Dat.	λεῷς	ἀνώγεῳς
Acc.	λεώς	ἀνώγεω
Voc.	λεῴ	ἀνώγεω

NOTE 1. Only a small number of words are declined in this manner, even by the Attics; and moreover, where this form exists among them, the common forms in -ος -ον are mostly in use at the same time. The peculiar forms of this Attic Dec. seem to have arisen from contraction; thus λαός—λώς, ἀνώγαον—ἀνώγων. For the sake of ease and euphony in pronouncing, the ε was thrown in before -ως -ων. The irregularity of the Attic form, both in declension and accentuation, is remarkable.

NOTE 2. A number of nouns (masc. and fem.) make their Acc. in -ω instead of -ων, as is noted in the Acc. of No. 1. The Gen. of such forms, in Homer, is -ωο.

NOTE 3. The singularity of the accentuation is, that proparoxytones (e. g. ἀνώγεων) preserve their accent unchanged throughout, (contrary to the usual laws of tone); and also that the Gen. sing. of oxytones retains the *acute* on the ultimate (e. g. λεώ), where we might expect the circumflex. See § 7.

Note 2. It would seem that the Attic Gen. -ω, and the ω generally as here employed, were not *practically* long in quantity.

NOTE 4. The neuter plural -ω seems to be a contract of -ωα. But the accentuation has no respect to this.

§ 24. *Third Declension.*

(1) The peculiarity of this Declension, as it now develops itself, is, that the ground-form or Nom. case exhibits, in only a few instances, the real form of the original root. The addition of ς as a sign of masc. or fem. gender in most cases; the prolongation of the final vowel of the root in many others; and lastly the omission of a final consonant in some neuter nouns; (and all this in order to make out the *present* ground forms); conceal the original root by the changes which they occasion. *But the Gen. singular resumes and develops the original form of the root;* and this form may therefore be easily known by merely subtracting -ος from this Genitive.

NOTE. The addition of the gender-sign ς, and the change of quantity in the end-vowel, belong only to masc. and fem. nouns; but the omission of final consonants of the root, takes place occasionally here in nouns of all genders. The *neuter* Nom., however, for the most part exhibits simply the pure root, or at least this root with some slight changes.

FORMATION OF THE NOM. CASE.

(2) NOUNS MASC. AND FEMININE may be divided into three distinct classes as to the manner of forming the Nom. case, when the root ends with a consonant. (*a*) Those which add ς (the gender-sign) to it. (*b*) Those which prolong a final ε or ο of the root, i. e. change them into η and ω. (*c*) Those which preserve the root unchanged in the Nominative.

(*a*) The Nom. takes the additional ς, when the original root ends in either of the mutes; also in many cases when it ends in ν or ντ.

(1) *When the root ends in either of the mutes;* then these mutes undergo the respective changes before the ς, which are indicated in § 10. R. 6.

E. g. (*a*) In roots with final π, β, or φ, only π can be admitted before ς; so that we must have λαῖλαψ (ψ=πς), λαίλαπ-ος· χάλυψ, χάλυβ-ος· κατῆλιψ, κατήλιφ-ος. (*b*) In roots with κ, γ, χ, only κ can be sounded; so κόραξ (ξ=κς), κόρακ-ος· φλόξ, φλογ-ός· ὄνυξ, ὄνυχ-ος. (*c*) The T class, i. e. τ, δ, θ, are thrown out; as φῶς, φωτ-ός· λαμπάς, λαμπάδ-ος· κόρυς, κορυθ-ός. In all these cases, the Gen. (subtracting -ος) gives the original form of the root, and the Nom. shows what effect the final supervening ς has upon that form.

NOTE. When the root ends in -λ, the ς is merely added; as ἅλς, ἁλ-ός.

(2) *When the root ends in -ν or -ντ,* in many cases the ς is added. When this is done, the ν is in general simply thrown out without further change; but -ντ is not only thrown out, but the end-vowel of the root is prolonged as a compensation, in case it was short.

E. g. ῥίς, ῥιν-ός· δελφίς, δελφῖν-ος· (ι long throughout); γίγᾶς, γίγαντ-ος· ὀδούς, ὀδόντ-ος, (vowels lengthened in the Nom.)

NOTE. There is no fixed rule to determine in all cases when a Nom. (with a root in -ν or -ντ) will be formed in this way, or when in the way of merely prolonging the final vowel of the root and retaining the ν; see (*b*) below. But the general principles are, that (1) The end vowel ο or ω takes ν after it; some exceptions, as ὀδούς above, see § 35. 2. (2) Nouns with ε or η take ν. (3) Participles with α, ε, υ, take ς. (4) Nouns and adjectives with α, ι, υ, take ς.

(*b*) When nouns form their Nom. by lengthening the final ε or ο of the root, this root ends in -ν or -ντ; in a few cases also it ends in -ρ. A τ at the end of the root is of course rejected; for a word cannot end in τ.

E. g. ποιμήν, Gen. ποιμέν -ος· δαίμων, δαίμον-ος· λέων, λέοντ-ος· ῥήτωρ, ῥήτορ-ος.

(c) A third class neither receive the ς nor change their final vowel. They end in -ν -ντ, or -ρ; and the Nom. and the root are one and the same; excepting that in words ending with -ντ the τ must of course be omitted at the end.

E. g. παιάν, παιᾶν-ος· αἰών, αἰῶν-ος· θήρ, θηρ-ός· Ξενοφῶν, Ξενοφῶντ-ος.

NOTE 1. In general the *original* vowel of the root is long here. In most cases, also, the ending is -ν or -ρ, which need no change.

NOTE 2. The student will find no trouble in distinguishing this class from any of the preceding, because the Gen. case will develop the nature of it at once. The declension is easy and obvious, inasmuch as merely the case-endings are to be added to the ground-form.

(3) NOUNS NEUTER. These often have the pure root for their ground-form or Nom. case; and when they have τ final in the root, they either omit it in the Nom. or else substitute -ρ or -ς in its place.

E. g. πεπέρι, Gen. -ος· ἄρσεν, -ος· σῶμα, σώματ-ος· χαρίεν, χαρίεντ-ος· ἧπαρ, ἥπατ-ος· τέρας, τέρατ-ος.

NOTE 1. A few neuters have -κτ final, which are dropped in the Nom.; as γάλα, γάλακτ-ος.

NOTE 2. For the most part, the *neuters* in -ν or -ντ are adjectives or participles. When the root of neuters ends, as it usually does, in ν or ρ, or in a vowel, no change is needed for the Nom.; but when it ends it τ, this of course must fall out. Of the mutes, only τ ends the root of neuter nouns.

N. B. *The account given above of ground-forms belongs mostly to nouns the final letter of whose root is a* CONSONANT. *The nouns with a final* VOWEL *mostly belong to what are called the* CONTRACTS *of Dec. III., and will be exhibited in the sequel.*

Formation of the other Cases.

(4) In general the case endings (see § 18. 4) are merely appended to the root simple or modified; but the Voc. has no appropriate and uniform case-ending to distinguish it.

The statement here made is evident at once to the reader, so soon as he casts his eye over the paradigms that follow. But some of the cases have occasional peculiarities, which need to be noted.

NOTE 1. FORMATION OF THE ACC. SINGULAR. Nouns whose root ends in a *consonant* form the Acc. regularly in –α; but (a) Barytone nouns, i. e. not accented on the ultimate, *when they have either of the* T *class of mutes for the final letter of the root*, may take the regular form, or an apocopate one ending with -ν; e. g. χάρις, χάριτα or χάριν· ἔρις, ἔριδ-α or ἔριν· ὄρνις, ὄρνιθ-α or ὄρνιν. But this same class of words, when *monosyllabic* or *oxytone*, form only the regular Acc.; e. g. πούς, πόδ-α· ἐλπίς, ἐλπίδ-α. But κλείς has κλεῖδα and κλεῖν. (b) Words ending in -ις -υς -αυς -ους, simply add -ν to the Acc.; e. g. πόλις, πόλιν· βότρυς, βότρυν· ναῦς, ναῦν· βοῦς, βοῦν.

§ 24. NOUNS: DEC. III.   49

NOTE 2. FORMATION OF THE VOC. SINGULAR. (1) The general piinciple is, that *the Voc. assumes the form of the simple root.* This takes place, (a) Of course in all cases where the Nom. exhibits the root. (b) Where the end-vowel of the root has been lengthened in the Nom., the Voc. shortens it; e. g. δαίμων, δαῖμον· μήτηρ, μῆτερ. EXCEPTIONS are *oxytone* nouns (not adjectives) which retain, in the Voc., the long vowel of the Nom. ; e. g. Nom. and Voc. ποιμήν. But πατήρ, ἀνήρ, σωτήρ, make Voc. πάτερ, ἄνερ, σῶτερ, and are anomalous. (c) When this class of words have dropped an -ν or -ντ in the Nom., the Voc. assumes the short vowel and the ν, or merely omits the τ, which cannot stand at the end of a word; c. g. μέλᾶς (μέλαν–ος), Voc. μέλαν· γίγᾶς (-αντος), Voc. γίγαν· χαρίεις (-εντος), Voc. χαρίεν. (d) Nouns in -ις -υς -αυς -ευς -ους omit the formative ς in the Vocative, and assume the root ; e. g. μάντις, μάντι· πρέσβυς, πρέσβυ· γραῦς, γραῦ· βασιλεύς, βασιλεῦ· βοῦς, βοῦ.

(2) The Vocative, on the contrary, *conforms to the Nom.*, not only when the latter exhibits the simple *root* (see *a* in No. 1), but, (a) In most words where the root ends with a consonant, which cannot stand at the end of a word and must be dropped, or else it takes ς after it, provided the final vowel of the root has not been changed in the Nom.; e. g. Nom. and Voc. φώς (root φωτ·) N. V. νίψ (νιφ·) N. V. σάρξ (σαρκ·) N. V. ὤψ (ωπ.) (b) In oxytones with prolonged vowels in the Nom. ; e. g. N. V. ποιμήν. (c) All participles of Dec. III. have the same Nom. and Vocative.

(3) Nouns in -ω -ως fem. (Gen. -οος) make the Voc. anomalously in -οῖ ; e. g. ἠχώ, ἠχοῖ· αἰδώς, αἰδοῖ.

NOTE 3. FORMATION OF THE DATIVE PLURAL. As this ends in -σι which is added to the *root*, nothing more is needed than the remark, that the same changes occur before σ here, in respect to preceding *mutes*, or -ν -ντ, as take place before ς in the Nominative ; e. g. λαμπάσι for λαμπάδσι, γίγᾶσι for γίγαντσι, ὀδοῦσι for ὀδόντσι, etc. PECULIARITIES : If the Nom. sing. have the diphthongs -αυς -ους, -ευς, the Dat. plural retains them ; e. g. γραυσί, βουσί, βασιλεῦσι.

N B In these general rules for the formation of the cases, some of the principles are applicable, as the reader will see, to nouns whose root has a *vowel* before the Gen. ending -ος But most of these latter nouns have some *peculiarities;* and these will be developed in the sequel.

Accentuation.

NOTE 4. The general rule is, (a) That *all words not monosyllabic in their Nom. case, retain the accent on the same syllable which has it in that case, whenever this can be done.* But,

(b) Monosyllabic words (*participles* excepted) accent the *ultimate* of the Gen. and Dat. of all numbers; see in the Par. ῥίς, θήρ. Ten nouns of this class, however, acute the *penult* in the Gen. sing. and dual ; e. g. φῶς, οὖς, παῖς, etc. Gen. plur. φώτων, ὤτων ; παίδων, παίδοιν, etc. instead of φωτῶν seq. Most of monosyllabic *contracts*, however, are exempt from the general rule as to Gen. and Dative. Participles of this class are also exempt ; e. g. ὤν, ὄντος, ὄντι, etc. Πᾶς conforms to the rule in the sing. number, but not elsewhere, e. g. παντός, but πάντων. Γυνή and κύων follow the rule of monosyllabic words.

(c) There are many anomalies in the accentuation of some nouns be-

7

§ 24. Nouns : Dec. III.

longing to Dec. III. (1) All *syncopated* nouns, in general, throw back as far as possible the accent in the Voc.; see Syncop. Nouns of Dec. III. *c.* Some of them have other irregularities, which are noticed below. (2) The Attic endings -ως -ων have no influence on the accent. (3) Monosyllabic nouns with -ς final in the Nom., and -ν in Acc., and all monosyllabic neuters, *circumflex* the Nom.; other monosyllabic nouns acute it; e. g. μῦς, νοῦς, τὸ πῦρ, but μήν, etc. Κλείς is an exception to the first class. (4) Neuter nouns of more than one syllable throw back the accent as far as they can. For a full account, see large Grammars, specially Kuhner I. § 292.

(5) The *paradigms* which will exemplify the preceding statements, are here arranged in accordance with them.

Sing.	No. 1 ό,	No. 2 ό,	No 3. ή,	No 4. ή,	No. 5 ό,	No. 6. ό,	No. 7. ό,
Nom.	λαῖλαψ	κόραξ	λαμπάς	ῥίς	γίγας	δαίμων	ῥήτωρ
Gen.	λαίλαπος	κόρακος	λαμπάδος	ῥινός	γίγαντος	δαίμονος	ῥήτορος
Dat.	λαίλαπι	κόρακι	λαμπάδι	ῥινί	γίγαντι	δαίμονι	ῥήτορι
Acc.	λαίλαπα	κόρακα	λαμπάδα	ῥῖνα	γίγαντα	δαίμονα	ῥήτορα
Voc.	λαῖλαψ	κόραξ	λαμπάς	ῥίν	γίγαν	δαῖμον	ῥῆτορ
Dual							
N. A. V.	λαίλαπε	κόρακε	λαμπάδε	ῥῖνε	γίγαντε	δαίμονε	ῥήτορε
G. D.	λαιλάποιν	κοράκοιν	λαμπάδοιν	ῥινοῖν	γιγάντοιν	δαιμόνοιν	ῥητόροιν
Plur.							
Nom.	λαίλαπες	κόρακες	λαμπάδες	ῥῖνες	γίγαντες	δαίμονες	ῥήτορες
Gen.	λαιλάπων	κοράκων	λαμπάδων	ῥινῶν	γιγάντων	δαιμόνων	ῥητόρων
Dat.	λαίλαψι	κόραξι	λαμπάσι	ῥῖσι	γίγασι	δαίμοσι	ῥήτορσι
Acc.	λαίλαπας	κόρακας	λαμπάδας	ῥῖνας	γίγαντας	δαίμονας	ῥήτορας
Voc.	λαίλαπες	κόρακες	λαμπάδες	ῥῖνες	γίγαντες	δαίμονες	ῥήτορες

Sing.	No. 8 ό,	No. 9. ό,	No.10. ό,	No.11. τό,	No.12 τό,	No.13. τό,
Nom.	ποιμήν	αἰών	θήρ	σῶμα	φρέαρ	τέρας
Gen.	ποιμένος	αἰῶνος	θηρός	σώματος	φρέατος	τέρατος
Dat.	ποιμένι	αἰῶνι	θηρί	σώματι	φρέατι	τέρατι
Acc.	ποιμένα	αἰῶνα	θῆρα	σῶμα	φρέαρ	τέρας
Voc.	ποιμήν	αἰών	θήρ	σῶμα	φρέαρ	τέρας
Dual						
N. A. V.	ποιμένε	αἰῶνε	θῆρε	σώματε	φρέατε	τέρατε
G. D.	ποιμένοιν	αἰώνοιν	θηροῖν	σωμάτοιν	φρεάτοιν	τεράτοιν
Plur.						
Nom.	ποιμένες	αἰῶνες	θῆρες	σώματα	φρέατα	τέρατα
Gen.	ποιμένων	αἰώνων	θηρῶν	σωμάτων	φρεάτων	τεράτων
Dat.	ποιμέσι	αἰῶσι	θηρσί	σώμασι	φρέασι	τέρασι
Acc.	ποιμένας	αἰῶνας	θῆρας	σώματα	φρέατα	τέρατα
Voc.	ποιμένες	αἰῶνες	θῆρες	σώματα	φρέατα	τέρατα

Explanation of Paradigms. Nos. 1—3 exhibit the manner in which words, whose root ends in one of the mutes (text 2. *a.* 1), are formed and declined.—Nos. 4, 5 show the same, when the root ends in -ν -ντ, and takes -ς in the Nom.; see text 2. *a.* 2.—Nos. 6, 7 illustrate text 2. *b.*—No. 8 illustrates text 2. *b* in connection with text 4. Note 2. *b. Exc.*—Nos. 9, 10 illustrate text 2. *c.*—Nos. 11—13 illustrate text 3 (nouns neuter).

NOTE 1. When a vowel precedes the Gen. ending -ος, and is such as cannot coalesce by contraction with any of the case-endings, or such as that

§ 25. Contract Nouns of Dec. III.

usage does not make it to coalesce, the noun is regularly declined, and does not properly belong to the *contracts* of Dec. III. The declension of such words is too obvious to need special paradigms; e. g. κίς, κίος, κίι, κῖν, κί or κίς, Plur. κίες, etc. So θώς, θωός, θωί, θῶα, θώς, Plur. θῶες, θώων, etc. In like manner some nouns in -ις -υς are declined in the sing., without contraction, as ἰχθύς -υος -υι -υν -υ· πολίς -ιος -ιι -ιν -ι, etc., although by common usage they are more frequently contracted in some of these cases.

NOTE 2. A great number of anomalies belong to this declension; as any one may see by consulting the larger grammars. A good lexicon will note them; and in general they make no special difficulty. It may be proper, however, to note one here which is common, and of some extent, viz. that a number of fem. nouns in -ων, Gen. -ονος -ωνος not unfrequently omit the ν of this ending, and then contract; e. g. εἰκών, contr. Gen. εἰκοῦς, Acc. εἰκώ, Acc. plur. εἰκοῦς. Such contractions are common in the comp. degree of adjectives ending in -ων -ον, which belong to Dec. III. see § 28.

§ 25. Special Forms of Dec. III. (*Contracts*).

In this designation are comprised those nouns in general which have -ος pure in the Gen., i.e. those nouns whose declension-endings are preceded by a *vowel*. Most of these are subject to peculiar modifications, inasmuch as some of their cases are *contracted*.

The reader has already seen, in Note 1. above, that some of such nouns, viz. with -ος pure in the Gen., are simply declined throughout. Where such is the case, nothing special belongs to their development. It is on account of the CONTRACTED NOUNS of this general class, that the following separate forms of declension have been adopted.

FIRST *form of Contracts (of Dec. III.)*

(1) To this belong words ending in

$$\left. \begin{array}{ccc} -ης & -ες & -ος \\ -ω & -ως & \end{array} \right\} \begin{array}{l} \text{Gen. } -εος \\ \ldots -οος \end{array}$$

Of these -ης is masc. and fem.; -ες -ος neut.; -ώ -ώς fem.

Sing.	No 1 ἡ,		No. 2. τό,		No. 3 ἡ,	
Nom.	τριήρης		τεῖχος		ἠχώ	
Gen.	τριήρεος	τριήρους	τείχεος	τείχους	ἠχόος	ἠχοῦς
Dat.	τριήρεϊ	τριήρει	τείχεϊ	τείχει	ἠχόϊ	ἠχοῖ
Acc.	τριήρεα	τριήρη	τεῖχος		ἠχόα	ἠχώ
Voc.	τριῆρες		τεῖχος		ἠχοῖ	
Dual						
N. A. V.	τριήρεε	τριήρη	τείχεε	τείχη	ἠχώ	
G. D.	τριηρέοιν	τριηροῖν	τειχέοιν	τειχοῖν	as Dec. II.	
Plur.						
Nom.	τριήρεες	τριήρεις	τείχεα	τείχη	ἠχοί	
Gen.	τριηρέων	τριηρῶν	τειχέων	τειχῶν	as Dec. II.	
Dat.	τριήρεσι(ν)		τείχεσι(ν)			
Acc.	τριήρεας	τριήρεις	τείχεα	τείχη		
Voc.	τριήρεες	τριήρεις	τείχεα	τείχη		

NOTE 1. (*a*) The forms in -ης -ες belong to *adjectives*. Kühner regards the ς final here as a part of the *root*, and as falling out between vowels in the sequel of declension, and before -σι in the Dat. plural. It is practically more simple for the student to look upon the η in -ης as the prolonged ε of the root, and upon ς as *formative*; although this is not in exact accordance with preceding principles, inasmuch as the *neuter* (e. g. σαφές) exhibits the ς, and therefore it seemingly makes a part of the *root*. But must we assume the form τριήρε-σ-ος for the original Gen.? (*b*) It would seem that the neuters in -ος originally had -ες for their root, and have suffered a commutation of the final vowel ε for the fuller ο; e. g. τεῖχος=τεῖχες, Gen. τείχεος. (*c*) A few ending in -ας are declined after the model here.

NOTE 2. *There are some peculiar modes of contraction here*; e. g. Dual -εε into -η. Moreover when a vowel precedes the neuter plur. ending -εα, this last contracts into -ᾶ, as κλέε-α—κλεᾶ (from κλέος); but the Acc. is sometimes regular, as ὑγιέα—ὑγιῆ in the N. Test. Besides this, *the Acc. plur. contracted is always of the same form with the Nom. plur. contracted*, without regard to the full form.

NOTE 3. Feminines in -ω -ως, contract only in the *singular*. In the dual and plural they are *regular* nouns of Dec. II. The Acc. of nouns in -ω acutes the final ending of the contracted form, as ἠχώ; analogically it would be ἠχᾶ. But the contracted Acc. of nouns in -ως is regular here in respect to accentuation; e. g. αἰδῶ. There are very few of this class of nouns (in common Greek only one in -ως, viz. αἰδώς). The formation of the Nom. here is peculiar, being made from the short ο of the root and omitting the usual formative ς.

NOTE 4. PECULIAR CONTRACTIONS. Proper names ending in -κλεης suffer double contractions in the Dat. singular; e. g. Ἡρακλέης, Dat. Ἡρακλέεϊ, Ἡρακλέει, Ἡρακλεῖ.

NOTE 4. The neuters σέλας and δέπας (Gen. -αος) are declined according to the analogy of this declension; e. g. σέλας, σέλαος, σέλαϊ and σέλᾳ, etc. Dual σέλαε -οιν, Plur. σέλαα, σελᾶ -ων -ασι, etc. Most other nouns in -ας (which belong here) make the Gen. in -εος, as usual.

NOTE 5. The *masc.* nouns of Dec. III., which end in -ως, are *regularly* declined, excepting that the Acc. sing. is sometimes contracted; as ἥρως, Acc. ἥρωα—ἥρω. They do not properly belong to the present declension of *Contracts*.

§ 26. *Second form of Contracts (of Dec. III.)*

(1) This comprises nouns ending in -ις -υς masc. and fem., and -ι -υ neuter.

(2) The class in -ις -υς comprises, (*a*) Nouns with a *long* vowel in the endings -ῑς -ῡς. (*b*) Nouns with a short vowel in -ῐς -ῠς. The former class retain the vowel of their final syllable throughout; the latter, only in the Nom. Acc. Voc. singular.

(3) The endings -ῐς ῐς, also -ῐ -ῠ, out of the N. A. V. sing. substitute ε for the ῐ, ῠ of the final syllables.

(4) Nouns in -ις -ῡς long sometimes contract in the Dat. sing. (when

§ 26. Nouns: Contracts of Dec. III.

this is feasible), and in the Nom. plural, but more commonly only in the Acc. and Voc. plural, yet even here not uniformly. The other class, i. e. nouns with short vowels, are *generally* contracted in the cases just named; and moreover they receive the Ionic Gen. endings -ως -ων sing. and plur., without any influence upon the accent; comp. the like endings in Dec. I. II.

(5) The following paradigms will exhibit these varieties.

I. Nouns in -ις -υς -ι -υ.

Sing.	No. 1. ή,	No. 2 ό,	No. 3 τό,	No 4. τό,
Nom.	πόλις	πῆχυς	ἄστυ	σίναπι
Gen.	πόλεως	πήχεως	ἄστεος (-ως)	σινάπεος (-ως)
Dat.	πόλει	πήχει	ἄστει	σινάπει
Acc.	πόλιν	πῆχυν	ἄστυ	σίναπι
Voc.	πόλι	πῆχυ	ἄστυ	σίναπι
Dual.				
N. A. V.	πόλεε	πήχεε	ἄστεε	σινάπεε
G. D.	πολέοιν	πηχέοιν	ἀστέοιν	σιναπέοιν
Plur.				
Nom.	πόλεις	πήχεις	ἄστη	σινάπη
Gen.	πόλεων	πήχεων	ἀστέων	σιναπέων
Dat.	πόλεσι	πήχεσι	ἄστεσι	σινάπεσι
Acc.	πόλεις	πήχεις	ἄστη	σινάπη
Voc.	πόλεις	πήχεις	ἄστη	σινάπη

II. Nouns in -ις -υς.

	No. 5.				No 6.		
	Sing ό,	Dual	Plural.	Sing ό,		Dual.	Plural.
Nom.	κίς	N. A. V.	κίες	ἰχθύς	N. A. V.	ἰχθύες -ῦς
Gen.	κιός	κίε	κιῶν	ἰχθύος		ἰχθύων
Dat.	κιί	G. D.	κισί	ἰχθύϊ	G. D.	ἰχθύσι
Acc.	κίν	κιοῖν	κίας	ἰχθύν	ἰχθύοιν	ἰχθύας -ῦς
Voc.	κίς		κίες	ἰχθύ		ἰχθύες -ῦς

Note 1. *Explanations*. Nos. 1—4 exhibit the usual forms with ῐ, ῠ, short in the final syllable. Let it be observed, that the Dat. singular and also the Nom. Acc. Voc. plural, *usually* contract as in the paradigms. But it must also be noted, that sometimes in Attic, but specially in the Ionic and Doric, and in poetry, more or less of these forms are used as *uncontracted*, and consequently as declined in a regular way, (like κίς above). But even here, in this mode of declining nouns, those cases *may* occasionally contract which commonly suffer contraction in the other mode of declining. Thus we find πόλις -ιος -ιι (-ῖ) -ιν -ι, Dual -ιε -ιοιν, Plur. πόλιες (πόλῖς) -ίων -ισι—Acc. πόλιας (πόλῖς). There are many nouns in -ις, with Gen. -ος pure, which exhibit the like forms.

Note 2. Adjectives in -υς -εια -υ are declined like πῆχυς and ἄστυ, excepting that the Gen. sing. always ends in -ος, not in the Attic -ως.

Note 3. The class No. II. is not numerous. Monosyllabic roots here (such as κίς, μῦς, etc.) do not usually contract in the plural. Moreover, the long quantity of the ῑ and ῡ in the Nom. is preserved only in the Nom.

Acc. and Voc. singular. It is now maintained by Grammarians, that the Digamma belonged originally to nouns of this class, (e. g. Δίς=ΔιFς, ἰχ-θύς=ἰχθύFς, etc.), which being dropped the vowels became long in the cases just noted. The omission of the Digamma, however, did not influence the *case-endings* before which it fell out. But as such matters cannot be dwelt upon here, I must refer the reader to Kuhner, I. § 287. If we except a regard to the *quantity* of vowels here in the Nom. Gen. and Voc. singular, nothing important can be attached to the distinction made in the paradigms; for it is manifest, that a large class of nouns are often so declined as to preserve the final *ground-vowel* (in -ῖς -ῦς) throughout the other cases; and then, *the first and second classes adopt substantially the like mode of declension.*

NOTE 4. For the Acc. sing. in -ν of nouns in -ις -υς, see § 24. 4. Note 1. *b.*—For forms of the Voc., ibid. Note 2. *d.* The Nom. Acc. Voc., plural neuter in -η, are contracted from -εα the full form.

NOTE 5. Nouns in -ῖς -ῦς, with Attic Gen., are *proparoxytones*, e. g. πό-λεως, πόλεων. But the neuters in -ῐ -ῠ do not generally admit the Attic Gen., and are accented according to common analogy; e. g. ἄστεος, ἀστέων.

§ 27. *Third Form of Contracts (of Dec. III.)*

(1) This is made up, for the most part, by nouns in -ευς; it comprises also the few in -αυς -ους; in all of which the final ς is *formative*, and the *v*, which was originally sounded as F is dropped before the declension-endings beginning with a *vowel*.

(2) For convenience sake these may be divided into two classes:

(1) Nouns in -εύς; which drop the *v* in all cases, excepting Nom. Voc. sing., and Dat. plural; employ the Attic −ος (for -ος) in the Gen. singular; and contract the Dat. sing., and also the Nom. Acc. and Voc. plural.

(2) Nouns in -αυς -ους; which drop the *v* in like manner as the preceding class, with the exception of the Acc. sing.; have a Gen. sing. in -ος; and usually contract only in the Acc. plural.

First form -εύς		Second forms -αυς -ους.			
Sing. ό,	Plural.	Sing ό,	Plur.	Sing. ἡ,	Plur.
Nom. βασιλεύς	βασιλεῖς	γραῦς	γρᾶες	βοῦς	βόες
Gen. βασιλέως	βασιλέων	γραός	γραῶν	βοός	βοῶν
Dat. βασιλεῖ	βασιλεῦσι	γραΐ	γραυσί	βοΐ	βουσί
Acc. βασιλέᾱ	βασιλέας (-εῖς)	γραῦν	γραῦς	βοῦν	βοῦς
Voc. βασιλεῦ	βασιλεῖς	γραῦ	γρᾶες	βοῦ	βόες
Dual. βασιλέε		γρᾶε		βόε	
βασιλέοιν		γραοῖν		βοοῖν	

NOTE 1. The Acc. plur. *uncontracted*, in the first form with -εύς, is the *common* one; its contracted form (βασιλεῖς) is the same as the Nom.; see and comp. § 25. Note 2. This latter form occurs in the N. Test.; e. g. γονεῖς, γραμματεῖς. The -α ending, in the Acc. sing. and plur., is long.

NOTE 2. When -εύς is preceded by a *vowel*, it may contract also in the

§ 28. Nouns: Contracts of Dec. III.   55

Gen. and Acc. sing. and plural, as well as in the usual cases; e. g. χοεύς, χοέως -χοῶς, χοέα -χοᾶ, Plur. χοέων -χοῶν, χοέας -χοᾶς.

Note 3. To the second class in -αυς -ους belong but very few words, viz. γραῦς, ναῦς, and βους, χοῦς, ῥοῦς. Contraction, except in the Acc. plur. (where it is nearly universal), is here seldom to be found. The discrepancies in declension between this class of nouns and that in -ευς, are such as might occasion the former to be ranked somewhere else, or simply to be placed among the irregular nouns, as they have usually been. But Kuhner classes both together on the general ground, that both have a final formative ς, and both end in a υ which was once pronounced as a consonant, i. e. as F. The evidences of this are plain, when we compare ναFς, ναFός, ναFί, etc., with navis, navis, navi, etc.; also βόFς, βοFός, βοFί, etc. and bos, bovis, bovi, etc. So βασιλέFς, βασιλέFος, etc. In all such cases, the F falling out before the declension-endings beginning with a vowel, (which is the common usage), explains the forms as they now appear in the paradigm. For the form of the Voc., see § 24. Note 2. d; for Acc. see § 24. 4. Note 1. b. But nouns in -ευς do not follow the rule there specified.

Note 4. Nearly all the contracted or irregular forms, specially in poetry or in some of the dialects, occasionally appear as regular; e. g. Gen. βασιλέος, Nom. plur. βασιλέες, Acc. plur. βόας, sing. βόα, etc. So some of the uncontracted forms in the paradigm occasionally appear as *contracted*; e.g. βασιλέα-βασιλῆ.

§ 28. *Syncopated Nouns of Dec. III.*

(1) Most of these *contract* after syncope; but some do not, because they are not adapted to contraction. They may be arranged under three classes: (*a*) Neuters in -ας with Gen. -ατος. (*b*) Feminines in -ών with Gen. -ονος. (*c*) Several nouns in -ηρ Gen. -ερος.

(*a*) *Neuters in* -ας.

	Sing.	Dual.	Plural.
N. A. V.	κέρας	κέρατε -αε -ᾱ	κέρατα -αα -ᾱ
Gen.	κέρατος, (κέραης), κέρως	κεράτοιν -άοιν -ῷν	κεράτων -άων -ῶν
Dat.	κέρατι, (κέραϊ), κέρα		κέρασι

(*b*) *Feminines in* -ων -ονος.

Nom.	εἰκών		εἰκόνες
Gen.	εἰκόνος, εἰκοῦς	εἰκόνε	εἰκόνων
Dat.	εἰκόνι	εἰκόνοιν	εἰκόσι
Acc.	εἰκόνα, εἰκώ		εἰκόνας, εἰκοῦς
Voc.	εἰκόν		εἰκόνες

(*c*) *Syncopates in* -ηρ.

Nom.	πατήρ		πατέρες
Gen.	πατέρος, πατρός	πατέρε	πατέρων
Dat.	πατέρι, πατρί	πατέροιν	πατράσι
Acc.	πατέρα		πετέρας
Voc.	πάτερ		πατέρες

Explanations.

NOTE 1. Like κέρας are declined τὸ γέρας, τὸ γῆρας, and τὸ κρέας, i. e. they suffer the syncope of the τ and then contract throughout the dual and plural (Dat. plural excepted), and also in the Gen. and Dat. singular. But τὸ τέρας commonly suffers syncope, etc., only in the plural. In the N. Test. κέρας and τέρας never contract; but κρέας makes plur. κρέᾱ.

NOTE 2. Like εἰκών are declined a number of fem. nouns in -ων; e. g. ἀηδών, χελιδών, ἅλων, etc. Some of them syncopate and contract the Dat., as well as the Gen. and Acc.; e. g. ἀηδοῖ, χελιδοῖ, etc.

NOTE 3. Like πατήρ are declined μήτηρ, θυγάτηρ, ἀνήρ and some others. The peculiarity is, a syncope of the ε in the penult of the Gen. and Dat. singular, and the insertion of α in its room in the Dat. plural. In the word ἀνήρ, however, the ε is omitted in all except Nom. Voc. sing., and δ is put in its place; e. g. Gen. ἀνδρός, Plur. ἄνδρες, ἀνδράσι, etc. Another peculiarity is, that the Gen. and Dat., when syncopated, throw the accent upon the *ultimate*, excepting the Dat. plural; e. g. θυγατρός, θυγατρί. And so in other cases of syncope, which are occasional, but not exhibited in the paradigm; e. g. θυγατρῶν, but Dat. θυγατράσι. The Voc. shortens the ultimate, and throws back the accent as far as it can go.

NOTE 4. I have classed these *syncopates* together here, merely for convenience' sake. Still, there is a common principle of syncope running through the whole, which would justify the present arrangement on other grounds. Usually only the first class—in ας have been reckoned as the *fourth* of the Contracts; but Kuhner makes no separate declension of these nouns. A general similarity in contraction, however, and a thorough one in syncope, renders it desirable to place them together. Classifications of such a nature are indeed somewhat arbitrary; but they should be adapted to convenience. Other syncopates of Dec. III. occur; but the cases are of an isolated kind, and do not well admit of classification.

§ 29. *Anomalies in Declension.*

Whatever does not conform to the general laws of declension, as given above, may be called *anomalous*. The anomalous nouns may be divided into several classes; viz.

(1) Anomalous as to the case-ending.

E. g. Ἰησοῦς, Gen. Dat. Voc. Ἰησοῦ, Acc. Ἰησοῦν. Also Ἰωσῆς, Gen. Ἰωσῆ, Matt. 27: 56.

(2) Anomalous as to the ground-form.

E. g. γυνή, Gen. γυναικός, etc. So ὕδωρ, ὕδατος, etc.; γόνυ, γόνατος, etc. In all nouns of this sort, the oblique cases seem to come from a different ground-form, e. g. γυναίξ, ὕδατ, etc.

(3) *Heteroclites*, i. e. words declined in different ways.

E. g. ὁ μύκης, μύκητος (Dec. III.), also Gen. μύκου (Dec. I.). So χρώς, χρωτός and χροός, etc.; σκότος, σκότου and σκότους, etc.

§ 30. ADJECTIVES. 57

(4) *Metaplasm*, i. e. when a word has but one ground-form in use, but some of the derivate cases are formed in such a way as implies another and different ground-form.

E. g. Ἀίδης, Ἄιδος (and Ἀίδου), etc.; ὁ σῖτος, ὁ δεσμός, plur. σῖτα, δεσμά, etc.

(5) *Defectives*, i. e. those which are wholly wanting in some parts of their declension.

E. g. ὁ αἰθήρ, only in the sing. number; αἱ Ἀθῆναι, only in the plural, etc.

(6) *Indeclinables*; and such are a multitude of proper names.

E. g. specially those of Hebrew origin, in the Sept. and N. Testament; all nouns made by the Inf. mode; all cardinal numbers from 5 to 100; the names of alphabetic letters, as ἄλφα, etc.; some common nouns, as χρεών, δέμας, ὄφελος, etc.

NOTE. Anomalous in some respects more or less, are ἀνήρ, γάλα, γαστήρ, γέλως, γόνυ, γυνή, θρίξ, κέρας, κλείς, κύων, μάρτυς, ναῦς, ὄρνις, οὖς, παῖς, ὕδωρ, υἱός, φρέαρ, χείρ, all in the N. Test.; and many more in the classics. But as the lexicons now give all the requisite information, it is needless to detail the forms here.

ADJECTIVES.

§ 30. *Terminations and flexions of Adjectives.*

(1) Adjectives are so intimately connected with nouns, as qualifying them and being often used for them, that they partake of all the forms and genders of nouns, and are distinguished and declined by the same laws.

(2) TERMINATIONS. These are, (*a*) *Three;* which separately distinguish the masc., fem., and neuter genders. (*b*) *Two;* where the masc. and fem. are not distinguished by their ending; as is the case in Dec. II. and III. of nouns. (*c*) *One;* in which case the adjective is rarely employed in the neut. gender.

(3) FLEXION. In the *first* class, viz. those of three terminations, the masc. and neuter may be of Dec. II., or of Dec. III.; but the fem. is only of Dec. I. The *second* class belong only to Dec. II. or III., because they have no separate fem. form. The third class belong only to Dec. III., or to Dec. I. masculine.

§ 31. Adjectives of three terminations.

	No. 1.			No. 2			No. 3.		
Sing.									
Nom.	καλός	-ή	-όν	νέος	-α	-ον	βαρύς	-εῖα	-ύ
Gen.	καλοῦ	-ῆς	-οῦ	νέου	-ας	-ου	βαρέος	-είας	-έος
Dat.	καλῷ	-ῇ	-ῷ	νέῳ	-ᾳ	-ῳ	βαρεῖ	-είᾳ	-εῖ
Acc.	καλόν	-ήν	-όν	νέον	-αν	-ον	βαρύν	-εῖαν	-ύ
Voc.	καλέ	-ή	-όν	νέος	-α	-ον	βαρύ	-εῖα	-ύ
Dual.									
N. A. V.	καλώ	-ά	-ώ	νέω	-α	-ω	βαρέε	-εία	-έε
G. D.	καλοῖν	-αῖν	-οῖν	νέοιν	-αιν	-οιν	βαρέοιν	-είαιν	-έοιν
Plural.									
Nom.	καλοί	-αί	-ά	νέοι	-αι	-α	βαρεῖς	-εῖαι	-έα
Gen.	καλῶν			νέων			βαρέων	-ειῶν	-έων
Dat.	καλοῖς	-αῖς	-οῖς	νέοις	-αις	-οις	βαρέσι	-είαις	-έσι
Acc.	καλούς	-άς	-ά	νέους	-ας	-α	βαρέας	-είας	-έα
Voc.	καλοί	-αί	-ά	νέοι	-αι	-α	βαρεῖς	-εῖαι	-έα

	No. 4				No 5.	
Sing.						
Nom.	χαρίεις	-εσσα	-εν	μέλας,	μέλαινα,	μέλαν
Gen.	χαρίεντος	-έσσης	-εντος	μέλανος,	μελαίνης,	μέλανος, etc.
Dat.	χαρίεντι	-έσσῃ	-εντι			
Acc.	χαρίεντα	-εσσαν	-εν		No. 6.	
Voc.	χαρίεν	-εσσα	-εν	τέρην,	τέρεινα,	τέρεν
Dual.				τέρενος,	τερείνας,	τέρενος, etc.
N. A. V.	χαρίεντε	-εσσα	-εντε			
G. D.	χαριέντοιν	-έσσαιν	-έντοιν		No 7	
Plur				ἑκών,	ἑκοῦσα,	ἑκόν
Nom.	χαρίεντες	-εσσαι	-εντα	ἑκόντος,	ἑκούσης,	ἑκόντος, etc.
Gen.	χαριέντων	-εσσῶν	-έντων			
Dat.	χαρίεσι	-έσσαις	-εσι		No. 8.	
Acc.	χαρίεντας	-έσσας	-εντα	πᾶς,	πᾶσα,	πᾶν
Voc.	χαρίεντες	-εσσαι	-εντα	παντός,	πάσης,	παντός, etc.

CONTRACTED FORMS.

	No. 9					No. 10			
Sing.									
Nom.	χρύσεος	-οῦς ἑα*	-ῆ	εον	-οῦν	διπλόος	-οῦς ὁη	-ῆ	όον -οῦν
Gen.	χρυσέου	-οῦ ἑας	-ῆς	έου	-οῦ	διπλόου	-οῦ όης	-ῆς	όου -οῦ
Dat.	χρυσέῳ	-ῷ ἑᾳ	-ῇ	έῳ	-ῷ	διπλόῳ	-ῷ ὁῃ	-ῇ	όῳ -ῷ
Acc.	χρύσεον	-οῦν ἑαν	-ῆν	εον	-οῦν	διπλόον	-οῦν όην	-ῆν	όον -οῦν
Voc.	χρύσεε	ἑα	-ῆ	εον	-οῦν	διπλόε	όη	-ῆ	όον -οῦν
Dual									
N.A.V.	χρυσέω	-ώ ἑα	-ᾶ	έω	-ώ	διπλόω	-ώ όα	-ᾶ	όω -ώ
G. D.	χρυσέοιν	-οῖν ἑαιν	-αῖν	έοιν	-οῖν	διπλόοιν	-οῖν όαιν	-αῖν	όοιν -οῖν
Plur.									
Nom.	χρύσεοι	-οῖ ἑαι	-αῖ	εα	-ᾶ	διπλόοι	-οῖ όαι	-αῖ	όα -ᾶ
Gen.	χρυσέων	-ῶν				διπλόων	-ῶν		
Dat.	χρυσέοις	-οῖς ἑαις	-αῖς	έοις	-οῖς	διπλόοις	-οῖς όαις	-αῖς	όοις -οῖς
Acc.	χρυσέους	-οῦς ἑας	-ᾶς	εα	-ᾶ	διπλόους	-οῦς όας	-ᾶς	όα -ᾶ
Voc.	χρύσεοι	-οῖ ἑαι	-αῖ	εα	-ᾶ	διπλόοι	-οῖ όαι	-αῖ	όα -ᾶ

* I give this form according to analogy, and as Matthiae, Buttmann, Rost, and Kühner give it. Thiersch, Passow, Donnegan, etc., give the fem. -ίη here.

NOTE 1. (a) Adjectives in -ος, with three endings, have the fem. in -η; except (as in Dec. I.) the final syllable is preceded by a vowel, or by ρ, in which case it of course takes -α, usually long, like νέος -α -ον. Yet nouns in -οος take -η in the fem., unless ρ goes before; e. g. ὕγδοος -η -ον; but with ρ, like ἀθρόος -α -ον.

(b) ACCENTUATION. In this class, the fem. and neuter preserve the same place of the accent which it occupies in the Nom. masc., in all cases where this can be done, although the nature of the accent must be varied (e. g. καλός, καλή· κοῦφος, κούφη, etc.) as quantity dictates. The Gen. plural has only one form and one mode of accentuation; as the paradigms shew. (c) Most compound adjectives in -ος; also, by Attic usage, many other adjectives in -ιος -ιμος -ειος -αιος; have only two endings, see § 32.

NOTE 2. Let the student compare the masc. and neuter of No. 3 with the second form of contracts belonging to Dec. III. (πῆχυς, ἄστυ); and the fem. with Dec. I. in -α pure; in which case all will be plain. But there are some minute discrepancies; (1) The Gen. sing. is commonly -ος (not -ως Attic). (2) The neuter plur. -εα never contracts. (3) The fem. forms are regularly accented as nouns of Dec. I. of the like quantity; e. g. βαρεῖα, Gen. plur. βαρειῶν.

NOTE 3. In respect to Nos. 4—8, let the reader consult § 24. 2, as to the forms of the Nom., which spring from the root which is developed in the Genitive. The masc. and neuter are mere copies of Dec. III.; the feminine with its accentuation is modelled after Dec. I.; e. g. πάντων, πασῶν. But here too are some minute discrepancies; e. g. -εις -εντος makes the Dat. plural in -εσι (as χαρίεσι), not -εισι as we should expect, comp. § 24. 4. Note 3. But participles like to these adjectives make -εισι in the Dat. plural. N. B. No. 5 has only τάλας of like declension; No. 6 stands alone; No. 7 is followed only by some composites of the same class; and of No. 8 the same is true. But many participles are declined like Nos. 7 and 8.

NOTE 4. Nos. 9, 10, exhibit the Contracts of adjectives with three endings. In most cases they simply conform to contracts in Dec. II. and I. PECULIARITIES; (1) The contractions of -εος and -οος take the circumflex on the ultimate, without regard to the tone in the full form. (2) The contractions of -όη -όα are into -ῆ -ᾶ (not ὤ), contrary to usual custom (§ 13. 3. II. 1.); e. g. διπλόη -ῆ, διπλόα -ᾶ. Comp. Note 1 above for the fem. ending of -οος. If another vowel or an ρ precedes -εος, the fem. contract is -ᾶ; e. g. fem. ἐρέεα -ᾶ, ἀργύρεος -ᾶ.

§ 32. Adjectives of two terminations.

(1) These are, (a) A few of the primitive adjectives in -ος, noted in good lexicons. (b) Most compounds in -ος. (c) The greatest part of those in -ιος -ιμος -ειος -αιος. (d) Those which increase in the Gen., and therefore belong to Dec. III., and have a separate neuter form in the Nom.; e. g. adjectives ending in -ων -ον; -ην -εν; -ης -ες; -ις -ι; -υς -υ; -ωρ -ορ; -ους -ον. (e) Parisyllabics in -ως -ων and -ους -ουν, of Attic and contracted Dec. II.

§ 33. ADJECTIVES.

(2) There is little or no difficulty in declining these; as the fem. forms (being the same with the masculine) are omitted, and all the others are of Dec. II. or III.

Sing.	No. 1. neut.	No. 2.	neut.	No. 3.	neut.	No. 4. neut.
Nom.	ἔνδοξος -ον	ἀληθής	ές	σώφρων	-ον	ἵλεως -ων
Gen.	ἐνδόξου	ἀληθέος -οῦς		σώφρονος		ἵλεω
Dat.	ἐνδόξῳ	ἀληθέϊ -εῖ		σώφρονι		ἵλεῳ
Acc.	ἔνδοξον	ἀληθέα -ῆ	ές	σώφρονα	-ον	ἵλεων
Voc.	ἔνδοξε -ον	ἀληθής	ές	σῶφρον		ἵλεως -ων
Dual.						
N. A. V.	ἐνδόξω	ἀληθέε -ῆ		σώφρονε		ἵλεω
G. D.	ἐνδόξοιν	ἀληθέοιν -οῖν		σωφρόνοιν		ἵλεων
Plur.						
Nom.	ἔνδοξοι -α	ἀληθέες -εῖς ἔα -ῆ		σώφρονες -α		ἵλεῳ -ω
Gen.	ἐνδόξων	ὐληθέων -ῶν		σωφρόνων		ἵλεων
Dat.	ἐνδόξοις	ἀληθέσι		σώφροσι		ἵλεῳς
Acc.	ἐνδόξους -α	ἀληθέας -εῖς ἔα -ῆ		σώφρονας -α		ἵλεως -ω
Voc.	ἔνδοξοι -α	ἀληθέες -εῖς ἔα -ῆ		σώφρονες -α		ἵλεῳ -ω

NOTE 1. No. 1 presents simply the masc. and neut. forms of Dec. II. The *contract* forms of that declension are also imitated by a few adjectives compounded with πλοῦς and νοῦς; e. g. contr. form εὔπλους -ον -ῳ -ουν, Pl. εὔπλοι, neut. εὔπλοα (uncontracted), Acc. εὔπλους—εὔπλοα. The neut. plur. here in -οα does not contract; and the accentuation is peculiar, as the tone remains on the *penult* of all contracted forms; see § 22. Note 1. *b.*

NOTE 2. No. 2 presents the forms in the first of the Contracts, Dec. III., with the neuter gender. When a vowel precedes the ending -ης, then the ending -εα usually (not always) contracts into -ᾶ; as ὑγίεα -ᾶ, but sometimes ὑγιῆ, see § 25. Note 2.

NOTE 3. No. 3 in -ων -ον is a specimen of all adjectives that are of Dec. III. and declined according to its usages. The very few in -υς -υ are modelled after ἰχθύς, Form II. of the Contracts, and are *defectives.*

NOTE 4. No. 4 follows the Attic form of Dec. II. For the neut. plural -ω (not ῳ like the masc.), see § 23. Note 4. For the contracted forms of Dec. II., see Note 1 above.

§ 33. *Adjectives of one ending.*

(1) These are such as have not, or cannot form, any *neuter* termination. Of course, they are usually employed only with nouns masc. and feminine.

Yet in the cases where there is but one form for all genders, (e. g. in the Gen. and Dat.) they are sometimes united with nouns neuter. In all respects they are declined simply as nouns of Dec. I. and III.; and therefore need no paradigms.

(2) There are but comparatively few words of this class; and these have the followings endings, viz.

§ 35. PARTICIPIAL AND ADJECTIVE FORMS. 61

Common gender, Dec. I. μονίας -ον, ἐθελοντής -οῦ. Dec. III. φυγάς -άδος, ἀπιήν -ῆνος, ἡμινθής -ῆτος, ἀγνώς -ῶτος, ἦλιξ -ικος, παραπλήξ -ῆγος, μῶνυξ -χος, αἰγίλιψ -ιπος, ἄναλκις -ιδος, σύγκλυς -υδος, etc. Some, moreover, are used only in the masculine; as γέρων, πρέσβυς, πένης, and others.

§ 34. *Anomalous Adjectives.*

(1) Two of these are very common, viz., μέγας and πολύς. They are declined thus:

Nom. Voc. μέγας   μεγάλη   μέγα | πολύς   πολλή   πολύ
Acc.   μέγαν   μεγάλην μέγα | πολύν   πολλήν πολύ

All the other cases are declined regularly, as if they came from μεγάλος and πολλός. Two original forms seem to be intermixed in these declensions. So the epic of πολύς has a Gen. πολέος, Nom. plur. πολέες -εῖς, etc., shewing a ground-form of Dec. III.

§ 35. *Adjectives and Participles compared.*

(1) ADJECTIVES indicate *quality* or *attribute* simply, without reference to time; PARTICIPLES, while they express the like ideas, convey also the adsigmfication of *time*, in respect to the existence or exertion of quality or attribute. Kühner, in reference to this, styles them *energic adjectives*.

(2) All participles and most adjectives partake of *declension* and *motion*; i. e. they have case-endings, and endings to distinguish the different genders, (which last is technically called *motion*).

All participles have *three* forms for the different genders. But adjectives of the second class have only two, and of the third class but one.

(3) The Vocative of participles is every where like the Nominative, and so differs here from many nouns and adjectives.

(4) For convenience sake the Participles may be divided, as to the mode declension, into three classes; viz.

(1) Such as belong to Dec. III. and I. and insert ντ before -ος of the Gen.; of course these prolong the vowel of the ground-form (§ 24. 2. *a.* 2.); e. g.

(*a*) τύπτων -ουσα -ον, Gen. -οντος -ούσης -οντος. (*b*) στελῶν -οῦσα -οῦν, Gen. -οῦντος -ούσης -οῦντος, (so the contracts and second futures). (*c*) διδούς -οῦσα -ούν, Gen. -όντος -ούσης -όντος, (of the 3d conj. of verbs in μι). (*d*) τύψας -ασα -αν, Gen. -αντος -άσης -αντος. (*e*) τυφθείς -εῖσα -έν, Gen. -έντος -είσης -έντος. (*f*) δεικνύς -ῦσα -ύν, Gen. ύντος -ύσης -ύντος, (4th of verbs in μι).

NOTE. In all these cases, ντ of the Gen. being omitted in the ground-form makes the vowel of that ground-form long, if it be not already so.

Before ς final and formative in the Nom., ε goes into ει, ο into ου; before ν final, ο goes into ω. The double-timed letters (α, υ) are made long, when standing before the formatives ς and ν.

(2) Such as belong to Dec. III. and I., and insert τ before the Genitive; viz. τετυφώς -υῖα -ός, Gen. -ότος -υίας -ότος. Usually ν is the final formative in participles, when ο precedes; but this tense is an exception; see § 24. a. 2. Note 1.

(3) Such as are of Dec. II. and I.; e. g. τυπτόμενος -η -ον, Gen. -ου -ης -ου, etc.; and all regular participles Pass. and Midd., excepting the Aorists of the Passive.

REMARK. These include all the varieties of participial declension; and they are so plain as to need no further explanation. As they all have *three* terminations, they of course are to be compared with Class I. of the Adjectives

§ 36. *Comparison of Adjectives.*

(1) Usually there are reckoned three degrees of comparison, viz. the *positive, comparative,* and *superlative.* But some adjectives from their nature do not admit of the forms of comparison.

Properly speaking, the *positive* is not a degree of *comparison*; it is simply an absolute assertion of quality. But it is not important here to insist on this.

(2) The usual comparison-endings may be ranged under two classes; viz., I. Those in -τερος -α -ον, comp.; -τατος -η -ον, superlative. II. Those in -ίων -ιον, comp.; -ιστος -η -ον superlative.

I. *Comparison by* -τερος -τατος.

(*a*) Most adjectives in -ος, with a *long* penult syllable, drop the ς and merely add the comparison endings; e. g. βέβαιος, βεβαιότερος, βεβαιότατος.

NOTE. It is enough for the application of this rule, if the penult be long merely by position; and even a mute and a liquid will constitute such position and make the rule applicable; e. g. πικρός, πικρότερος, πικρότατος.

(*b*) If the penult be *short*, the ο is prolonged; e. g. σοφός, σοφώτερος, σοφώτατος.

(*c*) Such as are of Dec. III., and end in -υς -υ; -ης -ες; -ας -αν; -αρ; usually add the comparison endings to the simple root. E. g. γλυκύς (-υ), γλυκύτερος, γλυκύτατος· ἀληθής (-ες), -έστερος -έστατος· μέλας (-αν), -άντερος -άντατος· μάκαρ -άρτερος -άρτατος.

(*d*) Most other adjectives of Dec. III. assume their original form, and then add -έστερος -έστατος, or -ίστερος -ίστατος, the -εσ- or -ισ- being euphonic.

E. g. σώφρων, σωφρονέστερος -έστατος· ἀφῆλιξ, ἀφηλικέστερος -έστατος· ἅρπαξ, ἁρπαγίστερος -ίστατος. Those in -εις -εν drop the ν of the simple

§ 36. Comparison of Adjectives.

root, and take σ before the usual endings; as χαρίεις (-εν), χαριέστερος, -έστατος.

II. *Comparison by* -ίων -ιστος.

(4) Usually this is adopted only by a few adjectives ending in -υς and -ρος; and then, by casting away these final syllables and receiving the comparison-forms in the room of them.

E. g. γλυκύς, γλυκίων, -ιστος· αἰσχρός, αἰσχίων -ιστος.

NOTE 1. Only a very few in -υς belong here; for most adjectives of this class are compared as in *c* above. Only a small number in -ρυς also belong here.

NOTE 2. Even some adjectives in -ος form comparisons in this way; e. g. κακός, κακίων, -ιστος· φίλος, φιλίων -ιστος· ὀλίγος, ὀλίγιστος· μέγας, μέγιστος.

III. *Anomalies in the comparison of Adjectives.*

(5) Adjectives in -στενος -κενος (with short penult) take either ω or ο in the comparison; e. g. στενός, -οτερος or -ωτερος, etc.

(6) Adjectives in -οος -οῦς often receive -έστερος -έστατος for the comparison-forms; e. g. ἁπλόος -ἁπλοέστερος -έστατος. But they may also exhibit -ώτερος -ώτατος.

(7) Some adjectives in -ος cast away the -ος, and then affix the comparison-endings; e. g. γεραιός, γεραίτερος -αίτατος· φίλος, φίλτερος, φίλτατος. In like manner,

(8) Some in -ος drop this syllable and then assume -αίτερος -αίτατος· -έστερος -έστατος· or -ίστερος -ίστατος, (instead of the usual -ότερος -ότατος); e. g. μέσος, μεσαίτερος -αίτατος· ἄφθονος, ἀφθονέστερος -έστατος· πτωχός, πτωχίστερος -ίστατος.

(9) Some few adjectives make the comparative degree in -σσων or -ττων; e. g. ταχύς, θάσσων· βαθύς, βύσσων· βραδύς, βράσσων· παχύς, πάσσων· μακρός, μάσσων· ἔλαχυς, ἐλάσσων· (Attice ττ), and some others.

(10) Adjectives anomalous in various respects, are the following; viz.,

	No. 1.			No. 2.	
ἀγαθός	ἀμείνων	ἄριστος	(πρό)	πρότερος	πρῶτος
	κρείττων	κράτιστος	(ὑπό)	ὕστερος	ὕστατος
κακός	χείρων	χείριστος	(ὑπέρ)	ὑπέρτερος	ὑπέρτατος
	κακίων	κάκιστος	(ἐξ)		ἔσχατος
μέγας	μείζων	μέγιστος			
ὀλίγος	μείων	ὀλίγιστος		No. 4.	
πολύς	πλείων	πλεῖστος	(κλέπτης)		κλεπτίστατος
καλός	καλλίων	κάλλιστος	(ἑταῖρος)		ἑταιρότατος
ῥᾴδιος	ῥάων	ῥᾷστος	(βασιλεύς)		βασιλεύτερος
	No. 3.		(κύων)		κύντερος
ἔσχατος	ἐσχατώτερος	ἐσχατώτατος	(κέρδος)	κερδίων	κέρδιστος
πρῶτος		πρώτιστος			

NOTE 1. To some of the irregular adjectives under No. 1. belong, by the arrangement of the lexicons and grammars, a great many more forms of comp. and superlative than I have exhibited. There are also a greater number of these adjectives, than are here presented. But as they belong not to N. T. usage, and may be found in Buttmann, and in other grammars, I purposely omit them. The adjectives under No. 2. show the manner in which the higher degrees of comparison may be formed from *particles*. No. 4. shows the manner in which they may be formed from *nouns*. No. 3. the manner in which another grade of comparison may be, and sometimes is, made from the common superlative, for the sake of high intensity of expression.

NOTE 2. In respect to the many adjectives which will not admit of the *forms* of comparison, the Greeks add (as we do in English) adverbs, etc., which serve the purpose of expressing gradation; e. g. δῆλος *evident*, μᾶλλον δῆλος *more evident* or *specially evident*, δῆλος μάλιστα *most evident* or *altogether evident*, etc.

§ 37. *Declension of the comparative degree.*

(1) The few comparatives which end in -ων -ον are capable of contraction in the Acc. sing., and in the Nom., Acc. and Voc. plural. This is done by dropping the ν, and then contracting the vowels thus brought together in the usual way; comp. 28. 1. *b*.

	Sing.		*Dual.*	*Plural.*			
Nom.	μείζων	-ον		μείζονες	μείζους	-ονα	-ζω
Gen.	μείζονος		μείζονε	μειζόινων			
Dat.	μείζονι		μειζόνοιν	μείζοσι			
Acc.	μείζονα	μείζω -ον		μείζονας	μείζους	-ονα	-ζω
Voc.	μεῖζον			μείζονες	μείζους	-ονα	-ζω

§ 38. *Numerals, Ordinals, etc.*

(1) Only the first four of the original cardinal numbers are declinable; all the rest (from 5 to 10 inclusively, and round numbers of tens, i. e. 20, 30, etc.) up to 100 are *indeclinable*. The round numbers of hundreds, thousands, etc., are regularly declined as adjectives of three terminations; e. g. διακόσιοι -αι -α (200), etc.

(2) The first four cardinal numbers are irregular in their declension; and for convenience' sake they are here subjoined.

Nom.	εἷς	μία	ἕν	τρεῖς	τρία
Gen.	ἑνός	μιᾶς	ἑνός	τριῶν	
Dat.	ἑνί	μιᾷ	ἑνί	τρισί	
Acc.	ἕνα	μίαν	ἕν	τρεῖς	τρία
Nom.	δύο	(δύω)		τέσσαρες	-α
Gen.	δυοῖν	(-εῖν -ῶν)		τεσσάρων	
Dat.	δυοῖν	(δυσί)		τέσσαρσι	(τέτρασι)
Acc.	δύο			τέσσαρας	-α

NOTE. The irregularity of the accent on μιᾶς, etc., δυοῖν, etc., should be noted. The word δύο is not unfrequently used as *indeclinable*, and so in all the cases without variation.

(3) *The Ordinals* are all adjectives of *three* endings and regularly declined, as πρῶτος -η -ον· δεύτερος -α -ον, etc.

(4) *The Multiplicatives* (διπλοῦς, τριπλοῦς, etc.) take the contracted form of πλόος (i. e. πλοῦς of Dec. II.) for their ending, and decline according to this. For accent, see § 22. Note 1. *b*.

(5) *The numeral Adverbs*, beyond ἅπαξ, δίς, τρίς, are formed by the addition of -κις to the numerals; e. g. πεντάκις, ἑκατοντάκις, χιλιάκις, etc.

NOTE. The Greeks, moreover, could with entire ease designate abstract number, i. e. the quality of three, seven, etc., (quasi *threeness, sevenness*), by adding the termination -ας; e. g. τριάς, ἑβδομάς, *triad, hebdomade*, etc.

PRONOUNS.

§ 39. *Personal Pronouns*.

(1) The usual forms of the personal pronouns are the following:

Singular.

	No. 1.	No. 2.	No. 3.
Nom.	ἐγώ	σύ	
Gen.	ἐμοῦ μοῦ	σοῦ	οὗ
Dat.	ἐμοί μοί	σοί	οἷ
Acc.	ἐμέ μέ	σέ	ἕ

Dual.

| N. A. | νώϊ νώ | σφώϊ σφώ | σφωέ σφέ |
| G. D. | νῶϊν νῷν | σφῶϊν σφῷν | σφωίν σφίν |

Plural.

Nom.	ἡμεῖς	ὑμεῖς	σφεῖς, Neut. σφέα
Gen.	ἡμῶν	ὑμῶν	σφῶν
Dat.	ἡμῖν	ὑμῖν	σφίσι
Acc.	ἡμᾶς	ὑμᾶς	σφᾶς, Neut. σφέα.

NOTE 1. In the *singular*, all the oblique cases of each of these three pronouns are enclitic, (excepting the dissyllabic ἐμοῦ, ἐμοί, ἐμέ, which are never so). Moreover, *all* the forms of No. 3 are enclitic, excepting the contracted forms σφεῖς, σφῶν, σφᾶς. But prepositions with tone require the accent on σοῦ, σοί, σέ, οἷ, σφίσι, e. g. παρὰ σοῦ; but the same prepositions usually take the fuller forms of the oblique cases of ἐγώ, which forms are not enclitic, as πρὸς ἐμοῦ. The *toneless* prepositions (ἐκ, εἰς, ἐς, ἐν) are

66 § 40, ETC. PRONOUNS.

connected with *enclitic* forms throughout; e. g. ἔκ μου, ἔν σοι, etc.; and even other prepositions are sometimes used in the same way; e. g. πρός με, περί μου. Emphasis, also, or antithesis, restores the accent to the enclitics; e. g. ἐμὲ ἢ σέ; *me* or *thee*?

NOTE 2. The Nom. of the 3d person is supplied by αὐτός, which originally was demonstrative = *ipse, self*, etc.; but in later times it is often employed as a pronoun personal, although in general of the *emphatic* cast. Kühner derives it from αὖ and τός, i. e. *again this*, q. d. *the same*. The original Nom. of οὗ etc. seems to have been ἴ or ἷ; comp. the Eng. *he*, Lat. *is*, Goth. *is*, Sanscrit *ig-am*, of the same meaning, and radically of the same sound. In the N. Test. the forms in No. 3 are not to be met with; instead of them αὐτός is usually employed.

NOTE 3. The *dialectical* variations of the *forms* of almost all these pronouns are very numerous; see in Buttmann and Kühner. But they are not found in the N. Test.

NOTE 4. The ground of the circumflex accent on nearly all the plural forms seems to be, that they are abridged from the older and fuller forms, e. g. ἡμέες, ὑμέες, σφέες, etc. See in Thiersch's Gr. Gramm. § 77.

§ 40. *Relative Pronouns.*

(1) These are ὅς, ἥ, ὅ, *qui, quae, quod;* and ὅστις, ἥτις, ὅ τι, *quicunque, quaecunque, quodcunque.*

	Singular.			Dual.			Plural.		
Nom.	ὅς	ἥ	ὅ				οἵ	αἵ	ἅ
Gen.	οὗ	ἧς	οὗ	ὧ	ἅ	ὧ	ὧν		
Dat.	ᾧ	ᾗ	ᾧ	οἷν	αἷν	οἷν	οἷς	αἷς	οἷς
Acc.	ὅν	ἥν	ὅ				οὕς	ἅς	ἅ

The other relative (ὅστις) is declined by combining the forms of τίς with those just exhibited.

§ 41. *Demonstrative Pronouns.*

(1) The article ὁ, ἡ, τό, and the pronominal intensive form of it ὅδε, ἥδε, τόδε, are often used as *demonstrative* pronouns; for such was the article in its original usage. For declension, see the article in § 19.

NOTE. It is easy to account for the softening of this *demonstrative* into the article which *specificates, distinguishes, points out emphasis*, etc., as the latter has a kindred use with the former. The τ seems to be the formative characteristic of the article and of most demonstrative words, e. g. τό, τοῦ, etc.; οὗτος=ὁ τός· αὐτός=αὖ and τός, etc. For the use of ὁ, ἡ, τό, as *article*, see Syntax.

(2) The demonstrative pronoun οὗτος, *this, that*, is thus declined:

Singular.

Nom.	οὗτος αὕτη τοῦτο	Dat.	τούτῳ ταύτῃ τούτῳ
Gen.	τούτου ταύτης τούτου	Acc.	τοῦτον ταύτην τοῦτο.

Dual.

N. A.	τούτω ταύτα τούτω	G. D.	τούτοιν ταύταιν τούτοιν.

Plural.

Nom.	οὗτοι αὗται ταῦτα	Dat.	τούτοις ταύταις τούτοις
Gen.	τούτων	Acc.	τούτους ταύτας ταῦτα.

NOTE. Kühner derives this from ὁ and τός, with ν inserted for the sake of euphony. Τός seems to be the old form of a demonstrative.

(3) The other demonstrative, ἐκεῖνος -η -ο, *that one, he, it,* etc., is regularly declined as an adjective; excepting that the *neuter* of the Nom. and Acc. has the ending -ο (not -ον).

§ 42. *Definitive Pronouns.*

These are αὐτός with αὐτός=ὁ αὐτός.

Αὐτός is declined regularly like adjectives in ος -η -ον, excepting that the neuter of the Nom. and Acc. sing. ends in -ο. The Gen., etc., of αὐτός is written ταὐτοῦ, ταὐτῷ, ταὐτόν, etc. (not as τούτου, τούτῳ, τοῦτον, from οὗτος), the *coronis* being designed to show that there is here a crasis of vowels. The Gen. etc. of this αὐτός is also entirely distinct from αὑτοῦ, etc., the contracted form of ἑαυτοῦ, etc.; see § 44. The neuter of αὐτός may however be ταὐτόν, as well as ταὐτό.

NOTE. Αὐτός, used as a *definitive*, in the Nom. signifies *self;* with the article, *the same* or *the self-same;* but the oblique cases of this pronoun usually signify *him, her, it,* etc. But even the Nom. also often stands for *he,* etc., with emphasis; see § 39. Note 2.

§ 43. *Indefinite and Interrogative Pronouns.*

(1) These are τίς, τί and δεῖνα, *some one, something, a certain one,* etc. The former is thus declined:

	Singular.		*Dual.*	*Plural.*		
Nom.	τίς,	τί	τινέ	τινές	τινά	(ἄττα)
Gen.	τινός	(του)	τινοῖν	τινῶν		
Dat.	τινί	(τῳ)		τισί		
Acc.	τινά			τινάς	τινά	(ἄττα)

NOTE 1. All these are *enclitics;* and, excepting in the Nom. sing., the accentuation (always on the *ultimate*) differs every where from that of τίς τί *interrogative,* which always has the *acute* placed on the *ground-syllable,* e. g. τίνος, τίνι, etc. Ἄττα is Attic, for ἅ τινα; and it is not enclitic.

NOTE 2. The forms του, τῳ, are often employed instead of Gen. τινος, Dat. τινι, the usual enclitics.

(2) Δεῖνα is used but once in the N. Testament. It is declin-

ed thus: δεῖνα, δεῖνος, δεῖνι, etc., regularly (the Nom. excepted) as Dec. III. Sometimes it is used as indeclinable.

(3) THE INTERROGATIVE PRONOUNS are τίς, τί, *who? what?* always with the acute, and retaining the accent throughout on the first syllable, as they are *never* enclitic. The Gen. and Dat. apocopate forms are τοῦ, τῷ, which can be distinguished from the article only by the sense.

§ 44. *Reflexive Pronouns.*

These are ἐμαυτοῦ -ῆς, etc., *myself*; σεαυτοῦ -ῆς, etc., *thyself*; ἑαυτοῦ -ῆς -οῦ, etc., or contr. αὑτοῦ -ῆς, etc., *himself*, etc.

NOTE. As these pronouns are employed only when the subject of a sentence (Nom. case) is the same person as the object (oblique case), the Nom. of such reciprocal forms must of course be excluded from use. The composition of the words is plain, viz. ἐμέ, σέ, ἕ, joined with αὐτός. The *composite* forms for the first and second persons are used only in the Singular; the plur. separates the elements, e. g. ἡμῶν αὐτῶν, ὑμῶν αὐτῶν, etc. Of course these have no *neuter* form. But the 3d pers. (ἑαυτοῦ, etc.) has a neuter Acc. ἑαυτό, *itself*; it has also a plur. in the composite form, e. g. ἑαυτῶν, ἑαυτοῖς, etc. Finally, the αὐτός in the composition here does not even generally retain its specific and intensive meaning in the *composite* forms, but these forms may frequently be rendered as a simple pronoun, specially in the contracted αὑτοῦ=ἑαυτοῦ which is very common. When emphasis is specially intended, the words are separated; e. g. ἐμὲ αὐτόν, etc. Kühn., I. § 337. 3. N. B. ἑαυτοῦ, etc. although properly of the *third* pers. only, is frequently employed for other persons; e. g. John 12: 8. 18: 34; and so in the Classics, Winer, § 22. 5.

§ 45. *Reciprocal Pronoun.*

This of course belongs not to the singular, as more than one must necessarily be included. It is regularly declined; but it has no Nom. or Vocative. It is compounded of ἄλλοι ἄλλων, etc.

	Dual.			Plural.
G. D.	ἀλλήλοιν	-αιν -οιν	Gen.	ἀλλήλων
			Dat.	ἀλλήλοις -αις -οις
Acc.	ἀλλήλω	-α -ω	Acc.	ἀλλήλους -ας -α

§ 46. *Pronominal Adjectives.*

These are easily and obviously formed; e. g. ἐμός -ή -όν · σός -ή -όν · ἡμέτερος -α -ον, etc.

NOTE. The third pers., ἑός -ά -όν (more usually ὅς, ἥ, ὅν Att.) does not appear in the N. Test. Instead of these forms we have αὐτός or αὑτός, mostly employed in the Gen. in the room of the pronominal adjective forms. The other pronoun adjectives are unfrequent also in the N. Test., the pronouns (Gen.) being more usually employed in their room. For ἑός or ὅς, we find ἴδιος, *his own*, sometimes used in the N. Test.; e. g. in Matt. 22: 5.

§ 47. *Correlatives.*

These are not properly pronouns, but a kind of pronominal adjectives which serve to show the mutual relations of things to each other, in respect to size, shape, condition, age, etc.

They are of three endings, and are regularly declined. Those beginning with π are distinguished only by the *accent;* the others are distinguished by beginning with τ and ο.

E. g. πόσος, *how great?* etc., ποσός, *of a certain magnitude,* etc.; ποῖος, *how situated?* etc., ποιός, *in a certain condition,* etc.; πηλίκος, *how old?* etc., πηλικός, *of a certain age,* etc. The *demonstratives* and *relatives* of this kind are τόσος, *so great,* etc. ὅσος, *so great as,* etc.; τοῖος, *so situated,* etc., οἷος, *so as, in such condition as,* etc.; πηλίκος, *so old,* etc., ὁπηλίκος, *as old as,* etc. These two latter classes have also several intensive forms.

§ 48. *Pronouns with paragogic forms.*

These are very common.

(*a*) The compound relatives, ὅστις, etc., often add οὖν, or δή, or δήποτε; as ὁστισοῦν, *whoever,* etc.; ὁστισδήποτε, *whosoever,* etc. (*b*) The simple relatives often take πέρ; as ὅσπερ, οἷόσπερ, etc. (*c*) In the Greek ι paragogic is often used, (always with the accent upon it); e. g. οὑτοσί, αὑτηί, τουτί, ὁδί (ὅδε), ἐκεινονί, τοσουτονί, etc. (*d*) The comedians sometimes add γι or δι; as τουτογί, τουτοδί.

VERBS.

§ 49. *Nature, Kinds, and Attributes of Verbs.*

(1) Verbs express *action* of some kind; and this may be, (*a*) *Within the subject;* as κεῖσθαι, ἀνθεῖν, (to lie, to bloom), when the verb is INTRANSITIVE. (*b*) *It may proceed from one agent* (subject), *and operate on another* (object); when the verb is TRANSITIVE.

(2) INTRANSITIVE VERBS in their full extent comprise, besides those simply neuter or intransitive, (1) *Reflexive verbs,* which are such as designate action that proceeds from an agent and returns to himself; as τύπτεσθαι (Mid.) *to smite one's self.* (2) *Passive verbs,* where the *subject* of the verb is at the same time the *object* of the action designated by it, which action proceeds from another; e. g. οὗτοι τύπτονται, *these are beaten,* i. e. by some other than themselves.

NOTE. Some verbs designate *reciprocal* action, i. e. that which proceeds from more than one subject, and is mutually directed toward each; as διαλέγεσθαι, *to hold mutual conversation*. These may be classed among the intransitives, as an offspring of *reflexive* verbs; from which, however, they are specifically distinct.

(3) To a verb belong distinctions of MODE, TENSE, PERSON, NUMBER, and VOICE.

§ 50. *Modes.*

(1) These are the Indicative, Subj., Opt., Imp., and Infinitive.

(2) The Indicative (as its name imports) declares or affirms what is known or regarded as matter of fact or reality.

(3) The Subjunctive expresses that which is supposable, possible, probable, or desirable, in reference to the future when it may be realized.

(4) The Optative expresses what is regarded as supposable or desirable, without definite reference to the fact whether it may be realized or not.

NOTE 1. In other words: The *Subjunctive* expresses possibility, or design, or desire, which is *objective*, i. e. has relation to facts or events that may take place; the *Optative* expresses *subjective* possibility, i. e. a supposition or desire which is merely the act of the mind, without reference to actual decision or realization. Such is the statement made by Kühner and others. But Kühner also ranges both these Modes substantially under one *genus*, viz. the CONJUNCTIVE. The Subj. is regularly and generally connected with the *primary* tenses of the Indic.; the Opt. with the *historical* ones; e. g. πάρειμι ἵνα ἴδω · but πάρην ἵνα ἴδοιμι. The fuller development must be reserved for the Syntax.

NOTE 2. Nothing is more common than the Indic. connected with particles which in themselves imply uncertainty; e. g. with εἰ and ἄν. But in such cases, what is said by the verb is *assumed* as a fact, without inquiring whether it actually is or is not so; e. g. εἰ τοῦτο λέγεις, ἁμαρτάνεις, where the fact of *saying*, whether real or not real, is virtually assumed, i. e. 'assuming that you say this, you are in an error.' So εἰ ἐβρόντησε, καὶ ἤστραψε, i. e. 'assuming that it has thundered, it has also lightened.' So the *Fut.* tense Indic. assumes the future reality of what is declared. But the Subj. and Opt. do not actually *assume*; they merely express supposition, expectation, possibility, desire, etc. Minuter information must be reserved for the Syntax. It is sufficient to remark here, that *may, can, might, could, should, would*, etc., are auxiliaries in English which correspond in the main to the shades of meaning conveyed by the Opt. and Subjunctive.

(5) The Imperative mode expresses command or desire.

(6) The Inf. mode expresses action without limitation of person or number, and partakes of the nature of a noun as well as of a verb.

§ 51. Verbs: Tenses.

NOTE 3. Besides the *modes*, as thus stated, there are also attached to the verb *participial* forms, which partake of the nature of adjectives inasmuch as they signify attribute or condition, but also of verbs inasmuch as they designate the relation of time.

§ 51. *Tenses.*

(1) By the *tenses* of a verb are meant the various forms which it assumes, in order to mark the relations of time in which an action takes place.

(2) Time is naturally divided into Present, Past, and Future. But each of these may be *absolute* or *relative*; absolute, when no reference is made to other events; relative, when such reference is made.

NOTE 1. E. g. γράφω, *I write* or *am writing*, simply indicating the present act; but γράφω ἐν ᾧ σὺ παίζεις, *I write while you play*, is a relative Present. So the Future, γράψω, *I will write*, absolute; but relative, γράψω ἐν ᾧ σὺ παίξει, *I shall write when you will be playing*; and the like of the Past. The Greek furnishes only one and the same form for the Pres. and Fut. absolute and relative; excepting that the Paulopost Future may be regarded as relative. When *speedy* future action is designated, μέλλω is joined to the verb.

NOTE 2. The *Past* makes nicer distinctions. Here absolute time is expressed only by the Aorist; while relative time is marked by the Imperf., Perf., and Pluperfect. The distinctions between these relative tenses, will appear in the sequel.

(3) THE PRESENT expresses action now doing and not completed.

NOTE. General truths or maxims; that which takes place always and uniformly; in a word, whatever is usually done, takes place, or exists; is commonly expressed by the Present; e. g. ἀγαθός ἐστιν ὁ θεός· ὁ ἥλιος λάμπει· Πολλῶν κακῶν αἴτιός ἐστιν ὁ πόλεμος.

(4) THE IMPERFECT is to the past, what the relative Present is to the time now being, i. e. it denotes *action continued and not completed while something else took place*. It is in its proper nature a relative tense, not an absolute one.

E. g. ἔγραφον τὴν ἐπιστολὴν ἐν ᾧ σὺ ἔπαιζες, *I was writing the letter while you were playing*, (for so the defects of our vernacular oblige us to express the idea). The leading characteristic of the Imperf. is, that it expresses *action in progress* or *development*, and usually in reference to something else that was done, or to be done, in past time.

(5) THE PERFECT, on the other hand, expresses the *completion* of an action previous to the time in which it is spoken of, i. e. it expresses *completion in relation to the present time*; and

usually it conveys the idea of *continuance* or *permanence* in the state designated.

E. g. γέγραφα, *I have written*, j. e. finished writing, before the time in which this is said; not *I wrote* some time or other, like the Aorist. It is of course a *relative* Praeterite.

NOTE. In speaking of past actions, however, the Greeks usually employ the Aorist, unless, (*a*) They wish to designate specially a relation of the action to the present time of the speaker; or, (*b*) To designate not merely what is completed, but also what is *abiding* or *continued* in its consequences or operations. To this last circumstance we are to look, in order to explain a great portion of the Perf. tenses which are employed. On this common ground the Pres. and Perf. often meet, and become nearly synonymous.

(6) THE PLUPERFECT stands related to the Perfect, as the Imperf. does to the Present; the Perf. designates action completed before the present time, while the Pluperf. designates *action completed before something else in the past time was done or took place*.

E. g. ἐγεγράφειν τὴν ἐπιστολὴν ἐπεὶ σὺ ἦλθες, *I had written the letter when you came*.

NOTE. It is, however, only when there is a special design to mark the relation between past actions, or else to designate *permanence* or *continued development*, that the Pluperf. is employed. The Aoristic forms are therefore the more common ones in the simple narration of successive events.

REMARK ON THE PRAETERITE RELATIVE TENSES. There are two classes; (1) The Imperf. designating action in time past *continued*, but not completed. (2) The second class comprises those tenses which denote *completed* action in time past; and this class is subdivided into, (*a*) The Perfect, designating action completed before the *present* time. (*b*) The Pluperf., designating action completed before some period in *past* time. This is a very minute and tenuous division of praeterite tenses; and it shews great perfection of development in the Greek verb.

(6) THE AORIST (I. and II.) merely designates *past actions* or *events*, without any relation to other periods of time or action.

E. g. ἔγραψα τὴν ἐπιστολήν, *I wrote the letter* simply, no matter at what period in the past time, for it belongs to the very nature of the Aorist (i. e. *the unlimited*) to leave this undefined.

NOTE. That this should be the usual tense employed in a narration of the past, is obvious from its peculiar nature. That it often is interchanged with the Imperf., Perf., and Pluperfect, and is mingled with them in the same paragraph, arises not from mere confusion of tenses or views, in the writer, but from the design of the writer or speaker to portray events in different attitudes, now as absolute, and then as relative; and particularly, now as momentary, and then as in the progress of development; now as drawn by a mere outline, and then as in an expanded picture.

§ 52. VERBS: TENSES. 73

(7) THE SIMPLE FUTURE (I. and II.), like the Present, may be employed as absolute or relative; (the Paulopost Fut. is relative only). It simply designates action as future, when employed in its absolute sense; in its relative one it marks future action as contemporary with some other action.

E. g. γράψω, *I will write*, viz. at some future period undefined; γράψω ἐν ᾧ σὺ ἐλεύσῃ, *I will write when you shall come*, (relative).

NOTE. As the Aorist spreads over all the past, so the Future tense extends over all the future, and consequently often designates *repeated* or *habitual* future action. From its nature, which seems to imply that which must and certainly will take place, the idea of *necessity, must, ought*, etc. is frequently attached to this tense.

(8) THE PAULO-POST FUTURE (Futurum exactum) is to future time nearly what the Pluperf. is to the past. It designates *action that will have been completed after something yet future has taken place*. At the same time it designates a relation to the present time of the speaker, inasmuch as it marks something which is future in respect to that present time. The idea of *completed action remaining permanent in its consequences and operations*, is usually an appropriate character of this tense, as well as of the Perf. and Pluperfect.

E. g. "If such a guardian over the Commonwealth shall be appointed, τελέως κεκοσμήσεται, *it will have been perfectly set in order*." So ἀεὶ τῆς σῆς φιλίας μεμνήσομαι, *I shall always continue to be mindful of your friendship*, the Fut. exactum making the declaration more intensive than the ἀεὶ makes it.

NOTE. Only a small class of verbs usually form this tense; and where other Futures are lacking, or gone into desuetude, this is sometimes employed in the sense of a simple active or passive Future.

N B For a minute account of the attributes of the Tenses, the reader is referred to the Syntax, where the subject is amply exhibited.

§ 52. *Limited use of the Tenses.*

(1) No verb actually employs *all* the tenses of which it is susceptible. Only a moderate number of tenses are in common use; and with respect to the biform tenses (e. g. Fut. I. II. Aor. I. II.), sometimes one form and sometimes another belongs to prevailing usage, even in cases where the sense may be the same.

(2) The forms of the Imperf., and of the Pluperfect (I. and II.) belong, according to the usual arrangement, only to the Indic. mode.

(3) The Subj. and Imper. modes exclude the Future, in classic Greek.

NOTE. But in the N. Test. we have κανθήσωμαι 1 Cor. 13: 3; κερδηθή–
σωνται 1 Pet. 3: 1; ἀρκεσθησώμεθα 1 Tim. 6: 8; all of Fut. I. pass. Subj.
mode.

(4) The Perfect is seldom employed in the Opt. and Subjunctive;
seldom also in the Imper., excepting in verbs whose Perfect has
the sense of the Present.

(5) Two Futures of the same verb do not occur either in the
Act. or Middle voice.

NOTE. Verbs whose character is a *liquid*, form Fut. II. only; other
verbs have only Fut. I. The exceptions to both of these usages are so rare
as to show that they are mere anomalies.

(6) The 3d Future or Paulo-post belongs to the Passive voice
only.

NOTE. Even here it is rare. Verbs with a *liquid* for their character exclude it; and rarely is it found in those which have a temporal augment, i. e.
which begin with a vowel.

(7) Aorist II. throughout the three Voices is confined to a
small circle of Verbs, as it can be formed only from the simple
root of an original verb.

NOTE. Mr. Sophocles (Gramm. § 105) states the number in the Act. voice
to be 89. This is too limited; but it is easy to see that the number must be
small from the following considerations: (1) *Verba pura*, i. e. those whose
ending in the Pres. (-ω) is preceded by a vowel or diphthong, exclude all
tempora secunda, and of course Aor. II. (2) Only *primitive* verbs can form
Aor. II.; of course it is wanting in all Derivatives, e. g. such as end in -άζω
-ίζω -αίνω -ίνω, and such as are compounds. Of primitives themselves
only a small number form it. (3) Verbs with character τ, δ, θ, do not form
it, except in some cases in epic poetry. (4) Verbs with Liquids rarely admit it. (5) Verbs in –μι exclude it from the Passive. (6) Such simple
verbs as must make the Imperf. and Aor. II. alike, do not form the latter
in the active voice, (they may have it in the Passive); not even in cases
where difference in the *quantity* of the root-vowel might distinguish them;
e. g. γράφω, Imperf. ἔγραφον, Aor. II. Act. wanting, Pass. Aor. II. ἐγράφην·
κλίνω, Imperf. ἔκλινον (ῐ), with only Pass. Aor. II. ἐκλίνην (ῑ).

(8) The Perfect II. is subject to the same narrow limitations
nearly throughout; and of course the Pluperf. II. (its derivate)
must be classed with it in this respect.

NOTE. Mr. Sophocles states the number of Perf. II. at 87 (in § 100);
which is too small. He represents the Perf. of Verbs in -φω -χω as Perf.
II.; which is plainly an error resulting from his imperfect rule of formation.

(9) Verbs with Aor. II. active and middle have no Aor. II.
passive; and *vice versâ*.

NOTE. The probable reason of this is, that the Aor. II. pass. may, and often does, convey the like meanings with the Aor. II. of the other voices. It is of an active form, after the analogy of Aor. II. belonging to verbs in -μι.

(10) The case is rare where the Aorist employs both forms in the same voice.

NOTE. When both are so used, either (1) They have different meanings, e. g. transitive and intransitive, etc. ; or, (2) Belong to different dialects or times, or different species of composition; or, (3) One form supplies defects in another.

The same remarks, in a good measure, may be applied to the use of Perf. I. and II. Seldom do both appear in the same voice, unless the sense of them is distinct.

§ 53. *Classification and Distinction of the Tenses.*

(1) Two Classes are made by grammarians ; (1) The PRIMARY TENSES, which are the Present, Future, and Perfect ; (2) The HISTORIC TENSES, which are the Imperfect, Pluperfect, and Aorists.

NOTE 1. *Primary* or leading tenses the first class are called, because they appear fitted to be considered as the *ground-forms* of all the others; but the name is not given, be it specially noted, in respect to their relative importance, nor their actual precedence even in the order of time. The *historic* tenses are so named, because they are the usual ones employed in narrations respecting past events. They have frequently been called *secondary* tenses, because this naturally distinguishes them from the *primary*. But this method of naming is very inconvenient, inasmuch as the word *secondary* is often needed to denote Fut. II., Aor. II., and Pluperf. II. By this name, or by the equivalent technical one, *tempora secunda*, these three last named tenses are often designated in the present work.

NOTE 2. Neither the name *historic*, nor *secondary*, is exactly accurate ; for in history the Perf. is often employed as well as the other Praeterites, and *secondary*, if applied either to rank or period of origin or actual derivation, would convey a meaning that it would be difficult to vindicate. It matters not, however, when (as here) mere *technical* use is concerned ; for this is definite, and it is such as is here set forth.

NOTE 3. All tenses designating *past* time, are occasionally, and may conveniently be, designated by the generic appellation, PRAETERITES.

(2) The two classes of tenses (primary and historic) are separated from each other by marked distinctions of formation, both as to their *endings* and their *beginnings*. This is best of all explained by a paradigm of the endings.

§ 53. VERBS: TENSES.

Paradigm of Tense endings.

ACTIVE.		PASSIVE.	
Primary.	*Secondary.*	*Primary.*	*Secondary.*
Pres. -ω	Imperf. -ον	Pres. -ομαι	Imperf. -ομην
Fut. 1. -σω	Aor. 1. -σα	Fut. 1. -θήσομαι	Aor. 1. -θην
Fut. 2. -ῶ	Aor. 2. -ον	Fut. 2. -ήσομαι	Aor. 2. -ην
Perf. 1. -κα, ά	Pluperf. 1. -κειν, ειν	Fut. 3. -σομαι	Pluperf. 1. -μην
Perf. 2. -α	Pluperf. 2. -ειν	Perf. -μαι	Pluperf. 2. -wanting

MIDDLE.

Primary.	*Secondary.*
Fut. 1. -σομαι	Aor. 1. -σάμην
Fut. 2. -οῦμαι	Aor. 2. -όμην

NOTE 1. (*a*) In the Middle, the Pres. and Perf. (primary tenses) are of the same form as in the Passive. So also in the *historic* class of tenses the Imperf. and Pluperf. are the same as in the Passive. The reader will perceive, at once, the striking difference between the two *classes* of the tenses; the historic tenses of the Act. (Aor. 1. excepted) all end in -ν; of the Pass. and Mid. all in -ην; while the primary tenses *never* end in this way. (*b*) Besides this, there is another marked characteristic in most cases, viz., in the Indic. the historic tenses all take the augment ε at the beginning (omitted in the Paradigm in order to simplify it); the primary tenses omit this ε, excepting that the Perfect takes a *reduplication*, which remains in all the modes. (*c*) In the primary tenses, the 3d pers. dual ends in the same manner as the 2d pers. (-ον -ον); in the historic tenses it is -ον -ην. (*d*) The 3d pers. plur. of the primary tenses ends in -σι; but in the secondary ones, the same person ends in -ν. (*e*) In the Pass. and Mid. the primary tenses end in -μαι -σαι (ῃ) -ται, etc.; the historic in -μην -σο -το, etc.

NOTE 2. If the reader will compare the Paradigm of the Verbs, he will see that the Subj. mode follows the manner of the *primary* tenses, in respect to the *personal* endings of the verbs, as stated in *c*, *d*; the Optative the manner of the *historical* ones. There are many other resemblances of the like kind, also, in the general structure of these modes. Hence it is, that recent grammarians (e. g. Kühner) call the Subj. *the Conjunctive of the primary tenses,* and the Optative *the Conjunctive of the historic tenses;* not without some good reason.

NOTE 3. TENSE-ENDING, employed as a general appellation, means all which is *suffixed* to the root of the verb in order to form the different tenses, persons, numbers, etc., of any verb. But these again may be analyzed, and will be found to consist of different materials; viz.

(1) When a CONSONANT immediately follows the root of a verb, that consonant is called the TENSE-CHARACTER; (after the analogy of the character-letter in a verb). This belongs only to a part of the tenses, e. g. Fut. 1., Aor. 1., Perf. and Pluperf. I., etc. This *tense-character* remains the same in all the persons of any particular tense.

(2) That VOWEL in the tense-ending which immediately follows the tense-character, or (where this latter is wanting) which immediately follows

§ 53. VERBS: TENSES. 77

the root of the verb, is called the MODE-VOWEL, and sometimes the *union-vowel*. This is mutable, and its different phases distinguish the different modes. A brief statement will exhibit these phases with their various uses.

Indicative; primary tenses, ω, ο, ει, ε; historic, ο, ε; (Act. and Pass.)
Subjunctive; Act. ω, η, ῃ; Pass. ω, η   *Optative;* οι, αι
Imperative;   ε   *Infinitive;* ει, ε, (η)
Participle;   ω, ο, (ει)

To these, however, must be added some peculiar *mode-vowels* mostly of the Aorist; viz., Aor. I. and Perf. I. II. Act. -α -ε; Aor. I. Midd. -ᾰ; Aor. I. Act. and Midd. of the Opt., -αι; Aor. I. Act. Midd. Imper. -ο -α; Inf. of same -α; Part. of same -α (ει). The Pluperf. has ει, rarely ε. This view gives the *original* mode-vowels; which in a few cases have been changed by contraction, e. g. 2d pers. singular of Present, τύπτῃ fiom τύπ-τεσαι, etc.

EXPLANATIONS. (1) The original *mode-vowel* of the Indicative is ε in all cases, except when the personal endings begin with μ or ν, before which ο is the mode-vowel. Two of the present mode-vowels, viz. ω (1st pers. sing.) and ει (3d pers. sing.), are the prolonged ο and ε; prolonged because in the first pers. Pres., μι (in the original τύπτομι) is dropped in order to shorten the form, and ο is changed into ω as a compensation; and ε (in the original τύπτετι or τύπτεσι) is for the like reason changed into ει, because the τι or σι is dropped. So ου in the 3d pers. plur. is ο prolonged because the ν is dropped. In the second pers. sing., τύπτεις, -εσι going into εις, just as μεγίων (comp. of μέγας) goes into μείζων, ἀμενίων into ἀμεί-νων, and θορέσκω into θρώσκω.

(2) As to all the *derived* modes; the Subj. merely prolongs the ε and ο of the Indic.; the Opt. in the way of distinction, takes the diphthongs οι, αι; the Imper. generally ο, but the Aor. Midd. has α; the Inf. ει is a contraction from the old -έμεναι -μεν -ναι (so frequent in Homer), and in contract verbs and in Aor. II. of verbs in general there is a contraction of the root-vowel with this abridged ending, which makes such forms as θελεῖν, τυπεῖν, etc. The η of the Inf. Pass. Aor. I. II., arises from the coalescence of the vowel which here stands attached to the root, (these tenses being formed after the analogy of Aor. 2 of Conj. I. of verbs in μι), with the usual vowel of the Inf. ending. In the Participle, the ω is a prolonged ο after the manner of masc. nouns in Dec. III., § 24. 2. a. 2. b. In Part. Aor. I. II. pass. (τυφθείς, τυπείς), the ει is made from ε (the neuter is τυφθέν) by the dropping of the ντ in the root of the part. form.

(3) The foregoing ingredients being abstracted, the real and proper *personal-endings* remain. In some cases they have indeed disappeared, in the present form of the verb; but most of them appear in some of the dialects, or in the archaeisms of the Greek. Originally they all began with a *consonant*. That the student may see the result of recent investigation in respect to this subject, I subjoin them in the briefest manner possible.

§ 53. Verbs: Tenses.

	Active.		Passive and Middle.	
	(A) *Primary*, Indic. and Subj.	(B) *Historical*, Ind. and Opt.	(A) *Primary*, Ind. and Subj.	(B) *Historical*, Ind. and Opt.
Sing. 1	(μι)	ν	μαι	μην
2	(σι, σθα)ς	ς (σθα)	σαι, η	σο, ο
3	(τι, σι)		ται,	το
Dual.			(μεσθον) μεθον	(μεσθον) μεθον
2	τον	τον	σθον	σθον
3	τον	την	σθην	σθην
Plur. 1	(μες) μεν	(μες) μεν	(μεσθα) μεθα	(μεσθα) μεθα
2	τε	τε	σθε	σθε
3	(ντι) σι, σιν	ν, σαν	νται (αται)	ντο (ατο)

	Imperative.		Imperative.
Sing. 2	(θι) 3 τω		2 σο, ο. (3 σθω)
Dual. 2	τον -των		2 σθον -σθων
Plur. 2	τε -τωσαν		2 σθε -σθωσαν, σθων

The correspondent endings of the Inf. mode (*personal* they cannot strictly be) are -ν -αι -ναι Act., -σθαι Pass. The *root-ending* of the Participle is -ντ -οτ Act., and -μενος -η -ον Passive.

In those cases where a formative personal ending is wanting in common use, in the above paradigm, it is to be understood that it has fallen off in the somewhat later form of the Greek language. Originally, for example, -μι belonged to the Pres.; as τύχωμι, ἔδωμι, etc., in Homer, and also the verbs in -μι -ίστημι, etc., show. So of the 3d pers. sing. Act. -τι -σι; Theocritus has ἐθέλητι, and forms like ἐθέλησι are frequent in the epic dialect. The 1st pers. dual has no separate form in the Act., but it is the same as the 1st pers. plural. For a full development of this subject, see Kuhner I. § 114 seq. In cases like τύπτ-ω, τύπτ-ει, the personal ending has disappeared, and only the mode vowel is retained in the usual flection.*

Such are the distinctions between the *endings* of the different tenses, and

---

* That the reader may see the striking resemblance between the old Greek forms, and those of Sanscrit and the Latin, I here subjoin a specimen, viz. the old Greek verb δάμνημι (=δαμνάω, *to subdue*, etc), in the Aeolic

Greek.	Sanscrit.	Latin
δάμναμι	damyami	damno
δάμνας	damyasi	damnas
δάμνατι	damyati	damnat
	damyawas	
δάμνατον	damyathas	
δάμνατον	damyatas	
δάμναμες	damyamas	damnamus
δάμνατε	damyatha	damnatis
δάμναντι	damyanti	damnant.

It is impossible to compare this, for a moment, without perceiving that the same essential ingredients are exhibited in nearly or quite all of the personal-endings. The Greek, indeed, has not, like the Sanscrit, a separate first pers. dual in the active; and the Latin, also, has no dual. But for the rest, comparison is itself both argument and conviction.

of the component parts of those endings. We must now consider, in the second place, the distinction between the two classes, as made by

§ 54. *The Augment.*

(1) This word is employed by grammarians in a *technical* sense, and does not mean every and any accession to the original root of a verb, but an accession at the *beginning* of it, (viz. ε), as a characteristic of certain tenses, etc.

NOTE. In the use which I here make of the word, I distinguish it from *reduplication* (§ 55), which is also an addition to the beginning of a word; for I employ it as always meaning either the prosthetic ε, or its equivalent in the prolonged time of a vowel, in case the verb begins with a vowel that may be prolonged.

(2) *Augment syllabic or temporal.* When a verb begins with a *consonant* the augment ε makes a syllable by itself, and is therefore called the *syllabic* augment. But when a verb begins with a *vowel*, this ε is made to coalesce with that vowel and thus to prolong its sound; and from this circumstance it is called the *temporal* augment. Both of these species of augment *are limited to the Ind. mode only.*

(3) SYLLABIC AUGMENT. All verbs beginning with a *consonant*, take this augment in all the historic tenses.

E. g. τύπτω, ἔ-τυπτον· γράφω, ἔ-γραψα ἐγεγράφειν, etc.

NOTE 1. But frequently the verbs μέλλω, βούλομαι, δύναμαι, (specially in the Attic), take η instead of ε for the syllabic augment; e. g. ἠμέλησα, ἠβουλήθην, ἠδυνάμην, etc. This usage is occasionally found in the N. Testament.

NOTE 2. The syllabic augment in the Pluperf. is not unfrequently omitted by the Attics; it is in fact the prevailing usage of the N. Testament. Even the Imperf. and Aor. are sometimes used in poetry without it; and in prose χρῆν often stands for ἐχρῆν.

(4) TEMPORAL AUGMENT. When verbs begin with a vowel or diphthong, the prosthetic ε is made in most cases to coalesce with them; e. g.

(*a*) The temporal augment causes a change in the first syllable of verbs beginning with α, ε, o, αι, αυ, οι, and ῐ, ῠ. E. g.

α goes into η, as ἄγω, ἦγον   o — ω, as ὁμιλέω, ὡμίλεον
αι — η, as αἰρέω, ᾕρεον   οι — ῳ, as οἰκτίζω, ᾠκτιζον
αυ — ηυ, as αὐλέω, ηὔλεον   ῐ — ῑ, as ἱκετεύω, ἱκέτευον
ε — η, as ἐλπίζω, ἤλπιζον   ῠ — ῡ as ὑβρίζω, ὕβριζον

In the four last cases here noted, it will be seen that *coalescence* rather than contraction, takes place. At all events, these cases are aside from the common laws of contraction; see § 13.

NOTE 1. A small class of verbs beginning with ε, e. g. ἔχω, ἐάω, ἕλκω, ἕρπω, ἐθίζω, ἕπομαι, ἐργάζομαι, and a few others (noted in the lexicons), take ει (instead of the usual η) for their augmented syllable; as Imperf. εἶ-χον from ἔχω; Perf. εἴργασμαι from ἐργάζομαι, etc.; thus following the usual contraction of εε into ει.

NOTE 2. *Variable usage.* Verbs beginning with ᾰ, αυ, οι, followed by a vowel, *usually* reject the augment; and οι not unfrequently rejects it, even when followed by a consonant. When they do admit the augment, it is usually in the manner above represented; but in a few cases the *syllabic* augment is used instead of the temporal; e. g. ἄγνυμι, Aor. II. pass. ἐάγην· and so ἑάλωκα, etc.

(*b*) Verbs beginning with η, ω, ει, ευ, ου, ῑ, ῡ, generally admit of no augment, inasmuch as the first syllable is already prolonged.

NOTE 3. Yet the Attics, in the case of ευ, frequently admit it. Occasionally, also, some of the other classes of verbs here specified admit it; e. g. ὠθέω, ἐώθουν; and so the irregular Perfects ἔοικα, ἔολπα, ἔοργα.

NOTE 4. In a very few cases, a double and even triple augment is admitted; e. g. the verbs ὁράω and ἀνοίγω take both the syllabic and temporal augment in some of their tenses: Imperf. ἑώρων, ἀνέῳγον, Aor. 1. ἀνέῳξα, Perf. ἀνέῳχα, ἑώρακα, etc. Some of the derivates of ἀνοίγω have, in the N. Test., even a *triple* augment; e. g. ἠνεῴχθη, ἠνεῴξεν. A syllabic augment is found in κατεάγωσι, John 19: 31, 3 plur. 2 Aor. pass. of κατάγνυμι; and a double one in ἀπεκατεστάθη, Matt. 12: 13; in ἠνείχεσθε, 2 Cor. 11: 1; and in some other cases.

N. B. The temporal augment in poetry and in the Ionic is not unfrequently omitted.

GENERAL REMARK. In all cases of augment, it is easy to see that there is but one simple principle, viz., the addition of ε; and *all the changes made by augment have reference merely to the various modes of adding this prosthetic ε*; which either makes a syllable by itself, or is contracted with the succeeding vowel, or else assimilates and coalesces—as the case may require.

§ 55. *Reduplication.*

(1) When verbs begin with a *single* consonant, or with a mute followed by a liquid, the Perfect and its derivatives (Pluperf. and Paulo-post Future) receive a REDUPLICATION at the beginning, which consists of the vowel ε with the first consonant of the original verb prefixed. *This reduplication extends through all the modes*

E. g. τύπτω, τέ-τυφα, ἐ-τε-τύφειν, τε-τύψομαι· γράφω, γέ-γραφα.

(2) EXCEPTIONS. (*a*) Verbs beginning with a double consonant, or with two consonants which are not a mute and a liquid, take only the syllabic augment.

E. g. σπείρω, ἔσπαρκα· ξενόω, ἐξένοχα· ψάλλω, ἔψαλκα· ζηλόω, ἐζήλωκα.

NOTE. *Exceptions:* μνάω makes μέμνημαι, and κτάομαι makes κέκτημαι,

§ 56. Verbs: Reduplication.   81

contrary to this rule. Moreover verbs with γν, γλ, βλ, (i. e. with a mute and a liquid), reject reduplication; e. g. ἐγνώρισμαι, etc. In a few cases the two last admit it.

(b) Verbs beginning with ρ admit no reduplication, but receive the syllabic ε and double the ρ.

E. g. ῥάπτω, ἔῤῥαφα. In like manner they double it in all the augmented secondary tenses; as Imperf. ἔῤῥαπτον, etc. Yet in the N. Test. it is sometimes single, as ἐράντισε, Heb. 9: 19, so 2 Cor. 11: 25. Heb. 10: 22. Matt. 26: 67. The like is found in Greek poetry, and sometimes in prose.

(c) Five verbs beginning with a liquid take ει instead of reduplication.

E. g. λαμβάνω, εἴληφα· λαγχάνω, εἴληχα· λέγω (I gather), εἴλεγμαι· ῥέω, εἴρηκα· μείρομαι, εἵμαρται. Even Aor. 1 retains the ει in John 8: 4, κατειλήφθη; and so in old Ionic.

Remark. It should be noted, that the Pluperfect has in reality a double accession, viz. the *syllabic* augment and also the *reduplication*, when verbs begin with a consonant.

§ 56. *Attic reduplication.*

(1) This is so called, not because it is used nowhere but in the Attic dialect (for it is even most common in the old epic dialect), but because the Attics frequently employed it, and for the sake of distinction. It consists mostly in repeating the two first letters of a Verb, which begins with the vowel α, ε, or ο, before the usual forms of the Perfect; and it remains through all the modes.

E. g. ἀγείρω, ἀγ-ήγερκα· ἐμέω, ἐμ-ήμεκα· ὀρύττω, ὀρ-ώρυχα· ὄζω (=ὄσ-δω), ὄδ-ωδα.

Note. In case the root is dissyllabic, and the second syllable is *long*, this reduplication *shortens* it; e. g. ἀλείφω, ἀλ-ήλιφα· ἀκούω, ἀκ-ήκοα· ἐλεύθω, ἐλ-ήλυθα, etc. Exception: ἐρείδω, ἐρ-ήρεικα.

(2) In the epic, the 2 Aor. frequently has the Attic reduplition; in which case the temporal augment is prefixed to the *reduplication*, while the radical part omits it.

E. g. ἄρω, Aor. 2 ἤραρον· ἄγω, ἤγαγον· φέρω (ʼΕΓΚΩ) ἤνεγκον. The two last are used even in common prose, and frequently in the N. Test.

§ 57. *Augment in compound verbs.*

(1) General Rule. When a verb is compounded with a separable preposition, the augment comes between this and the verb; but when it is compounded with other words, the augment is usually (not always) prefixed.

E. g. προσφέρω, προσέφερον. The final vowel of prepositions (where they have one) is dropped in such cases; e. g. ἀποπέμπω, ἀπέπεμπον; excepting in περί and πρό, as περιβάλλω, περιέβαλλον· προπέμπω, προέπεμπον, (usually with crasis in the case of πρό, as προὔπεμπον). As to denominative verbs, i. e. those derived from nouns, the augment usually *precedes*, as ἀντιδικέω (from ἀντίδικος), ἠντιδίκουν· μυθολογέω, ἐμυθολόγουν.

NOTE 1. Usage is not invariable in these cases. Some verbs closely compounded with prepositions receive augments like simple verbs; e. g. καθίζω, ἐκάθιζον, etc. Some adopt both forms; e. g. καθεύδω, ἐκάθευδον and καθηῦδον.

NOTE 2. Several verbs with prepositions take a double augment; e. g. ἀνέχομαι, ἠνειχόμην· ἐνοχλέω, ἠνώχλουν. So also διακονέω (as if it were a compound), ἐδιηκόνουν, δεδιηκόνηκα.

(2) Verbs compounded with εὖ and δυσ- take the temporal augment *after* these, if a vowel follows which is capable of it; otherwise (i. e. if an immutable vowel or a consonant follows), the augment stands at the beginning of the word.

E. g. εὐεργετέω, εὐηργέτησα· δυσαρεστέω, δυσηρέστουν; on the other hand, εὐτυχέω, ηὐτύχησα· δυστυχέω, ἐδυστύχησα· δυσωπέω, ἐδυσώπουν.

§ 58. *Person and Number of Verbs.*

In the Greek verb *three* persons, sing., dual, and plural, are designated. But the 1st pers. Dual of the Active has no separate form for itself, and coincides with the first pers. of the plural.

NOTE. The Dual is not a thing of *necessity*, like the sing. and plural; for most languages have it not. The older Greek frequently employs it; the latter, more seldom; the modern, not at all. When in common use, it was at the option of the writer or speaker. In what manner the several persons and numbers are distinguished, we have already seen in § 53, *Parad. of personal-endings.*

§ 59. VOICES.

(1) These are the *Active, Passive,* and *Middle.*

NOTE 1. The word *voice* means, of itself, merely *sound* or *word.* But being joined with the adjectives *active, passive,* or *middle,* it designates the various modes in which a word is inflected, in order to give it the various meanings designated by these words. The most recent grammarians substitute *form* for voice. Sometimes they employ the Latin *genus* in the same sense.

(2) The ACTIVE VOICE denotes action which proceeds from the subject (Nom.) of the verb. When this action terminates on another and different object, the verb is *transitive;* when it is confined within the agent or subject of the verb, it is *intransitive.*

§ 60. Verbs: Voices. 83

E. g. τύπτει *he beats* [some one]; but χαίρει *he rejoices*, ἀνθεῖ *it blooms*. This latter sense (intransitive), however, is not confined to the active only; the middle voice frequently expresses it.

(3) The PASSIVE VOICE is a form of the verb designed to signify, that the *subject* of the verb is also the *object* of the action indicated by it.

E. g. τύπτομαι, *I am beaten;* in which case the action terminates on the subject of the verb, while the agent is not brought to view. On the contrary, the active voice transitive presents the agent himself as the subject of the verb, and indicates, by some complement that follows it, the object on which the action designated terminates. In order that the passive voice should be definitely marked, it is furnished with forms differing from those in the active voice; and when the agent is to be designated from which the action proceeds, this is done in Greek by a noun in the Gen. with ὑπό, πρός, or παρά before it, or by a noun in the Dative without any preposition.

(4) The MIDDLE VOICE is distinguished from the Active by its forms, and generally by its signification; from the Passive, in part by its forms, but more particularly by its significations. It usually has an *intransitive, reflexive,* or *reciprocal* sense.

NOTE. It is customary to represent the Middle Voice as principally, if not entirely *reflexive.* Yet there are but very few forms where it is directly so, like λούομαι, *I wash myself,* etc. In most cases, where the peculiar sense of the Middle Voice is exhibited, it designates the doing of something *for one's self, for his own advantage, gratification, use,* etc., or *by his own desire, command, procurement,* etc. The *reciprocal* meaning is naturally connected with the reflexive; the intransitive meanings, and in some cases even the transitive ones, cannot well be translated so as to distinguish them from the like ones in the Active. But see Synt. for further development.

§ 60. *Similarity of Voices in some Tenses and Meanings.*

(1) The Greek has not developed separate forms for all the tenses of each Voice; particularly is this the case with the Middle, according to the usual place assigned it.

(2) *The same forms of Pres., Imperf., Perf., and Pluperf., belong to the Passive and Middle.* The sense demanded by each passage is the only means of distinguishing the one from the other.

NOTE. But in the Fut. and Aorists each of these Voices has its own proper development; so that these forms in the Middle are usually either reflexive or intransitive and *not passive.* In poetry, where the shorter forms of Fut. Midd. are frequently convenient, they are often used in a *passive* sense; but not elsewhere. In a few cases, e. g. σχέσθαι, κατέσχετο, ἐλίποντο, etc., Aor. II. seems to be *passive;* but it may be otherwise rendered; see Kühner II. § 400.

§ 60. Verbs: Voices.

(3) Aor. I. pass. is sometimes employed in a reflexive and intransitive sense; particularly where appropriate forms of the Middle are wanting, or are less euphonic.

E. g. φοβηθῆναι *to fear*, πορευθῆναι *to depart*, κοιμηθῆναι *to sleep*; ἀσκηθῆναι *to exercise one's self*, εὐωχηθῆναι *to feast one's self*, κατακλιθῆναι *to lay one's self down*, etc. In its *intransitive* senses Aor. I. pass. differs not substantially from the like meanings in the Aor. Act. and Midd.; in its *reflexive* senses it agrees with the Aor. Middle. In fact, intransitive and reflexive meanings are more often conveyed, on the whole, by the pass. Aorists, than by the Middle ones; Kühn. § 86.

(4) Aor. II. pass. is so often *intransitive*, that this is its predominant meaning, and would fairly entitle it to be ranked (like Perf. II.) under the *active* voice.

Note. (*a*) This intransitive sense often approaches more nearly to the Act. than to the Passive, and the verb may then be translated accordingly. Very often the Aor. I. Act. has a transitive sense, and Aor. II. pass. a corresponding intransitive one; e. g. ἔφηνα *I showed*, ἐφάνην *I appeared*, etc. In the English language, however, we are compelled to translate many verbs here *passively*, which in the Greek have merely intransitive meanings. (*b*) The very form and flexion of this tense throughout show that it is formed after the analogy of Aor. II. Act. of verbs in -μι; see Kuhner § 402.

Remark. Although Aor. I. II. Mid. are not used *passively*, yet since the common ground of *intransitive* and *reflexive* meaning is occupied here by Aor. I. II. both Mid. and Pass., it must depend more on special usage, the choice of the writer, and the demands of the context, than on the form of the tense, what meaning shall be given to these respective tenses in any particular instance.

(5) As both the Act. and Mid. may also have an *intransitive* meaning, so the act. and midd. Voice must often occupy common ground.

Note. This is not in reality so fully true of the Greek, as of our own language which is employed to translate it. Very many Greek verbs are employed in a *reflexive* sense, which we cannot so translate; and this, because our idiom is so different. In this way many intransitive verbs, in Greek, necessarily appear simply passive or active in our own language. Hence, while we need not say that the Act. and Middle are often really commuted in Greek, yet we may say, that by reason of our own idiom we are often obliged to translate them as if they were equivalent. Particularly is it the case, that *the Fut. Middle is employed in a like sense, or in the same sense, as the Fut. Active*, when the Fut. act. is obsolete, or rare, and also in many of the commonly occurring irreg. verbs; specially is this the case in the N. Test.; e. g. θαυμάσομαι, γελάσομαι, ἄσομαι, ἔσομαι, βήσομαι, λήψομαι, γενήσομαι, ὄψομαι, χαρήσομαι, ἐλεύσομαι, and many others.

General Remarks. It follows, of course, from the above view of several tenses in the different voices, that much was left to the choice of the writer or speaker, when he wished to convey *intransitive* meanings. He might select either Voice. Yet usage in many cases had limited one sense to one form of the Aor. or Fut., and another to another; and with this he must comply. But a range so ample in choice must well suit the purposes of poetry and rhetoric.

§ 61. *Deponent Verbs.*

(1) With the phenomena of the preceding Section, may be classed the so called DEPONENT VERBS, i. e. those which, with a pass. or midd. form, may have an active, passive, or medial signification.

(2) Some of these verbs, in some of the tenses, have both the pass. and midd. forms, and with these connect their appropriate signification; while in other cases the meaning is not determined merely by the form.

E. g. δέχομαι, ἐδεξάμην *I received*, ἐδέχθην *I was received*; and so in many verbs. Yet this is not so in all; e. g. μέμψασθαι and μεμφθῆναι *to find fault with.* The Pres., Perf., and Pluperf. are of course but of one form, and they vary as the case requires in respect to meaning.

NOTE. The *active* sense, even *transitive*, is not unfrequent, although the latter is not very common; e. g. δέχομαι [τι] *I take* [something]; ἐργάζομαι [τι] *I perform* or *produce* [something]. The *neuter* or *intransitive* sense, however, is the most common, when these verbs have an active meaning; and this is, indeed, their predominant meaning in the earlier Greek, but not in the later. This agrees well, as we have seen, with the nature of the Mid. voice.

§ 62. *Pure and impure, i. e. simple and augmented, Roots of Verbs.*

(1) A great number of verbs in the Greek language appear, in the Present and Imperf., in a form augmented, i. e. fuller than that which the other tenses naturally derived from the Present would lead us to suppose they originally had. Whatever may have been the reality in the case, it greatly aids us in the analysis and synthesis of verbs, to assume the fact in question. The simple root thus assumed is usually named THEME.

E. g. all the other tenses of τύπτω, appear to be derived from the simple root τύπω. In most cases, indeed, the *simple* form of the Present (where an augmented one is in use), is no longer extant as being actually employed. But still, in a few cases two forms are in actual use; e. g. λείπω and λιμπάνω, ἔδω and ἐσθίω, λανθάνω and λήθω, τρέπω and τράπω, etc. On this ground, and principally because of its great utility to the learner of grammar, *simple* roots are supposed by grammarians to have existed, where *augmented* ones only are found to be now actually employed. The derivate tenses can then be formed with great ease, when the *theme* or *simple root* is once known, or assumed.

NOTE. Sometimes more than one theme must be assumed; e. g. εὗρον, εὑρήσω, themes ΕΥΡ, ΕΥΡΕ.

§ 62. Verbs: Simple and Augmented Roots.

(2) The forms of verbs that are original and simple, are technically called PURE ; the augmented forms (by way of distinction) IMPURE. The latter belong only to the Pres. and Imperfect.

NOTE. Beyond these tenses, verbs in many cases drop the adscititious part of the Present; the *secondary* tenses always come from the *pure* theme ; the others are of a mixed character, varying with the different kinds of verbs.

(3) The impure forms may be made so by the addition of a consonant to the pure root, or by the prolongation of the vowel in that root.

(A) *By the addition of a Consonant.*

(4) The mass of simple and *original* verbs which receive accession in the Present by the addition of consonants, may be classed as follows :

(*a*) *Verbs with character* πτ.* Here the τ is added in order to make the *augmented* form ; and the *simple* character may be either π, β, or φ.

E. g. Τύπτω from τύπω, κρύπτω from κρύβω, ῥάπτω from ῥάφω. The reason why the original root is obscure in the Present of the second and last of these examples, is, that the adjectitious τ in each case causes a change in the preceding β and φ, i. e. it turns them into π; see § 10, R. 2. The β and φ of the root of course go into π before the -σω of the Fut. § 10, R. 6.

(*b*) *Verbs with* σσ *or* ττ (*sometimes* ζ). These have κ, γ, or χ, but mostly γ, for their simple character ; yet a few with character τ, δ, θ, assume this form in the Present.

NOTE 1. Here the original and simple *character* is wholly obscured in the Present; and the student can know which of all the letters just named constitutes it, only from some of the derivate tenses which develope it. Thus πράσσω is the augmented form of πράγω, φρίσσω of φρίκω, βήσσω of βήχω; all of which must have a common character in the Future, viz. κ before the formative -σω (κ in combination with σ and by an orthographical abridgment is written ξ=κς); see § 10, R. 6. The true roots therefore must be found by the aid of the 2 Aor. or 2 Perfect.

NOTE 2. As to the others, very few cases exist of the Present with σσ or ττ, having a simple character τ, δ, or θ. Of these, πλάσσω, Fut. πλάσω · πάσσω, Fut. πάσω, etc., are examples. Here we know from the Future with merely -σω (and not -ξω), that the *character* of the root could have been neither κ, γ, or χ, because these would make κσ=ξ. But whether the root has τ, δ, or θ, cannot be determined merely by the Future; for before the ending of the Future (-σω), each of these letters would fall out, § 10, R. 6. Other tenses of course must determine, e. g. λίσσομαι, Aor. II. ἐλιτό-

---

* *Characteristic letter* or *character* (χαραχτήρ) of a verb, is the technical name which is given to one or more consonants or vowels that *immediately* precede the final -ω of the 1st pers sing Present; e. g. in λέγω, τι'πτ-ω, τάσσ-ω, λύ-ω, τιμά-ω, φοιτεύ-ω, — γ, πτ, σσ, υ, α, ευ, are *characters* of their respective verbs.

§ 63. Verbs: Formation of Tenses. 87

μην; or if there are none, it can be determined only by correlative nouns, etc., which may lead to the knowledge of it.

(c) *Verbs with character* ζ=σδ. Most of these have δ for their character in the simple root; but some have γ; a very few γγ.

E. g. φράζω from φράδω, ὔζω from ὔδω; but also κράζω from κράγω. A great proportion (but not all) of verbs in -άζω -ίζω have δ for their simple character. Most verbs in -ζω, which designate *tone* or *sound* (as κρώζω, στενάζω, etc.) have γ for their simple character. A few, such as ἁρπάζω, βαστάζω, etc. form the Fut. both in -σω and -ξω, and of course have either δ or γ as a simple character. A small number have γγ as their original character; e. g. σαλπίζω, Fut. σαλπίγξω=σολπίγγ-σω, etc.

(d) Liquid Verbs. These have λλ or μν in the augmented form, while the simple theme has only λ and μ.

E. g. στέλλω, στελῶ· τέμνω, τεμῶ. Nearly all the original liquid verbs are prolonged in this way, or by protracting the vowel of the root, as noticed below.

Gen. Remark. In all these classes of verbs, the *ground-form* is a model only for the Present and Imperf. of all the voices. Fut. 1 in -ψω (=πσω) always shows that the simple character of the root must have been π, β, or φ; Fut. 1 in -ξω (=κσω) shows that the root must have had κ, γ, or χ in it; Fut. 1 in -σω, shows that either τ, δ, or θ was in the root, and has been thrown out (§ 10. R. 6); or else that the verb belongs to the class of *verba pura*, e. g. such as λύω, λύ-σω, etc. The student will see by this, that Fut. 1, (and of course all the tenses derived from it and conforming to it, i. e. Aor. 1, and Perf. with Pluperf. 1), cannot be relied on to trace any thing more than merely the *class* of mutes to which the character of a verb belongs. Which of the three letters in that class was the actual one in the root, must be decided either by Aor. 2, Perf. and Pluperf. 2, or else by some of the kindred derivates, such as nouns, adjectives, etc., coming from the original stock or root. The 2 Aor., and Perf. with Pluperf. 2, are all the tenses that necessarily retain the *original* character of the verb, in each of the three classes of mutes; all the other tenses either follow the ground-form where the character is obscured, or are changed by accession, or else are modelled after Fut. 1, which, as we have just seen, but partially developes the original character.

(B) *By the prolongation of vowels.*

(5) In many impure roots the vowels are *prolonged*, but not altogether in the usual method. The true roots of those which have prolonged vowels, are disclosed by Aor. II. in some one of its forms; or, in Liquids, by Fut. II.

Illustration. As Aor. II., which can be formed only from *original* (not from derived) roots, develops the true vowel of the primitive root, in all those cases where there has been no *vowel-exchange* (see No. 6 below), by comparing this with the actual Present, the nature and extent of the prolongation in question is easily found. It is as follows: viz. the vowels of

Aor. II., (Fut. II. of liquid verbs), and of course of the simple and original theme, are lengthened in the augmented Present, E. g.

α into η, as ἔλαθον, λήθω
αι — ἐφάνην, φαίνω
ει — ἐφθάρην, φθείρω
δ ει — κτενῶ, κτείνω

ι into ει — ἔλιπον, λείπω
ῐ — ἐτρίβην, τρίβω
ῠ — ἔφυγον, φεύγω
ῠ — ἐφρύγην, φρύγω

General Remark on finding the simple root. In respect to some of the diphthongs and prolonged vowels, only the *tempora secunda* will decide with certainty; as is plain from the table above. But where two consonants appear as *character*, reject the second. But in ζ (=σδ) reject the first; and so when ευ, ει, come before a *mute*, reject the first vowel.

(6) In many cases Aor. II. and Perf. II. take a *vowel* different from that in the simple root. But this belongs to the formation of the *derivate* tenses, and will be considered in the sequel.

NOTE. In such cases, it is evident that the *tempora secunda* would not be the exact index of the simple root. It is important, therefore, to know what these cases are; and the sequel will disclose them.

§ 63. *Formation of the Tenses.*

(1) Strictly speaking, every tense has its own appropriate formation and characteristics, and is not dependent on, or derived from, any other tense.

It would be scientifically correct, therefore, to point out the manner in which each appropriate tense-ending and augment (where the latter is employed) is united with the root, either in its augmented or simple state, and there to leave the matter; as Kühner has done. But the mass of learners would not be able to avail themselves so well of this method, as of the ordinary one of tracing an analogy and connection between diverse tenses. As this method of proceeding is wholly arbitrary, so far as it respects the derivation of one tense from another, it is obvious that only the most plain and facile method should be adopted. With this artificial connection, however, many things of fundamental importance respecting the real development of the tenses are of necessity intermingled; so that this part of grammar, in its present shape, can not well be neglected.

(2) From some classes of verbs certain tenses are wholly excluded; in others partially admitted. The rules given for the formation of all tenses, can of course apply only where any particular tense is admissible.

E. g. The whole class of *verba pura* (contracts and others) admit no *secondary* tenses, i. e. no Fut., Aor., Perf., or Pluperf., second. *Derivative* verbs are almost equally exclusive. Liquid Verbs admit no Paulo-post.

Formation of the primary Tenses in the Active.

(3) *The Present* is formed by annexing ω to the root either simple or augmented.

§ 63. VERBS: FORMATION OF TENSES, ACT. 89

E. g. λύ-ω, τύπτ-ω. The old pronominal formative -μι is here dropped in verbs with -ω final, and the ω is only the mode-vowel (o) prolonged.

(4) THE FIRST FUTURE is formed by adding -σω to the *simple* root; and when the character is a mute, by subjecting that mute to such changes as the σ in the formative syllable requires.

NOTE 1. The Future of verbs with λ, μ, ν, ρ for their character, and of contracts in -άω, -έω, -όω, are not here included, as they have peculiarities of their own which will be stated in their proper place.

NOTE 2. ILLUSTRATIONS. (1) All *verba pura* (not contracts) merely append -σω to the root; e. g. λύω, λύσω· κελεύω, κελεύσω, etc. (2) All verbs with a simple and original consonant for their character in the Present, merely add -σω and conform or drop the consonant, as the σ may require; e. g.

No. 1.	No. 2.	No. 3.
λείπω, λείψω	πλέκω, πλέξω	ἀνύτω, ἀνύσω
θλίβω, θλίψω	λέγω, λέξω	σπεύδω, σπεύσω
γράφω, γράψω	τεύχω, τεύξω	πείθω, πείσω

In No. 1., all the mutes of course go into π before σ in -σω; in No. 2, they all go into ξ; in No. 3, they are all thrown out; see § 10. R. 6. The student will see, of course, that the Futures in each of these classes assume respectively the very same form; and consequently, all the derivates from the Future do the same; so that it matters not for any of these, which of the mutes is the character in the root, as the shape of the Future and its derivates does not depend on the quality or individual species of the mute, but on the *class* to which it belongs. (3) The same thing is true in regard to all verbs with character πτ (§ 62. 4, *a*); with σσ or ττ (§ 62. 4. *b*); with ζ (§ 62. 4. *c*). The student has merely to find the simple mute that is in the original root, by the rules given him in § 62. 4, and then the Fut. is formed exactly as above.

NOTE 3. The Fut. I. and II. seems to be formed by the aid of the old Fut. of εἰμί, viz. ἔσω; sometimes by dropping the ε of this, as in the examples above; sometimes by dropping the σ and contracting the ε-ω, as Fut. II. of Liquids (e. g. στελῶ); sometimes by the coalescence of the ε in ἔσω with the character-vowel of the verb, as φιλ-ησω=φιλε-έσω, etc.; and lastly by prolonging the ε in εσω, e. g. ἕψω, ἑψήσω.

(5) THE ATTIC FUTURE. Futures of three or more syllables, having α, ε, or ι, before the ending -σω, reject the σ, and then are contracted (if capable of contraction) in the usual way.

NOTE. This form of the future is called *Attic*, because it is principally used in this dialect. Its formation and accentuation are for the most part obvious; e. g. βιβάζω, βιβάσω, (βιβάω) contr. βιβῶ, βιβᾷς, βιβᾷ, etc., as in the contract verbs. So τελέω, τελέσω, (τελέω) τελῶ, τελεῖς, τελεῖ, etc., as in the second class of contract verbs. But verbs in -ίζω cannot properly *contract*, and therefore they merely assume the accentuation of contracts; e. g. κομίζω, κομίσω, κομιῶ, κομιεῖς, κομιεῖ, κομιοῦμεν, etc. The Fut. Middle is formed after the same analogy; e. g. βιβᾶσι, βιβᾷ, βιβᾶται, etc.; τελοῦμαι, τελεῖ, τελεῖται, etc.; κομιοῦμαι, κομιεῖ, κομιεῖται, etc. Polysyllabic verbs in -ίζω, and verbs in -έω with Fut. -έσω, *usually* take this Future, (in

§ 63. VERBS: FORMATION OF TENSES, ACTIVE.

the N. Test. verbs in -ίζω nearly always); but verbs in -άζω more seldom have it. It is not employed in the Optative.

(6) THE FIRST PERFECT is the usual one; and ordinarily it has for its radical character the same form as the radical part of the Future, both as to vowels and consonants, with the exception that it aspirates the two first classes of mutes (π, β, φ—κ, γ, χ,) before its ending -α. Its distinctive character, therefore, consists in its reduplication, and in the tense-ending -α in verbs π, β, φ, —κ, γ, χ, and -κα in other verbs.

NOTE 1. ILLUSTRATIONS. (a) When the simple character is π, β, φ, or κ, γ, χ, the student has merely to find his Future, by the rules in No. 4, and then the *radical* part of this (rejecting the -σω) with reduplication added, etc., and the making such changes in the mute-character as the final -α requires (§ 10. R. 5), will constitute the form of the Perfect. E. g.

τύπτω, τύψω, τέτυφα   πλέκω, πλέξω, πέπλεχα
λέπω, λέψω, λέλεφα   λέγω, λέξω, λέλεχα
τρίβω, τρίψω, τέτριφα   τεύχω, τεύξω, τέτευχα
γράφω, γράψω, γέγραφα   τάσσω, τάξω, τέταχα, etc.

It is obvious in all these cases, that the mutes in the Future become aspirated in the Perfect, merely by reason of the final -α, § 10. R. 5.

(b) In all other cases the Perfect receives the ending -κα; e. g. in verba pura, as τίω, τέτικα· λύω, λέλυκα· δακρύω, δεδάκρυκα· and so where τ, δ, or θ, was the original character, as φράζω (φράδω), πέφρακα· πείθω, πέπεικα, etc.

NOTE 2. A few of the 1st Perfects, having the vowel ε in their root, change it for o; e. g. πέμπω, πέπομφα· τρέπω, τέτροφα· κλέπτω, κέκλοφα. In this respect Perf. I. imitates Perf. II.; but the number of cases is very small where such vowel-changes take place.

NOTE 3. In the N. Test. (and also in the Sept.), the 3d pers. plur. of the Perfect sometimes ends in -αν; e. g. ἔγνωκαν, εἴρηκαν, ἑώρακαν. This is sometimes found in other Greek.

(7) THE SECOND PERFECT (formerly called Perfect Middle), is commonly made by prefixing the usual reduplication, adding -α (not ά) to the *original* root, and more usually by retaining or making a long vowel in the root-syllable.

NOTE. In respect to the *vowel-changes* in the root-syllable, Perf. II. has several developments diverse from each other.

(a) Liquids with α (long merely by position) and αι, take η in Perf. II.; e. g. θάλλω, τέθηλα· φαίνω, πέφηνα.

(b) *Mutes and Liquids* with ε in the root, and also Liquids with ει, take short o in the Perfect, (contrary to analogy in other cases); e. g. τρέφω, τέτροφα· δέρω, δέδορα· φθείρω, ἔφθορα. Where the original root has o, it remains; as κόπτω (κόπω), κέκοπα.

(c) *Mutes* with ει, take οι; e. g. λείπω, λέλοιπα· εἴδω, οἶδα.

(d) But where a long vowel or diphthong already stands in the ground-

§ 63. VERBS: FORMATION OF TENSES, ACTIVE. 91

form of the Present, change (excepting in cases above noted) is unnecessary; e. g. λήθω, λέληθα· φεύγω, πέφευγα. Yet, in cases such as the last, in the Perfect Passive ευ sometimes shortens into v; e. g. πέφυγμαι. For changes made by Attic reduplication, see § 56. 1. Note 1.

N. B. For the limited use of Perf. II., see § 52. 8.

Historic Tenses in the ACTIVE.

(8) THE IMPERFECT is formed from the Present, by dropping -ω final, suffixing -ον, and prefixing the augment.

In the Alexandrine dialect, the 3d pers. plur. of the several tenses in -ον, i. e. Imperf. and Aor. II., is often made by -οσαν; e. g. Aor. II. ἤλθοσαν, ἐφάγοσαν, κατελίποσαν, ἐκρίνοσαν, etc. In the N. Test. (and Byzantine historians) the like forms occur; e. g. Imperf. ἐδολιοῦσαν Rom. 3: 13; εἴχοσαν (for εἴχον) in some Codd. John 15: 22; Aor. II., παρελάβοσαν 2 Thess. 3: 6.

(9) PLUPERF. I. is formed from the Perfect, by dropping the final -α, suffixing -ειν and prefixing (but not usually in the N. Test.) the augment. Pluperf. II. is formed in the same way from Perf. II.

(10) THE FIRST AORIST is formed from the Future, by dropping its final -ω, suffixing -α, and prefixing the augment.

NOTE 1. The most easy and obvious mode of forming Aor. I. is, by supposing the old Aor. I. of εἰμί, viz. ἔσα, to be suffixed; which appears, as the case may require, in the form -εσα, -εα or -α. Accordingly ἐτύπεσα, ἔχεα, ἔνεγκα [root ἐνεγκω], are easily accounted for on this ground; and so with Aor. I. of the liquid verbs.

NOTE 2. Assuming the principle of formation in the text, it must be noted, that Liquids have merely -α (not -σα) in Aor. I.; and a few others (see in Note 1) anomalously follow this analogy.

(11) AORIST II. is formed from the simple root, by suffixing -ον, prefixing the augment, and shortening the penult; as τύπτω (τύπω) ἔτυπον.

NOTE 1. Such is the general principle; but still, this comprises only a moderate number of verbs, viz. those which have two character-consonants, or a prolonged vowel, in the root. In case of a prolonged vowel,

In Mutes, η } go into ἄ. E. g. λήθω, ἔλαθον
In Liquids, αι ει }   πταίρω, ἔπταρον· κτείνω, ἔκτανον.
In Mutes, ει —— ἴ   λείπω, ἔλιπον
           ευ —— ὔ   φεύγω, ἔφυγον.

Only a few anomalous cases present a *long* penult here; e. g. εὗρον, ἦλθον, ἔβλαστον, ἔπαρδον, εἶπον, etc.

NOTE 2. A large portion of Aorists II., both mute and liquid, have ε in a *monosyllabic* root, and require a change of this into α in Aor. II. E. g. τρέπω, ἔτραπον· τέμνω, ἔταμον, etc. But in the Passive this vowel-change

§ 64. VERBS: FORMATION OF TENSES, PASSIVE.

is sometimes neglected; e. g. *ἐβλέπην*, etc., (§ 64. 8. Note 3); and sometimes even in the Act. and Midd. voices, as *πίπτω* (*πέτω*), *ἔπεσον* · *θείνω*, *ἔθενον* · *γίνομαι* (*γένω*), *ἐγενόμην*, etc.

NOTE 3. It follows of course from the general principle of formation stated in the text, that verbs with *double* character, e. g. *πτ, σσ, ττ*, etc., must divest themselves of this, in order to form Aor. II. which can be formed only from the *simple* root. See § 62. 4. Also ib. No. 5. Gen. Remark. Of verbs *κ, γ, χ*, only verbs with *γ* form Aor. II.; and verbs *τ, δ, θ*, do not form it at all.

N. B. In respect to the very limited number of verbs which can form an Aor. II., see § 52. 7. But a considerable number form Aor. II. *passive*, which are not susceptible of an Aor. II. Act.; see § 52. 7. 6.

REMARK. In the Alexandrine dialect, and also in the N. Test., the Aor. 2 (at least forms substantially belonging here) assumes the ending of Aor. 1 (-*α*); e. g. in the Sept., *εἴδαμεν, ἔφυγαν, εὗραν, παρῆλθαν, ἐφάγαμεν, ἐλθάτω*, and so very often, both here and in the Apocrypha. In the N. Test. we find (at least in some very good Codd.) *ἤλθατε*, Matt. 25: 36; *ἐξῆλθατε*, Luke 7: 24; *παρελθάτω*, Matt. 26: 39; *ἐξείλατο*, Acts 7: 10. 12: 11; *ἀνείλατο*, Acts 7: 21; *ἐξεπέσατε*, Gal. 5: 4; *ἔπεσαν*, Rev. 7: 11; *εὑράμενος*, Heb. 9: 12. It should be noted that the 2d pers. sing. does not adopt these peculiar forms, nor the Infin. mode, nor the participles, in the N. Testament. The like forms are found in some of the poets, e. g. in Orpheus; and in some of the classics; also, some forms in Aor. 2 retain an *σ*, like Aor. I.; e. g. *ἔπεσον, ἶξον, ἐβήσετο, ἐδύσετο*, etc.

(12) Fut. II. is formed only in *liquid verbs;* under which head will be found an account of it.

§ 64. *Formation of Primary Tenses in the* PASSIVE.

(1) THE PRESENT (passive and middle) is formed from the Present active, by dropping the final -*ω* and annexing -*ομαι*; as *τύπτω, τύπτομαι*.

(2) THE FUTURE (I. and II.) is formed from Aor. I. and II. passive, by dropping the final -*ν*, annexing -*σομαι*, and omitting the augment.

E. g. *ἐτύφθην, τυφθήσομαι* · *ἐτύπην, τυπήσομαι*. The reader will call to mind, that this is a mere expedient hit upon by grammarians in tracing the analogy of forms; and so he will not object to this derivation, the fact that the Futures are in their nature *primary* tenses.

NOTE. It should be remembered here, that Fut. II. pass. cannot be formed from any verbs which cannot form an Aor. II., either Act. or passive; and of course that it must be very limited in its use. But there are not a few verbs which exhibit Fut. I. and II.; in which case there is a choice very convenient in poetry. Sometimes usage has made a slight difference in the sense of the two, Fut. II. inclining more to the intransitive sense. Specially is Fut. II. employed where the form of Fut. I. is unwieldy, or contrary to euphony.

§ 64. Verbs: Formation of Tenses, Passive.

(3) The Perfect (passive and middle) is formed from the Perf. I. active, by retaining its reduplication, and by μαι added to the *root* instead of the Act. -ά or -κα.

Such is the general principle; but in its development it makes some apparent variety in the formation of this tense; e. g.

(*a*) *Verbs with* π, β, φ—κ, γ, χ, (i. e. those which make final -φα or -χα in Perf. I. Act.), here conform the character-letter before the endings -μαι, -σαι, -ται, etc., agreeably to the principles laid down in § 10.

E. g. τέτυφα, pass. τέτυμμαι, (φ assimilated, § 10. R. 7); τέτυψαι, (φ into π, § 10. R. 6); τέτυπται, (φ into π, § 10. R. 2); τετύμμεθον (as in the first instance); τέτυφθον, (φ retained because of the θ in the ending, § 10. R. 2); τέτυφθε, (σ dropped in the ending -σθε, § 10. R. 17). The 3d pers. plur. is usually a *participial* form joined with εἰσί.

(*b*) *Verbs with Perf. I. act. in* -κα are either (1) Pure Verbs; (2) Verbs with τ, δ, θ; or, (3) Liquids.

(1) Pure Verbs. Here the general principle is, that verbs with a *long* vowel in Fut. I. Act. simply add, in the passive, the tense-endings -μαι, σαι, etc., to the root; but verbs with a short vowel in Fut. I. act. insert σ before the tense-endings. E. g. τιμήσω, τετίμημαι· τίσω, τέτιμαι, etc.; on the other hand, τελέω, τελέσω, τετέλεσμαι· σπάω, σπάσω, ἔσπασμαι, etc.

Exceptions. These are not a few; (*a*) Some verbs with Fut. I. act. *long* penult, both *contracts* and other *verba pura*, take σ before the passive, contrary to the rule; e. g. ἀκούσω [-ομαι], ἤκουσμαι· χράω, χρήσω, κέχρησμαι, etc. (*b*) *Vice versa*, some with *short* Fut. I. act. do not take σ in the Perf. pass.; e. g. γαμέσω, γεγάμεμαι· κρίνω, κρῖνω, κέκριμαι. (*c*) There is even a third class, which vibrate between both methods; e. g. γεύω, δράω, δέδραμαι and δέδρασμαι, etc. See the full exhibition in Kühner, § 136. Usage and the lexicons, therefore, rather than any fixed principle, must decide as to the form of the Perf. passive in Verba Pura.

(2) Verbs τ, δ, θ, (which letters of course are dropped in Fut. I., Perf. I. act., § 63. 4. Note 2) here compensate the dropping of these letters by inserting σ before the tense-endings; e. g. πείθω, πέπεισμαι· φράζω [=φράσδω], πέφρασμαι. But when any of the tense-endings begin with σ, this adjectitious σ is omitted; e. g. 2nd pers. πέπεισαι (not πέπεισ-σαι)· πέπεισθε (not πέπεισ-σθε); § 10. R. 17.

(3) Liquid Verbs in general drop the -κα of Perf. act. and simply add -μαι, -σαι, -ται, etc. But verbs in -αίνω -ύνω usually drop the ν and take σ in its room; e. g. φαίνω, πέφασμαι· μολύνω, μεμόλυσμαι. Sometimes the ν assimilates; as ξαίνω, ἔξαμ-μαι.

N. B. When a tense-ending beginning with σθ follows a *liquid* letter of the verb, the σ falls out, e. g. ἀγγέλλω, Perf. Inf. ἠγγέλ-θαι (not ἠγγέλ-σθαι); and so of course in declining, as ἤγγελ-θον, ἤγγελ-θε, not -σθον -σθε.

(*c*) *Vowel changes.* Liquid Verbs, with ε in the pure *monosyllabic* root, exchange it for α in the Perf. act. and pass.; as στέλλω, ἔσταλκα, ἔσταλμαι· φθείρω, ἔφθαρκα, ἔφθαρμαι, etc. Even the mute verbs, στρέφω, τρέπω, τρέφω, imitate this in the Pass, e. g. ἔστραμμαι, etc.

N. B. *Polysyllabic* verbs do not admit such an exchange of vowels; e. g. ἀγγέλλω, ἤγγελμαι, ε retained.

(4) THE THIRD FUTURE (Paulo-post Future, *Futurum exactum*) is formed most conveniently from the 2nd person of the Perfect, by dropping -σαι and suffixing -σομαι; as τέτυψαι, τετύψομαι.

NOTE. When a vowel precedes the ending -σομαι it is generally *long* here, although it may have been shortened in the Perfect. Verbs λ, μ, ν, ρ, never have this Future; and verbs with *temporal* augment rarely have it. The nature of its signification would naturally refer its derivation to the Perf.

Historical Tenses of the PASSIVE.

(5) THE IMPERFECT (passive and middle) is formed from the Present by dropping -μαι, suffixing μην, and prefixing the augment; as τύπτομαι, ἐτυπτόμην.

(6) THE PLUPERFECT (pass. and middle) is formed from the Perfect in the same manner; as τέτυμμαι, ἐτετύμμην.

(7) AOR. I. may be formed from the root of the verb, by suffixing -θην and prefixing the augment.

NOTE 1. Of course Mutes at the end of the root must conform to the formative-ending -θην, e. g. τύπτω (τύπω) ἐτύφθην· λέγω, ἐλέχθην, etc.; see § 63. 4. Note 2.

NOTE 2. It should be specially noted here, that *in general Aor. I. pass. follows the analogy of the* PERFECT PASSIVE, *both as to the insertion of σ before the tense-ending, and as to the quantity of its penult vowel*. (*a*) In VERBA PURA the exceptions are a few as to the σ; e. g. πέπαυμαι, ἐπαύσθην, and so with some four other verbs. The *root-vowel* here, in the Perfect and Aor. I. remains the same in all regular forms; but αἰνέω, ποθέω, δέω, αἱρέω, and some few others, have η in the Perf. and ε in Aor. I.; e. g. δέδημαι, ἐδέθην, etc. (*b*) The few Perfects passive of *Mutes*, which undergo vowel change in their root (§ 64. *c.*) do not continue this change in Aor. I.; e. g. ἔστραμμαι, ἐστρέφθην, etc. Verbs τ, δ, θ, which take σ in the Perf. (§ 64. 3. *b.* 2.) retain it in Aor. I. (*c*) Aor. I. of verbs in -μι takes a *short* vowel. (*d*) *Liquids* which have a monosyllabic root with ε, and exchange this for α in the Perf. act. and pass. (§ 64. *c.*), preserve this α in Aor. I.; e. g. στέλλω, ἔσταλμαι, ἐστάλθην, etc.

REMARK. It is evident from these phenomena, that we must not regard the rule in the text [No. 7] as developing all of even the essential circumstances which often combine in the formation of Aor. I. Hence some grammarians have preferred to derive it from the Perf. pass.; but this, in many cases, is also accompanied with difficulties.—One can hardly fail to remark, also, how different from other tenses in the Pass., are the modes of inflection in Aor. I. and II.; for they resemble altogether Aor. II. of the active voice of verbs in -μι. In their meaning, also, there is much more latitude than is usual in most other tenses.

(8) Aor. II. pass. assumes the form of Aor. II. active of verbs in -μι. For convenience sake we may say: It is formed from Aor. II. active, by substituting -ην for -ον.

§ 65. VERBS: FORMATION OF TENSES, MIDDLE. 95

NOTE 1. It follows, of course, that Aor. II. pass. can be formed only from *simple* roots, like Aor. II. active. Pure and derivative verbs; those with character τ, δ, ϑ; verbs in -μι; and mostly liquid verbs; reject this tense. But verbs in -μι admit Aor. II. act. (not passive); while, on the other hand, such simple roots as would make, in the active Voice, the Imperf. and Aor. II. in the same way, do *not* admit Aor. II. active, but employ Aor. II. passive; e. g. γράφω, Aor. II. ἐγράφην· κλίνω, ἐκλίνην. Here the Imperf. and Aor. II. act. would be of the same form.

NOTE 2. *In no case do Aor. II. act. and pass.* coexist, for where the passive form is used, the active is wanting; and so, *vice versa*. The true reason of this seems to be, that the pass. form supplies the place of the active, by its intransitive and reflexive meanings. It is on this ground, that Kuhner (§ 86) assigns this tense a place in the *active* voice, averring that it bears the same relation to the transitive Aor. I. there, which Perf. II. bears to Perf. I.

NOTE 3. *Vowel-exchanges.* In general these are the same, and regulated by the same laws as those noted under Aor. II. *active;* e. g. τρέπω, ἐτράπην· δέρω, ἐδάρην· στέλλω, ἐστάλην, etc. There is, however, a considerable number of verbs which actually employ no Aor. II. act., that still form Aor. II. pass. *without the usual exchange of vowels;* e. g. βλέπω, ἐβλέπην (not ἐβλάπην)· λέγω, ἐλέγην, etc. (Even in the act. and midd. Voices there are a few cases of the same nature; see § 63. 11. Note 2). *Polysyllabic* roots of course exclude this exchange of vowels. One obvious reason of the usage in question is, that the ending -ην here makes the distinction from the Imperf. active so plain, that the usual vowel-exchange of the act. voice is unnecessary.

§ 65. *Primary Tenses in the Middle Voice.*

(1) The PRESENT and PERFECT are the same as the passive.

(2) The first Future is formed from Fut. 1 act., by exchanging -ω for -ομαι; e. g. τύψω, τύψομαι.

NOTE. Verbs λ, μ, ν, ρ form a peculiar Future here, (see § 66. 2), which has unfortunately been called Fut. II. It is no secondary tense, but a *primary* one, differing from the common Futures of other verbs (just as the Attic Fut. differs from them), and formed on the same principles as the Attic. For the formation of this, see § 66. 2.

Historic Tenses in the Middle Voice.

(2) The IMPERFECT and PLUPERFECT are the same as in the the Passive.

(3) Aor. 1 is formed from Aor. 1 active, by adding μην; as ἔτυψα, ἐτυψάμην.

(4) Aor. 2 is formed from Aor. 2 active (real or assumed), by dropping -ον and suffixing -όμην; as ἔτυπον, ἐτυπόμην.

NOTE. Only in a very few cases does this Aor. II. coexist with an Aor. II. passive; but it is often coexistent with Aor. II. active and is formed as if it were derived from it. Of course it is subject to like *limitations*, as to its use, with Aor. II. active.

§ 66. *Formation of Tenses in verbs* λ, μ, ν, ρ.

(1) These verbs differ from other barytone verbs in some important particulars, having some forms of tenses altogether peculiar, and some specialities in regard to others.

(2) The so-called Fut. I. is never found here in the active voice. Instead of this a circumflexed and abridged Fut. II. (so called) is always employed; which resembles the Attic Fut. in some of the barytone verbs, (§ 63. 5). It is formed by suffixing -ῶ circumflexed to the root, shortening the vowel in the last syllable of the *root* when it is long, and, dropping its augmentary consonant.

E. g. ψάλλω, ψαλῶ· κρίνω, κρινῶ, etc. As the pure and simple root is the ground of this peculiar Future, it presupposes the like simplifications of the augmented Present, so far as they are needed, as take place to form Aor. 2. active; but the *vowel exchanges* of the latter are not included in this; e. g. φαίνω, φανῶ· σπείρω, σπερῶ· στέλλω, στελῶ, etc.

NOTE 1. The circumflexed -ῶ in this Fut. seems plainly to come from ἕσω, midd. ἕσομαι (Fut. of εἰμί), which drops the σ and then contracts in the Act. and Middle into -ῶ -οῦμαι. Hence the circumflex accent, and also the mode of inflection, viz., -ῶ -εῖς -εῖ -εῖτον, etc. -οῦμαι -εῖ -εῖται, etc. In the common Future of other verbs, such contraction does not take place, but -σω -σομαι are employed, in which merely the ε is dropped.

NOTE 2. As this is a *primary* tense, it must not be at all confounded with the *tempora secunda*, which imply that two forms of the same tense exist, or may exist, in the same voice, e. g. Aor. I. and II., Perf. I. and II. But in the passive Voice *there may be two Futures* here, as in other verbs; yet *no Fut. III. or Paulo-post Future is made by liquid verbs.*

NOTE 3. Some verbs λ, ρ, form Futures in poetry with -σω; e. g. κείρω, κέρσω, ἄρω, ἄρσω, κέλλω, κέλσω, etc.; but these and the like are exceptions to common usage.

(3) AORIST I. is formed from Fut. II. by substituting -α for -ῶ, and making the penult *long*.

Of course the ending here is not -σα (as elsewhere), but -α simply; e. g. τιλῶ, ἔτιλα· κρινῶ, ἔκρινα. In this tense, in order to make the penult *long*, ε of the Fut. goes into ει, and α usually into η; as μενῶ, ἔμεινα· φανῶ, ἔφηνα. But verbs in -ιαίνω -ραίνω, take ᾱ long here instead of η. Others in -αίνω -αίρω, vary between α and η, in different dialects and at different periods. Short ῐ and ῠ of the Present here become ῑ and ῡ.

(4) AORIST II. is formed from Fut. II., by dropping -ῶ, suffixing -ον, and prefixing the augment; as βάλλω, βαλῶ, ἔβαλον.

NOTE 1. Here the usual vowel-exchange of Aor. II., when the simple

§ 66. Verbs: Formation of Tenses, Liquids. 97

root is *monosyllabic* and has ε in it, claims its full place; see § 63. 11. Note 2. But polysyllabic roots with ε do not admit this exchange; e. g. Fut. ἀγγελῶ, Aor. II. ἤγγελον.

Note 2. In this class of verbs, Fut. II. is taken as the more convenient index of the simple root, because Aor. II. is not frequent here. Hence, to derive Aor. II. from Fut. II. here, means nothing more than that the proper means is employed to ascertain the simple root, viz. by appealing to Fut. II., and then the Aor. is formed in the same way as in mute verbs.

(6) Perf. I. act., (and along with this, its derivatives the Perf. pass. and Aor. I. pass.), follow the *penult* vowel of Fut. II.; vowel-exchanges in appropriate cases being excepted.

In other words; as in *verba muta* the Perfect usually follows the model of the Future, so here the *simple* form of Fut. II. goes over to the Perfect.

Note 1. To liquid verbs, also, the vowel-exchange common to Aor. II. extends; as it does, moreover, to the Perf. and Aor. II. passive; see § 64. 3. *b. c.* Of course liquid verbs with ε in the Fut. of a monosyllabic root, change it for α; e. g. στέλλω, στελῶ, ἔσταλκα· πείρω, περῶ, πέπαρκα, etc. So in the Perf. and Aor. I. pass.; e. g. ἔσταλμαι, ἐστάλθην· φθείρω, φθερῶ, ἔφθαρκα, ἔφθαρμαι, ἐφθάρθην.

Note 2. Verbs in -νω sometimes retain the ν, and sometimes omit it, in Perf. 1 active, and in the derivate tenses (Perfect and Aor. 1 passive). When it is retained, it is of course written γ (=ng) before -κα; as φανῶ, πέφαγκα. Several verbs in -νω usually (not always) omit the ν in the Perf., etc.; as κρινῶ, κέκρικα, κέκριμαι, ἐκρίθην· and so with κλίνω, πλύνω, τείνω, κτείνω. Before the ending -μαι, ν either assimilates, as Fut. ξηρανῶ, ἐξέραμμαι; or goes into σ, as Fut. φανῶ, πέφασμαι. Usage and lexicons only can determine such cases.

Note 3. The Perfect of verbs in -μω is formed as if from verbs in ἐω; e. g. νέμω, νεμῶ, νενέμηκα, etc. This is sometimes the case, also, with some verbs in -νω; e. g. μένω, μεμένηκα. All these various ways of modifying the Perf. result from an attempt to get rid of the harsh sound of ν and μ before the Perf. ending -κα.

(7) Perf. II. Like Aor. I. here, and Perf. II. of Mutes (§ 63. 7. Note *a*), the Perf. II. usually *prolongs* the penult; but when a root-monosyllabic in Fut. II. has ε in it, this goes here into ο; comp. ut supra.

Perf. II. is formed only in a few cases in liquid verbs. It differs from the Perf. II. of *verba muta* dissyllabic when ει is in the ground-form; for in the *Liquids* we have, as in the rule above, σπείρω, ἔσπορα, but in *Mutes* we find it thus: λείπω, λείψω, λέλοιπα. See § 63. ut supra.

§ 67. Classification of Verbs.

A formal division of these has not been hitherto made, although it has in some measure been necessarily anticipated. But hitherto the principles developed were intended to be *general*, so far as the nature of them would permit. We now come to *the more distinct development of each class of verbs*, so that the learner may more plainly apprehend the grounds of distinction heretofore necessarily adverted to and recognized.

(1) The primary division of Verbs is into VERBS PURE and IMPURE, i. e. verbs which have a *vowel* or *diphthong* before -ω of the Present, or which have a *consonant*.

(2) Pure verbs are subdivided into CONTRACTED and UNCONTRACTED; the contracts are those which have α, ε, or ο, before the ending -ω; the uncontracted, those which have other vowels or diphthongs.

(3) Impure Verbs are also subdivided, viz., into MUTE VERBS and LIQUID VERBS. The former have some one of the nine Mutes for their *character;* the latter, some one of the Liquids, λ, μ, ν, ϱ.

In respect to *accentuation*, all verbs are called *barytones* which have not the circumflex on the final syllable of the Present, i. e. all but the Contracts are called *Barytones*.

§ 68. *Pure Verbs.*

It would be the most easy method for the learner, who is a novice, to begin with the uncontracted verbs of this class. But as brevity must be here consulted in the paradigms, I have merely exhibited a synopsis of these in the sequel, because *Verba pura* form no *secondary* tenses, and therefore are not appropriate to a *full* exhibition of forms. The *Contracts* are purposely deferred to another occasion, on account of their peculiar difficulty.

The reason why pure verbs are more easy and obvious to the tyro is, that they unite with the tense-endings without changing their root or stem; while other verbs, (e. g. *verba muta*, as must have been noticed in the rules above given for the formation of the tenses), undergo a great variety of changes. Some peculiarities, first of pure verbs in general, and then specially of the Contracts, will be noticed when we come to treat particularly of the latter.

§ 69. *Paradigm of* MUTE VERBS.

The student has already been advertised, that he must not expect to find any verb which actually exhibits all the possible tenses and modes of the Greek language. E. g. τύπτω, which from the nature of its form is adapted to give as full an exhibition as any verb, is wanting in Fut. II. act. and midd., which belong only to *liquid* verbs. In the Paradigm of Liquids these will be exhibited. *Vice versa* in Liquids Fut. I. act. and midd. is wanting; and in pure verbs no *tempora secunda* are formed.

In the *Synopsis* that follows, I have placed the.*Imper.* next in order after the Indic., merely because the greater part of the grammars in present use among us have done so, and consequently this order is more familiar to most students. In Germany, recent grammarians place the Subj next to the Indicative. It is a matter of little consequence which order is adopted, if the nature of the case is well understood.

NO. I. (SYNOPSIS.)

ACTIVE VOICE

Tense.	Indic.	Imp.	Opt.	Subj.	Inf.	Part.
Pres.	τύπτω	τύπτε	-οιμι	τύπτω	-ειν	-ων
Imp.	έτυπτον					
Fut.	τύψω		-οιμι		-ειν	-ων
Aor. 1	έτυψα	τύψον	-αιμι	τύψω	-αι	-ας
Perf. 1	τέτυφα	-ε	-οιμι	-φω	-έναι	-ώς
Plup. 1	ἐτετύφειν					
Perf. 2	τέτυπα	-ε	-οιμι	-πω	-έναι	-ώς
Plup. 2	ἐτετύπειν					
Aor. 2	έτυπον	τύπε	-οιμι	-τύπω	-εῖν	-ών

PASSIVE VOICE.

Pres.	τύπτομαι	-ου	-οίμην	-ωμαι	εσθαι	-όμενος
Imp.	ἐτυπτόμην					
Fut. 1	τυφθήσομαι		-οίμην		-εσθαι	-όμενος
Fut. 2	τυπήσομαι		-οίμην		-εσθαι	-όμενος
Perf.	τέτυμμαι	τέτυψο			-ύφθαι	-υμμένος
Plup.	ἐτετύμμην					
Fut. 3	τετύψομαι		-οίμην		-εσθαι	-όμενος
Aor. 1	ἐτύφθην	τύφθητι	-είην	τυφθῶ	-ῆναι	-θείς
Aor. 2	ἐτύπην	τύπηθι	-είην	τυπῶ	-ῆναι	-είς

MIDDLE VOICE.

Fut. 1	τύψομαι		-οίμην		-εσθαι	-όμενος
Aor. 1	ἐτυψάμην	τύψαι	-οίμην	τύψωμαι	-ασθαι	-άμενος
Aor. 2	ἐτυπόμην	τυποῦ	-οίμην	τύπωμαι	-έσθαι	-όμενος

No. II. Paradigm of the barytone

INDICA-

Tense.	1st pers.	Singular. 2.	3.
Pres.	τύπτω	-εις	-ει
Imp.	ἔτυπτον	-ες	-ε
Fut. 1	τύψω	-εις	-ει
Aor. 1	ἔτυψα	-ας	-ε
Perf. 1	τέτυφα	-ας	-ε
Plup. 1	ἐτετύφειν (-εα -εας etc.)	-εις	-ει
Perf. 2	τέτυπα	-ας	-ε
Plup. 2	ἐτετύπειν (-εα -εας etc.)	-εις	-ει
Aor. 2	ἔτυπον	-ες	-ε

SUBJUNC-

Pres.	τύπτω	-ῃς	-ῃ
Aor. 1	τύψω	-ῃς	-ῃ
Perf. 1	τετύφω	-ῃς	-ῃ
Perf. 2	τετύπω	-ῃς	-ῃ
Aor. 2	τύπω	-ῃς	-ῃ

OPTA-

Pres.	τύπτοιμι	-οις	-οι
Fut. 1	τύψοιμι	-οις	-οι
Aor. 1	τύψαιμι	-αις	-αι
		-ειας	-ειε
Perf. 1	τετύφοιμι	-οις	-οι
Perf. 2	τετύποιμι	-οις	-οι
Aor. 2	τύποιμι	-οις	-οι

IMPERA-

Pres.		τύπτε	-έτω
Aor. 1		τύψον	-άτω
Perf. 1		τέτυφε	-έτω
Perf. 2		τέτυπε	-έτω
Aor. 2		τύπε	-έτω

INFINITIVE.

Pres.	τύπτειν
Fut.	τύψειν
Aor. 1	τύψαι
Perf. 1	τετυφέναι
Perf. 2	τετυπέναι
Aor. 2	τυπεῖν

§ 69. Paradigm of Mute Verbs.

verb τύπτω in the Active (Mutes).

TIVE.

Dual. 2.	3.	1.	Plural. 2.	3.
-ετον	-ετον	-ομεν	-ετε	-ουσι
-ετον	-έτην	-ομεν	-ετε	-ον
-ετον	-ετον	-ομεν	-ετε	-ουσι
-ατον	-άτην	-αμεν	-ατε	-αν
-ατον	-ατον	-αμεν	-ατε	-ασι
-ειτον	-είτην	-ειμεν	-ειτε	-εισαν
-ατον	-ατον	-αμεν	-ατε	-ασι
-ειτον	-είτην	-ειμεν	-ειτε	-εισαν
-ετον	-έτην	-ομεν	-ετε	-ον

TIVE.

-ητον	-ητον	-ωμεν	-ητε	-ωσι
-ητον	-ητον	-ωμεν	-ητε	-ωσι
-ητον	-ητον	-ωμεν	-ητε	-ωσι
-ητον	-ητον	-ωμεν	-ητε	-ωσι
-ητον	-ητον	-ωμεν	-ητε	-ωσι

TIVE.

-τον	-την	-μεν	-τε	-εν
-τον	-την	-μεν	-τε	-εν
-τον	-την	-μεν	-τε	-εν
				-ειαν
-τον	-την	-μεν	-τε	-εν
-τον	-την	-μεν	-τε	-εν
-τον	-την	-μεν	-τε	-εν

TIVE.

-τον	-των		-ετε	-τωσαν or -όντων
-τον	-των		-ατε	-άτωσαν, etc.
-τον	-των		-ετε	-τωσαν, etc.
-τον	-των		-ετε	-τωσαν, etc.
-τον	-των		-ετε	-τωσαν, etc.

PARTICIPLES.

Pres.	τύπτων	-ουσα	-ον
Fut.	τύψων	-ουσα	-ον
Aor. 1	τύψας	-ασα	-αν
Perf. 1	τετυφώς	-υῖα	-ός
Perf. 2	τετυπώς	-υῖα	-ός
Aor. 2	τυπών	-οῦσα	-όν

§ 69. Paradigm of Mute Verbs.

No. II. Paradigm of

INDIC-

Tense.	Singular.			Dual.		
	1.	2.	3.	1	2.	3.
Pres.	τύπτομαι	-η (ει)	-εται	-όμεθον	-εσθον	-εσθον
Imp.	ἐτυπτόμην	-ου	-ετο	-όμεθον	-εσθον	-έσθην
Fut. 1	τυφθήσομαι	-η (ει)	-εται	-όμεθον	-εσθον	-εσθον
Fut. 2	τυπήσομαι	-η (ει)	-εται	-όμεθον	-εσθον	-εσθον
Perf.	τέτυμμαι	-υψαι	-υπται	-ύμμεθον	-υφθον	-υφθον
Plup.	ἐτετύμμην	-υψο	-υπτο	-ύμμεθον	-υφθον	-ύφθην
Fut. 3	τετύψομαι	-η	-εται	-όμεθον	-εσθον	-εσθον
Aor. 1	ἐτύφθην	-ης	-η		-ητον	-ήτην
Aor. 2	ἐτύπην	-ης	-η		-ητον	-ήτην

SUBJUNC-

Pres.	τύπτωμαι	-η	-ηται	-ώμεθον	-ησθον	-ησθον
Aor. 1	τυφθῶ	-ῇς	-ῇ		-ῆτον	-ῆτον
Aor. 2	τυπῶ	-ῇς	-ῇ		-ῆτον	-ῆτον
Perf.	τετυμμένος ὦ	ῇς etc.				

OPTA-

Pres.	τυπτοίμην	-οιο	-οιτο	-οίμεθον	-οισθον	-οίσθην
Fut. 1	τυφθησοίμην	-οιο	-οιτο	-οίμεθον	-οισθον	-οίσθην
Fut. 2	τυπησοίμην	-οιο	-οιτο	-οίμεθον	-οισθον	-οίσθην
Fut. 3	τετυψοίμην	-οιο	-οιτο	-οίμεθον	-οισθον	-οίσθην
Aor. 1	τυφθείην	-ης	-η		-ητον	-ήτην
Aor. 2	τυπείην	-ης	-η		-ητον	-ήτην
Perf.	τετυμμένος εἴην	...εἴης	...εἴη	...εἴητον	...εἴητον	...εἰήτην

IMPER-

Pres.		τύπτου	-έσθω		-εσθον	-έσθων
Perf.		τέτυψο	-ύφθω		-υφθον	-ύφθων
Aor. 1		τύφθητι	-ήτω		-ητον	-ήτων
Aor. 2		τύπηθι	-ήτω		-ητον	-ήτων

INFINITIVE.

Pres.	τύπτεσθαι
Fut. 1	τυφθήσεσθαι
Fut. 2	τυπήσεσθαι
Perf.	τετύφθαι
Fut. 3	τετύψεσθαι
Aor. 1	τυφθῆναι
Aor. 2	τυπῆναι

§ 69. Paradigm of Mute Verbs. 103

the Barytone Passive (Mutes).

ATIVE.

	Plural.	
1.	2.	3.
-όμεθα	-εσθε	-ονται
-όμεθα	-εσθε	-οντο
-όμεθα	-εσθε	-ονται
-όμεθα	-εσθε	-ονται
-ύμμεθα	-υφθε	τετυμμένοι εἰσί
-ύμμεθα	-υφθε	τετυμμένοι ἦσαν
-όμεθα	-εσθε	-ονται
-ημεν	-ητε	-ησαν
-ημεν	-ητε	-ησαν

TIVE.

-ώμεθα	-ησθε	-ωνται
-ῶμεν	-ῆτε	-ῶσι
-ῶμεν	-ῆτε	-ῶσι

TIVE.

-οίμεθα	-οισθε	-οιντο
-οίμεθα	-οισθε	-οιντο
-οίμεθα	-οισθε	-οιντο
-οίμεθα	-οισθε	-οιντο
-ημεν	-ητε	-ησαν
-εῖμεν	-εῖτε	-εῖεν
-ημεν	-ητε	-ησαν
-εῖμεν	-εῖτε	-εῖεν
τετυμμένοι εἴημεν, etc.		

ATIVE.

	-εσθε	-εσθωσαν or ἔσθων
	-υφθε	-ὑφθωσαν or ὕφθων
	-ητε	-ήτωσαν
	-ητε	-ήτωσαν

PARTICIPLES.

Pres.	τυπτόμενος	-η	-ον
Fut. 1	τυφθησόμενος	-η	-ον
Fut. 2	τυπησόμενος	-η	-ον
Perf.	τετυμμένος	-η	-ον
Fut. 3	τετυψόμενος	-η	-ον
Aor. 1	τυφθείς	-εῖσα	-έν
Aor. 2	τυπείς	-εῖσα	-έν

No. II. Paradigm of the Barytone Middle (Mutes).

INDICATIVE.

Tense.	Singular. 1.	2.	3.	Dual. 1.	2.	3.	Plural. 1.	2.	3.
Fut. 1	τύψομαι	-ῃ (ει)	-εται	-όμεθον	-εσθον	-εσθον	-όμεθα	-εσθε	-ονται
Aor. 1	ἐτυψάμην	-ω	-ατο	-όμεθον	-ασθον	-άσθην	-όμεθα	-ασθε	-αντο
Aor. 2	ἐτυπόμην	-ου	-ετο	-όμεθον	-εσθον	-έσθην	-όμεθα	-εσθε	-οντο

SUBJUNCTIVE.

Aor. 1	τύψωμαι	-ῃ	-ηται	-όμεθον	-ησθον	-ησθον	-όμεθα	-ησθε	-ωνται
Aor. 2	τυπῶμαι	-ῃ	-ηται	-όμεθον	-ησθον	-ησθον	-όμεθα	-ησθε	-ωνται

OPTATIVE.

Fut. 1	τυψοίμην	-οιο	-οιτο	-οίμεθον	-οισθον	-οίσθην	-οίμεθα	-οισθε	-οιντο
Aor. 1	τυψαίμην	-αιο	-αιτο	-αίμεθον	-αισθον	-αίσθην	-αίμεθα	-αισθε	-αιντο
Aor. 2	τυποίμην	-οιο	-οιτο	-οίμεθον	-οισθον	-οίσθην	-οίμεθα	-οισθε	-οιντο

IMPERATIVE.

Aor. 1		τύψαι	-άσθω		-ασθον	-άσθων	-ασθε	-άσθωσαν or -άσθων
Aor. 2		τυποῦ	-έσθω		-εσθον	-έσθων	-εσθε	-έσθωσαν or -έσθων

INFINITIVE.

Fut. 1 | τύψεσθαι
Aor. 1 | τύψασθαι
Aor. 2 | τυπέσθαι

PARTICIPLES.

τυψόμενος | -η- | -ον-
τυψάμενος | -η- | -ον-
τυπόμενος | -η- | -ον-

§ 69. Notes on Mute Verbs. 105

No. III. Paradigm of inflections in the Perfect Passive.

INDICATIVE.

1. Verba Pura; πεπαίδευμαι -σαι -ται. μεθον -σθον -σθον. μεθα -σθε -νται, or (usually) πεπαιδευμένοι εἰσί, sometimes πεπαιδεύαται.
2. Verbs π, β, φ; τέτριμμαι -ψαι -πται. ἴμμεθον -ιφθον -ιφθον. ἰμμεθα -ιφθε -ιμμένοι εἰσί (τετρίφαται); ground-form τρίβω.
3. Verbs κ, γ, χ; τέταγμαι -αξαι -ακται. ἄγμεθον -αχθον -αχθον. ἄγμεθα -αχθε -αγμένοι εἰσί (τετάχαται); ground-form τάσσω, root τάγω.
4. Verbs τ, δ, θ; πέπεισμαι -εισαι -εισται. εἰσμεθον -εισθον εισθον. εἰσμεθα -εισθε -εισμένοι εἰσί (πεπείθαται); ground-form πείθω.

IMPERATIVE.

πεπαίδευσο, πεπαιδεύσθω, etc. τέτριψο, τετρίφθω, etc. τέταξο, τετάχθω, etc. πέπεισο, πεπείσθω, etc. ἔσταλσο, ἐστάλθω, etc.

The form of the participles is already given in the 3d pers. plur. of the Perf. above.

I. Illustrations of No. I. (Synopsis). It will be understood, of course, that where tenses are here omitted in any particular mode, they are not formed there in this species of verbs; and where they are *wholly* omitted, (as Fut. II. act. and mid.), they are not formed by *mute* verbs, of which τύπτω is an exemplification. Where the accent does not appear on the *tense-ending*, it must be understood to lie further back.

II. Notes on the Paradigm of the Verb, and Illustrations. The design of the following remarks is to aid the student in recalling certain principles of inflection; to explain more fully some things which have merely been hinted; and to suggest some other things which have not hitherto been developed, and which may now be better understood by the aid of the Paradigm.

(1) The reader will see, that *no separate 1st pers. dual exists in the* Active. It is here of the same form with the 1st pers. plural. He will note also, that in all the *primary* tenses the two duals are alike; in all the historic ones, they end in -τον -την. Moreover, all the primary tenses end in -σι (-σιν) in the 3d pers. plural; and all the historic ones in -ν; § 53. 2. Note 1.

(2) In the Subj. mode, all its *duals* follow the analogy of the *primary* tenses (-τον -τον). The ι subscript found here in the 2d and 3d pers. sing. throughout, is occasioned by prolonging the ε in the mode-vowel (ει) of the Indic., which of course makes it η for the Subj., and thus it designates the distinction between the two modes. The Subj. has also this peculiarity, that *all its tenses are declined after the same model*, viz. all like the Present of the same mode.

(3) In like manner the Opt. throughout is all declined *uniformly*, with the exception of Aor. 1, where merely the penult vowel differs. The *dual* throughout conforms to that of the historic tenses (-τον -την); and the 3d pers. plural in like manner ends in -ν.

(4) The Imper. is uniform throughout in its flexions; except that in Aor. 1, the vowel in the derived forms conforms to the ending of the same tense in the Indic., e. g. τύψον, τυψάτω, etc., with α.

14

§ 69. Notes on Mute Verbs.

(5) The ending of the 2nd pers. sing. passive (*η*) is a contracted form of the old termination -*εσαι*, which by dropping *σ* makes -*εαι*, contr. *ῃ*. For this *η* the Attics more commonly, and also the κοινή διάλεκτος often, employ -*ει*; as the paradigm shows. *βούλει, οἴει, ὄψει* (for *βούλῃ, οἴῃ, ὄψῃ*) have even become exclusive. In the Attic (circumflexed) Future, the same peculiarity is common. In the N. Test. we find this ending; e. g. *βούλει, ὄψει, παρέξει,* etc., all 2nd pers. sing. (*ει* for *η*).

Vice versa; the old form of the 2d pers. in -*σαι* sometimes appears in the N. Testament, e. g. ὀδυνᾶσαι Luke 16: 25, καυχᾶσαι Rom. 2: 17, al., κατακαυχᾶσαι Rom. 11: 18. Even among the Attics some examples of this kind may be found; Buttm. Ausf. Sprachl, § 87. Anm. 8.

(6) In nearly (if not quite) all the cases where a circumflex appears on an ultimate syllable in the ground-form, etc., there is a contraction at the basis of the form; e. g. Attic Fut. τελῶ from τελέω, which last is made by dropping the *σ* from the ultimate of the Future (§ 63. 5); and so the Fut. of verbs λ, μ, ν, ρ (§ 66. 2. Note 2.), στελῶ, from στελέω, and this from στελέσω. Moreover the two Aor. pass. Subj., which have -ῶ -ῇς -ῇ, are contracted forms from the old or Ionic -*έω -έῃς -έῃ*, etc.; or they may be regarded (as they are by Kuhner § 199) as formed after the analogy of the Subj. of verbs in -*μι*, whose forms are the result of the like contraction. As to Inf. Aor. 2 τυπεῖν with circumflex, it is disputed whether this is the result of contraction, or of design to make distinction merely by accent. The actual existence, however, of such forms as βαλέειν (=βαλεῖν) favours the former opinion; see under *e* in No. 7 below.

(7) Various dialects have given many additional forms to several of the tenses besides those exhibited in the paradigm. For example; (*a*) Imperf. and Aor. 1, 2, have an *iterative* (intensive) form in -*σκον -σκομην* in the Indic., without any augment; as τύπτεσκον for ἔτυπτον, etc. (*b*) The Pluper. 1 and 2 has Ionic endings -*εα -εας -εε*, instead of -*ειν -εις -ει*; also -*η* is substituted by the Attics for the Ionic -*εα*, as ᾔδη for ᾔδειν, etc. (*c*) The 3d pers. plur. of the *primary* tenses has in Doric -*οντι -αντι* for -*ουσι -ασι*; as τυπτόντι, τέτυφαντι, etc. (*d*) The Subj. act. 1st pers. sing. has sometimes in Homer the paragogic -*μι*, as ἀγάγωμι; 2nd pers. sing. often and in almost all writers -*σθα* for -*ς*, as ἐθέλῃσθα; 3d pers. sing. -*σι -σιν*, Dor. -*τι*, as λάβῃσι, ἐθέλῃτι. (*e*) The Infs. act. in -*ειν*, viz. Pres. and Fut. 1 and Aor. 2, and -*ναι* of the Perfect, have, in Homer and in the older Greek, the old forms also, viz., -*έμεναι -μεναι*, or the abridged forms of these, viz. -*εμεν* -*μεναι*. The Aor. pass. has -*ήμεναι -ῆμεν* for the usual ἦναι. From the form -*εμεν*, by syncope of the *μ*, come the endings -*εεν -ειν -εῖν* employed in several tenses. Other Infinitives remain unchanged. For many lesser and merely dialectical changes, the larger Gr. grammars must be consulted.

(8) In Aor. 1 of the Opt. act. the student will perceive, under 2nd and 3d pers. sing. and 3d pers. plural, secondary forms (τύψειας, τύψειε, τύψειαν) which are called Aeolic, but *which are more usual than the regular forms.*

(9) The secondary and syncopated forms in the plur. of the passive Aorists, Opt., (τυφθεῖμεν, etc., τυπεῖμεν, etc.) *are more common than the regular ones.* The 3d plur. syncop. is almost exclusively used.

(10) The Imper. 3d plur. (τυπτόντων) in the act. voice, and Imp. 3d plur. pass. (τυπτέσθων), were the *more usual* forms among the Attics; and are also found in other dialects.

§ 70. SYNOPTICAL PARADIGMS OF MUTE VERBS. 107

III. NOTES ON PARADIGM III. OF THE FORMS OF THE PERFECT. (1) The main object here is to exhibit the various ways in which the different *mutes* are changed, before the endings -μαι -σαι -ται, etc.; see in § 10. But there are other objects; as the sequel will show.

(2) In the 3d plur. here may be seen the forms πεπαδεύαται, τετρίφαται, τετάχαται, πεπείθατοι. In these, the old poetry, the Ionics, and even the Attic poets, substituted α for the ν of the common ending, and thus made a declension-ending in the verb itself, without the use of the participle. Regularly the 3d plur. Perf. would always end in -νται (as in πεπαίδευνται, which is placed here merely in order to illustrate this); but when a *consonant* in the root precedes, this is impracticable. Hence the participial form on the one hand (the usual one), and the above peculiar form on the other which dispenses with the ν and puts a vowel in its room.

(3) The Pluperf. pass. 3d plur. ending in -ντο, and the Opt. tenses pass. which end in the same manner (-ντο), are sometimes subjected to the same changes; e. g. τυπτοίατο for τύπτοιντο, etc. The Ionics even substitute -έατο for the ending of the secondary tenses in -οντο.

(4) In those Perf. passives which come from verbs τ, δ, θ, and where σ in the Perf. is a compensation for the omitted τ, δ, or θ, (§ 64. 3. *b* 2), such σ is dropped in these peculiar forms, and the mute is restored; e. g. πείθω, πέπεισμαι, 3d plur. πεπείθαται (with θ restored) instead of πέπεινται, etc.

§ 70. *Synoptical Paradigms of mute Verbs in* -ω.

(1) In order to render more complete the exhibition of these verbs, the following Synopsis is subjoined; which may be easily understood with a little explanation. No. I. exhibits verbs of the π, β, φ class, viz. λείπω with prolonged vowel (ει) in the root, and ῥάπτω with root-character φ. On account of the ρ, (which is purposely chosen in order to exhibit its various phenomena), it is specially defective in secondary tenses. At the bottom are such tenses of τρίβω (with character β), as depend on the *character* for a development distinct from that of those with character π as in τύπτω; see § 62. 4 etc.

No. II. exhibits verbs of the κ, γ, χ class, many of which (with γ simple character) assume σσ -ττ in the Present. The verb πλέκω has the κ character; ἄρχω has a χ; τάσσω (τάττω) has originally γ; and finally κράζω has a character γ, and its leading peculiarities are placed at the bottom of the page. Only a few verbs are of this last species.

No. III. exhibits verbs of the τ, δ, θ class, with characters pure and impure; e. g. ψεύδω, πείθω, have δ, θ, for their pure character, while φράζω (=φράσδω) has the double letter ζ=σδ for the augmented present, and δ in the pure root. Those with a letter of the *T* class for their character, and which make the Pres. in -σσω (ττω), are few. I have put an exemplar at the bottom of the page, viz. πάσσω, 1 Fut. of which (πάσω not πάξω) shows that its *character* is of the *T* class of mutes. The *tempora secunda* are scarcely found in this class, excepting in a few cases in poetry. An example of possible formation is πείθω, as exhibited in the paradigm.— Of the ending -ζω here, only a very few verbs are exemplifications, and these vibrate between the γ character and the τ one; e. g. ἁρπάζω at the bottom of the page. So βαστάζω, μύζω, παίζω, and a few others.

§ 70. Synop. Paradigms of Mute Verbs.

Synoptical View

		No. I. Veibs τ, β, φ, πτ.		AC- No. II. Veibs κ, γ, χ.
Tenses.				
Pres.	λείπω	ῥάπτω	πλέκω	ἄρχω
Imp.	ἔλειπον	ἔρραπτον	ἔπλεκον	ἦρχον
Fut. 1	λείψω	ῥάψω	πλέξω	ἄρξω
Aor. 1	ἔλειψα	ἔρραψα	ἔπλεξα	ἦρξα
Perf. 1	λέλειφα	ἔρραφα	πέπλεχα	ἦρχα
Plup. 1	ἐλελείφειν	ἐρράφειν	ἐπεπλέχειν	ἤρχειν
Perf. 2	λέλοιπα			
Plup. 2	ἐλελοίπειν			
Aor. 2	ἔλιπον			
Fut. 2				

PAS-

Pres.	λείπομαι	ῥάπτομαι	πλέκομαι	ἄρχομαι
Imp.	ἐλειπόμην	ἐρραπτόμην	ἐπλεκόμην	ἠρχόμην
Fut. 1	λειφθήσομαι	ῥιφθήσομαι	πλεχθήσομαι	ἀρχθήσομαι
Fut. 2	λιπήσομαι	ῥαφήσομαι	πλακήσομαι	
Perf.	λέλειμμαι	ἔρραμμαι	πέπλεγμαι	ἦργμαι
Plup.	ἐλελείμμην	ἐρράμμην	ἐπεπλέγμην	ἤργμην
Fut. 3	λελείψομαι		πεπλέξομαι	
Aor. 1	ἐλείφθην	ἐρράφθην	ἐπλέχθην	ἤρχθην
Aor. 2	ἐλίπην	ἐρράφην	ἐπλάκην	

MID-

Fut. 1	λείψομαι	ῥάψομαι	πλέξομαι	ἄρξομαι
Aor. 1	ἐλειψάμην	ἐρραψάμην	ἐπλεξάμην	ἠρξάμην
Aor. 2	ἐλιπόμην			
Fut. 2				

τρίβω, ἔτριβον   κράζω, κράξω, P. II. κέκραγα
ἐτρίβην, τριβήσομαι   A. II. ἔκραγον

§ 70. Synop. Paradigms of Mute Verbs.

of Verba Muta.

TIVE.

No. II.		No. III.	
σσ (ττ), ζ.		τ, δ, ϑ, σσ (ττ), ζ.	
τάσσω	ψεύδω	πείϑω	φράζω
έτασσον	έψευδον	έπειϑον	έφραζον
τάξω	ψεύσω	πείσω	φράσω
έταξα	έψευσα	έπεισα	έφρασα
τέταχα	έψευκα	πέπεικα	πέφρακα
έτετάχειν	έψεύκειν	έπεπείκειν	έπεφράκειν
τέταγα		πέποιϑα	
έτετάγειν		έπεποίϑειν	
		έπιϑον	

SIVE.

τάσσομαι	ψεύδομαι	πείϑομαι	φράζομαι
έτασσόμην	έψευδόμην	έπειϑόμην	έφραζόμην
ταχϑήσομαι	ψευσϑήσομαι	πεισϑήσομαι	φρασϑήσομαι
ταγήσομαι		πιϑήσομαι	
τέταγμαι	έψευσμαι	πέπεισμαι	πέφρασμαι
έτετάγμην	έψεύσμην	έπεπείσμην	έπεφράσμην
τετύξομαι		πεπείσομαι	πεφράσομαι
έτάχϑην		έπείσϑην	έφράσϑην
έτάγην	έψεύσϑην	έπίϑην	

DLE.

τάξομαι	ψεύσομαι	πείσομαι	φράσομαι
έταξάμην	έψευσάμην	έπεισάμην	έφρασάμην
		έπιϑόμην	

πάσσω, πάσω   άρπάζω, άρπάσω
(πεπακα) πέπασμαι   and άρπάξω

§ 71. *Liquid Verbs*, i. e. *with* λ, μ, ν, ρ, *character.*

(1) By recurring to § 66. 2. Note 2, it will be seen, that Liquids form no Fut. III. pass., and seldom a Perf. II. active. The forms of Aor. I. and Perf. II. act. are those which claim some particular attention on the ground of discrepancy from most other verbs; but more especially Fut. II. (so called) act. and middle. All the various phenomena are explained in § 66. No. 1 exhibits a prolonged vowel in the Present; No. 2, a polysyllabic verb with augmented character-consonant, and excluding the exchange of vowels in Aor. 2 active and Perf. and Aor. I. passive; Nos. 3 and 4 show what vowel-changes take place in *monosyllabic* roots with ε, in the appropriate tenses. No. 5. exhibits the manner in which the circumflex Fut. (act. and midd.) is declined; which is the same as the Attic Future.

(2) Verbs in -νω of course put γ for ν when κ follows; e. g. φαίνω, πέφαγκα, § 10. R. 12. But often this is avoided; see § 66. 6. Note 2, 3.

(3) (*a*) In verbs -αίνω -ύνω, the ν is exchanged for σ, when the tense-ending begins with μ; or else the ν assimilates; e. g. φαίνω, πέφασμαι · ξηραίνω, ἐξήραμμαι. (*b*) When the tense-endings which begin with σθ follow a Liquid, the σ is dropped, e. g. πέφασμαι, πεφάσμεθον, πεφαν-θον (not πεφαν-σθον); and so in other cases, as ἠγγέλ-θαι (not -σθαι) Inf. Perf. Pass. In No. 6, the two Perfects pass., one from φαίνω with σ (in the room of ν) before μ, the other from τείνω without any σ (see *a* above), afford an exemplification of the different modes of declining this peculiar tense, in accordance with these rules.

Synopsis of Verbs λ, μ, ν, ρ.

	(1)	(2)	(3)
Pres.	φαίνω	ἀγγέλλω	στέλλω
Imp.	ἔφαινον	ἤγγελλον	ἔστελλον
Fut. 2	φανῶ	ἀγγελῶ	στελῶ
Aor. 1	ἔφηνα	ἤγγειλα	ἔστειλα
Perf. 1	(πέφαγκα)	ἤγγελκα	ἔσταλκα
Plup. 1	(ἐπεφάγκειν)	ἠγγέλκειν	ἐστάλκειν
Perf. 2	πέφηνα		
Plup. 2	ἐπεφήνειν		
Aor. 2		ἤγγελον	
Pres.	φαίνομαι	ἀγγέλλομαι	στέλλομαι
Imp.	ἐφαινόμην	ἠγγελλόμην	ἐστελλόμην
Fut. 1	φανθήσομαι	ἀγγελθήσομαι	σταλθήσομαι
Fut. 2	φανήσομαι	ἀγγελήσομαι	σταλήσομαι
Perf.	πέφασμαι	ἤγγελμαι	ἔσταλμαι
Plup.	ἐπεφάσμην	ἠγγέλμην	ἐστάλμην
Aor. 1	ἐφάνθην	ἠγγέλθην	ἐστάλθην
Aor. 2	ἐφάνην	ἠγγέλην	ἐστάλην
Fut. 2	φανοῦμαι	ἀγγελοῦμαι	στελοῦμαι
Aor. 1	ἐφηνάμην	ἠγγειλάμεν	ἐστειλάμην
Aor. 2		ἠγγελόμην	

§ 72. Pure Verbs. 111

(4) φθείρω, φθερᾶ (ἔφθαρκα), ἔφθορα.
(5) Active Future, στελῶ -εῖς -εῖ-εῖτον -εῖτον -οῦμεν -εῖτε -οῦσι, Opt. and Inf. are regular. Part. στελῶν -οῦσα -οῦν, etc. Future Middle, στελοῦμαι -εῖ (ῆ) -εῖται -ούμεθον -εῖσθον -εῖσθον -οῦμεθα -εῖσθε -οῦνται.

(6) *Perfect Passive of Liquid Verbs.*

(a)	(b)
πέφασμαι	τέταμαι
πέφανσαι	τέτασαι
πέφανται	τέταται
πέφασμεθον	τετάμεθον
πέφαν-θον	τέτι-σθον
πέφαν-θον	τέτα-σθον
πεφάσμεθα	τετάμεθα
πέφαν-θε	τέτα-σθε
πεφασμένοι εἰσί	τέτανται

PURE VERBS.

§ 72. *Peculiarities of pure Verbs.*

We come next to such verbs as have a *vowel* or *diphthong* for their character, and are named Pure on this account. These are divided into *contracted* and *uncontracted*, or (to name them from their accentuation) *perispomes* and *barytones*.

(1) This class of verbs form no *tempora secunda*.

(2) When either of the short vowels (ᾰ, ε, ῐ, ο, ῠ) is the character, the *derived* tenses usually *prolong* this vowel.

E. g. τιμάω, τιμήσω· φιλέω, φιλήσω· χρυσόω, χρυσώσω· τίω, τίσω· δακρύω, δακρύσω; and so of other tenses. The ground of this, see in § 54. 4. Note 5.

Note 1. Short ᾰ in the Pres. usually makes η (as above) in the other tenses; but if ε, ι, or ρ, precedes it, then it goes into ᾱ long; e. g. ἐάω, ἐάσω· μεδιάω, μεδιάσω· φωράω, φωράσω, etc. But χράω, χρήσω, conforms to the general rule.

(3) Exceptions. There is a considerable number of verbs, in each of the classes specified in No. 2, which retain the *short* vowel in the derived tenses; some others retain it in part, and prolong it in another part.

E. g. (*a*) *Many verbs in* -αω *retain short* ᾰ, which have a liquid before the character ᾰ; as γελάω, γελάσω· δαμάω, δαμάσω· περάω, περάσω, etc., with some others. (*b*) *A considerable number in* -εω; e. g. ἀλέω, ἀλέσω· τρέω, τρέσω; while several verbs vibrate between both methods, as αἰνέω, αἰνέσω and αἰνήσω, and in like manner καλέω, αἱρέω, γαμέω, δέω, ποθέω, πονέω, adopt a different usage in different tenses, as καλέω, καλέσω, κέκληκα, etc.

(c) In -οω; only ἀρόω makes ἀρόσω, etc., with short ŏ. (d) In -ίω; only χρίω, φθίω, with ῖ short in the derivates; and here some of the tenses have the vowel prolonged. (e) In -ΰω; but few retain the short vowel uniformly, such as ἀνύω, ἀρύω, πτύω, etc. Most verbs here vibrate in different tenses between the long and short vowel; e. g. λύω, λύσω, λέλυκα, λέλυμαι, and so with δύω, θύω, μύω, ἐρύω, and some others.

NOTE. As the usage differs so much here in different verbs, in respect to employing a long or short vowel; and in the same verb varies in different tenses; it is evident that *practice* only can effectually guide the learner here.

(4) In those verbs which retain the *short* vowel of the character in their derivate tenses, the Perf. pass., (with Plup., Aor. I., and Fut. I. pass., which conform to it), takes σ before the tense endings.

E. g. τελέω, τελέσω, τετέλεσμαι, ἐτετελέσμην, ἐτελέσθην, τελεσθήσομαι; on the contrary, τιμάω, τετίμη-μαι, ἐτιμήθην, τιμηθήσομαι, etc.

NOTE. But here, too, there are many EXCEPTIONS. (a) Some with long vowels and even dipthongs in the derived tenses, take σ (against the general rule) in the tenses named; e. g. ἀκούω, ἤκουσμαι, ἠκούσθην · χράω, χρήσω, κέχρησμαι; and so of several other verbs. (b) Some vibrate between both usages; e. g. γεύω, γέγευμαι, ἐγεύσθην · δράω, δέδραμαι, δέδρασμαι, etc., with several others: while some omit σ in the Perf. and take it in Aor. I., as παύω, πέπαυμαι, ἐπαύσθην, with some others. (c) Finally, some with a *short* vowel in the derived tenses *omit* the σ, (contrary to the rule above); e. g. αἰνέω, αἰνέσω, ᾔνεμαι, ᾐνέθην, and the like with αἱρέω, δέω, γαμέω, χέω, and some others.

(5) ANOMALIES. The verbs καίω, κλαίω, δαίω make the Fut. in αυ; e. g. καύσω, κλαύσομαι, etc.

§ 73. CONTRACT VERBS.

(1) Such are all verbs in -ω which have ᾰ, ε, ο, for their character. The contraction is limited to the Pres. and Imperf. tenses, because in these only the *vowel-character* of the root comes in contact with a vowel of the tense ending.

(2) The formation of the derived tenses is mostly *regular*, and has already been given in § 72.

(3) The contractions are made in accordance with the rules in § 13, and by these the student can explain them all.

NOTE. As a mere *technical* guide, however, in order to aid the memory, the following hints may be worth attention.

1. *Verbs in -άω.* (a) The α is dropped before the O class of vowels (ο, ω, οι, ου), all of which then become or remain ω. If ι was connected with the O class, it is then subscribed under this ω; as τιμάοιμι, τιμῷμι. (b) The α expels the E class (ε, η, ῃ) that follows it, and receives ι under it, in case it was connected with this E class; as τιμάει, τιμᾷ · τιμάῃς, τιμᾷς.

§ 74. SYNOPSIS OF PURE VERBS. 113

2. *Verbs in -έω.* (a) The ε falls out before all long vowels and all diphthongs. (b) εε goes in ει; εο into ου; as φιλέεται, φιλεῖται· φιλέομεν, φιλοῦμεν.

3. *Verbs in -όω.* (a) Short ο falls out before the prolonged O class (ω, οι, ου); while οο and οε contract into ου, as χρυσόομεν, χρυσοῦμεν· χρυσόετον, χρυσοῦτον. (b) The short ο of the root expels η of the ending, and then goes into ω; as χρυσόητον, χρυσῶτον. (c) Short ο before ει or η expels the E (short and long), and receives the ι into a diphthong with itself; e. g. μισθόεις, μισθοῖς· μισθόης μισθοῖς.

NOTE. The Infinitive τιμᾶν is from τιμάεν (old form); and χρυσοῦν from χρυσόεν, (id.)

(4) The Attic and common dialect usually employ the contracted forms; the Ionic uses the uncontracted ones in -έω, but not usually in -άω -όω.

EXCEPTIONS. *Monosyllabic* roots in -έω contract, by usage, only in cases where the ending is -εει -εε, (and then into -εῖ); thus πλέω, πλέομεν, πλέουσι, Subj. πλέω, πλέῃς, πλέῃ. πλέωμεν, etc., uncontracted; but πλεῖς, πλεῖ, πλεῖτε, etc., contracted. And thus in respect to πνέω, θέω, and the like.

§ 74. *Synopsis of Pure Verbs.*

ACTIVE.

Pres.	λύω	παιδεύω	τιμάω-ῶ
Imp.	ἔλυον	ἐπαίδευον	ἐτίμαον-ων
Fut. 1	λύσω	παιδεύσω	τιμήσω
Aor. 1	ἔλυσα	ἐπαίδευσα	ἐτίμησα
Perf. 1	λέλυκα	πεπαίδευκα	τετίμηκα
Plup.	ἐλελύκειν	ἐπεπαιδεύκειν	ἐτετιμήκειν

PASSIVE.

Pres.	λύομαι	παιδεύομαι	τιμάομαι-ῶμαι
Imp.	ἐλυόμην	ἐπαιδευόμην	ἐτιμαόμην-ώμην
Fut. 1	λυθήσομαι	παιδευθήσομαι	τιμηθήσομαι
Perf.	λέλυμαι	πεπαίδευμαι	τετίμημαι
Plup.	ἐλελύμην	ἐπεπαιδεύμην	ἐτετιμήμην
Fut. 3	λελύσομαι	πεπαιδεύσομαι	τετιμήσομαι
Aor. 1	ἐλύθην	ἐπαιδεύθην	ἐτιμήθην

MIDDLE.

Fut. 1	λύσομαι	παιδεύσομαι	τιμήσομαι
Aor. 1	ἐλυσάμην	ἐπαιδευσάμην	ἐτιμησάμην

§ 75. Paradigm of Contracts.

§ 75. Paradigm of ACTIVE.

		Present. τιμ-		φιλ-		χρυσ-	
Ind.	S.	άω	-ῶ	έω	-ῶ	όω	-ῶ
		άεις	-ᾷς	έεις	-εῖς	όεις	-οῖς
		άει	-ᾷ	έει	-εῖ	όει	-οῖ
	D.	άετον	-ᾶτον	έετον	-εῖτον	όετον	-οῦτον
		άετον	-ᾶτον	έετον	-εῖτον	όετον	-οῦτον
	P.	άομεν	-ῶμεν	έομεν	-οῦμεν	όομεν	-οῦμεν
		άετε	-ᾶτε	έετε	-εῖτε	όετε	-οῦτε
		άουσι	-ῶσι	έουσι	-οῦσι	όουσι	-οῦσι
Subj.	S.	άω	-ῶ	έω	-ῶ	όω	-ῶ
		άῃς	-ᾷς	έῃς	-ῇς	όῃς	-οῖς
		άῃ	-ᾷ	έῃ	-ῇ	όῃ	-οῖ
	D.	άητον	-ᾶτον	έητον	-ῆτον	όητον	-ῶτον
		άητον	-ᾶτον	έητον	-ῆτον	όητον	-ῶτον
	P.	άωμεν	-ῶμεν	έωμεν	-ῶμεν	όωμεν	-ῶμεν
		άητε	-ᾶτε	έητε	-ῆτε	όητε	-ῶτε
		άωσι	-ῶσι	έωσι	-ῶσι	όωσι	-ῶσι
Opt.	S.	άοιμι	-ῷμι	έοιμι	-οῖμι	όοιμι	-οῖμι
		άοις	-ῷς	έοις	-οῖς	όοις	-οῖς
		άοι	-ῷ	έοι	-οῖ	όοι	-οῖ
	D.	άοιτον	-ῷτον	έοιτον	-οῖτον	όοιτον	-οῖτον
		αοίτην	-ῴτην	εοίτην	-οίτην	οοίτην	-οίτην
	P.	άοιμεν	-ῷμεν	έοιμεν	-οῖμεν	όοιμεν	-οῖμεν
		άοιτε	-ῷτε	έοιτε	-οῖτε	όοιτε	-οῖτε
		άοιεν	-ῷεν	έοιεν	-οῖεν	όοιεν	-οῖεν
Imp.	S.	αε	-α	εε	-ει	οε	-ου
		αέτω	-άτω	εέτω	-είτω	οέτω	-ούτω
	D.	άετον	-ᾶτον	έετον	-εῖτον	όετον	-οῦτον
		αέτων	-άτων	εέτων	-είτων	οέτων	-ούτων
	P.	άετε	-ᾶτε	έετε	-εῖτε	όετε	-οῦτε
		αέτωσαν	-άτωσαν	εέτωσαν	-είτωσαν	οέτωσαν	-ούτωσαν
Inf.		άειν	-ᾶν	έειν	-εῖν	όειν	-οῦν
Part.	M.	άων	-ῶν	έων	-ῶν	όων	-ῶν
	F.	άουσα	-ῶσα	έουσα	-οῦσα	όουσα	-οῦσα
	N.	άον	-ῶν	έον	-οῦν	όον	-οῦν

Imperf. ἐτίμ- ἐφίλ- ἐχρύσ-

Ind.	S.	αον	-ων	εον	-ουν	οον	-ουν
		αες	-ας	εες	-εις	οες	-ους
		αε	-α	εε	-ει	οε	-ου
	D.	άετον	-ᾶτον	έετον	-εῖτον	όετον	-οῦτον
		αέτην	-άτην	εέτην	-είτην	οέτην	-ούτην
	P.	άομεν	-ῶμεν	έομεν	-οῦμεν	όομεν	-οῦμεν
		άετε	-ᾶτε	έετε	-εῖτε	όετε	-οῦτε
		αον	-ων	εον	-ουν	οον	-ουν

§ 75. Paradigm of Contracts.

Contract Verbs.

PASSIVE.

τιμ-		φιλ-		χρυσ-	
άομαι	-ῶμαι	έομαι	-οῦμαι	όομαι	-οῦμαι
άῃ	-ᾷ	έῃ	-ῇ	όῃ	-οῖ
άεται	-ᾶται	έεται	-εῖται	όεται	-οῦται
αόμεθον	-ώμεθον	εόμεθον	-ούμεθον	οόμεθον	-ούμεθον
άεσθον	-ᾶσθον	έεσθον	-εῖσθον	όεσθον	-οῦσθον
άεσθον	-ᾶσθον	έεσθον	-εῖσθον	όεσθον	-οῦσθον
αόμεθα	-ώμεθα	εόμεθα	-ούμεθα	οόμεθα	-ούμεθα
άεσθε	-ᾶσθε	έεσθε	-εῖσθε	όεσθε	-οῦσθε
άονται	-ῶνται	έονται	-οῦνται	όονται	-οῦνται
άωμαι	-ῶμαι	έωμαι	-ῶμαι	όωμαι	-ῶμαι
άῃ	-ᾷ	έῃ	-ῇ	όῃ	-οῖ
άηται	-ᾶται	έηται	-ῆται	όηται	-ῶται
αώμεθον	-ώμεθον	εώμεθον	-ώμεθον	οώμεθον	-ώμεθον
άησθον	-ᾶσθον	έησθον	-ῆσθον	όησθον	-ῶσθον
άησθον	-ᾶσθον	έησθον	-ῆσθον	όησθον	-ῶσθον
αώμεθα	-ώμεθα	εώμεθα	-ώμεθα	οώμεθα	-ώμεθα
άησθε	-ᾶσθε	έησθε	-ῆσθε	όησθε	-ῶσθε
άωνται	-ῶνται	έωνται	-ῶνται	όωνται	-ῶνται
αοίμην	-ῴμην	εοίμην	-οίμην	οοίμην	-οίμην
άοιο	-ῷο	έοιο	-οῖο	όοιο	-οῖο
άοιτο	-ῷτο	έοιτο	-οῖτο	όοιτο	-οῖτο
αοίμεθον	-ῴμεθον	εοίμεθον	-οίμεθον	οοίμεθον	-οίμεθον
άοισθον	-ῷσθον	έοισθον	-οῖσθον	όοισθον	-οῖσθον
αοίσθην	-ῴσθην	εοίσθην	-οίσθην	οοίσθην	-οίσθην
αοίμεθα	-ῴμεθα	εοίμεθα	-οίμεθα	οοίμεθα	-οίμεθα
άοισθε	-ῷσθε	έοισθε	-οῖσθε	όοισθε	-οῖσθε
άοιντο	-ῷντο	έοιντο	-οῖντο	όοιντο	-οῖντο
άου	-ῶ	έου	-οῦ	όου	-οῦ
αέσθω	-άσθω	εέσθω	-είσθω	οέσθω	-ούσθω
άεσθον	-ᾶσθον	έεσθον	-εῖσθον	όεσθον	-οῦσθον
άεσθων	-άσθων	εέσθων	-είσθων	οέσθων	-ούσθων
άεσθε	-ᾶσθε	έεσθε	-εῖσθε	όεσθε	-οῦσθε
αέσθωσαν	-άσθωσαν	εέσθωσαν	-είσθωσαν	οέσθωσαν	-ούσθωσαν
άεσθαι	-ᾶσθαι	έεσθαι	-εῖσθαι	όεσθαι	-οῦσθαι
αόμενος	-ώμενος	εόμενος	-ούμενος	οόμενος	-ούμενος
αομένη	-ωμένη	εομένη	-ουμένη	οομένη	-ουμένη
αόμενον	-ώμενον	εόμενον	-ούμενον	οόμενον	-ούμενον

ἐτιμ-		ἐφιλ-		ἐχρυσ-	
αόμην	-ώμην	εόμην	-ούμην	οόμην	-ούμην
άου	-ῶ	έου	-οῦ	όου	-οῦ
άετο	-ᾶτο	έετο	-εῖτο	όετο	-οῦτο
αόμεθον	-ώμεθον	εόμεθον	-ούμεθον	οόμεθον	-ούμεθον
άεσθον	-ᾶσθον	έεσθον	-εῖσθον	όεσθον	-οῦσθον
αέσθην	-άσθην	εέσθην	-είσθην	οέσθην	-οίσθην
αόμεθα	-ώμεθα	εόμεθα	-ούμεθα	οόμεθα	-ούμεθα
άεσθε	-ᾶσθε	έεσθε	-εῖσθε	όεσθε	-οῦσθε
άοντο	-ῶντο	έοντο	-οῦντο	όοντο	-οῦντο

§ 76. *Notes on Contract Verbs.*

(1) Instead of the forms of the Opt. Pres. exhibited in the paradigm, the Attic usually, and other dialects occasionally, employed, particularly in the singular, a *contracted* form with the ending -ην instead of -μι, which is regularly declined; e. g. τιμῴην -ῴης -ῴη ῴητον -ῴητον ῴημεν -ῴητε -ῴησαν. So φιλοίην -ης, -η, etc.; χρυσοίην -ης -η, etc.

(2) The Subj. and Opt. Perf. pass. of κέκτημαι, μέμνημαι, is formed in a regular way; as Subj. κέκτωμαι, Opt. κεκτῄμην and -ῴμην; Subj. μεμνωμαι, Opt. μεμνῄμην and -ῴμην, etc. In general, these tenses are formed in the Contracts as elsewhere, viz. by a Part. and the verb εἰμί.

(3) The epic and the different dialects made minute changes almost without number in the contracted verbs; which can be learned only from the lexicons, larger grammars, and practice.

(4) Some verbs in -άω (e. g. ζάω, πεινάω, διψάω, and some others) take η instead of ᾱ in the contracted forms of αε, αει; as ζάω -ῶ, ζάεις -ῇς (not ζᾷς), ζάει -ῇ (not ζᾷ), etc.; Imperf. contracted, ἔζης, ἔζη, etc.

(5) Five verbs in -έω signifying constant motion, have an anomalous Fut. -είσω; viz. πλέω, ῥέω, θέω, νέω, πνέω, Fut. πλεύσω, ῥεύσω, etc.; χέω, Fut. χεύω.

§ 77. *Accentuation of Verbs.*

The minute detail of this would be out of place here; the leading principles will be very briefly stated.

(1) GENERAL RULE. The accent is placed as far back as the nature of syllables will permit.

(2) When an accented *augment* falls away, the accent goes upon the next succeeding syllable, as ἔβαλε, βάλε; and if this be the only remaining syllable of the word, it takes the circumflex, as ἔβη, βῆ.

(3) The circumflexed forms of various tenses are to be regarded as contracts (-έω into -ῶ); and so of circumflexed temporal augments, as ἀνῆπτον=ἀνέαπτον.

Exceptions from the general principle in No. 1.

(4) ACCENT ON THE ULTIMATE. (1) Aor. II. act. in the Inf. and Participle; also Aor. II. midd. Imper. e. g. γενοῦ. (2) In the Imper. of Aor. II. act. (contrary to common usage elsewhere), εἰπέ, ἐλθέ, εὑρέ, (Att.) λαβέ, ἰδέ, are oxytones. (3) All participles in -ς with Gen. -τος, excepting those of Aor. I. active; e. g. τετυφώς, τυπείς, ἐκβάς, διδούς, etc.; but Aor. I. τύψας, etc.

(5) ACCENT ON THE PENULT. (*a*) In the passive Perf. Inf. and Part.; as τετύφθαι, τετυμμένος. (*b*) In all the usual Infinitives

in -ναι; as τετυφέναι, τυπῆναι, τιθέναι. (c) In Aor. I. Inf. and Part. active, as τύψαι, τύψας; also in Aor. II. midd., as τυπέσθαι. (d) In all the Optatives in -οι -αι, as φυλάττοι, φυλάξαι. (e) In 3d plur. pres. of verbs in -μι, as τιθεῖσι, διδοῦσι, etc.

(6) COMPOUND VERBS. Here, (a) The accent can never go farther back than the augment, while this augment is retained, as ἀνέσχον; but if it be dropped the accent may recede, as προσέβη, πρόσβη.

(b) When a preposition is united with a verb, the accent cannot recede beyond its usual place on the preposition; e. g. παράσχες, ἐπίθες.

NOTE 1. If two prepositions are prefixed, the accent cannot recede beyond the second; e. g. συνέκδος.

NOTE 2. With the above exceptions, the accent in compound verbs falls as far back as quantity will allow; e. g. πρόσφερε, σύνοιδα, ἔκφευγε, etc. Even in Aor. II. Mid. and Act., where some simple verbs are oxytones, (4. 2. sup.) *compound* ones throw back the accent in the Imper.; as ἔξελθε, ἐπιλάθου. Verbs in -μι have various usage here.

(7) PARTICIPLES. The accent in the ground-form is retained in *all* cases throughout on the *same* syllable, when quantity permits; as φυλάττων, φυλάττουσα, φυλάττον, etc.

VERBS IN -μι.

§ 78. *Distinguishing traits of these verbs.*

(1) These are various; (a) They receive the tense-endings in the Indic. without the union-vowel common to other verbs; the character-vowel of the root belonging to, or assumed by, the Verb, being itself made subservient to the union.

(b) Some of the tense-endings are peculiar to these verbs; e. g. -μι -σι, 1st. and 3d. person singular.

(c) Only the Pres. and Imperf. of these forms are common to all the Voices; Aor. II. is formed in the Act. and Mid., but scarcely ever in the Passive. These are all the tenses which are peculiar to these verbs.

NOTE. Only ἵστημι, τίθημι, δίδωμι, and ἵημι, form all of even these tenses. Most verbs of this class employ only parts or fragments of certain tenses with these irregular formations, making up the rest by regular formations from regular kindred roots, either actual or assumed.

(d) They are all *augmented* forms; and most of them have

§ 78. Verbs in μι.

a kind of reduplication at the beginning, as well as an extension in the middle of the root; as will be seen in the sequel.

(2) Verbs in -μι are divided into two classes, viz. (1) Those which come from roots of the contract *verba pura*, most of which assume a prosthetic syllable in the formation; (2) Those which are derived from various sources and receive the epenthetic -ννυ or -νυ before the tense-endings.

(3) CLASS I. These nearly all come from roots -άω -έω -όω; and the monosyllabic roots generally have a formative reduplication, and all have a prolonged vowel.

E. g. στάω, ἵστημι· θέω, τίθημι· δόω, δίδωμι; here ᾰ and ῐ of the roots go into η in the new formations, and ο into ω, thus making a prolonged vowel. THE REDUPLICATION is governed by the following laws, viz. (a) In roots with a simple consonant for the first letter, or with a mute and a liquid, the first consonant united with ι is prefixed; e. g. θέω, τί-θημι (τ not θ, § 10. R. 4); δόω δί-δωμι· χράω, κί-χρημι. (b) When the root begins with an aspirated vowel, or with στ or πτ, the ι is prefixed, with the rough breathing instead of a consonant before it; e. g. ἕω, ἵημι· στάω, ἵστημι· πτάω, ἵπταμαι.

NOTE 1. The original root must be *monosyllabic* in order to admit this reduplication. Other roots exclude it; e. g. δάμνημι from δαμάω, ἴλημι from ἱλάω, πέρνημι from περνάω, etc. excepting only ὀνίνημι. Four monosyllabic roots also exclude it, viz. those of εἰμί, εἶμι, φημί, and ἔχρην (Imperf.)

NOTE 2. One verb with root ἰ, viz. εἶμι (*to go*), and some few with υ in the root, belong to verbs in -μι, as ἐρύω, ἔρυμαι (Midd.); but these are too few to vary the common classification.

NOTE 3. The *original* root may easily be found in this class of verbs, by rejecting reduplication and tense-endings, and then shortening the vowel which precedes the latter.

(4) CLASS II. This consists of verbs which insert ννυ or νυ before the tense-endings, and then (like Class I.) attach the latter without the usual union-vowel. This class forms no Aor. II.

NOTE 1. (a) When the root ends in a *vowel*, the epenthetic ννυ is added; e. g. σκεδά-ω, σκεδάννυμι· κορέ-ω, κορέννυμι· στρό-ω, στρώννυμι, etc. (b) When it ends in a *consonant*, νυ is inserted; e. g. ΔΕΙΚ, δείκνυμι· ΟΜ, ὄμνυμι.

NOTE 2. Even in the Pres. and Imperf., specially in the latter, forms from a regular Present, e. g. like δεικνύω, etc., are in use, and oftentimes predominate.

(5) PROLONGATION OF THE ROOT-VOWEL. (*a*) This takes place in the Act. voice and *singular* number only, in the Indic. mode of verbs *belonging to Class I.*, and belongs to the three tenses of these verbs; but Conj. I., i. e. such verbs as end in -αω, makes Aor. II. long in the Indic., Imper., and Inf. *throughout*. Beyond

the singular number, the *short* root-vowel is in other cases employed as the union-vowel.

E. g. ἵστησι, ἱστᾶτον, ἱστᾶμεν, etc.; δίδωσι, δίδοτον, δίδομεν; and so of the other tenses, with the exception above named, viz. ἔστην, ἔστητον, ἔστησαν, etc. But Aor. II. Inf. has an extended vowel in all the forms; e. g. στῆναι, θεῖναι, δοῦναι.

NOTE. The model of this Aor. II. (ἔστην) *with a long vowel throughout*, is followed exactly by Aor. I. II. pass. of verbs in -ω, even in the Imper. and Inf. of these tenses.

(*b*) *Verbs of Class II.* (1) Those with epenthetic ννν retain the *short* vowel of their root throughout; excepting that those with *o* go into ω. (2) Verbs with epenthetic νυ (i. e. those with a consonant-character), *prolong* the vowel that precedes the νυ.

E. g. of the first species, σκεδάννυμι, κορέννυμι; and with ο, στρώννυμι, etc. Of the second, with a consonant-character, ΠΑΓ, πήγνυμι· ΔΕΚ, δείκνυμι· ΖΥΓ, ζεύγνυμι. Some, however, insert νη instead of prolonging the vowel; e. g. ΔΑΜ, δάμνημι· ΠΕΡ, πέρνημι.

(6) The Subj. mode employs the common union-vowels of other verbs, viz. ω, η; but these *coalesce* with the character-vowel of the root in a peculiar manner.

E. g. -αη -αη make ῇ, ῇ by coalescence, (and not ᾶ, ᾷ as in the Contracts, (but comp. ζάω, ζῇς, ζῇ, etc.); and οη makes ῷ (not οῖ); e. g.

full form	contr.	full form	contr.	full form	contr
ἱστάω	ἱστῶ	διδόω	διδῶ	τιθέω	τιθῶ
ἱστάῃς	ἱστῇς	διδόῃς	διδῷς	τιθέῃς	τιθῇς
ἱστάηται	ἱστῆται	διδόῃ	διδῷ	τιθέῃ	τιθῇ

Aor. 2 Subj. follows the same model; and so do Aor. I. II. pass. Subj. of all regular verbs as τυφθῶ -ῇς -ῇ, etc.; τυπῶ -ῇς -ῇ, etc.

(7) The Optative, which elsewhere has οι for its union-vowel, here substitutes the short vowel of the root in the place of the ο, and then assuming -ην in the act. as its ending, declines regularly with the usual tense-endings. The like with the ending -μην in the Passive.

E. g. ἱσταίην -αίης, etc.; τιθείην -είης, etc.; διδοίην -οίης, etc.; so Aor. II. σταίην, θείην, δοίην· ἱσταίμην, τιθείμην, etc., Passive.

NOTE. Verbs in -υμι almost exclusively form both the Subj. and Opt., as if from regular roots; e. g. δεικνύω -ῇς -ῇ, etc.; δικνύοιμι -οις -οι, etc. A few examples there are, where the υ unites with the mode-vowel, as in Class I., and contraction takes place.

(8) THE INF. takes -ναι formative throughout; in the Present, -ναι is preceded by the *short* vowel of the root, but Aor. II. *prolongs* the vowel before it; see in paradigm.

(9) *The Participles* all take -ς in the ground form, (with a preceding -ντ implied, as the Gen. shows), and consequently the root-vowel that precedes them is extended before this ς; § 24. 2. *a.* 2.

NOTE. In the same manner are formed the participles of Aor. I. II. pass. of verbs in -ω; e. g. τυφθείς, τυπείς.

(10) THE PASSIVE AND MIDDLE VOICES preserve the *short* vowel of the root throughout the Indic., and use it as the union-vowel in all the modes excepting the Subj. and Optative. In the latter it coalesces with the union-vowel, as described in Nos. 6, 7.

NOTE 1. Only the 2nd pers. sing. has a peculiar tense-ending, with variations; see in the Par.—The verbs τίθημι and ἵημι make Perf. act. and pass. τέθεικα, τέθειμαι · εἷκα, εἷμαι; contrary to the general rule above.

(11) As to the formation of the other tenses of these verbs, which tenses are regular, the usual rules of forming them in *verba pura* must be applied in respect to the prolongation of vowels in derived tenses, etc.

NOTE. Three verbs, viz. τίθημι, δίδωμι and ἵημι, form a peculiar Aor. I., viz. ἔθηκα, ἔδωκα, and ἧκα. But this extends not beyond the Indic. mode. The Perf. of τίθημι and ἵημι is also irregular; see No. 10. Note.

GENERAL REMARKS. The first class of verbs here, (-αω -εω -οω) form no Aor. II., Fut. II., or Fut. III., *passive.* The second class form very rarely the Aor. II. active, and as rarely Aor. II. and Fut. II. passive.

§ 79. *Notes on the Verbs in -μι.*

(1) The Paradigms show peculiar variations of forms, here in many cases, which should be specially noted; e. g. in the Imperf. act., in the Opt. also, and in the Imper. of the same voice both Pres. and Aor. II.; in the Passive 2nd pers. sing. Pres. of Indic. and Imper., and of the Imperf.; also in the Middle, Aor. II. Indic. and Imperative.

(2) In the Imperf. sing. act. all the verbs in -μι (the first conj. only excepted, viz. ἵστημι) usually have forms like the barytones in -ω; and the 2d and 3d pers. sing. are *generally* of this kind. Even in the case of ἵστημι, the Ionic has such forms in the Imperf., e. g. ἵστων, ἵστας, ἵστα, etc. In the Present, the 1st pers. sing. is generally of the form in -μι; the other persons often take the barytone form, i. e. they appear as if coming from ἱστάω, τιθέω, διδόω, etc.

(3) In the Subj. mode throughout, act. and passive, the accent does not fall back as in regular verbs, *but remains on the syllable that follows the root*; e. g. τιθῆτον (not τίθητον), διδοῖτον (not δίδοιτον), ἱστῶμαι (not ἵστωμαι), διδῶσθον (not δίδωσθον), etc. This comes from *contraction*; see § 78. 6.

(4) The preceding remarks apply to the usual Subj., when it is actually formed from verbs in -μι. But the Attics often formed and accented both

§ 78. NOTES ON VERBS IN -μι.

the Subj. and Opt., Pres. and Aor. II. of the verbs τίθημι, δίδωμι, and ἵημι, as if they were from the roots τίθω, δίδω, ἵω; e. g. τίθωμαι, τιθοίμην -τί-θοιτο· δίδωμαι, διδοίμην -δίδοιτο· ἵωμαι, ἱοίμην -ἵοιτο· Aor. II. πρόσθω-μαι, προσθοίμην -πρόσθοιτο, etc. In all such cases, the regular union-vowel of verbs in -ω is employed, and the accentuation therefore accords with the usual one in those verbs. The Opt. of ἵσταμαι (pass.) imitates this accentuation; e. g. ἵσταιο, ἵσταιτο; and so also is the Opt. of δύναμαι accented, and of other verbs declined like ἵστομαι in the pass. and mid. forms.

NOTE. The usual accentuation of the common Opt. *pass.*, τιθεῖο, τιθεῖτο· διδοῖο, διδοῖτο, etc., instead of τίθειο etc., δίδοιο, etc., is wrong, because here the *root-vowel* simply takes the places of the common mode or union-vowel, and the quantity remains as in regular verbs, there being no contraction; see Kuhner § 205. Anm. 1.

(5) The Imper. Aor. 2 middle puts a circumflex on the simple forms, in the 2d pers. sing., which only a *dissyllabic* preposition moves back; e. g. θοῦ and also ἐνθοῦ, but κατάθου. Out of the 2d pers. sing., the accentuation is as usual; c. g. ἔνθεσθε, κατάθεσθε, etc.

(6) The peculiar accentuation of the 3d plur. Pres. Ind. of the Act., viz. ἱστᾶσι, τιθεῖσι, etc., arises from the old ending here -νσι, (ἵστανσι, τίθενσι, etc.), which the Attics changed by substituting α for the ν. We have then, (Attice) ἱστάασι, τιθέασι, διδόασι, etc. (forms sometimes found in the N. Test.), and by contraction the usual forms in the Paradigms.

(7) The dialects occasion a great variety of changes in these irregular verbs. Some of these are, (a) Prolongation of forms; e. g. θῶ, Ion. θέω, Epic. θείω: so στῶ, στέω, στείω, etc.; δῶ, δώω, Opt. δῴη for δοίη in the N. Test., etc. (b) The Inf. in -μεν -μεναι, as τιθέμεν, τιθέμεναι, for τιθέναι; δόμεν, δόμεναι, for δοῦναι, etc. (c) So ἐτίθεα (Ion.) for ἐτίθην, ἐτίθεν (epic) for ἐτίθεσαν, διδόντι (Dor.) for διδοῦσι, τιθέαται (Ion.) for τίθενται, etc.

GENERAL REMARKS. I. It is now generally agreed among recent grammarians, who have made extensive research, that the forms in -μι approach nearest of all to the original and most ancient Greek. The Aeolic and Doric present most forms of this kind; and these dialects are regarded as the best index of the ancient Greek.

REM. II. The number of verbs in -μι, in the common language, is not great. (1) Of CLASS I., (which have a short vowel for their character to which the personal terminations are directly attached), there are, according to Kuhner, 20 of the ᾰ class act. and 11 deponent; 7 of the ε class; one in ἰ (εἶμι to go); two of the ο class (δίδωμι and ὄνομαι); and 7 of the ῠ class (c. g. εἴρυμι, κίνυμαι, etc.) (2) CLASS II.; roots ending in a short vowel, (ᾰ, ε, ῐ, ο) to which -νυ is attached, 17; roots ending in a consonant followed by -νυ, of the mute character 14, of the liquid 9. *Most* of these, however, belong only to the poetic idiom, or to some of the dialects. Some few of nearly all the classes are in common use.

§ 79. Paradigm of the

INDICATIVE, etc. (Present.)

Pres.	ἵστημι	-ης	-ησι	-ατον	-ατον	-αμεν	-ατε	-ᾶσι	Att.
	τίθημι	-ης	-ησι	-ετον	-ετον	-εμεν	-ετε	-εῖσι or -ἐᾶσι
	δίδωμι	-ως	-ωσι	-οτον	-οτον	-ομεν	-οτε	-οῦσι or -όᾶσι
	δείκνυμι	-υς	-υσι	-υτον	-υτον	-υμεν	-υτε	-ῦσι or ὑᾶσι

SUBJUNCTIVE.

Pres.	ἱστῶ	-ῇς	-ῇ	-ῆτον	-ῆτον	-ῶμεν	-ῆτε	-ῶσι
	τιθῶ	-ῇς	-ῇ	-ῆτον	-ῆτον	-ῶμεν	-ῆτε	-ῶσι
	διδῶ	-ῷς	-ῷ	-ῶτον	-ῶτον	-ῶμεν	-ῶτε	-ῶσι
	δεικνύω	-ύῃς	-ύῃ	-ύητον	-ύητον	-ύωμεν	-ύητε	-ύωσι

OPTATIVE.

Pres.	ἱσταίην	-ης	-η	-ητον / -αῖτον	-ήτην / -αίτην	-ημεν / -αῖμεν	-ητε / -αῖτε	-ησαν / -αῖεν
	τιθείην	-ης	-η	-ητον / -εῖτον	-ήτην / -είτην	-ημεν / -εῖμεν	-ητε / -εῖτε	-ησαν / -εῖεν
	διδοίην	-ης	-η	-ητον / -οῖτον	-ήτην / -οίτην	-ημεν / -οῖμεν	-ητε / -οῖτε	-ησαν / -οῖεν
	δεικνύοιμι	-οις	-οι	-οιτον	-οίτην	-οιμεν	-οιτε	-οιεν

IMPERATIVE.

Pres.	ἵσταθι / ἵστη	-άτω	-ατον	-άτων	-ατε	-τωσαν or -άντων
	τίθετι / τίθει	-έτω	-ετον	-έτων	-ετε	-τωσαν or -έντων
	δίδοθι / δίδου	-ότω	-οτον	-ότων	-οτε	-τωσαν or -όντων
	δείκνυθι / δείκνῡ	-ύτω	-υτον	-ύτων	-υτε	-τωσαν or -ύντων

INFINITIVE.

Pres.
ἱστάναι
τιθέναι
διδόναι
δεικνύναι

PARTICIPLE.

Pres.
ἱστάς -ᾶσα -άν
τιθείς -εῖσα -έν
διδούς -οῦσα -όν, Gen. ὄντος, etc.
δεικνύς -ῦσα -ύν

§ 79. Verbs in -μι. (*Active.*)

Verbs in -μι.

INDICATIVE, ETC. (IMPERF. and AOR. II.)

	ἵστην	-ης	-η	-ατον	-άτην	-αμεν	-ατε	-ασαν
	ἐτίθην	-ης	-η	-ετον	-έτην	-εμεν	-ετε	-εσαν
	ἐτίθουν	-θεις	-ει					
Impf.	ἐδίδων	-ως	-ω	-οτον	-ότην	-ομεν	-οτε	-οσαν
	ἐδίδουν	-ους	-ου					(ἐδίδουν)
	ἐδείκνυν	-υς	-υ	-υτον	-ύτην	-υμεν	-υτε	-υσαν
	ἐδείκνυον	-υες	-υε					

INDICATIVE.

	ἔστην	-ης	-η	-ητον	-ήτην	-ημεν	-ητε	-ησαν
Aor. 2	ἔθην	-ης	-η	-ετον	-έτην	-εμεν	-ετε	-εσαν
	ἔδων	-ως	-ω	-οτον	-ότην	-ομεν	-οτε	-οσαν

SUBJUNCTIVE.

	στῶ	-ῇς	-ῇ	-ῆτον	-ῆτον	-ῶμεν	-ῆτε	-ῶσι
Aor. 2	θῶ	-ῇς	-ῇ	-ῆτον	-ῆτον	-ῶμεν	-ῆτε	-ῶσι
	δῶ	-ῷς	-ῷ	-ῶτον	-ῶτον	-ῶμεν	-ῶτε	-ῶσι

OPTATIVE.

	σταίην	-ης	-η	-ητον	-ήτην	-ημεν	-ητε	-αῖεν or -ησαν
Aor. 2	θείην	-ης	-η	-ητον	-ήτην	-ημεν	-ητε	-εῖεν or -ησαν
	δοίην	-ης	-η	-ητον	-ήτην	-ημεν	-ητε	-οῖεν or -ησαν

IMPERATIVE.

	στῆθι*	-ήτω	-ῆτον	-ήτων	-ῆτε	-ήτωσαν, etc.
Aor. 2	θές (θέτι)	-έτω	-ετον	-έτων	-ετε	-έτωσαν, etc.
	δός (δόθι)	-ότω	-οτον	-ότων	-οτε	-ότωσαν, etc.

INFINITIVE.   PARTICIPLE.

	στῆναι		στάς -ᾶσα -άν
Aor. 2	θεῖναι	Aor. 2	θείς -εῖσα -έν
	δοῦναι		δούς -οῦσα -όν Gen. -όντος

* In the N. Testament ἀνάβα, κατάβα here, from βῆμι; so ἀνάστα, etc. Such abridged forms are common.

§ 79. Verbs in -μι. (Passive.)

Passive (Present and Imperfect).

INDIC-

Pres.
ἵσταμαι	-σαι	-ται	-άμεθον
τίθεμαι	ἵστᾳ -σαι τίθῃ	-ται	-έμεθον
δίδομαι	-σαι	-ται	-όμεθον
δείκνυμαι	-σαι	-ται	-ύμεθον

SUBJUNC-

Pres.
ἱστῶμαι	-ῇ	-ῆται	-ώμεθον
τιθῶμαι	-ῇ	-ῆται	-ώμεθον
διδῶμαι	-ῷ	-ῶται	-ώμεθον
δεικνύωμαι	-ῇ	-ηται	-ώμεθον

OPTA-

Pres.
ἱσταίμην	-ο	-το	-αίμεθον
τιθείμην	-ο	-το	-είμεθον
διδοίμην	-ο	-το	-οίμεθον
δεικνυοίμην	-ο	-το	-οίμεθον

IMPER-

Pres.
	ἵστασο ἵστω	-άσθω
	τίθεσο τίθου	-έσθω
	δίδοσο δίδου	-όσθω
	δείκνυσο	-ύσθω

Imperf.
ἱστάμην	-ασο (-ω)	-ατο	-άμεθον
ἐτιθέμην	-εσο (-θου)	-ετο	-έμεθον
ἐδιδόμην	-οσο (-δου)	-οτο	-όμεθον
ἐδεικνύμην	-υσο	-υτο	-ύμεθον

INFINITIVE.

Present
ἵστασθαι
τίθεσθαι
δίδοσθαι
δείκνυσθαι

§ 79. Verbs in -μι. (Passive.)

Passive (Present and Imperfect).

ATIVE.

-ασθον	-ασθον	-άμεθα	-ασθε	-ανται
-εσθον	-εσθον	-έμεθα	-εσθε	-ενται
-οσθον	-οσθον	-όμεθα	-οσθε	-ονται
-υσθον	-υσθον	-ύμεθα	-υσθε	-υνται

TIVE.

-ῆσθον	-ῆσθον	-ώμεθα	-ῆσθε	-ῶνται
-ῆσθον	-ῆσθον	-ώμεθα	-ῆσθε	-ῶνται
-ῶσθον	-ῶσθον	-ώμεθα	-ῶσθε	-ῶνται
-ησθον	-ησθον	-ώμεθα	-ησθε	-ωνται

TIVE.

-αισθον	-αίσθην	-αίμεθα	-αισθε	-αιντο
-εισθον	-είσθην	-είμεθα	-εισθε	-ειντο
-οισθον	-οίσθην	-οίμεθα	-οισθε	-οιντο
-οισθον	-οίσθην	-οίμεθα	-οισθε	-οιντο

ATIVE.

-ασθον	-άσθων	-ασθε	-άσθωσαν, etc.
-εσθον	-έσθων	-εσθε	-έσθωσαν, etc.
-οσθον	-όσθων	-οσθε	-όσθωσαν, etc.
-υσθον	-ύσθων	-υσθε	-ύσθωσαν, etc.

-ασθον	-άσθην	-άμεθον	-ασθε	-αντο
-εσθον	-έσθην	-έμεθα	-εσθε	-εντο
-οσθον	-όσθην	-όμεθα	-οσθε	-οντο
-υσθον	-ύσθην	-ύμεθα	-υσθε	-υντο

PARTICIPLES.

Present
- ἱστάμενος -η -ον
- τιθέμενος -η -ον
- διδόμενος -η -ον
- δεικνύμενος -η -ον

§ 79. Verbs in -μι. (Middle.)

MIDDLE VOICE.

INDICATIVE, Aor. II.

Aor. 2	ἐστάμην*	-ασο (ω)	-ατο	-άμεθα	-ασθον	-ασθον	-αντο
	ἐθέμην	-εσο (ου)	-ετο	-έμεθα	-εσθον	-εσθε	-εντο
	ἐδόμην	-οσο (ου)	-οτο	-όμεθα	-οσθον	-οσθε	-οντο

SUBJUNCTIVE.

Aor. 2	στῶμαι	-ῇ	-ῆται	-ώμεθα	-ῆσθον	-ῆσθε	-ῶνται
	θῶμαι	-ῇ	-ῆται	-ώμεθα	-ῆσθον	-ῆσθε	-ῶνται
	δῶμαι	-ῷ	-ῶται	-ώμεθα	-ῶσθον	-ῶσθε	-ῶνται

OPTATIVE.

Aor. 2	σταίμην	-ο	-το	-αίμεθα	-αῖσθον	-αῖσθε	-αῖντο
	θείμην	-ο	-το	-είμεθα	-εῖσθον	-εῖσθε	-εῖντο
	δοίμην	-ο	-το	-οίμεθα	-οῖσθον	-οῖσθε	-οῖντο

IMPERATIVE.

	στάσω	-ασθω	-ασθον	-άσθων	-ασθε	-άσθωσαν, etc.
	στά·					
	θέσο	-έσθω	-εσθον	-έσθων	-εσθε	-έσθωσαν, etc.
	θοῦ					
	δόσο	-όσθω	-οσθον	-όσθων	-οσθε	-όσθωσαν
	δοῦ					

INFINITIVE.

Aor. 2
στάσθαι
θέσθαι
δόσθαι

PARTICIPLES.

Aor. 2
στάμενος -η -ον
θέμενος -η -ον
δόμενος -η -ον

* Aor. II. of ἵστημι is not used at all. It stands here merely as an exemplar

§ 80. Formations of some tenses of verbs in -ω after the model of verbs in -μι.

(1) About 25 verbs with root-character ἄ, ε, ἴ, ο, or ὔ, form Aor. II. act. throughout all the modes, entirely after the model of Aor. II. of ἵστημι. Several of these are in common use.

F. g. Βαίνω (ΒΑΩ), Aor. II. ἔβην -ης -η -ητον -ήτην -ημεν -ητε -ησαν. Sub. βῶ. Opt. βαίην. Imp. βῆθι. Inf. βῆναι. Part. βάς.

Γιγνώσκω (ΓΝΟΩ), Aor. II. ἔγνων -ως -ω -ωτον -ώτην -ωμεν -ωτε -ωσαν. Subj. γνῶ. Opt. γνοίην. Imp. γνῶθι. Inf. γνῶναι. Part. γνούς.

Δύω, Aor. II. ἔδυν -υς -υ -υτον -ύτην -υμεν -υτε -υσαν, (ῦ). Subj. δυῶ. Opt. δύην (for δυίην). Imp. δῦθι. Inf. δῦναι. Part. δύς.

So σβέννυμι (ΣΒΕΩ), Aor. II. ἔσβην -ης, etc.; φθάνω (ΦΘΑ), Aor. II. ἔφθην -ης -η, etc. Other examples in verbs of frequent use, are διδάσκω (ΔΑΕ), ἐδάην· καίω (ΚΑΕ), ἐκάην· ῥέω (ΡΥΕ), Fut. ῥυήσομαι, Aor. II. ἐρρύην· Χαίρω (ΧΑΡΕ), Aor. II. ἐχάρην -ης -η, etc.; φύω, Aor. II., ἐφῦν, etc. Most of the others exhibit only some portions of Aor. II., e. g. the Indic., or an Infin. Part., etc. (Kuhner, § 228 seq.)

NOTE. How exactly Aor. I. II. *passive* of verbs in -ω are copied after the same model, we have already seen, § 78. 5.

(2) Aor. II. *Middle* of more than 30 verbs in -ω, is formed with the like analogy to Aor. II. Midd. of verbs in μι.

As these are used only in the epic and Attic poetry, it would be out of place to exhibit them here. The design in mentioning them is, to show the reader the *extent* of such formations.

(3) There are many examples in poetry, where the Perf. and Pluperf., (and even the Pres. and Imperf.), are formed after the like analogy.

See Kuhner § 235—§ 242. As these are not in common use, I forbear to produce them, except merely a few samples; e. g. δέδια, γέγαα, ἕσταα, from which comes ἑσταώς, contract ἑστώς· ἐδεδίειν, etc. Pres. τάνυται for τανύεται, from τανίω· Imperf. ᾠμην for ᾠόμην, from οἴομαι. The peculiarity is, that the *root-vowel* supplies the place of the mode-vowel, and thus makes their formation like that of verbs in -μι.

§ 81. ANOMALOUS VERBS IN -μι.

(1) The three principal ones are from the old roots ἕω, *to send, place, clothe;* ἔω, *to be;* and ἴω, *to go.* They assume respectively the ground-forms ἵημι, εἰμί, and εἶμι (see § 78. 3. Note 1, 2.); and in many of their derivate forms, they either coincide, or approximate very nearly to each other. Hence the importance of paradigms for the learner.

NOTE. I have given the usual derivation here of εἰμί *to be;* but Kühner makes the root to be εσ, and apparently with good reasons.

I. Ἵημι from ἕω to send, etc.

ACTIVE VOICE.

Ind. Pres. ἵημι -ης -ησι -ετον -ετον ʽ-εμεν -ετε -ᾶσι or εἷσι. Subj. Pres. ἰῶ -ῇς -ῇ, etc. Opt. Pres. ἰείην -ης, etc. Imp. Pres. ἵει (ἵεθι) ἱέτω, etc. Inf. ἱέναι. Part. ἱείς -εῖσα -έν. Imperf. ἵουν (ἵειν), ἵεις, etc. (as if from ἱέω). Also ἵην -ης, etc. 3d pers. plur. ἵεσαν. Indic. Fut. ἥσω. Aor. 1. ἧκα (ἕηκα). Perf. εἷκα, Pluperf. εἵκειν. Aor. 2, (no sing.); plural, ἕμεν, ἕτε, ἕσαν, or (with augment) εἷμεν, εἷτε, εἷσαν. Subj. ὦ -ῇς, etc. Opt. εἵην -ης, etc.; and plur. contracted, εἷμεν, εἷτε, εἷεν. Imper. ἕς (ἕθι), ἕτω, etc. Inf. εἷναι. Part. εἵς, εἷσα, ἕν.

PASSIVE.

Pres. ἵεμαι. Imperf. ἱέμην. Perf. εἷμαι. Pluperf. εἵμην. Aor. 1. ἕθην (εἵθην). In the N. Test., ἀφέωνται (Doric) 3d plur. Perfect pass. for ἀφεῖνται, from ἀφίημι.

MIDDLE.

Ind. Fut. ἥσομαι. Aor. 1. ἡκάμην. Aor. 2. ἕμην (εἵμην). Subj. ὦμαι. Imper. οὗ. Inf. ἕσθαι. Part. ἕμενος -η -ον.

NOTE 1. The *simple* verb ἵημι is seldom used; but the compounds ἀνίημι, ἀφίημι, ἐφίημι, μεθίημι, ξυνίημι προΐημι, ὑφίημι, etc., occur so often, that it becomes indispensable for the student to be acquainted with the inflections of the simple verb. After these all the compounds are modelled of course, with such exceptions as inserting or omitting the necessary aspirates, etc., necessarily occasion.

II. Verbs εἰμί to be, and εἶμι to go.

(2) These are most easily distinguished, where they nearly resemble each other, by their *accentuation*; and the best method of learning them, is to place them by the side of each other.

Indic. Pres.	εἰμί, εἶς or εἶ, ἐστί	ἐστόν, ἐστόν	ἐσμέν, ἐστέ εἰσί	
	εἶμι, εἶς or εἶ, εἶσι	ἴτον, ἴτον	ἴμεν, ἴτε, ἴᾱσι	
Subj. Pres.	ὦ, ᾖς, ᾖ, etc.			
	ἴω, ἴῃς, ἴῃ, etc.			
Opt. Pres.	εἴην, εἴης, εἴη, etc.			
	ἴοιμι, -οις -οι, etc., or ἰοίην -οις -οι, etc.			
Imper. Pres.	ἴσθι (ἔσο), ἔστω (ἤτω), ἔστον, etc.			
	ἴθι ἴτω, ἴτον, etc.			
Inf. Pres.	εἶναι			
	ἰέναι			
Part. Pres.	ὤν, οὖσα, ὄν, ὄντος, etc.			
	ἰών, ἰοῦσα, ἰόν, ἰόντος, etc.			
Imperf.	ἦν, ἦς, ἦ or ἦν ἦτον, etc. 3 plur. ἦσαν			
	ᾔειν -εις -ει -ειτον, etc. 3 plur. ᾔεσαν ʻAtt. ᾔα -εις, etc.			

§ 81. ANOMALOUS VERBS IN -μι.

Fut. (of εἰμί to be), ἔσομαι, ἔσῃ (-ει), ἔσεται, in prose ἔσται, ἐσόμεθον, etc. Imperf. (middle) from εἰμί to be, ἤμην. Fut. middle (of εἶμι to go), εἰσομαι, Aor. 1 εἰσάμην.

NOTE. I. Of both these verbs there is a great variety of forms in the poets, dialects, etc., which the lexicons now exhibit, and also the larger grammars; e. g. (from εἰμί to be) Subj. ἔω, ἔῃς, etc. : Opt. ἔοιμι, etc. Imper. ὄντων (for ἔστωσαν); Inf. ἔμεν, ἔμεναι, ἔμμεναι, etc., (for εἶναι); Part. ἐών -οῦσα, etc. IMPERF. ἔα, ἦα, ἔον, ἔσκον, ἤμην, ἔην.

NOTE 2. The Imperf. of εἶμι (to go) has also ἤια, or ἤιον -ες -ε, etc. This is the only verb in -μι from a root ἰ, i. e. from a root whose only letter is Iota. Its Pres. εἶμι has the sense of the Fut. I will go, i. e. I am going, iturus sum.

(3) The verb εἰμί (to be) is an *enclitic* in the Present, *the* 2d *pers. sing. excepted.* Εἰμί is an enclitic, however, only when it stands in a proposition where it connects a subject (expressed or implied) and a predicate.

NOTE. When it merely asserts existence, e. g. θεὸς ἔστιν, it takes the accent, but generally transfers it (in the 3d pers. sing.) to the first syllable of the word. The same transfer takes place, when ἐστί stands at the beginning of a sentence, or after the particles οὐκ, μή, ὡς, ἀλλ', εἰ, καί, μέν, ὅτι, πού, and the pronoun τοῦτ', e. g. οὐκ ἔστι, τοῦτ' ἔστι, etc. Elsewhere, however, when it is *prevented* simply by the state of the preceding word, etc., from being enclitic, it retains its tone on the ultimate, as in the paradigm; e. g. λόγος ἐστί, ἀγαθός δ'ἐστί.

III. Other irregulars in -μι, viz. φημί, κεῖμαι, οἶδα.

(4) Φημί is declined in the main like ἵστημι ; but differs in regard to its accentuation in the Present, where (like εἰμί) it is an *enclitic*, and when accented places the tone on the *ultimate*. But the 2d pers. sing. (φῄς) is *not* enclitic.

NOTE. 1. The Subj. is φῶ, Opt. φαίην, Imper. φάθι, Inf. φάναι, Part. φάς. The Imperf. is ἔφην -ης -η -ατον -άτην, etc.; also (by *aphaeresis*) the Imperf. sing. 1st and 3d pers. is ἦν, ἦ (for φῆν, φῆ). But Kühner derives the latter from the root ἄω (to sound), Pres. ἦμι, Imperf. ἦν, ἦ. Fut. of φημί, φήσω, Aor. I. ἔφησα.

(5) Κεῖμαι (root κείω) is reckoned by most grammarians as a deponent (Midd.), and a Pres. tense, etc., is assigned to it. Kühner assigns to it the Perf. without reduplication, having the sense of the Present.

It is declined as a Perf., κεῖμαι -σαι -ται -μεθα -σθε -νται. But the Subj. has κέωμαι -η -ηται, etc. as from κέω. So Opt. κεοίμην -ο -το, etc. Other forms follow the root κείω, e. g. Imper. κεῖσο, Inf. κεῖσθαι, Part. κείμενος· Imperf. ἐκείμην, Plup. ἐκείμην, Fut. κείσομαι.

(6) Οἶδα is an anomalous Perf. 2 (in reality from εἴδω), used like the Present as to sense. By the older grammarians this word is derived from ἴσημι.

It is declined thus: οἶδα, οἶσθα (for οἴδασθα), οἶδε· ἴστον -ον· ἴσμεν, ἴστε, ἴσᾱσι. But in most other modes the ει of the root appears; as Subj. εἴδω, Opt. εἰδείην, (Imp. ἴσθι, ἴστω, etc.) Inf. εἰδέναι, Part. εἰδώς -υῖα -ός. Plup. 2, ᾔδειν -εις -ει, etc.; or ᾔδη -ης -η, ᾔσμεν, ᾖστε, ᾖσαν, contracted out of ᾔδεα, etc. The singular forms here are Attic.

Class of Anomalous Verbs in the N. Test.

(7) In all the late grammars there is a large class of anomalous verbs inserted. This indeed is very useful and convenient for beginners; but such verbs may be found equally well in the better lexicons. As I aim at brevity, where there is no important sacrifice to be made by it, I shall simply name the defective verbs of the N. Test. here, remitting the reader to the most recent lexicons of Wahl, Bretschneider, and Robinson, which will give him the synopsis which he needs of these verbs.

The principal defective verbs in the N. Test. are ἄγω, αἱρέω, ἀκούω, ἁμαρτέω, ἀνέχομαι, ἀνοίγω, ἀπαντάω, ἀποκτείνω, ἀπόλλυμι, ἁρπάζω, αὐξάνω, βασκαίνω, βιόω, βλαστάνω, γαμέω, γελάω, γίγνομαι, δίδωμι, διώκω, δύω, εἴδω, εἴπω, ἐκχέω, ἐπαινέω, ἐπιορκέω, ἔρχομαι, εὑρίσκω, ζάω, ἥκω, θάλλω, καταάγνυμι, κατακαίω, καταλείπω, κεράννυμι, κερδαίνω, κλαίω, κλέπτω, κράζω, κρέμαμαι, κρύπτω, νίπτω, οἰκτείρω, ὀμνύω, ὁράω, παίζω, πέτομαι, πίνω, πίπτω, ῥέω, σαλπίζω, σημαίνω, σπουδάζω, στηρίζω, φαγεῖν, φαίνω, φαύσκω, φέρω, φύω, χαίρω, χαρίζομαι, ὠθέω, ὠνέομαι. See a minute account of these in Winer's N. Test. Gramm. § 15.

Several of these, however, can hardly be called defective verbs, when compared with a multitude of others in the Greek language. But as there is more or less of irregularity attached to them in *some* respects, they are here classed together.

§ 82. *Verbal Adjectives or Verbals.*

(1) In general, verbs may form two classes of these, viz., (*a*) Those ending in τός -τή -τόν. (*b*) Those ending in τέος -τέα -τέον.

NOTE. The first class have either simply a *passive* meaning, as λεκτός *spoken;* or else (more usually) they designate *possibility of action*, etc., as αἱρετός *eligible*, ὁρατός *visible,* etc. Sometimes they have an *active* meaning, as μενετός *waiting;* and lastly, at times although rarely, the same meaning as verbals in -τέος, e. g. βιωτόν ἐστι one must live, ὑποπτός *suspicandus.* The second class (in -τέος) denote *what must be done,* or *what is wished or desired;* as αἱρετέον *capiendum, eligendum;* γραπτέος *scribendus.*

(2) The most convenient rule for forming these, is to take Aor. 1 passive as the root; then reject the ending -θην and the augment ε, and you have the *stem;* to this append -τός or τέος,

§ 83. SYNCOPE AND METATHESIS OF VERBS. 131

and change the *aspirate* of the stem into a *tenuis*, that it may correspond with the τ of the ending; § 10. R. 2.

E. g. λέγω, ἐλέχϑην, λεκτός· στρέφω, ἐστρέφϑην, στρεπτός· φιλέω, ἐφιλή-ϑην, φιλητέος· παίω, ἐπαύσϑην, παυστός· ἵστημι, ἐστάϑην, στάτος, στατέος, etc.

§ 83. Change of forms in Verbs by Syncope and Metathesis.

I. SYNCOPE.

(1) A number of verbs (several of them in common use) vary in some degree their forms by syncope, i. e. by omitting a vowel between two consonants; specially when these are a mute and a liquid which may easily combine.

E. g. (a) ἦλϑον, from ἤλυϑον, Aor. II. of the old root ἐλεύϑω· πέτομαι to *fly*, Fut. πτήσομαι (for πετήσομαι), Aor. ἐπτόμην· ἐγείρω, Aor. ἠγρόμην (diphthong ει omitted); πέλομαι, Imperf. ἔπλην. In particular do those which receive the prosthetic *reduplicative* syllable, (like that which verbs in -μι receive), suffer such a syncope: e. g. γίγνομαι for γι-γένομαι· μίμνω for μι-μένω· πιπράσκω for πι-πέρασκω· πίπτω for πι-πέτω, Aor. II. ἔπεσον (=ἔπετον), etc. So in Aor. II. with reduplication; as τέτμον for τε-τέμον, from τέμνω.

(b) Here also may be most conveniently arranged many cases which some grammarians rank under *metathesis*; e. g. δμάζω, Perf. δέδμηκα—δμήμαι, ἐδμήϑην, (for δέδαμηκα, etc.) In the same way, καλέω, κέκληκα, ἐκλήϑην· κάμνω, κέκμηκα· τέμνω, τέτμηκα· βάλλω, βέβληκα, Aor. II. ἔβλην (poet.), Fut. βλήσομαι (poet.); σκέλλω, ἔσκληκα, Aor. II. ἔσκλην.

II. METATHESIS.

(2) By this is here meant *the transposition of a vowel and a liquid*. This is not unfrequent, and seems to be practised for the purposes of euphony.

E. g. δαρϑάνω, ἔδραϑον· πέρϑω, ἔπραϑον· δέρκομαι, ἔδρακον· ϑνήσκω, root ΘΑΝ, Aor. II. ἔϑανον· πέρϑω, Aor. II. ἔπραϑον· τέρπω, Aor. II. ἐτράπην, etc.

NOTE. Of the existence and tendency of the phenomena here described, there can be no good reason to doubt. In most languages, the liquids, or mutes followed by liquids, exhibit a tendency to syncopated forms. Short vowels, in such cases, are easily and rapidly passed over, and finally are omitted. But still, neither Syncope nor Metathesis, as exhibited above, are very extensive in Greek; and a majority of the cases belong to poetic license in changing forms. But to form a new root, as some lexicographers have done, e. g. κλέω for κέκληκα, etc., betrays a singular oversight in respect to an obvious usage. See Kuhner, § 178. § 179.

§ 84. ADVERBS.

(1) Adverbs are properly such *indeclinable* words as designate relations of *time, place, way, manner, measure*, etc., to a predicate expressed by a verb, or by an adjective with the verb of existence.

E. g. ἦν ἐκεῖ, *I was there*; ἦλθε νύκτωρ, *he came by night*; ἐποίησε καλῶς, *he did well*; πάνυ σμικρός, *very small*, etc.

NOTE. In cases almost without number, nouns with or without prepositions, participles, etc., are used for the same or the like purpose as proper adverbs; e. g. εἶπε μετ' ὀργῆς, *he spoke indignantly*; εἶπε γελῶν, *he spoke laughingly*, etc.

(2) Adverbs may be *classified* according to the various relations which they sustain.

E. g. (1) Of place; as οὐρανόθεν, *from heaven*; πανταχῇ, *every where*. (2) Of time; as νύκτωρ, *by night*; νῦν, *now*. (3) Way and manner; as καλῶς, *well*; οὕτως, *so as*. Connected with these latter are, (4) Those of modality, viz. of affirmation or negation, of certainty, uncertainty, positiveness, or conditionality; as ναί, οὐκ, μήν, δή, ἴσως, πάντως, ἄν, πού, etc. (5) Of frequency or repetition; as τρίς, αὖθις. (6) Of intensity; as μάλα, πάνυ, πολύ, etc.

(3) Adverbs are formed in various ways. (*a*) The principal part of them are from adjectives, and end in -ως.

From the nature of adverbs we might naturally expect such an origin. The easiest method of formation is to change -ων of the Gen. plur. in adjectives into -ως, and follow the accentuation of the adjective; e. g. καλῶν, καλῶς· σωφρόνων, σωφρόνως· ταχέων, ταχέως· ἁπλῶν, ἁπλῶς, etc.

(*b*) Participles Perf. pass. or midd., having the nature of adjectives, form adverbs in the same way.

E. g. τεταγμένος, τεταγμένως· κεχαρισμένος, κεχαρισμένως, etc.

(*c*) Many adverbs are formed from nouns and adjectives in those particular cases which are adapted to express the relation demanded; and also with prepositions in connection.

(1) Nouns; as δωρεάν, *freely*; σπουδῇ, (lit. with pains-taking), *scarcely*; ἀρχήν, *at first*. (2) Adjectives; where the *neuter* gender is chosen for an adverb, either singular as ταχύ, μικρόν, or plural, as ταχά, μικρά, σαφά, κρυφά, etc. The singular is most common in prose for the positive and comparative degree; but the superlative degree usually is made by the plural forms. (3) By prepositions combined with nouns; as προὔργου, *profitably*; παραχρῆμα, *immediately*. Sometimes the accentuation is changed by such a union; as ἐκποδών, ἐπισχερώ, not ἐκ ποδῶν, ἐπὶ σχερῷ.

(*d*) Most of the peculiar endings of adverbs, except -ως, are now traced

§ 84. ADVERBS. 133

by grammarians to peculir flexions of these words in the ancient language. E. g.

(1) GENITIVE. Such as end in -ης -ου; as ἑξῆς, αἴφνης, etc.; πού, ὅπου, ὑψοῦ, τηλοῦ, etc.; Gen. of Dec. I. II. In the Gen. of Dec. III., ἐντός, ἐκτός, (ἐν, ἐξ). Such as end in -ξ are contracted Genitives of Dec. III., as πύξ, from πυκός, by dropping the ο of the final syllable; so λάξ, ἅπαξ, ὀδάξ, etc. with Gen. -κος abridged.

(2) DATIVE. This includes the old *Ablative* and *Locative* cases, and therefore makes a variety of endings, most of which, however, are very obvious. (a) In ι; as ἕκοντι, αὐτοχειρί, αὐτονυκτί, etc.; *locative*, ὑψί, ἶφι, ἄγχι, etc. Sometimes with paragogic ν or ς; as πάλιν, μόγις, etc. (Dat. of Dec. III.) (b) In -εί -ί; as ἀμελεί, ἀμαχεί, ἀμισθί, πανοικί, etc., mostly from adjectives in -ος -ης. So local adverbs; as ἐκεῖ, αὐτεῖ, etc. (Dat of Dec. III.) (c) In -ω; as ἄνω, κάτω, ἔσω, etc. (Dat. of Dec. II.) (d) In -οῖ; as οἴκοι, πεδοῖ, ποῖ, (like the old Dat. in μοί, σοί, etc.) (e) In -αι; χαμαί, παλαί, ὑπαί, etc. (Dat. of Dec. I.) (f) In -η -ᾶ; as κρυφῇ, πεζῇ, εἰκῇ, ἰδιᾷ, δημοσίᾳ, etc. (Dat. *instrumentalis*). (g) In -ε; as τῆλε, ὀψέ, αὖτε, etc. (old Ablative).

(3) ACCUSATIVE. (a) In -ην -αν; as πρώην, πέρην, μακράν, λίαν, etc. (Dec. I.) (b) In -ον; as πλησίον, σήμερον, etc. (Dec. II.) (c) In -δην -δον -δα; as ἱπποτροχάδην, χανδόν, ἀποιστιαδά, (Dec. I. II. III.) (d) In -ᾶ; as τάχα, σάφα, λάθρα, κρύφα, etc., (Dec. II. III. neut. plural.) (e) In -υ -υς; εὐθύ, εὐθύς, ἀντικρύ, (Acc. neut. sing., sometimes with paragogic -ς).

NOTE. To adverbs are attached, sometimes, the endings -θεν, -δε, (-σε, -ζε), -θι, to denote *whence, whither, where*; as οὐρανόθεν *from heaven*; οἰκόνδε *homewards*; ἐκεῖσε *thither*; ἄλλοσε *elsewhere*; Ἀθήναζε *toward Athens* (-ζε when the word ends with -ας); ἐκεῖθι *there*; ἄλλοθι *elsewhere*, etc. But as nearly all such endings are also attached to nouns, pronouns, etc., they cannot be considered as mere *formatives* of adverbs.

(4) COMPARISON OF ADVERBS. (1) Those with -ως (derived from adjectives) make their comparative degree in the neuter singular of the adjective, and their superlative in the neut. plural.

E. g. σοφῶς, σοφώτερον, σοφώτατα· σαφῶς, σαφέστερον, σαφέστατα. ἡδέως, ἥδιον, ἥδιστα, etc. Sometimes -ως is retained in the comp. degree; e. g. χαλεποτέρως, ἐχθιόνως, etc.

(2) Those in -ω retain this throughout; and most other adverbs imitate this.

E. g. ἄνω, ἀνωτέρω, ἀνωτάτω· κάτω, κατωτέρω, κατωτάτω; and so τηλοῦ, τηλοτέρω, τηλοτάτω· ἔνδον, ἐνδοτέρω, ἐνδοτάτω. Sometimes the method in No. 1 is adopted; as ἐγγύς, ἐγγύτερον, ἐγγύτατα.

NOTE. A few are irregular in their comparison; as ἄγχι, ἆσσον, ἄγχιστα· μάλα, μᾶλλον.

§ 85. PREPOSITIONS.

(1) Prepositions are words which originally denoted, in respect to nouns or pronouns, the relations of *space* to the action

designated by a verb. Subsequently their office extended to the designation of *time* and *causality.*

E. g. ἔστη παρὰ τῷ βασιλεῖ he stood *by* the king; ἦλθεν ἐν ἐκείνῃ τῇ ἡμέρα he came *on* that very day; ἀπέφυγεν ὑπὸ δέους he fled *because of* fear.

(2) The so called *primitive* prepositions are the following eighteen; viz., ἀμφί, ἀνά, ἀντί, ἀπό, διά, εἰς, ἐν, ἐξ, ἐπί, κατά, μετά, παρά, περί, πρό, πρός, σύν, ὑπέρ, ὑπό. These are all *oxytones;* and these only are united with verbs without changing their form.

NOTE. When the dissyllabic prepositions here enumerated (ἀμφί, ἀνά, ἀντί, διά excepted) *follow* the word which they govern, (this is called *anastrophe*), they shift their accent to the first syllable; e. g. τούτου πέρι. The otherwise toneless prepositions (εἰς, ἐς, ἐν, ἐκ), in such a case receive an accent, as πλήθους ἔκ. So, also, when they are used as adverbs; e. g. ἐγὼ πάρα *I am present,* for ἐγὼ πάρειμι· αὐτὸς πέρι, sc. περίεστι.

(3) The prepositions in most common use may be classed according to their regimen; viz.,

(*a*) Such as govern the Gen. only; viz., ἀντί, ἀπό, ἐκ (ἐξ), ἕνεκα, πρό.

(*b*) The Dat. only; viz., ἐν, σύν, (ξυν).

(*c*) The Acc. only; viz., ἀνά, εἰς (ἐς).

(*d*) Such as govern the Gen. and Acc.; viz. διά, κατά, ὑπέρ.

(*e*) Such as govern the Gen., Dat., and Acc.; as ἀμφί, ἐπί, μετά, παρά, περί, πρός, ὑπό.

REMARK ON INTERJECTIONS.

As these words are mere exclamations of grief, joy, etc., and are immutable, there need nothing be said in respect to them here. It is well however to remark, that ὦ before the Vocative has the circumflex; but employed as an exclamation it takes the acute (ὤ); yet there is no uniformity here in the various editions.

§ 86. *Formation of derived or secondary words.*

(1) The most recent grammarians of distinction regard the *verbs* in Greek as, in general, the *roots* or *primitive forms* of the language. Such is acknowledged to be the fact in regard to most of the so called Oriental languages. It seems, in the main, to be true of the Greek.

(2) Most, if not all, really original roots are *monosyllabic,* and

begin or end with a short vowel or simple consonant, or else with two consonants one of which is a liquid.

E. g. λύ-ω, τύπ-ω, τάγ-ω, κρύβ-ω, ἄρχ-ω, κάμπ-ω, etc. So στά-ω, θέ-ω, δό-ω, etc., as roots of verbs in -μι.

(3) In derivatives from such roots, the vowel is often lengthened, changed, etc., and the consonants often augmented; as we have already seen in respect to the augmented forms of verbs, etc.

NOTE. Most of the primitive forms have disappeared; and the reason of this seems to be, the desire of obtaining more *euphony* than a monosyllabic language is capable of. Longer words, if they do not exhibit as much of energy, afford more of euphony and melody to the ear, than short ones.

I. DERIVATE VERBS.

(4) THESE COME FROM OTHER VERBS, by adding the endings -άζω -ίζω -ύζω, also -σκω and -σείω, to the original forms.

NOTE. (a) In the three first cases, the meaning is generally rendered intensive or frequentative; e. g. αἰτέω *I ask*, αἰτίζω *I beg*; στένω *I sigh*, στενάζω *I sigh often and deeply*, etc. (b) The ending -σκω is either inceptive or factitive; inceptive, as ἡβάω *I am young*, ἡβάσκω *I am becoming young*; γενειάω *I am bearded*, γενειάσκω *I am becoming bearded*, etc.; factitive, as μεθύω *I am drunk*, μεθύσκω *I make drunk*; πίνω *I drink*, πιπίσκω *I make to drink*; so διδάσκω *I make to learn*, i. e. I teach, βιώσκομαι *I make to live*, etc. (c) The ending -σειω is attached to the Future tense of a root, and in its meaning is desiderative; e. g. γελάσω, *I will laugh*, γελασείω, *I am inclined to laugh*; πολεμισείω *I desire to fight*, etc.

(5) FROM NOUNS AND ADJECTIVES; in which case is suffixed to the root one of the following endings, viz., -έω -εύω -άω -άζω -όω -ίζω -αίνω -ύνω. Between these classes, however, there are, as in No 4, some distinctions as to meaning; e. g.

(a) VERBS IN -έω -εύω, (formed from nouns, etc., of every kind of ending), usually express *the state*, or *action*, or *practice of that which the original noun designates*.

E. g. βασιλεύς *a king*, βασιλεύω *to reign*; δοῦλος *a servant*, δουλεύω *to serve*; κοινωνός *a partaker*, κοινωνέω *to participate*, etc.; πόλεμος *war*, πολεμεῖν *to practice war*; αὐλός *a flute*, αὐλεῖν *to play on the flute*; ἵππος *a horse*, ἱππεύειν *to ride on horseback*, etc. In general, endings of this sort are *intransitive*; but not without some exceptions, as φίλος, φιλέω *I love*.

(b) VERBS in -άω -άζω. These naturally spring from nouns in -α -η, of Dec. I.; but some others are included. They mostly signify *the possession of some quality or attribute*; or *the practice of that* which the noun designates.

§ 86. FORMATION OF DERIVATES.

E. g. κόμη *hair*, κομᾶν *to have long hair*; λίπος *fat*, λιπᾶν *to be fat*; βοή *cry*, βοάω *to cry out*; τιμή *honour*, τιμᾶν *to do honour*; δόξα *glory*, δοξάζω *to glorify*, etc. When verbs in -άζω are formed from proper names, they mean, *to act* or *think like the person named*; e. g. Δωριάζω (from Δωριεύς) *to act* or *think like a Dorian*.

(c) Verbs in -όω, mostly from forms of Dec. II.; in -ίζω from all the declensions; in -αίνω, mostly from adjectives; in -ύνω, only from adjectives; all have predominantly a *factitive* (Heb. Hiphil) meaning.

E. g. (a) In -όω; as δοῦλος *a slave*, δουλόω *to enslave*; χρυσός *gold*, χρυσόω *to gild*; πῦρ *fire*, πυρόω *to put into the fire*; πτέρον *wing*, πτερόω *to furnish with wings*; σταυρός *a cross*, σταυρόω *to crucify*. (b) In -ίζω; as ἁγνός, ἁγνίζω *to make pure*; αἷμα *blood*, αἱματίζω *to make bloody*, etc. (c) In -αίνω; as λευκός *white*, λευκαίνω *to make white*; κοῖλος *hollow*, κοιλαίνω *to make hollow*, etc. (d) In -ύνω; as ἡδύνειν *to make sweet*, from ἡδύς *sweet*; σεμνύνειν *to make venerable*, from σεμνός *venerable*, etc.

NOTE 1. But this class of derivate verbs, particularly in -ίζω -άζω, are not confined solely to the meanings here designated. For the most part the context will guide the reader, when a departure from the ordinary meaning becomes necessary.

NOTE 2. Besides the classes above noted, there are verbs (from adjectives of Dec. I.) in -ώσσω (ώττω), which are usually *intransitive* or *factitive*; as ὑπνώσσω *I sleep*, νεώσσω *I make young*; and verbs in -άω -ιάω (from all declensions), which are *desideratives*, as θανατιάω *I wish to die*, ὠνητιάω *I wish to buy*, etc.

REMARKS. *Comparison of verbal forms in the N. Testament*. Some derivate forms are more frequent here than in classic Greek; viz., (1) *Forms in* -όω; which stand sometimes where we might expect forms in εύω, e. g. δεκατόω (classic, δεκατεύω); or in -ίζω, as ἀφυπνόω (class. ἀφυπνίζω): or in -ύνω, as κραταιόω (class. κρατύνω); or -εω, as σθενόω (class. σθενέω). (2) *Forms in* -ίζω are very frequent, and arise from roots of all kinds, even the most diverse; e. g. δειγματίζω from δεῖγμα, πελεκίζω from πέλεκυς, αἱρετίζω from αἵρεσις, etc. (3) *Forms in* -άζω and -εύω, though unusual, occur; e. g. νηπιάζω, σινιάζω, etc.; μεσιτεύω, μαγεύω, etc. (4) *Verbs in* -θω, are rather more frequent than usual; e. g. νήθω, κνήθω, ἀλήθω, etc. (5) *Verbs in* -σκω are rare, and some of them are factitive; e. g. μεθύσκω *to make drunk*, γαμίσκομαι in the common *passive* sense.

II. *Derivate Nouns.*

(6) The number of derivates of this class from verbs is so great, and the modes of derivation so various, that *fully* to classify them would scarcely be practicable. The leading classes, however, may be named.

(a) CONCRETES *from Verbs and Nouns*. Masc. -εύς, Fem. -εια -ισσα; -της -της -τωρ, fem. -τρια -τρις -τις -ις -τειρα; -ων, fem. αινα; -ως, fem. -ωίς -ωίνη; also fem. -σσα (-ττα), -σα (-τα). All these are usually con-

§ 86. Formation of derivates.

cretes, i. e. names of active agents. Sometimes they are used in a kind of tropical sense for *things*; e. g. ζωστήρ *girdle*, i. e. the girder.

(*b*) Abstracts ; *with occasional variations of meaning, as the context may demand.* (1) From Verbs ; such as end in -σις -σια -μη -η -σ ; masc. -μός -ος (-ου) -τος (-του) ; neut. -μα -ος (-οις). Beside these, some merely add ς to the root of a verb, and change ε in a *monosyllabic* root into o, (as is usual in some derivative forms of verbs); e. g. φλόξ=φλόκς from φλέγω *to burn ;* others add to the root the endings -τύς -ονη -μονή -ωλή -ωρή -δών e. g. ὀρχηστύς, ἡδονή, πλησμονή, εὐχωλή, ἀλεωρή, ἀλγηδών, etc.

Note. The leading terminations need no examples for illustration here as they occur every where. The general laws of formation may be briefly stated. (1) To the pure root -σις or -σία is added ; as λύσις from λύ-ω, ξή-ρα-σία from ξηραίνω. (2) The ending -μος usually inserts σ before it, when it is from *pure* verbs ; but sometimes also, τ, δ, or ϑ ; as χρησμός from χράω, and so ἀρδμός, ἐρετμός, σταϑμός, etc. (3) When *contract* verbs are the roots, the final short vowel is lengthened in the nouns, as we might expect ; e. g. τίμησις, τύφλωσις, etc. (4) In nouns -μος -ος -η -α, the ε in the root of monosyllabic verbs goes into o ; as γόνος and γονή from γένω, σπορά from σπείρω, στολμός from στέλλω. When the root is *polysyllabic*, this rule does not apply ; as ἀγερμός from ὑγείρω. (2) Abstracts from adjectives ; (*a*) In -ία ; as σοφία from σοφός, ἀλήϑεια from ἀληϑής. (*b*) In -σύνη ; as σωφροσύνη from σώφρων, δικαιοσύνη from δίκαιος. (*c*) In -της (-τητος); as ἰσότης from ἴσος. (*d*) In -ος (-εος); as ψεῦδος from ψευδής. (*e*) In -ας (-αδος); as μονάς from μονός, etc. ; and so δυάς, τρίας, etc.

(*c*) *Several special classes of Nouns.*

(1) Gentilia, i. e. names of persons taken from the country to which they belong. These end in -ευς, fem.-ις; -ίτης, fem.-ιτις; -άτης, fem.-ατις; -ήτης and -ώτης ; as Εὐβοεύς, Δωρίς; Συβαρίτης -τις ; Σπαρτιώτης -τις ; Γήτης (fr. Γος), etc.

(2) Patronymics, i. e. names from ancestors; mostly in -ίδης -ιάδης, fem. -ις -ας; in poetry -ίων -ιώνη; e. g. Πελείδης, *son of Peleus*, Τελεμωνιάδης, *son of Telamon*, etc.

(3) Diminutives; with endings -ιον -άριον -ρίδιον; -υλλίς -ύλλιον -ύδριον -ύφιον; -ις -ίσκος -ίσκη -ιδεύς; as παιδίον *a little child*, βιβλίον *a small book*, βιβλαρίδιον *a very small book ;* etc. These endings beginning with υ belong to the conversation and comedy dialect, with few exceptions.

Note. The ending -ιον not unfrequently is employed merely as a neut. formative ending, without the diminutive sense ; as ϑηρίον *beast*, βιβλίον *book*, ὅριον *boundary*, etc.

(4) Names of locality ; -ιον -ών are the usual ones ; as ἐργαστήριον *workshop*, Θησεῖον *temple of Theseus*, ἀνδρών *men's chamber*, δαφνών *laurel-grove*, etc.

(5) Names of instruments or means; principally in -τρα -τρον, as ἀκέστρα *sewing-needle*, δίδακτρον *reward for teaching*, etc.

Remarks on N. Test. usage. Verbal derivations are, (1) The ending -μος, which is extended to several cases not extant in the classics; e. g. πειρασμός, ἐνταφιασμός, ῥαντισμός, etc. (2) The endings -μα -σις are pe-

§ 86. FORMATION OF DERIVATES.

culiarly prevalent; the first, as in βάπτισμα, ῥάπισμα, ᾔττημα, αἴτημα, etc., mostly (but not altogether) of an *abstract* meaning, i. e. *nomina actionis*, like the Inf. mode; the second (-σις), as δικαίωσις, βίωσις, specially in the Ep. to the Hebrews, which also are *nomina actionis*. (3) The ending -μονή is also used with an *abstract* meaning; as in πλησμονή, πεισμονή, etc. (4) *Concretes*, i. e. words designating *agents*, from verbs in -άζω -ίζω -ύζω, have nothing peculiar in the N. Test., excepting some new formations; e. g. βαπτιστής, Ἑλληνιστής, etc.

Adjective derivations are, (5) Nouns in -της -οτης, from adjectives in -ος, etc., as ἁγιότης, τελειότης, τιμιότης, used as *abstracts*. (6) Some nouns in -συνη and -ία, of the like signification; as ἐλεημοσύνη, μεγαλωσύνη, etc.; so ἐλαφρία, etc. (7) Nouns in -ήριον are neuters from adjectives.

III. *Derivate adjectives.*

(7) ADJECTIVES FORMED FROM VERBS are numerous; and the endings of them are usually appended to the simple root of the verbs. They have various significations; e. g.

(*a*) Those in -ικός -ιμος -σιμος denote *fitness* for that which the verb describes; e. g. γραφικός *fit for engraving* or *painting*, χρήσιμος *useful*, ἰάσιμος *curable*, etc.

(*b*) Those in -ος -νύς -λος -ωλος -ηλος -αρος -τός -τέος -μων -ης (-ες) -ας, have a great variety of meanings, transitive and intransitive; specially -ος -νός -τός -άς have frequently a *passive* meaning, as λοιπός *left*, στυγνός *hated*, γραπτός *written*, λογάς *chosen*, but most of them are not confined to this. So varied is the use, that rules cannot designate exactly the limits.

(8) ADJECTIVES FROM NOUNS AND ADJECTIVES. This common ground of origin is not very extensive; for most adjectives come either from verbs only, or from nouns only. The meanings of this class is too various to be designated.

The usual endings are -ιος -ικός, also (in connection with preceding vowels) -αιος -ειος -οιος -ῳος -υιος. Many of these express the *way* and *manner* of action, etc.; those in -κός denote what belongs to the essence or peculiar character of an object, as δουλικός, βασιλικός, etc.

(9) ADJECTIVES FROM NOUNS.

(*a*) Those in -εος -ινος denote the *material* out of which any thing is made; as χρύσεος *of gold*, ξύλινος *wooden*, etc. (*b*) Those in -ινός are indicative of *certain portions of time*; as ἡμερινός *daily*, χθεσινός *of yesterday*. (*c*) Those in -εις (-εντος) -ρος -ερος -ηρος -αλέος denote *fulness* or *abundance* in the quality designated; as χαρίεις *full of grace*, αἰσχρός *hateful*, φθονερός *envious*, ῥωμαλέος *powerful*. (*d*) Those in -ώδης denote *likeness, resemblance*; as φλογώδης *flamelike*, αἱματώδης *bloodlike*. (*e*) *Gentilia* end in -ιος -κος -ικος -ηνός -ανός -ῖνος; as Κορίνθιος, Θηβαϊκός, Κυζικηνός, etc. (*f*) Those in -ειος denote *personal qualities*; as ἀνδρεῖος, γυναικεῖος, etc. (*g*) Those in -ήριος are transitive; as σωτήριος *saving*.

REMARKS ON N. TEST. USAGE. (1) The contested adjectives περιούσιος, ἐπιούσιος, probably come from the participial forms περιοῦσα, ἐπιοῦσα; like ἑκούσιος from ἑκοῦσα. (2) The contested readings σάρκινος and σαρκικός, in 1 Cor. 3: 1. Heb. 7 : 16, can hardly be doubtful. Σάρκινος would mean *made of flesh* which would not be apposite ; see *a* above. Endings however occur in -ινος, in the N. Test., which have relation to *time* ; e. g. ὀρ- θρινός, πρωϊνός, which are later forms of Greek in place of the earlier ones in -ιος.

As to verbals in -τος (§ 82), πείθος *persuasive*, in 1 Cor. 2: 4, is a contested form ; but it may mean *persuasive*, as may be seen in § 82. 1. Note. So ἀπείραστος (James 1: 13) is capable of an *active* signification ; and πα- θητός (Acts 26 : 23) agreeably to Gr. idiom may mean *must suffer* ; ib.

§ 87. *Formation of composite words.*

(1) The Greek language possesses a facility in this respect, and uses a liberty, of which scarcely any other language is susceptible. In this way the power and significance of expression is exceedingly increased, diversified, and variously modified, in a manner that cannot well be imitated by any translations into another language. Even two and three prepositions, may be thrown into a single word, to modify and vary the sense of the original root.

E. g. φεύγω to *fly*, ὑπεκφεύγω to *flee away privately*, καταφεύγω to *fly to a place of refuge*; λαμβάνω to *take*, καταλαμβάνω to *overtake*, προκαταλαμβάνω to *anticipate*, etc.

Note. *Prepositions* may be prefixed to verbs, nouns, adjectives, and even adverbs ; but when thus employed they acquire the nature of adverbs. *Adverbs*, also, may be prefixed in like manner ; most of which are separable words, and may be written independently. But there are several which never appear except in composite words ; viz. δυς, α privative (before a vowel ἀν), *a* intensive or collective, and ἡμι *half* (as ἡμίφλεκτος *half-burned*); poetic, νη, νω, αρι, ζα, δα. The two first are the only usual ones. It is remarkable that *a* should be employed in two senses so different ; e. g. privative, ἀδύνατος *impossible*, ἀτιμία *dishonour* ; intensive and collective, ἀτενής *very intent*, ἄσκιος *thick-shaded*, and also ἄκοιτις *bed-fellow*, ἀδελφός *brother*, (from δελφύς *mother's womb*). Doubtless these two were derived from different sources; the first perhaps from ἀνά, ἄν *without*, answering to our inseparable *un*, as in *undoubted*, etc. ; the second Hartung derives from the Sanscrit *sa*, which marks *union* and *intensity* ; Hart. Gr. Part. L. p. 227, and so Kühner, § 380, Anm. 3.

(2) If no *cacophony* arises from the simple junction of two words without change, they are brought together unaltered.

E. g. πολυφάγος, παλαίφατος, etc.

But if the consonants (mutes, etc.), at the end of one word and the beginning of the other, require a change, this is made agreebly to the laws in § 10.

E. g. πάμφορος (παν, § 10. R. 11) ; ἐγκαλέω (ἐν, § 10. R. 12), etc. But,

(3) Most usually *o* is taken after the *root* of nouns in the first

part of the word, and ε, σ, σι, after the root of verbs. These epenthetic letters or syllables, stand between the first and second word in the composition.

E. g. *παιδ-ο-τρίβης* a teacher of youth, *σωματ-ο-φύλαξ* body-guard; *τελε-σ-φόρος* bringing to an end (*τελέω*), *παυ-σί-χολος* anger-stilling (*παύω*).

(4) When an *indeclinable* word forms the first part of any composite word, it remains in general unchanged; but if it is a preposition, and ends in a vowel, this is elided or not, according as the first syllable of the next word is a vowel or a consonant.

E. g. *ἀγχύ-αλος, παλαι-γενής*; but *ἀνέρχομαι* (*ἀνά* with elision), *προάγω, περιάγω* (for *πρό* and *περί* see § 8. 3. Note 2); *ἐλλείπω* (*ἐν*, § 10. R. 13), *συμφέρω* (§ 10. R. 11), etc. *Πρό*, however, although it does not suffer elision sometimes makes a *κρᾶσις* (§ 8. 4) with the vowel of the succeeding word; as *προῖχω* for *προέχω, προῦπτος* for *πρόοπτος*. *Ἀμφί* also often retains its final *ι*; as *ἀμφίαλος, ἀμφίετες*, etc.

REMARKS ON N. TEST. USAGE. (1) Composites whose *first* part is a noun or adjective, are very frequent; e. g. *δικυιοκρισία, καρδιογνώστης. δεσμοφύλαξ*, etc. (2) On the other hand, such as place the *verbal* part first, are also to be found; as *ἐθελοθρησκεία*, etc. (3) The negative α is not unfrequent; the intensitive α is found in *ἀτενίζω*, and a few other words. (4) In those words where the *verbal* part stands last, the verbs (as in other Greek) retain their own forms in *loose* composition, and change or modify them in *close* composition; see § 88.

NOTE. Proper names, which are compounded, are often contracted in the N. Testament; e. g. *Ἀρτεμᾶς* for *Ἀρτεμίδωρος, Δημᾶς* probably for *Δημήτριος, Λουκᾶς* for the Latin *Lucanus*. Some names of this kind are even written without the circumflex accent; as *Ἀντίπας* for *Ἀντίπατρος, Σίλας* for *Σιλουανός*, etc.

§ 88. *Loose and close composition of words.*

(1) Such are the names given to the composition of a verb, etc., when the form remains unchanged, and when it undergoes a modification by a new derivation or at least a new ending.

(2) The 18 primitive prepositions (§ 85. 2), when compounded with a verb, are merely prefixed without changing or modifying the form of the verb; i. e. they are in this case used in an *adverbial* way, and really constitute a separate part of speech, although written in conjunction with the verb. This is what is called *loose* composition.

NOTE. For example, we might write *εὐπράττειν* for *εὖ πράττειν*; and so *κακοποιεῖν* for *κακῶς ποιεῖν*; and the like to this was often done in earlier poetry. In the same way we write *ὑπολαμβάνω*, when we might write *ὑπὸ λαμβάνω*, etc. And so the poets often write, using *Tmesis*, i. e. a division of words, in respect to verbs compounded with the original prepositions.

§ 88. Composite Words. 141

(3) To constitute the *close* composition, viz. that by which the several parts of a compound verb do really become one word, there must be a new derivation through the medium of a compound noun. The ending is usually in -έω ; but the composite words are very various, from which these *secondary* verbs are derived.

E. g. from ἔργον and λαμβάνω comes the compound noun ἐργολάβος, and then the new or secondary verb is derived from this, in the way stated above, i. e. by suffixing -έω, as ἐργολαβέω ; and so εὐεργετεῖν from εὐεργέτης, δυσαρεστεῖν from δυσάρεστος, ἀφειδεῖν from ἀφειδής ; and ἀντιβολεῖν from ἀντιβολή, is an instance (with some others), where composition, even with a *primitive* preposition, follows the like model.

(4) In the composition of nouns only the *close* connection exists, as the parts are never separated by Tmesis.

The modifications of nouns (including adjectives) in consequence of composition, are very various. (a) More generally compound words, whose *latter* part is a *noun*, signify the *object* and not the *subject* of the quality, action, etc., expressed by the word; e. g. δεισιδαίμων *one who fears demons*, not ' demons who are fearful.' (b) When the *latter* part is a *verb* and the first part a noun, the first part designates the object or direction of the action, etc., indicated; e. g. ἱπποτρόφος *one who raises horses*, (not 'a horse which feeds'). (c) But *adjectives* in composition often retain their principal meaning, which is simply modified by the word admitted into composition ; e. g. πιστός *credible*, ἄπιστος *incredible*.

Note 1. Adjectives in -υς, when they are to form such compounds, usually adopt the ending ης; e. g. ἡδύς, but in composition, ἀηδής.

Note 2. In a few cases of nouns in composition, they retain their principal meaning with mere modification by the word received ; as ξένος *a guest*, πρόξενος *a public guest*, etc.

Note 3. The modifications of nouns and adjectives, when euphony requires some change in their form in order to be compounded, are very various, as the case may require ; e. g. ἄδακρυς from δάκρυ, ἄτιμος from τιμή, εὔγεως from εὖ and γῆ, λειπόνεως from λείπω and ναῦς, κακοήθης from κακός and ἦθος, σώφρων from σωφός and φρήν, εὐπάτωρ from εὖ and πατήρ, etc.

Note 4. But when a compound noun is to be formed by the help of a *verb*, the verb usually stands *last ;* as ἐργολάβος, ἱπποτρόφος, etc. For the meaning, see No. 4. b above.

General Remark 1. In respect to the changes suffered by the second or last word in composition, it should be noted, that when this word begins with α, ε, ο short, η or ω is usually assumed in the room of them in the composite word ; e. g. ὑπήκοος from ὑπανούω, εὐήνεμος from εὖ and ἄνεμος, δυσήλατος from δυς and ἐλαύνω, ἀνώμοτος from α and ὄμνυμι, etc.

General Remark 2. A very large portion of words in Greek is compounded either in the close or loose way, and verbs almost without number are *derivates* in the manner stated under No. 3. The lexicons are just beginning to designate such formations ; but the work, as yet, is very imperfectly done. It is matter of much interest to accurate study, that it should be thoroughly accomplished.

Accentuation of compound words.

(5) **General Rule.** The accent is thrown as far back as possible.

E. g. ὁδός, σύνοδος· παῖς, ἄπαις, etc.

EXCEPTIONS. (*a*) Adjectives in -ης (-ες) are usually *oxytone*; as ἀπαθής, προσφιλής, etc. But there are many exceptions; as εὔηθες, etc. (*b*) Verbals in -ά -η -ής -ήρ -εύς -έος, and also nouns in -μος, do not change the tone by composition; as ἐπιτομή, συγγραφεύς, etc.; so παροξυσμός, etc.

(6) Compound words (e. g. προσδοκητός) that are oxytone, when re-compounded, follow the general rule; as ἀπροσδόκητος.

(7) Words compounded with a verb *transitive* for their last part, usually accent the *penult* (when short) if the signification is *active*; and the *antepenult*, if it be *passive*.

E. g. μητροκτόνος *matricide*, μητρόκτονοι *destroyed by the mother*.

NOTE 1. But if the penult be long and the meaning *active*, the word becomes oxytone; as ὁδηγός *a guide*. Some words, however, accent the antepenult; as πτολίπορθος, ἡνίοχος, etc.

NOTE 2. When verbs *intransitive* form the last part of a word, the general rule (with little exception) is followed; e. g. αὐτόμολος, αἱμόρροος, etc.

PART III.

SYNTAX.

[There are various methods of arranging a Syntax; but the most facile is, to treat of the parts of speech in the natural order in which they would occur to the mind, the noun with its various adjuncts coming first, then the verb with its various moods, tenses, regimen, etc; and lastly the various particles which serve as a modification of these. Special peculiarities of phraseology, etc., may then be annexed.]

ARTICLE.

§ 89. *The Article; its nature and leading use.*

(1) The article is a declinable part of speech, which, when employed, is usually prefixed to nouns, adjectives, or participles, for the purpose of specification or emphasis.

NOTE 1. *Specification* may be, (*a*) Either on account of *individuality*, i. e. when one individual is distinguished from others of the same species, or when one species or genus is distinguished from other species or genera; or, (*b*) It may be on account of quality, attributes, condition, actions, circumstances, etc., in which case the quality, attributes, etc., are as it were *individualized* or *specificated*, when the article is employed. E. g. ὁ ἀετός *the eagle*, when one is distinguished from several of the same kind; ὁ ἀετός or οἱ ἀετοί, when either the singular or plural is used *generically*, so as to distinguish this species of birds from other species. Specifications on the ground of attributes, etc., are such as follow; viz., εἰσὶν οἱ λέγοντες *there are* [some] *who say*, where this class of persons is distinguished by the particular action attributed to them in λέγοντες. So οὐκ ἔστι ὁ ἡγησόμενος *there is no one who will lead*, where the action of *leading* is made to distinguish the individual who performs it; so ὁ σπείρων *the sower*, ὁ πειράζων *the tempter*, etc., in which latter cases we convert the participles into mere nouns in translating them, while the article directs the reader to note the *distinctive* quality or trait of the agent named. The cases of specification, which belong to the class just named, are almost without number; e. g. ὁ ἀγαθός or οἱ ἀγαθοί, ὁ κακός or οἱ κακοί; and so οἱ φιλοσοφοῦντες, οἱ ἀποφυγόντες, οἱ δοκοῦντες, etc. Almost all adjectives and participles are capable of such a use, because they are *attributives;* and so, likewise, a multitude of attributive nouns, as ὁ βαπτιστής, ὁ βασιλεύς, ὁ ἡγέμων, ὁ χιλίαρχος, etc.

N. B. In cases where *specification* is not intended, the article is omitted; and then we may translate by, or without, our indefinite article *a* (*an*), as our idiom may require. The N. Test. Greek sometimes employs the numeral εἷς (*one*) as an indefinite article; e. g. Matt. 8: 19, προσελθών εἷς γραμματεύς—*a scribe*. So in John 6: 9. Matt. 21: 19. Rev. 8: 13. So אֶחָד is frequently employed, in the later Hebrew. In a like sense τις is often used.

NOTE 2. The article, it should be understood, is not rigidly confined to nouns, adjectives, and participles; but when adverbs, the Inf. mode, a part of a sentence, etc., take the place of nouns or adjectives, i. e. become nouns or adjectives *ad sensum*, then the article may be, and often is, prefixed to them.

NOTE 3. The *demonstrative* and *pronominal* use of the article will be treated of in the sequel; see § 94.

(2) *Use before leading nouns.* (*a*) It is usually placed before nouns that designate any thing *single*, or *monadic* in its kind, or which is deemed by the speaker or writer to be so. Adjectives and participles, with the meaning of nouns, follow the same rule.

E. g. ὁ οὐρανός, ἡ γῆ, ὁ ἥλιος, ἡ σελήνη, ἡ δικαιοσύνη, ἡ φιλοσοφία, ἡ ἀρετή, τὸ καλόν, τὸ κακόν, ὁ σπείρων, etc.

Under this head may be ranked not only the use of the article for designating *individuality*, i. e. a single individual as distinct from others of the same species, but all those cases where a whole species or genus is regarded as a *unity* in distinction from other classes of beings; see No. 1. Note 1, above.

NOTE 1. Cases of *distributive* meaning, with the article, may be explained on the ground of *individuality*; e. g. Xen. Anab. I. 3. 21, "Cyrus promised ... three half-Dories τοῦ μῆνος τῷ στρατιώτῃ, *each month to each soldier*."

NOTE 2. When *parts* of an assumed *totality* or *unity* are enumerated, the article is usually *omitted*, although each of these parts may embrace a whole species, and each would demand the article, when considered in another relation; e. g. γυναῖκες καὶ παῖδες· ἀδελφοὶ καὶ ἀδελφαί, etc. Here the idea of specific differences seems to be merged by the consideration of union in one whole, and so the article which notes the specific difference is omitted. But where the writer means that each class shall be *distinctly* noted, he of course employs the article before them; and such are perhaps a majority of the cases.

NOTE 3. Nouns which in common cases are *specific* and would take the article, omit it when they are used in an abstract or indefinite sense; e. g. ἡγεῖσθαι θεοίς *to believe in gods*; ἰέναι ἐπὶ δεῖπνον *to go to supper*; γράψαι ἐπὶ μισθῷ *to write for reward*. With all these and the like words, the article would of course be employed where individual specification was intended.

(*b*) But on the very ground that many nouns, etc., are so definite in their nature as to leave no room for mistake, or on the ground that they have by usage acquired as it were the force

§ 89. SYNTAX: ARTICLE.   145

of proper names, the article is often omitted where it might be inserted.

E. g. in the N. Test. it is often omitted in ἥλιος, γῆ, οὐρανός, θάλασσα, νύξ, ἀγορά, ἀγρός, θεός, πνεῦμα ἅγιον, πατήρ, ἀνήρ, πρόσωπον, ἐκκλησία, δεῖπνον, θάνατος, θύρα, νόμος, νεκροί, κόσμος, διάβολος, ὥρα, ἀρχή, κύριος· also δικαιοσύνη, ἀγάπη, πίστις, κακία, πλεονεξία, ἁμαρτία, etc. These, although *monadic*, are more or less frequently employed *without* the article, as may be seen by reference to the Greek Concordance. The like usage exists in the Classics.

NOTE 4. On the ground of *single* objects may be placed the proper names of persons, countries, cities, rivers, etc.; which, as is universally acknowledged, employ or omit the article, with few exceptions, almost *ad libitum scriptoris*. In the N. Test., the names of *countries* and *rivers* more frequently take the article than the names of *towns*. The names of *persons* vary so much, that no general principle can be stated; for different writers have different usages. Where the names are indeclinable, it might naturally be expected that the article would be added in order to distinguish the case; and this often happens, but not always; see in Matt. 1: 1—16, where throughout vs. 2—16 both usages are developed. And the like, often elsewhere. The usual custom is, to employ the article with proper names, in case the person, etc., spoken of has been, or is now specially designed to be, the subject of the writer's consideration; as ὁ Σωκράτης ἔφη, i. e. the Socrates whom I am now considering.

NOTE 5. Connected with the principle above stated, but somewhat diverse in its nature, is *the omission of the article before abstract nouns in general*. An abstract idea, in its very nature, is divested of *individuality*, and therefore dispenses with the article; e. g. σοφία *wisdom*, etc. But if a distinction is to be made between *one class* of abstracts and *another*, then of course the article is employed to mark it; e. g. ἡ φιλοσοφία as a science distinguished from other sciences. If, moreover, the writer wishes to mark the *totality* or *whole compass* of any science, etc., and not simply its abstract nature, the article is employed, as in other like cases; e. g. Phaedo, p. 69, ἡ φιλοσοφία καὶ ἡ δικαιοσύνη καὶ ἡ ἀνδρία καὶ αὐτὴ ἡ φρόνησις, μὴ καθαρμός τις ᾖ; i. e. *philosophy* as a science, *justice* as practical virtue, etc. How much more exact the Greek is than our own language, in such cases, is plain to the considerate reader.

NOTE 6. On the like ground with the preceding cases stand words designating *material substances* simply considered; e. g. γάλα *milk*, ὕδωρ *water*, etc., without the article. But when considered in relation to the speaker, they become individualized and take the article, as δός μοι τὸ γάλα; and so when they are considered as a whole species in distinction from other things, as τὸ γάλα ἐστὶν ἡδύ *milk is sweet*.

(3) When a word, not definite and specific in itself, is rendered so by some adjunct, (pronoun, adjective, participle, noun, noun with a preposition, etc.), it may, like monadic nouns, admit or reject the article.

E. g. in Matt. III. we find in quick succession and with the article, ταῖς ἡμέραις ἐκείναις, τῇ ἐρέμῳ τῆς Ἰουδαίας, ἡ βασιλεία τῶν οὐρανῶν, τὴν ὁδὸν κυρίου, τὰς τρίβους αὐτοῦ, τὸ ἔνδυμα αὐτοῦ, τὴν ὀσφῦν αὐτοῦ, ἡ τροφὴ αὐτοῦ, τὰς ἁμαρτίας αὐτῶν, etc.; most of these nouns, being in their own nature indefinite, are here made specific by the adjuncts united with them, and are so marked

On the contrary, ἐπὶ πρόσωπον αὐτῶν, Matt. 17: 6; ἐν βραχίονι αὐτοῦ, Luke 1: 51; ἐν δεξιᾷ αὐτοῦ, Eph. 1: 20; ἀπὸ ὀφθαλμῶν σου, Luke 19: 42; νοῦν κυρίου, 1 Cor. 2: 16; ἐν πόλει Δαυίδ, Luke 2: 11; ἡμέραν κρίσεως, 2 Pet. 2: 9; πρώτην φυλακήν, Acts 12: 10; all without the article. And thus, very often elsewhere. This is less frequent in the Classics, but still it may often be met with.

(4) When from the nature of the case the speaker or writer can be supposed to mean only *one* particular object, the article is *usually* prefixed; although even here, in some instances where there is no danger of mistake, the article is sometimes omitted.

NOTE 1. The cases of this nature may be resolved principally into two leading classes; viz. either, (a) *Well known or celebrated objects*; e. g. τὸ ποτήριον, in Matt. 26: 27, means *the cup* by which drink was usually served at the table; τὸν νιπτῆρα in John 13: 5, *the wash-bason* which was usually placed in a guest-chamber; τῷ ὑπηρέτῃ in Luke 4: 20, *the servant* who usually waited in the synagogue; τοὺς ἀγγέλους in James 2: 25, the well known *spies*, etc. Cases of this nature are very frequent, and are not always to be judged of by the knowledge which the *reader* may possess. Enough that the objects were *well known*, or *definitely conceived of*, by the writer and his cotemporaries.—Somewhat different from this are two cases, not unfrequent; viz. (1) Merely *implied* antithesis occasions the use of the article; and then special stress is of course laid upon the noun which it accompanies; as John 7: 24, τὴν δικαίαν κρίσιν κρίνατε *judge the righteous judgment*, in opposition to that which is unrighteous. When antithesis is *expressed*, of course it justifies the same usage in respect to the article; as πόλεμος οὐκ ἔστιν ἄνευ κινδύνων, without the article; but when spoken in the way of *contrast*, the usage would be different, as ὁ πόλεμος οὐκ ἄνευ κινδύνων, ἡ δὲ εἰρήνη ἀκίνδυνος. (2) In like manner things necessary or appropriate to any particular occasion or end, often take the article; as Xen. Anab. vii. 6. 23, " he ordered to send on Xenophon to the army τοῖς ἵπποις *with the* [necessary] *cavalry*." Ib. 6. 23, " he must then take τὰ ἐνέχυρα the [necessary] *pledges*." (3) Diverse still are other cases, such as Acts 26: 24, 'Festus spake μεγάλῃ τῇ φωνῇ *with a* [the] *loud voice*.' 1 Cor. 11: 5, 'prophesying ἀκατακαλύπτῳ τῇ κεφαλῇ, *with* [the] *uncovered head*.' Heb. 7: 24, 'hath ἀπαράβατον τὴν ἱεροσύνην [the] *unchangeable priesthood*.' So Rev. 2: 18. 4: 7. Mark 8: 17. Matt. 13: 4. Heb. 5: 14. Here *voice, head, priesthood*, etc. are *definite*, as belonging to specific individuals, etc. See Wm. Gram. § 17. 2.

(b) *Objects that have already been mentioned*, either directly or indirectly; e. g. directly, as Matt. 1: 20 ἄγγελος, 1: 24 ὁ ἄγγελος; Matt. 2: 1 μάγοι, 2: 7 τοὺς μάγους; Matt. 13: 25 ζιζάνια, 13: 26 τὰ ζιζάνια; Luke 9: 13 πέντε ἄρτοι καὶ ἰχθύες δύο, 9: 16 τοὺς πέντε ἄρτους καὶ τοὺς δύο ἰχθύας; and so often, every where. *Indirect* mention also authorizes the use of the article; e. g.

§ 89. Syntax: Article. 147

Eph. 6: 12, ἡ πάλη the contest, viz., the one implied by what is said in vs. 10, 11; τὴν οἰκίαν, Acts 9: 17, refers to what is said in v. 11; τὸν ἄγγελον, Acts 11: 13, refers to the ἄγγελος mentioned in Acts 10: 3, 22. The article in such cases is *demonstrative* in its nature.

Note 2. The reader must not suppose the above rules in *a, b*, to be imperious in all cases. Whenever a speaker or writer chose to employ a word, which had been already mentioned, in a sense less specific, or when (from the nature of the case) there was no danger in respect to its being regarded rightly as specific, he could omit the article; e. g. Matt. 13: 27, ζιζάνια, which had been already twice mentioned, but which in this case required a sense less specific.

(5) The *subject* of a proposition, (*a*) More usually takes the article, and the *predicate* omits it. But, (*b*) Sometimes the reverse of this is the case. (*c*) Sometimes both subject and predicate take it, and sometimes omit it.

E. g. (*a*) θεὸς ἦν ὁ λόγος, John 1: 1, where ὁ λόγος is the subject; ὁ μισῶν τὸν ἀδελφὸν αὐτοῦ, ἀνθρωποκτόνος ἐστί, 1 John 3: 15; and thus in a multitude of cases, because in general the subject of a proposition is specific, and the predicate is not so, but is designed merely to mark quality, state, condition, character, etc., without individuality in the mode of expression. (*b*) Often a pronoun demonstrative or personal without the article, (sometimes other words), is employed as the Nom. or subject, while the predicate has the article; as αὕτη ἐστὶν ἡ ἀγγελία, 1 John 3: 11; οὗτός ἐστιν ὁ τέκτων, Mark 6: 3; ὑμεῖς ἐστε οἱ λαλοῦντες, Mark 13: 11; et saepe alibi. So also in the Classics; as εἰρήνη ἐστὶ τὸ ἀγαθόν. Phaed. of Plato, p. 78, ταῦτα μάλιστα εἶναι τὰ ἀσύνθετα, *these things most of all must be* [the] *uncompounded*. (*c*) The third case is very common; e. g. ἡ ἁμαρτία ἐστὶν ἡ ἀνομία, 1 John 3: 4; ἡ ἐντολὴ ἡ παλαιά ἐστιν ὁ λόγος κ. τ. λ. 1 John 2: 7; ἡ κεφαλὴ ὁ Χριστός ἐστι, 1 Cor. 11: 3; ἡ δὲ πέτρα ἦν ὁ Χριστός, 1 Cor. 10: 4; ἡ ζωὴ ἦν τὸ φῶς, John 1: 4; and thus in a multitude of cases. On the contrary, both subject and predicate sometimes omit the article, as πολλοὶ γάρ εἰσι κλητοί, Matt. 20: 16; Id. 22: 14; so in the classics: αἰτία τούτων φύσις ἀγαθή, Ael. Animal. III. 24; and thus the proverbs, πάντων χρημάτων μέτρον ἄνθρωπος, and καλὸς θεσαυρὸς . . . χάρις ὀφειλομένη. — All the usages under No. 5, are common to the Classics.

From facts such as these, it appears that the subject and predicate, *as such*, neither take nor reject the article; but the addition or omission of it depends entirely on the nature of the words employed, i. e. on the fact, whether they are designed to be specific or otherwise.

(6) Nouns in apposition, explanatory of a preceding noun, usually take the article; but sometimes it is omitted.

E. g. Ἀγρίππας ὁ Βασιλεύς, Ἰωάννης ὁ Βαπτιστής, etc. But on the other hand; Σίμων Βυρσεύς, Acts 10: 32; Ἄννα προφῆτις, Luke 2: 36; Γάιος Δερβαῖος, Acts 20: 4; Τιβερίου Καίσαρος, Luke 3: 1; Φαραὼ Βασιλέως, Acts 7: 10, etc. Both of these usages are common in the Classics. In cases where the object of the noun in apposition is to mark something specific and individual, which is altogether appropriate to the person or thing named, the article is employed; but when there is no special design of this nature, it may be omitted, as in Θουκυδίδης 'Αθηναῖος, Βρέννος Γαλατῶν βασιλεύς, etc. Very generally *when the explanatory noun in apposition takes the article, the preceding proper name omits it*; see above. Of course it is omitted in the first noun, when it is wanting in the second; see above. But in a few cases both nouns take the article; e. g. ὁ Κροῖσος, ὁ τῶν Λυδῶν βασιλεύς. Here, and in such cases, special emphasis, or demonstrative meaning, is attached to the *first* noun. In like manner, ἐγὼ ὁ τλήμων and ἐγὼ τλήμων; in the first case, an intensity is expressed by ὁ τλήμων, quasi *the wretched one*.

The names of rivers, mountains, countries, and islands, are sometimes put between the article that belongs to the apposition-noun and that noun itself; as ὁ Ἅλυς ποταμός, *the Halys river*; τὸ Σούνιον ἄκρον, *the Sunium summit*; ἡ Δῆλος νῆσος, *the Delos island*, etc. In such cases the two nouns must be of the same gender, and then this position of the words makes them, as it were, one compound word.

Participial nouns in apposition always take the article; and generally the nouns also which precede them; e. g. οἱ Φοίνικες—οἱ κτίσαντες τὴν νῆσον.

• (7) Verbs signifying *to be* or *to call*, usually take *anarthrous* nouns, i. e. nouns without the article, after them; but this custom is not uniform.

E. g. ἐν σῶμά ἐστι, ἓν πνεῦμά ἐστι, οὐκ ἔστι φόβος, Matt. 5: 9 υἱοὶ θεοῦ κληθήσονται, Matt. 23: 10 μηδὲ κληθῆτε καθηγηταί; and thus often. On the contrary; λέγεται ὁ ἄψινθος, Rev. 8: 11; καλεῖται ... ὁ λόγος τοῦ θεοῦ, Rev. 19: 13. So Xen. Cyrop. III. 3, 4, ἀνακαλοῦντες τὸν εὐεργέτην τὸν ἄνδρα τὸν ἀγαθόν. See also Anab. VI. 7. Matth. Gramm. § 268. Examples of the article after the substantive verb, see above under No. 5. In such cases, where the article is employed, it of course is emphatic, i. e. it attributes the meaning of the noun joined with it in a peculiar sense to the individuals in question. This usage is not unfrequent in the Classics.

(8) When the *gender* of nouns connected together in the same case is *different*, if the article stands before the first noun, it is commonly inserted before the second, etc.; but this practice is not uniform.

E. g. τὰς σεβομένας γυναῖκας ... καὶ τοὺς πρώτους τῆς πόλεως, Acts 13: 50; ἐν τοῖς παραπτώμασι καὶ τῇ ἀκροβυστίᾳ, Col. 2: 13; τὸ δίκαιον καὶ τὴν ἰσότητα, Col. 4: 1; et alibi saepe. Yet the contrary usage exists; e. g, τὰ ἐντάλματα καὶ διδασκαλίας, Col. 2: 22: εἰς τὰς ὁδοὺς καὶ φραγμούς, Luke 14: 23; τὴν δύναμιν καὶ πλοῦτον, Rev. 5: 12; Luke 1: 6. 23: 49, et al. So Plato: οἱ παῖδές τε καὶ γυναῖκες· ὁ σωφρονῶν καὶ σωφρονοῦσα, et al. In all cases of this nature, the use of the article before the second noun, etc., depends on the degree of *distinction* which the writer means to make between the different classes named. If this is a prominent object, the article is employed in each case; otherwise it is omitted in the subsequent nouns, etc.

(9) Nouns connected in the same case and the same gender,

§ 90. SYNTAX: ARTICLE. 149

usually omit the article after the first noun ; but not unfrequently they insert it.

E. g. μετὰ τῶν πρεσβυτέρων καὶ γραμματέων, Mark 15 : 1 ; διὰ τῆς φιλοσοφίας καὶ κενῆς ἀπάτης, Col. 2 : 8 ; ἐπὶ τῇ θυσίᾳ καὶ λειτουργίᾳ, Phil. 2 : 17, et alibi saepe. And the like in respect to adjectives and participles ; e. g. τὸν ἅγιον καὶ δίκαιον, Acts 3 : 14 ; and so Acts 2 : 20, etc. Participles ; οἱ ... λατρεύοντες καὶ καυχώμενοι ... καὶ ... πεποιθότες, Phil. 3 : 3 ; and so in John 21, 24, et al. saepe.

Yet the contrary usage is almost equally common ; e. g. οἱ ἀρχιερεῖς καὶ οἱ ὑπηρέται, John 19 : 6 ; τῷ ἀνέμῳ καὶ τῷ κλύδωνι, Luke 8 : 24. Luke 11 : 37, et al. saepe. The general principle seems to be, that where the particulars belong to one genus, the article is not repeated ; but where they are entirely separate, it is inserted. Yet this principle is very often violated ; as appears by the examples above, and as is manifest from the best Greek writers ; see Matth. Gramm. § 268. Anmerk. 1. Here, as in No. 8, the use of the article depends on the degree of *distinctiveness* to be given to each particular.

GENERAL REMARK. Such are the general principles respecting the article, when employed, or not employed, as connected with the leading or principal noun or nouns in a sentence. The subordinate uses of it remain to be developed. In the mean time the student should note, that the Greeks have three distinct methods of exhibiting their views in regard to the *definiteness* or *indefiniteness* of any object. For example ; ζῶον means *animal*, i. e. every and any animal ; τὸ ζῶον means *the animal*, i. e. a specific individual in a certain condition or with certain particular attributes ; ζῶόν τι means *an animal*, i. e. a particular beast, or an individual beast, considered simply as individual, but not as distinguished by particular attributes or conditions, etc. In the latter case τις, τι, is usually employed in order to denote *simple individuality;* and in the N. Test., sometimes, εἷς, see No. 1. Note 1. N. B. But sometimes, even here, emphasis occasions the use of the article with the noun which τις qualifies ; as ὁ κύριός τις, Soph. O. C. 288. τοὺς αὐτοέντας τινάς, O. R. 107.

§ 90. *Article with adjectives.*

(1) An adjective qualifying any noun may be placed either *between* the article and its noun, or *after* the noun. In the last case the general rule is, that if the noun has the article, the adjective must adopt it.

E. g. τὸ ἅγιον πνεῦμα, οἱ ἀληθινοὶ προσκυνηταί, etc. More usually the adjective is placed *after* the noun ; as ἡ ζωὴ ἡ αἰώνιος, ἡ πόλις ἡ μεγάλη, ὁ ἄνθρωπος ὁ ἀγαθός, etc. Cases of both kinds occur every where, and more examples are unnecessary.

(2) Different from the cases in No. 1, are all those cases in which the adjective is the *predicate* of a sentence. Here it usually and naturally dispenses with the article, and more commonly (not always) precedes the noun or pronoun to which it bears a relation.

§ 90. SYNTAX: ARTICLE.

E. g. *καλὸς ὁ νόμος· οὐ καλὸν τὸ καύχημα· τοῦτό ἐστι καλόν.* As the adjective in this case does not in reality agree with the noun expressed, it may be of a different number or gender, when the writer pleases; like the Latin: *Varium et mutabile semper femina*, and so the Greek *πονηρὸν μὲν γυνή.*

NOTE 1. In nearly, if not quite, all the cases in which the noun has an article, and the adjective has not the position, or the adjunct article, described in No. 1, it must be regarded as a *predicate.* E. g. *τὸ γὰρ πνεῦμα ἅγιον*, (so Griesbach and Schott), Luke 12:12. 1 Cor. 10: 3, *τὸ αὐτὸ βρῶμα πνευματικόν . . . . τὸ αὐτὸ πόμα πνευματικόν*; Gal. 1:4, *τοῦ ἐνεστῶτος αἰῶνος πονηροῦ*; 1 John 5: 20, *ἡ ζωὴ αἰώνιος.* See also above, No. 4. Note 1. *a.* 3. In the classics a larger number of the like constructions are found, which are copiously exhibited in Matthiae's Gramm. § 277. *b.* Some of these are as follows; 'It is proper for me to speak *μὴ ἐπὶ τοῖς ἔργοις καλοῖς concerning works which are not good,'* Eurip. Pheniss. 540; *ὁ μάντις τοὺς λόγους ψευδεῖς λέγει,* Soph. Oedip. Tyr. 526; *πονηροῖς καὶ τοῖς λόγοις καὶ τοῖς πράγμασι χρώμενοι* Isoc. [Orell.] § 208. So in Buttmann (§ 125. Note 3), *ὅλην τὴν νύκτα· ἔχει τὸν πελέκυν ὀξύτατον· ἐπ' ἄκροις τοῖς ὄρεσι· ᾔδετο ἐπὶ πλουσίοις τοῖς πόλεσι.* In such cases the adjective may precede or follow the noun with the article. In these and all the like cases, Matthiae, Buttmann, Kuhner, and others, think the adjective is a kind of *predicate;* e. g. "the prophet speaks words *which are false;*" "making use of words and actions *which are bad;*" "he has an axe *which is very sharp,*" etc. But if we may solve these cases in such a way, why may we not do the same in respect to all other adjectives, especially such as *follow* the noun, e. g. *ὁ ἄνθρωπος ὁ ἀγαθός, the man who is good?* Moreover how shall we render *ὅλην τὴν νύκτα,* following the principles of these grammarians? *The night which is whole*, i. e. unbroken, undivided, would not give the sense of the Greek, which means 'the whole time of the night season without any subtraction.' Are not cases of this nature, in respect to adjectives, like those of participles, which, placed before or after the noun with the article, may take or omit the article, just as the writer means to make them more or less prominent and distinctive? If this principle may be applied to adjectives, all will be at least intelligible. But now, exactly the contrary meaning is elicited by the principles of the grammarians named; and perhaps with good reason in most cases; for most of the adjectives so arranged seem to be emphatic, as the reader may see for himself.

In particular, adjectives of *quantity, space*, and the like, are wont to obtain the anarthrous state in question; e. g. such as *πᾶς, ὅλος, μέσος,* which rarely indeed stand between the article and its noun. Such cases, however, seem to be merely idiomatic. But in regard to most adjectives in the condition now under consideration, Kuhner states the general principle to be, that *the writer means to give them a* PREDICATE SENSE, *and thus to throw them into a kind of subordinate clause,* instead of uniting them into one compound idea with the noun. It is not by the *nature of the case* only that we are to judge of them, but by the design of the writer. Quite different is the solution of Winer, § 12. 1. *a.*

(3) The article with adjectives, which are not connected with any noun expressed, indicates that they are employed as *nouns.* It is regulated by the usual principles of specification.

E. g. ὁ ἀγαθός, οἱ κακοί, οἱ θνητοί, and particularly the neuter sing., and often the plural, as τὸ καλόν, τὸ κακόν, τὸ γνωστόν, τὰ ἀναγκαῖα, τὰ ἀόρατα, etc. The neuter thus employed is very often used in the place of *abstract* nouns; and often also for adverbs.

NOTE. The article here, as in the case of nouns, can be omitted if the expression is designed to be indefinite; e. g. Odys. θ', 195, ἀλαός *a blind man.*

§ 91. *Article with Participles.*

(1) When participles are employed as mere adjectives, in respect to meaning, the construction of them, in regard to the article, is substantially the same with that of adjectives.

E. g. (*a*) They are placed *between* the article and its noun; as ὁ τεχθεὶς βασιλεύς, Matt. 2:2; τοῦ φαινομένου ἀστέρος, Matt. 2:7; τῆς μελλούσης ὀργῆς, Matt. 3:7; τὸν λεγόμενον Πέτρον, Matt. 4:18; et al. saepe. (*b*) More usually they are placed *after* the noun, and take the article when the noun has it; e. g. ὁ ἄρτος ὁ ζῶν *the living bread*, John 6:51, comp. v. 57, ὁ ζῶν πατήρ. Matt. 10:6, τὰ πρόβατα τὰ ἀπολωλότα *the lost sheep*, etc. Neuter intransitive and passive verbs form most of the participles used as adjectives.

(2) *Participles retaining the meaning of verbs* are subject to a different construction; and for the most part the so-called article, when attached to them, is to be translated by *he who, who, whoever, they who, that which*, etc. No certain rule can be given here, inasmuch as it generally depends on the intention of the writer, as to the *prominence* which he designs to give to the participial word, whether the article is inserted or omitted.

ILLUSTRATIONS. Several classes may be here distinguished. (*a*) Where the Participle forms the *subject* or *object* of a sentence; in which case it takes the article in order to give it somewhat of the nature of a noun; e. g. ὁ ποιήσας τὸ ἔλεός [ἔστι πλησίον], Luke 10:37. In 11:23, ὁ μὴ ὤν— ὁ μὴ συνάγων; v. 40, ὁ ποιήσας, etc. John 6:35, ὁ ἐρχόμενος—ὁ πιστεύων, etc. Rom. 10:5, and in like manner every where. Here we translate ὁ by *he who, whoever,* etc., and subjoin a *verb* ; and we do so, because our idiom differs from the Greek. When participles are the *object* of a sentence, the principle is the same; e. g. " I will in no wise cast out τὸν ἐρχόμενον πρός με," John 10:37. Id. saep. al.

NOTE. But here also, as in the case of adjectives, if the object be not *specific*, the article may be omitted, even according to the best Greek usage; e. g. βοήσας *one who cries, a crier*, Odys. ε, 473; νοήσας *an intelligent person*, Hes. Ἐργ. init.: ὁμολογῶν *any one who confesses*, Lys. p. 104. 28; and Plato even commingles both constructions in the following sentence; διαφέρει δὲ παμπολὺ μαθὼν μὴ μαθόντος, καὶ ὁ γυμνασάμενος μὴ γεγυμνασμένου *he differs much who has learned, from him who has not learned, and he who has practised, from him who is not practised.* Matth. § 556. 4. So in Rom. 10: 14, 'How shall they hear χωρὶς κηρύσσοντος.'

(b) Where the subject or object of the sentence is otherwise designated, i. e. is a noun, pronoun, etc., the practice is various, as the part. (the participial-adjectives excepted) then comes near to the nature of a verb. (1) The subject or object may have or omit the article, while the participle is *anarthrous*; e. g. ὁ ἰσχυρὸς καθωπλισμένος φυλάσσῃ, etc. Luke 11: 21. V. 22, ὁ ἰσχυρότερος ἐπελθὼν νικήσῃ, etc. V. 24, τὸ ἀκάθαρτον πνεῦμα ... ζητοῦν ... καὶ μὴ εὑρίσκον. V. 53, οἱ γραμματεῖς ... ἐνεδρεύοντες, etc. John 6: 14, 19. Rom. 10: 12. Acts 23: 27. 3: 26. 21: 8. Such is the great majority of cases. But cases where the article is omitted in *both* words are frequent; e. g. Rom. 11: 21, πρὸς λαὸν ἀπειθοῦντα καὶ ἀντιλέγοντα. Luke 11: 17, πᾶσα βασιλεία ... διαμερισθεῖσα, etc. Luke 10: 25. Acts 1: 15; and so whenever the subject is designed not to be specific. (2) The participle may take the article, while the subject either has it, or rejects it; as οἱ ὀφθαλμοὶ οἱ βλέποντες, Luke 10: 23; οἱ ἄνθρωποι οἱ περιπατοῦντες, Luke 11: 44; τὸ αἷμα ... τὸ ἐκχυνόμενον, Luke 11: 50. John 6: 22, 27, 33, 44, 50. The subject is anarthrous in Luke 11: 10, πᾶς ὁ αἰτῶν; 11: 45, διδάσκαλε, ταῦτα λέγων, etc. John 6: 45. Rom. 10: 4, 11, et al. saepe. Generally some pronoun, or πᾶς, or τίς, is the subject or object in such cases, i. e. where the noun, etc., omits the article and the participle takes it.

REMARK. In a great number of instances, a Participle of the Nom. case merely supplies the place of a verb, and is used to designate *preparatory* action; see § 140. 3. Of course it is *anarthrous* here, where the *subject* is a noun or pronoun expressed or understood. But the great mass of cases in which the Part. has an *article*, (excepting those which supply the place of nouns or adjectives), is of such a nature that the article must be rendered *he who, who, whoever, that which*, etc., and such are to be regarded as being thus made *prominent* by the article, and in a measure disjoined from the nouns, etc., with which they are construed. Of course, the case No. 1 above presents the less emphatic use of the participle; No. 2, the more emphatic one. See an example of both in 1 Pet. 5: 10. The reader will not fail to remark, that such being the case, the article before participles of this class produces an effect just the reverse of that which is produced when it is employed with adjectives. Is there not something yet undeveloped, respecting the use of the article in senses so opposite?

§ 92. *Article before other adjuncts to principal Nouns.*

(1) A multitude of leading nouns have other adjuncts besides adjectives and participles, which *qualify* them, or are *exegetical* in their nature; and thus these adjuncts *partake of the nature of adjectives*. Such adjuncts, when connected with *prepositions*, are disposed of in the same way as adjectives, in regard to the article.

E. g. (a) Such adjuncts may be put between the article and the noun; as τὸ ἐν ἀνθρώποις κακόν· ταῖς ἐν διασπορᾷ φυλαῖς· τὰ ἐν σαρκὶ ἔθνη, etc. In all such cases the adjuncts are, to all intents and purposes, adjectives *ad sensum*. (b) They are put *after* the principal noun, and usually (but not always) with the article before them when the noun has the article; as τῆς

§ 93. Syntax: Article. 153

διακονίας τῆς εἰς τοὺς ἁγίους, 2 Cor. 8: 4; τοῖς ... ἀδελφοῖς τοῖς ἐξ ἐθνῶν, Acts 15: 23; James 1: 1. Rom. 4: 11, et saepe alibi. (c) The adjunct sometimes has the article when the principal noun omits it; and vice versa; e. g. πίστει τῇ εἰς ἐμέ, Acts 26: 18; ἔργων τῶν ἐν δικαιοσύνῃ, Tit. 3: 5; 2 Tim. 1: 13, et saepe al., see Winer § 19. 4. *Vice versa*; τῶν συγγενῶν μοῦ κατὰ σάρκα, Rom. 9: 3; τὰ ἔθνη ἐν σαρκί, Eph. 2: 11; 2 Cor. 7: 7. Col. 1: 4. 1 Cor. 10: 18. And so Polyb. III. 48. 11, τὴν ἀλλοτριότητα πρὸς ʽΡωμαίους, et al. saepe.

NOTE 1. It will be understood, of course, that where the principal noun *omits* the article, the adjunct more commonly omits it also; as εἰς μετάληψιν μετὰ εὐχαριστίας, 1 Tim. 4: 3; 1 Tim. 1: 5. Rom. 14: 17, et al. saepe. But exceptions to this, as in (c) above, are by no means rare.

(2) The most common adjunct of all is the **Gen.** *case*, as connected with the principal noun. The usage here differs somewhat from that described in No. 1. E. g.

(1) *The Gen. is usually put after the principal noun without repeating the article which belongs to the principal noun;* as ὁ λόγος τοῦ θεοῦ (not ὁ τοῦ θεοῦ); and thus in cases without number. But, (2) We find also (although not often in the N. Test.) such constructions as repeat the article of the principal noun; e. g. ὁ ἀνὴρ ὁ τῆς Κυθήρης (Anac.); ὁ δῆμος ὁ ʼΑθηναίων, Plat. Gorg. p. 481; τὰ τείχη τὰ ʼΑθηναίων, id. p. 455, et al. saepe. . So in the N. Test.; 1 Cor. 1: 18, ὁ λόγος ὁ τοῦ σταυροῦ; Acts 13: 22, Δαβὶδ, ὁ τοῦ ʼΙεσσαί. John 19: 25. Matt. 4: 21. 10: 2. Mark 3: 17, etc.; nearly always for the sake of emphasis or distinction. (3) Not unfrequently the Gen. is placed between the article of the governing noun and that noun itself; e. g. τὰ τῆς πόλεως πράγματα, etc. ; but this is not a usual construction in the N. Testament.

NOTE 1. Usually *both* nouns, in such cases, have or omit the article. But this is not a necessary rule; for *often the first noun is anarthrous, while the second noun has the article; and sometimes vice versa*; e. g. ἐν μέσῳ τῶν ἀκανθῶν, Luke 8: 7; ἡδονῶν τοῦ βίου, Luke 8: 14; Luke 8: 41. Phil. 2: 25, et al. saepe. In the examples above, viz. τὰ τείχη τὰ ʼΑθηναίων, ὁ δῆμος ὁ ʼΑθηναίων, etc., the noun in the Gen. omits the article; and so in some other cases where proper names are not concerned; e. g. συνέκαλεσε, καὶ ἱππέων καὶ πεζῶν καὶ ἁρμάτων τοὺς ἡγεμόνας, Cyrop. vi. 3. 8. It does not seem to depend merely on the *relation* of the two nouns, whether they shall both take or both reject the article; but on the nature of each noun by itself, and on the particular design of the writer as to specification in respect to either noun.

NOTE 2. The construction in No. 3 is sometimes carried so far in the classics, that three articles are brought together; e. g. τὴν τοῦ τῷ ὄντι ῥητορικοῦ ... τέχνην· τὰ τῆς τῶν πολλῶν ψυχῆς ὄμματα, Plato. This involute construction is not at all predominant in the N. Test.; the writers of which generally prefer the most simple and obvious position of their words, and plainly seek for no effect resulting from mere artificial harmony of arrangement.

20

§ 93. *Special usages of the article.*

(1) Οὗτος, ἐκεῖνος, and αὐτός, used as *pronominal adjectives*, require the noun (some *proper* names excepted) to which they belong, to take the article, throughout the N. Test.

NOTE 1. In the classics, nouns thus connected sometimes take and sometimes omit the article, specially in poetry; see Matth. § 265. 1. § 266.

NOTE 2. When the noun is the *predicate* of a sentence, and the pronoun the *subject*, the article may of course be dispensed with; as ταῦτα τέκνα τοῦ θεοῦ these [are] *the children of God*, Rom. 9: 8. Comp. Gal. 3: 7. 1 Thess. 4: 3. Luke 1: 36, et alibi.

(2) *Ἕκαστος*, in the N. Test., used as an *adjective*, expels the article; see Luke 6: 44. John 19: 23. Heb. 3: 13, al.

NOTE. The Greeks, on the other hand, sometimes admitted the article in this case; see Matth. § 265. 5.

(3) *Τοιοῦτος* admits or rejects the article, as the nature of the noun is definite or indefinite.

E. g. 2 Cor. 12: 2, 3. John 4: 23. Mark 9: 37. Excluded in Matt. 9: 8. Mark 6: 2. Acts 16: 24, et al. Same usage in the classics.

(4) *Πᾶς* in the singular, (*a*) Requires the article with its noun when it indicates *totality*, i. e. a *tout ensemble*. (*b*) It excludes it, when *each* is the idea conveyed by it.

E. g. πᾶσα ἡ ἀγέλη, Matt. 8: 32. 21: 10. Mark 4: 1, et al. saepe. (*b*) E. g. πᾶς ἄνθρωπος, πᾶσα πόλις, etc.; see Matt. 3: 10. 13: 47. Luke 3: 5, et al. saepe.

NOTE. Proper names under (*a*) do not always take the article; as πᾶσα Ἱεροσόλυμα, Matt. 2: 3. Acts 2: 36. On the other hand, when a *participle* is employed in the room of a noun, in the case (*b*), the article remains; as πᾶς ὁ ὀργιζόμενος, Matt. 5: 22; πᾶς ὁ βλέπων, Matt. 5: 28; and so in innumerable cases, both in the N. Test. and in the classics. It is the participle which demands the retention of the article in such cases, in order that this article should mark its nature as a noun, adjective, etc.

(*c*) A *definite* noun, joined with the plural (*πάντες*, etc.), requires the article; before an indefinite one the article is omitted.

E. g. inserted in such cases as Matt. 2: 16. 4: 24. Mark 5: 12, et saepe alibi. On the contrary, omitted in such cases as Rom. 5: 12. Gal. 6: 6. 1 Tim. 2: 4, et al. saepe. The presence of *πάντες*, etc., then, does not seem to affect the omission or insertion of the article before the noun; this depends on the nature of the noun itself.

NOTE. The position of *πᾶς* etc., and *πάντες* etc., varies in a few cases; e. g. πᾶσα ἡ πόλις, ὁ πᾶς νόμος Gal. 5: 14, τέκνων αὐτῆς πάντων Luke 7: 35; but in almost all cases this adjective *precedes* the noun to which it belongs.

The like position (*before* the noun) does ὅλος always take in the N. Test.; and very often ἐκεῖνος, in like manner.

(5) The pronominal adjectives ἐμός, σός, ἡμέτερος, etc., usually require the article, because of their *definitive* nature.

But sometimes it is omitted, where the nature of the case shows that the writer does not desire to particularize; as ἐμὸν βρῶμά ἐστιν, John 4: 34.

(6) Adverbs often take the article and thus become adjectives, or supply the place of nouns.

E. g. οἱ πάλαι [ἄνθρωποι], ἡ αὔριον [ἡμέρα], ἡ ἄνω [πόλις], etc.

(7) The Infinitive mode when used *substantively*, usually takes the article; in which case this mode is employed as an indeclinable noun, in all the usual cases of a noun.

(8) The article τό is put before a word, phrase, etc., quoted; as τὸ ʽΙλλάς the [word] *Hellas* ; or before a phrase or sentence, the whole of which is employed as *subject* or *object* in a sentence.

E. g. 'There arose a dispute among them, τὸ τίς ἂν εἴη μείζων αὐτῶν,' Luke 9: 46; 'And they sought . . . τὸ πῶς ἂν ἔλωσιν αὐτόν,' Luke 22: 2. So Rom. 8: 26. Acts 4: 21. 22: 30. Mark 9: 23. Luke 1: 62. 22: 23. 1 Thess. 4: 1. In such cases, τό is equivalent to *videlicet, namely*, etc.

§ 94. *Article as a pronoun.*

(1) The simple article as a *pronoun demonstrative*, is employed rarely in the N. Test.; but the sense of a *demonstrative* attaches to it in cases such as ὁ μέν . . . ὁ δέ, or ὅδε and οἵδε, or οἱ ἐκ νόμου, τὰ περὶ ὑμῶν, and the like.

In Acts 17: 28, τοῦ γὰρ γένος ἐσμέν (from Aratus) means: *We are the offspring of* THIS ONE, i. e. τούτου τοῦ θεοῦ. But in general the demonstrative is made as above. Oftentimes ὁ δέ alone is equivalent to οὗτος; as ὁ δὲ ἀποκριθείς, Matt. 15: 24, 26. 12: 39, 48, al. saepe. Again: οἱ, etc., with the Gen. dependent on it, or followed by a noun with a preposition, is often used as a kind of demonstrative; e. g. οἱ τοῦ Ζεβεδαίου, John 21: 2; τὰ τῆς σαρκός, Rom. 8: 5. Luke 2: 49. Matt. 16: 23, et al. saepe; and so οἱ ἀπὸ τῆς Ἰταλίας, οἱ ἐκ περιτομῆς, etc., i. e. *they* or *those of Italy*, etc.

(2) The use of ὁ, ἡ, τό, *as a proper relative pronoun* in the N. Test., is denied by late critics. Matthiae limits this use to the Ionic and Doric writers, and to the tragedians in the Attic, § 292; and Winer does not recognize it in the N. Testament, § 20. 3.

NOTE. Separate from its connection with participles, I am not aware of any instance in which the article is employed as a simple *relative* pronoun, in the N. Testament. But here, whatever may be said as to the nature of the *Greek* idiom itself in respect to ὁ, ἡ, τό, before participles, in translating such phrases into English, or Latin, we are obliged to render the article as if it were a *relative* pronoun; e. g. ὁ θεὸς, ὁ καλέσας ἡμᾶς, God, who called us; ὁ θεὸς, ὁ ἀφορίσας με, God, who separated me, etc.; and thus of nearly all the participles that bear a *verbal* sense and have the article prefixed. It would not be strictly correct, as a matter of mere grammar, to name the article in such cases a *relative* pronoun; but it constitutes an idiom so peculiar that *we* can express the sense of it only by translating it as a *relative*. Evidently something more remains to be done, in order to cast satisfactory light upon the differences (as grammarians now represent the matter) between the insertion and omission of the article in connection with adjectives, and the same in connection with participles. At present the theory is not only *diverse* in regard to this subject, but on some points it seems to be directly contradictory.

NOUNS.

§ 95. *Number and Gender of nouns.*

(1) In cases almost without number, in the Old Test. and in the New, also in all classic authors, the singular number of nouns and pronouns stands *generically* for a whole class; i. e. (as we say), it is a noun or pronoun of *multitude*.

E. g. James 5: 6, 'ye have killed τὸν δίκαιον;' 2: 6, 'but ye have dishonoured τὸν πτωχόν;' 1 Pet. 4: 18, 'if ὁ δίκαιος scarcely be saved, where will ὁ ἀσεβὴς καὶ ἁμαρτωλός appear?' Pronouns (which of course occupy the place of nouns) conform every where, *pro re natâ*, to this usage.

Note. Of course, a verb, adjective, or participle, may be in the *singular* or *plural* when connected with a noun, etc., of multitude.

(2) *Vice versâ*, the plural form is often used where only an individual, or a particular thing is meant.

E. g. (*a*) In a multitude of cases where the plural form of nouns is employed to designate a single object; as οὐρανοί, αἰῶνες, ἀνατολαί, δυσμαί, τὰ δεξιά, τοῖς κόλποις Luke 16: 23, ἐξ αἱμάτων ἐγεννήθησαν John 1: 13, (probably referring to the blood of both parents), τὰ ἐγκάνια, γενέσια, ἄζυμα, αἱ γραφαί, and the like. Usage only can determine the extent of this idiom; but in many cases such plurals depend on the *whole* being regarded as *made up of various parts* or *ingredients*.

(*b*) In many special cases, where *emphasis* is designed to be given to the expression, or *generality* of idea to be expressed; as Heb. 9: 23, κρείττοσι θυσίαις, spoken of the death of Christ; John 9: 3, ἔργα θεοῦ, the peculiar or miraculous work of healing the blind; Heb. 7: 6, ἐπαγγελίας, the special promise respecting the Messiah; 2 Cor. 12: 1, ὀπτασίας καὶ ἀποκαλύψεις, the heavenly vision related in the sequel; James 2: 1, ἐν προσωποληψίαις, partiality of any kind; and so oftentimes, both in the New and Old Testament. Cases like this last, viz. of *abstract* nouns in the plural

§ 95. SYNTAX: NOUNS. 157

necessarily denote the various developments or exhibitions of the qualities named.

(c) Where the thought is designed to be *general* only, the *plural* is not unfrequently used, when strictly speaking the subject or agent is only one; e. g. Matt. 26 : 8, οἱ μαθηταὶ αὐτοῦ ... λέγοντες, but in John 12: 4, εἷς ἐκ τῶν μαθητῶν αὐτοῦ, Ἰούδας ... λέγει, etc., for here Matthew relates the fact in a general way, while John specificates; so Matt. 27 : 44, οἱ λησταὶ ... ὠνείδιζον, but Luke 23 : 39, εἷς δὲ τῶν ... κακούργων ἐβλασφήμει ; Matt. 20 : 30—34 δύο τυφλοί κ. τ. λ., Mark 10 : 46—52, Βαρτίμαιος ὁ τυφλός, and Luke 18 : 35—43 τυφλός τις, where the former evangelist relates the occurrence in a more general way, Mark specificates a noted individual, and Luke particularizes but does not specificate. So John 20 : 1, 11, 18, speaks of Mary Magdalene only as going to the sepulchre, while Mark 16 : 1, 2. Luke 24 : 1, 9, 10, speak of her and several others, and Matt. 28 : 1, 7, 8, of Mary Magdalene and another Mary; in Matt. 8: 28 seq. two demoniacs are mentioned, while in Mark 5:1 seq., Luke 8: 26 seq., only one is named. Comp. also Mark 7: 17 with Matt. 15: 15; Matt. 14: 17 and Mark 6: 38 with John 6: 8, 9; Matt. 24: 1 with Mark 13: 1; Matt. 27: 37 with John 19: 19; Matt. 27: 48 and Mark 15: 36 with John 19: 29. So in Luke 22: 67, λέγοντες, when, in all probability, one only is meant; see also the same idiom in John 11: 8. Luke 20: 21, 39. 24: 5 (εἶπον). Matt. 15: 1, λέγοντες. 15: 12 (εἶπον). In John 6: 45. Acts 13: 40, we have ἐν τοῖς προφήταις ; Matt. 24 : 26, ἐν τοῖς ταμείοις, when, evidently, only a particular passage of Scripture, and a particular recess is meant; so ἐπεκάθισεν ἐπάνω αὐτῶν, Matt. 21: 7, where only one can be meant, unless, with Euthymius, we refer αὐτῶν to ἱμάτια. The reader is particularly desired to collate all these passages; for the subject is of great importance in respect to the conciliation of one part of Scripture with another.

NOTE 1. In classical Greek a multitude of the like idioms occur. Matthiae says (§ 293), that '*expression in the plural serves to give emphasis to general expressions.*' So τὰ φίλτατα for *mother, spouse,* etc.; so δώματα—κάρηνα Ὀλύμπου, etc. So also, Eurip. Hipp. 11, Hippolytus is called Πιτθέως παιδεύματα *the pupil of Pittheus ;* Hesiod. Sc. H. 312, τρίπος ... κλυτὰ ἔργα. The exchange of ἐγώ and ἡμεῖς, and of corresponding verbs, occurs times without number in the classics. Matthiae, moreover, lays it down as a principle, that, 'in the Greek language, more than in any other (has he studied the Hebrew?) there is a passing from the plural to the singular, and *vice versâ ;* and also, that the *plural* may receive attributives or definitives [i. e. verbs, participles, adjectives, etc.] in the *singular* number, § 293. Hence a verb in the *singular* is sometimes employed after a Nom. in the plural; or a participial noun singular, or a common noun singular, stands connected with a plural verb. In like manner the singular of nouns is often put where we might expect the plural.' Such being the case in the Classics, why should we imagine that the N. Test. writers have departed from the idiom of the Greek language, when examples of this kind are now and then found among them?

NOTE 2. It follows of course, that the rule respecting *the agreement of a verb, adjective, etc., with a noun in regard to number, is by no means universal.* Nouns or pronouns generic, although in the singular, may be construed *ad sensum*, and therefore take a plural verb, etc.; and *vice versâ*, those plurals which designate *single* things, or an *entirety* of several parts combined together, may have a singular verb, etc. In the Classics examples without number may be found of the *constructio ad sensum*, where the *meaning* (and not the form) of words is principally regarded. See in Kühner, § 418. *a, b*, etc.

(3) The neuter gender is not unfrequently used in reference to *persons*, where the expression is designed to be of a general nature.

E. g. πᾶν ὅ, John 17: 2, in reference to the elect; so αὐτοί . . . ἓν ὦσιν, John 17: 21; τὸ κατέχον, 2 Thess. 2: 6, for the masc. see v. 7; comp. also 1 Cor. 1: 27, 28. Heb. 7: 7. 1 John 5: 4, et al. So frequently, in classical Greek; e. g. τὸ μειράκιον, τὸ γυναίκιον, τὰ παιδικά, τὰ ἀνθρώπια, etc. for *youth, women, children, men*, etc.

NOTE. Whenever *constructio ad sensum* takes place, the gender or number of the word employed is overlooked, and the verb, adjective, etc., accords with the real gender or number of the *thing* or *person* intended to be expressed; thus τὰ παιδικά ἐστι καλός.

§ 96. *Nature and meaning of Case.**

(1) It seems to be now generally agreed among grammarians of the higher class, that the germ of the several cases in Greek, is to be found *in the sensible relations of space to material objects*. Strictly considered, the Nom. and Voc. are not cases; but real cases are made by variations from these, or at least from the Nominative. In this light case is here considered.

(2) The relations of space to objects are twofold; first as in motion, secondly as at rest. The first comprises two particulars, viz. (*a*) Motion *from* an object. (*b*) Motion *toward*, or *over* an object. The second comprises the notion of an object *at rest* in a certain place.

(3) The Gen. case, in its *first* and *original* meaning seems to have sprung from the idea of motion *from* an object, and so to answer the question, *Whence?* The Acc. denotes the idea of motion *toward* or *over* an object, and answers the question, *Whither?* The Dative originally designated the *where* of an object, i. e. it designated rest or continuance in any place.

NOTE. By subdivisions of one or more of these, some languages, e. g. the Latin, has made more cases than three. But originally these seem to comprise the whole ground. The three cases may be named, (as they have recently been for the purpose of designating their origin), the *whence-case* (Gen.), the *where-case* (Dat.), and the *whither-case* (Acc.)

(4) Transferring the relations just specified from *space* to *time*, (a transfer very natural and often found in all languages), we have the Gen. marking

---

* This subject has recently been discussed in a most ample manner. by Hartung, Ueber Bild und Bedeutung der Casus, 1831 ; Wulner, Bedeut der sprachl. Casus. 1827 ; K F. Becker, Organismus der Sprachen, etc., Heiling, Syntax der Deutschen Sprache; and Kühner, ausfuhrl Griech. Gramm § 503 seq.

§ 96. SYNTAX: CASES. 159

the time from which any thing, event, etc., is to be dated; the Acc. marking *the time unto* or *through which* any thing is developed; and the Dat. designating *the time in which* any thing happened.

(5) Those relations being, in the next place, carried over to *causality*, will of course denote, (*a*) The Gen., *the source from which any thing springs*, viz. the ground, reason, origin, or author of the same. (*b*) The Acc. *the whither of action*, i. e. the effect, consequence, etc. of it, or the object on which it terminates. (*c*) The Dat., *the delaying or continuance of action on or in a thing* (*the where*) and therefore the means or intermediate process by which any thing is accomlpished.

(6) *The way and manner* of any action, etc., may be expressed by either of these cases, according to the writer's design to refer this manner to the *whence*, the *where*, or the *whither*, of any action, event, etc.

(7) *Rise of prepositions.* It is easy to see that, only the more general purposes of speech could be well subserved by marking these general relations. Something more definite was needed to designate such space-relations, as *above, below; within, without; before, behind; on this side, on the other side; to, from; thereto, therefrom; forwards, backwards; over here, over there*, etc. For distinction's sake these minuter relations are now named *dimension-relations*, in order to separate them from the more general relations of space as marked merely by cases. To mark definitely these *dimension-relations*, prepositions were originally introduced.

(8) Once introduced, and the convenience of them being so obvious, the general power of case *retreated* and the sway of prepositions *advanced*. At last *case* came to be employed, more usually, only to designate mere *causal* relations; although even in the latter stages of Greek, many vestiges of the ancient usages still remain.

NOTE. *Causal relations*, as the phrase is now employed, means the relation of *agency* or *influence of an internal nature*, i. e. such as the springing from, or else affecting, any being, object, etc. The Gen. indicates the *source* of influence or causality, and the Acc. the *object* of it, viz., that which is affected by it. The Dat. leans to the expression of *locality*, and indicates cause, therefore, only in the secondary sense of *end in view, means, instrument, way and manner*, etc. The development of the Greek language corresponds with the view given above. Older writers make use of fewer prepositions; the later ones employ them much oftener.

(9) It is easy to see by this account of the general nature of case and of the prepositions, that the necessities of a language would of course occasion enlargements of some of these principles, or, in other words, occasion it to shoot out branches from this trunk and main limbs. Accordingly we shall see, in the particular syntax of the Gen. Dat. and Acc., that there are divergencies from the leading principles, which at times it is difficult for us to trace; but, in the main, all moves on in conformity with these general views.

GENERAL REMARKS. The idiom of the Greek differs widely, in some respects, from that of the English, in the use of verbs and cases connected. To a very great extent the Greek employs the *Gen.* after verbs, adjectives, and participles; but as thus employed it was not by them regarded as a *passive* subject of influence or action, but as an *active* agent, causing or giving occasion, in one sense or another, to the action, influence, etc., designated by the verb, adjective, etc., connected with it. Hence verbs, etc., thus employed before the Gen., are to be regarded, so far as *Greek* usage in this particular instance is concerned, as *intransitive*, or *reflexive*, or *passive*. This accounts for the frequency with which the *middle* voice is employed before the Genitive. When influence is exerted which merely *passes over* to some object, this object is designated by the Acc. case and not by the Genitive, i. e. the Acc. points out the object on which the action or influence terminates, (the *whither-case*). In English we have little, comparatively, to correspond with some part of the Greek usage of the Genitive after verbs; e. g. the Greeks would say: ἀπολαύειν τινός, θιγγάνειν τινός, ἀκούειν τινός, ἐρᾶν τινος, etc., which we must translate, *to enjoy any thing, to touch any thing, to hear any thing, to love any one*, etc. Which is the more philosophical? Doubtless the Greek; for enjoying, touching, hearing and loving, are matters of *our own* experience, and do not directly affect the objects which occasion these internal sensations. These views, moreover, are fundamental as distinguishing the nature of the Gen. and Acc. cases. The former is *active*, i. e. according to the Greek method of conception; the latter denotes the *passive* subject of influence. That the Greeks often used the Dat. and also the Acc. after the same verb which at times takes a Gen., is no objection to this view; for different nouns have different meanings, and therefore imply different relations; and besides this, the effort to attain variety of expression would give rise to many such interchanges as these. It does not follow, when I say: *He tasted of honey*, and *he tasted honey*, that there is no difference in the *mode of expression* minutely considered, although the general idea may be and is the same. The Greeks could say: ἐρῶν τινος or τινα, and we can say, in a like way: *to be in love with any one*, or *to love any one*. Yet the expressions are not in all respects exactly equivalent.

§ 97. *Nominative and Vocative.*

(1) THE NOM. CASE usually constitutes the subject of a sentence, i. e. of some verb expressed or implied. But,

(2) The Nom. in some cases is used *absolutely*, i. e. independently of the construction which follows it, both in the N. Test. and in classic writers.

E. g. ὁ Μωϋσῆς οὗτος ... οὐκ οἴδαμεν τί κ. τ. λ, Acts 7 : 40 ; ὁ νικῶν, ποιήσω αὐτὸν κ. τ. λ, Rev. 3 : 12. Also Luke 13 : 4. 1 John 2 : 27. Matt. 10 : 32. 12 : 36. Mark 9 : 20, et al. See Matth. § 311.

(3) The Nom. form is often used as a Vocative, both in the N. Test. and elsewhere.

E. g. ἡ παῖς, ἐγείρου, Luke 8 : 54. Mark 9 : 25. Matt. 27 : 29. Mark 10 : 47, et saepe al. Matth. § 312.

(4) The Nom. stands in Greek *after*, as well as before, such verbs as merely constitute a *copula* in a sentence, and even when this Nom. is not the subject of the sentence.

§ 99. SYNTAX: GEN. CASE. 161

NOTE 1. The student is already acquainted with the well known leading constituents of a sentence, viz., the subject and predicate, which last may be either a verb, or an adjective, noun, etc., with the copula or verb of existence. Most verbs of course serve the double purpose of copula and predicate, i. e. they not only assert, but assert some particular quality, action, state, etc. But there is a considerable class of verbs, which usually serve merely as the copula of a sentence, and do not contain in themselves any completed declaration of attribute, action, state, etc. All these usually take the Nom. case after them. Such verbs are not only εἰμί, ὑπάρχω, γίνομαι, but also, φύω, κυρέω, κυλέομαι, φωνέω, ἐπικαλέομαι, προσαγορεύομαι, ὀνομάζομαι, λέγομαι, ἀκούω, αἱρέομαι, ἀποδείκνυμαι, χειροτονέομαι, κρίνομαι, δοκῶ, φαίνομαι, ἔοικα, νομίζομαι, ὑπολαμβάνομαι, κρίνομαι, δηλόομαι, μένω, καθίστημι, and others. It must not be supposed that all these verbs in all their voices, etc., take a Nom. after them; nor in all the meanings which they bear; but in those cases in which they serve as a *copula* only, they take the Nom. after them; e. g. ἐγώ εἰμι θεός · φωνεῖτέ με, ὁ διδάσκαλος, John 13: 13; λέγεται, ὁ ἄψινθος, Rev. 8:11; φίλος ... κόσμου ἐχθρὸς τοῦ θεοῦ καθίσταται, James 4: 4, et sic. al. saepe. Rost § 100, Anm. 1. Matth. § 307.

NOTE 2. When a name is given in connection with ὄνομα, it may be done in three ways; e. g. τό ὄνομα αὐτῆς, Μαριάμ · or ᾗ ὄνομα, Μαριάμ · or ὀνόματι Μαριάμ. In the last case, the proper name stands in apposition with some preceding noun, and ὀνόματι is the Dat. of circumstance, as ἑκατοντάρχῃ ὀνόματι Ἰουλίῳ, Acts 27: 1. Luke 1: 5. Ἄνδρα ὀνόματι Ἀνανίαν, Acts 9: 12.

5. When an epexegetical clause is added to a preceding clause which contains an *oblique* case, the clause added sometimes begins with a Nom., as if it were a part of a new sentence, instead of adopting the oblique form merely for the sake of apposition.

E. g. Il. ζ. 395, θυγάτηρ μεγαλήτορος Ἠετίωνος, Ἠετίων ὅς ἔναιεν κ. τ. λ. Il. κ. 437, τοῦ δὲ καλλίστους ἵππους ἴδον ἠδὲ μεγίστους· λευκότεροι χιόνος, θείειν δ᾽ ἀνέμοισιν ὁμοῖοι. Plato, Soph. p. 266. τίθημι δύο διχῇ ποιητικῆς εἴδη · θεία μὲν καὶ ἀνθρωπίνη κατὰ θάτερον τμῆμα. Ib. p. 218. τί δῆτα προσταξαίμεθ᾽ ἂν εὔγνωστον μὲν καὶ σμικρόν ... ; οἷον ἀσπαλιευτής, κ. τ. λ. See copious citations of the like kind, in Bernhardy. Synt. p. 68 seq. Such a construction often occurs in the Apoc., and has been sometimes put to the account of solecism. With how much reason, the reader may now judge. See Rev. 1: 5.

(6) THE VOCATIVE is used either with or without the ὦ.

E. g. Matt. 15: 28, ὦ γύναι! Acts 21: 20, ἀδελφέ, and saepe al. So in the classics; Matth. § 312. 4.

GENITIVE.

§ 98. *Nature and uses of the Genitive.*

(1) The fundamental idea of this case has already been shown (in § 96); it is *the whence-case*. This general idea may be ap-

21

plied to *space, time,* and finally to *causality* or *originating source* in its most extensive sense. It is with the latter that we are principally concerned.

NOTE 1. The name *Genitive* (i. e. gignit) shows well the true nature of this case. In some sense, direct or indirect, real or supposed, does this case, in nearly all its developments, correspond with this name.

NOTE 2. The *primary* uses of the Gen., in relation to *space* and *time,* have for the most part yielded to the interposition of prepositions, such as ἀπό, ἐκ, etc.; while the secondary uses, such as *causality, source, occasion,* etc., are widely diffused. Yet after verbs signifying *separation* or *division,* we shall see, in the sequel, that enough of usage remains to indicate clearly the primary *space-relations* of the Genitive.

(2) The Gen. and Acc. are, in their very nature, *the opposite of each other* as to meaning. The Gen. indicates the *source* of any thing, i. e. that from which influence, quality, attribute, action, etc., proceeds, and implies that this influence, etc., terminates elsewhere, i. e. out of itself; the Acc. marks the *object* on or in which the influence, action, etc. terminates. In its nature the Gen. implies some *active* influence, it is *causal* in some sense or other; the Acc., on the contrary, designates an object that *passively* receives such influence.

NOTE. Hence so many Genitives are used with verbs designating some *affection of the mind,* such as *love, hatred, remembering, forgetting,* etc.; for these, and all such verbs, must in their true nature be *intransitive,* since what the mind itself experiences does not affect external objects.

§ 99. *The Genitive after Nouns.*

I separate this case from that of verbs, adjectives, etc , because the importance of it deserves special and separate notice The frequency of it, moreover, is so great, that a good acquaintance with it becomes indispensable to the interpreter.

(1) The general idea of the Gen. after nouns, or words equivalent to nouns, is that of *source.* In other words; it designates *that on which something else* (marked by the preceding noun) *depends,* or by which it is *modified* in respect to its nature, condition, attributes, etc.

These modifications, in all of which the Gen. expresses some *source* of influence, control, quality, condition, etc., are very numerous and diversified, and can hardly be reduced to a complete and orderly summary. The following specifications, however, may aid the student in comprehending the leading ones:

(*a*) The Gen. of possession or property; as ὁ οἶκος τοῦ βασιλέως· ἡ χεὶρ τοῦ Κυρίου.

(*b*) The Gen. of cause, source, occasion, etc., (Gen. *auctoris*); e. g. φόβος θεοῦ, *the fear which God inspires ;* ἡ κακία τῶν πονηρῶν, *the vexation which*

§ 99. Syntax: Gen. case. 163

wicked men occasion. Most of such expressions are also capable of another sense which is *subjective,* viz., ' the fear which one has of God, the injury which one does to evil men,' etc. But in many cases only one sense is admissible, as υἱὸς πατρὸς ἀγαπητοῦ · ὁ καρπὸς τοῦ δένδρου, etc. So in the classics ; κύματα παντοίων ἀνέμων, *waves occasioned by various winds ;* πένθος δαιμόνων, *grief occasioned by the gods.* See Matth. § 375.

(c) The Gen. of object; as παραβολὴ τοῦ σπείροντος, *the parable respecting the sower ;* Luke 6 : 7, κατηγορίαν αὐτοῦ, *accusation against him ;* Acts 4 : 9, εὐεργεσία ἀνθρώπου, *beneficence toward the man ;* 1 Cor. 1 : 18, ὁ λόγος ὁ τοῦ σταυροῦ, *doctrine respecting the cross ;* John 17 : 2, ἐξουσίαν πάσης σαρκός, *power over all flesh ;* Rom. 13 : 3, οὐκ εἰσὶ φόβος τῶν ἀγαθῶν ἔργων, *are not a terror in respect to good works ;* see also Matt. 14 : 1, ἀκοὴν Ἰησοῦ; Luke 6: 12. 2 Cor. 10 : 5. Mark 11: 22, πίστιν θεοῦ, *faith in God,* or *faith which God requires ;* Rom. 3 : 22. Gal. 2 : 16, et al. saepe. This is a wide field for the interpreter, and it needs much caution and discrimination to traverse it with good success.

(d) The Gen. of subject; as ὀργὴ θεοῦ, *the wrath which God feels ;* ἡ ἀγάπη τοῦ θεοῦ, *the love which God feels.* This class of cases might possibly be ranked under *a,* but the relation oftentimes is somewhat discrepant.

(e) The Gen. of material ; as στέφανος χρυσοῦ, ἄγαλμα λίθον, etc. ; not common in the N. Test., but very common in the classics.

(f) The Gen. of quality ; as Rom. 1 : 26, πάθη ἀτιμίας, *base passions ;* Acts 7 : 2, ὁ θεὸς τῆς δόξης, *the glorious God ;* and thus often, both in the O. and N. Test., in which cases the noun in the Gen. supplies the place of an adjective.

(g) The Gen. of place ; us in Matt. 1: 11, 12, μετοικεσία Βαβυλῶνος, *the carrying away to Babylon ;* Matt. 10 : 5, ὁδὸς ἐθνῶν, *the way to the Gentiles.*

(h) The Gen. of time ; Jude ver. 6, κρίσιν μεγάλης ἡμέρας, *judgment at the great day ;* Heb. 6 : 1, τὸν τῆς ἀρχῆς τοῦ Χριστοῦ λόγον, *instruction at the beginning of a Christian course of life.* So νυκτός, *by night ;* χειμῶνος, *during the winter ;* τῶν προτέρων ἐτέων, *in former years,* with a preceding noun (χρόνος, etc.) implied.

(2) Many shades of more remote relations and connections still, are expressed occasionally by the Genitive.

E. g. Col. 1: 20, αἷμα τοῦ σταυροῦ, *blood shed upon the cross ;* 2 Cor. 11: 26, κίνδυνοι ποταμῶν, *dangers on the waters* or *occasioned by the waters ;* John 5 : 29, εἰς ἀνάστασιν ζωῆς, *to the resurrection that is connected with happiness ;* Mark 1 : 4, βάπτισμα μετανοίας, *baptism which obligates to repentance ;* Rom. 7 : 2, νόμος τοῦ ἀνδρός, *the law which binds to the husband ;* Rom. 7 : 24, σῶμα θανάτου, *the body which occasions death ;* Rom. 6 : 6, σῶμα τῆς ἁμαρτίας, *the body which leads to sin ;* Luke 11: 29, τὸ σημεῖον Ἰωνᾶ, *the sign which happened to Jonah,* (Gen. of *similitude*) ; Philem. ver. 9, δέσμιος Χριστοῦ, *a prisoner for the sake of Christ ;* James 2 : 5, οἱ πτωχοὶ τοῦ κόσμου, *poor in respect to the present world ;* and so in a great variety of other cases. Some of these examples might be ranked under some of the divisions already named above ; but in general, they are not of so direct a nature.

Note 1. Such examples as Μαρία Ἰακώβου, Ἰούδας Ἰακώβου, etc., are elliptical; for either γυνή, μήτηρ, πατήρ, υἱός, or ἀδελφός, etc., must be understood, according to the nature of the context. So ὁ Ἰανώβου, ἡ Ἀλεξάνδρου, οἱ Χλόης, etc., υἱός, θυγάτηρ, οἰκεῖοι, etc., being understood.

Note 2. Three Genitives in succession are sometimes connected; e. g. in 2 Cor. 4:4. Eph. 4:13, et al. Sometimes the Gen. is separated from the noun that governs it; as in Phil. 2:10. 1 Tim. 3:6. Heb. 8:5. Sometimes (although seldom) of two genitives, one belongs to *persons* and another to *things*; as in Acts 5:32. Phil. 2:30. 2 Pet. 3:2. Heb. 6:1.

Note 3. When the Gen. stands *before* the governing noun, either (a) It belongs to several nouns; as Acts 3:7. Or, (b) It is emphatic; as in 1 Cor. 3:9. Acts 13:23. Heb. 10:36. Phil. 2:25, et saepe alibi.

Note 4. The so called *periphrasis of the Gen.* by a noun with ἐκ, περί, ἀπό, κατά, etc., is seldom, if ever, to be regarded as a simple Gen., but as a mode of expression designed to give a somewhat different shade to its meaning.

GENERAL REMARK. All these and the like Genitives may be considered in the simple light of ATTRIBUTIVES, ɪ. e. *they all attribute to the preceding noun some modification which is occasioned by them, which they designate, or of which they are the source or cause.* Thus in the case (c), τοῦ σπείροντος limits and modifies παραβολή; in the case (e), χρυσοῦ modifies στέφανος; and so of the others. In the case (a), the *king* has the control or ownership of the *house*, quasi, it depends on him. In (g), Βαβυλῶνος modifies and distinguishes μετοικεσία. And thus of the Genitives (in h) designating *time*; e. g. ἡμέρας distinguishes κρίσιν by a peculiar attribute. The use of the Gen. in the way of thus modifying, completing, defining, or qualifying the noun which precedes it, and is said to govern it, is of almost unlimited extent, and far exceeds the boundaries of the Gen. after verbs. *Any substantives, and most adjectives, may be placed in the connection now in view, whenever a noun in the Gen. may be needed in order to complete or limit and define the idea which is to be conveyed.*

§ 100. *Genitive after Verbs.*

(1) The general principles developed in § 96 respecting the nature of the Gen., may for the most part be obviously applied to the case now before us. Yet custom has extended the use of the Gen. so far, that it is difficult, in some cases, to make the application of the theory plain and palpable. A few exceptions, however, if they are indeed such, would not set aside general principles that are plain.

(2) The general idea of *proceeding from, depending on,* and as intimately connected with this, *the ground, source, reason, cause,* or *occasion,* of the action, etc., expressed by a verb, is designated by the Gen. In a word, wherever the verb needs something to define the nature, cause, source, occasion, etc., of the action which it expresses, the Genitive may make that explanation.

§ 100. SYNTAX: GEN. AFTER VERBS. 165

NOTE. From this general view it is easily understood, that whatever belongs to any one as attribute, property, duty, power, may take the Genitive; for all these things *proceed from*, or *depend on*, the agent or thing in question. So *parts* depend on *the whole*; and the latter, as the *source*, is marked by the Genitive. Even *time* and *place* may be considered as attributes of any particular thing, and accordingly they may take the Genitive.

(3) The student will more easily obtain a view of the Gen. as used after verbs in Greek, if he compares the very numerous class of verbs in English, which are in like manner followed by the Genitive.

E. g. The verbs ἀκούω and γεύομαι (verba sensûs) govern the Genitive; and in English we often say: *hear of, taste of.* Often too we leave out the *of*; and so does the Greek, for ἀκούω and nearly all other verbs which govern a Gen. may and do sometimes govern other cases, i. e. the Acc., or Dat., as may be necessary. Compare our English, *thought of, smell of, eat of, take of, give of, partake of, drink of, to be of, to be glad of, to be full of, to be emptied of, to complain of, to accuse of, to convince of, to buy of, to sell of, to learn of, to rob of, to make of, to require of, to take hold of, to beg of,* and so of a multitude of other verbs. In nearly all these cases, there is an agreement with the Greek idiom as to the Genitive; and also in the fact, that nearly all these verbs, and most others which govern the Gen., may also govern other cases. But when they do, the shade of the idea conveyed is different from that which the Gen. expresses.

(4) Conveniently for the learner, may the regimen of the Gen. be *classified* according to the leading idea which belongs to the meaning of respective verbs.

I. Class. Those which have relation to Space; (whence-Case).

(5) Verbs of *removing, separating, disjoining, departing*; verbs of *loosing, refraining, abstaining,* and *ceasing from*; those which signify *to keep off, to avert, to deliver* or *free from*; also *to miss of, to stray from; to differ from, to deviate; to rob of* [any thing], *to want,* i. e. to come short of [any thing]; take the Genitive after them of the thing from which removal, separation, etc., is made.

In other words; the *source* from which these actions commence, or which occasions removal, distance, departure, etc., is indicated by the Gen., which thus marks the source or cause of action. Even in our English idiom the custom is mostly the same, in cases of the like nature; inasmuch as we say: *loose from, separate from, keep from* or *off, rob of, to be in need of,* etc. Such cases are so plain, that illustrations are hardly needed. A very few may suffice; e. g. τῆς γῆς ἀπιέναι, to depart *from the country*; διαφέρει ὁ ἄνθρωπος τῶν ἄλλων ζώων, man differs *from other animals*; ὀλίγου δεῖ, there is need *of a little,* etc.

NOTE 1. As marking the relation of space, δεξιᾶς—ἀριστερᾶς (χειρός), *on the right, on the left*, seems to belong to the same category as the preceding cases. Usually, however, a preposition (ἐκ) is employed in these cases.

NOTE 2. *Nouns, adjectives* and *adverbs*, expressive of the ideas of separation, division, removal, etc., take the Gen. after them in like maner.

(6) Verbs of *beginning* or *commencing* take a Genitive, in order to indicate the source or starting point of action.

E. g. μολπῆς ἐξάρχειν *to begin with a song;* ὑπάρχειν εὐεργεσίας *to commence with beneficence*, etc.

II. Relation of the Genitive to time.

(7) This is more usually marked by *prepositions*, both in the classics, and in the N. Testament. Yet frequently we find the Gen. marking time without a preposition.

E. g. νυκτός *by night*, τοῦ σαββάτου *on the sabbath*, ὄρθρου βαθέος *very early*, τοῦ λοιποῦ *for the future*, χείματος *in the winter season*, ὀλίγον χρόνου, πολλῶν ἡμερῶν, δέκα ἐτῶν, προτέρων ἐτῶν, etc.; and thus, often. In all these cases, it is easy to perceive the analogy between distance as to *space* (No. 5), and distance as to *time*. Both stand on the same general basis.

III. Causal relation of the Genitive.

(8) This, in the *generic* sense here designated, is of wide extent, and comprises a large portion of the Genitives which are put after Verbs. It comprises, (*a*) The idea of originating. (*b*) Of acquiring, or possessing. (*c*) Of comprising and comprehending. (*d*) Of supporting, nourishing, or filling. All of these and the like verbs may be regarded as *marking* or *manifesting action*, in some respect or other, occasioned by the subjects that are designated by the Genitive.

(*e*) In some measure distinct from these is the Genitive of *reason* or *ground* (indirect cause), which merely *calls forth* action in an agent; (*f*) Also the Genitive of *mutual relations*, in which one thing is the occasion or condition of the other.

(9) (*a*) GENITIVE OF ORIGIN OR AUTHOR. Verbs signifying *to take rise, originate, beget*, or *produce*, take the Genitive.

E. g. πατρὸς ἀγαθοῦ εἰμι· ἐσθλῶν γένεσθαι· αὐτοῦ ἔφυν ἐγώ *I sprung from him*, etc.

(*b*) THE GENITIVE OF POSSESSION OR PROPERTY is mostly placed after εἶναι and γίνεσθαι.

The verbs εἰμί and γίνομαι are principally employed here, for the obvious reason that other verbs designate *action, state*, etc., which would be inappropriate to the purpose under consideration. As examples: τοῦτ' ἔστιν Ἰωάννου, *this is John's;* πολλῆς ἀνοίας ἐστί, *it belongs to consummate*

§ 100. Syntax: Gen. After Verbs. 167

folly; ἐστὶν δικαίου ἀνδρός, *it belongs to a good man*, or *a good man must, should, may, can*, etc., *do* thus and so. And so of γίνομαι which is often equivalent, in this connection, to εἰμί. Very commonly the noun in the Gen. has some adjective of quality with it; as in the last example above.

(10) (c) Genitive of that which comprises or comprehends. When a *partitive* sense is intended, the *whole* which comprises or comprehends all the parts, is often put in the Genitive after a variety of verbs. This is called the *Genitive partitive*, because it relates to a partitive sense. This includes,

(1) Verbs *to be, to become*; as οἳ ἀνεπίληπτοι—οὗτοι τῶν γεραιτέρων γίνονται, *the blameless—these become a part of the more venerable.* "They think death τῶν μεγίστων κακῶν εἶναι *to be among*, or *a part of, the greatest evils.*" This head might also be ranked under (b). In phrases of this kind, ἐκ often stands before the Genitive.

(2) *To put, place, reckon, count, constitute* one as a part of such or such a class; as θὲς ἐμὲ τῶν πεπεισμένων, *put me down as one of the persuaded;* αὐτὸν ἀριθμήσει τῶν φιλτάτων τέκνων, *he will count him as one of the most beloved children.*

(3) Verbs signifying *to participate, share, communicate, possess in common*; e. g. μετέχειν τιμῶν *to share the honours*; κοινωνεῖν τῆς δυνάμεως *to participate of the power*; τῶν κρεῶν διαδιδόναι *to impart some of the meat.* Any verbs whatever, even those which are usually construed with the Acc., may take a Genitive where a *partitive* sense is meant to be conveyed; as Odys. ὁ, 98, ὀπτῆσαι κρεῶν *to roast* [some] *flesh*; Thucyd. II. 56, τῆς γῆς ἔτεμον *they destroyed* [a part of] *the country*; Plato, Symp. p. 213, λαβόντα τῶν ταινιῶν *taking* [some] *fillets*; Soph. Oed. Tyr. 709, μαντικῆς ἔχον τέχνης *having* [something] *of the prophetic art*, etc. Matth. § 323. See Acts 27: 36. Matt. 16: 28. Luke 9: 27. 14: 24, al.

(4) Verbs which, either in a *physical* or *mental* sense, signify *to touch, come in contact with, grasp, comprehend, lay hold of*; also verbs of *binding* or *connecting together*; e. g. ἅπτεσθαι τῆς χειρός · ἔλαβεν αὐτὸν τῶν ποδῶν, *he took him by the feet*; ἐρχώμεθα τοῦ ἔργου, *let us approach the undertaking*; φρενῶν ἀνθάπτεται, *it touches* or *takes hold of the mind*, etc. Mark 9: 27. Acts 3: 7. Heb. 12: 20. Luke 8: 54.

(5) *To acquire, to obtain*; so τυγχάνειν χρημάτων, *to acquire property*; λαγχάνειν εὐτυχίας, *to have good luck*, etc.

(6) *To feel after, reach after, rush towards, strongly desire, long after, aim at*; mostly, both in a physical and mental sense; e. g. ὀρέγεσθαι τοῦ καλοῦ, *to desire good*; ὁρμᾶν τῶν Τρώων, *to rush upon the Trojans*; ἐπιστρέφεσθαί τινος, *to regard any thing* (turn towards it); Ἕκτωρ Αἴαντος ἀκόντισε, *Hector aimed his dart at Ajax*.

(7) *To meet, to approach*; as ἀντιᾶν μάχης, *to meet the contest*; ἀντιβολῆσαι τάφου, *to approach the tomb*.

Note. 1. It is difficult to discern in many of these verbs, their relation to a *partitive* Genitive. The truth is, they are only secondarily and distantly connected with such a meaning. E. g. verbs of *touching, grasping*, etc., usually refer of course only to a *part* of the object touched, grasped, etc.;

then with *grasping*, etc., is associated the ideas of obtaining, acquiring; *mental* grasping is desiring strongly; approaching objects, rushing towards them, aiming at them, etc., are all indications of a state of mind desirous to have control of them, etc. Such is the present theory of these Genitives among grammarians. It is too subtile for general apprehension; but, be it true or false, the state of facts is not altered by it.

(11) (*d*) GENITIVE OF MATERIAL. This is of wide extent, and comprises all those cases, *where the Gen. points out the object by or of which any thing is constituted; which fills any thing; is in any way partaken of, or perceived by the senses or by the mind; or which is the subject of discourse, judgment, knowledge,* and the like. E. g.

(1) *Material for making and forming;* e. g. 'They pave the way λίθου with stone.' 'They make shields χαλκοῦ with brass.'

(2) *The material which fills any thing;* e. g. 'He fills the cup οἴνου with wine;' 'The books γέμει τούτων τῶν λόγων, are full of these discourses.' See in John 2: 7. Acts 5: 28, al.

(3) *To eat, drink, enjoy, satisfy one's self;* and tropically, *to have enjoyment in, to profit by, to reap advantage from;* e. g. πίνειν οἴνου, *to drink of wine;* φάγειν σαρκός, lit. *to eat of meat;* ὄνασθαι τῆς φιλοσοφίας, *to profit by philosophy,* etc. Matt. 16: 1 8. Mark 9: 1.

(4) Verbs of sense, such as *to smell, to hear;* also verbs of mental sense, i. e. of *perceiving, knowing, supposing, imagining, reflecting, learning, apprehending,* etc.; e. g. ὄζειν μύρου, *to smell of ointment;* ἄκουέ μου, *hear me;* γνωσόμεθα ἀλλήλων, *we shall know each other;* μανθάνεις μου, *thou apprehendest me;* ἐννοῶ τοῦ ῥηθέντος, *I am considering what has been said,* etc. So in Matt. 17: 5, αὐτοῦ ἀκούετε, Luke 2: 46. John 3: 20, al. saepe.

(5) Verbs of *judging, proving, affirming, and telling;* as οὕτως κρίνεις εὐδαιμονίας, *dost thou so judge of good fortune?* τοῦ πατρός τί φῇς; *what dost thou affirm of the father?* εἰπέ μοι τοῦ υἱοῦ, *tell me of the son;* ''There is no time τοῦ λέγειν τούτων *to speak of these matters.*'

(6) Verbs signifying *to praise, blame;* as μέμφεται τοῦ υἱοῦ αὐτοῦ, *he blames his son;* ἐπαινεῖ τοῦτο Σωκράτου, *he praises this quality of Socrates.* In most cases, however, the Acc. of that which is praised, etc., is also connected with such Genitives.

(12) (*e*) GEN. OF GROUND OR REASON, i. e. that which occasions or calls forth action, etc. This, (as is intimated §100. 8. *e*), is somewhat different from the preceding Genitives, inasmuch as here the thing designated by the Genitive is considered as rather the *occasion* of action, than as the direct and efficient cause.

This distinction, however, is too subtile to be easily perceived and made out in many cases But in others it is sufficiently plain The real *facts* in regard to the construction itself are unaffected by this

(1) Here belong *verbs signifying any affection of the mind;* e. g. such as *to desire, long after; care for, look after; to be pained for, mourn over,*

compassionate; to be angry or displeased, to envy; to admire, wonder at; to remember, forget, be cognisant of or ignorant of, to be expert or inexpert; to possess capacity, ability, or *aptitude.*

In all these, the objects that follow in the Gen. are regarded as the exciting cause of the state of mind which the verb designates, or as the source from which knowledge, experience, etc., spring, or the occasion of them, etc. Such examples, however, as *being ignorant of,* or *inexpert,* (which are mostly made by adjectives and participles), are more easily solved by the Gen. which designates *relation,* viz. *in respect to,* etc.

E. g. ἐπιθυμεῖ τοῦ καλοῦ · πεινῇ τῶν ποτῶν, *he longs after drinks;* φροντίζει τῆς ἀρετῆς · ἀλγεῖν τύχης πονηρᾶς · οἰκτείρω τοῦ πάθους, *I pity the suffering;* χολοῦσθαι τοῦ ἀνδρός, *to be angry at the man;* φθονεῖ τινι τῆς σοφίας (with Dat. of person); θαυμάζω σε τῆς σοφίας (Acc. of person); μιμνήσκειν τοῦ πατρός · ἐπιλανθάνει τοῦ φθόνου · ἐπιστάμενος τῆς τέχνης · ἀνεπιστήμων τῆς τέχνης, *ignorant of the art;* and so with other adjectives and participles denoting fitness etc. In the N. Test., μνημονεύετε τῆς γυναικὸς Λώτ, Luke 17: 32. Acts 11: 16. 2 Pet. 3: 2, al.; ἐπιλαθέσθαι τοῦ ἔργου ὑμῶν, Heb. 6: 10; οὐ ... ἀγγέλων ἐπιλαμβάνεται, Heb. 2: 16 (figuratively interpreted); μὴ τῶν βοῶν μέλει; 1 Cor. 9: 9. Acts 18: 17, al.; καλοῦ ἔργου ἐπιθυμεῖ, 1 Tim. 3: 1; ἐπισκοπῆς ὀρέγεται, 1 Tim. 3: 1. Heb. 11: 16.

(2) Verbs signifying *retribution, revenge, complaint, accusation, condemnation;* e. g. τίσασθαί τινα κακότητος (Acc. of person); *ἐδίωξαν* τυραννίδος · γράφεσθαί τινα παρανόμων, *to enter complaint against any one because of offences;* δικάζουσι ἀχαριστίας, *they condemn ingratitude,* etc.

NOTE 1. In the classics, verbs signifying *to eat, drink,* or *make an offering* or *a libation,* in honour of a god, put the name of the divinity in the Gen., as σπεῖσον ἀγαθοῦ δαίμονος, *make a libation in honour of the good demon.*

NOTE 2. When the Inf. mode, connected with a clause, expresses a *cause* or *ground* like the cases above, the Gen. of it with τοῦ is the usual construction.

(3) Several intransitive verbs, (particularly ἔχειν, ἥκειν, and εἶναι), joined with such adverbs as modify their meaning so that it expresses *state, condition,* etc., take the Gen. as indicating that to which this state, condition, etc., has respect.

The adverbs are usually εὖ, καλῶς, μετρίως, ὡς, πῶς, ὅπως, ᾖ, ὅπῃ, οὕτως, ὧδε, or ὡσαύτως; e. g. ὡς ποδῶν εἶχον, *as they were able in respect to their feet,* i. e. as fast as they could run; εὖ ἔχειν φρενῶν, *to be sound in respect to understanding;* Eurip. El. πῶς ἀγῶνος ἥκομεν; *how do we come off as to the contest?* Καλῶς κεῖται τοῦ ἡλίου, *it lies well in respect to the sun;* Matth. §§ 337, 338. This is a construction deserving of particular attention, as it seems to develope prominently the nature of the Genitive.

(12) (*f*) THE GENITIVE OF MUTUAL RELATION. By this is meant, that Gen. which expresses the idea of a state or condition which is mutually relative and dependent. Thus *to be master* implies a correlative, viz. *to be servant; to surpass* or *exceed* implies *something surpassed* or *exceeded,* etc.

§ 100. Syntax: Gen. after Verbs.

Under this generic head are ranged many verbs which imply relative and mutual action or condition; also verbs, nouns, etc., indicating *comparison, superiority, diversity,* etc.; and finally the so called Gen. of *price* or *value,* is also ranged under the same category; e. g.

(1) Verbs signifying *to command, govern, lead, guide,* and the like; and of course verbs signifying *to be subject, to be overcome, to be inferior;* as ἀνάσσει Αἰγύπτον· ἄρχει τούτων· ἡττᾶσθαι τῶν ἐπιθυμιῶν, *to be overcome by lusts; κρεισσόνων νικώμενοι, overcome by superiors.* So in the N. Test.; e. g. Rom. 14: 9. 2 Cor. 11: 24. 1 Tim. 2: 12. James 2: 6. Acts 18: 12, etc.

(2) Verbs signifying *to have the preference, to exceed, to be preeminent, to excel,* etc.; e. g. ἀριστεύει τῶν ἄλλων· τοῦτο ὑπερβάλλει τοῦ κακοῦ· ὑπερέχει τῶν πολλῶν, *he stands preeminent among the many,* etc.

(3) Verbs indicating *diversity, distinction, unlikeness,* etc.; e. g. διαφέρει ἄλλος ἄλλου, *one differs from another.* Moreover, the comparative degree of adjectives, or any of its equivalents, more usually stands before *Genitives of* comparison; see Syntax on comparative degree.

(4) The Genitive of *price* or *value* is preceded by verbs signifying *to buy, sell, exchange, estimate, value, prize,* etc.; e. g. Matt. 10: 20, ἀσσαρίου πωλεῖται, *it is sold for a farthing;* Matt. 26: 9, πραθῆναι πολλοῦ, *be sold for much.* 1 Cor. 6: 20. Rev. 6: 6. So πόσου ἂν πρίαιο; *for how much could you purchase it?* τιμᾶσθαι πολλοῦ, *highly to prize;* ποιεῖσθαι πολλοῦ, *highly to esteem* or *to value much;* ψυχῆς ἂν ἀλλαξαίμην, *I would exchange my life* [for it].

NOTE. In these last cases, the purchase, estimation, etc., of objects, is brought about by the worth, price, value, etc.; so that a *mutual* relation is assumed. Such is the recent solution of grammarians. To me it seems more simple and easy to say, that a thing is *bought, sold,* etc., *on account of* the price; and that it is *prized, valued,* etc., *in regard to,* or *for the sake of,* the consideration designated by the Genitive.

GENERAL REMARKS. (1) In nearly all the cases, under this head, where a verb takes the Genitive after it, as noted in the examples above brought to view, another and different construction is often found, viz *that with a preposition before the Genitive,* which marks more precisely and emphatically the relation intended. Earlier writers are more sparing of the prepositions; later ones, and with them the N. Test. writers, abound more in the use of them.

(2) A great proportion of the verbs governing the Gen. may also govern the Acc. or Dative, *pro re natâ;* but then the mode of expression, and the shade of meaning also, is in the latter case somewhat different. The Gen. indicates that which, in some sense or other, is the cause, ground, reason, or motive, of action, and NOT *that which is the* PASSIVE *recipient of action or influence.* The Acc. is the appropriate case to designate the latter. When the Gen. stands after a verb, the indication is, that the subject of the verb is the object of the action, influence, etc., designated by the Genitive, and so the Genitive in fact requires verbs to be used in a really *intransitive* or *passive* sense.

(3) In many of the cases where a Genitive of the *thing* follows a verb, it is accompanied by an Acc. or Dat. of the person affected by the action of the verb; e. g. θαυμάζω σε τῆς σοφίας· ζηλῶ σε τοῦ πλούτου· φθονῶ σοι τῆς σοφίας· μέλει μοί σου, etc. Such cases afford no serious difficulty; but they can be learned, in their full extent, only by practice.

(4) Such Genitives as designate *the way and manner* of any thing, are generally attended with prepositions; and when this is not the case, they may for the most part be solved by some of the preceding principles. The *causal* Genitive, in a nearer or more remote sense, is of great extent. The Genitive which im-

§ 101. SYNTAX: GEN. AFTER VARIOUS WORDS. 171

plies *connection* or *relation*, and so some sort of *dependence*, in one sense or another, and where we may supply before it, *in respect to, in regard to*, is almost of equal extent.

§ 101. *Genitive after partitives, adjectives, and participles.*

(1) *Partitives* of all classes, from their very nature (viz. as designating a *part* or *portion* of), may take the Gen. after them, in order to indicate the *whole* to which they stand related.

E. g. (*a*) Ὁ μὲν ... ὁ δέ; as τὰ μὲν τῶν ὄντων ... τὰ δὲ τῶν ὄντων. (*b*) *Demonstratives*, as οὗτος, etc; as τοῦτο ἀνάγκης. (*c*) Participles, which (with the article) denote a particular class of men; as οἱ καταφυγόντες αὐτῶν. (*d*) Adjectives, which denote *classes* of men, etc., as ὀλίγοι, πολλοί, πλεῖστοι, οἱ χρηστοί, etc.; as ὀλίγοι ἀνθρώπων, οἱ χρηστοὶ τῶν ἀνθρώπων, ὁ ἥμισυς τοῦ χρόνου, etc. And so even in the singular number of the adjectives; as τάλαινα παρθένων. (*e*) Interrogatives; as τίς θεῶν; (*f*) Names of towns belonging to a country; as Βηθλεὲμ τῆς Ἰουδαίας. (*g*) Adverbs of place; as ἄλλοθι γαίης, *in another part of the country;* ποῦ γῆς; *in what part of the world?* (*h*) Adverbs of time; as ὀψὲ τῆς ἡμέρας, *in the evening;* πηνίκα τῆς ἡμέρας; *at what time of the day?* (*i*) Superlatives, (which of course indicate a *part* only); as ἔχθιστος βασιλέων. Also, of course, such adjectives, adverbs, etc., as have a superlative meaning; e. g. ἔξοχος, ἔξοχα, etc.

(2) Adjectives, (including participial adjectives), which convey a meaning like that of the several classes of verbs mentioned in § 100, may take the Genitive after them. E. g.

Adjectives and participials signifying *division, separation, distinction, difference, likeness,* or *unlikeness, privation* (many with *α* privative); *agreement* or *disagreement, participation, conjunction, union, community, connection, proximity; plenty* or *fulness* and *want* or *deficiency, superiority* or *inferiority, worth* or *want of worth; knowledge* or *ignorance, skill* or *want of skill, experience* or *inexperience, ability* or *inability, fitness* or *unfitness;* those which signify *any affection of the mind;* also to be *fortunate* or *unfortunate;* in a word, any adjectives holding such a relation to the noun that follows, as may be expressed by IN RESPECT TO, IN REGARD TO; take the Genitive after them. E. g. ἀλλοῖον ἐπιστήμης, *a different thing from knowledge;* ἀνήριθμος ἡμερῶν, *unnumbered in respect to days* (*α* privative); ὅμοιός μου, *like me;* συγγενὴς αὐτοῦ, *his relative;* μεστὸς οἴνου· ἐπιστήμων τέχνης· ἐγκρατὴς ἐπιθυμιῶν· τάλαινα τῶν ἀλγέων, etc.

NOTE. These cases are so plain and so numerous every where, that particular illustration at length is not needed, after all that has been said above. Almost all these cases are made plain by supposing the relation designated by *in respect to, in regard to*. Adjectives with a *partitive* sense are frequent, in a great variety of forms; but these are mainly comprised under No. 1 above.

(3) The comparative degree of adjectives takes the Genitive after it.

NOTE. This comes under the head of *mutual relation*, or of *exceeding*, *excelling*, etc. Of course all adjectives in the *positive* state, which imply a comparative meaning, may govern the Genitive case; e. g. δεύτερος οὐδενός· περισσὰ τῶν ἀρκούντων. The usual comparative is thus: ὁ υἱὸς μείζων ἐστὶ τοῦ πατρός; but frequently the same idea is conveyed by ἤ (*than*), and then the same case stands after ἤ as before it, e. g. ὁ πατὴρ μείζων ἤ ὁ υἱός.

(4) Participials, inasmuch as they retain the nature of the verbs from which they are derived, may take the Gen. whenever it sustains the appropriate relation to them.

E. g. φοίνικος . . . πεποιημέναι, *made of palm-wood*, Xen. Cyrop. V. 7. 22; πληγεὶς θυγατρὸς τῆς ἐμῆς, *smitten of my own daughter*, Eurip. Orest. 491. So ἐπιστάμενος τῆς σοφίας, etc.

§ 102. *Genitive after Adverbs.*

(1) Adverbs are so obviously of the nature of adjectives, that we might naturally expect the Genitive to follow them, in cases like those where it follows adjectives. Such is the fact;

E. g. in respect to adverbs of *separation, division*, such as ἄνευ, χωρίς, δίχα, πλήν, etc.; of *connection*, such as ἑξῆς, ὄπισθεν, μεταξύ, etc.; of *direction*, aim, εὐθύ, μέχρι, etc.; of *nearness, proximity*, such as ἐναντίον, πλήσιον, ἐγγύς, ἐνώπιον, etc.; signifying *affection of the mind*, such as οἴμοι διωγμῶν· φεῦ τοῦ ἀνδρός, etc., (although these last may perhaps be called *interjections*); and so of many others.

NOTE. Hermann proposed that all such adverbs as govern cases should be called *prepositions*, when they are found in such a connection; but many of them will scarcely come within the strict definition of prepositions.

§ 103. *Accusative after Verbs.*

I place this case next after the Gen., because it is of a nature *directly opposite*, and therefore may be the better understood by being brought into contrast. The sequel will show what is here meant.

(1) The Acc. case marks the *end* or *object* on which the action expressed by the verb terminates. It is always to be viewed as *recipient*, and not as agent.

On the other hand; *the Genitive marks a cause, an influence, an agent, by which the subject of the verb is affected.* Transitive, in the proper sense, no verb governing the Gen. can be, as represented by the Greek language, for the subject of the verb is the *recipient* of action, influence, etc. ; *transitive* a verb must be, as employed by the Greeks, when it governs an Acc., although in its nature, and in other connections it may be intransitive; e. g. in νόσον νοσεῖν, lit. *to be sick a sickness*, the verb νοσεῖν, although in itself plainly intransitive, still designates that efficiency in this case which makes or occasions νόσον. And so of many other verbs.

§ 103. Syntax: Acc. after Verbs. 173

Note. The Acc. before the Inf., which often marks the proper *agent* of the Inf., does not come under the present category.

(A) *Space relations of the Accusative.*

(2) The original meaning of the Acc. case, (the *whither* in respect to *space*), has been but partially retained in later usage, inasmuch as prepositions are now more usually employed. Still, enough of the ancient usage remains, viz. the designation of *space-relations*, to exhibit clearly the idiom of the Greek. Verbs of *motion, coming, going*, etc., precede this Acc.

E. g. ἔβαν νέας, *they went to the ships;* ἄστυ μολεῖν, *to go to the city*, (quasi to go *ship-wards, city-wards*); ἱκώμεθα δόματα, *let us go home;* ἔπλευσε πύργους, *he sailed to the towers,* et sic al. In N. Test. Acts 27: 2, πλεῖν τοὺς κατὰ τὴν Ἀσίαν τόπους, *to sail to the places lying along the Asian region.*

Note. The simple limit of time, *to which* any thing may extend, is not usually designated by the Acc. except it be with prepositions. The adverbial τὸ τέλος, τὸ τελευταῖον, etc., is however of such a nature. But the idea of time as a *space passed over,* is often put in the Acc., as we shall see in the sequel.

(B) *Causal Relations of the Accusative.*

(3) Such is the general designation of those relations in which the Acc. marks *the result of any agency* or *influence,* or *the objects on which these are exerted.* This extensive category may be considered under two heads; (I.) The Acc. of that which is actually *produced* or *caused* by the action designated through the verb. (II.) That which is in any way *affected* or *modified* by it, or is supposed to be so affected or modified.

(4) I. Produced or caused. Here the Greeks use an almost unlimited license. What some incautious writers have called *Hebraism,* in the N. Test., viz. the case where a verb is followed by its correlate noun, or by an equivalent, is far more frequent even in the best Greek writers than in the Hebrew.

E. g. βουλὴν βουλεύειν—ἁμαρτάνει ἁμαρτίαν—πράξεις πράττειν—ἄρχειν ἀρχήν—δουλείας δουλεύειν—πόλεμον πολεμεῖν—νόσον νοσεῖν—μέριμναν μεριμνᾶν—and so often and every,where. In the N. Test., Luke 2: 8, φυλάσσοντας φυλακάς—8: 5, σπεῖραι τὸν σπόρον—John 7: 24, . . . κρίσιν κρίνετε—1 Tim. 1:18. 6: 12. Mark 4: 41. Rev. 17: 6, et sic al.

Note 1. The same idiom appears in cases where an *equivalent* for the correlative noun is employed in its stead; e. g. ἐκοιμήσατο ὕπνον—ἔκειρε φόνον, lit. *he cut a slaughter;* καλεῖν ὄνομα, etc.

Note 2. It matters not here, whether the verb is in itself transitive or intransitive; for the latter class of verbs are even the most frequently employed in such phraseology.

(5) Kindred to this is the use of the verb and Acc., where the

action does not properly pass to the Acc., but this case is employed to designate the *result* of the action. Properly such cases involve a kind of *constructio pregnans*.

E. g. νικᾶν μάχην, to win a battle (as we express it); νικᾶν ναυμαχίας, to win a naval action. So θύειν εὐαγγέλια—γενέθλια—γάμους, to make a sacrifice on account of good news—birth-days—weddings, etc.; πέμπειν ἑορτήν, to make a procession on account of a feast.

NOTE 1. With some variations, but still as marking effects or consequences, we have such constructions as ῥέειν ὕδωρ—Ἄρεα πνεῖν, to breathe Mars—πῦρ πνεῖν—βλέπειν Ἄρεα—κυάνεον λεύσσων, looking grim—ὀδύρματα γοημέναι, to weep lamentations, etc. A very wide range is taken by poets and orators in the use of such expressions.

NOTE 2. Even the Acc. to mark *an end designed* or *intended*, may sometimes be found; e. g. ἐλθεῖν ἀγγελίην, to come for the sake of delivering a message; δικαστήριον συναγαγόντες, assembling in order to constitute a tribunal, Herod. 6: 85.

(6) ACC. OF OBJECT WROUGHT UPON OR AFFECTED. This has an almost boundless extent, and belongs of course to all nouns following *purely transitive* verbs. But the Greek language goes far beyond the English idiom in respect to the Acc., employing it after a multitude of verbs, where we employ prepositions, adverbs, etc., to mark relations. Only such peculiarities need to be here noticed, inasmuch as the other cases are too plain and frequent to need illustration.

NOTE 1. In such cases as *to profit, injure, reproach, sadden, heal, buffet, worship, persuade*, and many others, our English idiom, like the Greek, takes the Acc. But in verbs like εὐσεβεῖν, ἀσεβεῖν, λοχᾶν (*insidiari*), δορυφορεῖν, ἐπιτροπεύειν, εὐεργετεῖν, κακουργεῖν, ἀποδιδράσκειν, ἀποφεύγειν, θαῤῥεῖν, λανθάνειν, φθάνειν, ἀφαιρεῖσθαι, στερεῖν, ἐνδύειν, ἐκδύειν, and many others of a similar character, where the Greeks employ the simple Acc., we are obliged to use prepositions and adverbs. Yet most of these verbs admit of constructions after them like ours; and they sometimes govern other cases besides the Accusative.

NOTE 2. In order to show to what almost boundless limits such a loose usage of the Acc. was extended by the Greeks, take the following samples; e. g. verbs of *feasting, offering, dancing,* etc., in honor of any one, take the Acc. in order to designate the individual; e. g. Φοῖβον χορεύων, lit. *choiring Apollo*, i. e. celebrating Apollo by choirs; ἑλίσσετε... Ἄρτεμιν, *dance in honor of Diana*. So the Acc. marks the godhead by which one swears; e. g. ὄμνυμι Ἄρτεμιν—νὴ Δία—μὰ Δία, etc. See James 5: 12.

NOTE 3. *Verbs expressive of feeling and affection* often put the object toward which these are directed in the *Acc.*, thus seeming to mark it as influenced by the action of the verb; e. g. ἀλγεῖν αὐτόν, *to grieve for him* (as we must say); and so with αἰσχύνεσθαι, αἰδεῖσθαι, χαίρειν, θάμβειν, ἐλεεῖν, ἐκπλήττεσθαι, and the like, as αἰσχύνομαι αὐτόν, *I am ashamed of him*, etc. Such verbs, however, more frequently and appropriately take the *Genitive*; although many of this nature, even in the N. Test., take the Accusative.

§ 104. Syntax: Acc. after Verbs.

(7) On like grounds with the above usage stands the following viz. *after verbs of motion* we often find the Acc. of the thing on or over which the motion takes place.

E. g. βαίνειν ὁδόν—ἕρπειν ὁδόν—στείχει πύργον—μολεῖ γέφυραν, *he passes the bridge*—ἄγειν ὁδούς *to conduct over the roads*—πλέων τὴν θάλασσαν, etc. Often, however, our English idiom accords with the Greek here. In Greek poetry, verbs of a class opposite to this, viz. verbs of *rest*, sometimes take the Acc.; e. g. καθίζων τρίποδα—σέλμα σεμνὸν ἧμαι, *I sit* [on] *a venerable throne*, etc.

(8) So *time passed through* or *occupied* takes the Acc.; specially after verbs designating motion or rest.

E. g. κείμεθα δύο νύκτας, *we stay two nights;* ἔβη τρεῖς ἡμέρας—γεγαμημένη ἐννάτην ἡμέραν, *married nine days ago*, etc.

(9) *Measure both of distance and weight* is put in the Acc., after the verbs which naturally precede them.

E. g. ἐπορεύσατο δύο σταδίους, *he went two stadia;* δύναται ἑπτὰ μνέας, *it amounts* or *is equivalent to seven pounds*, etc.

(10) THE ACC. OF SPECIAL LIMITATION. This follows intransitive verbs and adjectives, in order to mark the object towards which action, influence, or attribute is directed.

E. g. κάμνειν τοὺς ὀφθαλμούς—ὑγιάνειν τὰς φρένας—ἀλγεῖν τοὺς πόδας, which we express by *diseased as to the eyes*, etc. So in adjectives of a similar nature; e. g. πόδας ὠκύς—ἀγαθὸς τέχνην—δεινοὶ μάχην, etc. Oftentimes, moreover, the like relation is expressed by prepositions; and often, also, by the Dative.

NOTE. Under this category may be ranked such expressions (adverbially employed) as εἶρος, ὕψος, βάθος, i. e. *as to breadth—height—depth*, etc. So τὸ ἐνάντιον, τἆλλα, λοιπόν, πότερον, οἷον, πολλά, and the like when used adverbially.

§ 104. *Verbs governing two Accusatives.*

(1) In this regimen the Greek extends far beyond our English idiom, and embraces many forms of expression which we can scarcely imitate even by periphrasis. E. g.

(*a*) Verbs governing correlate nouns, or their equivalents, even when these verbs are in their nature intransitive, may take *two* Accusatives; e. g. φιλίαν μεγάλην φιλεῖ αὐτόν—μὲ ἐγράψατο ταύτην τὴν γραφήν—ἢν ἔπεα πτερόεντα προσηύδα, *whom he addressed* [with] *winged words;* καλεῖ με τοῦτο τὸ ὄνομα, etc.

(*b*) Verbs signifying *to do* or *speak good* or *evil; to make, choose, appoint, nominate; to regard as, declare, represent as, suppose, deem, consider, acknowledge; to say, call, name, blame, praise; to give, take, receive; to produce, increase, form, teach, bring up*, etc., may take *two* Accusatives, where the one denotes the object affected, and the other the effect produced by the action of the verb.

E. g. ποιεῖ αὐτὸν ἀγαθά ... κακά—αὐτοὺς πολλᾶ τε καὶ κακὰ ἔλεγε—τοὺς φίλους ἐποίησε πλουσίους—αὐτὸν καλεῖ ἀγαθόν—αἱρεῖται αὐτὸν στρατηγόν— αὐτὸν νομίζει ἀγαθόν—τοῦτον τὸν ἄνθρωπον ποιοῦσι βασιλέα—τοιαῦτα τίθεται γέλωτα—αὐτὸν παιδεύει σοφόν, etc. Here one of the Accusatives expresses a *predicate* of the object affected; and therefore this Acc. is usually called the *Acc. of predicate*. This usage is frequent in the N. Test.; e. g. John 6: 15. Acts 20: 28. Heb. 1: 2. James 5: 10, al. saepe.

(c) Verbs of *asking, beseeching, desiring, seeking after, inquiring for;* also of *teaching, and remembering* ; take a double Acc.

E. g. αὐτὸν αἰτεῖ ἄρτον—αὐτὸν ἐξέταζε θυγατέρα—πολλὰ διδάσκει με— ἀναμνήσω ὑμᾶς καὶ τοὺς κινδύνους

(d) Verbs signifying *to divide* or *distribute* into parts; *to rob* or *plunder;* *to hide* or *conceal.*

E. g. τέμνει αὐτὸ μέρη, he cuts it into parts; ἀποστερεῖ με τιμήν, he robs me of honour—αὐτὸν κρύπτει πολλά, etc;

(e) Verbs of *counselling, persuading, warning, demanding, compelling* to any thing, etc., take two Accusatives.

E. g. πείθει σε ταῦτα—μὲ ἐπαρεῖς ταῦτα; *Will you excite me* [to] *these deeds ?*—τοῦτο ἀναγκάζει με, *he forces me* [to] *this.*

(2) Of a cast somewhat different are another class of verbs, wheie *both Accusatives, which follow, express objects merely influenced or affected,* the one a person, the other a thing.

(a) Verbs signifying to *put on* or *off;* e. g. παῖδα μέγαν ἐκδύσας χιτῶνα, παῖδα μικρὸν ἀμφιέννυσι ταῦτον τὸν χιτῶνα, *he took off a coat from the larger child, and put the same coat upon the small child.*

(b) Even *person* and *space* or *time* are sometimes ranged under this category; e. g. ἀνάγω σε τὴν ὁδόν—ῥίζας ὀρύσσοντες τὸ θέρος, *digging roots through the summer.*

(c) In a few cases, two Accusatives of *things* are placed together in such a regimen ; e. g. ὑπερενέγκειν τὰς ναῦς τὸν ἰσθμόν, *to transport ships over the isthmus.*

NOTE. What is called by grammarians σχῆμα καθ᾿ ὅλον καὶ μέρος, (i. e. where the *whole* is named, and then a *part* is put in apposition as explicative), belongs to No. 1. *b* above; e. g. αὐτὸν ἐκάλυψε τοὺς ὀφθαλμούς— κρύψον με πόδα.

§ 105. *Accusative with the Passive Voice.*

(1) The general principle here is, that where verbs govern two Accusatives, the one of a *person* and the other of a *thing,* the Passive retains the latter.

E. g. διδάσκω ὑμᾶς παραδόσεις, but Pass. παραδόσεις, ἃς ἐδιδάχθητε, 2 Thess. 2: 15. *Πλήττει αὐτὸν τὴν κεφαλήν,* but Pass. πληγεὶς τὴν κεφαλήν.

§ 106. SYNTAX: DAT. AFTER VERBS. 177

NOTE. The like construction with the Passive exists in cases where the active verbs govern an Acc. and Dat., when the Acc. is retained ; e. g. πεπίστευμαι εὐαγγέλιον, Gal. 2: 7. So 1 Cor. 9: 17. Rom. 3: 2. 1 Thess. 2: 4. 1 Tim. 1: 1. Tit. 1: 3.

REMARK. The true solution of most cases of the nature now under consideration, seems to be, that the so-called *passive* verb is in its real nature *reflexive*, i. e. of the Middle voice; e. g. κόπτονται τὰ μέτωπα, i. e. *they let their foreheads be beaten.* So Kuhner, § 565.

§ 105. *Other uses of the Accusative.*

The Acc. is often used *adverbially*, particularly in respect to adjectives, participial adjectives, etc. Often it is used independently of any connection with verbs, when it is called *the Acc. absolute.* But these uses are elsewhere explained. See, for *adverbial* use, § 84. *d.* 3 ; for Acc. *absolute*, § 114. 4.

§ 106. DATIVE AFTER VERBS.

(1) The Dative is specially named, by recent grammarians, *the space-case*, because it not only designates the *where* of objects, but even in most of its causal meanings it exhibits merely the *external* and *more remote* relations, and not (like the Gen. and Acc.) the internal and immediate ones.

NOTE 1. (*a*) The Dative is not confined to the simple relation *where* or *wherein*, although this meaning takes the lead in point of antiquity. When it has such a meaning, it is called, in order to distinguish it, the *local* Dative. (*b*) When the Dative refers to *persons*, it may designate (in a modified sense), the *whence*, or the *whither* respecting them. This is its most frequent use, and here it is by way of eminence named simply *the Dative.* (*c*) The Dative, in reference to the *whence* of *things* (not of persons), has generally an *instrumental* sense, and is called *the instrumental case*, or *the instrumental Dative.*

NOTE 2. The distinction between the relation of the Gen. and Dative to the *whence*, is rather subtile, and in some cases it would be difficult to make it palpable. But in general it may be thus stated. The *Genitive* (designating whence, origin, source of influence, etc.) denotes the agency, influence, etc., itself *as a cause or agent in operation ;* while the *Dative* in respect to the whence, source, etc., *denotes only the where of its commencement*, the place in which it begins, the source or the where of its origin, and not the agency itself as continuing in action. So in regard to the *whither* as designated by the Acc. and the Dative; the Acc. denotes the tendency or momentum or influence itself, as well as the *whither* or direction of it ; the Dative designates the *whither* of the influence merely, i. e. it contemplates it merely in relation to its ultimate object, or, in other words, in relation to the place or object to which it finally attains. The Dative then, in relation to the *whence* and the *whither*, marks the *where* of the *commencement* and the *end* of motion, influence, etc.

23

178   § 106. SYNTAX: DAT. AFTER VERBS.

REMARK 1. In many cases it would be difficult to make a plain application of these general principles, because usage has made so many branches and minute subdivisions of the Dative. Still, the *where* and the *wherein* are predominant qualities of the Dative, in a more or less palpable form, to a very great extent. The *whence* and the *whither*, as marked by this tense, are blended in some measure with the preceding main relation.

REMARK 2 The *instrumental* Dative is much narrower in Greek than one might expect. The Genitive as designating *source, cause, occasion*, etc , and designating them in the lively manner of representing them as actual agents, has encroached upon what would otherwise be the natural domain of the Dative.

[A] *The Dative of proper locality.*

(2) Not unfrequently, in more ancient usage, is the *place where* put in the Dative.

E. g. *αἰθέρι ναίων, dwelling in the air ; ἥμενος κορυφῇ Ὀλύμποιο, sitting on the summit of Olympus.* In later Greek, prepositions, such as ἐν, ἀνά, περί, ἐπί, etc., are usually employed to mark such relations.

(3) Kindred to the merely *local* sense is that of the Dative which designates the *being with* or *by*, or *a community* or *association with*, any thing.

E. g. *ἀνθρώποις ἀεὶ ὁ πονηρὸς ... κακός, among men,* etc. *ὁ Θρῃξὶ μάντις, the soothsayer among the Thracians ; ὡς πλήθει, so among the mass ; αὐτοῖς ἰόντες, going in company with them ; αὐτοὺς αὐτοῖς μελάθροις διεφθαρμένους, them destroyed together with their houses ;* and often thus. So *ἦλθε στρατῷ—πλήθει, he came with an army—with a multitude,* etc.

(4) This original relation of space is transferred to *time* also, and here the Dative designates rather *a point of time*, than a continuance or extension of it.

E. g. 'he came *τρίτῃ ἡμέρᾳ, on the third day ;*' 'he will come *τῇδε νυκτί, this very night.*' The Acc. of time differs from this ; e. g. 'they stayed *τὴν ἐπιοῦσαν ἡμέραν, through the following day.*' The Gen., e. g. *ἐμαχέσαντο ταύτης τῆς ἡμέρας*, would present a still different view, where time is spoken of as a kind of *sustainer* of the fight, as having a kind of agency in it. But sometimes the Dative is loosely employed for duration ; e. g. *μακρῷ χρόνῳ*, Soph. Trach. 599.

(5) Another branch of this *local* Dative is, that which designates the *things that surround* one when he acts, or (as we say) *the circumstances* in which he acts.

E. g. ' we sailed to the port *ἀνέμῳ καλῷ, accompanied by a fair wind ;*' 'she bore thee *κακῇ αἴσῃ, with an unlucky omen.*'

[B] *The usual and proper Dative.*

(6) This is employed to designate the *direction* of any action or influence, the *where* to which it tends, and not (like the Acc.) the action or influence as having already reached its destiny and affected the object. Here *persons* are principally concerned.

§ 106. Syntax: Dative after Verbs.

In the words of the older grammarians : " The person (or thing) *to* or *for* which any thing is, or is done, demands the Dative." But the Acc. denotes the person or thing which any action or influence has already reached, and which it has affected.

(7) This *direction* may be one that has immediate respect to *space*.

E. g. he lifted up his hands πᾶσι θεοῖς, *toward all the gods* ; Σαμίοις ἦλθε, *he went toward Samos*; ἀναβλέπει αὐτῷ, *he looks toward him*. In prose, prepositions are more commonly employed to designate this relation.

Note. Most *local* adverbs have the Dative form ; which is easily explained on the above ground.

(8) *The appellation*, causal dative, given by recent grammarians, must be understood in a *modified* sense. It does not express, like the *local* Dative, a mere proximity of space, or a mere external relation of space, but *a tendency of action, influence, etc., in a certain direction*. When this tendency and direction merely are noted, a great variety of verbs may take the Dative after them. E. g.

(a) Verbs significant of *association, intercourse, communication, imparting, participation*, etc., in a good or bad sense.

E. g. ὁμιλεῖν τινι—λαλεῖν τινι—μετέχειν τινί—λοιδορεῖσθαι τινί—προσεύχεσθαί τινι, etc. So with adjectives of the like meaning ; e. g. κοινός, σύμφωνος, συγγενής, etc.

Note. This idea of *influence directed in a certain way*, seems to lie at the basis of such regimen as that of verbs of *reigning, commanding*, etc., when they take (as they sometimes do) the Dative.

(b) Verbs signifying *to meet, approach, move towards*, and sometimes *to retreat* ; also *to contend, strive with*, and *rival* ; often take the Dative. In all these cases, the *direction* of the action is a plain element of the construction.

E. g. ἐγγίζει αὐτῷ—ὑπαντᾷ αὐτῷ, *he meets him* ; ὑπείκει αὐτῷ, *he yields to him* ; μάχεται αὐτῷ, *he contends with him* ; ἀείδει αὐτῷ, *he rivals him in song*, etc.

(c) Kindred to these, are the Datives of *following, accompanying, serving*, and *obeying*. The direction of the movement, service, etc., is marked by the Dative.

E. g. ἀκολούθει αὐτῷ—εἰσακούω αὐτῷ—διαδέχεται αὐτῷ—δουλεύω αὐτῷ.

(d) Verbs of *giving* and *taking away* ; of *commanding* and *exhorting* ; verbs signifying *fitness, propriety*, or *to be becoming* ; take the Dative.

E. g. δὸς βιβλίον αὐτῷ—ἀφαίρεται βιβλίον αὐτῷ—κελεύω σοι—παραινέω σοι—δεῖ αὐτῷ—πρέπει αὐτῷ, etc.

(e) Verbs of *pleasing* and *displeasing* ; *envying* and *being angry with* ; of *assenting to* or *objecting*, of *praising*, and *blaming* ; of *helping, injuring, defending*, and *profiting* ; govern the Dative.

E. g. ἀρέσκει αὐτοῖς—φθονεῖ αὐτῷ—χολοῦται αὐτοῖς, *he is angry with them* ;

180   § 106. Syntax: Dative after Verbs.

συναινεῖ μοι, he assents to me ; βοηθεῖ αὐτῷ—ἀμύνειν αὐτῷ—λυσιτελεῖ αὐτοῖς, he profits them ; λυμαίνει αὐτοῖς, he injures them, etc.

(*f*) From the two examples last exhibited may be gathered the *principle* which pervades an extensive use of the Dative, viz. that after all words which designate action, influence, etc., that will redound to the *profit*, *gain*, or *honour* of any one, or to his *injury*, *loss*, or *disadvantage*, the person concerned is put in the Dative. This is called, *Dativus commodi et incommodi*.

E. g. πράττω ταῦτα σοι, *I do these things for your advantage*; σιωπῶ σοι, *I am silent for your sake* ; δέχομαι τοῦτο αὐτοῖς, *I take this for their good*; πέφευγέ μοι ἐλπὶς σωτηρίας, *the hope of safety for me has fled* ; χαλεπόν ἐστί μοι, *it is troublesome to me*; so αἰσχρόν μοι—ἐνάντιόν μοι—λύπη ἐγένετό μοι, etc. Verbs, nouns, or adjectives, may take the Dative after them, when such a relation is intended to be designated.

General Remark The *causal* sense in verbs ranged under *a–f*, is to be understood mostly as being only *indirect* and *remote;* (immediate and direct cause is marked by the Genitive) In nearly all of these classes of verbs the *direction* or *tendency* of the action, feeling, affection, etc , is manifestly designated by the Dative Of course the Dative is not to be considered at all in the light of an Acc , viz. as merely marking the *passive object* of influence, action, etc , for verbs governing the Dative, so far as this tense merely is concerned, are not to be regarded as transitive. *Proper transitive verbs of course require the Accusative ;* e g. ταῦτα ποιεῖ αὐτοῖς, where ταῦτα is the passive object, and αὐτοῖς points out the direction, aim, or purpose of the action.

(9) Dative of possession. This points out a *relation* of the thing possessed to the owner, or the respect in which the thing is to be regarded.

E. g. ἐστὶ αὐτῷ—αὐτοῖς πολλά εἰσιν—ἐγένετο αὐτῷ ὄνομα, etc.

Note. The Gen. is more often employed to designate *possession* than the Dative; but its shade of meaning is different from that of the Dative. The Gen. designates the possessor as exercising an *active influence* over the thing possessed ; the Dative indicates *the being with* the owner and being of course under his control.

(10) *Dative signifying* in respect to, in regard to. This Dative is frequent, and of wide extent. Leading particulars only can be specified.

(*a*) It serves to express a *limitation* of the general idea contained in the predicate ; e. g. 1 Cor. 14: 20, " Be not children ταῖς φρεσίν, *in respect to understanding*, but be ye children τῇ κακίᾳ, *in respect to malice*." Rom. 4: 20, ἐνεδυναμώθη τῇ πίστει, *he was strong in regard to faith*; so Phil. 2: 7. Acts 7: 51. Rev. 4: 3. Heb. 5: 11, and saepe al.

(*b*) It often expresses *the principle, rule,* or *guiding influence,* according to which, or in accordance with which, any thing is done, etc. E. g. Acts 15: 1, " Except ye be circumcised τῷ ἔθει Μωϋσέως, *in accordance with the Mosaic rites*." 2 Pet. 2: 21, " The prophecy came not θελήματι ἀνθρώπων, *according to the will of men*." Job 3: 3. 2 Macc. 6: 1.

(*c*) A more extensive use still of this Dative is, to designate persons to whose *consideration, act of comparing, estimation,* or *judgment,* any thing is submitted, and by whom a decision, etc., is made. E. g. σοὶ συμφωνεῖ

§ 106. Syntax: Dative after Verbs. 181

τοῦτο; does this harmonize, in your opinion? ὡς καλός μοι ὁ πατήρ, how lovely is the father in my view; μοὶ ἀγαθά εἰσι, in my view they are excellent; σοὶ νικήσουσι, in your judgment they will be victorious.

(d) Here I would also rank the frequent use of the Dative after words expressing *likeness* or *unlikeness*, *equality* or *inequality*, *agreement* or *disagreement*; e. g. ἔοικε αὐτῷ, he is like to him, i. e. in respect to him; ἴσος αὐτῷ, equal to him, i. e. in regard to him; διάφορος αὐτῷ, different in respect to him; σύμφωνος αὐτῷ, accordant in regard to him, etc.

Note 1. Very often a participle, or a noun with a participle or adjective, denotes the *state* or *condition* of a person *in respect to whom*, or *in regard to whom*, any thing is said or done; e. g. βουλομένῳ, in regard to him who is willing; αὐτῷ ἐλπομένῳ, in respect to him who is hoping. The particle ὡς is often prefixed in such cases, to moderate the tone of the expression; e. g. ὡς πιστεύοντι, as to one who believes, i. e. who seems to believe.

Note 2. There are many other minute shades of meaning in the Dative, which are not included in these specifications. But these will serve to guide the student in most of the cases of this nature which occur.

[C] *Dative instrumental.*

(11) The Dative proper and usual, i. e. the Dative of person, as we have seen (No. 6), stands nearly related to the *whither* (the Acc.) of objects, although plainly distinguishable from it. The *instrumental* Dative stands related, in a similar way, to the Genitive or the *whence* case; but it is easily distinguishable from it.

The Genitive designates *active* and *immediate* authorship, influence, etc.; but the instrumental Dative, as the very name imports, only *secondary* or *intermediate* influence. Instruments must be used by others, and hence they are of course but *secondary* causes. The *space relation*, viz. the idea of *being with*, *near by*, etc., seems to be plain in most of the cases which rank under this category; for it is action, cause, influence, etc., considered in their *external* relations and as instruments, etc., to which this Dative has respect. With this view of the subject it is easy to see, that a variety of particulars must be comprehended under this category. E. g.

(12) (a) Ground or reason. The instrumental Dative designates a *ground* or *reason* on which any action or feeling is based, or which gives occasion to it; particularly in cases of *mental* affection.

E. g. φόβῳ ἀπελθεῖν, to depart through fear; "They were broken off τῇ ἀπιστίᾳ, through unbelief," Rom. 11: 20. "Ye have obtained mercy τῇ τούτων ἀπιστίᾳ, through the unbelief of those, Rom. 11: 30. Gal. 6: 12. So οὗτοι χαίρουσίν σοι, these exult on your account; ἀγανακτεῖ τῷ θανάτῳ αὐτοῦ, he grieves because of his death.

(13) (b) The means and instrument are put in the Dative.

E. g. σκήπτρῳ ἐλάσασκε, he smote with the sceptre; ἀκοντίζει αἰχμῇ, he

§ 106. Syntax: Dative after Verbs.

pierces with a spear; διώξομαι τῷ ἵππῳ, *I will pursue with the cavalry;* ἀνατρέψω αὐτὸν τῇ ῥώμῃ μου, *I will turn him back by my strength;* διαφέρειν φρονήσει, *to excel by virtue of sober consideration,* etc.

NOTE. Rarely are *persons* designated as means or instruments, etc.

(14) (c) THE WAY AND MANNER, with which, in which, or after which, any thing is done, etc., is designated by the Dative.

E. g. 1 Cor. 11: 5, 'praying ἀποκαταλύπτῳ τῇ κεφαλῇ, *with uncovered head;*' John 21: 8, πλοιαρίῳ ἦλθον, *they came in a small boat.* 2 Cor. 1: 15. Rom. 4: 20. Φοιτῶσι σιγῇ, *they march in silence;* and so δίκῃ, ἐπιμελείᾳ, δημοσίᾳ, ἰδίᾳ, πέζῃ, διχῇ, etc.; used adverbially as indicating manner, etc.

(15) (d) THE MEASURE, PRICE, AND WORTH, are sometimes put in the Dative, as indicating the means by which, or according to which, action, etc., is determined.

E. g. οἰνίζοντο χαλκῷ καὶ σιδήρῳ, *they procured wine by brass and iron;* ζημιοῦν τινα χιλίαις δραχμαῖς, *to fine any one a thousand drachmas;* μείζων πολλῷ—ὀλίγῳ—ἀριθμῷ, etc.

NOTE. So also in respect to the object *by which* any thing is *judged, estimated, decided,* etc.; as σταθμώμενος τοῖς λεγομένοις, *judging by the things that are said;* γιγνώσκω τοῖς λόγοις σου, *I perceive by thy words;* τῇ σῇ ἐσθῆτι εἰκάζω, *I conjecture by your dress,* etc.

(16) (e) THE MATERIAL is sometimes put in the Dative, as inindicative of *means.*

E. g. τὸ ἅρμα χρυσῷ καὶ ἀργύρῳ εὖ ἤσκεται, *his chariot is well ornamented with gold and silver.*

General Remarks.

(a) In nearly all of the cases where the Dative is used after verbs, other constructions are occasionally, and some of them often, employed, viz. those in which a preposition is interposed in order to designate the relation; e. g. ὑγιαίνειν τῇ πίστει and ἐν τῇ πίστει; διαφέρειν τινί and ἕν τινι; βαπτίζεσθαι ὕδατι and ἐν ὕδατι; λέγειν τινί and πρός τινα; μάχεσθαί τινι and πρός τινα; and so of most of the other verbs. The Greek language affords wide scope for variety in the modes of expression.

(b) Many of the verbs which take a Dative after them do also *demand* an Accusative; for all verbs really *transitive* must of course have an Acc. (expressed or implied) which they govern; and then in the way of *complement,* or in order to show the *direction* of any action, influence, etc., they may, and often do, take a *Dative.* Verbs which admit of but one tense, i. e. the Dative, must, as there employed, be *intransitive;* for the Dative designates not the object *passively* affected by action, influence, etc., but only the direction of it, the *where* to which it tends, or the *whence* (external, local *whence*) from which it commences. A different *shade* of idea, then, is given by the Dative, from that which is given by the Gen. or Acc.; although for *substance* the idea may be the same in all three cases. In this way a great variety of expression becomes practicable and easy.

§ 107. *The Dative after adjectives, adverbs, and certain classes of nouns.*

(1) Adjectives, adverbs, and some nouns, signifying *society, conjunction, community, participation, intercourse,* and the like, take the Dative after them.

E. g. κοινὸς αὐτῷ—σύμφονος αὐτοῖς—σύμμιγδα ἄλλοις θεοῖς, lit. *commingled with other gods*—κοινῶς αὐτοῖς, *in common with them;* ἔχει ἡ φύσις αὐτῶν κοινωνίαν ἀλλήλοις, *their nature has mutual connection.*

(2) The same classes of words also govern the Dative, when they designate *proximity, over against, approach, contest, following, accompanying,* and the like.

E. g. πλήσιος *near*, ἐναντίος *over against*, ἐγγύς, πέλας, etc., take the Dative after them. So ἔρις Ἥρᾳ Παλλάδι, *Juno had a strife with Minerva.* So with διάδοχος, ἐξῆς, and the like.

(3) *Likeness* or *unlikeness, equality* or *inequality, agreement* or *disagreement,* expressed by the same classes of words, take the Dative.

E. g. ὅμοιος, ὁμοίως, and ὁμοιότης—ἴσος, ἴσως, and ἰσότης, etc.

(4) In general, adjectives, adverbs, or nouns, with a sense kindred to that of verbs which govern the Dative, may take the Dative after them, whenever the writer chooses to employ this construction.

NOTE. Many constructions of this nature may be explained, on the ground that the Dat. indicates the relation of *belonging to, appropriate to, designed for, having respect to, on account of, in the view of,* etc.; e. g. παρακέλευσις τῷ ἀγαπῶντι—ὕμνοι θεῷ—ἐμοὶ αἴτιοί εἰσι, *in my opinion they are culpable,* etc.

(5) *The Dative of instrumentality* may be put after adjectives and even nouns.

E. g. ποσὶ ταχύς, *swift by means of his feet;* κίνησις τῷ σώματι, *motion by means of the body;* πράξεις βίᾳ, *deeds done by violence,* etc.

§ 108. CASES AFTER PREPOSITIONS.

The *Syntactical* consideration of prepositions renders it necessary to premise some general remarks respecting this part of speech, in order to aid the student in understanding this somewhat difficult subject.

(1) We have seen that *cases* have their origin in the *relations of space,* § 96. So is it, also, with all the *original* and proper prepositions; for they primarily relate to *modifications of space.*

NOTE 1. It is now made sufficiently plain by recent grammarians, that

§ 108. SYNTAX: CASES AFTER PREPOSITIONS.

all the *original* Greek prepositions were at first mere *adverbs of place*. Accordingly Kühner has shown, in his admirable development of their meaning (Gramm. §§ 596—618), that their *primary* signification accords with this view of the subject; and he has given us (§ 618) examples from leading Greek authors of the use of nearly all the prepositions in the simply *adverbial* sense, besides many preceding illustrations in regard to their *local* sense when joined with nouns. *The difference, and the only difference, which can now be really made between prepositions and adverbs, is, that the former relate to and qualify* NOUNS, *while the latter relate to and qualify* VERBS *or* ADJECTIVES.

NOTE 2. Illustration of the relations to *space*: ἦλθε ἐκ τῆς πόλεως, he came FROM *the city*; ἔβη εἰς τὴν οἰκίαν, he went INTO *the house*; οἰκεῖ ἐπὶ τῷ ὄρει, he dwells ON *the mountain*.

(2) Prepositions, in themselves, even when they are placed before different cases, seem to retain *substantially* their original meaning; but this is necessarily modified by the cases with which they are connected.

E. g. παρά means *near by, with*; so ἦλθε παρὰ τοῦ βασιλέως, lit. he came from the *near* of the king; ᾔει παρὰ τὸν βασιλέα, lit. he went into the *near* of the king; ἔστη παρὰ τῷ βασιλεῖ, lit. he stood in the *near* to the king.

NOTE 1. Of course the meaning of several prepositions is such, that they cannot stand before all the cases. Hence it follows, that some are associated with the Gen., or Dat., or Acc. only; some with the Gen. and Acc.; and some with all three cases.

(3) Prepositions, in their *original* meaning, do not strictly relate to the simple *whence*, and *whither*, and *where*, for these relations are expressed by the *cases* themselves; but they designate what grammarians now name *dimension-relations*.

E. g. they designate such relations as *with, near, by, on, in; before, behind; above, below; out of, into; to, from; through, around*, etc., differing from the simple relations which respect motion or rest, and are designated by *whence, whither, where*. These latter relations are shown by the aid of the *cases merely*. Yet in translating the Greek, we cannot exhibit this matter in a true light, because our idiom will not express what the Greek expresses.

(4) The relations of *space*, which prepositions originally designated, are easily and naturally transferred to *time*; and finally they came to be employed in expressing all the various relations of *causality*, either as to the source, manner, or direction of agency, influence, etc. In the progress of time the divisions of meaning became so various and nice, that it is difficult, in many cases, to trace a relation to the original *space-meaning*.

NOTE 1. In most cases the relation to *space* is sufficiently plain to an attentive reader; e. g. μάχεσθαι περί τινος, lit. to fight *about* or *around* one, viz. so as to guard and defend him, but secondarily, as we now employ the

§§ 108—112. SYNTAX: CASES AFTER PREPOSITIONS. 185

phrase, *to fight for one*, or *on his account*. The easy transition from relations of *space* to those of *time* may be illustrated thus: πρὸ τῶν πυλῶν ἔστη, *he stood before the gates* (space), πρὸ τῆς ἡμέρας ἀπῆλθεν, *he went away before the day* (time); ἐκ τῆς πόλεως ἀπέφυγε, *he fled from the city* (space), ἐκ τοῦ πολέμου ἐγένετο εἰρήνη, *immediately after the war came peace* (time); ἐν ταύτῃ τῇ χώρᾳ, *in this region* (space), ἐν τούτῳ τῷ χρόνῳ, *at this time* (time), etc.

NOTE 2. The original *space-relation*, as a basis, may be easily discovered in a great variety of phrases which now designate *causal* relations; e. g. πράττεταί τι ὑπό τινος—πρὸς τινος—παρά τινος—ἔκ τινος—διά τινος, something is done *by, with, near, from, through*, some one, i. e. by one as agent; with his concurrence and aid; by his immediate influence or agency, or as proceeding from him, i. e. from him as the real source and author; by him as instrument or means, etc. All these shades of difference in meaning evidently have their bases in the original *space-relations* of the words in question.

§ 109. *Prepositions before the Genitive only.**

(1) These are ἀντί, πρό, ἀπό, ἐκ (ἐξ).

The relation of ἀπό and ἐκ to *source*, (the *whence*), is obvious. Ἀντί and πρό, as indirectly designating *dependence*, are employed in like manner with the Genitive.

NOTE. Many adverbial words, such as δίκην, δέμας, χάριν, ἕνεκα, ἕκητι, etc., are also constructed with the Gen., as a species of improper prepositions; see § 102. 1.

§ 110. *Prepositions before the Dative only.*

(1) These are ἐν, σύν (ξύν.)

These obviously accord with the nature of the Dative (the *where*). So the adverbial ἅμα.

§ 111. *Prepositions before the Acc. only.*

(1) These are ἀνά, εἰς, (ἐς), ὡς (*to*).

These plainly relate to the *whither*, i. e. they indicate a meaning appropriate to the Acc. case. Ἀνά, *up toward, up on, throughout;* (in older poets sometimes found with the Dative in the sense of *on*); εἰς (ἐς) *toward, to, unto, into.*

§ 112. *Prepositions before the Gen. and Accusative.*

(1) These are διά, κατά, ὑπέρ.

With the Gen. διά, originally and *locally*, meant *through* and *therefrom*; with the Acc., only *through*. Κατά with Gen., *from above downwards*; with

---
* Only the so called *original* prepositions are here and in the sequel taken into consideration.

§ 113. Syntax: Cases after Prepositions.

Acc., *towards*, from a more elevated object. ‘Υπέρ with Gen., *over away*; Acc., *over*, *clear over* or *thoroughly over, beyond*. The derived or secondary meanings correspond with these distinctions, in many cases; in some it is difficult to distinguish the correspondencies.

§ 113. *Prepositions with the Gen., Dat., and Accusative.*

(1) These are ἀμφί, περί, ἐπί, μετά, παρά, πρός, and ὑπό.

(*a*) Ἀμφί and περί are scarcely distinguishable in their original meanings. With the Gen. *around*, *the surroundings*, as dependent on the object which they encompass; Dat. *around*, as the place *where*, i. e. near to something; the Acc. marks the *around* of objects to which any thing or person moves, advances, tends, etc. (*b*) Ἐπί with the Gen., *on*, something as bearing or sustaining the action indicated by the verb; Dat. *on*, as the place of delay, rest, stay, etc.; Acc. *on* as the *where* of motion, etc., ἀναβαίνειν ἐπὶ θρόνον. (*c*) Μετά with Gen., *with*, i. e. *communion, participation*; with the Dat., *with* in the sense of resting in the same *place*; the Acc. notes the direction of action, etc., to the *midst* or the *within* of any thing. (*d*) Παρά, πρός, the first relates more to the *external* relations, the second to the *internal*. With Gen., *near*, *next to*, so that the Gen. means from or out of the *near*; Dat., *in the near*, spoken of staying, resting, etc.; Acc. motion, etc., *toward the near* or *before the near*, etc, (*e*) ‘Υπό, with Gen. *from under*, *out of* or *away from the under*; with Dat. *under* as the place of rest, e. g. ὑπὸ γῆς εἶναι; with Acc., motion, etc., *toward the under*, e. g. ἰέναι ὑπὸ γαῖαν, *to go under ground*.

General Remark. It will readily be seen, that I have aimed here only at giving the *original space-relations* of the proper prepositions. The *time-relations* and the *causal relations*, are also given in Winer, Kühner, and others, but as the lexicons now give these meanings, they may well be dispensed with in a grammar. Here only so much is given as will serve to lead the student to some proper knowledge of the original source and design of the prepositions. For brevity's sake, I have omitted exemplification, for the most part, as every good lexicon will furnish it. It is plain enough, that the same preposition, when employed before different cases, retains substantially the same meaning in itself; but as it is joined with different *cases*, these modify the meaning so that we are, in translating, obliged to express the various relations by various phraseology. For example, (as before given), παρά, *near to*, may be before the Gen., as " he came παρὰ τοῦ βασιλέως, *from near* the king;" so, " he went παρὰ τὸν βασιλέα, *to the near* of the king," and " he stood παρὰ τῷ βασιλεῖ, *in the near* of the king." While the preposition in itself remains the same, the relations of the *near* are altered by the *cases* themselves with which the preposition is connected.

Note 1. Prepositions are not only connected with *adverbs* when the latter have the sense of nouns, as εἰς νῦν, ἐκ τότε, etc. but are often conjoined or combined in one word, as ὑποκάτω, ὑπεράνω, ἔμπροσθεν, ἔκπαλαι, etc.

Note 2. Constructio pregnans made by some prepositions. (*a*) *After verbs of motion*, frequently the Dative with ἐν, (sometimes with ἀμφί, περί, ἐπί, πρός, ὑπό, but not often), follows in the same sense as the Acc. with εἰς. Such constructions involve the idea of *resting* or *abiding in a place*, as the sequel of going to it; e. g. John 5: 4, 'an angel κατέβαινε ἐν τῇ κολυμβήθρᾳ, *went down to* [and took his station] *in the pool*; Luke 7: 17, 'a report ἐξῆλθεν ἐν ὅλῃ τῇ Ἰουδαίᾳ, *went into* [and spread] *in all Judea*,'

§ 114. Syntax: Cases after Prepositions. 187

So Rom. 5: 5. Matt. 10: 16, et al. The same usage is very common in the classics; e. g. Thucyd. 4: 42, ἐν Ἀμπρακίᾳ ... ἀπῄεσαν, they went [and abode] in Amprachia; Ael. V. Hist. 4: 18, 'Plato κατῆλθε ... ἐν Σικελίᾳ, came to [and abode] in Sicily,' and saep. al.; see Winer's Gramm. § 54. 4. Kuhner, § 621. a. b. As the direct antithesis of this, (b) Verbs of rest often take the Acc. with εἰς after them, so as to denote the coming to a place, as well as staying in it; e. g. Matt. 2: 23, κατῴκησεν εἰς πόλιν Ναζαρέθ, i. e. [he came to] and dwelt in the village Nazareth; John 9: 7, νίψαι εἰς τὴν κολυμβήθραν, [go to] and wash in the pool; Mark 2: 1. John 1: 18. So in the classics; e. g. λῖς ἐφάνη εἰς ὁδόν, a lion [came into] and showed himself in the path; Odys. δ. 51, ἐς θρόνους ἕζοντο, [they mounted] and sat upon thrones; and al. saepe. See Winer and Kuhner, ut supra. In such constructions, brevity and energy of expression are conspicuous. See Rob. Lex. under ἐν and εἰς.

NOTE 3. The same prepositions are occasionally connected in the same sentence and with the same nouns, sometimes with *different* and designedly opposite senses, (e. g. with the Gen. and Acc.); and at other times, merely for rhetorical effect, or to designate an idea considered *in all and every respect*; see in Gal. 1: 1, οὐκ ἀπ' ἀνθρώπων, οὐδὲ διὰ ἀνθρώπου, ἀλλὰ διὰ Ἰ. Χριστοῦ. So in Rom. 3: 22. 11: 36. Eph. 4: 6. Col. 1: 16, al.; and in like manner in the Classics.

NOTE 4. When several nouns in succession follow, before which the same preposition is designed to stand, it is repeated in case there is any special cause for *marked distinction and emphasis*; and omitted more usually in other cases. See in Luke 24: 27. 1 Thess. 1: 5. Luke 13: 29. Phil. 1: 7. Rom. 4: 10. John 4: 23. Luke 21: 26. Acts 15: 22. 16: 2, et al. saepe. So in the classics; Kuhner, § 625.

NOTE 5. The simple *adverbial* use of the primitive prepositions is unusual in the N. Test.; 2 Cor. 11: 23, ὑπὲρ ἐγώ, I am *more*, is an example. In the classics, μετὰ δέ, *but afterwards*, πρὸς δέ, *and besides*, and the like, are frequent. But the use of prepositions with appropriate nouns, to supply the place of adverbs and adjectives, is almost too common to need exemplification; e. g. δι' ὑπομονῆς, *patiently*; δι' ἀφροσύνης, *imprudently*; εἰς τὸ παντελές, *perfectly*; ἐξ ἀδίκου, *unjustly*; ἐν ἀληθείᾳ, *truly*; ἐπ' ἐλπίδι, *assured*; ἐν τάχει, *shortly*.

§ 114. *Regimen by Verbs compounded with prepositions.*

(1) Compound verbs may be divided into two classes; (1) Such as have so entirely combined the prepositions with them as to make in reality but one word and designate but one simple idea, e. g. μεταδιδόναι *to impart*, προάγειν *to precede*, ἀποδεκατοῦν *to tithe*; or those where the preposition is used *adverbially* and designates *intensity*, as ἐπιζητεῖν, διατελεῖν, συντελεῖν, etc. (2) Those which retain the power of the preposition as such, and generally demand a correspondent case.

NOTE. It is only with the latter that we are here concerned. The *former* class often take a case after them which is in conformity with the adverbial preposition. Yet it is not the preposition itself, but the meaning of the verb considered as a whole which regulates such instances; for often the case that follows, differs from that which the preposition alone would govern.

(2) *Usually* a preposition, compounded with a verb, governs the *same case* as when standing alone.

NOTE 1. *Usually* is all that can be said; for the exceptions are many. Thus, (a) Verbs with πρό, ἀπό, ἐκ, take the Gen.; but with ἀντί, the Dat. or Gen. (b) Verbs with σύν, the Dat.; with ἐν, Dat. and Acc. (c) With εἰς, the Acc.; with ἀνά, Acc. and Gen. (d) With κατά, ὑπέρ, Acc. and Gen.; with διά, Acc. and Dat. (e) With ἀμφί, παρά, Acc.; περί, Acc. and Gen.; ὑπό, Dat. and Acc.; μετά, Gen. and Dat.; ἐπί, Acc., Gen., Dat.; πρός, Dative. Even here the practice is not uniform.

(3) Besides the *usual* regimen mentioned in No. 2, it is very common for compound verbs either to repeat after them the same preposition which they contain, or else to employ another one of equivalent or kindred meaning.

E. g. (a) The same preposition; as ἀποβαίνειν ἀπό—ἐκκόπτειν ἐκ—εἰσφέρειν εἰς—ἐπιτιθέναι ἐπί—προσπίπτειν πρός, etc. (b) A kindred preposition; as ἀναβαίνειν πρός—ἐκπορεύεσθαι ἀπό—ἐμβαίνειν εἰς—καταβαίνειν ἀπό —προσμένειν ἐν, etc.

NOTE 1. Which of these various ways of construction in Nos. 2, 3, is the most common to any verb, can be decided only by a Concordance or a registry of usage. Enough, as it respects the *principles* of Syntax, for the student to know, that either of them may be employed, although some verbs seldom employ any other construction than that designated in No. 2.

GENERAL REMARK. As compound verbs, even when the meaning of the *preposition* is in general distinctly preserved, are not always employed in the same sense, so, when the sense varies, the regimen may vary, according to the real meaning of the verb. In other words; the *general* principle of conforming the regimen to the prepositions, is *by no means universal*.

§ 115. *Cases absolute.*

(1) CASES ABSOLUTE mean those cases which are not connected or interwoven with the texture of a sentence, according to the usual laws of grammatical construction.

(2) THE NOMINATIVE not unfrequently stands as absolute.

E. g. Acts 7: 41, ὁ Μωϋσῆς οὗτος ... οὐκ οἴδαμεν τί γέγονεν αὐτῷ, *this same Moses* ... we know not what has become of him; Rev. 3: 12, ὁ νικῶν, ποιήσω αὐτὸν στύλον, κ. τ. λ., *as to the conqueror*, I will make him a pillar, etc. Acts 20: 3. John 7: 38. 1 John 2: 27, al. saep. So, often, in the heathen classics, and in the Hebrew language. Participles, also, not unfrequently follow a like construction; see § 171. 1.

(3) THE GENITIVE ABSOLUTE. This is very frequent, and is employed in a variety of ways.

(a) Principally it is employed, where a clause is inserted, in which *the agent differs from the principal agent of the sentence*. E. g. αὐτοῦ ἐνθυμηθέντος, ἰδοὺ ἄγγελος Κυρίου κ. τ. λ. Matt. 1 : 20. 2 : 1, et passim both in the N. Test. and classics. (*b*) But sometimes the agent is the *same* in both cases ; e. g. μνηστευθείσης τῆς μητρὸς αὐτοῦ ... εὑρέθη ἐν γαστρὶ ἔχουσα, Matt. 1 : 18. This latter construction is not very common ; but it occurs in the classics occasionally.

(3) THE DATIVE ABSOLUTE. This is sometimes employed instead of the Genitive.

E. g. Matt. 8: 1, καταβάντι αὐτῷ, *having gone down;* Matt. 21 : 23, ἐλθόντι αὐτῷ, *when he had come.* So also in the classics ; περιϊόντι τῷ ἐνιαυτῷ, Xen. Hist. Graec. III. 2. 25; νότῳ ... ἀέντι, Theoc. 13. 29. This construction, however, is not frequent.

(4) THE ACCUSATIVE ABSOLUTE. In some cases, the Accusative appears to stand as *absolute*, i. e. as unconnected with any regimen of a verb. But in the N. Test., most of these admit of solution, by supposing an *elliptical* construction.

E. g. Rom. 8 : 3, τὸ ἀδύνατον τοῦ νόμου may be considered as absolute, or we may supply ἐποίησε ὁ θεός. See also Acts 26 : 3. Eph. 1 : 18. Luke 24: 46. Rev. 1 : 20 ; 21 : 17, with suggestions by Winer, § 32. 7.

NOTE. Kühner distinctly acknowledges such a construction, § 566, § 670, and produces examples from the classics. He justifies it by saying, that 'any object of interest to the speaker's feelings may be proposed as the subject of consideration, by marking it with the Accusative form.' Under the so-called *Anacolutha*, we shall find *participles* not unfrequently used in the way here specified.

GENERAL REMARK. It appears, then, that *all* the cases may be employed, and are occasionally employed, as *absolute*. The Vocative is so in its own nature, and by *usage* all the other cases are occasionally dissociated from their common grammatical connections and relations. A proper knowledge of this fact may serve to free the N Test. writers, in many cases, from the charges of solecism and ignorance of Greek construction, which have not unfrequently been made against them. The Syntax of the *Participle* will give still more information respecting the usages noted in this section; see § 171 seq.

§ 116. *Apposition of Nouns.*

(1) *Apposition* means the placing of one noun by or with another, and in the like predicament, in order to designate some *attribute* or *modification* of that other.

E. g. Ἡρώδης, ὁ βασιλεύς—Σωκράτης, ὁ σοφός.

NOTE 1. As a matter of course, *the like case, number, and gender*, in both nouns, are required, unless special reasons, (as in the case of attributive adjectives) may exist for varying any of these. Where such reasons do exist, (and they are not unfrequent), this general principle is not adhered to.

NOTE 2. Attributive Adjectives which *follow* their noun, are (for substance) to be considered as in *apposition* with it. Moreover a *pronoun* may take a noun after it in apposition, as well as a noun; e. g. ὑμεῖς, οἱ σοφοί —ἐκεῖνος, ὁ βασιλεύς.

(2) Not only single words, but whole clauses, single or successive, may constitute apposition.

E. g. 'I beseech you to present your bodies, θυσίαν ζῶσαν, ἁγίαν, εὐάρεστον τῷ θεῷ, τὴν λογικὴν λατρείαν,' Rom. 12: 1; where the three last clauses, or the last alone, may be regarded as in apposition with θυσίαν. So 1 Tim., 2: 6, 'Who gave himself, ἀντίλυτρον ὑπὲρ πάντων, τὸ μαρτύριον καιροῖς ἰδίοις,' where the last clause is the apposition to ἀντίλυτρον. A peculiar case exists in Mark 7: 19, καὶ εἰς τὸν ἀφεδρῶνα ἐκπορεύεται, καθαρίζον πάντα, where καθαρίζον (neut. part. in the Nom. case) is in apposition with the whole of the preceding clause. See a peculiar case of suspension in 2 Tim. 1: 3—5.

NOTE. *Use of the Article in apposition.* For this, the reader is referred to § 89. 6, where he will find the usage developed.

(3) Apposition, for *substance*, may be made by a *Gen.* case, following the noun to be qualified. The *number* of the latter noun in apposition, also, occasionally differs from that of the main one.

E. g. in Latin, Hebrew, and English, we have *city of Rome* ; in the two former, *river of Euphrates.* So in Greek also, there seems to be some instances in which the Gen. is equivalent in sense to a noun in usual apposition : as 2 Cor. 5: 5, τὸν ἀρραβῶνα τοῦ πνεύματος, *the Spirit as a pledge.* Rom. 8: 23, τὴν ἀπαρχὴν τοῦ πνεύματος, *the Spirit as first fruits.* Comp. also Rom. 4: 11, σημεῖον... περιτομῆς. Acts 4: 22. 1 Pet. 3: 7. Col. 3: 24. Rom. 8: 21. 2 Cor. 5: 1. Heb. 6: 1. 12: 11. Eph. 4: 9 (perhaps). See Winer, § 48. 2.

In respect to number ; 1 John 5: 16, καὶ δώσει αὐτῷ ζωήν, τοῖς ἁμαρτάνουσι μὴ πρὸς τὸν θάνατον, where αὐτῷ and ἁμαρτάνουσι are in apposition, (constructio ad sensum.)

(4) *Attraction* not unfrequently changes the case of nouns in apposition.

E. g. 1 John 2: 25, αὕτη ἐστὶν ἡ ἐπαγγελία ἣν αὐτὸς ἐπηγγείλατο, ἡμῖν, τὴν ζωὴν τὴν αἰώνιον, where ἣν puts ζωήν into the Acc. by attraction, while in reality it is in apposition with ἡ ἐπαγγελία. So Phil 3: 18. Plat. Phaed. p. 86. Hipp. maj. p. 281.

REMARK I. The natural position of the noun in apposition is in *immediate* connection with the leading noun ; but, (*a*) Sometimes an intervening clause comes between them ; e. g. in James 1: 7. 2 Pet. 2: 6. (*b*) Sometimes the subordinate word precedes ; as in Tit. 1: 3, κατ᾽ ἐπιταγὴν τοῦ σωτῆρος ἡμῶν θεοῦ, where θεοῦ immediately follows ἐπιταγήν as to the *logical* connection. So 1 Tim. 2: 3. 2 Tim. 1: 10. Luke 1: 26. 2 Pet. 1: 11. 2: 20. 1 Cor. 11: 3, al.

§ 117. SYNTAX: ADJECTIVES. 191

REMARK II. Perhaps apposition is more frequent in the N. Test. than many critics seem to suppose. Comp. Rom. 8: 23. Eph. 1: 7. 2: 15. Col. 1: 14. Luke 2: 30, 32. Rom. 9: 16. 1 Cor. 11: 10. Heb. 12: 22.

N. B. A peculiar usage takes place when a possessive prenominal adjective has a noun in apposition ; for the pronoun-adjective agrees in *form* with the principal noun, while its noun in apposition takes the *Genitive* ; e. g. ἐμὸς, τοῦ ἀθλίου βίος, meaning *the life of wretched me*, or *of me a wretch*, i. e. ἐμοῦ τοῦ ἀθλίου. The reason of this is, that ἐμός (adj.) signifies the same in substance as ἐμοῦ (pron.) would in the latter construction.

§ 117. ADJECTIVES.

The cases which are governed by adjectives have already been treated of in connection with the regimen of cases by verbs, viz *the Genitive after adjectives*, § 101; *the Dative*, § 107, *the Accusative*, § 103 10. It remains here to notice some other circumstances which are matters of interest in regard to this part of speech.

Concord of Adjectives.

(1) The general rule respecting adjectives as united to nouns, etc., is, that they must agree with them in *gender* and *number;* but to this there are not a few exceptions.

NOTE. An adjective *agrees* with a noun, when it is so combined with it as to form one whole, which, without the adjective, would be imperfectly or incompletely expressed. On the other hand, the adjective is a *predicate* in a sentence, when the expression of the noun, etc., is complete without it, and the adjective only adds some new limitation or modification.

(2) Concord merely *ad sensum* and not as to form, is frequent in respect to adjectives.

E. g. (a) In respect to gender; as τὰ στρατεύματα . . . ἐνδεδυμένοι, Rev. 19: 14 ; τὰ λοιπὰ ἔθνη . . . ἐσκοτισμένοι, Eph. 4: 17; φωναὶ μεγάλαι . . . λέγοντες, Rev. 11: 15. And so, frequently, in the classics. (b) In regard to number; τὸ πλῆθος . . . χαίροντες, Luke 19: 37 ; ὁ λαὸς . . . ἔκθαμβοι, Acts 3: 11. So in the classics ; e. g. τὴν πόλιν . . . ὄντας, Thucyd. III. 79, and the like oftentimes ; see Matth. § 434.

NOTE. In Rev. 14: 19, we find τὴν ληνὸν . . . τὸν μέγαν ; but ληνός is itself of the common gender ; Sept. Gen. 30: 37, 42.

Repetition.

(3) When the same adjective is repeated before nouns of *different* gender which are connected, and *precedes* these nouns, it is conformed in each case to the gender of the respective nouns ; but if both nouns are of the *same* gender, it is commonly inserted but once.

E. g. πᾶσα δόσις . . . καὶ πᾶν δώρημα, James 1: 17 ; ποταποὶ λίθοι καὶ ποταπαὶ οἰκοδομαί, Mark 13: 1. Acts 4: 7. On the contrary, where the adjective is not repeated; πολλὰ τέρατα καὶ σήμεια, Acts 2: 43; ποικίλαις νόσοις καὶ βασάνοις, Matt. 4: 24. 13: 32. 9: 35. al. Exceptions to the first rule, however, may be seen in Luke 10: 1. 2 Thess. 1: 4. al. The same usages are found in the classics.

(4) An adjective which in reality qualifies several connected nouns, if inserted but once, may take the gender and number of either of the nouns which it qualifies; but commonly it conforms to its proximate noun.

E. g. ἔρις τε φίλη, πόλεμοί τε μάχαι τε, Il. ε, 891. But also ἄγγεα πάντα, χαυλοί τε σκαφίδες τε, τετυγμένα, Odyss. ι, 222.

NOTE. In names of persons the masc. takes precedence of the fem.; the fem. of the neuter; e. g. ὁ ἀνὴρ καὶ ἡ γυνὴ ἀγαθοί εἰσι—γυναῖκες καὶ παιδία καλαί εἰσι. In the successive names of *things*, when the gender differs, no regard is paid to *gender*, but the attribute is *neuter* plural; e. g. λίθοι καὶ ξύλα καὶ κέραμος ... οὐδὲν χρήσιμα.

N. B. In respect to the relative *position* occupied by adjectives, see § 90. 1. seq.

Various uses of adjectives.

(5) With the article they are often employed, (more commonly in the singular but sometimes in the plural), as *abstract nouns*.

E. g. τὸ ἀσθενὲς ... [τῆς ἐντολῆς] Heb. 7: 18; τὸ μωρὸν τοῦ θεοῦ, and τὸ ἀσθηνὲς τοῦ θεοῦ, 1 Cor. 1: 25. Rom. 2: 4. Heb. 6: 17. 2 Cor. 4: 17. 8: 8. So τὰ ἀόρατα [τοῦ θεοῦ], Rom. 1: 20. This idiom is very common in the Greek writers, especially in the philosophical ones.

(6) On the contrary, the place of an adjective is frequently supplied by a noun in the Gen. which qualifies the preceding noun on which it depends. Such a Gen. is called *attributive*; see § 99.

E. g. τοῖς λόγοις τῆς χάριτος, Luke 4: 22; οἰκονόμος τῆς ἀδικίας, *unjust steward*, Luke 16: 8; υἱὸς τῆς ἀγάπης, *beloved son*, Col. 1: 13. Luke 18: 6. Rev. 13: 3, et al. saepe.

NOTE. The *frequency* of this in the N. Test. may be called *Hebraism*; for although this idiom is by no means foreign to the classic Greek, it is more common in the poets than in the prose writers; see Matth. § 316. f.

(7) But sometimes the *principal* noun (and not the one which designates qualification), is put in the Genitive.

E g. ἐπὶ πλούτου ἀδηλότητι, *in riches that are deceitful*, or *in deceitful riches*, 1 Tim. 6: 17; ἐν καινότητι ζωῆς, *in a new life*, Rom. 6: 4; ἐνέργειαν πλάνης, *strong delusion*, 2 Thess. 2: 11. So not unfrequently in the Hebrew SS.; Heb. Gramm. § 440.

NOTE. When a pronoun or pronominal adjective, etc., follows two words connected as in Nos. 2, 3, it usually relates to *both* as one whole; as τῷ ῥή-

§ 118. SYNTAX: ADJECTIVES. 193

ματι τῆς δυνάμεως αὐτοῦ, by his powerful word, Heb. 1:3. Rev. 3:10. 13:3. Sometimes, however, such pronoun or adjective is more appropriately connected only with one of the words; e. g. Rom. 7:24. Acts 13:26.

(8) In a few cases, the *feminine* of adjectives seems to stand for the *neuter*; according to the Hebrew idiom.

E. g. αὕτη and θαυμαστή in Matt. 21:42. Mark 12:11. But this is a citation from Ps. 118:22. (Sept.); and in the Sept. such an idiom is not unfrequent, while in the N. Test. it is scarcely to be found.

(9) The *frequent* expression of the sense of adjectives, by the use of υἱός, τέκνον, etc., before abstract nouns, is properly *Hebraistic*.

E. g. υἱοὶ ἀπειθείας · τέκνα φωτός—ὑπανοῆς—ὀργῆς—κατάρας. The Greeks use παῖδες ἰατρῶν—δυστήνων, etc., where however the Gen. is not an *abstract* noun. Expressions like the above are common in most languages; but their frequency is peculiar to the Hebrew and its cognate dialects.

(10) Neuter adjectives, either singular or plural, with or without the article, are often used in an *adverbial* manner.

E. g. πρῶτον, τὸ πρῶτον, *first*; αἰνά, *dreadfully*; μικρά, σοφώτατα, αἴσχιστα, etc. See § 84. 3. c. 2.

§ 118. *Comparative and Superlative degree of Adjectives.*

Comparative.

(1) The usual form of the comparative requires the Genitive after it; see § 101. 3.

(2) The comparative degree is often expressed in the N. Test., by the positive form of the adjective connected with ἤ, *than.*

E. g. καλόν σοι ἐστί ... ἤ, etc., *it is better for thee ... than*, etc., Mark 9:43. So Mark 9:45. Matt. 18:8, 9, al. The same usage is occasionally found in the classics: as ἐμοὶ πικρός ... ἢ κείνοις κ. τ. λ, Soph. Ajax. 981. Comp. Luke 15:7. 18:14. Gen. 28:36. 1 Cor. 14:19, for the like expressions; which are very common in the Sept., and are a close copy of the Hebrew comparative. When ἤ is thus employed, *the word which follows is in the same case as that which precedes.*

NOTE. The older grammarians say, that μᾶλλον is to be supplied by the mind before ἤ in all cases of this nature. Recent-grammarians do not deem this to be necessary; see Kuhner, § 747.

(3) The positive degree followed by παρά or ὑπέρ, is sometimes employed to designate the sense of the comparative. E. g.

(a) *Παρά*; as ἁμαρτωλοὶ παρὰ πάντας τοὺς Γαλιλαίους, greater sinners, or sinners above, more than, Luke 13:2. Rom. 14:5. In Heb. 1:9, the same

25

sense is made by παρά after nouns. The same preposition, moreover, is very common after the *comparative* degree; as πλέον παρά, Luke 3: 13; διαφορώτερον παρά, Heb. 1: 4. (*b*) Ὑπέρ; which is employed in the same way as παρά; e. g. Luke 16: 8. Heb. 4: 12. In all these respects, parallels are found in the classics. Other prepositions are found in them also, before the Genitive of comparison, e. g. such as ἐπί, πρό, ἀντί; see Kühner, § 588.

(4) The comparative is sometimes used, when the thing with which it is compared is merely *implied*, but not expressed.

E. g. Acts 17: 21, τι ... καινότερον, *something more recent* than even what was called *new*; Acts 25: 10, κάλλιον, *better* than I; 2 Cor. 7: 7, μᾶλλον χαρῆναι, *rejoice still more* than I did before, viz. on the arrival of Titus. So in Phil. 1: 12. Acts 27: 13. John 13: 27. Heb. 13: 19. Matt. 11: 11, al., examples of the like kind may be found; and so in the classics, Matth. § 457.

NOTE 1. Μᾶλλον and ἔτι, put before the comparative, make an *intensive* sense; as μᾶλλον περισσότερον, *the more abundantly*, Mark 7: 36. Phil. 1: 23. So ἔτι μᾶλλον, *still more*, Phil. 1: 9. Heb. 7: 15. The same usage is found in the classics.

NOTE 2. For πρότερον (compar.) πρῶτον seems to be used in John 1: 15. 15: 18. Comp. Heb. 8: 7. Acts 1: 1.

(5) An imperfectly expressed, but concise and energetic comparison is made, by comparing a thing with a person, when, strictly speaking, the comparison is with something which belongs to the person.

E. g. μαρτυρίαν μείζω τοῦ Ἰωάννου, *testimony greater than John's*, i. e. greater than that of John, John 5: 36. Matt. 5: 20. Comp. 1 Cor. 1: 25. This construction is frequent in the classics; Herod. II. 134. Matth. § 453.

Superlative.

(6) The so called *superlative degree* may be either *comparative* or *absolute*. In the comparative sense, other objects are actually compared with it, and the precedence over them is marked by the form of the superlative. In the absolute sense, the superlative stands alone, and may designate a degree absolutely the highest; or may constitute merely a highly energetic mode of expression.

NOTE. The comparative Superlative usually takes the Gen. after it of the object with which the comparison is made; e. g. πάντων ἀνθρώπων ἄριστος.

(7) Besides the usual superlative forms, this degree is sometimes expressed by the positive joined with a noun which designates the class of persons or things to which it belongs.

E. g. εὐλογημένη σὺ ἐν γυναιξίν, lit. *thou art the blessed one among women,* i. e. *most blessed of women art thou,* Luke 1: 28. This is like the He-

§ 119. Syntax: Numerals. 195

brew בְּרוּכָה בְנָשִׁים; but examples of the like kind are not wanting in the Greek classics, e. g. ὦ φίλα γυναικῶν, Eurip. Alcest. 473; ὦ σχέτλι ἀνδρῶν, most miserable man! Aristoph. Ran. 1081; ὅετὸς ὠκὺς ἐν ποτανοῖς, the eagle is the swiftest of the winged, Pind. Nem. III. 76.

(8) The Heb. superlative, such as קֹדֶשׁ קָדָשִׁים, is found in but very few cases in the N. Test.; even the classic Greek is not wanting in the like expressions.

E. g. ἁγία ἁγίων, Heb. 9: 3; βασιλεὺς βασιλέων, Rev. 19: 16. In Soph. Elect. 849, we find δειλαία δειλαίων; Oed. R. 446, ἀῤῥήτ᾽ ἀῤῥήτων; Aeschyl. Supp. 524, ἄναξ ἀνάκτων. So also, κακῶν κάκιστος—μακάρων μακάρτατος, and the like, which are very common in the poets.

NOTE 1. The so called superlatives made by θεοῦ, κυρίου, etc., appear to be all capable of solution in another way; e. g. αὔξησιν τοῦ θεοῦ, an increase of which God is the author, Col. 2: 19; σάλπιγξ θεοῦ, the trumpet which God will order to be sounded, 1 Thess. 4: 16. So in Luke 1: 15. 2 Cor. 1: 12. Rev. 21: 11. 15: 2. Ἀστεῖος τῷ θεῷ, fair in the view of God; see § 106. 10. c.

NOTE 2. Superlatives are often made more intense by adverbs or intensive conjunctions; e. g. by καί (intensive), πολύ, μακρῷ, μέγα, ἔξοχα, ὡς, ἐν τοῖς, etc.

NUMERALS.

§ 119. *Use of Ordinal and Cardinal Numbers.*

(1) For the ordinal πρῶτος, the cardinal εἷς is constantly employed, in designating a day of the week.

E. g. πρωΐ τῆς μιᾶς τῶν σαββάτων, *early on the first day of the week*, Mark 16: 2. Matt. 28: 1. John 20: 19. Acts 20: 7, al. The Greeks employ εἷς, in such cases, only when δεύτερος, ἄλλος, etc., follow. The N. Test. usage is therefore Hebraistic.

(2) Cardinal numbers repeated denote *distribution;* as in Hebrew.

E. g. δύο δύο, *two and two* or *two by two*, Mark 6: 7. The Greeks would say: δύο κατὰ δύο, or δύο ἀνὰ δύο; and like the latter is Luke 10: 1. But occasionally the Greeks employ an idiom like the Hebrew; e. g. Aeschyl. Pers. 915, μυρία μυρία, i. e. *by myriads*.

NOTE. The formulas, ἀνὰ εἷς ἕκαστος, Rev. 21: 21; εἷς καθ᾽ εἷς, Mark 14: 19. John 8: 9; ὁ καθ᾽ εἷς, Rom. 12: 5; are peculiar. The usual Greek is, ὁ καθ᾽ ἕνα.

(3) Ordinals of the neuter gender are sometimes used *adverbially.*

E. g. τρίτον, δεύτερον, *thrice, twice,* etc.

GENERAL REMARK. Numerals in their nature, approach very near to one class of the adjective pronouns, e. g. ἕκαστος, ἕτερος, ἄλλος, ὅσος, τόσος, etc., which might well be reckoned among numerals.

PRONOUNS.

§ 120. *General principles respecting gender and number.*

(1) It is a general law respecting pronouns of every kind, that they should conform, as to *gender*, to the noun which is their correlate. But concord in this respect is often merely *ad sensum*.

E. g. 'Teach πάντα τὰ ἔθνη, baptizing αὐτούς,' masc. pronoun, because ἔθνη designates *men*, Matt. 28: 19 ; τεκνία μου, οὓς πάλιν ὠδίνω, where οὓς refers to τεκνία for the like reason, Gal. 4: 19 ; 'There is παιδάριον ἓν here, ὅς κ. τ. λ.' (in the better Codd.), John 6: 9. So in 2 John v. 1. Acts 15: 17. Mark 5: 41. Rom. 2: 14, 26. Rev. 17: 16. This is frequent in classic Greek ; Matth. § 434.

(2) Plural pronouns are often employed, when the correlate noun is *nomen multitudinis* in the singular number, but has a *collective* sense.

E. g. λαὸν ... αὐτῶν, Matt. 1: 21; ἐν μέσῳ γενεᾶς ... ἐν οἷς, Phil. 2: 15; τῇ ἐκκλησίᾳ ... αὐτῶν, 3 John v. 9 ; τοῦ σκότους ... ὑπ᾽ αὐτῶν, Eph. 5: 11, 12 ; κατὰ πᾶσαν πόλιν, ἐν αἷς κ. τ. λ. The adjectives *each*, *every*, are collectives in their own nature, and therefore they cause the noun with which they are joined to partake of this sense. So כֹּל and אִישׁ in Hebrew, are followed often by a plural verb.

(3) On the contrary ; pronouns in the *singular* are often used in a *generic* sense, i. e. as collectives or in the place of nouns of multitude.

In the O. Test. this occurs times without number ; it is not unfrequent in the N. Testament.

§ 121. *Use of personal pronouns.*

(1) Personal pronouns, specially in the oblique cases, are more frequent in the N. Test., than is usual in classic Greek.

NOTE. The ground of this seems to be like that in the case of prepositions, which also are employed in the N. Test. with unusual frequency. A definiteness is thus given to the expression in Greek, such as a foreigner would very naturally seek for, because it made the language more intelligible to him ; and in respect to the Greek, all the Hebrews were in a sense *foreigners*. Seldom indeed is the pronoun omitted, where we might expect it ; e. g. Acts 13: 3. Mark 6: 5. 1 Tim. 6: 2.

(2) Personal pronouns are not usually added to verbs as the *subjects* of them, i. e. as Nom. case. When they are, emphasis or distinction is generally intended.

E. g. σύ in Luke 17: 8; ὑμεῖς in Mark 6: 37. So also in Mark 13: 23.

§ 121. Syntax: Pronouns. 197

1 John 4: 19, et al. saepe. But in some cases, it is difficult to make out an emphatic meaning; e. g. ὑμεῖς in Mark 13: 9; ἐγώ in Eph. 5: 32. In a few cases, in the same sentence, one verb has a pronoun expressed and another has not; e. g. in Luke 10: 23, 24, ἅ βλέπετε... ἅ ὑμεῖς βλέπετε. See also 2 Cor. 11: 29.

(3) In some cases the noun itself is repeated, where we might naturally expect the pronoun.

E. g. in Luke 3: 19, Ἡρώδης; and so πρόσωπον in 2 Cor. 3: 7; see also John 10: 41. In some cases of this nature, there is an emphasis or significance attached to the repetition of the noun; e. g. John 4: 1. Matt. 10: 23. Luke 12: 8. 9: 26. John 6: 40, et saep. al.

(4) Αὐτός is often a *demonstrative* pronoun; but it is also employed, specially in its *oblique* cases, as a *personal* pronoun.

Note 1. Αὐτός, when joined with a noun or pronoun as a kind of pronominal *demonstrative*, means *self*; and with the article, *self-same, the same*; as ὁ πατὴρ αὐτός, ἐγω αὐτός, οἱ ὑπὸ τῆς υὑτῆς μητρὸς τραφέντες, *those who have been nourished by the same mother*; οἱ Πέρσαι καὶ αὐτοί, *even the Persians themselves*, etc. When thus employed, it may stand either *before* a noun and its article, as αὐτὸς ὁ ἀδελφός; or between the article and its noun, as τὸ αὐτὸ χωρίον; or *after* the noun, when the intention of the writer is to render its meaning (*self*) emphatic, as οἱ Πέρσαι καὶ αὐτοί.

Note 2. Αὐτός, meaning *he*, is employed in the room of the antiquated pronoun of the third person. It is derived from αὖ *again*, and τός *the same*. Throughout the N. Test., and usually in the later Attic writers, it is employed instead of the old pronominal adjective, ὅς, ἥ, ὅν, *his, hers, its*; or else the compound ἑαυτοῦ (αὑτοῦ), etc., takes its place; see No. 1 above. The position of some grammarians, viz., that αὐτός in the Nom. is never a simple substantive pronoun, does not seem to be correcct; see Kuhner, § 342. 4.

Note 3. The noun to which αὐτός relates when it is employed as a pronoun, is sometimes a collective one in the *singular*; as in Matt. 4: 23, αὐτῶν refers back to Γαλιλαίαν (the country, for its inhabitants). So in Matt. 9: 35. Luke 4; 15, al.; (constructio ad sensum). Not unfreqeently αὐτός stands related to some noun merely implied by the nature of the case or by the context; as in Luke 1: 17, 'He shall go before αὐτοῦ, *him*,' viz. the Messiah, not mentioned in the preceding discourse; αὐτοῦ in 1 John 2: 12, in reference to Christ. So αὐτοῦ in 2 John v. 6; and in many cases the reference is more or less obscure, and can be made out only by the context.

Note 4. Αὐτός, as a pronoun, is not unfrequently repeated in cases where its use would seem to be *pleonastic*; e. g. ἐξελθόντι αὐτῷ ἐκ τοῦ πλοίου, εὐθέως ἀπήντησεν αὐτῷ, Mark 5: 2. So Mark 9: 28. Matt. 26: 71. Rev. 6: 4, al. But such constructions, following clauses with a participle, are common in the classics. More pleonastic still would seem to be the following constructions, with clauses containing the relative pronoun; viz., οἷς ἐδόθη αὐτοῖς ἀδικῆσαι κ. τ. λ, Rev. 7: 2; ἣν οὐδεὶς δύναται κλεῖσαι αὐτήν, Rev. 3: 8; so Mark 7: 25. 13: 19, comp. Rev. 12: 14, ὅπου and ἐκεῖ.

This is very common in the Sept. and in the Hebrew; but it is also found in classical Greek, Xen. Cyrop. I. 4. 19. Diod. Sic. I. 97. XVII. 35. See many examples of the pleonastic repetitions of personal pronouns, in Matth. § 465. 4. Sometimes this repetition seems to be for the sake of emphasis, and sometimes for the sake of greater perspicuity.

(5) Ἑαυτοῦ (Attice αὑτοῦ) is a compound of ἕ and αὐτός, and is used only in the *oblique* cases. But, as used in the N. Test., it is not limited to the *third* person, as its etymology would seem to indicate.

NOTE 1. It is sometimes applied to the 1 pers. plural, as in Rom. 8: 23. 1 Cor. 11: 31. 2 Cor. 1: 1, 9, al; sometimes to the 2nd pers. plural, as in John 12: 8. Phil. 2: 12. Matt. 3: 9, al; sometimes to the 2nd pers. sing., as in John 18: 34. The same usage is found in the classics.

NOTE 2. Αὐτοῦ, etc., the Attic form, is used in a multitude of cases where αὐτοῦ, etc., might have been employed. It often depends merely on the mode of expression which the writer deems the more eligible, and not on any substantial difference of meaning, whether the one or the other is employed. Hence the continual discrepancies of the Codices, in relation to these words. *Generally, where the pronoun refers to the principal subject of the sentence*, ἑαυτοῦ (αὑτοῦ) *is employed*; see Rost's Grammar, § 99. 2.

§ 122. *Possessive pronouns.*

(1) The *possessive pronominal adjectives* are not very frequent in the N. Testament. Instead of ἐμός, σός, etc., the Gen. of the personal pronoun, μοῦ, σοῦ, etc., is more commonly employed.

NOTE. This is the case also in the classics. When possessive pronouns are employed, their position is like that of adjectives in general. The pronouns employed instead of them may *precede* or *follow* the noun, e. g. ἡμῶν ἡ σωτηρία, Rom. 13: 11: μοῦ τὴν χαράν, Phil. 2: 2: and often so in the writings of Paul, Luke, and John. The other construction, such as ὁ θεός μου, ἡ πίστις ὑμῶν, etc., is too common to need examples. The first of these constructions is generally deemed *emphatic*; but instances occur, where no particular emphasis seems to be apparent.

(2) The meaning of possessive pronouns may be *subjective* or *objective*.

E. g. ὁ σὸς πόθος may mean *the desire which you have*, or *the longing* of another *after you*. So τὴν ἐμὴν ἀνάμνησιν, *the remembering of me*, Luke 22: 19; τῷ ὑμετέρῳ ἐλέει, *through mercy bestowed on you*, Rom. 11: 31. See 2 Tim. 4: 6. 1 Cor. 15: 31. So ἡ ἡμέτερα εὔνοια may mean *our own benevolence*, or *benevolence towards us*. The like in the Greek classics.

(3) The Dative of pronouns often supplies the place of a possessive pronoun.

E. g. μητήρ μοι, *my mother*; οἱ ἡμῖν σύμμαχοι, *our allies*; σοὶ ἐχθροί, *thine enemies.* The true solution of such cases seems to be either thus: *a mother in respect to me,* or μήτηρ ἥ ἐστί μοι. See § 106. 9.

(4) The place of the possessive pronominal adjective, or of the pronoun in its stead, is sometimes supplied in the N. Test. by ἴδιος,

E. g. εἰς τὸν ἴδιον ἀγρόν *to his field,* Matt. 22: 5; τοὺς ἰδίους δούλους, *his servants;* where to say, *his own* field, *his own* servants, does not seem to be the intention of the writer. See also 1 Pet. 3: 1, and comp. Prov. 27: 8. Jos. 7: 10 in the Sept. In the classics, no certain example of such usage has been produced.

§ 123. *Demonstrative pronouns.*

(1) The demonstratives οὗτος, ὅδε, ἐκεῖνος, (αὐτός), are sometimes put immediately before the verb, even after the subject of the sentence has already been specified, in order to give emphasis to the expression.

E. g. '*He* who endureth to the end, οὗτος σωθήσεται.' Matt. 24: 13. See Matt. 6: 4. Mark 7: 15, 20. 12: 40, et al. saepe.

(2) Οὗτος (in distinction from ὅδε) more usually refers to a *preceding* noun, ὅδε to something which *follows;* but at other times οὗτος refers to a more distant object, ὅδε to a nearer one. Οὗτος (in distinction from ἐκεῖνος) refers to what immediately precedes, ἐκεῖνος to that which is more remote.

NOTE 1. Yet none of these usages are invariable; for there are cases where they are relinquished. Not unfrequently, (as in respect to αὐτός as a pronoun), the subject referred to is remote, or merely implied, or simply something which the nature of the topic under discussion suggests. See Acts 4: 11, οὗτος. 1 John 5: 20 is a doubtful case, so far as οὗτος is concerned. See also Acts 8: 26. 7: 19. 2 John v. 8.

NOTE 2. The usual place of οὗτος is *before* the noun to which it has relation (when adjectively used); that of ἐκεῖνος, *after* the noun. But the reverse of this sometimes happens in both cases.

(3) Some one of the demonstrative pronouns is omitted, but still implied, in innumerable cases where the relative pronoun is employed; which latter seems often to include the demonstrative along with it.

E. g. ἀγόρασον ὧν χρείαν ἔχομεν, *buy* [those things] *of which we have need,* i. e. ἀγόρασον [τὰ ἐκεῖνα] ὧν κ. τ. λ, John 13: 29; 'How shall they call εἰς ὃν οὐκ ἐπίστευσαν,' i. e. εἰς [ἐκεῖνον] ὃν οὐκ κ. τ. λ, Rom. 10: 14; 'What fruit had ye ἐφ' οἷς νῦν ἐπαισχύνεσθε,' i. e. ἐπ' [ἐκείνοις] οἷς νῦν κ. τ. λ, Rom. 6: 21; ἄρας ἐφ' ὃ κατέκειτο, i. e. [ἐκεῖνο] ἐφ' ὃ κ. τ. λ, Luke 5: 25. Comp. John 6: 29. 2 Cor. 5: 10. The same idiom is frequent in the classics.

(4) The demonstrative τοῦτο is often employed before ἵνα, ὅτι,

and the like particles, when that which follows them is intended to be made particularly emphatic.

E. g. εἰδὼς τοῦτο, ὅτι κ. τ. λ, 1 Tim. 1: 9; οἶδα τοῦτο, ὅτι κ. τ. λ, Acts 20:29. So εἰς τοῦτο... ἵνα κ. τ. λ, Acts 9:21; εἰς τοῦτο γὰρ... ἵνα κ. τ. λ, Rom. 14:9, and so, very often, in all parts of the N. Test., and sometimes in the classics.

NOTE. The neuters ταῦτα, τοῦτο, etc., are often used *adverbially*. Τούτων appears, also, to be employed in the same way as the singular number, in 3 John v. 4; and so ταῦτα in John 15:17.

§ 124. *Relative Pronouns*.

(1) As a general principle, the relative agrees with its antecedent in *gender* and *number*; but there are not a few exceptions to this.

(*a*) *Exceptions as to number.* (1) A *plural* pronoun not unfrequently is related to an antecedent in the *singular*, when the pronoun designates not an individual but a species or genus; e. g. ἀνδρὶ καλῷ... ἐν οἷς οὐδαμοῦ σὺ φανήσῃ γεγονώς, *a good man* (generic)... *among whom* etc., Demosth. pro Cor. Ἄλλο τι ἢ ἐν οἷς ζῶμεν, Thucyd. III. 38. (2) On the other hand, when the antecedent is *plural* the relative is frequently *singular*, if it has a *collective* sense; i. e. such relatives as ὅστις, ὃς ἄν, etc. Thus Il. λ. 367, νῦν τοὺς ἄλλους ἐπείσομαι, ὅν κε κιχείω, *now will I pursue others, whomsoever I may catch.* Thucyd. VII. 29, 'Slaying πάντας, ὅτῳ ἐντύχοιεν, *all, whomsoever they might overtake*.' So also the relative may be singular, when the antecedent is a plural with the meaning of a singular; e. g. οἰκτρὰ πεπόνθαμεν, ἢ κενὴν κατέσχον ἐλπίδα, WE *have suffered pitiably* WHO (sing.) *have cherished a vain hope.*

NOTE. Cases of this nature are very plain, merely resolving themselves into the principle which respects nouns of *multitude* or *collective* nouns.

(*b*) *Exceptions as to gender.* (1) Particularly is the *neuter* gender singular employed for the relative, when it is designed to express a *generic* sense, whatever the gender of the antecedent may be; e. g. Mark 12:42, ἔβαλε λεπτὰ δύο, ὅ ἔστι κοδράντης, *she cast in two mites, which make a farthing.* So Xen. Mem. III. 9. 8, φθόνον δὲ σκοπῶν, ὅ τι εἴη, *considering envy, whatever it may be.* In particular, if an epexegetical noun is joined to an antecedent, the pronoun relative to that antecedent very often conforms to the *second* noun; e. g. τῷ σπέρματί σου, ὅς ἐστι Χριστός, Gal. 3:16. See also Mark 15:16. Eph. 1:14. 3:13. 6:17. 1 Tim. 3:15. Phil. 1:28. 1 Cor. 4:17.

NOTE. Often a *neuter* relative relates to the whole of a preceding clause or sentence, which contains masc. or fem. nouns. Sometimes it relates merely to a single word, which, as such, is about to be explained; e. g. John 1:42, τὸν Μεσσίαν, ὅ ἐστι μεθερμηνευόμενον, Χριστός; and so in Σαλήμ, ὅ ἐστι κ. τ. λ, Heb. 7:2. Matt. 27:33. Mark 12:42. John 1:39, 43.

(*c*) *Cases of a complex nature.* (1) Two or more nouns of the same gender usually take a relative of the same gender and plural number; but

§ 124. Syntax: Attraction of Pronouns. 201

when *things* are designated by the nouns, the relative is often in the *neuter*; e. g. 'Seeing him adorned ὑπογραφῇ of the eyes, and ἐντρίψει of colouring, and with ornamental κόμαις, ἃ δὲ νόμιμ' ἦν κ. τ. λ, Xen. Cyr. I. 3. 2. (2) If the antecedents are of *different* gender, the masc. is preferred for the relative; but the *neuter* is used when *things* are designated; 'We have assembled for a matter πολέμου τε καὶ εἰρήνης, ἃ ἔχει κ. τ. λ, Isoc. de Pac. p. 159. (3) In sentences with a copula (εἰμί) and a predicate *noun*, the relative frequently agrees with the latter instead of conforming to the antecedent; e. g. ἡ μὲν ὁδός ... τὸ καλέεται Πηλούσιον στόμα, *the way ... which is called Pelusian outlet*, Her. II. 17. This is very common; specially when the relative *follows* the predicate; e. g. 'Justice among men—how should it not be καλόν, ὃ πάντα ἡμέρωκε, which [viz. justice, δίκη] *softens every thing*, etc.

Attraction of the Relative pronoun.

(2) The case of the relative is sometimes determined by the verb with which it is connected. But the usual custom of the classic Greek, and the predominant one in the N. Test., is, *to make the case of the relative accord with that of the antecedent*, when that antecedent is in the *Gen*. or *Dative*, and the verb connected with the relative would require this to be in the *Accusative*. This is called Attraction.

E. g. ἐπὶ πᾶσιν, οἷς ἤκουσαν, Luke 2: 20; ἐπίστευσαν ... τῷ λόγῳ, ᾧ εἶπεν, John 2: 22; περὶ πάντων τῶν ἔργων ... ὧν ἠσέβησαν, Jude v. 15. So in Acts 3: 21, 25. 10: 39. 7: 17. 22: 10. James 2: 5. 1 Pet. 4: 11. John 15: 20. 21: 10, et al. saepe. If the pronoun thus *attracted* has predicates of any kind, they suffer attraction in the same manner, i. e. they still agree with the attracted pronoun.

Note 1. In most parts of the N. Test. this usage is very common, or rather, it is the regular one. But in Matthew it never occurs; and in Mark but once, 7: 13, other passages having various readings. In the Apoc., only one or two cases of attraction are found.

Note 2. The word, whether a noun or demonstrative pronoun, etc., which is the antecedent, is often *omitted*, while the relative assumes the same case that it would have assumed, provided the antecedent had been expressed; e. g. μεμνημένος ὧν ἔπραξε, i. e. μεμνημένος [τῶν πραγμάτων] ὧν ἔπραξε. So οἷς ἔχω, χρῶμαι, *the things I have, I use*, for χρῶμαι [τούτοις] οἷς ἔχω; and with still greater latitude, as δεινότερά ἐστιν ... ὧν εἴρηκα, *they are more dreadful than the things which I have said*, for δεινότερά ἐστιν [ἐκείνων] ὧν εἴρηκα. Comp. Heb. 5: 8. Rom. 15: 18.

Note 3. In a very few cases, the Dat. and Nom. (i. e. cases which would regularly be in the Dat. or Nom.) suffer attraction; e. g. ὄφελες τιμῆς ... ἧσπερ ἀνάσσεις κ. τ. λ, instead of ἧπερ ἀνάσσεις, etc., Odyss. ω. 30. So Herod. I. 68, οὐδὲν εἰδότες τῶν ἦν περὶ Σάρδις κ. τ. λ, i. e. ο. εἰδ. [τούτων] ἃ ἦν, etc.

(3) *Vice versâ*, the noun sometimes conforms to the case in which the relative is put by the proper regimen of the verb.

E. g. (a) When the noun precedes, as τὸν ὄρτον ὃν κλῶμεν, 1 Cor. 10: 16; λίθον ὃν ἀπεδοκίμασαν, οὗτος κ. τ. λ, Matt. 21: 42; παντὶ ᾧ ἐδόθη πολύ, Luke 12: 48. 1: 72, 73. (b) When the noun follows; as ὃν ἐγὼ ἀπεκεφάλισα Ἰωάννην, οὗτος κ. τ. λ, Mark 6: 16; εἰς ὃν παρεδόθητε τύπον διδαχῆς, Rom. 6: 17. Philem. v. 10. Both usages occur in the classics. Comp. Heb. 5: 8.

NOTE. This *inverted attraction* (as it is called) takes place principally when the noun thus attracted would otherwise be in the Nominative or Accusative. A unity of construction is thus effected in a way like to that described in No. 2 above.

GENERAL REMARK. The usage of *attraction* is evidently the result of an effort to amalgamate *adjective* clauses, i e. such as are introduced by a relative pronoun, into a unity like that which an adjective agreeing with its preceding noun would express. Instead, however, of turning the clause into such a shape, the relative is preserved, but made (as to its case) to imitate an adjective which might stand in the room of the relative clause.

§ 125. *Interrogative and Indefinite Pronouns.*

(1) INTERROGATIVES. The interrogatives τίς, τί, are employed in questions *direct* and *indirect ;* and also in some cases where the Greeks would employ ὅ τι.

E. g. δοθήσεται ὑμῖν . . . τί λαλήσετε, *what ye shall say, shall be given to you,* Matt. 10 : 19 ; ἑτοίμασον τί δειπνήσω, *prepare that which I may eat,* Luke 17 : 8. Mark 6 : 36. So Xenophon ; οὐκ ἔχω τί μεῖζον εἴπω, *I have nothing more important which I could say,* Cyrop. VI. 1, 48.

(2) In the N. Test., ἵνα τί is frequently employed in an interrogative sense, *why ? wherefore ?*

E. g. Matt. 9 : 4. 27 : 46. Luke 13 : 7. al. It is also employed in the same way in the Greek classics.

REMARK. The student will remember that the interrogatives τίς, τί, always have the acute accent, which is retained on the *first* syllable in the oblique cases. By this the *interrogatives* are distinguished from the *indefinite* pronouns ; and the accentuation is retained in the singular usage noted above.

(3) INDEFINITES. Τὶς, τὶ (indefinite), are sometimes added to nouns, in order to express the idea of *a certain, a kind of*, etc.

E. g. ἀπαρχήν τινα, *a kind of first fruits,* James 1 : 18.

(4) Sometimes they are joined to numerals; and sometimes to adjectives.

In the first case, they mean *a certain,* or *about so many ;* as δύο τινάς, Acts 23 : 23. So ἡμέρας ἑβδομήκοντά τινας, *some seventy days.* With adjectives they have a kind of *intensive* meaning, as φοβερά τις ἐκδοχὴ κρίσεως, *a certain terrible expectation of punishment,* Heb. 10 : 27 ; μέγας τις, *some great affair, some important personage,* Acts 8 : 9. 1 Cor. 3 : 7. Gal. 2 : 6, al.

§ 126. *Hebraism as to the designation of certain pronouns.*

(1) The usual classic words οὐδείς, μηδείς, *no one*, are sometimes expressed in the manner of the Hebrew כֹּל — לֹא, οὐ — πᾶς; yet with this modification, that the negative particle (οὐ or μή) is closely joined with the verb of the sentence, and not with πᾶς.

E. g. οὐκ ἄν ἐσώθη πᾶσα σάρξ, lit. *then could not be saved all flesh*, i. e. *no flesh* or *no man could be saved*, Matt. 24 : 22 ; οὐ δικαιωθήσεται πᾶσα σάρξ *no flesh*, i. e. *no man*, *shall be justified*, Rom. 3 : 20. Eph. 5 : 5. 1 John 2 : 21. John 3 : 15. 1 Cor. 1 : 29. Acts 10 : 14. Rev. 7 : 1. See the like idiom, also, in Matt. 10 : 29. Luke 1 : 37.

NOTE. Different from this is the case, where the negative particle is immediately connected with πᾶς ; for then the meaning is as in other languages, i. e. *not every one*, (q. d. only some of). E. g. οὐ πᾶς ὁ λέγων · κύριε, κύριε, κ. τ. λ, *it is not every individual who addresses me with Lord ! Lord !* etc., Matt. 7 : 21 ; οὐ πᾶσα σάρξ ἡ αὐτὴ σάρξ, *not all flesh is the same flesh*, i. e. there are different kinds of flesh, etc., 1 Cor. 15 : 39. So οὐ πάντες in Matt. 19 : 11. Rom. 9 : 6. 10 : 16. When a verb is *omitted* by ellipsis, οὐ, may stand before πᾶς and yet mean *no*, *none ;* e. g. in Rev. 7 : 16.

REMARK. There is no serious difficulty in the mode of expression stated in the text above. For example, John 2 : 21, ὅτι πᾶν ψεῦδος ἐκ τῆς ἀληθείας οὐκ ἔστι, *for every lie is not of the truth*, must of course be equivalent to *no lie is of the truth*. But in the classics this mode of expression is not found ; nor is it frequent in the N. Testament.

(2) *The one and the other*, in classic Greek, may be expressed by εἷς μέν, εἷς δέ; but in the N. Test. we find εἷς . . . καὶ εἷς.

E. g. Matt. 20 : 21. 27 : 38. Mark 4 : 8. et al. The Heb. idiom, אֶחָד ... וְאֶחָד, seems to be the basis of the N. Test. mode of expression. Sometimes we find ὁ εἷς . . . ὁ εἷς — ὁ εἷς . . . ὁ ἕτερος.

SYNTAX OF SIMPLE SENTENCES.

§ 127. *Component parts of a simple sentence.*

(1) *A sentence* means the union of a *substantive* and *verbal* idea in one expression, so as to exhibit their mutual relation and dependence. It consists, therefore, of a *subject* and *predicate*.

In other words, there must be *something* in respect to which an affirmation or negation is made (subject); and also an affirmation or negation of some action, energy, quality, etc., must be made (predicate), in order to constitute a sentence.

(2) SUBJECT. The subject of a verb must always be a *noun*, or an equivalent for a noun.

EQUIVALENTS may be, (*a*) Pronouns; as ἐγώ, ὑμεῖς, etc. (*b*) An adjective or participle used as a noun; e. g. ὁ σοφός, τὸ καλόν, ὁ σπείρων, οἱ φιλοσοφοῦντες. (c) An adverb used as a noun; as οἱ νῦν, οἱ τότε. (d) A preposition with its appropriate case used as a noun; as οἱ ἀμφὶ Σωκράτην, οἱ ἐκ πόλεως. (e) The Inf. mode, with or without adjuncts; as διδάσκειν καλόν ἐστιν· ἀποθανεῖν ὑπὲρ τῆς πατρίδος καλόν ἐστιν. (f) Any particular object whatever as a letter, word, part or whole of a sentence, phraseology, etc., quoted as such, may be the subject of affirmation, etc., and therefore the subject of a verb; e. g. τὸ τύπτω ῥῆμά ἐστι, the [word] τύπτω *is a verb.*

(3) Ellipsis of the Subject. Although a verb must always have a subject, yet this is *not* always expressed, but generally omitted in certain classes of expressions.

(a) The subject is omitted when it is indefinite; e. g. εὖ ἔχει, *it is well*; ἐδήλωσε δέ, *it is clear*. (b) When the verb can naturally be applied only to one subject, or when it implies the subject within itself; as ὕει, *it rains*; βροντᾷ, *it thunders*, etc., where ὁ Ζεύς or ὁ θεός is the implied subject; so οἰνοχοεύει, *one pours out wine*, sc. ὁ οἰνοχόος, or ἐπεὰν θύῃ, *whenever one may sacrifice*, sc. ὁ θυτήρ; in which cases the verb furnishes the subject by suggesting the correlate noun. (This idiom is frequent in Hebrew). (c) Not unfrequently the *sense of the passage in its connection* suggests a subject to the mind of the reader, which is not expressed; e. g. 'Insurrections came, and from these murders, and from murders ἀπέβη εἰς μοναρχίαν, i. e. [this affair] *terminated in monarchy;*' so ἦν ἐγγὺς ἡλίου δυσμῶν, i. e. ἡ ἡμέρα; again, 'I will go to the *palace*, καὶ ἢν μὲν ὀνθίστηται, *and if one shall present himself,*' i. e. if ὁ βασιλεύς etc. (d) In like manner τίς (the indefinite pronoun) is often omitted, and must be supplied by the reader; e. g. 'It is unbecoming to act injuriously, ὁτιοῦν ἂν πάσχῃ, *whatever one may suffer*, i. e. whatever [τίς] *any one*, etc.

Note. Strictly considered, some subject must always be implied to every verb. Yet an *indefinite* expression of mere agency is most appropriately made without naming a subject.

(4) Predicate. This must always be a verb, or its equivalent.

(a) *A verb*; e. g. τὸ ῥόδον θάλλει. (b) Its equivalent; which is the copula εἰμί (*to be*), with an adjective, noun, pronoun, etc., following it; e. g. ὁ ἄνθρωπος θνητός ἐστιν—ὁ Κῦρος ἦν βασιλεύς=ὁ Κ. ἐβασίλευε—τὸ πρᾶγμά ἐστι τόδε, *the matter is this.*

Note. The copula (εἶναι) signifies not *action* but mere existence, when thus employed, and so an adjective, noun, etc., must be added, in order to make up the deficiency in the meaning of the verb and fully to indicate what is designed to be predicated. Other verbs, such as ὑπάρχω, γίνομαι, τυγχάνω, φῦναι, and κυρεῖν, are sometimes employed merely in the sense of a *copula*, i. e. they are sometimes equivalent to εἶναι. When εἰμί, however, merely *asserts existence*, as ἔστι θεός, it is then employed in like manner with other verbs, i. e. it predicates some particular thing of its subject.

(5) Ellipsis of the predicate Copula, εἶναι. This is very

§ 128. Syntax: Subject and Predicate. 205

frequent, but it is mostly confined to the *present* tenses of the verb and its participle.

(a) Omitted in general sentences, proverbs, etc.; e. g. θνητὸς ὁ ἄνθρωπος. (b) After verbals, and adjectives designating necessity, duty, readiness, ability, etc.; e. g. ἀγωνιστέον ἡμῖν—ἕτοιμος δοῦναι—πρόθυμος εἰδέναι —ἀνάγκη θανεῖν. (c) In relative clauses, after ὁ, οἱ, etc., εἶναι is very often omitted.

NOTE. The Subj. mode rarely omits the copula; so with the Inf. and the Imper.; the Opt. never; but the Part., *very frequently*.

REMARK *on the Ellipsis of subject and predicate.* As we have seen above, the subject is often omitted, because it is well known, or may be easily made out. So the *Copula* meiely may, as is evident, be often omitted; but the real and substantial part of the *predicate* can never be omitted, unless it has just been repeated, and suggests itself as a matter of course; comp. in 2 Cor. 1:6. 1 John 2:9. Rom. 8:4. 11:6; specially John 4:12.

§ 128. *Relation between subject and predicate, or agreement between a verb and its subject or Nominative.*

(1) *General Rule.* (a) A verb (predicate) agrees with its noun in *number* and *person.* (b) In sentences with εἰμί as copula, the adjective or noun, which follows as predicate, must agree with the subject in *gender, number,* and *case.*

E. g. ἐγὼ γράφω—ὁ Κῦρος ἦν βασιλεύς. Examples occur every where, so that further illustration would be useless. See a full exhibition of the same *case* after a copula (verb) as before it, in § 97. 4. Note 1.

(2) EXCEPTIONS to the general rule, however, are apparently very many; and they need some special illustration.

1. Constructio ad sensum.

(a) *As to number.* Nouns of multitude, i. e. generic nouns, in the *singular*, often take a plural verb, adjective, participle, etc.; e. g. ὁ ὄχλος . . . εἰσι, John 7: 49; τὸ πλῆθος οἴονται—στρατὸς ἀπέβαινον, et sic passim. Matt. 21: 8. Luke 9: 12. 'In John 6: 2, both singular and plural are united; and so elsewhere.

NOTE. Kindred to this is the case of *distributives*, which, not unfrequently, take a *plural* verb; e. g. John 16: 32, σκορπισθῆτε ἕκαστος; and so Acts 2: 6. 1J: 29. Rev. 5: 8. The same in the Classics, as to ἕκαστος, ἑκάτερος, πᾶς, ἄλλος, and the like; and so in Hebrew often, in respect to אִישׁ, אָדָם, etc.

(b) *Constructio ad sensum as to gender and number* often occurs in sentences with a copula expressed or implied; e. g. τὸ γυναίκιόν ἐστι καλή, lit. *womanhood is beautiful;* τὰ παιδικά ἐστι καλός, lit. *childhood is beautiful.* Often in respect to pronouns; as, 'when it was told at Sparta, αὐτοῖς ἔδοξε, it seemed good *to them*,' i. e. to the Spartans, etc.

NOTE. The neuter articles, τό and τά, with a Gen. plural after them,

§ 128. Syntax: Subject and Predicate.

take a *plural* predicate; as τὸ τῶν θηρίων ... ἐλευθηρώτερα. In a compound subject made up of two cases, the *case* of the one part may be followed, and the *gender* and *number* of the other (principal) part; as πλῆθος τῶν ἱππέων ... ἐπιόντες, the last word has a Nom. case like πλῆθος, but a plural number like ἱππέων. This is a *mixed* constructio ad sensum.

II. Real discrepancies between the subject and predicate.

(3) These are numerous, and they assume a variety of forms; e. g.

(a) Masc. and fem. subjects may have (with a copula) a predicate adjective, etc., in the *neuter* singular or plural; e. g. ὁ πόλεμος φοβερόν—ἡ πόλις φίλτατον—ἱκανὸν ἡ ἐπιτιμία, 2 Cor. 2: 6. Such constructions are very frequent; comp. "varium et mutabile semper femina." With a pronoun; τοῦτο τυραννίς, etc. In the *plural*; οὐ δεινὰ τοῦτο πάσχειν—δῆλα ὅτι γέγονε; specially in the case of verbals in -τέος and -τός, as ἐστὶν αὐτῷ πιστά *one must trust him*, ἀμυντέα ἐστὶν αὐτῷ, *one must help him*. And so often with ταῦτα, τάδε; as ἀρχὴ οὐκ ἔστιν ταῦτα, *government is not this*. In all such cases the *generic* idea is designated by the neuter singular, and the same idea in all its compass by the neuter plural.

(b) Predicate nouns, concrete or abstract, (the names of *persons* excepted), are often of different *gender*, and sometimes of a different *number*, from that of the subject; as σοὶ ἐγὼ ἔσομαι ὄνειδος—Ἄργεος ἄκρα Πελασγοί, *the Pelasgians were the most distinguished* (lit. summits) *of Argos*. So the neuter plurals (used as nouns) τὰ πρῶτα, τὰ πάντα, τὰ φίλτατα; and so θρέμμα, κήδευμα, etc.

(c) Neuter plurals often take a verb singular; e. g. τὰ ζῶα τρέχει—δῶρα οὐκ ἔχει ὄνησιν, *gifts have no advantage*. So with participles, as δόξαν ταῦτα, *these things having seemed proper*.

But this usage has many limits; (1) Nouns denoting *persons* or *living beings* usually (not always) take the *plural*; Matt. 12: 21, ἔθνη ἐλπίουσι; τὰ δαιμόνια πιστεύουσι καὶ φρίσσουσι, James 2: 19. Mark 5: 13. Rev. 11: 18. 16: 14, al. But the *sing.* is found in Luke 4: 41. 8: 30, 38. 13: 19, al. So in the classics. (2) Where the whole compass of the subject, or the subject in all its individual particulars, is to be made emphatic, a *plural* predicate is used after neuter plur. subjects; e. g. φανερὰ ἦσαν ... ἴχνη πολλά, Xen. Anab. I. 7, 17; ἐπειδὴ ἐπῆλθον Ὀλύμπια, *when the Olympiac feasts came on*. Specially is the plural used when *numerals* belong to the subject, as ἦσαν δύο τείχη—ἐγένοντο ἑκατὸν τάλαντα. The poets (not Attic) often use the plural out of these limits; the general rule is not without many exceptions.

(d) In a few cases masc. and fem. subjects in the *plural* take a verb singular; e. g. ἔστι ἑπτὰ στάδιοι—ἦν τρεῖς κεφαλαί. But this is confined to ἐστί and ἦν when thus (as it were *impersonally*) used; comp. the French, *il est des hommes*, etc.

NOTE. Besides the discrepancies above noted, in classic Greek a dual may have a plural predicate, and *vice versâ*. So the dual δύω may have a plural noun with it; and *fem.* duals may take a masc. attributive. But these cases do not concern the N. Test. Greek, as it does not employ the dual.

§ 128. Syntax: Subject and Predicate. 207

(4) A verb which is a mere copula may conform to the subject or to the predicate.

E. g. ἡ περίοδος ... εἰσὶ στάδιοι ἕξ, the circuit is [are] six stadia; τὸ λειπόμενον γίγνονται λόγοι.

(5) There are, moreover, several peculiarities in respect to subject and predicate, which deserve to be specially noted. Such are the following:

(a) Frequently the verb goes from the singular to the plural; and vice versâ; e. g. εἴ τις ἡγεῖται... ἔχει... ἀγνοοῦσι, Xen. Mem. II. 3. 2. Vice versâ, οἱ ἰατρευόμενοι χαίρουσι... μεγάλου γὰρ κακοῦ ἀπαλλάττεται, Plat. Gorg. p. 478. In such cases the singular designates each individual of the whole mass. This is very frequent in Hebrew.

(b) Masc. predicates are sometimes joined with fem. subjects, when there is no special design to distinguish sex; e. g. ἀδελφαὶ ... καὶ τοσαῦται, ὥστε εἶναι ... τοὺς ἐλευθέρους, Xen. Mem. II. 7. 2.

(c) *The first person plural* is often employed in the same sense as the *first person singular*; specially when the plural may be naturally interpreted as including both an individual and those who are his associates; e. g. ἄρξομαι ... ἵνα πρεσβεύωμεν, Plat. Sympos. p. 186. So, often, in the N. Test.; specially in the writings of Paul, who is continually making transitions of this nature.

(d) The Imper. sing. is sometimes employed where the subject is plural; e. g. εἰπέ, τί πάσχετε; James 4: 13, ἄγε νῦν οἱ λέγοντες, also 5: 1. In such cases, the Imper. is a kind of *interjection*.

Verb or predicate with several subjects.

(6) *Several subjects of different persons* are thus arranged; the first person has precedence over the others; the second over the third; and the verb takes the plural form.

E. g. ἐγὼ καὶ σύ—or ἐγὼ καὶ ἐκεῖνος—or ἐγὼ καὶ σὺ καὶ ἐκεῖνος—γράφομεν. So ἐγὼ καὶ ἐκεῖνοι γράφομεν; σὺ καὶ ἐκεῖνος—or σὺ καὶ ἐκεῖνοι—γράφετε. So ἡμεῖς καὶ ἐκεῖνοι γράφομεν—ὑμεῖς καὶ ἐκεῖνοι γράφετε, etc.

NOTE. But sometimes the *number* of the person conforms to the *prominent* subject; sometimes to the *nearest* one; as θεοὶ κἀ γὼ ἐμηχανησάμην, Eurip. Med. 1020. Οὔτε σὺ οὔτ᾽ ἂν ἄλλος δύναιτο.

(7) Several subjects of the same person regularly demand a plural predicate; but often a singular one is employed; E. g.

(a) The verb at the *head* of a sentence, or at the *close*, conforms to the subject which is proximate; as οὐκ ἔγνω Ἰωσὴφ καὶ ἡ μήτηρ αὐτοῦ, Luke 2: 43. John 4: 12. Πένητες καὶ δῆμος πλέον ἔχει, Xen. So often in Cicero, and not unfrequently in our English version of the SS. (b) Sometimes the verb conforms to the *prominent* subject; as βασιλεὺς καὶ οἱ σὺν αὐτῷ ... εἰσπίπτει. (c) Names of *things*, of different gender, take a plural verb, when a *distinction* is intended to be marked: a singular one, when a *unity of the*

§ 129. Syntax: Verbs distiuguished.

whole is designated. If all the names are *neuter*, the verb is usually in the singular. (*d*) Subjects with ἤ ... ἤ (*or* ... *or*), also with οὔτε ... οὔτε, may take a sing. or plur. verb ; a sing. one when separation is really meant, as ἢ οὑτός ἀληθῆ λέγει; a plural one when the same predicate is in the same manner applied to both, as εἰ Ἄρης ἄρχωσι ... ἢ Φοῖβος Ἀπόλλων.

GENERAL REMARK. Few of the rules respecting the concord of the subject and predicate are uniformly observed. The rules of Greek usage in this respect are far less rigid and exact than those of the modern English language. In fact, they closely resemble the Hebrew.

SYNTAX OF VERBS.

§ 129. *Distinctions in the nature of different Verbs.*

(1) A verb signifies *action* in its most enlarged sense, either external or internal.

(2) *Ideas of space*, which arise from our sense of *motion*, seem to lie at the basis of the different classes of verbs as distinguished by their respective kinds of meaning.

E. g. (*a*) Action considered in the relation of *whither*, is designated by a *transitive* verb, which requires an object to be placed after it (either expressed or implied), which object marks the *whither* of the action, as τύπτω τὸν παῖδα. Kindred to this is the marking of the *effect* of action, e. g. γράφω τὴν ἐπιστολήν. (*b*) Action considered in the relation of *whence*, requires a verb *passive*, i. e. one the subject of which is affected by the action of another agent; e. g. τύπτομαι ὑπό τινος. (*c*) Action may be regarded in the light of *where*; and then the verb must be *intransitive*, inasmuch as the action which proceeds from the subject of the verb, terminates within the same subject; e. g. τὸ ῥόδον ἀνθεῖ — ἥδομαι (Midd.)

(3) Besides the general distinctions of transitive, intransitive, and passive, there are subordinate classes of verbs distinguished by the names, *reflexive, reciprocal,* and *causative*.

(*a*) *A reflexive verb* is one which marks an action as proceeding from an agent and returning to him again, i. e. as exercising an influence over him ; e. g. τύπτομαι (Midd.) *I beat myself;* κομίζομαι, *I procure for myself.* Here the sense is the same as if the active voice were employed with a pronoun relating to the agent in the Acc.; e. g. μέ or ἐμαυτόν ; while in many other cases, the sense is the same as that of a verb in the active voice with an Acc. of the thing and the Gen. or Dative of the person; e. g. ἀμύνομαι τοὺς πολεμίους *I keep off the soldiers from me* = ἀμύνω τ. πολ. ἐμοῦ. So κομίζομαι πολλὰ χρήματα,=κομίζω μοι πολλὰ χρήματα, *I procure much property for myself.* This kind of verb belongs to the *Middle Voice*.

(*b*) Kindred to this class of verbs are those named RECIPROCAL. These indicate reflexive action extended mutually to *two* subjects; as τύπτονται, *they beat each other* ; μάχονται, *they fight each other.*

(*c*) A peculiar species of the transitive verb is the so-named CAUSATIVE. Verbs of this class designate action upon an object which occasions that

§ 129. SYNTAX: KINDS OF VERBS.

object to exercise *intransitive* action, i. e. action upon itself; e. g ἐγείρω, *I waken*, i. e. I cause one to awake, (the *awaking* is intransitive action); ὄλλυμι, *I destroy*, i. e. I cause that one should perish; παύω, *I make one to cease*, etc. These correspond to the Hiphil conjugation of the Hebrews.

NOTE. The Greek language has not *distinct* forms for all the classes of verbs. The *active* voice designates a transitive, and often intransitive and causative sense; the *middle* voice frequently designates an intransitive, as well as reflexive sense. The passive voice has distinct forms, as to a few tenses; and so the middle voice; but in the Pres., Imperf., Perf. and Pluperf., these two voices can employ only one and the same form.

(4) It seems most probable, that originally the active voice had only a *transitive* sense, and the middle voice an *intransitive* one; but at present these forms are extended much beyond the ancient limits.

NOTE. Thus the verbs in -μι, (which retain most of all the *antique* usage), are all *transitive* in their present tenses, (εἰμί and εἶμι excepted); while the verbs in -ω (which are more recent), are both transitive and intransitive; yea, in very many cases, the same verb has both senses. Moreover the forms of the middle voice, in at least half of its tenses, are common to this voice and to the passive, while the middle was probably the more ancient voice.

(5) The lines of distinction between verbs as *transitive* and *intransitive*, in Greek, cannot be very definitely drawn from the general nature of any verb. Almost any verb whatever is capable of being employed in both senses; and each case must be determined in and by itself, whether the action is transitive or intransitive.

NOTE. This may seem strange to a mere English reader; because our vernacular is more definite in respect to the usage in question. But in Greek, nothing is more frequent than the exchange of meanings in regard to this particular. For example:

(a) *Intransitive* verbs often put on the nature (1) *Of transitive ones*; e. g. βαίνειν πόδα—νόσον νοσεῖν, etc.; see § 103. 4. (2) *Of passive ones*; e. g. ἐκπίπτω ὑπό τινος—τετελεύτηκε ὑπὸ τοῦ ἐχθροῦ. Here, in the first case (No. 1), an Acc. or *object* being supplied, the verb must of course be transitive; in the second (No. 2), the agent being supplied, it is evident that the subject of the verb is not the agent, and therefore he must be the *patient*, i. e. the verb becomes passive in its meaning. This usage of intransitive verbs in a *passive* sense is of wide extent, and deserves special notice. It is quite common in Hebrew.

(b) Transitive verbs, specially such as indicate motion, are often employed in an *intransitive* sense; e. g. ἐκβάλλειν *to spring forth;* ὑπερβάλλειν *to excel;* and κλίνειν *to decline;* and so of a multitude of others. So also in English; *I move, I turn, I change, I advance*, et al. multa, are both transitive and intransitive.

REMARK I. Two very plain principles are applicable to all these cases, viz, first, that almost any verb whatever may, in the Greek language, have an Acc. after it, and then of course it becomes *transitive*; and secondly, that most verbs may be used in an *intransitive* sense, and are so of course when no object of their action is supplied or intended. The inference of course is, in such a case, that the subject of the verb is the *object* of the action, or (in other words) that the verb is *intransitive*

REMARK II It would seem that the *Tempora Secunda* were the original tenses, which were often, and more usually, employed in the *intransitive* sense. The necessity of a *transitive* sense occasioned the formation anew of other tenses; which, for the most part, are employed in the *transitive* sense, provided the Tempora Secunda still remain in use. The latter, in such cases, more usually have an intransitive sense, e. g Aor. II. and Perf. II. active, Aor. II. passive and middle.

§ 130. *Voices, with their respective meaning.*

For the definitions of these, and the leading distinctions, the reader is referred to § 59. The substance will be here repeated very briefly, in order to facilitate an understanding of the subjects developed in the sequel.

(1) The *active* voice designates action which proceeds from the subject of the verb, and which may terminate either on a different object or upon itself; (verbs transitive, and neuter or intransitive).

E. g. τύπτω τὸν παῖδα—ἀλγέω.

(2) When the subject of the verb is represented as the *passive recipient* of the action expressed by it, the form of the verb is *passive*.

E. g. τύπτομαι, *I am beaten*, i. e. by some other person.

(3) When the subject of the verb is represented as both *agent* and *recipient*, then the verb is said to be of the middle voice.

E. g. τύπτομαι, *I beat myself*, (the latter pronoun being unnecessary in the Greek).

REMARK. It is obvious that *intransitive* active verbs, *which confine the action to the agent or subject*, are very nearly allied to verbs of the middle voice which do the same. But the middle voice more fully and of itself indicates the reflexive meaning; and moreover it is often so used as to govern nouns in a transitive way, which stand connected with it, when its design is to point out the *ultimate object* of an action; e. g. τύπτομαι, *I beat myself*; κομίζομαι χρήματα, *I acquire wealth for myself*. Here, *for myself* is implied by the form of the verb, while, in this second example, the verb also takes an Acc. after it.

§ 131. *Various meanings of the Middle Voice.*

(1) The general design is, *to mark action which terminates on the subject of the verb ; on something which belongs to this subject ; or on some object that stands nearly connected with this subject.*

§ 131. Syntax: Voices of Verbs. 211

It is evident that this last category must open a wide field for the employment of the middle voice; and such is the fact according to Greek usage.

(a) *Action terminating on the subject himself.* (1) Some verbs are *necessarily* confined to the middle form here, having no active form, or none employed in the like sense; e. g. ἥδομαι *laetor;* στέλλεσθαι *to depart,* (στέλλειν means *to send away*). Like to this last verb are a large class which are *transitive* in the active voice, and have there a different sense from the Middle, as φαίνεσθαι *to appear,* (φαίνειν *to show*); ἵστασθαι *to stand,* (ἱστάναι *to station*), etc. So it is also with some which are *intransitive* in the active voice, but *reflexive* in the Middle; as βουλεύειν τινί *to give counsel to any one,* βουλεύσασθαι *to determine for one's self.* Here also belong many so called *deponent* verbs.

(2) Sometimes the Middle is employed where the same sense might be, and usually is, indicated by the *active* voice with its attending pronoun; e. g. τύπτομαι *I beat myself,* but one might say also, τύπτω ἐμαυτόν; ἐπαινεῖται *he praises himself,* which is usually expressed by ἐπαινεῖ ἑαυτόν. If we except a few verbs, like λούομαι, κείρομαι, ἐνδύεσθαι, and the like, which have immediate respect to one's own person, almost always the *active* voice (with a pronoun) is employed to make out a *reflexive* sense, in those cases where the meaning of the verb is not essentially changed by being employed in the middle voice. It is to that class of verbs, then, that we are principally to look for examples of the middle voice, where this voice has a different meaning from the active; for then the active voice will not afford the meaning demanded.

(b) The middle voice designates *action upon something which* BELONGS TO *the subject of the verb*; e. g. νίπτομαι τοὺς πόδας, *I wash my feet,* (the Middle verb indicating this relation of πόδας to *me*); τύπτομαι τὴν κεφαλήν, *I beat my own head.* But there are also other and different shades which may be marked; e. g.

(c) It expresses *action on objects in one's possession,* or *objects which affect one's self*; e. g. παρέχεσθαί τι, *to give out of one's own property or possession;* θέσθαι νόμον, *to make a law which will include one's self,* (θεῖναι νόμον, act., would mean *to legislate for others*); ἀποδείκνυσθαι ἔργον, *to exhibit one's own doings;* ἀποφαίνεσθαι γνώμην, *to show one's own opinion;* λύεσθαί τι, *to ransom something for one's self,* (λύειν τι, merely *to ransom any thing*). Some other shades of meaning, also, may be ranked here; e. g.

(1) Here may be classed the *reciprocal* verbs, which, in order to complete their action, imply that *others must be within the sphere of the agent's influence*; e. g. verbs of contending, rivalling, conversing with, reproving, embracing, kissing, greeting, thrusting at, etc., as μάχεσθαι, ἀγωνίσεσθαι, λοιδορεῖσθαι, ὁμολογεῖσθαι, συμβολεύεσθαι, etc.

(2) Also action which must bring things within the sphere of one's own influence, or remove them out of this sphere; e. g. παρασκευάσασθαι τὰ ἐπιτήδεια, *to prepare things necessary for one's self*; ποιεῖσθαι εἰρήνην, *to make peace for one's self*; αἱρεῖσθαί τι, *to take away any thing for one's self,* etc. So, to remove out of the sphere of one's own influence; as ἀπόσασθαι κακά, *to ward off evil from one's self*; παραιτεῖσθαι κακόν, *to deprecate evil*

§ 131. Syntax: Voices of Verbs.

in respect to one's self; ἀπόδοσθαί τι, to sell any thing from one's own possession, etc.

NOTE. Verbs with a *causative* or *permissive* sense are frequent in the middle voice. They may have respect either to *one's own person*, or to *objects within his influence*. (1) His own person; as κείρασθαι, *to let one's self be shaved*; διδάξασθαι τοὺς παῖδας, *to procure teachers for one's own children*, etc. (2) Objects within one's sphere, or to be brought within it, or removed out of it; c. g. πρεσβεύομαι αὐτόν, *I employ him on an ambassy for myself*; παραγράφεσθαι νόμους, *to cause the laws to be inscribed*; ἀρέσασθαί τινα, *to cause one to be appeased*; καταδικάσεσθαί τινα, *to procure one's condemnation*; παραθέσθαι τράπεζαν, *to cause a table to be set for one's self*; γήμασθαι τὴν θυγατέρα, *to give one's daughter away in marriage*.

REMARK I. The *reflexive* meaning, (as will be seen by several examples in the note above), is often so weakened, that it is scarcely (if at all) perceivable, and may be resolved into some thing that has a bearing either more or less direct on the *advantange* or *disadvantage* of the subject or agent, or is connected with his concerns. Hence, in a few cases, even a *pronoun* is put after a verb of the middle voice, to render more emphatic the relation of the action; e. g. ἐμαυτῷ θρεψαίμην, Soph. O. T. 1143. So σεαυτὸν ὑποκηρυξάμενος, Plato. But this is not usual.

REMARK II. In a multitude of cases it is comparatively a matter of indifference whether the *active* or *middle* voice is employed, and this may depend merely on the *subjective* views of the writer; e. g. μισθὸν φέρειν *to receive a reward*, where the sentiment would be *generic*, while μισθὸν φέρεσθαι would show that the reception had particular respect to the subject of the verb. On the shade of meaning, then, which the writer means to convey, would depend the one voice or the other; and so in a multitude of cases where the general meaning would be *substantially* the same, whether the active voice was employed or the middle.

REMARK III. The older Greek employs oftentimes the middle voice to designate *intransitive* meanings, and in particular to express *the operations of our senses*, internal or external. Hence, in Homer, ἀκούει and ἀκούετο, ἰδεῖν and ἰδέσθαι, γηρεύειν and γηρεύεσθαι, et al. sim., in the like sense. Hence (as a relic of this more ancient usage) we often find, specially in respect to *intransitive* verbs and those expressive of external or internal sense, the Future middle employed as a Future active, i. e. instead of it; see § 60. 5.

REMARK IV. From this usage of employing the middle voice in an *intransitive* sense and also as a *reflexive*, originated, in all probability, the frequent employment of it in a *figurative* or *secondary* sense, as having reference (in a reflexive way) to the *internal senses*. Thus, σκοπεῖν *to see*, *speculari*, σκοπεῖσθαι *to consider*, i. e. to look at internally; ὁρίζειν *to fix bounds*, but ὁρίζεσθαι *to decide* or *determine*; σταθμᾶν *to weigh off*, σταθμᾶσθαι *to weigh* or *deliberate upon internally*, etc. Specially do verbs ending in -εύω (which designate, in the *active*, the being in such or such a state or condition), signify, in the Middle, *acting the part* or *endeavouring to act the part, of those who are in such or such a state or condition*; e. g. πολιτεύω *I am a citizen*, πολιτεύομαι *I live and act as a citizen*; πονηρεύω *I am base*, πονηρεύομαι *I behave myself basely*; ταμιεύω *I am a manager*,

§ 133. SYNTAX: VOICES OF VERBS. 213

ταμιεύομαι *I act the part of a manager*, etc. In many verbs of such a nature, the active form is gone into desuetude, and only the middle (deponent) remains; in others, both forms are employed with a difference of meaning.

REMARK V. As the *intransitive* sense is one so common to the Middle, and also is conveyed by the Active, here is room, in very many cases, for *choice*; and this may depend on euphony, more current usage, rhythm (in poetry), or the taste of the writer, etc. In some cases the distinctions are very tenuous; e. g. στρατεύειν to make war (said of the State), στρατεύεσθαι *to take the field* (said of the soldiers).

§ 132. *Peculiar Tenses of the Middle Voice.*

(1) The Pres., Imperf., Perf., Pluperf., and Paulo-post, are common to the Passive and Middle, and can be understood in their true sense only by virtue of the context, the nature of the case, etc. But,

(2) The Aorists and Futures Middle, (the same verb has only *one* Future), bear the appropriate sense of the Middle, i. e. either reflexive or intransitive, and are not usually susceptible of a *passive* sense, except in an indirect way.

NOTE 1. Still there are cases where a verb has no other Fut. but the Fut. middle; and then it may be used *passively*, or *actively*. The poets, moreover, for the sake of rhythm, not unfrequently use this Fut. instead of the passive one. But common usage demands a passive Fut. for a passive meaning.

NOTE 2. The Aorist I. Midd. is not at all employed in a *passive* sense. Usually it designates an operative and energetic meaning; while Aor. II. Middle more commonly has an *intransitive* sense. This agrees well with the usual distinction between the *Tempora Secunda* and the *Tempora Prima*.

§ 133. *Uses of the Passive Voice.*

(1) It seems prob.. '`, that the present arrangement of a full (original) passive Voice, . `ur Greek Grammars, is not in accordance with the primitive st.   `·re of the Greek language. The middle Voice seems to have b.   `·terior.

So Kühner, § 401; and he has illus.   :d confirmed his positions by many proofs. The most striking are , .n cases as the following: τύπτεται πληγὰς πολλάς, *he is beaten many stripes*; ἐσθῆσθαι ἐσθῆτα, *he is clothed with clothing*, etc. Here, when we assume a Middle sense, we can solve the regimen of the Acc. at once, because it may take an Acc. of the *thing* after it. Thus, *he suffers many stripes to beat him, he permits clothing to be put on him*, etc., would solve the enigma of a voice apparently passive still governing one of the two cases which the Act. voice governs. So φθονοῦμαι *I experience envy*, ἐπιβουλεύομαι, *I suffer plotting*, πιστεύομαι *I receive credit*, and the like. In a multitude of cases, this manner of viewing the subject will explain the apparent enigma of the syntax.

(2) Aor. I. and II. Passive seem to have stood related to each other, more anciently, as *passive* and *intransitive*. In later usage this distinction is not observed with any strictness.

Kuhner ranks Aor. II. passive as *a simple intransitive of the active voice*, formed after the model of verbs in -μι. Plainly, in many cases, this is correct; e. g. *ἐξέπληξα* (Act.) *I terrified*, *ἐξεπλάγην I feared*; *ἔφηνα I showed*, *ἐφάνην I appeared*; *ἔστησα I placed*, *ἔστην I stood*. Hence the principle laid down (§ 64. 8. N. 2.), that no Aor. II. *active* is formed, when Aor. II. passive is employed; for obviously it is then superfluous, inasmuch as the Aor. II. passive (so called) performs the part of Aor. II. act. intransitive.

NOTE. In process of time the difference between Aor. I. and II. passive seems to have been much weakened; for Aor. I. is now often found with a reflexive or intransitive meaning, and Aor. II. has often an intransitive sense which is equivalent to a *passive* one.

§ 134. *Use of Deponent Verbs.*

(1) These, having no *active* form, employ the middle and passive forms in a reflexive, intransitive, or passive sense.

NOTE. When they form an Aor. I. middle, they are called *middle deponents*; when they form Aor. I. passive, *passive deponents*.

(2) Not unfrequently the reflexive sense is so weakened in them, that they must be translated as merely *transitive*.

E. g. *δέχομαί τι—ἐργάζομαί τι—βιάζομαί τινα*, etc. Not improbably the *active* forms once existed in most or all verbs of this kind. Hence the *passive* forms of these verbs may easily be supposed to have a passive meaning; which is often the case. When they form both Aor. I. middle and Aor. I. pass., the latter of course is really passive in its meaning. The Pres., Imperf., and Fut., more seldom have a *passive* meaning, for they incline to the meaning of the middle voice.

TENSES OF VERBS.

§ 135. *Nature and design of the Tenses.*

(1) The basis of these is, *expression of the relations of time*.

(2) These relations may be divided into two kinds; (*a*) The mere relation to the present time of the speaker. (*b*) The relation to some other action or thing in time past, present, or future.

(3) In relation to present time of the speaker, things are designated as taking place *now*, or in *past time*, or in *future*. In such a case, merely the simple relation of *time* is designated without reference to other *events*; and the tenses which designate it, (Present, Aor., and Future), are therefore, when thus employed, named ABSOLUTE TENSES.

§ 135. SYNTAX: TENSES OF VERBS. 215

E. g. γράφω, ἔγραψα, γράψω, uttered simply in relation to the present time of the speaker, are in this sense called *absolute* tenses.

(4) But time may also be referred to other things or events; and one may represent any thing as taking place in the present, past, or future of those events. The tenses employed in such a case are called *relative*; and for the most part, they are tenses appropriate solely to the purpose of marking these relations.

(5) *The relative tenses* are naturally divided into three classes, to each of which belongs an appropriate manner of expression.

ILLUSTRATION. (a) If we affirm something to have been done in TIME PAST, and this time is designated as being related to something else which took place in time past, then there may naturally arise three views of the thing affirmed to have been done, viz., it was done *at the same time* when something else took place; or it was done *before* that something else took place; or it was to be done *after* that something else took place. These three relations are expressed by the Imperf., the Pluperf., and the Fut. with μέλλω; e. g. ἔγραφον τὴν ἐπιστολὴν ἐν ᾧ σὺ ἔπαιζες, *I wrote the letter while you were playing*, where the *past* is the scene of action for both predicates, but the *writing* is contemporary (*present*) with the playing. Again; ἐγεγράφειν τὴν ἐπιστολὴν ὅτε σὺ ἦλθες, *I had written the epistle when you came*, where the scene of both events is laid in the past, but the writing was completed before the coming took place. Finally, ἔμελλον γράφειν ὅτε σὺ ἦλθες, *I was about to write when you came*, where the scene is still in the past, but the writing is designated as taking place *after* the coming.

(b) In the same manner the PRESENT may become a *relative* time, by referring to *actions done* or *things existing*, during that same present time. The principal thing to be affirmed may be done *during* that same present time, or *before* it, or *after* it. E. g. γράφω τὴν ἐπιστολὴν ἐν ᾧ σὺ παίζεις, *I am writing my letter while you are playing*, where both actions are present, but the main action stands related (as to time) to a subordinate one, and so distinguishes this Present from the absolute Present, which merely expresses time without relation to another action or event. Again: γέγραφα τὴν ἐπιστολήν, *I have written the epistle*, i. e. I have completed it, viz. before the time in which I am speaking; (for the Perfect, from its very nature, is only a *relative* tense). So the *Future* relative, μέλλω γράφειν, *I am about to write, I intend to write*, i. e. I have this intention now while I am speaking.

(c) If the speaker chooses his scene of action in the FUTURE, then a principal action of that future may be done *during* some subordinate one, or *before* it, or *after* it. E. g. γράψω τὴν ἐπιστολὴν ἐν ᾧ σὺ παίξει, *I shall write while you are at play*, where relative *contemporaneous* action is palpable, while both actions are yet placed in the *future*. So ἡ ἐπιστολὴ γεγράψεται ὅταν σὺ παραγένῃ, *the letter will have been written whenever you may come*, where the main action is already *past* in respect to the subordinate one, while both are still placed in the *future* of the person who speaks. Again; μελλήσω γράφειν ὅτε ὁ πατήρ μου παραγενήσεται, *I shall write when my father shall come*, where both actions are future, but the main action is moreover future in relation to the subordinate one.

REMARKS. It appears, then, that while there are only three *absolute* tenses for past, present, and future, there are nine *relative* ones, i. e. three in respect to a point of time combined with action in the past; three in the same respect as it regards the present; and three as it regards the future.

(*a*) THE ABSOLUTE TENSES are the Present, Aor., and Future. Of these the Present and Future are also employed to mark the *relative* present and future and as well as the absolute; but the Aorist designates in itself only the *absolute* past, having no relation to other things or events, but merely expressing *past action as such*.

(*b*) THE RELATIVE TENSES, on the other hand, have, for the most part, exclusively appropriate forms; e. g. the Imperf., the Perf., and Pluperf., are all *relative merely ;* while the *Futures relative* are often made by μέλλω in combination with the Infinitive, as μέλλω γράφειν, ἔμελλον γράφειν, μελλήσω γράφειν. The whole may be rendered more perspicuous by a tabular view.

I. *Time absolute.*

Present.	Past.	Future.
γράφω	ἔγραψα	γράψω

II. *Time relative.*

Contemporaneous	γράφω	ἔγραφον	γράψω
Antecedent	γέγραφα	ἐγεγρόφειν	γεγραφὼς ἔσομαι
Future	μέλλω γράφειν	ἔμελλον γράφειν	μελλήσω γράφειν

What is meant by *contemporaneous, antecedent,* and *future*, in this tabular view, has already been explained above. These respective tenses are so named in their relation, or because of their relation, to some other action or event in the past, present, or future.

(6) As to the *primary Tenses,* i. e. the Pres., Fut., and Perfect, although they are often employed (the Perf. always) as *relative* tenses, yet *their relation is confined merely to one point,* viz. to the present time of the speaker and the action of speaking; but the *relative historical Tenses,* on the other hand, i. e. the Imperf., Pluperf., and Paulo-post Future, always presuppose some other and different action or event, either expressed or implied, to which they stand related.

NOTE. The design of this remark is to show, that all the *primary* tenses, even when *relative,* are still distinguished in their use, in one respect at least, quite plainly from the relative *historic* tenses. The distinctions as to the nature of the tenses in general, have already been noted in § 51 and § 53. Whatever else is necessary to a more particular view, will be developed in the sequel.

§ 136. *Distinctions and Use of the Tenses.*

(1) THE PRESENT. Strictly speaking, the Present designates only the moment in which the speaker is making his declaration;

§ 136. SYNTAX: TENSES OF VERBS.   217

and merely so considered, it would have a *relative* sense. But the Greeks also employ it in a much wider sense, i. e. as embracing greater or smaller periods of time. So we speak, in English, of the *present* month, year, century, etc. In this extended sense of *present*, the tense in question is very often employed.

(*a*) Proverbs, maxims, general and universal truths, what is usual, constant, invariable, etc., is commonly expressed in the present tense, by virtue of such an extended use; e. g. ὁ ἥλιος λάμπει—ὁ ἄνθρωπός ἐστι θνητός—ἀπ᾽ ὄρους νεφέλη ἔρχεται, etc.

(*b*) In narration, past events are frequently spoken of as if they were *present* before the view of the speaker, in which case the *present* tense is of course employed. This is found every where among the Greek historians, and is very frequent in the N. Test.; e. g. John 1:29, 'John βλέπει seeth Jesus coming to him, καὶ λέγει.' 1:44. [Nathaniel] εὑρίσκει . . . καὶ λέγει; and the like every where, but specially in John's Gospel, and in the Apocalypse.

NOTE. In such cases writers take the liberty of employing interchangeably the Pres. and Praeterite forms even in the same sentence; see in Mark 2:4. 4:38. 5:15. Luke 23:12. John 1:42, 43, 44. 5:14. 4:29. 18:28, et al. saepe. So in the Classics; see Winer 41. 2. *b*.

(*c*) ThePresent is sometimes employed for the Future; specially (1) Where the mere *futurity* of the action is not intended to be made particularly prominent; e. g. Matt. 26:2, 'Ye know that after two days γίνεται is the passover, and the Son of Man παραδίδοται, is betrayed, in order that he may be crucified.' John 14:3, 'If I go away, πάλιν ἔρχομαι.' Matt.17:11. Luke 12:54. See examples from the Classics in abundance, Kuhner § 437. *a*. (2) But particularly, where *certainty* of action is intended to be designated, *the Present may be used for the Future.* This might be applied to the cases above; and it is founded, indeed, in the nature of things. If that which is in reality *future*, is announced as now *present*, this speaks loudly for the assumed certainty of the thing. So the heathen oracles often employed the Present, in order to announce prediction. The Heb. Present participle is used in cases without number as a future in *-rus* in Latin. So in John 4:21, 23, ἔρχεται ὥρα, designating the proximate and certain future. The like is often found.

(*d*) Inasmuch as the Present denotes *unfinished* action, it is sometimes employed in the sense of *design, purpose, intention* to do a thing, or the *effort* to do it; e. g. 'My dishonoured house you are destroying . . . παῖδά τ᾽ ἀποκτείνεις, and *you are intending* or *endeavoring to kill my child*, Odyss. π. 431. Ἐγὼ ἔριν λύουσα (Pres. Part.) ἔπεισα . . . παῖδα, *I designing to end the strife*, or rather, *endeavoring to end the strife, have persuaded*, etc., Eurip. Phoen. 81.

NOTE. As a peculiar Present, may be noted the use of this tense when it involves along with it something of the past which still continues; e. g. John 8:58, 'Before Abraham was, ἐγὼ εἰμί, *I am*,' i. e. I was and still am. Comp. Jer. 1:5 (Sept.). John 15:27. Acts 25:11. John 8:14, ἔρχομαι.

(2) THE IMPERFECT. (I.) The stand-point of this tense is in the

§ 136. Syntax: Tenses of Verbs.

past, primarily denoting *unfinished action*, or *action which is going on while something else is being done*.

Illustration. The Imperfect stands related to some point in *past* time, as the relative Present does to the *present* moment. Both signify *action going on and unfinished;* both have reference to something else which is taking or has taken place; but the Imperf. refers to the past, and the Present to the moment of speaking. E. g. *ἔγραφον τὴν ἐπιστολὴν ἐν ᾧ σὺ ἔπαιζες, I wrote the letter while you were playing.* But the subordinate clause may also have a Pluperfect or an Aorist in it in such cases, as well as the Imperf.; e. g. *ὅτε ἐπελήλιθησαν* or *ἐπῆλθον* or *ἤρχοντο, οἱ Ἕλληνες ἐμάχοντο.* See in Luke 14: 17. 24: 32. 6: 19. John 5: 16. 12: 6, al. saep.

(II.) From this *leading* use of the Imperf. naturally flow several other kindred uses, which must here be particularized.

(*a*) *It designates continued and repeated action in past time;* but still it is mostly action related, in respect to time, to some other predicate. This is its principal use in the N. Test.; e. g. John 3: 22, 'There Jesus *διέτριβε μετ᾿ αὐτῶν καὶ ἐβάπτιζε,*' denoting continued habitual action. So in cases almost without number; e. g. Rom. 15: 22. 1 Cor. 10: 4. 13: 11. Acts 13: 11. Matt. 13: 34. Luke 8: 31, 41. 17: 28, al. saep.

Note. The Aorist also denotes *often repeated* action in the past. Kuhner says that the Imperf. is distinguished from it by *always* having a relation to another predicate in the past time, while the Aorist is absolute and simply expresses repetition. In most cases this is true; but in some it would be very difficult to make this out with definite and satisfactory evidence. In fact, this seems to be a point in which the Aorist and Imperf., plainly as they differ from each other for the most part, come very near if not entirely together and are hardly to be distinguished; e. g. examine the use of the Aor. in such cases as these, viz. ὁ *Σωκράτης ἐδίδαξε ἀμίσθι—οἱ Πέρσαι ἐπολέμησαν τροθύμως*—where the *habit* of teaching and making war are plainly signified. See James 1: 11, 24. Eph. 5: 29.

(*b*) From the general nature of the Imperf. it is adapted to designate *action commenced but not completed*, and often, as we might suppose, it is employed in this way; e. g. Matt. 3: 14, ὁ *δὲ Ἰωάννης διεκώλυεν αὐτόν, forbade him,* i. e. at first, but afterwards he yielded. So *ἐβουλόμην, I would,* i. e. if it could have been so; so Rom. 9: 3, *ηὐχόμην, I wished,* i. e. if it could have been so; and in like manner Eurip. Iph. T. 26, '*Coming to Aulis . . . ἐκαινύμην ξίφει, I was killing,* i. e. I was preparing to kill him, but Diana stole away the sword.' See Kuhner, § 438. 4.

Note. The use of the Imperf. in hypothetical or conditional sentences, where it implies a *negative*, stands closely allied to the shade of meaning in *b*; e. g. *εἰ τοῦτο λέγεις, ἡμάρτανες ἄν, if you should say so, then you would err,* where the implication is: You do not say so, and therefore do not err.

(*c*) The Imperfect sometimes includes the Present with it; e. g. *οὐκ ἄρα ἀγαθὸς ... Περικλῆς ἦν ἐκ τούτου τοῦ λόγου,* 'then Pericles *was* [and *is*] not good.for this reason,' Plat. Gorg. p. 516. See examples in Kuhner, § 438. 4.

(*d*) In a narration of the past, the Imperf. is often exchanged with the Aorist, although it still retains its own appropriate meaning; see Luke 8: 23. James 2: 22, and also No. 5. *b*. 1, in the sequel here.

§ 136. Syntax: Tenses of Verbs. 219

(3) THE PERFECT. This expresses an *action done or completed before the time present of the speaker*. Specially is it employed, when the consequences of that action are intended to be represented as continuing or abiding.

NOTE 1. It matters not whether the action is in fact just completed, or was done long ago. The speaker, who uses the Perfect, means merely to declare completion antecedent to the present moment in which he is speaking.

NOTE 2. The Greeks in general did not make frequent use of this form, specially in narration, (Herodotus is an exception), but more usually presented a picture of the past under the *Aorist* form, as this tense is the more current and less embarrassed with any special relations. Yet in *two* cases the Perfect has always maintained a predominant place; viz.

(*a*) When a relation to the present time was to be marked as emphatic and important, then of course this tense *must* be employed, as neither the Aorist nor any other tense beside the Perfect would mark this in such a manner.

(*b*) When not only the previous happening of an event, but also its *enduring and present effects* are designed to be marked; e. g. Luke 4: 6, ἐμοὶ παραδίδοται [ἡ ἐξουσία], *to me has been* [*and still is*] *committed*, etc. Luke 5: 32, οὐκ ἐλήλυθα καλέσαι δικαίους, *I have not come* [*and am not here*] *to call*, etc. Gal. 2: 7, πεπίστευμαι τὸ εὐαγγέλιον. *I have been* [*and am*] *entrusted with the gospel.* See also Acts 8: 14. Mark 10: 40. 11: 21. 16: 4. John 12: 7. 13: 12. Rom. 3: 21. 5: 2, al. saepe. The same in the Classics; see Kühner, § 439. *b*. Winer, § 41. 4.

NOTE. In Rev. 5: 7, εἴληφε seems to be merely *aoristic* in its meaning. See also 2 Cor. 21: 25. Heb. 11: 28. Vide Winer, § 41. 4. Occasionally the same in the classics, specially the later ones; see Winer ibid.

(*c*) In several verbs, the Perfect is employed so as to supply the place of the Present; e. g. κέκτημαι, οἶδα, ἕστηκα, κέκριγα, ἑώρακα, δέδοικα, τέθνηκα, τεθαύμακα, βέβηκα, εἴωθα, and others; see Kühner, § 439. Anm. 2. The ground of this is plain; e. g. 'I have acquired and do possess; I have known and still know; I have taken my stand and remain; I have cried and still cry; etc.' When thus employed as a Present tense, these Perfects may denote habitual and repeated action, as ἀργυρότοξ, ὃς Χρύσην ἀμφιβέβηκας, Il. α. 37.

(*d*) The Future is sometimes *energically* designated by the Perfect; e. g. 'If he shall fall, τέθνηκα ἐγώ, *I am dead*,' i. e. I shall be dead as soon as the fall happens, Soph. Elect. 690. Rom. 14: 23, 'If he eat, κατακέκριται, *he has been condemned*,' i. e. so soon as the eating takes place the act of condemnation is already passed. So in John 14: 7. The *energic* nature of the declarations here is plain. Especially is the Imper. Passive Perfect, 3d person employed in this way with great force; e. g. πεπειράσθω, *let trial have been made*, i. e. make and complete it forthwith; τετάχθω, *let the arrangement have been made*, i. e. complete it forthwith.

(4) THE PLUPERFECT. This marks *action completed antece-*

dent to a period in past time; just as the Perfect marks it as antecedent to the present time.

E. g. *ἐγεγράφειν τὴν ἐπιστολήν, ἐπεὶ ὁ πατὴρ ἦλθε*. The clause denoting the period of past time may have a verb in the Imperfect, Aorist, or Pluperfect.

NOTE 1. The same laws regulate the use of this tense in reference to the *past* time, as regulate the Perfect in reference to the *present* time. The Pluperfect is used to mark the relation when it is *emphatic*, or to designate an action *which was permanent in its consequences.*

NOTE 2. When the Perfect has the sense of the Present, the Pluperfect of course has the sense of the Imperfect.

(5) THE AORIST. This designates action simply as past, without relation to any other event in the past or present.

E. g. *ἔγραψα τὴν ἐπιστολήν*, I wrote the letter, no matter how long ago, or how recently. From the nature of the Aorist, it follows, of course, that it is the appropiate tense;

(a) For designating the momentary past, i. e. the mere happening of an event, without reference to its duration.

(b) The Aorist is also the usual tense in narration; but it is often exchanged with other praeterite tenses, (although it is generally in itself neither equivalent to them, nor they to it), for the sake of variety and of animated description. E. g.

(1) *With the Imperfect.* There are two ways of narrating; the one is simple description or narration, the other portrays or as it were paints; the first merely announces that such or such a thing took place, the other holds it up before you and lets you see it in progress. The Aorist performs the first office, the Imperfect (denoting *continued* action) the last. The interchange of these in narration makes a pleasing variety of light and shade. E. g. Cyrop. I. 4. 1, *τοιαῦτα μὲν δὴ πολλὰ ἐλάλει ὁ Κῦρος· τέλος δὲ ἡ μὲν μητὴρ ἀπῆλθε, Κῦρος δὲ κατέμενε, καὶ αὐτοῦ ἐτρέφετο, many such things, moreover, did Cyrus say* [Imperf. *ἐλάλει*, said at one time and another]; *at last his mother went away* [*ἀπῆλθε*, Aor. momentary action, not repeated or continued], *but Cyrus remained* [*κατέμενε*, Impeif. continued to stay], *and there was he brought up*, [*ἐτρέφετο*, continued action]. It is by such an exchange of tenses in narration, that appropriate action in each case can be distinctly and vividly marked.

NOTE. It matters not whether, in all cases, the actions, etc., marked by the predicate, are of such a nature as in themselves to justify the use of the Imperf. or of the Aorist. It is enough that *the writer means* to present them in the respective light in which he places them, by employing these respective tenses.

(2) *The Aorist is exchanged with the historical Present.* This Present describes *continued* action; therefore, when the writer employs the *historical* Present, he presents the passing scene before the eye, as if he himself were present to behold it. In this way the vivacity of narration is greatly heightened. E. g. [*Ἕλληνες*] *ἀναλαμβάνουσι τὰ ὅπλα, καὶ οἱ Συρακούσιοι*

§ 136. SYNTAX: TENSES OF VERBS.   221

αἰσθάνονται καὶ ἐπαιώνισαν, [The Greeks] *resume their arms, and the Syracusans perceive it, and they raised a shout.* In this way, the Aorist and Present are often commingled in the same sentence. Yet the shade of meaning in each is in fact separate, and is designed to be so.

(3) *The Aorist is exchanged with the Perfect and Pluperfect.* Either of these tenses denotes *action which is past*; but the Perfect and Pluperfect usually denote *continued* consequences and influences, the first as to what was previous to the present time, the second as to what was previous to some point in past time.

NOTE. But here some latitude must be given to the use of the Aorist. E. g. John 18: 24, 'Annas ἀπέστειλεν αὐτόν κ. τ. λ, had sent him, etc.' Matt. 14: 3, 4, ἔδησεν ... ἔθετο *had bound ... had put.* Acts 1: 2, οὓς ἐξελέξατο, *whom he had chosen.* 9: 35. John 4: 45, 46. 11: 30. 13: 12. 19: 23. Luke 19: 15. 24: 1, al. saepe. In cases like these we must translate by the Pluperfect. Yet, even here, it may be supposed that the writer himself regarded the facts in question in an absolute way, and so employed the Aorist, although we naturally construe them as being *relative*, and thus substitute the Pluperfect. So Winer, in § 41. 5. So also, in respect to the Aorist for the Perfect, Winer interprets ἐπεχείρησαν in Luke 1: 1; ἐποίησας in Luke 2: 48; ἠγόρασα in Luke 14: 18, 19; ἔλαβον in Phil. 3: 12; ἐδόξασα ... ἐτελείωσα in John 17: 4, et al. simil. But this seems to be somewhat like straining the matter, and cooping up the Aorist too rigidly within technical theory. That all the tenses are occasionally employed with some latitude of usage, seems undeniable to an observing reader.

(c) *Action frequently repeated or customary,* in times past, is also designated not unfrequently by the Aorist.

In respect to the difference between the Imperf. (which designates *continued* action in time past) and the Aorist, see above No. 2. II. *a*. Note. An overwhelming mass of examples as to the Aorist, with this sense, may be found in Kuhner, § 442. 1. But Winer (§ 41. 5. 6. 1) seems disposed to doubt this usage in the N. Testament. What then can we fairly make of ἀνέτειλεν ... ἐξήρανε, in James 1: 11 ? Or of the like in 1 Pet. 1: 24? See also James 1: 24. But we may go almost any where into narrative and find examples which nothing but a strained construction can exempt from the meaning in question ; e. g. I open my N. Test. at John IV. and at v. 12 we find ἔπιε (Aor II.), which surely does not mean one act ; v. 20, προσεκύνησαν certainly means *habit of worshipping,* and so elsewhere. I see no room for doubt here, moreover, inasmuch as the classical usage of this kind is so common.

NOTE. Kindred to this usage is that of employing the Aorist in *comparisons*. The object in comparison is to render plainer something which is apparently obscure, by introducing a like thing which is already plain by reason of *frequent* and *familiar repetition* or occurrence. Hence, together with the Pres. and Fut., the Aorist is also introduced by the Greek into comparisons. See Il. γ. 33—36; also π. 436. Kühner § 442. 2.

(d) *The Aorist is sometimes employed in respect to the Future,* in order to denote the certainty that an event will take place. E. g. Rev. 10 : 7, 'When the angel *shall* sound the trumpet, καὶ ἐτελέσθη τὸ μυστήριον τοῦ θεοῦ, lit. *then has the mytsery of God been completed,* i. e. forthwith and surely it will be comple-

§ 136. SYNTAX: TENSES OF VERBS.

ted. So Eurip. Med. 78, 'If we must add the endurance of a new evil to the old one, *ἀπωλόμεσθ' ἄρ'*, *we have been undone*,' i. e. we shall forthwith be ruined. See a mass of examples in Kuhner, § 443. 2.

GENERAL REMARKS (*a*) The Aorist is often employed, both in the principal and subordinate parts of sentences, where the Imperfect, Perf, or Pluperf, might have been used; i e. it is employed when no special emphasis is intended to be laid on the *continuance* of an action (Impert), or on its *abiding consequences* in respect to time present (Perfect), or in regard to a point in time past (Pluperf.). So Kuhner acknowledges, § 444, and so every attentive reader must acknowledge, who can easily find examples of no unfrequent occurrence

(*b*) The reader will of course understand, that Aor. I. and II are both included in all of the preceding principles, as there is no difference between them in any of the respects which have been the subject of remark.

(6) THE AORIST IN THE DERIVED MODES, i. e. in the Opt., Subj., Imper., and Infinitive. Here the nature of the case makes some difference, and requires some distinction of usage. Facts correspond ; for,

(*a*) In part, the Aorist in these four derived modes designates action simply past or finished; in like manner as in the Indicative. But,

(*b*) More generally, mere [momentary] action, without any reference to the relation of time or the length of time, is designated by the Aorist in these modes; so that this tense is not within any strict limit of time but truly *aoristic.*

Examples of this may be found on all sides, where the Aor. Subj., Inf., etc., takes its hue as to *time* merely from the context, not from the nominal nature of the tense as here employed. *In general, when continued action is intended, the Present tense of these modes is employed; but where mere action, simply considered, is to be designated, the Aorist is the appropriate tense, in the derived modes.* Even such verbs as *wishing, asking, commanding,* etc., which naturally claim a future sense after them, may take an Inf. Fut., Pres., or Aor., just as the writer designs to convey the idea of a future relation, or of continued action, or merely an idea of action simply considered without reference to time or frequency.

(7) THE FUTURE sustains, as we have seen (§129. 5), a twofold relation, *absolute* and *relative*. The absolute Future merely signifies that something will take place; the relative, that it will take place while something else is done.

E. g. *γράψω, I will write—when*, or *where*, is not said; Fut. relative, *γράψω ἐν ᾧ σὺ παιξεῖ, I will write while you are at play.* The same form is here used in both cases. Yet most of the relative Futures are made by *μέλλω* and the Infinitive mode. See in § 129. 5. The future relative is of course limited to a definite time; not so with the Fut. absolute, for,

(*a*) It *often designates repeated action* in future time. It does this in the same manner, with respect to the future, as the Aorist does in respect to the past, see No 5, 3. c. above. E. g. *αὐτὸς ἐλέησει, he will be compassionate; οὗτοι εὐεργετήσουσι, these will be beneficent;* et al. saepe.

(*b*) The Future often expresses *obligation, necessity, duty,* and may be translated by the auxiliaries, *may, must, ought, can,* etc. E. g. Luke 3: 10,

§ 136. Syntax: Tenses of Verbs. 223

τί οὖν ποιήσομεν; *What now must we do?* Rom. 10 : 14, πῶς οὖν ἐπικαλέσονται; *how shall they call upon him*, etc. In *questions* this is a predominant sense. But in *commands* it is equally so ; e. g. οὐ φονεύσεις, *thou must not kill*; so οὐ μοιχεύσεις, οὐ ἐπιορκήσεις· ὑποδώσεις τῷ κυρίῳ τοὺς ὅρκους σου, al. saepe.

(c) The relative Future with μέλλω and the Inf. mode, is employed in reference either to the present, or to a point of time past, or future ; e. g. μέλλω γράφειν, *I am intending to write immediately;* ἤμελλον γράφειν, *I was going to write*, viz. ὅτε ὁ ἑταῖρος παρῆλθε, i. e. *when a friend came in;* μελλήσω γράφειν ὅταν ὁ ἑταῖρος παραγένηται, etc.

Note. In the classics, the Fut. is often employed as a softened and polished mode of expression for indicating *present* intention, etc. E. g. βουλήσομαι, *volo*, i. e. si licet ; so ἐθελήσω, προθυμήσομαι, etc.

General Remarks. The Future is not rigidly confined to the rules here developed. In Rev 4 · 9, δώσουσι . πεσοῦνται extend to habitual *action*, viz. which was, is, and will be, (like the Hebrew Future) , Luke 1 · 37, ἀδυνατήσει has a like sense. Kindred to this is the use of the Future in supposed cases that may at any time occur , e g James 2 10, ὅστις ὅλον τὸν νόμον τηρήσει, πταίσει δὲ ἐν ἑνί, and so in the formulas, ἐρεῖ τις or ἐρεῖς οὖν 1 Cor. 15 35 Rom. 9. 19. Like to this is Luke 11 5, τίς . ἕξει καὶ πορεύσεται ,

N B In the active and middle voices there is but *one* Future, (either Fut 1. or II. as the nature of the verb may be) , and in the Passive, where are two Futures, there is no difference between them as to the relations of time.

(8) The Paulo-post Future or Futurum Exactum. This has a double relation ; (1) To the Present of the speaker, inasmuch as what it designates is future in respect to that Present. (2) To another event in the Future, in regard to which it designates what is past.

E. g. 'If such a guardian shall watch over it, the republic τελέως κεκοσμήσεται, *will have been perfectly arranged*,' Plat. Repub. vi. p. 506. This form is unusual in the N. Testament.

Note 1. For this tense is frequently substituted a participle with the verb εἶναι; e. g. ἐσόμεθα ἐγνωκότες, *we shall have known*. The Paulo-post Fut. is formed from the Perf. passive, and is compounded, therefore, of a past and a future.

Note 2. By Attic usage, the Paulo Post Fut. has, in several verbs, the sense of the Fut. passive simply. But this is mostly where the Perfect of those verbs is used in the sense of the Present tense.

Note 3. Immediate accomplishment, without delay after the action has taken place to which this Fut. relates, is often signified by it ; e. g. φράζε, καὶ πεπράξεται, *speak, and it will have been done*, i. e. it will be forthwith done.

General Remarks on all the Tenses. By far the greater part of the instances in which they are employed, exhibits the *regular* and *normal* use, in accordance with the general principles respecting them. But cases occur, not unfrequently, as the preceding account of usage fully shows, in which all the tenses are employed (so to speak) *tropically*, i. e. out of their customary meaning. In these cases, (which are as natural as the use of *words* in a tropical sense), the reader generally finds but little embarrassment; inasmuch as the context nearly always supplies him with the means of interpretation. But it is highly important that he should know the facts respecting *tropical* usage (sit venia verbo), and within what limits they are comprised; and also that the student should understand the ground or reason of this usage. Otherwise, he will be prone to make all manner of conjectures, and talk at large about *enallage* of the tenses (as many of the older critics have done), or devise crude and offensive theories which can never be supported. It were easy to verify all this, by pointing to examples. But the task would be invidious. Then, and only then, can the considerate philologist feel safe, when he knows that his interpretation is conformed to the *usus loquendi.* That allows a *tropical* use of the tenses; and this being conceded, the only question then is: Within what limits? The preceding rules are designed to answer this question.

To say simply, that *one tense is used for another*, is not saying much to the purpose; less still is it to the credit of the writer. But to show that there is some common ground which different tenses may occupy, some in their *ordinary* and some in a *tropical* sense, is doing what may give satisfaction to the mind of an intelligent reader.

MODES OF VERBS.

§ 137. *General principles in respect to Modes.*

(1) We may contemplate events in three different ways, viz. as *actual*, as *possible* or *conditional*, or as *desirable*. On these three different methods of regarding them are founded the *modes* of representing action.

(2) The Indic. mode designates events regarded as *actual;* the Subj. and Optative as *possible* or *conditional*, and sometimes as *desirable* in reference to some conditionality; the Imper. expresses simple *desire* in the shape of command.

(3) The possible, conditional, or desirable, which is expressed by the *Conjunctive* (generically so named), may be divided into two kinds, viz. that which respects the *present* or *future*, and that which respects the *past*. The first of these is designated by the Subjunctive mode, the last by the Optative.

Explanation. Inasmuch as possibility or conditionality, which respects the present or future, may be realized by events that will happen, the Subj., which expresses these, approaches nearer to the Indic. than the Optative. This is the distinguishing trait of the Subjunctive, viz. *possibility that something may be realized.* On the other hand; as the Opt. expresses possibility or conditionality in respect to *past* events, and these having once taken place cannot occur so as to be realized, the office of the Optative is mainly to designate *mere supposition* or *assumption,* without the conjoint idea of looking for or expecting realization.

NOTE. An action in itself conditional may still be regarded by the speaker as *something which will never take place.* The Greek has forms to

§ 138. SYNTAX: MODES OF VERBS. 225

express such peculiar conditionality, and at the same time to signify the judgment or opinion of the speaker as to the event; and these forms are the relative tenses, viz. the Imperf. and Pluperf., and the Aorists. These, which are usually accompanied with appropriate particles of conditionality, designate the opinion of the speaker that the conditional action or event will not take place; e. g. εἰ τοῦτο ἔλεγες, ἡμάρτανες ἄν, *if you should say this, you would commit an error*, in which the direct implication is: 'You have not said it, [as I believe], and so you have not committed an error.'

MODES IN INDEPENDENT SENTENCES.

§ 138. *Indicative mode Independent.*

(1) This affirms or declares whatever is regarded as matter of fact.

E. g. τὸ ῥόδον ἀνθεῖ—ἀνθήσει—ἤνθησε. So in εἰ τοῦτο λέγεις, ἁμαρτάνεις, although the fact of speaking is not asserted, yet it is assumed as a fact in order to make a deduction from it, viz., ἁμαρτάνεις. So the *erring* is not directly asserted here as a matter of fact, but it is assumed as a matter of fact on the like ground with the assumption in λέγεις. The sentiment may be thus expressed in other words; 'Assuming as a fact that you have said this, it follows that you have erred.'

(2) The Future Indicative would seem, at first, to be inconsistent with the nature of this mode, which asserts what is already regarded as a reality. Yet the Fut. Indic. is designed to indicate what is assumed, or what, it is believed, will certainly become a matter of fact.

A future *certainty* comes naturally to be regarded as a reality; and so, the Indic. Fut. may express this idea. As kindred to this, the classic writers frequently make use of the Future as a kind of moderate or courteous Imperative; e. g. τούτου φείσεσθε, *ye will spare this person*, i. e. I expect or wish or desire you to spare him, with the confident expectation that this will be done. This adds a shade to the colouring of the diction, which the proper Imper. is not competent to furnish.

(3) The Indic. Imperfect is used frequently in a moderated or conditional sense, in cases where the English idiom employs a *potential* mode.

NOTE 1. Usually this method of employing the Imperf. requires ἄν; but ἄν is omitted in those cases where the apodosis is not actually dependent on the protasis; e. g. καλὸν ἦν αὐτῷ εἰ οὐκ ἐγεννήθη, Mark 14: 21, lit. *it was good*, etc. So 2 Pet. 2: 21. 2 Cor. 12: 11. Matt. 25: 27. So in Gal. 4: 20, ἤθελον δὲ παρεῖναι πρὸς ὑμᾶς ἄρτι, καὶ ἀλλάξαι τὴν φωνήν μου, *I would be present with you*, etc., i. e. did circumstances permit, I would, etc. The implication of course is, that circumstances do *not* permit; and still more also, viz. that the desire remains unchanged. So in Acts 25: 22, ἐβουλό-

29

§ 138. Syntax: Modes of Verbs.

μὴν καὶ αὐτὸς τοῦ ἀνθρώπου ὀκοῦσαι, *I could wish myself to hear the man*, i. e. if circumstances permitted. Here the speaker does not mean to say merely, that he was once desirous to hear him, but now was not desirous; nor that he *might* now hear him, but still he would not, (which would be ἐβουλόμην ἄν); but to express a desire to hear him which circumstances only (and not his own inclination) prevented. And so, in that much controverted passage in Rom. 9:3, ηὐχόμην γὰρ αὐτὸς ἐγὼ ἀνάθημα εἶναι ἀπὸ τοῦ Χριστοῦ, etc., *I could wish*, etc. i. e. 'Were it possible that I might be an ἀνάθημα in the room of my brethren, I would be so; but it is not possible.' To substitute ηὐχόμην ἄν or εὐχοίμην ἄν here, as some have proposed to do, would destroy the present meaning, inasmuch as it would make the apostle say: 'I might wish to become an *anathema*, or I might be one, but I will not.'

NOTE 2. The importance of this principle in the Greek idiom, is fully manifest from the controversies which have arisen about passages which exhibit the kind of usage now under consideration, particularly Rom. 9:3. But it is now well established among grammarians, that specially verbs which signify *necessity, inclination, duty, propriety, possibility, liberty*, etc., omit ἄν in all those cases where the writer does not mean to represent the necessity, propriety, desire, etc., as conditionally dependent on the meaning of the adjunct clause (expressed or implied) which is connected with them. So χρῆν, ἔδει, ὤφελον, καλὸν ἦν, ἐξῆν, ἔμελλες, ἐβουλόμην, εἰκὸς ἦν, προσῆκε (Acts 22:22), and the like, very often omit ἄν, and by omitting it make the Imperfect (and sometimes the other historic tenses) to say, that such or such a thing was or is proper, becoming, desirable, etc. unconditionally; for ἄν would imply that it was so only in case some implied or expressed condition was fulfilled. It must still be understood, that the Greek writer did not mean to make the expressions in question *entirely* absolute, i. e. to dissever them from all conditions expressed or implied, but only to express the necessity, propriety, desirableness, etc., in terms apparently absolute, *for the sake of giving intensity to his expression*. Plainly such is the effect; e. g. καλὸν ἦν αὐτῷ εἰ οὐκ ἐγεννήθη, where the form of the expression (καλὸν ἦν) seemingly does not allow the κυλόν to depend on the εἰ οὐκ ἐγεννήθη as an indispensable condition. Had the latter been meant, ἄν must have been added to the ἦν in order to point out such a conditionality. Yet the *connection* of καλόν with εἰ οὐκ ἐγεννήθη must not be regarded as superseded; the καλὸν ἦν, (and so of all other like expressions in similar belongs only to an *energetic* or *intense* mode of declaration.

NOTE 3. Very often, in such expressions, the *protasis* is omitted; e. g. ἐξῆν ταῦτα ποιεῖν—καλῶς εἶχε ἡ παραμυθία—ἄξιον ἦν ἀκοῦσαι; i. e. *it might be lawful to do those things; consolation might be well; it might be proper to hear;* for so we must translate, although this does not reach the exact manner of the Greek. In Latin: *Licebat—bene erat—proprium erat*. Such is the case, in regard to several instances in Note 2.

NOTE 4. To all the above methods of expression ἄν might be, and often is, added; which then, of course, receive a modification, the apodosis being evidently made to depend on the happening or not happening of a condition designated by a protasis either expressed or implied.

NOTE 5. In all such conditional imperfects, (conditional in *fact*, but not

§ 139. SYNTAX: MODES OF VERBS. 227

fully in manner), *there is an implication of course of a negative nature as to the happening of the condition.* When, on the other hand, the idea is meant to be expressed, that the thing in question may happen, the Present is used; e. g. χρή, δεῖ, προσήκει, καλῶς ἔχει, etc. See on this whole subject, Winer § 42. 2; but more especially Kuhner, § 821.

§ 139. *Subjunctive Mode Independent.*

(1) Strictly speaking, this can never be independent; for the Subj. as its very name imports, is connected with some predicate which goes before it; yet, as the preceding clause is often omitted, (in some cases nearly always), the Subjunctive is spoken of by grammarians as standing in independent sentences.

The Subj. represents a predicate as related either to an act of conception in the mind of the speaker, or to the development of some mental conception; e. g. οὐκ οἶδα τί εἴπω, or λέγε τί εἴπω, *I know not what I can say—tell me what I may say.* But the protasis in such cases is often omitted, and then, as to *form* or *appearance*, the Subj. is placed in an independent sentence.

(2) The 1st pers. sing. and plural of the Subj., is employed in a *hortatory* sense, i. e. as expressing *desire, warning, requisition,* etc.

E. g. In the first person plural, as John 14: 31, ἄγωμεν ἐντεῦθεν, *let us go hence;* 1 Cor. 15: 32, φάγωμεν καὶ πίωμεν. So John 19: 24. Phil. 3: 15. 1 Thess. 5: 6, and often in the N. Test. and the Classics. So in the first person sing.; as φέρε, ἴδω, *come, let me see;* ἄγε δή, πειραθῶ, *come now, let me try.* In all such cases it is easy to see, that the expression is equivalent to 'I desire that we may go;' 'I wish that I may try,' etc.; and of course the predicate (Subj.) refers to a state of mind then existing in the speaker when he is supposed to utter the words.

NOTE. In the *second* and *third* persons the Optative is employed to express *hortatory* ideas; which are thus exhibited in the form of a *wish;* e. g. δοίη κράτος μέγα! *may he impart much strength!*

(3) The Subjunctive, in *all* its persons, is employed to express questions or doubts of mind in respect to future action; and it is then called the *Subjunctive deliberative.*

E. g. Mark 12: 14, δῶμεν ἢ μὴ δῶμεν; *shall we give, or shall we refuse to give?* τί δράσω; *what shall I do?* And so in indirect speech; as οὐκ οἶδα, πότερον εἴπωμεν ἢ σίγωμεν. So Luke 9: 54, θέλεις εἴπωμεν πῦρ κ. τ. λ. Often in the Classics with βούλει, as βούλει οὖν ... θῶμεν, etc., Plato; and so in other indirect speech of the like tenor. The adverbial ἄν is frequently added to the Subj. here.

NOTE 1. But when deliberation or doubt in *past* time is to be expressed, the *Optative* is employed instead of the Subjunctive; e. g. Il. α. 189 seq. 'He doubted ... ἠὲ χόλον παύσειεν ἐρητύσειέ τε θυμόν, *or restrain his rage and check his indignation.*'

NOTE 2. The Indic. Fut., (which is nearly allied to the Subj.), is also not unfrequently employed in questions; e. g. τί δράσομεν; This is common to the N. Test. and the Classics; but it is not very frequent.

§ 140. *The Optative Independent.*

I. *Without* ἄν.

(1) The same is true of the Optative as of the Subj. (§ 133. 1), i. e. it is in reality always *dependent;* but often it appears alone, or only with ἄν, and then it is named *independent*.

(2) The Optative in its primary meaning simply expresses *supposition,* or *an idea conceived in the mind without reference to its realization.* But many shades of particular meaning are deduced from this general and leading signification.

E. g. εἴη νῦν ... ἐδωδή, *let it be now that we have food,* etc., i. e. supposing this to be the case. Plat. Phaed. p. 87, 'The soul having perished, the body immediately ἐπιδεικνύοι *would show* its weakness, and quickly wasting away διοίχοιτο *would vanish.*'

(3) The expression of *wish* or *desire* is peculiarly appropriate to the Optative.

E. g. Acts 1:20, 'His bishopric λάβοι ἕτερος, *may another one take!* Acts 8:20, ' May thy money εἴη σοι εἰς ἀπώλειαν, *be for destruction to thee!*' Rom. 15: 5. 2 Tim. 2: 7. 4: 14. So μὴ γένοιτο! et al. saep.

NOTE 1. When a *negative* is expressed, μή is employed.

NOTE 2. When the speaker is fully persuaded that his wish cannot be accomplished, he employs *the historic tenses of the Indic.,* with the particles of wishing, as εἴθε, etc.; e. g. εἴθε τοῦτο ἐγένετο! *I wish this might take place,* [but I am persuaded it will not].

NOTE 3. A moderated *command* is often expressed by the Opt. of wishing; which is very natural, and is very near to our own idiom: 'Let such a thing be done!'

NOTE 4. Very naturally mere *desire, will, inclination,* without particular reference to the fact whether it may be fulfilled or not, is expressed by the Optative.

NOTE 5. Sometimes the Opt. is employed, in the Classics, in questions; as ποῖ τις φύγοι; *whither can one flee?*

II. *The Optative with* ἄν.

(4) In a conditional sentence, (be the condition either expressed or implied), ἄν may be employed with the Optative in the *apodosis;* which then marks the conditionality of the predicate expressed by the Optative.

E. g. εἰ τοῦτο λέγοις, ἁμαρτάνοις ἄν, *if you should say this, then you would err.* The *erring* is dependent entirely on the condition of *saying this;* and this connection and dependence is marked by the ἄν with the Optative. Very often the condition (protasis) is not expressed, but merely implied.

§ 141. Syntax: Imperative Mode. 229

(5) The Opt. with ἄν is used in polite and *moderated affirmations*, where positivity of manner is avoided; and so also in moderate or mild *commands, requests*, etc.

E. g. Οὐκοῦν ἡ ῥητορικὴ δημηγορία ἄν εἴη, rhetoric then would not seem to be harangue, i. e. it is not. For the moderated Imper. of command: λέγοις ἄν=λέγε; χωροῖς ἄν, you might go=go. The like in our own idiom, when we use the Subjunctive in such cases.

Note. When ἄν is employed in the Opt. of *question*, it designates that the predicate is conditional; e. g. 'If any one should see you, τίς ἄν δή τοι νόος εἴη;' i. e. *what would then be your mind?* So without protasis; ποῖ τις ἄν φύγοι; *whither could one flee?* This is a shade different from ποῖ τις φύγοι; *whither may one flee?* and from ποῖ τις οὖν φύγῃ; *whither shall one flee?*

(6) Frequently the Optative is employed in the expression of a *wish*, with πῶς ἄν prefixed.

E. g. πῶς ὂν ὀλοίμην; *how can I perish?* i. e. I would fain perish. Πῶς ἄν καλῶς διηγησαίμην; *how shall I relate it well?* i. e. I would fain relate it appropriately.

Remark 1. The Optative *without* ἄν is plainly stronger than *with* it; for ἄν makes the predicate dependent on some previous condition. Accordingly, in poetry the Opt. is often used without ἄν in order merely to express *supposition* or *conception* of the mind, and to express these in some measure *unconditionally*.

Remark 2. The Opt. with ἄν expresses a kind of *future* condition, and so approaches the Indic. Future. The difference between them is, that the latter expresses an *unconditional* and certain Future, the other a conditional one. These two Futures (so to call them) are sometimes joined in the same sentence, with different shades of meaning.

§ 141. Imperative Mode.

(1) This expresses *desire* or *wish* in the form of *command*.

E. g. δός μοι τὸ βιβλίον—γράφε τὴν ἐπιστολήν.

(2) Often times the Imper. form expresses *permission*.

E. g. 1 Cor. 7: 15, 'If the unbelieving depart, χωριζέσθω, *let him separate himself*.' So in 14: 38, 'If any one is ignorant, ἀγνοείτω, *let him be ignorant*.' In our own idiom, this *permissive* sense is universal (as to *form* of expression) out of the second person; e. g. Let him do, let them do, etc.

(3) When two Imperatives are used in succession with καὶ between them, the latter usually has a sense equivalent to a Future.

E. g. ἐρεύνησον καὶ ἴδε, *search and see*, i. e. search and you will see.

(4) In the place of an Imper., the Future is not unfrequently used in commands and requisitions.

230   § 142. SYNTAX: MODES OF VERBS.

E. g. μὴ φονεύσεις· μη μοιχεύσεις. So ἀγαπήσεις τὸν Κύριον, etc This is in fact the stronger mode of expression, inasmuch as the Future often expresses *obligation* as well as expectation. In Hebrew this is the usual method of announcing obligation.

(5) The Imper. Present usually denotes *continued* action ; while the Aorist designates action *speedily completed*, or *only once to be done.*

E. g. PRESENT; Rom. 11:20, μὴ ὑψηλοφρονεῖ, be *not high-minded* (either now or at any other time); 13:3, ἀγαθὸν ποιεῖ. James 5:12, μὴ ὀμνύετε. 1 Tim. 4:7. John 1:44. 7:24. 21:16. Mark 8:15. 9:7, 39, al. saep.— AORIST; Mark 2:9, ἆρον σου τὸν κράββατον. 1:41, καθαρίσθητι. 3:5, ἔκτεινον τὴν χεῖρα σου. 6:11. 9:43. John 2:7, 8. 14:28. Luke 20:23. Acts 3:4. Eph. 6:13, 17, al. saep. So in the Classics.

NOTE 1. Of course an Imper. can in its nature pertain only to the present or future. The Aorists and Perf., therefore, must here give up their *temporal* signification, and be employed only to express *modification of action.* Sometimes both Present and Aorist stand in the same sentence, with their appropriate meanings; e. g. John 2:16, ἄρατε ταῦτα ἐντεῦθεν, μὴ ποιεῖτε τὸν οἶκον τοῦ πατρός μου, etc., where the *taking away* is only one act, but the *not making*, etc., refers to a habitual course of conduct. 1 Cor. 15:34.

NOTE 2. While this principle is very *general* throughout the N. Test., there are a few cases in which it is apparently disregarded; e. g. John 15:4, μείνατε (Aor.) ἐν ἐμοί. 1 John 5:21, φυλάξατε ἑαυτούς κ. τ. λ, (here is *continued* action in both cases). Heb. 3:1. Mark 16:15. John 14:15. 1 Cor. 6:20, et al. But in such cases, the speaker or writer may have had a view to some immediate and specific action, and therefore might employ the Aorist, although the thing commanded may in itself be of universal obligation.

NOTE 3. The Perfect Imper. is used only where an action is demanded which in its consequences will appertain to the present time; e. g. Mark 4:39, πεφίμωσο, *be thou still* (and remain so); or such an Imper. may be regarded as simply an *intensive* expression demanding instantaneous obedience; comp. § 130. 3. *d.* I should be inclined to regard it as *intensive.*

(6) In negative or prohibitive forms of speech the Imperative takes μή; but only with the *Present.* When an *aoristic* sense is required here, it is made by the *Subjunctive* Aorist and μή.

E. g. μὴ ὀμνύετε· μὴ κρίνετε, etc.; but in the Aor. μὴ κρίνητε· μὴ δικάσητε· (Subj.), not μὴ κρίνατε—μὴ δικάσατε (Imper.)

§ 142. *Various Modes as affected by the* Use *of* ἄν.

(1) The general use of this particle may be thus stated : *ἄν is connected with a verb which stands in a clause expressive of conditionality*, i. e. of dependence on something else in order that the action designated by the verb may take place. "Ἄν is

§ 142. SYNTAX: MODES OF VERBS. 231

an appropriate mark or sign, that the verb stands in such a relation and does not absolutely assert, but only makes a *conditional* declaration.

The complete meaning of ἄν, as employed by the Greeks, can be designated by no one word in the English language, because we have no adequate correspondent particle. Sometimes *perhaps* may convey the sense; and often, in conditional sentences, we may put *then* in its room, in the apodosis; e. g. εἰ τοῦτο ἔλεγες, ἡμάρτανες ἄν, 'if you should say this, *then* you would err.' Yet ἄν does not of itself mean *then*, although the entire English sentence above (with *then*) corresponds in sense to the Greek one with ἄν. The simple truth is, that in the English language, the conditional tenses of our verbs answer for the most part the same purpose as the Greek verbs with ἄν. Even in Greek, *ἄν is in many cases omitted*, where it might be inserted; and this, because the modes there give *substantially* the same meaning without it. But ἄν makes conditionality more *explicit and prominent;* and on this account it is usually employed in cases of conditional assertion. Hartung (Gr. Partic. II. § 3) and Kuhner (§ 453. 2) suppose ἄν to be of the like meaning with the Latin dubitative *an*, and with the Greek ἄν in ἄνευ, and also with the inseparable negative ἄν which is prefixed to many words. This agrees well with the dubitative and conditional nature of the particle, as joined with verbs.

NOTE 1. Wherever ἄν is employed, either in the protasis or apodosis of a sentence, (for it is often found in the *protasis* as well as in the apodosis), it still marks *conditionality ;* i. e. εἰ ταῦτα λέγοις ἄν, ἅμαρτανοις ἄν, *should you say so, you would err*. Here εἰ . . . λέγοις ἄν is itself *conditional*, and is designed to be so. The meaning is '*should you*' (viz., either in case circumstances required it—opportunity offered—or you should deem it best —or one should demand it of you, etc.), '*say so, then,* etc.'

NOTE 2. In a great many cases the *protasis* is *not* expressed, when ἄν is employed in the apodosis, i. e. in such a clause as amounts to an apodosis; for the very fact that ἄν is used, is of course a plain indication that not a direct but a conditional assertion is made, or, at all events, that a declaration is made the import of which is to be modified by circumstances.

(2) *"Ἄν is employed in all the modes and tenses*, as occasion may require, excepting the Indic. Present and Perfect, and the Imperative.

NOTE 1. The nature of these tenses, (the present being what is now seen, and the Perfect what has been actually completed, and the Imper. what is absolutely demanded), of course excludes such conditionality and uncertainty as ἄν necessarily marks. The Mss. which occasionally join ἄν with these three forms, are now admitted to be *faulty*.

(a) *"Ἄν is employed with the Indic. Future ;* in which case it moderates the otherwise positive declaration of the Future; e. g. οὐχ ἥκει, οὐδ' ἄν ἥξει δεῦρο, *he is not come, nor* [in my judgment] *will he come now.*

(b) *It is used with the Indicative historic tenses, Imperf., Pluperf., and Aorists ;* e. g. with Imperf., as εἰ τοῦτο ἔλεγες, ἁμάρτανες ἄν. Cases like these denote a belief, that the action designated will not take place or has not taken place; comp. § 137. 3. Note. Here, as in many other cases, ἄν is sometimes omitted. *Ἄν is used with the Imperf., Aor., or Perf. bearing the sense of an Imperf.*; in which case ἄν is employed very often in clauses that denote the possible *frequency* or rather the *repetition* of an action at different times, viz. so often as circumstances may or might permit. *In these forms the condition (protasis) is often omitted*, and is to be supplied by the mind of the reader; e. g. εἶπεν ἄν, he was wont to say, i. e. so often as this or that happened, etc. 'Sometimes I had food, εἰ᾽ οὐκ εἶχον ἄν, then [as circumstances might be] *I had none.*' So in Luke 19:23. Matt. 25:27. Heb. 10:2. The protasis expressed, Luke 7:39. 17:6. John 5:46. 8:42. 9:41. 15:19. Gal. 1:10. Heb. 8:4, al. saepe.

It should also be noted here, that relative clauses introduced by ὅς, ὅστις, ὅσος, ὅπου, etc., take an *Indic.* (Praeter) with ἄν, whenever a matter of *real fact* is designated, which occurs merely *pro re natâ*; Acts 2:45, 'And they made distribution to all, καθότι ἄν τις χρείαν εἶχε, as [from time to time] *each one had need.*' So Acts 4:35. 1 Cor. 12:2. Mark 6:56.

NOTE. When the Aorist or Pluperf. stands in the apodosis, the *past* time is marked by them; Matt. 11:12, 'If the mighty works done among you had been done in Tyre and Sidon, πάλαι ἄν . . . μετενόεσαν, long ago . . . *they would have repented.*' 1 John 2:19, 'If they had been of us, μεμενήκεισαν ἄν μεθ᾽ ἡμᾶν, then would they have remained with us.' Comp. also 1 Cor. 2:8. Rom. 9:29. John 14:28. 18:30. Acts 18:14. Matt. 12:7, al. saepe.

But here ἄν is not unfrequently omitted; e. g. in John 9:33. Rom. 7:7. John 15:22. 19:11. Acts 26:32. The same in the classics, specially in the later ones.

(c) *With the Subjunctive;* which, from its very nature, being founded on what *may* be, or what one may hope for or expect to realize, and therefore *conditional*, unites well with ἄν. (1) In questions both direct and indirect; § 139. 3. e. g. (2) *Specially is ἄν with the Subj.* employed in conditional clauses thrown into the main discourse, and introduced by ἐάν=εἰ ἄν, ἐπεάν ὅταν, ὁποτάν, εὖτ᾽ ἄν, πρὶν ἄν, ἕως ἄν, ἔνθ᾽ ἄν, οὗ ἄν, ὅπου ἄν, οἷ ἄν, ὅποι ἄν, ᾗ ἄν, ὅπῃ ὄν, ὅθεν ἄν, ὁπόθεν ἄν, etc.; so also with ὅς ἄν, οἷος ἄν, ὁποῖος ἄν, ὅσος ἄν, ὁπόσος ἄν, etc. In all these and the like cases, *ἄν* expresses *conditionality*, i. e. the relation of a thing *conditioned* (sit venia) to something *conditioning*. But the latter is generally left to the reader's mind to supply, it being seldom expressed in *by-clauses* of this kind; yet the true nature of the sentence is not altered by this omission. It lies upon the very face of all such clauses, that they are *conditional*.

NOTE 1. Here, (a) The *Aor. Subj.* is employed, when possible *future* action is designated; e. g. Matt. 21:22, ὅσα ἄν αἰτήσητε, *whatever ye shall ask for.* Matt. 10:11. Mark 9:18. Acts 2:39. 3:22. Rom. 10:13, al saepe. (b) But *the Pres. Subj.* is employed, when any thing customary, frequent, or continuing, is to be designated; e. g. Col. 3:17, πᾶν ὅ τι ἄν ποιῆτε, *whatever ye may do* [at any time]. Gal. 5:17. 1 Thess. 2:7. Luke 9:46. John 5:19, al. saepe. So in the Classics.

NOTE 2. The examples similar to those in general under No. 2 above, which are found in the N. Test., are very numerous, specially after particles of *time*, and sometimes of *design* or *end;* e. g. Matt. 15:2. John 8:

§ 143. Syntax: Composite Sentences. 233

44. 1 Cor. 3 : 4. Luke 11 : 36. Matt. 10 : 11. James 5 : 7. Luke 9 : 27. Rev. 2 : 25, al. saepe.—Of design ; Luke 2 : 35. Acts 3 : 19.

Note 3. Here, also, ἄν is not unfrequently *omitted*, in most of these cases that have been specified.

(*d*) *"Ἄν is used with the Optative*, when the supposition (such is implied by the mode itself) is designed to be represented as *conditional* ; e. g. εἰ τοῦτο λέγοις, ἁμαρτάνοις ἄν, i. e. should you say so, on that condition I must suppose you to err. So when the condition is merely *implied* ; Acts 2 : 11, τί ἂν θέλοι τοῦτο εἶναι, *what can this mean*? [i.e. if indeed it has any meaning]. Acts 17 : 18. So also in indirect questions with the Opt. ; e. g. Acts 5 : 24. 10 : 17. 21 : 33. John 13 : 24. Luke 9 : 46. 6 : 11. 18 : 36, al.

(*e*) *"Ἄν may be joined with the Inf.*, when this designates a meaning equivalent to the definite modes and tenses with ἄν. Thus, εἴ τι ἔχει—εἴ τι εἶχε —εἴ τι ἔχοι, ἔφη, δώσειν ἄν—δοῦναι ἄν=εἴ τι ἔχει δώσει ἄν—εἴ τι εἶχεν ἐδίδου ἄν, etc.

(*f*) *The same is true of the Participle*, when it is employed as equivalent to definite modes and tenses with ἄν ; e. g. εὑρίσκω δὲ ὧδε ἂν γινόμενα ταῦτα, *but I find that these matters are probably so, if*, etc. So πολὺ ὄμεινον ἂν ἔχοντα, εἰ νόμων ἔτυχε=ἃ πολὺ ἄμεινον ἂν εἶχεν κ. τ. λ. Plat. Leg. vi. p. 781.

Remark I. *"Ἄν* is sometimes found *alone* ; but only when its accompanying verb is plainly implied ; e. g. 1 Cor. 7 : 5, 'Defraud not one another, εἰ μὴ ἂν ἐκ συμφώνου, i. e. εἰ μὴ ἂν [γένοιτο] ἐκ συμφώνου. So frequently in dialogue ; e. g. πῶς γὰρ ἄν ; πῶς δ' οὐκ ἄν ; ὡς ἄν, ὥσπερ ἂν εἰ, etc., in Plato.

Remark II. *Position of ἄν.* *"Ἄν* with a conjunction and the Subjunctive after it, attaches itself to the conjunction, and often coalesces with it ; e. g. ὅταν, ἐπάν—ὃς ἄν, πρὶν ἄν, etc. Usually, in other cases, it attaches itself to the verb ; e. g. λέγοιμι ἄν, or else it is joined to some emphatic word, as οὐκ ἄν, τί δ' ἄν, etc.

Remark III. *"Ἄν* is sometimes repeated in the same clause. In such a case, the first ἄν is merely *anticipative* of the nature of the sentence ; e. g. ὥστ' ἄν, εἰ σθένος λάβοιμι, δηλώσαιμ' ἄν. Here we should translate it but once ; e. g. *so that, should I receive strength, I might perhaps show*, etc.

General Remark The object here in view, in making a distinct representation of the nature and offices of ἄν, is to concentrate the information on this subject for the use of the student *"Ἄν* is employed with verbs in *simple* sentences, (which thus far have been the principal object of consideration), and also with verbs in *composite* sentences, which yet remain to be considered Its object and office every where, however, is *substantially the same;* and when the nature of it is well understood, and the extent of its usage, the right understanding of the clauses in which it is employed, is greatly facilitated.

SYNTAX OF COMPOSITE SENTENCES.

§ 143. *Nature of simple and composite Sentences.*

(1) A simple sentence consists merely of a subject and predicate.

E. g. λέγει, where the *form* of the verb indicates the subject (*he*), the verb itself designates the predicate. In αὐτός λέγει, the subject is designated in the way of emphasis.

(2) Two sentences, of the same tenor, may be joined in one by means of the simple conjunctions, τέ, καί, δέ, etc., and then the sentence is, as a *whole*, a *compound* one, consisting of *co-ordinate* members which are not dependent on each other.

E. g. τὸ ἔαρ ἦλθε, τὰ δὲ δένδρα θάλλει, *the Spring has come, and the trees bloom.* Here each of the members are coordinate, and each might form a complete sentence by itself. This kind of sentence expresses merely the *logical* relation of its two members, and not a mutual dependence in respect to construction.

(3) But a far more prevalent mode of forming composite sentences, is, to make one *principal* member of a sentence, and to arrange the rest as *subordinate* ones, dependent on and attached to the principal member. These constitute what may be called the *complementary* parts of a sentence.

Thus, τὰ δένδρα θάλλει, ὅτε τὸ ἔαρ ἦλθε, presents us with a simple leading sentiment, while the latter clause contains only a *complement* of the main sentence, designed to point out the *time* when the main action takes place, and to connect this with the main action. It is easy to perceive, therefore, that a *composite* sentence of this nature, i. e. with *dependent* clauses, must essentially consist of several sentences which might be announced distinctly, but which are combined in one sentence for the sake of brevity and of exhibiting mutual relation and dependence.

(4) The main sentiment, on which the subordinate clauses are dependent, is called the *leading* or *principal* clause or sentence; the dependent clauses are called *subordinate*, or *dependent* clauses or sentences, or *by-clauses*.

E. g. 'The man, who comes from the camp, proclaims that a victory, which was gained by night, when the enemy were asleep, has made our country master of all their military stores.' Here, *a victory has made our country master* is the leading or principal sentence; all the others are subordinate, inferior, and therefore merely *complementary*.

(5) Every *dependent* clause must, from its nature as a sentence in itself, of course have a *subject* and *predicate*, and so it might be expressed independently; but the nature of composite sentences (and such are now before us) requires a modification of such clauses, and this must be such as will designate *dependence* and *connection*.

Such a sentence may be likened to a tree with its branches or limbs. The leading clause is the trunk; on this are engrafted the limbs, (subordinate clauses); and from these may spring forth branches dependent on the limbs, (in which case the limbs themselves become, in relation to these branches, *leading sentences* or trunks). Every portion of a sentence, the

§ 144. SXNTAX: SUBORDINATE SENTENCES. 235

main verb excepted, may send out limbs and branches. Thus: *The rose blooms*, is simple; *the beautiful rose blooms*, has joined an attribute to the subject, which might be thus expressed: *The rose which is beautiful, blooms*. Even the main verb itself may be *modified;* e. g. *the rose blooms καλῶς well*, or *ἐν τῷ κήπῳ in the garden*. So the object of a sentence may have attributives; e. g. *he wrote a letter ; he wrote an excellent letter*, i. e. a letter, which is excellent; *he wrote a letter, which was sent to his friends, and which gave them much pleasure,* etc. The main verb can be modified as to manner, degree, time, place, etc.; but it does not and cannot properly *branch* out, like the subject and object of sentences.

(6) The essential parts of a full composite sentence are *subject, predicate, object, and attribute*,

NOTE. *The subject, predicate,* and *object* of a sentence are easily understood, after what has been said. But in a multitude of composite sentences an *attributive*, i. e. either an adjective, or a participle, or an equivalent, is inserted, which of itself is equivalent to a *dependent* clause, and which often gives rise to clauses dependent on it; e. g. 'Muse, sing for me of the man, πολύτροπον, ὃς μάλα πολλὰ πλάγχθη, *the much-wandering, who suffered very much*, etc. Here the attributive πολίτροπον enlarges itself into the subsequent branch. And thus often in respect to attributives, whether participles or adjectives.

REMARK. The Greek has much fewer *subordinate* clauses than the English. The principal reason of this lies in the power of the participle in the Greek. E. g. ἔαρος ἐλθόντος, ἀπῆλθε, which we thus express: 'When the spring was come, he departed.' So ταῖτα πράξας, ἀπέβη, which we translate: *When he had done these things, he departed*. So νικήσας τοὺς πολεμίους, ἀνῆλθε ; and in like manner are a multitude of sentences constructed in Greek. In regard to vivacity and neatness and brevity, as exhibited in such sentences, the English is greatly inferior to the Greek.

§ 144. *Classification of subordinate Clauses or Sentences.*

(1) Subordinate clauses are constituted either of such expressions as are equivalent to, and may be represented by, a noun, or an Inf. mode employed as a noun ; or such as may stand in the place of an adjective or participle ; or such as may be expressed by an adverb or participle employed in an adverbial sense. Such may be named *substantive sentences* or *clauses, adjective* or *relative sentences*, and *adverbial sentences*.

Illustration. 'That man is mortal, is certain' = the mortality of man is certain; the first clause, in the former case, constituting (like a noun) the subject of the sentence. 'All men know [this] that man is mortal,' where the subordinate clause stands as the Acc. after the verb, or in apposition with *this* implied. In like manner, a *by-clause* may stand as the representative of a Gen. case ; e. g. τοὺς αὑτῷ συνόντας ὁ Σωκράτης ὑπέμνησε [τούτου], ὅτι ὁ ἄνθρωπος θνητός ἐστιν, where the latter clause supplies the place of a Gen., being in apposition with τούτου implied. Again : ἐλυπήθη [τούτῳ], ὅτι ὁ ἄνθρωπος θνητός ἐστιν, where the latter clause supplies a Dative instrumental. The Acc. case is the one which is most frequently represented in this manner.

Adjective sentences are easily understood: e. g. 'the beautiful rose blooms,' we may express with an adjective by-clause, 'The rose blooms, which is beautiful.' So with a participle; e. g. οἱ ἀποφυγόντες πολέμιοι may be turned into οἱ πολέμιοι, οἳ ἀπέφυγον, the latter being the *by-clause*.

Adverbial clauses are such as are introduced by particles significant of *time, place, manner, degree,* etc. E. g. τὰ ἄνθη θάλλει, ὅτε τὸ ἔαρ ἦλθε, where the last clause is an *adverbial* one in respect to *time*. So ἕπεσθε, ὅποι ἄν τις ἡγῆται, *ye follow wherever any one may lead*, where the latter clause is adverbial in respect to *place*. So ἐπεὶ ταῦτα λέγεις, ἁμαρτάνεις, *inasmuch as you say so, you err*, where the by-clause is *causal*. Either adverbs or conjunctions may introduce such clauses.

§ 145. *Modes and Tenses of dependent clauses in general.*

(1) The general rules already given as to modes and tenses of simple sentences are applicable to *by-clauses*.

But the nature of subordinate clauses is sometimes such, (as we shall see in the sequel), that they differ from each other in regard to the use of particular modes and tenses. These differences will be pointed out, when each class comes to be considered.

(2) *General Rule for tenses.* Subordinate clauses stand related, as to *time*, to the principal sentence, and not to the present time of the speaker.

E. g. If the principal sentence exhibits a Pres., Perf., or Future, so does the subordinate one. But here the Aor. sometimes stands instead of the Perfect, and of course may be treated as one, § 136. 5. 3. If a Subj. mode is required in the by-clause with a Fut. sense, the Pres. or Aor. of the Subj. is of necessity used for such a future (the Subj. having no such tense); e. g. τοῦτο λέγω, ἵνα γιγνώσκῃς or ἵνα γνῷς. So if the principal sentence exhibits the (preterite) *historic* tenses, the by-clause will contain either the same or their equivalents; e. g. ἠγγέλλετο, ὅτι οἱ πολέμιοι ἔφευγον.

(3) EXCEPTIONS TO THE GENERAL RULE. Very often the by-clauses are constituted so as to have reference, not to the main clause, but to *the present of the speaker.*

Of course the *primary* tenses may be used in the by-clauses, in such cases, although the *historic* ones are in the main clause; e. g. οὗτοι ἔλεγον, ὅτι Κῦρος . . . τέθνηκεν. In fact this mode of representation arises from the speaker's assuming a position in past time corresponding with that indicated by the main verb.

Vice versâ, the *historical* tenses may be employed in by-clauses, when the *primary* tenses stand in the main ones; e. g. λέγουσι Πέρσαι, ὡς Δαρεῖος ἦν . . . ἐκαπήλευε . . . ἐμηχανήσατο, Herod, iii. 89. The like, when a by-clause

§ 145. Syntax: Subordinate Sentences. 237

stands in a mutual relation to another by-clause, or is in a *conditionated* part of a sentence, as φημὶ, ὅτι, εἰ τοῦτο ἔλεγες, ἥμαρτες ἄν.

Note 1. Sometimes ὅτι, etc. is omitted, and a by-clause appears in the same garb as a main one; e. g. ὁρᾶς, ἔφη, ... δίκαια δοκεῖ λέγειν. Sometimes εἰ (if) stands in the room of ὅτι; e. g. θαυμάζω, εἰ σὺ ταῦτα ποιεῖς, instead of ὅτι σύ, etc.

Note 2. The Greeks are not confined to any one mode of forming subordinate clauses. Thus they can say, with equal propriety: εἶπεν, ὅτι ὁ πατὴρ τέθνηκε, or εἶπεν, τὸν πατέρα τεθνηκέναι—ἀνήρ, ὃς μαλὰ πολλὰ ἐπλάγχθη, or μαλὰ πολλὰ πλαγχθείς—τὰ δένδρα θάλλει, ὅτε τὸ ἔαρ ἦλθε, or τοῦ ἔαρος ἐλθόντος, etc.

Note 3. Parenthesis, interjections, and Vocatives, are not *by-sentences*, in like manner with those described above; but they stand (as to construction) independent, although they are in unity (as to connection) with the sentence where they are employed.

§ 146. *Dependent substantive sentences : Classification.*

(1) These generally supply the place of a noun in the Acc., i. e. they designate the *complement* of a sentence. As such, they are divided into *those which designate the object of the* IMMEDIATE *action of the verb,* and *those which designate the* DESIGNED *operation or action of it.*

The first class are preceded by ὅτι, ὡς, (ὅπως), meaning *that ;* the second, by ἵνα, ὡς, ὅπως (μή lest), *so that, in order that,* etc., having what is named a *telic* signification, [from τελικός].

Note. In reality ὅτι is the neuter Acc. of the demonstrative ὅστις, and stands correlate to a preceding demonstrative usually not expressed but implied ; e. g. ἀκούω, ὅτι ἐλεύσεται, i. e. ἀκούω [τοῦτο], ὅτι etc. Ὡς and ὅπως correspond to the Latin *ut.* From the nature of this class of subordinates it is plain, that they must usually follow verbs of *sense* or *intellection,* such as ὁράω, ἀκούω, μανθάνω, etc. ; or else follow verbs expressive of a *development* of sensation or intellectual action, e. g. λέγω, δεικνύω, etc.

Construction of subordinate Clauses with ὅτι, ὡς, *etc.*

(1) The simple verb, as the case may require, may be in any tense of the Indic. ; but with ἄν, it must be in some of the *historic* tenses of the Indicative.

Note 1. The Indic. here designates, as usual, what is *actual* or *certain,* or is believed to be so. (*a*) It is *always* employed after the *Present* in the main clause, because what is present appears to be actual; e. g. λέγω, ὅτι νοσεῖς—ὅτι τοῦτο γενήσεται etc. (*b*) Usually, when the speaker relates what he himself has thought or said, because this appears to him as *actual ;* e. g. ἔλεξά ποτε, ὅτι οἱ Ἕλληνες νικήσουσι. The Opt. here (instead of the Indic.) would indicate an indetermination of mind, whether the thing stated would actually take place or not. (*c*) When the main clause affirms something

§ 147. Syntax: Subordinate Sentences.

which renders *certain* the action of the by-clause, the Indic. of affirmation is of course employed in the latter; as εὖ ᾔδει, ὅτι ἔπραξας. In one by-clause may be the Indic. and in another the Opt., or even in the same, just as *certainty* or mere *supposition* is intended to be expressed.

NOTE 2. Ἄν *here with the Indic.* differs not (as to meaning) from ἄν in other cases with the same mode. Ἄν of course marks the *conditionality* of the clause in which it is; e. g. εἰ ὁ πατὴρ ἠπίστει, δῆλον, ὅτι οὐκ ἂν τοῦτο ἐπέτρεπε.

(2) The verb may be in the Optative, without ἄν, or with ἄν, as the case may require.

NOTE 1. (a) The Optative is used when *uncertainty, possibility*, etc. are designated, or a mere supposition is made or an opinion stated; e. g. ἔδοξεν αὐτοῖς δηλῶσαι, ὅτι οὐ ταχέως αὐτοῖς βουλευτέον εἴη. (b) The Opt. with ἄν is used when the *supposition* expressed is made *conditional;* as εἰ αὐτῷ δοίη ἱππέας . . . ὅτι κατακαίνοι ἄν, etc.

REMARK I. Ὅτι is not only used in *indirect* quotations, as λέγει, ὅτι οὐ θέλει, etc., but often employed in *direct* ones, where merely the speaker's words are quoted; e. g. εἶπε, ὅτι Εἰς καιρὸν ἥκεις. So often in the N. Testament. In fact, almost all the quotations in the N. Test. are *direct*, so that ὅτι before them very often is susceptible of no translation, but is merely to be noted by a double comma in writing. See Matt. 2: 23. 5: 31. 21: 16. Acts 11: 3, al. saepe.

REMARK II. The Opt. is hardly to be found in the N. Test. in quotations, and indeed could not be employed usually, unless the quotations were *indirect;* which they are not.

REMARK III. The Acc. with Inf. may designate the same sense as ὅτι with its clause; e. g. ἀγγέλλει, ὅτι παῖς γέγονε—ἀγγέλλει, παῖδα γεγονέναι. Sentences therefore are not unfrequent, where both these modes of construction are exhibited in the same connection; and even where the construction with ὅτι is interrupted, it is sometimes resumed by a construction with the Infinitive. Kühner § 771. 5.

REMARK IV. Such verbs as μέμνημαι, οἶδα, ἀκούω, etc., may take ὅτε (*when*) instead of ὅτι *that;* e. g. μέμνημαι, ὅτε ἔλεξας. In such cases, τοῦ χρόνου seems to be implied after the principal verb.

So verbs signifying an *affection of the mind* often take εἰ (*if*) instead of ὅτι, when some uncertainty is designed to be implied; e. g. θαυμάζω, εἰ ταῦτα γίγνεται—οὐκ ᾐσχύνθη, εἰ τοιοῦτο κακὸν ἐπάγει. So after verbs signifying *to grieve, be offended* or *angry, to blame, love, envy*, etc. — In like manner ὡς sometimes stands in the place of ὅτι; e. g. θαυμάζω, ὡς ἡδέως καθεύδεις, *I wonder how you sleep sweetly.*

§ 147. *Subordinate substantive clauses with* ἵνα, ὡς, ὅπως (ὄφρα), μή.

(1) Such clauses indicate the *end* or *object* to be attained, in connection with the action of the principal verb; and so they are called FINAL CLAUSES, i. e. those which indicate the end to be accomplished.

§ 147. SYNTAX: SUBORDINATE SENTENCES.

The Latin *finis* of course explains the meaning of this appellative. "Οφρα is poetic only. *Μή*=Latin *ne* interrogative, but is often constructed in the same way as the other particles here named, and therefore is here considered.

(2) As the *end* or *design* must in its nature have reference to a *future*, and at the same time, not being yet actual, must have its basis in the will or idea, so the Subj. or Opt. modes are of course appropriate modes for *final* clauses.

(3) GENERAL RULE. *Primary* tenses in the main clause require the *Subjunctive* in the dependent clause; *historic* tenses in the main clause demand the *Optative* in the subordinate one.

E. g. Primary tenses; ταῦτα γράφω—γράψω—γέγραφα, ἵνα ἔλθῃς (Subj.) Historic; ταῦτα ἔγραφον—ἔγραψα—ἐγεγράφειν, ἵνα ἔλθοις (Opt.) So in the N. Test. very often, in regard to the Subj.; as Matt. 6: 2, ποιοῦσιν . . . ἵνα δοξάσθωσι. 2 Tim. 2: 4, 10. Luke 8: 12. Heb. 9: 15, al. saepe. The *Imperative* may precede, as well as the Indicative; e. g. Matt. 2: 8, ἀπαγγείλατέ μοι, ὅπως κἀγὼ προσκυνήσω αὐτῷ. 1 Tim. 4: 15.

But to both these rules there are not a few *exceptions*. E. g.

(*a*) *The Subjunctive sometimes follows the historic tenses;* (1) When the Aorist has the meaning of a Perfect, and expresses action that stands related to the present time of the speaker; as τίπτ᾽ αὖτ᾽ . . . ἤλυθες, ἵνα ἴδῃ, i. e. *why hast thou come* [and art present], *that thou mayest see*, etc. (2) When the writer transports himself into the past, and speaks as from a position there; or when he designs to present action as *continuing*, or as every now and then *recurring;* e. g. Σόλων ἀπεδήμησε . . . ἵνα μὴ . . . ἀναγκασθῇ λῦσαι, etc. 1 Tim. 1: 16, ἠλεήθην, ἵνα ἐν ἐμοὶ . . . ἐνδείξηται Ι. Χριστός, etc.; v. 20, οὓς παρέδωκα . . . ἵνα παιδευθῶσι, etc. Tit. 1: 5. 2: 14. Rom. 6: 4. 1 John 3: 5. 5: 13, al. saep.

NOTE. So far is the rule in No. 3 from being universal, that in fact the N. Test. exhibits *no* examples of the use of the *Optative* in such a connection, but every where employs the *Subjunctive*. The like construction is frequent in Plutarch, and is altogether predominant in Hellenistic Greek in general. The Optative, indeed, is quite in the back ground, in all Hebrew-Greek.

(*b*) *The Optative, on the other hand, sometimes in the classics follows the primary tenses;* (1) When the Present is merely a *historical* present, (= a Preterite). (2) When the speaker does not give his own view or design, but that of the agent; so that a kind of indirect quotation is made, in which the Opt. is very common. (3) When the speaker, although he employs the Present in the main clause, still takes his stand in the *past* and speaks accordingly; e. g. βαδίζω καὶ πονῶ . . . ἵνα μὴ ταλαιπώροιτο, etc. Aristoph. Ran. 24, where he is speaking of the past.

NOTE. The Opt., with or without ἄν in the *main* clause, would regularly be followed by the same mode in the *by-clause;* but when *probability of realization* is designed to be expressed, then the Subjunctive may stand in the by-clause.

§ 147. Syntax: Subordinate Sentences.

REMARK. When two or more *final* clauses follow each other, the one may have the Subjunctive and the other the Optative, just as the exigency of the sense requires.

(4) Both the Subj. and Opt. take ἄν here, when the writer designs to constitute a *conditional* clause.

NOTE. They are subject to the same general laws, in this case, as have been already stated. In the expression of a *wish*, ἄν may be joined with the Optative; e. g. ὡς ἄν γαῖα χάνοι! *May the earth open!* i. e. in case this is possible, (which the ἄν implies).

(5) Ὅπως and ὡς, (also ἵνα), may be followed by the *Indicative Future*.

This is not unfrequent in the classics, so far as ὅπως and ὡς are concerned. See abundance of examples in Kuhner, § 776. 1. Sometimes even ἄν is put with ὅπως before the Future. In the N. Test. we sometimes find the Future after ἵνα; e. g. Rev. 22: 14, μακάριοι . . . ἵνα ἔσται. John 17: 2, ἔδωκας αὐτῷ ἐξουσίαν . . . ἵνα . . . δώσει, etc. Other cases there are, but with various readings, as Rev. 6: 2. 13: 16. 1 Cor. 13: 3, al. As to ἵνα with the Future, in the classics, it is still a matter of dispute in regard to the readings.

REMARK The Future is so nearly allied to the Subj, that this idiom cannot appear strange The difference between the Fut Ind and the Subj, in this case, is, that the former expresses *more certainty* in respect to realization than the latter.

(6) In some cases the *final* particles stand before the *historic* tenses of the *Indicative*, when past actions are spoken of which ought to have taken place, or might have done so, but have not.

E. g. 'Why didst thou not seize and kill me forthwith, ὡς ἔδειξα μήποτε ἐμαυτὸν ἀνθρώποισι, etc., lit. *so that I had not disclosed myself to men*, from whom I sprung,' Soph. Oed. Tyr. 1377. 'Then I should not have been obliged to expose my wretched body, ἵνα ἦν τυφλός τε καὶ κλύων μηδέν, *that I might be blind and deaf*, or *so that I became blind*, etc. See many examples in Kuhner, § 778, who, however, does not explain this peculiarity with his usual success. The simple truth seems to be, that the writer takes his stand in the *past;* and not in the present; yet still he preserves the language of the Praeterite, but at the same time exhibits the *relative* condition of the by-clause to the main one, just as if he were speaking in the posture of the *present*. There is a grammatical inconsistency in this; but as a matter of fact it cannot be denied.

REMARK. *Special usage in the N. Test.* In 1 Cor. 4: 6. Gal. 4: 17, ἵνα is used before the Indic. *Present*, viz. φυσιοῦσθε, ζηλοῦτε. This is without established precedent; and both readings must be therefore somewhat doubtful. If correct, they must arise from the freedom of later usage in Greek.

§ 148. *Peculiar uses of μή in final sentences.*

(1) After verbs expressive of *doubt, questioning, consideration, deliberation, enquiry, solicitude, fear,* etc., the particle μή is often employed before *final* clauses.

In all these cases μή is in reality a mere *interrogative*, (like the Latin *ne*); e. g. ὀκνέω, μὴ μάταιος ἡ στρατεία ὑμῶν γένηται, lit., *I am troubled, whether* [that] *the expedition will be fruitless,* i. e. I am fearful that it will be fruitless; δείδω, μὴ ἀληθές εἶπεν, lit. *I fear, whether* [that] *he has spoken the truth,* which means, 'he has doubtless spoken the truth,' although, in our own idiom, the literal sense would appear to be of the contrary meaning. If in both cases we translate μή by *lest*, our own idiom will agree sufficiently well with the Greek.

NOTE. We have no particle which will correspond with μή in *all* the cases of using it. Sometimes it might be translated *lest;* then again *that, whether,* etc.; but oftener still we must modify the whole phrase, in order to express the sense conformably to our own idiom. The simple fact seems to be, that *in all cases where μή is employed in final clauses, a verb of the nature above described is either expressed or implied.* In most cases *brachylogy* leaves the verb unexpressed; but still it is implied.

(2) When the clause following μή is intended to denote that the thing spoken of is *certain, true,* etc., then the *Indic.* mode in any of the requisite tenses is employed.

E. g. φοβοῦμαι δέ, μή τινας ἡδονὰς ἡδοναῖς εὑρήσομεν ἐναντίας, *I fear lest we shall find some pleasures opposed to others,* i. e. undoubtedly we shall find etc. So φοβερόν, μὴ σφαλεὶς τῆς ἀληθείας . . . κείσομαι, *it is to be feared lest having missed the truth . . . I shall succumb,* i. e. I shall surely succumb in case I miss the truth.

(3) The Subj. or Opt. may be employed after μή, when the sense is that of *deliberation* and *reference to future decision,* or that of *indetermination* or *mere supposition.*

E. g. δείδω, μή ἕλωρ γένωμαι, *I fear lest I should become a prey,* i. e. I am doubtful whether this may or may not be the case. So in the Opt.; ὅρα, μὴ ὁ λόγος μάτην εἴη, *look well to it, lest what is said may be in vain.*

NOTE. When ἄν is added, it shows the *conditionality* of the clause in which it stands.

(4) In οὐ μή the same meaning of μή is in reality retained.

The particles οὐ μή are used either before the Subjunc., or the Ind. Future; very rarely in the Optative. The solution of the phrase lies in the fact, that all such phrases imply before them a verb, etc., of the character described in No. 1 above. Thus in Aristoph. Ran. 508: 'By Apollo, οὐ μή σε περιόψομαι ἀπελθόντα, [I fear] *not whether I shall see you off,* i. e. I have not the least doubt you will be off. So ἀλλ' οὐ μὴ οἷός τ' ᾖς, *but* [I fear] *not lest you may be able to do that,* i. e. certainly you can never do it. Ἀλλ' οὐ μὴ φῶμεν, but [I fear] *not lest we may say this*, i. e. but we cannot say so. How different this is from the common solution of οὐ μή, every well informed Greek scholar will readily perceive. In many cases, the Greek idiom here corresponds with our own; in many others, it is quite foreign to it.

REMARK. (*a*) After verbs of *fearing, solicitude*, etc., or other words of equivalent import, εἰ sometimes stands instead of μή; i. e. φόβος, εἰ πείσω· —φοβῶμεν, εἴ τις ... αἰσθήσεται. (*b*) After the same class of verbs we also find ὅπως μή, ὅπως, ὅτι, ὡς, or the Inf. with or without an article; all helping to make out variety of expression; e. g. δέδοικα δέ, ὅπως λάθω etc. —φοβοῦ, ὡς ἀπορήσεις—φοβοῦμαι τὸ ἀποθνήσκειν=μὴ ἀποθάνῳ, etc.

ADJECTIVE OR RELATIVE SENTENCES.

§ 149. *Manner in which dependent relative clauses are formed.*

(1) These clauses are so called because they stand in the place of a participle or an adjective, i. e. they convey an idea which might be expressed by a participle or adjective; see § 144.

E. g. οἱ πολέμιοι, οἳ ἀπέφυγον=οἱ ἀποφυγόντες μολέμιοι. So τὰ πράγματα, ἃ ὁ Ἀλέξανδρος ἔπραξε=τὰ ὑπὸ τοῦ Ἀλεξάνδρου πραχθέντα πράγματα, etc. While the idea is in substance the same in both forms, yet the mode of expression is quite different. It is those clauses which follow the relative pronoun in such cases, which constitute what are technically called *adjective sentences* or *clauses*, or, as I prefer naming them, *relative clauses*. These are the subjects of our present inquiry.

REMARK. Simple attributives are not usually expressed by *adjective* clauses; e. g. Δαρεῖος ὁ βασιλεύς. But when the attributive is to be made *emphatic*, then it is usually expressed by a *relative* clause; e. g. Δαρεῖος, ὃς βασιλεὺς ἦν. So participial attributives are made more emphatic, by being moulded into a *relative* clause.

(2) The relative clause stands related to the main one, and *vice versâ*, in various ways; which, however, do not affect the substance of the relation itself. E. g. the relative clause has respect,

(*a*) To a demonstrative pronoun (οὗτος, ἐκεῖνος, ὅδε, ὁ αὐτός, etc.); as οὗτος ὁ ἀνήρ, ὃν εἶδες. (*b*) To a noun with an article, (for this is in its nature demonstrative); as τὸ ῥόδον, ὃ ἀνθεῖ. The article always *implies* some relative clause after it; as τὸ ῥόδον καλόν ἐστιν, viz. τὸ ῥόδον, ὃ ὁρᾷς, or the like. (*c*) To a noun without the article; as ἀνήρ, ὃς καλός ἐστιν. (*d*) To a pronoun expressed, or implied in the verb; as καλῶς ἐποίησας, ὃς ταῦτα ἔπραξας, (σύ being implied). (*e*) To an adjective, supplying the place of a noun; as ἦλθον οἱ ἄριστοι ἦσαν, i. e. οἱ ἄριστοι [ἄνδρες].

REMARK I. Originally the relative pronouns were of a *demonstrative* nature; and so, even in later usage, they are often employed; as καὶ ὅς and *he*, ὃς μέν ... ὃς δέ, ὃς καὶ ὅς, ἦ δ' ὅς *said he*, etc.

§ 151. Syntax: Adjective Sentences. 243

Remark II. ὅς, ἥ, ὅ (relative) correspond to οὗτος, αὕτη, τοῦτο, and ὁ, ἡ, τό, demonstrative; so οἷος to τοῖος and τοιοῦτος—ὅσος to τόσος and τοσοῦτος, etc.

(3) The demonstrative in the *main* clause is very often *omitted*, because it may be easily supplied.

E. g. ἀγόρασον ὧν χρείαν ἔχομεν, John 13: 29, instead of ἀγόρασον [ἐκεῖ-'να] ὧν, etc. In such cases the relative answers to our English *what*=that which. So passim.

§ 150. *Verbs in relative clauses; person.*

(1) The person of the verb in the relative clause, must conform to the antecedent.

E. g. ἐγὼ, ὃς γράφω—σὺ, ὃς γράφεις—ἡμεῖς, οἳ γράφομεν, etc. The *Vocative*, when an antecedent, usually demands the second person in the verb of the relative clause, but not always; e. g. ἄνθρωπε, ὃς ἐποίησας, but also as ὦ φίλοι, οἳ πίνουσι.

N B. For the concord of the *relative* with its *antecedent*, see § 124. 1, respecting the relative pronouns; also for the so called *Attraction* of relatives, and of nouns connected with them, see § 124. 2.

§ 151. *Verbs with relative clauses; Modes.*

(1) As in the main clauses, so here, the Indic. is employed to indicate whatever is deemed *certain* and *actual*; and the Future of it often designates *what should take place*.

E. g. 'They choose leaders, οἳ τῷ Φιλίππῳ πολεμήσουσι, *who must or should make war with Philip*.'

Note. Even after negative particles the Indic. is used here, although the Latin employs the Subj.; e. g. οὐδεὶς, ὅστις μὴ ἱκανός ἐστι, 'there is no one who *is not* able, etc.'

(2) The Indic. of the *historic* tenses, with ἄν, is used when any thing is spoken of which would take place under a certain condition, but has not taken place because the condition is not fulfilled.

E. g. οἷς ἄν [λόγοις] ἔπεισα, εἰ ᾤμην δεῖν ἅπαντα λέγειν, (Apol. Soc.), where the implication is, that, not believing it proper to say any thing and every thing, he had not persuaded, as he might otherwise have done.

(3) The Subjunctive is used when the relative clause expresses what is set forth as probable or possible; and with ἄν, when this is *conditionally* so.

E. g. 'Men praise poetry most, ἥτις ... νεωτάτη ἀμφιπέληται, *which is most recent*, i. e. whenever it may be most recent=ἐὰν νεωτάτη ᾖ.

Note 1. In such cases the *primary* tenses of the Indic. stand in the main clause. When ἄν is added, it increases the indefinite nature of the assertion, making it more prominently conditional; e. g. 'The Pythoness ordered the Athenians to inflict punishments, τὰς ἂν αὐτοὶ Ἀθηναῖοι δικάσωσι, whatever the Athenians themselves should decide upon,' Her. VI. 139.

NOTE 2. Occurrences of undefined frequency, things taking place *so oft as*, etc., are expressed by the Subj. usually with ἄν; comp. in § 142. Note 1. *c*. 2. So when the relative clause is a member of a *comparison*, the Subj. is common.

NOTE 3. Ἄν very often amalgamates with the relative pronoun, adverb, etc.; as ὅταν, ἔπαν, ἐπειδάν, and the like. In poetry it is often omitted in such cases; in Attic prose, seldom.

§ 152. *Optative with relative or adjective Clauses.*

(1) The Opt. in relative clauses often differs very little from the Subjunctive, except that it follows the *historic* tenses in the main clause. As in other cases, it leans more to the side of mere *supposition* or *ideality* than the Subj., and so is often employed in the expression of *indefiniteness*, or of *undefined frequency*.

NOTE. When ἄν is added, then *conditionality* is implied, in addition to the general, undefined, and ideal nature of the Opt. expression. The Opt. without ἄν expresses a mere *supposition* more *definitely* than with it; for ἄν conjoins an additional conditionality with mode.

REMARK. *Relative clauses connected.* When two clauses have the same verb and the same regimen, the *relative* is *omitted* before the second clause. But if they have a different verb and different regimen, then the *relative* is usually *repeated*; e. g. ὁ ἀνήρ, ὅς παρ᾽ ἡμῖν ἦν καὶ ὃν πάντες ἐφίλουν. But here the second relative is sometimes omitted, and sometimes αὐτός or a personal pronoun is put in its place.

CAUTION The reader must not suppose that all the clauses which have a pronoun *apparently* relative, belong in reality to the *adjective* clauses in question; for the relative ὅς is frequently employed as a *demonstrative*, even in clauses which assign the *reason* or *ground* of any thing; in the resumption of a discourse which has been interrupted; and (in poetry) in addresses, questions, and commands. The nature of the sense renders it, for the most part, easy to decide respecting the quality of the apparent relative.

ADVERBIAL SENTENCES OR CLAUSES.

§ 153. *Nature and various classes of them.*

(1) The *designation* of these clauses is derived from the leading word that introduces them, which, in its nature, is either an *adverb*, or *of a meaning such as may be adverbially designated*. These clauses are not the *complement* of the verb in the main clause, but they express *something which limits, qualifies, or modifies that verb*.

E. g. ὅτε τὸ ἔαρ ἦλθε, τὰ ἄνθη θάλλει—ὡς ἔλεξας, οὕτως ἔπραξας. Here the first clause in each sentence is *adverbial*; and the sense of each might be differently expressed, viz. τοῦ ἔαρος ἐλθόντος—τοῦτο λέξαντος. The adverbs ὅτε and ὡς plainly qualify the clauses to which they belong, so as to make them expressive of the same sense that the participles would express.

NOTE. In reality all the adverbs thus introducing relative clauses, are in their own nature *relative*, and must therefore have some antecedent, either expressed, or (which is much more common) merely implied. E. g. ὅτε must (by implication at least) refer to τότε, ὡς to οὕτως, οὗ to ἐκεῖ, ἡνίκα to τηνίκα, πρίν to ἄν, etc. These *antecedents* (demonstrative adverbs), to which all *relative* adverbs must naturally refer, may be divided into several classes, viz. (1) Those of *place*. (2) *Of time*. (3) *Causality*. (4) *Way and manner*. (5) *Comparison*. Of each something must be said, in its appropriate order.

§ 154. *Adverbial clauses of place.*

(1) These designate the *where*, the *whence*, and the *whither*; and in respect to the use of *modes and tenses* after them, they agree with the corresponding adjective or relative clauses as set forth in the preceding sections.

Clauses expressive of the *where* begin with οὗ, ᾗ, ὅπῃ, ὅπου, ἔνθα, ἵνα (where); of the *whence* with ὅθεν, ἔνθεν; of the *whither* with οἷ, ὅποι, ᾗ, ὅπῃ.

NOTE. Adverbs *relative* are sometimes exchanged for demonstrative, (e. g. ὅθεν for οὗ, etc.), and *vice versa* by what is named *attraction;* Kuhner § 787. Anm. 6. § 789. Anm. 2.

§ 155. *Adverbial clauses of time.*

(1) These are naturally divided into those which express relation to *present, past,* and *future* time.

(a) Present; ὅτε, ὁπότε, ὡς, ἡνίκα, (relating to a *point* of time), and ἐν ᾧ, ἕως, [ὄφρα], (*duration* of time). (b) Past; ἐπεί, ἐπειδή (*after*), ἐξ οὗ, ἐξ ὅτου, ἀφ' οὗ, (*from which, since*).

(c) Future, or what is to follow; πρίν, πρὶν ἤ, ἕως, ἕως οὗ, εἰς ὅ, μέχρις, ἄχρις οὗ, μέχρις ὅτου, etc.

NOTE 1. Some of these adverbial conjunctives not unfrequently express other meanings than those which belong here; e. g. ὅτε, ὁπότε, ὡς, ἐπεί, etc. frequently are used with a *causal* meaning.

NOTE 2. All of these *relative* adverbs, significant of *time*, of course imply an *antecedent* which corresponds, and which (although usually not expressed) must in its nature be *demonstrative*. Thus ὅτε must refer to a τότε or its equivalent, ὄφρα to τόφρα, ἡνίκα to τηνίκα, πρίν to ᾗ, etc.

(2) The Indic. is used in these clauses in its usual way, i. e. whenever any thing deemed *real* or *actual* is designated.

NOTE. The conjunctive particle ἕως takes some *historic* tense of the Indic., when any thing that has not taken place, or cannot take place, is to be designated; e. g. ' Gladly would I talk with Callicles, ἕως αὐτῷ ... ἀπέδωκα, *until I had restored to him*, etc., implies that he had not been restored.

(3) The Subj. designates what is *possible, probable*, etc., which is to be decided by events yet to come; with ἄν, the *conditionality* of the action is more specifically stated.

There is nothing peculiar in the use of the Subj. here. It is frequently employed to designate events recurring *so oft as* this or that may happen; sometimes (in poetry) to express *comparison* or *similitude*, which is merely assumed and not stated as actual fact.

(4) The Opt. is employed in its usual way; and also, very often, in a sense almost identical with that of the Subj., although it differs in this respect, that it usually follows the *historic* (instead of the primary) tenses in the main clause.

NOTE. 1. *Undefined frequency* is indeed expressed often by the *Opt.*, as well as by the Subjunctive. But still, the prevailing use of the Opt. is, to express that which is merely *supposed*, and of course an *indefinite possibility* or *probability* without reference to any determination by future events. In this latter respect it differs from the Subjunctive.

NOTE. 2. The Opt. with ἄν merely makes palpable a *conditionality* which is attached to the predicate.

REMARK RESPECTING πρίν. This adverbial conjunctive may stand before the Indic. when facts are asserted; before the Subj. when a conditional clause follows a *primary* tense in the main clause; or before the Opt., when it follows a *historic* tense in the main clause. It also stands before the *Inf. mode*, either with or without ἤ after it.

§ 156. *Causal adverbial sentences.*

This designation must not be understood in a strict and confined sense, but in an *expanded* one, viz. as designating all such sentences as are introduced by adverbs conjunctive, which indicate *ground* or *reason* or *indispensable condition*, etc., i. e. such as are causal in a sense direct or indirect.

(1) Causal adverbial clauses may be divided into several classes; viz. (*a*) Those which assign the *ground* or *reason*. (*b*) Those which express *conditionality*.

(2) (*a*) THE GROUND OR REASON. These include, (a) Such *temporal* conjunctions as, by the connection in which they stand, become *causal* in their import.

E. g. ὅτε, ὁπότε, ὡς, ἐπεί, = *since*, in the connection now designated, e. g. μή με κτεῖνε, ἐπεὶ ἀδελφός σού εἰμι, *kill me not, since* (= *because*) *I am thy brother.* The same meaning for substance is given to ἐπειδή, ἐπείπερ, ἐπειδήπερ, intensives of ἐπεί, and signifying *for this very reason, since now*, etc. The temporal particles ὅτε, ὁπότε, ὡς, have rarely the *causal* meaning, and where they do have it, they seem to stand in the place of ὅτι. "Ὅπου may be added to these, when it signifies *quandoquidem*.

NOTE. Here the Indic. is the usual mode. The Opt. with ἄν is also employed, when *conditional supposition* is expressed; and the Ind. historic

§ 156. SYNTAX: ADVERBIAL SENTENCES. 247

tenses with ἄν, when it is implied that a thing has taken place, or could take place, only under certain circumstances. For the Indic., see the example above. For the *Optative ;* 'Now you may kill Hector, ἐπεὶ ἄν μάλα σοι σχεδὸν ἔλθοι, *since he may have come near enough to you,* Il. ι. 304. For the Indic. Praeterite thus: 'He has yielded... ἐπεὶ οὔ κεν [=ἄν] ἀνιδρωτί γ' ἐτελέσθε, *since* (otherwise) *the matter would not have been finished without sweat,*' Il. o, 228.

(b) Such adverbial conjunctives as stand for nouns, pronouns, etc., expressive of *ground* or *reason.*

These are ὅτι, διότι, διόπερ, οὕνεκα, etc. Of these, ὅτι is itself Acc. neut. of ὅστις ; διότι = διὰ τοῦτο ὅτι ; οὕνεκα = τούτου ἕνεκα ὅ. The correlative of these, in the leading clause, must be τούτῳ (Dat. instrumental), or διὰ τοῦτο, ἐκ τούτου, etc., either expressed or implied.

NOTE. *Modes* here are the same as in the preceding class (a).

(3) (*b*) CONDITIONAL ADVERBIAL SENTENCES. These are in their nature *hypothetical,* and are introduced by εἰ, ἐάν (=εἰ ἄν), ἤν (contract of ἐάν), or ἄν (a substitute for ἤν).

One might naturally expect that in all *hypothetical* sentences we should of course find only the Subj. or Opt. mode. But the Greeks have formed for these sentences some of the most minute shades of expression of which any language is capable. The εἰ or ἐάν which introduces them seems in itself to indicate the idea of *possibility,* while *the verbs that follow are designed to express the relation of the action designated to the apprehension or conviction of the speaker's own mind.* This will account for the apparent departure from ordinary constructions.

(4) Hypothetical sentences may be divided into *four* classes, each of which has its own peculiar construction and meaning.

I. *The Protasis.*

(1) The condition stated is regarded as a *thing certain* or *actual ;* in which case εἰ with any tense of the Indic. is employed.

E. g. εἰ τοῦτο λέγεις—ἔλεγες—ἔλεξας—λέξεις, etc. It matters not whether the thing is in reality certain or not; for the nature of the case refers it only to the *convictions of the speaker ;* and the *Indic.* shows that he assumes the thing as actual.

(2) The condition is stated as a thing *possible* or *probable, with the adjunct idea of its being realized by future circumstances.* Here the Subj. with ἐάν is employed.

E. g. ἐὰν τοῦτο λέγῃς, i. e. I do not know, or decide, or assume, that you say this, but I suppose it, and think it probable that the future will so decide it.

(3) The condition is stated as something which is merely *supposed* or *conjectured, without any reference in the mind to a future decision from circumstances.* Here the Opt. with εἰ is used.

E. g. εἰ τοῦτο λέγοις, i. e. I merely suppose the case to be that you say this. What will be matter of *fact,* I neither ask nor attempt to decide.

248 § 157. SYNTAX: ADVERBIAL SENTENCES.

(4) The condition is stated as something which the speaker believes has not happened, or will not, or cannot. Here the Ind. *historic* tenses with εἰ are employed.

E. g. εἰ τοῦτο ἔλεγες—ἔλεξας, i. e. I merely suppose the case that you said this, although I believe that you did not, and will not.

II. *The Apodosis.*

(5) Corresponding to these four respective *Protases* there must of course be so many *Apodoses* or reciprocal members, which state the *sequence* of each supposed case. These have as many gradations as the Protases, and generally correspond in mode and tense. E. g.

(1) *Certainty* in the apodosis is expressed by the *Indicative*; as εἰ τοῦτο λέγεις, ἁμαρτάνεις, i. e. assuming that you said this, it is certain that you err. Here, also, if the protasis be only a probability, the apodosis may still, if the speaker wishes it, be in the Indic.; as ἐάν τοῦτο λέγῃς, ἁμαρτάνεις, i. e. supposing (as is probable) you say this, then you are in error.

(2) *Probability*, to be determined by circumstances, would naturally require the Subj. in the apodosis; but in the N. Test. every where, and usually in the classics, the Ind. Future (nearly allied to the Subj.) is employed; e. g. ἐάν τις θέλῃ τὸ θέλημα αὐτοῦ ποιεῖν, γνώσεται, etc. John 7: 17. Matt. 28: 14. In Homer, however, the Subj. is not unfrequently employed in such an apodosis.

(3) *Mere supposition* in the apodosis takes the Optative with ἄν; e. g. εἰ τοῦτο λέγοις, ἁμαρτάνοις ἄν, should you say this, you would err.

(4) What is regarded as *impossible* or *improbable*, is expressed in the apodosis by the historic tenses of the Ind. with ἄν; e. g. εἰ τοῦτο ἔλεγες, ἡμάρτανες ἄν, if you had said this, it were erroneous, [the implication is, You did not say it, and therefore did not err].

(6) GENERAL PRINCIPLE. *In general, the mode and tense of the protasis is adopted also in the apodosis;* but this is far from being always the case. It becomes necessary, therefore, to point out the various phases which the protasis and apodosis here assume in their relation to each other.

Each of these, by itself, has already been illustrated above; where it has been shown, that the *protasis* of a conditional sentence may have four forms, and also the *apodosis* four forms. But the mode and tense of the protasis is not always followed by the same in the apodosis; for the speaker often wishes to express a shade of certainty or uncertainty in one member of a conditional sentence, which he does not express in the other. Hence the various combinations, which we must now notice.

§ 157. *Mutual relation of Protasis and Apodosis.*

(1) What is regarded as *certain* or *actual* is expressed, in the

§ 157. Syntax: Protasis and Apodosis.

protasis, by the Indicative of all tenses; in the apodosis it is expressed in the same way, or by an Imperative.

The meaning is, that any tense of the Indic., appropriate to the nature of the case, may be employed in either the protasis or apodosis. In other words, it is *not* necessary, when the protasis employs any one particular tense, that the apodosis should employ the same tense. Any other tense of the Indic. that is needed, may be employed; or an Imper. mode may be used in its room. E. g. the Present in both clauses: Matt. 19: 10, εἰ οὕτως ἐστίν ... οὐ συμφέρει. 1 Cor. 6: 2. Rom. 8: 25.—Present in one and Future in the other: Rom. 8: 11, εἰ τὸ πνεῦμα ... οἰκεῖ ... ζωοποιήσει. Matt. 17: 4. John 5: 47.—Present and Perfect: 1 Cor. 15: 16, εἰ νεκροὶ οὐκ ἐγείρονται, οὐδὲ Χριστὸς ἐγήγερται. 2 Pet. 2: 20.—Present and Imperative: εἰ θέλεις εἰσελθεῖν ... τήρησον τὰς ἐντολάς, Matt. 19: 17. 8: 31. 27: 42. al. In the same manner, the protasis may have a Praeterite and the apodosis a Present, Future, or Imperative mode, etc.; see Rom. 15: 27. 1 John 4: 11. John 13: 32. 15: 20. 18: 23. Rom. 11: 17, 18. So there may be a Future in both the protasis and apodosis, Matt. 26: 33. James 2: 11.

Note 1. In the N. Test. most of the cases of this nature are such as take the *Indic.* mode in both clauses. But the Greek is susceptible of a wider range of expression. An apodosis may be required which expresses mere *supposition*, and not what is viewed as actual; and then the Optative with ἄν is employed in it; e. g. εἰ τοῦτο λέγεις, ἁμαρτάνοις ἄν, *if you say this, I should suppose you to be in an error,* (a *softened* mode of expressing one's opinion, instead of employing the categorical Indicative). Here ἄν is sometimes *omitted;* and then mere *possibility* is signified, without reference to conditionality.

Note 2. In case the actual *consequence* of the condition is intended to be denied, or is strongly doubted, the apodosis takes a *historic* tense of the Indic. with ἄν.

(2) *Supposition,* or *possibility with the expectation of future realization,* takes the Subj. (either Pres. or Aor.) with ἐάν in the protasis, and usually (not always) the Indic. Future in the apodosis, or else the Imper. mode.

E. g. John 7: 17, ἐάν τις θέλῃ ... γνώσεται. Matt. 28: 14, ἐὰν ἀκουσθῇ τοῦτο ... πείσομεν. Matt. 5: 13. Rom. 2: 26. 1 Cor. 8: 10. So the Imperative also; as in John 7: 37. Matt. 5: 23. 10: 13. 18: 17. Rom. 12: 20.—But sometimes the *Present* (Indic.) is in the apodosis; e. g. Matt. 18: 13. 2 Cor. 5: 1. Rom. 7: 3, al., mostly in the sense of a Future, or with such a meaning as the Present has in general propositions. So also with the Perfect or the Aorist Indicative in the apodosis; e. g. Rom. 2: 25. 7: 2. 1 Cor. 7: 28.

Note 1. Ἄν is sometimes joined with the Fut. in the apodosis, and then such Fut. is conditional. Instead of the Fut. here, Homer often employs in the apodosis the Subj. Aor. or Present, with or without ἄν.

Note 2. When *supposition merely* is to be indicated by the apodosis, it takes the Opt. with ἄν; e. g. ἐὰν καταμέμφωμαι ἐμαυτόν, πῶς ἄν ... βιοτεύοιμι; *If I must condemn myself, how could I then live?*

§ 157. SYNTAX: PROTASIS AND APODOSIS.

NOTE 3. In epic, Doric, and Aeolic, *εἰ* stands in the protasis with the Subj., instead of *ἐάν*. Sometimes also in Herodotus and the tragedians; so too in the N. Test., e. g. Rev. 11: 5. Luke 9: 13. 1 Cor. 14: 5, with Var. On the other hand, *ἐάν* sometimes takes the *Indic.* mode after it in its various tenses, instead of the Subjunctive; as Rom. 14: 8, *ἐὰν ἀποθνή-σκομεν.* So Gal. 1: 8. John 8: 36. Luke 11: 12. 1 John 5: 15. See Job 22: 3. This is a *late* idiom; and it is still a contested one, as to some of the better classics. See Winer, § 42. c. Remarks.

(3) *Mere supposition,* without reference to realization, takes the Opt. with *εἰ* in the protasis, and usually the Opt. with *ἄν* in the apodosis.

E. g. *εἰ ταῦτα λέγοις, ἁμαρτάνοις ἄν. Εἴ τι ἔχοι, δοίη ἄν.*

NOTE 1. When the apodosis is designed to state any thing as *actual* or *certain,* then it takes the Indic. of any tense which is rendered necessary, viz. Pres. Fut., etc. E. g. *εἰ τοῦτο λέγοις, ἁμαρτάνεις—εἰ τοῦτο γένοιτο, ἔσται καὶ ἐκεῖνο.* Instead of the *Fut.* Indic. here, Homer often employs the Subj. with *ἄν.* To the Indic. Future, moreover, in other writers, *ἄν* is sometimes attached.

NOTE 2. (*a*) In the apodosis, the *historic* tenses of the Indic. are employed with *ἄν, when actuality is denied;* e. g. *εἰ οὐκ εἰδεῖεν τοῦτο ... ἴεντο ἂν ἐπὶ τοὺς πόνους,* i. e. =they did see this, and so did not go, etc. This form is not usual; but,

(*b*) Very often the Indic. Imperfect with *ἄν,* in such a conditioned sentence, shows *repeated action* in past time, but repeated only so often as the circumstances mentioned in the protasis permitted it to be repeated; e. g. *εἰ δέ τις αὐτῷ περί του ἀντιλέγοι. ἐπὶ τὴν ὑπόθεσιν ... ἐπανῆγεν ἂν πάντα τὸν λόγον, and if any one contradicted him respecting any matter ... he brought back the whole discourse to the fundamental principle,* i. e. so often as the first was done, so often he repeated the latter.

NOTE 3. The Opt. in the apodosis sometimes omits *ἄν.* Moreover, in many sentences which really belong here, the *protasis* is omitted, because it may be easily supplied; e. g. *ἡδέως ἂν ἀκούσαιμι, gladly would I hear him,* i. e. *εἰ γένοιτο.* So, *if I could, might it be allowed, should it be possible, should circumstances allow,* etc., are almost usually *omitted* in a protasis, while the apodosis is expressed.

Vice versâ, the apodosis is sometimes omitted; e. g. in expressions of *wish,* as *εἰ τοῦτο γένοιτο, might this happen,* scil. *εὐτυχὴς ἂν εἴην, then I should be lucky.*

(4) *Conditionality which the speaker believes will not take place,* or the actuality of which he disbelieves, is expressed by a *historic* tense of the Indic. in the protasis with *εἰ,* and usually by the same tense with *ἄν* in the apodosis.

E. g. *εἰ τοῦτο ἔλεγες, ἡμάρτανες ἄν, should you say this, you would err,* (but you do not say it, and therefore do not err). So often in the N. Test.; e. g. Luke 7: 39. 17: 6. John 5: 46. 8: 42. 9: 41. Matt. 11: 21. 12: 7. John 14: 28, al. saepe.

§ 157. Syntax: Protasis and Apodosis. 251

NOTE 1. Here, of the historic tenses, the Imperf. usually denotes *abiding* or *continuing action*; the Pluperf., action the *consequences of which continue*; the Aor., action *momentary*, or once for all.

NOTE 2. The Opt. with ἄν stands in the apodosis, when the possibility of what is there predicated is admitted; as εἴ τις τοῦτο ἔλεγε, ψεῦδος ἄν φαῖμεν, i. e. *we might say it was false*.

NOTE 3. THE PROTASIS, as in No. 3. Note 3 above, is frequently omitted here in short phrases, and where it is easily supplied by the mind; as ἐγὼ μὲν οὔ τ' ἂν ᾠόμην γενέσθαι, *I should not have thought it*, i. e. even had one told it to me, etc. So in formulas of wishing, THE APODOSIS may be omitted; as εἰ τοῦτο ἔγενετο, *if this had happened!* where εὐτυχής ἂν εἴην, *I had been lucky*, is implied.

NOTE 4. OMISSION OF ἄν IN THE APODOSIS. This is so frequent, that some special attention to it is needed. In the apodosis of such conditional sentences as exhibit a *historic* tense of the Ind., it seems to have been deemed sufficient, in a multitude of cases, for the *protasis* to take such a form as to show that the condition was *not* fulfilled, and consequently the apodosis must of course imply a *denial* of the reality of the thing predicated in it; and this, whether ἄν is inserted or omitted. When ἄν is omitted, the apodosis, so far as the manner of expression is concerned, stands free of conditionality, i. e. it is not expressed as if it were dependent on the fulfilment of the condition stated in the protasis, or it takes no notice of this in the manner of its construction. The Greeks seem to have employed this mode of construction as *energetic*; although we cannot make this apparent by any translation into English, because our language does not correspond here. E. g. εἰ ζῶν ἐτύγχανεν ὁ Ἀμύντας, ἐκεῖνον αὐτὸν παρειχόμην, *had Amyntas been alive, I should have produced him*; where ἄν is omitted in the apodosis, and the omission serves to throw energy into the predicate (*producing*), while still the form of the whole sentence, taken together, shows conclusively, that Amyntas was *not* alive, and therefore was *not* produced. So εἰ δὲ μήτε διδάσκαλον εἴχομεν ... οὕτω δὴ ἀνόητον ἦν δήπου ἐπιχειρεῖν, etc., *but if we have had no teacher ... so it were a foolish thing surely to undertake*, etc.; where ἄν is omitted, and the latter clause is intensive.

In particular, this omission of ἄν is common in the apodosis, when this contains verbs indicative of *necessity, propriety, expediency, possibility, liberty, inclination, duty*, etc., or the reverse of these; e. g. such verbs as χρῆν, ἔδει, ὤφελον, προσῆκε, εἰκὸς ἦν, αἰσχρὸν ἦν, ἔξην, καλῶς εἶχε, ἔμελλον, ἐβουλόμην, etc. In such cases the Greeks preferred to state actions that were *just, decorous, desirable*, etc., as unembarrassed with conditionalities although the contour of the sentence implies of course that the actions were not done. E. g. εἰ ... εἶπέ με τελευτήσειν ... χρῆν δή σε ποιέειν, *had he said that I should perish ...* [then] *was it necessary that you should do this*, Herod. I. 39, where ἄν is omitted after χρῆν. So εἰ μὲν αἰσχρόν τι ἔμελλον ἐργάσασθαι, θάνατον ἀντ' αὐτοῦ προαιρετέον ἦν [ἄν], *death was more eligible than this*.

In cases like these, *the protasis is* OFTEN *omitted*, when it may be easily supplied by an intelligent reader. Moreover, *in all these cases ἄν may be inserted, pro libitu scriptoris*. See Kühner, § 821, for an ample illustration of the whole subject.

NOTE 5. Such words as do in themselves convey the sense of ἄν, in apodoses of this nature, require of course the omission of ἄν, in order to avoid repetition; e. g. κινδευνεύω, ὀλίγου, μικροῦ, τάχα, *nearly, almost*. Such words of themselves show that the thing mentioned did not actually take place, and so virtually they supply the place of ἄν.

§ 158. *Some peculiarities of hypothetical sentences in general.*

(1) Ἄν *sometimes appears in the protasis, as well as in the apodosis;* but when it does, it shows that the protasis is itself in a *conditional* state, and depends on something else to be performed; εἰ ταῦτα λέγοις ἄν, *if you should say this*, i. e. if you should say it in case circumstances required, opportunity offered, demand should be made, etc.

(2) *In many cases the* PROTASIS *is omitted.* But here the context may supply it, or the nature of the phrase suggest it.

(3) *In some cases the* APODOSIS *is omitted;* e. g. in cases of wishing; in Siopesis, 1. e. suppression (by reason of feeling) of a part of a sentence; in which cases the context easily supplies it.

(4) The εἰ or ἐάν of the protasis is sometimes omitted, when other equivalent modes of expression compensate for it.

§ 159. *Adverbial sentences: Way and Manner.*

(1) These consist of such clauses as are introduced by ὥστε, (seldom ὡς); to which there must be a correspondent οὕτως (οὕτω) in the main clause, either expressed or implied.

E. g. οὕτω καλός ἐστιν, ὥστε θαυμάζεσθαι=θαυμασίως καλός ἐστιν. But here the reader must be advertised, that not all clauses with ὥστε are of this nature, for some of them constitute clauses *complementary* of a verb = Acc. case. The nature of each, considered by itself, will enable one easily to distinguish them.

(2) In these clauses, when that which is *actual* and *real* is to be designated, as usual, *the Indicative is employed.*

E. g. οὕτω κακῶς διακείμεθα, ὥστ᾽ ... οὐδὲν ... πρᾶξαι δυνάμεθα.

(3) Most usually the *Inf.* mode is employed after ὥστε; and in the following cases, viz.

(1) When an action is designated by it which proceeds *from the nature of the thing* designated in the main clause, or from this in conjunction with *design* or *intention;* as πεπαιδευμένος οὕτως, ὥστε μικρὰ... ῥᾳδίως ἔχειν ἀρκοῦντα, *so taught as easily to regard a little as sufficient,* i. e. this estimation flowed from the nature of his instructions. Σκοποῦντες καιρόν, εἴ τις παραπέσοι, ὥστε τοὺς ἄνδρας σῶσαι, *watching the opportunity, in case any might occur, in order that they might save the men* [design].

(2) When οὕτως is expressed in the main clause; or when ὥστε means *in such a way as;* the Inf. is usually employed after ὥστε. So also when the *intensity* of the predicate in the main clause is compared with some-

§ 160. SYNTAX: ADVERBIAL CLAUSES. 253

thing in the by-clause; as ἦν κακὰ μείζω, ἢ ὥστε ἀνακλαίειν, *the evils were greater than can be deplored.*

NOTE. Not unfrequently ὥστε is *omitted* before the Infinitive, inasmuch as this mode of itself designates *sequel* or consequence.

(3) When the main clause has an Opt. predicate, the subordinate one (with ὥστε) takes the Opt.; without ἄν, when *mere supposition* is expressed; with ἄν, when *conditionality* is added to this, in which case the main clause has the Indicative.

E. g. εἴ τις χρῷτο τῷ ἀργυρίῳ, ὥστε... κάκιον τὸ σῶμα ἔχοι, *if any one should use money, so that... he should make himself diseased,* etc.—ἰσχυρόν ἐστιν, ὥστ' οὐκ ἂν καταγείη, it [the vessel] *is strong, so that it cannot be broken,* i. e. without great force applied.

(4) *Parenthetic* clauses with ὡς and an Inf. are frequently employed, which, in *construction*, are independent of the main clause, but serve as a kind of limitation or modification of it.

E. g. ὡς ἔπος εἰπεῖν—ὡς γέ μοι δοκεῖν, *so to speak, as it seems to me,* etc. So ὡς ἐμὲ οὖ μεμνῆσθαι, *as I well remember.* Such clauses partake of brachylogy.

REMARK. Sometimes ὥστε is placed before an *Imper.;* but it does not make the Imper. deyendrnt on it, but rather implies some verb in the Inf. after it; e. g. ' Orestes is mortal, ὥστε, μὴ λίαν στένε, *so that* [I say] *do not mourn,* instead of saying: ὥστε μὴ λίαν στένειν.

§ 160. *Adverbial clauses of comparison.*

(1) These may respect comparison in regard to *quality* or *quantity.*

(2) (*a*) As TO QUALITY. Clauses of this nature are introduced by ὡς, ὥστε, ὥσπερ, ὅπως; which correspond to οὕτως, ὧδε, or ὡς, in the main clauses, either expressed or implied. The modes and tenses correspond with those of *adjective or relative clauses.* See § 149 above.

Here, (1) The Indic. is used to express definite certainty. (2) The Subj. with ἄν (sometimes without it) to express a relation of undefined frequency, i. e. *whenever,* etc, a thing is done. (3) The Opt., when a supposition or possibility is made to depend on something. E. g. δίδωσιν, ὅπως ἐθέλει—δίδωσιν, ὅπως ἂν ἐθέλῃ—δοκεῖ ὁμοίως λέγεσθαι ταῦτα, ὥσπερ ἄν τις... λέγοι, *as one might say,* Phaedo, p. 87.

NOTE. In comparisons, the Pres., Fut., or Aorist, is employed, as the writer has respect to the present, future, or past, in regard to the things which are said. Here the *modes* are regulated, as usual, by the nature of the declaration.

(3) (*b*) As TO QUANTITY. Here ὅσῳ (ὅσον) begins the by-clause; and the main clause contains τόσῳ, τόσον, τοσούτῳ, τοσούτον, either expressed or implied.

NOTE. But here, not unfrequently, τύσῳ, τοσούτῳ, etc., are omitted, and the relative ὅσῳ is the representative of *so much as*, or of *so much, as much*; just as ὅς, ὅ, comes in this way to mean *he who, that which*, etc.

INFINITIVE MODE.

§ 161. *Nature of Inf.; distinguished from the Participle.*

(1) The Inf. mode expresses *a verbal idea, independent of modal and personal relations.*

That it has no *personal* inflections, is evidence that in itself it is not designed to express personal relations. Equally clear is it, that it expresses no relations which are properly *modal*; e. g. it is not like *I say, I may say, I might say*, etc.; but expresses simply the abstract verbal idea of action, independent of such modifications. It is named *mode*, merely in the way of analogy. The appellation *Infinitive mode* of itself warns the reader, that the term *mode* is not to be taken here in its ordinary sense, viz. that of definite or limited modification.

NOTE 1. *Distinction between the Inf. and Participle.* As the Inf. is the representative of an *abstract* verbal idea, and therefore occupies in reality the place of a *noun*, so the Part. occupies the place of an *attributive adjective*, and is the representative of an *adjective* idea. The Inf. may be called *the noun of the verb*; the Participle may be named *its adjective*. The Part., however, is distinguished both from the real noun and adjective by two qualities, (1) *By an adsignification of time.* (2) *By its retaining the regimen of the verb.* Adjectives and even nouns, however, do also occasionally retain the regimen; yet only certain limited classes of them do this. With the *participle*, on the other hand, the principle is a *general* one. The *adjective* nature of the Part. is manifest, moreover, from the fact, that it has inflections in common with adjectives, and like them, is always an *attributive*.

NOTE 2. That the Inf. is in substance a *noun*, is manifest from the fact, that it may be the *subject* or *object* of a sentence, and that it takes the article, in all its cases, in like manner as a noun. Besides this, the Inf. is in all cases manifestly dependent on a finite verb, or on some word which bears a sense equivalent to such a verb. Strictly speaking, it is always in and of itself an *object*, i. e. a governed word in a sentence = Acc. case; but *practically* it often appears in other forms i. e. in other cases, by means of the *article*, like nouns in general. *It either designates something* DONE, ACCOMPLISHED, SUFFERED; *or else something* TO BE DONE, TO BE EFFECTED, i. e. END, DESIGN, CONSEQUENCE.

§ 162. [A] INF. MODE WITHOUT THE ARTICLE.

(1) This is distinguished from the Inf. with the article by the fact, that it is always dependant in such a way as to be the *object* of a sentence, i. e. it always points out something to *be done* or to *be aimed at*, and so can in reality be only in the *objective*

§ 162. SYNTAX: INFINITIVE MODE. 255

(i. e. Acc.) case, although in some instances it does not seem to be so; while the *Inf. with the article* is used as a simple *nomen verbale*, and may be employed in all the cases of a noun.

NOTE. In respect to most cases, this statement is very plain, e. g. ἐλπίζω νικήσειν, *I hope to conquer* = Spero victoriam, where something *to be done* is indicated; ἥκω μανθάνειν, *I come to learn* = ἥκω εἰς μάθησιν, where *design, purpose*, or *end*, is designated. But in sentences which have a *copula*, their construction with the Inf. in such a sense is not so apparent; e. g. οὔ τι κακὸν βασιλεύειν, *it is not a bad thing to reign, or to reign is no bad affair*. Here the Inf. is plainly the *subject* of the sentence; but still, it is *dependent* and expresses something to be done. So also μανθάνειν καλόν, which we may render *learning is good*; but here μανθάνειν still expresses an object *to be achieved*, or an end *to be attained*. By urging the subject a little farther, the true basis of the more difficult constructions will appear, and it will be seen that they are *breviloquent*, or that an ellipsis must be supposed; e. g. οὔ τι κακὸν [με, ὑμᾶς, ἡμᾶς, τινο, etc.] βασιλεύειν—so [με, ἡμᾶς, αὐτούς, τινα, etc.] μανθάνειν, καλόν ἐστι ; in which cases the *objective* nature of the Inf. is apparent.

(2) The Inf. without the article may be the *subject* of a sentence or proposition.

This is sufficiently illustrated above. But here the reader must distinguish this carefully from such subjects as designate *agents*. The Inf. alone, which designates abstract action (as above); the Inf. with adjuncts, as εἰσελθεῖν εἰς τὴν ζωὴν χωλὸν ἢ κυλλόν, καλόν σοί ἐστιν; yea, parts of sentences with other forms, or even whole sentences, *may be the subject of a verb that follows*; as, 'If he had not been born, καλὸν ἦν αὐτῷ; so 'Whether they depart or remain, whether they neglect this business or attend to it, οὐ διαφέρει, *makes no difference*.' 'That he said: I will not do this; that he has actually neglected to do it; yea, that he has made active opposition to it; *is well known*.' Such cases show how widely this principle is extended. So in the *formal* construction of a sentence, the Inf. often occupies the place of *subject*; yet its true nature is the designation of something *objective*, either to be accomplished or to be sought after. See Matt. 12: 10. 15: 26. 1 Thess. 4: 3. Eph. 5.12, al saepe. Much more frequent, however, is the use of the Inf. in the cases that follow, viz.

(3) The Inf., as immediately designating an *object*, follows large classes of verbs, with various shades of meaning.

(1) It follows verbs expressive of *effort, intention, will, purpose*, etc.; e. g. πειρῶμαι, ἐπιθυμῶ, βούλομαι, ἐάω, μηχανῶμαι, etc.; or the converse of these, as φοβοῦμαι, φεύγω, κατέχω, κωλύω, etc. In short, whatever verbs designate a *conatus* of body or mind, in any sense, may take the Inf. as their *complement*, i. e. in order to designate the object or end of the *conatus*.

NOTE 1. Sometimes, in order to render the expression of this complement *emphatic*, ὥστε is put before the Inf. mode; e. g. ἔπεισεν ὥστε ἄγειν.

NOTE. 2. *Oftentimes other constructions besides the Inf. are used in order to designate a complement* to verbs of this nature; viz. the Subj., Opt., or

Indic. Fut., with ὡς, ὅπως, ἵνα, etc. before them. E. g. 'My meat is, ἵνα ποιῶ, that I may do the will, etc. instead of ποιεῖν, etc. John 4 : 34. I am not worthy, ἵνα λύσω, that I should loose, etc.' John 1 : 27. Acts 27 : 42. John 9: 22. 11 : 37, al saep. So often in the classics; Kuhner, § 637. Anm. 4. Winer (§ 45. 9) has discussed and vindicated this usage, particularly in respect to ἵνα, at great length, and triumphantly. The N. Test., however, abounds more in it than the classics, and carries it further ; but the modern Greek introduces even the Inf. itself with νά (=ἵνα) before it.

(2) The Inf. follows verbs expressive of any *direct action of the mental faculty*, and also such as indicate the *outward expression of this action.*

E. g. νομίζω, ἐλπίζω λέγω, μανθάνω, et al. simil.

(3) It follows verbs signifying *ability, efficiency, power, aptness, capability,* etc.; also verbs of *choosing, nominating, educating, teaching, showing, urging,* and the like.

These are all so plain, and so frequently to be met with, that no examples are needed. It is enough to remind the reader, that all such verbs, being imperfect as to the full expression of an idea or sentence, need a *complement* in order to make the sentence complete and intelligible, and the Inf. mode supplies that complement.

NOTE. Here also ὥστε is not unusual before the Inf., in the way of emphasis ; e. g. ἱκανός ὥστε λέγειν.

(4) Adjectives, participials, and even abstract nouns, take an Inf. after them in the way of *complement*, i. e. to show the object, tendency, or design, of the action, etc., which is designated by them.

E. g. ἄξιος θαυμάζεσθαι—ἥδιστον πίνεσ-θαιπίνεσθαι—φόβος ἀκοῦσαι—θυῖμα ἰδέσθαι—ἕκων εἶναι—etc. Any adjectives or nouns, which in their nature are significant of something that needs a *complement* in order to complete the idea, may take an Inf. for this purpose ; *and this more commonly* WITHOUT, *but sometimes* WITH, thed efinite article. The article designates specification or emphasis.

NOTE 1. The Inf. *active* or *middle* is often used here where we should translate *passively*, e. g. ὁ χῶρος . . . ἐπιτήδεος ἐνδιατάξαι τε καὶ ἐξαριθμῆσαι τὸν στρατόν, *a place fit for the army to be marshalled and numbered*, or *for one to marshall*, etc. Herod. VII. 59. So ῥᾴδια ποιεῖν, *easy to be done*, or *for one to do.* At other times, a *personal* pronoun is to be supplied from the context; as ῥηίτεροι πολεμίζειν ἦσαν Ἀχαιοί, *the Grecians were easy* [for us] *to conquer*, Il. σ. 258.

NOTE. 2. Even the substantive verbs εἶναι and πεφυκέναι, may be followed by the same construction as the adjectives and nouns designated above require ; e. g. ἀμύνειν εἰσὶν καὶ ἄλλοι, *there are others to defend* ; ἔφυν οὐδὲν πράσσειν κακῶς, *I was born to do nothing badly.*

(5) The Inf. alone, or the Inf. with other adjuncts intimately connected, is often employed, (after verbs, adjectives, or nouns) , for the purpose of *defining, limiting, explaining, specifying, showing the sequel, operation, or effect of*, etc. ; thus constitut-

§ 162. SYNTAX: INFINITIVE MODE. 257

tuting, in the widest sense, the *complement* in sentences where it is used.

E. g. ἄριστος θείειν, *preeminent as to the race;* ἄλκιμος μάχεσθαι, *brave as to the combat;* τύχη οἱ ... τελευτῆσαι εὖ τὸν βίον, *it was his fortune ... to end life well,* where the last clause explains τύχη. So ἔχων ὦτα ἀκούειν, *having ears to hear,* i. e. ears adapted to hear, or made for the purpose of hearing, Luke 8 : 8 ; ἐξουσία γυναῖκα περιάγειν, *power to lead about a wife,* where the Infin. περιάγειν defines the nature of the power, 1 Cor. 9 : 5 ; ἃ παρέλαβον κρατεῖν, *which they have received in order to retain* or *hold fast,* Mark 7 : 4 ; ἔδωκαν αὐτῷ πιεῖν ὄξος, *they gave him vinegar to drink,* i. e. that he might drink it, Matt. 27 : 34 ; οὐ μετενόησαν δοῦναι αὐτῷ δόξαν, *they did not repent to give him glory,* i. e. so as to give him glory, Rev. 16 : 9 ; ἤλθομεν προσκυνῆσαι αὐτῷ, *we have come in order to worship him,* Matt. 2 : 2. Rev. 14 : 15, ἡ ὥρα θερίσαι, *the hour proper for reaping;* Rev. 12 : 2. 2 Pet. 3 : 1, 2. 1 Cor. 1 : 17. 10 : 7. Matt. 11 : 7. 20 : 28. Luke 1 : 17. John 4 : 15, al. saepe. See Matth. § 532. d., for evidences of the like usage in the classics. In fact, the use of the Inf. in them is even more lax than in the N. Testament ; see Winer, § 45. 3.

NOTE 1. In cases where *design* is to be indicated by the Inf., it often takes ὥστε before it ; e. g. καταργηθῆμεν ἀπὸ τοῦ νόμου ... ὥστε δουλεύειν, *in order that we might serve,* etc., Rom. 7 : 6. Luke 9 : 52. 2 Cor. 3 : 7, al. saepe. Once ὡς is used for ὥστε, Acts 20 : 24 ; so also occasionally in the classics, Rost, § 125. 8. Kühner § 642. a. Anm. 1.

REMARK. *Inf. with the article in the place of the Inf. without it.* In nearly all the instances where the Inf. is usually employed without the article, in case the writer means to *give a particular emphasis* or to *specify,* he may employ the article. In the tragic poets this is very common ; but it is also usual elsewhere.

§ 163. *Infinitive used for the Imperative.*

(1) Since the Inf. is so intimately connected with verbs signifying *desire, wish, request,* etc., it is natural to conclude, that in brachylogical expressions of command these verbs may be omitted, and *the Inf. only be expressed;* and such is the fact.

E. g. ' Whoever may ask for these, τούτῳ ἀποδοῦναι, *give to him;* Herod. vi. 86. Τοῦτον, τοίνυν ... φάναι, *say this now.* In the classics this is not unfrequent ; see Kühner § 644. a. In the N. Test., however, this usage is not frequent ; Phil. 3 : 16, στοιχεῖν seems to belong here ; and perhaps Apoc. 10 : 9, δοῦναι ; and Col. 4 : 6, εἰδέναι.

NOTE. The classics often use the Inf. in formulas where *wish, supplication, entreaty, invocation,* etc., should be designated ; Kühner, ubi sup. b. c. The Inf., also, like the Fut. Indic., sometimes expresses *what ought to be done;* e. g. γυμνὸν σπείρειν, γυμνὸν δὲ βωτεῖν, i. e. *one must sow naked, and also plough naked;* Hesiod. Opp. 391.

33

§ 164. *Cases after the Infinitive.*

The Inf. after another verb may have the *same* subject (agent) as its preceding Verb ; or it may have a *different* one.

(1) When it has the *same* subject, that subject is of course understood to be in the Nominative, although not expressed, and any adjuncts, adjectives, participles, etc., relating to the same subject must usually be in the same case.

E. g. ἐλπίζω διαπορευόμενος θεάσασθαι ὑμᾶς, *I hope, when I pass through, to see you*, i. e. I, passing through, hope etc. Rom. 15: 24 ; δέομαι τὸ μὴ πάρων θαρρῆσαι, *I pray that when present I may not be bold*, i. e. ἐγὼ δέομαι πάρων κ. τ. λ, *I pray that I when present* etc., 2 Cor. 10 : 2. Rom. 1 : 22. Acts 14 : 10. So in the classics; ἔφασκες εἶναι δεσπότης · ἔπεισα αὐτοὺς εἶναι θεός, *I have persuaded them that I am a god*.

NOTE. Where the subject of the Inf. and of the preceding verb is one and the same, it is not usual to repeat it before the Inf. ; e. g. ὁ φίλος ἔφη σπουδάζειν. i. e αὐτὸν σπουδάζειν ; see also the examples under No. 1. above. Yet where emphasis is demanded, the subject may be repeated, and then it is put in the Acc. case, like the examples under No. 2 ; e. g. ἐγὼ ἐμαυτὸν οὐ λογίζομαι κατειληφέναι, Phil. 3 : 13. So καὶ μ' οὐ νομίζω παῖδα σὸν πεφυκέναι, *I do not think myself to have been born your child*, Eurip. Alc. 657 ; and thus not unfrequently in the classics. Winer, p. 265. Rost, p. 507. Yet sometimes the *Nom.* is employed even here ; see Kühner § 646. 2.

(2) When the Inf. has a *different* subject from that of the preceding verb, that subject is regularly put in the Accusative.

E. g. βούλομαι προσεύχεσθαι τοὺς ἀνθρώπους, *I desire that men should pray*, 1 Tim. 2 : 8. 2 Pet. 1 : 15. 1 Cor. 7 : 10. Acts 14 : 19, al. saepe.

NOTE 1. Verbs of all kinds, whether governing the Gen. or Dat., or both, when they take an *object* after them and also the Inf. mode, *usually put that object in the Acc. only*. Yet in some cases the Gen. or Dat. of *object* follows the leading verb ; and even then, another attributive or explanatory word connected with it, and naturally assuming the same case, still assumes the *Acc.* by reason of the influence of the Inf. mode ; e. g. Ἀθηναίων ἐδεήθησαν σφίσι βοηθοὺς γενέσθαι, *they besought the Athenians, to be helpers to them*, where βοηθούς of course is to be referred to Ἀθηναίων. So with the Dative ; e. g. σοὶ ἔστι, ἢ καταδουλῶσαι, ἢ ἐλευθέρας ποιήσαντα . . . λιπέσθαι etc., *it is for thee to enslave, or having made free . . . to leave a memorial*, etc., where ποιήσαντα refers to σοί. So, often, in the classics ; see Kühner, § 648. a. b.

NOTE 2. So, also, *peculiar regimen* may not only change the *case* of the subject, and throw it out of the usual construction, i. e. out of the Acc., but also put an adjunct word in the same unusual case ; e. g. κρεῖττον ἦν αὐτοῖς, μὴ ἐπεγνωκέναι τὴν ὁδὸν κ. τ. λ, where αὐτοῖς is put in the Dat. after κρεῖττον, while, so far as the Inf. is concerned, αὐτούς would be the regular construction, 2 Pet. 2 : 21. So in the classics : δός μοι φανῆναι ἀξίῳ, *help me to appear worthy* ; ὑμῖν . . . ἔξεστι εὐδαίμοσι γενέσθαι, *it is permitted to you*

§ 165. Syntax: Infinitive Mode. 259

to be fortunate; ἅπασι συνέπεσεν... γένεσθαι λαμπροῖς. *it has happened to them all... to become conspicuous.* So, also, as to the Genitive; ἐδέοντο αὐτοῦ εἶναι προθύμον, *they besought him to be ready;* εἰρήσεις... τυράννους... διαφθαρμένους... ὑπὸ ἑταίρων... δοκούντων φίλων εἶναι, where φίλων conforms to the preceding noun (ἑταίρων).

Remark. All cases of this nature, in which the *subject* of the Inf. is thrown out of the Acc. into another oblique case, and where adjunct words (as above) conform to that other oblique case, are called cases of ATTRACTION, because the predicate or adjunct word is attracted to the same case with its principal noun or pronoun. Yet attraction, although admissible at the pleasure of an author, is not always practised; e. g. Herod. III. 36, ἐνετείλατο τοῖς θεράπουσι, λαβόντας μιν ἀποκτεῖναι, *he commanded the servants, that they should take and kill him,* where the writer might have said λαβοῦσι, but he has followed the usual construction, viz. the Acc. case. Often is the regular construction (the Acc.) adopted for the *adjunct* word, where the subject is so remote from the Inf., that attraction would make the sense obscure. See above, in Note 1.

(3) Passive or impersonal verbs, also adjectives or nouns with the verb *to be,* and which yield a like sense, take the *Acc.* after them of the word, which, *logically* considered, is the *subject* of the sentence.

E. g. λέγεται τὸν βασιλέα... ἀγαγεῖν, *it is said that the king leads;* Herod. III. 9. So ἀγγέλλεται τὸν Κῦρον νικῆσαι=ἀγγέλλουσι, etc. The true logical meaning is developed by a different form, which is by no means unfrequent, viz., ὁ Κῦρος ἀγγέλλεται νικῆσαι, where the real subject of the sentence is apparent.

Note. The like construction follows such verbs also as ὁμολογεῖται, πέπρωται, ἔοικε, προσήκει, πρέπει, δονεῖ, συμβαίνει, and also such expressions as ἐστὶν ἀγαθόν—καλόν—φίλον—ἐπεικές; μοῖρά ἐστιν—οὐκ ἔστιν, etc.

Remark. Impersonal constructions are *frequently* modified so as to become personal ones; e. g. the meaning of δίκαιόν ἐστί με ταῦτα πράττειν, is frequently expressed by δίκαιός εἰμι τοῦτο πράττειν. So δίκαιός εἰμι εἶναι ἐλεύθερος=*it is proper that I should be free.* So with ἄξιος, δυνατός, χαλεπός, ἐπίδοξος, etc.

§ 165. [B] Infinitive Mode with the Article.

(1) The article has the effect of transforming the Inf. mode into a noun, which can be employed in all the cases (the Voc. excepted) of other nouns, and with the like significancy.

Note. Still, this *verbal* noun does not lay aside its power to *govern cases* which follow it, in the same manner as the *finite* verb of the same root does; e. g. τὸ ἐπιστολὴν γράφειν.

(2) In this way the Inf. with adjuncts may be made the subject or object of a sentence, by a unity which is given to a composite expression of this nature in consequence of the article.

E. g. *Subject;* as τὸ θνήσκειν τινὰ ὑπὲρ τῆς πατρίδος, καλόν ἐστιν, that one should die for his country, is good. Here, although the first clause is composite, yet it is *as a whole* the subject of the main predicate, καλόν ἐστιν. It should be noted also, that θνήσκειν requires its subject (τινα) to be in the *Acc.*, as usual; for this rule is not dispensed with because of the article. So this Inf. may constitute the *Acc.* or *object* of a sentence; as οὐδεὶς φοβεῖται αὐτὸ τὸ ἀποθνήσκειν, no one fears mere dying; πολὺ μᾶλλον δεῖταί τὸ ζῆν, much rather is he afraid of living. Here *prepositions* may be joined with the Inf., when it has an article; as διὰ τὸ φιλομαθὴς εἶναι—πρὸς τὸ θεαθῆναι αὐτούς, Matt. 6: 1—μετὰ τὸ ἐγερθῆναί με, Matt. 26: 32, al. saep.

(3) The Gen. case, or the Infin. with τοῦ before it deserves special notice. It is more frequent in the N. Test., than any other case of the Inf. when employed as a verbal noun.

(1) The Inf. with τοῦ stands after words which usually govern the Gen., whether these are nouns, adjectives, or verbs; as οὐκ ἔχομεν ἐξουσίαν τοῦ μὴ ἐργάζεσθαι, 1 Cor. 9: 6. ὁ καιρὸς τοῦ ἄρξασθαι, 1 Pet. 4: 17. ἕτοιμοι τοῦ ἀνελεῖν, Acts 23: 15. ἔλαχε τοῦ θυμιάσαι, Luke 1: 9. See 1 Cor. 10: 13. Acts 15: 23. Luke 22: 6. Phil. 3: 21. 2 Cor. 8: 11. Rom. 7: 3, al. saepe. See Kuhner, § 651. 3. *b.* Matth. Gramm. 1256.

(2) More particularly is this form of Inf. employed to designate *design, purpose, object in view,* etc.; e. g. 'A sower ἐξῆλθεν τοῦ σπεῖραι, went forth in order to sow,' Mark 4: 3. 'Satan hath made demand for you τοῦ σινιάσαι ὡς τὸν σῖτον, that he may sift you as wheat,' Luke 22: 31. 'Lo! I come τοῦ ποιῆσαι, in order to do thy will,' Heb. 10: 7. See also Acts 26: 18. 18: 10. Rom. 6: 6. Acts 21: 12. James 5: 17. Eph. 3: 17. Col. 4: 6. Heb. 11: 5, al. saepe. So in the Classics; but not to the same extent. See Kuhner ut supra.

NOTE. Not all Infinitives with τοῦ are to be construed in this way. Verbs of *removing, preventing, hindering,* etc., govern the Gen. of the Inf. nominascens, in the same manner as they govern nouns in the Genitive; e. g. Rom. 15: 22, ἐκοπτόμην ... τοῦ ἐλθεῖν. Acts 10: 47, τίς δύναται κωλῦσαι ... τοῦ μὴ βαπτισθῆναι. Acts 14: 18, μόλις κατέπαυσαν ... τοῦ μὴ θύειν. 1 Pet. 3: 10. Luke 24: 16, al. So in the Classics.

(3) It is also employed in a *laxer* sense, in a kind of *epexegetical* way, or as an equivalent for an Inf. with ὥστε; and sometimes it is scarcely to be distinguished from the common Infinitive without the article; e. g. Acts 7: 19, 'The same dealt hardly with our fathers τοῦ ποιεῖν, *so that they might make* their children outcasts, etc.' Still more lax is the use in Acts 3: 12, 'Why wonder at *us*, as if, by our own power or piety, we had made τοῦ περιπατεῖν αὐτόν, *this man to walk;*' where the force of τοῦ can hardly be discerned. In Luke 1: 77—79 we find ἑτοιμάσαι ... τοῦ δοῦναι, and ἐπιφᾶναι ... τοῦ κατευθῦναι, in the same connection and regimen, without any sensible difference in the Inf. meanings. In the Sept., the Inf. with τοῦ is of most frequent usage, and with many shades of meaning; and oftentimes it is not perceptibly different in sense from the Inf. without τοῦ. So in the later Greek. An instance of the Inf. in Rev. 12: 7, Μιχαὴλ καὶ οἱ ἄγγελοι αὐτοῦ τοῦ πολεμῆσαι, has as yet found no adequate solution; see Winer, § 48, 4 sub fin.

(4) The Dative case of the Inf. mode, with an article, is employed in a sense like that of the Dative of nouns; but it is less frequent than the other cases of the Infinitive.

E. g. 'I had no quietude in my mind τῷ μὴ εὑρεῖν Τίτον, *because I did not find Titus,*' 2 Cor. 2: 12. So τῷ ζῆν ἔστι τι ἐνάντιον, ὥσπερ τῷ ἐγρηγορέναι τὸ καθεύδειν, *there is something opposite to living, as sleeping* [is] *to waking,* Plato, Phaed. p. 71.

NOTE. Here *prepositions* often govern the Dative; as ἐν τῷ καθεύδειν, Matt. 13: 25. Luke 1: 8. Gal. 4: 18. Acts 3: 26, al. Ἐπὶ τῷ δικαίως χρῆσθαι, Plato.

GENERAL REMARK. When prepositions are employed before the Inf, *the article must be inserted.*

§ 166. *Use of* TENSES *in the Infinitive.*

(1) The Present, as elsewhere, denotes continued and repeated action.

E. g. ἐμὲ δεῖ ἐργάζεσθαι τά ἔργα, etc., John 9: 4. 7: 17. 16: 12. Acts 16: 21. Gal. 6: 13, al. saepe.

NOTE. After μέλλω the Inf. Present is frequent, specially in the Evangelists. The Aor. and Fut. are also employed; but the Aor. mostly designates actions which are *temporary;* see Rev. 3: 2, 16. 12: 4. Gal. 3: 23. Acts 11: 28. 27: 10. In the classics, the Fut. is the most usual after μέλλω.

(2) The Aorist is usual when mere *temporary* action is designated; as is also the case with this tense in the definite modes.

This distinction, however, is not very scrupulously observed, either in the N. Test. or in the Classics; see and comp. Matt. 24: 24 and Mark 13: 22, also Mark 13: 3 and Luke 8: 5. For the classics, see Winer § 45. 8 sub med.

(3) The Inf. Perfect is used to denote action *completed,* and also permanent in its consequences.

E. g. in Acts 16: 27. 26: 32. 27: 9, 13. Rom. 15: 9. 2 Pet. 2: 21.

PARTICIPLE.

§ 167. *Nature and construction of the Participle.*

(1) The Participle is employed as an *attributive,* i. e. *it attributes action, state, quality, condition, etc., to some person or thing,* and always is to be connected with a person or thing either expressed or implied.

NOTE 1. Hence it partakes of the nature of an *adjective;* and like the adjective it is often employed in an *adverbial* way. It differs, however, from the adjective, in the fact that it is significant of time (and therefore

§ 167. SYNTAX: PARTICIPLE.

has *tense*), and also retains the usual regimen-power of the verb to which it belongs.

NOTE 2. The Inf. mode, on the other hand, designates in and of itself *an object to be attained* or *sought after*, and does not depend for its significancy on any noun to which it attributes quality or condition. In most cases, the Part. and Inf. can not be exchanged for each other without materially changing the *form* of the sentiment; but in some cases the same idea, for substance, may be expressed by either form. Thus ἥκω μανθάνειν cannot be expressed by ἥκω μανθάνων; the first indicates *design to do something*, the last affirms the fact that the agent is already, or has already been, doing it. But ἥκω μαθησόμενος would indicate substantially the same idea as ἥκω μανθάνειν, although there is still even here, a shade of difference; for the Inf. expresses predominantly *object, end*, while the Part. Fut. designates the idea simply, *that the agent will learn something*.

(2) The Participle being in its nature an *attributive*, and having reference to some person or thing, it must, like an adjective, of course agree in gender and number and case with its noun.

E. g. ἀκούω αὐτοῦ διαλεγομένου—χαίρω σοι ἐλθόντι—ὁρῶ ἄνθρωπον τρέχοντα. Like adjectives, however, it varies occasionally from this general principle; and it does so for the same reasons; see § 117. 2 seq.

(3) A participle may agree with the *subject* of a sentence, or with the *object*. The two cases require a different construction.

(*a*) *With the subject*; where, in case this subject is not repeated after the verb in the form of an object, (and such repetition is not usual), the Part. takes the Nominative case; e. g. οἶδα θνητὸς ὤν, i. e. [ἐγὼ] θνητὸς ὢν οἶδα. Where the subject is repeated in the form of an *object*, the Part. conforms; e. g. οἶδα ἐμὲ θνητὸν ὄντα.

In such cases the Part. of εἶναι is frequently omitted; e. g. σὲ δηλώσω κακόν [sc. κακὸν ὄντα].

(*b*) *With the object*; as ὁρῶ ἄνθρωπον τρέχοντα, etc. So if the object be in the Gen. or Dative, the Part. of course conforms.

(4) Some verbs, from their very nature, do not admit the Part. after them, but demand an Infin. complement; others exclude the Inf. and take a Participle. Many admit both.

This of course depends on the nature of the Infin., or of the Part., as adapted to complete the sentence begun by any verb. To make an enumeration of these verbs, respectively, would occupy too much room, and be a somewhat useless, at any rate an almost endless, task. Kühner has made out a large list (§§ 657—664); but of course it must be incomplete. Nor is it of any serious advantage. It is enough in regard to the *object* which follows a verb, that it is of such a nature that a *participial attribute* can be attached to it. If this be the fact, then it can take a participle.

NOTE. 1. The affirmation made by some critics, that the Part. is in some cases equivalent to the *Inf. mode*, or to a *definite mode*, is not accurate, nor well grounded. E. g. οὐκ ἐπαύοντο διδάσκοντες (Acts. 12: 18) is said

§ 168. SYNTAX: PARTICIPLES. 263

to be equivalent to οὐκ ἐπαύοντο διδάσκειν. But this is not the case. In the first instance the meaning is: 'They teaching, i. e. already having acted and still acting the part of teachers, ceased not to perform the same duty;' in the second: 'They refused to abandon the business of teaching in future.' The shade of meaning, therefore, in each is evidently different.

Here too some nice distinctions are sometimes made; e. g. ἀκούω αὐτοῦ διαλεγομένου, I hear him [with my own ears] discoursing; ἀνοίω καλὸν αὐτὸν εἶναι, I hear [from others] that he is good. So εὗρον αὐτὸν ἔχοντα, I found him possessing, i. e. that he was a possessor, (indicating condition); εὗρον αὐτὸν ἔχειν, I found that he possessed, designating an act in regard to a particular thing.

So, where the sense for substance is the same, whether a Part. or a finite verb is employed, there is still a shade of difference in the manner of the enunciation; e. g. ἐλθὼν εἶδε, and ἦλθε καὶ εἶδε. In the former the minute shade of meaning is: 'When he had come he saw:' in the latter: 'He came and saw.' The first denotes the state of the agent, as having arrived before he saw; the second merely asserts the fact that he came, and then saw.

NOTE 2. In general, verbs signifying any action of the outward or inward senses, any development of these senses, or any affections of the mind; verbs of permitting, bearing, waiting, tiring, beginning, ceasing, prospering, excelling, failing, being inferior, undertaking, ἔχειν denoting condition, etc., are among those which specially stand connected with participles.

§ 168. *Object and manner of using the Participle.*

(1) The wide extent of this usage strikes every reader of a Greek book. In general, the *subordinate* action designated in any composite sentence, is, or may be, expressed by a Participle.

In this way, clearness, precision, distinctiveness, and energy of expression, are attained in a high degree; while the *main* action, being thus separated from the *subordinate*, is rendered much more prominent. Thus *preparatory* or *introductory* action is mostly designated by the Participle; e. g. ἐλθὼν εἶδε· ἀποκριθεὶς εἶπε· ἀκούσας ἐθαύμασε· where, as to the subordinate sense, one might say ἦλθε καὶ εἶδε, etc. The advantage of the Part. is, that it varies the construction, and avoids the use of the conjunction which must be inserted between verbs.

Note 1. Two or more participles may be used, in such a connection, without any intervening καὶ; as καταβὰς ... προσελθὼν ἀπεκύλισε τὸν λίθον, Matt. 28:2; ἀκούων ... πεσών ἐξέψυξε, Acts 5:5; Luke 9:16. 16: 23. 23:48. Mark 1:41, al. The omission of καί denotes that all the participles are closely allied to one and the same final and principal action. Sometimes one Part. is before the principal verb, and another after it; as ῥίψαν ... ἐξῆλθεν ... μηδὲν βλάψαν, Luke 4:35. 10:30. Acts 14:19. al.

NOTE 2. There are a few cases, on the contrary, in which the *principal* action is designated by the Part.; while the verb joined with it has only a *subordinate*, and often an *adverbial* sense. Such secondary verbs are τυγχάνω, λανθάνω, φθάνω, διατελέω, διαγίνομαι, διάγω, δίειμι, χαίρω, and οἴχομαι; e. g. οἳ ἔτυχον παρόντες, *who were present*, where ἔτυχον is a mere helping verb; διατετέλεκα φεύγων τὸ μανθάνειν, *I always avoid learning;* οἱ θεοὶ χαίρουσι τιμώμενοι, *the gods gladly receive honour;* ὃς ἂν φθάνῃ εὐεργετῶν, *whoever first shows favour,* etc.

NOTE 3. In some cases it is a matter of indifference, as to the sense, which of two verbs is used as a participle; e. g. ἥκω καλῶς ποιῶν, or καλῶς ποιῶ ἥκων, et al. saepe.

§ 169. *Participles as expressing adverbial relations.*

(1) This is an important and widely extended office of the Participles, and may be compared with the *gerund* in the Latin language. The Participle thus employed, may, therefore, be named the *gerundial participle.*

Its nature and use will be made plain in the sequel. It needs only to be remarked here, that the participle used as a mere *complement,* and annexed to the idea of a person or thing, differs specifically from this.

(2) *Gerundial Participles* may express. (*a*) Adverbial relations of *time.* (*b*) *Causal* and *conditional* relations. (*c*) Relations of *way* and *manner.*

(3) (*a*) RELATIONS OF TIME. Here the Participle contains in itself the adsignification of time, which may be *adverbially* expressed.

E. g. τὰ χρήματα ἀναλώσαντες ... τούτων οὐκ ἀπέχονται, WHEN *they have spent their property ... they do not abstain from these.* Οὐχὶ μένον σοι ἔμενε; WHILE *it remained, was it not thine own?* Acts 5:4. So 1 Thess. 3:6, al Often so in the Classics.

NOTE 1. The Greeks, in some cases, carry this use of the Part. so far, that it seems to lose its ordinary meaning and to designate *time* principally; e. g. ἀρχόμενος, *in the beginning;* τελευτῶν, *finally, at last;* διαλείπων τὸν χρόνον, lit. *intermitting the time* = *after sometime;* ἀνύσας, lit. *hastening* = quickly, immediately.

NOTE 2. Frequently adverbs expressive of *time* are joined with participles of this nature; which of course gives to them a more emphatic sense.

(4) (*b*) CAUSAL AND CONDITIONAL RELATIONS. In these is a great variety of shades which are to be determined in the context.

E. g. Acts. 4:21, 'They set them at liberty, μηδὲν εὑρίσκοντες, *because they found nothing,*' etc.' Heb. 8:4, 'Then he would not have been a priest, ὄντων τῶν ἱερέων etc., *inasmuch as there are priests* etc.' Rom. 7:3, 'So that she will not be an adulteress, γενομένην ἀνδρὶ ἑτέρῳ, *in case she should marry another man;* [conditional]. See also 1 Thess. 3:5. 1 Tim. 3:10. 4:4. 6:8. John 12:37, 'They believed not on him, τοσαῦτα αὐτοῦ σημεῖα πεποιηκότος, *although he had done so many miracles.*' Κρατῶν δὲ ἡδονῶν ... ὁ Ἔρως ἂν σωφρονοῖ, *Love would behave soberly ... in case it*

§ 170. Syntax: Participles. 265

should refrain from pleasures ; [conditional]. So also as *means ;* e. g. ληϊζόμενοι ζῶσι, *they live by robbing.*

Note. Here also particles, such as καί, καίτοι, καίπερ, ὅμως, ἔπειτα, etc., are often added, which render the relation more emphatic.

(5) (*c*) Way and Manner. Here the Greek has peculiar power, employing this idiom with striking significancy.

E. g. γελῶν εἶπε, *he said laughingly ;* λαθών εἶπε, *he spake secretly.* So φθάσας, *quickly ;* ἐχών, *so,* 1. e. being in such a state ; φερών *impetuously,* ἄγων = *with,* as ἵππον ἄγων ἦλθε. In these and many other participles of a similar nature, it is plain that the *adverbial* signification is the predominant part of the meaning.

§ 170. *Special uses of the Participle.*

(1) It is often, with the article, a mere *nomen agentis.*

E. g. ὁ σπείρων, ὁ κλέπτων, ὁ νικῶν, etc. In this case, it may have the usual regimen of nouns or pronouns ; e. g. τὸ ὑμῶν συμφέρον, *your profit.* And here the article is omitted, when the sense is designed to be *indefinite ;* comp. § 90. 3. Note.

(2) Very often, with the article, participles retain the essential force of verbs and must be so rendered in our language.

E. g. ὁ πράσσων ταῦτα, *he who does these things,* where ὁ = ὅς and πράσσων governs the Acc. case. So ὁ διώκων ἡμᾶς ποτέ, νῦν εὐαγγελίζεται etc., *he who once persecuted us* etc. Gal. 1: 23. Such a use of the participle is also common, when it follows and qualifies an oblique case ; e. g. 'Inherit τὴν βασιλείαν τὴν ἡτοιμασμένην, etc. *the kingdom which has been prepared,* etc.

(3) Participles are often joined with ὡς, which makes their meaning *subjective* rather than *objective.*

The meaning is, that ὡς qualifies them so that they merely declare the opinion, supposition, conclusion, etc., of the agents to which they refer ; or else merely what is probable or apparent, in distinction from what is real and matter of fact. E. g. 'Artaxerxes took hold of Cyrus, ὡς ἀποκτενῶν, *as if he was about to kill him ;*' 'Overlooking other cities, ὡς οὐκ ἂν δυναμένους βοηθῆσαι, *as if,* or *as believing that, they were unable to assist ;*' ὡς ἀπιόντες, *as desirous to go away ;*' 'They punish him who withdraws, ὡς παρονομοῦντα, *inasmuch as they consider him as a transgressor ;*' 'The Athenians made ready, ὡς πολεμήσοντες, *expecting to engage in a war ;*' Luke 16: 1, ὡς διασκορπίζων, *as one supposed to waste ;* ὡς ἀποστρέφοντα, *as one supposed to pervert,* etc., Luke 23 : 14, al. But this idiom, so common in the classics, is not very frequent in the N. Testament.

Note. The particle ὡς, in the sense above described, may be joined with a Part. in any of the cases ; also with the Part. as standing in the Gen. or Acc. *absolute.* Moreover ὥστε, ἅτε, οἷον, or οἷα (*as*), sometimes take the place of ὡς.

(4) Participles are frequently joined with verbs of existence

(εἰμί, γίγνομαι, τυγχάνω), and then stand in the room of a finite verb.

This we can fully appreciate, inasmuch as we can say in English with equal propriety, *I do*, *I am doing*, *I write*, *I am writing*, *I have been writing*, etc. So the Greeks; 'The stars of heaven ἔσονται ἐκπίπτοντες, lit. *shall be falling*, i. e. shall fall, Mark 13: 25. Luke 5: 1. 2 Cor. 5: 19. Mark 15: 43. Luke 24: 32. 1: 22. 5: 10. Acts 1: 10, al. saepe. The examples in the N. Test. appear to be mostly (if not all) of the Pres. tense of the Part. ; but still, it is the *helping verb* which designates the time. In the classics other tenses are employed, as κρατήσας ἦν, Herodian. The later classics abound in this idiom ; the early ones more rarely employ it.

NOTE The verbs γίγνομαι, ὑπάρχω, τυγχάνω, are employed in the same manner as εἰμί, with participles. Also the verbs ἥκω (*to arrive*), εἶμι (*to go*), ἔρχομαι (*to come*), are frequently joined in like manner with participles. So ἔχω is also used ; in which case its only force seems to be, to give the idea of *permanency* to the meaning of the participle ; e. g. θαυμάσας ἔχω, *I have wondered*, i. e. have long been wondering.

§ 171. *Participles in the Case Absolute.*

(1) *Where the Part. has a subject of its own, which is different from the subject or object of the principal verb, it is called* THE CASE ABSOLUTE.

Such is the general fact in regard to *cases absolute*. We shall see, however, in the sequel, that this case is also employed in not a few instances, where the *subject* of the Part. absolute is the *same* as that of the verb in the main clause.

(2) Generally participles thus conditioned express a relation either of *time* or *cause* ; and therefore (as the Gen. is adapted to the expression of these) they are put in the Genitive.

E. g. αὐτοῦ εἰπόντος, πάντες ἐσίγων, *while he was speaking, all were silent* ; θεοῦ διδόντος, οὐδὲν ἰσχύει φθόνος, *when God permits, envy avails nothing* ; 'The city was not the richer, προσόδων αὐτῇ πλειόνων γενομένων, *because it had many sources of revenue* ; οὕτω, τοῦ αἰῶνος προκεχωρηκότος, *thus, because his age was advanced*, he went etc.

NOTE 1. When the agent or object of the verb and of the Part. is the same, then the Part. stands in the same case with such object or agent; (*a*) The *agent* or Nom. of the verb being also the subject of the Part., the Part. of course usually takes the Nom. case ; as αἰσχύνομαι ταῦτα ποιῶν or ποιήσας, *I am ashamed that I do, or have done, these things* ; διαβεβλημένος οἱ μανθάνεις ; *being calumniated dost thou not perceive it* ? So in the Pass. voice ; ἐξελήλεγκται ἡμᾶς ἀπατῶν, *he is convicted of deceiving us* ; ἠγγέλθη ὁ Φίλιππος τὴν Ὄλυνθον πολιορκῶν, *it was announced that Philip was besieging Olynthus*, lit. *Philip, besieging Olynthus, was announced* ; in which the Greek form of expression has the advantage over ours in point of brevity and energy. 1 Cor. 14: 18. Acts 16: 34.

§ 172. Syntax: Participles. 267

(b) When the Part. refers to the *object* of the verb, its accord with this in respect to gender, number, and case, is a matter of course, a few peculiar cases only excepted; e. g. 'The Persians relate τὸν Κῦρον ἔχοντα ᾳ ὕ- σιν etc., *that Cyrus had a disposition*,' i. e. they tell of Cyrus as one having etc. So in the Gen. and Dative; ᾐσθόμην αὐτῶν οἰομένων εἶναι σοφωτα- των, *I perceived that they deemed themselves to be very wise ;* οὐδέποτε μετα- μέλησέ μοι σιγήσαντι, *I never repent of having kept silence*. So in Luke 8: 46. Acts 24: 10. 2 John v. 7.

(c) In case the verb has a reflexive pronoun after it, differing in case from the subject or Nom., the Part. may be in the Nom. or in the same oblique case as the reflexive pronoun; e. g. σύνοιδα ἐμαυτῷ σοφος ὤν, or σοφῷ ὄντι.

(3) DATIVE ABSOLUTE. As the Dative also is sometimes used in designating *time, cause, occasion*, etc., so the case absolute of participles is sometimes made by the Dative.

E. g. καταβάντι αὐτῷ, *when he had descended*, Matt. 8; 1; ἐλθόντι αὐτῷ, *when he had come*, Matt. 21: 23. But this is rare in the N. Testament. In the Greek classics it is also rare; but still it is clearly an idiom belonging to the Greek; Matth. § 562. 2. Kühner, § 669.

(4) THE ACC. ABSOLUTE is not unfrequent in the Classics. Generally it is made *by participles belonging to impersonal verbs.*

E. g. δόξαν αὐτοῖς, *it having seemed good to them ;* προσῆκον, *since it is becoming ;* αἰσχρὸν ὄν, *it being shameful ;* τοὺς βοῦς θάπτουσι, τὰ κέρατα ὑπερ- έχοντα, *they bury the oxen, the horns sticking out ;* ταῦτα γενόμενα, πένθεα με- γάλα . . . καταλαμβάνει, *these things being done, much grief seized*, etc., Herod. ii. 66; δόξαντα δὲ ταῦτα καὶ περανθέντα . . . ἀπῆλθε, *these things being decided and completed . . . he went away.* This usage in respect to single participles of impersonal verbs, i. e. participles without a subject expressed, is very common, the Gen. being but rarely employed here; Kuhner, § 670.

(5) EVEN THE NOMINATIVE is sometimes found in the *absolute* state.

E. g. 'That he might have twelve years instead of six, αἱ νύκτες ἡμέραι ποιεύμεναι, *the nights being computed as days ;* 'After these things they departed,'Ἀργεῖοι μὲν καὶ οἱ σύμμαχοι ἐντόνως καὶ ὀργῇ χωροῦντες, Λακεδαιμό- νιοι δὲ βραδέως, *the Grecians and their allies going vigorously and with indignation, but the Lacedemonians slowly ;* ἐκεῖνοι δὲ εἰσελθόντες . . . εἶπεν ὁ Κρι- τίας, *when they had gone*, . . . *Critias said.* See Kühner, § 678. Rost, § 131. 5, 6. Matth. § 564.

§ 172. *Peculiar Anomalies of the Participle.*

(1) *The Nominative case* is sometimes assumed by the Part., when the noun, etc., to which it belongs is in the Gen., Dat., or Accusative.

E. g. IN THE GENITIVE; as παθοῦσα δ᾽ οὕτω . . . οὐδεὶς ὑπὲρ μου . . .

μηνίεται, where παθοῦσα belongs to μού; Δαρείου ἡ γνώμη ἔην ... εἰκάζων, where εἰκάζων belongs to Δαρείου.

In the Dative; as ἔδοξεν αὐτοῖς ... ἐπικαλοῦντες, where the Part. belongs to αὐτοῖς, Thucyd. iii. 36. So ἕρως ἐνέπεσεν πᾶσιν ... εὐέλπιδες ὄντες, where the latter clause belongs to πᾶσιν.

In the Accusative; as αἰδώς μ᾽ ἔχει ... τυγχάνουσα, where the Part. refers to μέ. So τὰ πολλὰ δὲ πάλαι προκόψασα ... οὐ .. με δεῖ, the Part. referring to μέ. See Kühner, § 667.

Note. Not unfrequently the *Nom.* of a Part. may be formed without any finite verb; and in some of these cases it seems to supply the place of a finite verb. But such Nominatives are in reality to be construed *variously*, viz., (a) As standing in an elliptical clause in which the main verb is to be mentally supplied. (b) As being used in the way of case absolute. (c) As implying the verb *to be*, so as to form a verb compound; see § 170. 4.

(2) The Genitive of the Participle is often found not only in the place of other tenses which it might regularly have, but employed also as *a Gen. absolute having the same subject or object as the main verb.*

(a) *Gen. absolute instead of the Nominative.* E. g. πόλις κεῖται ... ἐούσης τετραγώνου, *a city was founded ... being square,* Herod. i. 78. Κῦρος προηγόρευε ... αὐτοῦ διαβησομένου, *Cyrus exhorted ... being himself ready to go,* Ib. 208. Μή τι πάθω ὑπό σου, ὡς ἀδικηκότος ἐμοῦ μεγάλα, *let me not suffer by you, I being already much injured,* Xen. Cyr. vi. 1. 37.

(b) *Gen. absolute instead of the Dative.* E. g. τὸν ... χρῆν, ἐμεῦ αἰσχρὰ ... πεπονθότος, τιμωρέειν ἐμοί, *I must needs punish him, having myself suffered shameful treatment;* where ἐμοί is the subject of the sentence, Herod. iii. 65. So διαβεβηκότος ἤδη Περικλέους ... ἠγγέλθη αὐτῷ ... *Pericles having already passed through ... it was told him,* Thucyd. i. 114.

(c) *Gen. absolute instead of the Accusative.* Herod. ix. 99, ἀπικομένων Ἀθηναίων ... τούτους λυσάμενοι, *the Athenians having already come ... they* [the Samians] *dismissed them;* where the *object* of the main verb (τούτους) designates the Athenians. Thucyd. v. 56, ἦλθον ἐπὶ τὴν Ἐπίδαυρον, ὡς ἐρήμου οὔσης, *they came to Epidaurus, being as it were deserted.*

Note. Often are all these anomalies to be found in Thucydides; occasionally elsewhere. For a full supply of examples, see Kühner, § 681.

(3) The Accusative of the Participle is sometimes employed, when the same Part. relates to a noun in a different case.

E. g. πέπαλταί μοι φίλον κέαρ τόνδε κλύουσαν οἶκτον, *my dear heart beats, whilst I hear this moaning;* where κλύουσαν refers to μοί, Aesch. Choeph. 396. Id. Pers. 909, λέλυται γὰρ ἐμοὶ γυίων ῥώμη, τήνδε ἡλικίαν ἐσιδόντα ἀστῶν, *the strength of my limbs fails me, while I look upon the mature state of the city.*

Note. Sometimes a sentence commences with an *Acc.*, when the verb which follows governs another case; which is to be solved by a reference to a preceding construction, or to some rhetorical reason, or else is to be regarded in the light of a case absolute. See examples in Kühner, § 632. 2, 3.

§ 173. Syntax: Participles. 269

GENERAL REMARKS. The *concord* of the Participle with its noun, as it would seem plain from the preceding view, is not to be viewed as subject to any strictness of rule. On the contrary, nearly every possible variety of departure from this is found in the Greek language; the departures being far more numerous and striking, than in the case of *adjectives*. The general reason of this seems to be, the *verbal* quality which the Part retains, notwithstanding it is an attributive. Possessing this, it often breaks the bands of *grammatical concord*, and assumes (one might almost say) a place independently, just as if it were in fact a verb.

§ 173. *Participial use of the tenses.*

(1) The *Present* Part. designates not merely something now present, but also what is now commencing and is to be continued, or what is immediately to commence.

The first needs no examples. As to the other meanings, they may be illustrated very easily: e. g. ἀποθνήσκων, *moriturus, dying* in the sense of being already *in extremis*. Matt. 26: 28, τὸ αἷμα .... τὸ ἐκχυνόμενον, *the blood ... which is about to be shed*. So διδόμενον, in Luke 22: 19; κλώμενον, in 1 Cor. 11: 24. These cases may also be solved, by considering the Part. as expressing what is *mentally* regarded as present. Rom. 15: 25, διακονῶν. 1 Pet. 1: 7.

(2) The Pres. Part. is often employed in the sense of the Imperfect.

E. g. ἐρευνῶντες, *who searched*, 1 Pet. 1: 11 ; 'I saw seven angels, ἔχοντας πληγάς, *who had plagues,* Rev. 15: 1, 6. Acts 21: 16. 25: 3. Matt. 14: 21. In particular, the Part. Pres. is often connected with a verb Praeterite, in order to designate something done, etc., at the time when another thing was done which the principal verb announces ; e. g. ' on the following day, ὤφθη αὐτοῖς μαχομένοις, *he showed himself to them when they were contending*,' Acts 7: 26. 18: 5. Heb. 11: 22. Luke 5: 18, al. saepe.

NOTE. Very often is the Part. ὤν employed in the sense of the Imperf., when it stands connected with a verb in the Praeterite ; e. g. John 1: 49. 5: 31. 21: 11. Acts 7: 2. 11: 1. 18: 24. 1 Cor. 8: 9, al.

(3) *Perf. participle and Aorist.* The Perf. is used to note things done, the result of which is somewhat *permanent*, or the consequences of which continue; the Aorist, on the other hand, is usually employed *where a thing is done once for all*, and is not designedly represented as continuing in its consequences.

E. g. *Perfect*; Heb. 2: 9. John 19: 35. Acts 22: 3. 1 Pet. 1: 23. 2: 4. Rev. 9: 1. *Aorist*; Rom. 8: 11. 16: 22. Acts 9: 21, al. saepe.

NOTE. The Pluperf. sense of a Part. is sometimes made by the Part. Perf. John 13: 2. Acts 18: 2. 28: 11 ; but more often by the Part. Aorist, as in Matt. 2: 13. 22: 25. Acts 5: 10. 13: 51, al.

(4) The Future Part. is seldom employed, except after verbs of *motion* ; and there it is very common.

E. g. ἔρχομαι φράσων, *I am come to tell*; σέγε διδάξων ὥρμημαι, *I hasten to teach you*. So 'Bring him before the judges, δίκην δώσοντα, *that he may receive retribution*.'

NOTE. The Part. Aorist, although it does not stand for the proper Future Part., may still represent the meaning of the *Futurum exactum*; so Mark 13:13, ὁ ὑπομείνας etc., *he who shall have endured*.

§ 173. *Alleged Hebraism in the use of Participles.*

This consists in employing the Part. with a verb of the same root in a definite mode, in the room of the Heb. Inf. with a definite mode.

E. g. ἰδὼν εἶδον, εὐλογῶν εὐλογήσω, πληθύνων πληθυνῶ, βλέποντες βλέπετε, etc.; forms of speech which are very frequent in the Septuagint. It is however the *frequency* only of this idiom which may be called Hebraism in the Sept.; for such phrases are found, not only in the Greek poets, but in the prose-writers; Winer, § 46. 8. See numerous examples also, in Matth. § 553.

IMPERSONAL VERBS.

§ 174. *Manner in which these are employed.*

The Greeks usually employ the 3d pers. plural or sing. of these verbs; and sometimes the 2nd pers. singular. In the N. Test., the 3d pers. plural is the more usual form.

E. g. John 15:6. 20:2. Mark 10:13. Matt. 7:16. Luke 12:20, 48, et al. saepe. The 3d pers. sing., φησί, is used in 2 Cor. 10:10. So the passive γέγραπται, λέγεται, etc., are naturally employed in the same impersonal way.

NOTE 1. In the Hebrew the same custom prevails. The 3d pers. sing. and plural, also the 2nd pers. sing., are used in an impersonal way, or with indefinite Nominatives; Heb. Gramm. § 500.

NOTE. 2. Not unfrequently the 3d pers. plural, used *impersonally*, may be conveniently rendered as a *passive* verb; e. g. Luke 16:9, δέξωνται ὑμᾶς, [they] *may receive you*, i. e. ye may be received; al. saepe.

INTERROGATIVE SENTENCES.

§ 175. *Nature and variety of these sentences.*

(1) Interrogative sentences or clauses may be divided into two kinds, viz. (*a*) Such as are *independent* of any other construction. (*b*) Such as are *dependent* on a foregoing clause. The first is named the *direct*-interrogative; the second, the *indirect*.

§ 175. SYNTAX: INTERROGATIVE SENTENCES. 271

E. g. *Has my friend come?* is independent and direct; while 'I know not *whether my friend has come*,' is dependent and indirect.

I. Direct Interrogatives.

(2) Interrogatives are frequent, where there is no written symbol of them, or none except the *order* of the words.

E. g εὕδεις, Ἀτρέος υἱέ; *dost thou sleep, son of Atreus?* τὸ βάπτισμα Ἰωάννου, ἐξ οὐρανοῦ ἦν; *The baptism of John, from heaven was it?* Luke 20: 4. Gal. 9: 10. Rom. 2: 4, al. saepe. So οὐκ ἐθέλεις ἰέναι; *wilt thou not go?* Here, as usually elsewhere, the word on which the main question turns, stands *first* in the interrogative part. On this word the stress of voice is to be laid; and by this stress the *question* is to be made out.

(3) The Greek, beyond almost any other language, abounds in interrogatives, either pronouns, pronominal adjectives, or adverbials respecting time, place, quality, quantity, way and manner, etc.

(a) Pronominal interrogatives; τίς, τί, ποῖος, πόσος, etc. (b) Adverbials; πῶς, πῇ, ποῦ, πόθι, πόθεν, πόσε, etc.; also ἦ, ἆρα, ἆρ᾽ οὐκ, ἆρα μή, μή, μῶν=μὴ οὖν, οὐ, οὐκοῦν, οὐ μέντοι, οὐ δή, ἀλλά, ἀλλ᾽ ἦ, and many others.

NOTE 1. Τίς, τί, very frequently connect themselves with particles which give a colouring to the interrogation; e. g. τίς ποτε, τίς τε, τίς ἄρα, τί οὖν, τί δή, τί μήν, τί καί, τί δέ, etc. So ποῖος ἄρα, πῶς ἄρα, etc.

NOTE 2. Γάρ often stands connected with the interrogative particles, with a kind of *illative* meaning, and also as an indication of surprise; e. g. πῶς γὰρ σοι δώσουσι γέρας; *how then shall they give a reward to you?* So πῶς γάρ; *how then?*=it cannot be; πῶς γὰρ οὔ; *how then not?* i. e. how can it be otherwise.

NOTE 3. Peculiar idiom is τί μαθών=*what do you mean*, viz. by doing so and so; and τί παθών, *what ails you*, viz. that you do so and so.

NOTE 4. ἦ ῥα, i. e. ἆρα (Att.), expresses *doubt, uncertainty, surprise, astonishment*, etc. Ἆρα οὐ indicates expectation of an *affirmative* answer; ἆρα μή. of a *negative* one.

NOTE 5. Ἀλλά stands at the head of an interrogative made in the way of *objection* to another's views. Εἶτα and ἔπειτα stand in interrogatives of irony, or wonder.

GENERAL REMARK. The *particles* that may be coupled with interrogatives, are many, and are thus employed in all their various senses, in order to give light and shade to a vivid part of language, viz. interrogations.

(4) Two successive questions, mutually connected or related, are often asked, for which there are appropriate particles.

E. g. in Homer, ἦ ... ἦ; in the Attic, πότερον ... ἤ; (once in John 7: 17) ἆρα ... ἤ; μῶν ... ἤ.

II. *Indirect Interrogatives.*

(5) These are in themselves *substantive* sentences or clauses, although they have the form of adverbial ones; and they constitute either *subject* or *object*.

E. g. εἰ τοῦτο ποιήσεις, οὐκ οἶδα, *I know not whether you will do this*, where the first clause in the Greek is the *object* of οἶδα. So εἰ τοῦτο ποιήσεις, οὐ δῆλόν ἐστι, *whether you will do this, is not certain*, where the first clause is in reality the *subject* of ἐστί.

(6) Usually the compound interrogatives introduce indirect questions; but sometimes the common ones also; e. g.

Usually ὅστις, ὁποῖος, ὁπόσος, ὅπως, ὅπου, ὅπη, and the like, commence such interrogative sentences; but ὅς, οἷος, ὅσος, ὡς, are occasionally employed. E. g. οὐκ οἶδα ὅστις ἐστί — οὐκ οἶδα ὅπως τὸ πρᾶγμα ἔπραξε; so with the simple interrogatives, ὃν δὲ τρόπον, καὶ δι' οἴων κακουργημάτων ... ἄξιόν ἐστιν ἀκοῦσαι, *it is worth hearing, in what manner, and by what malpractices, he accomplished this*.

(7) Questions indirect are made often by εἰ, although it is more appropriate to the double questions.

So after verbs of *considering, advising with, seeking, inquiring, attempting, knowing, saying*, and the like; e. g. φράσαι, εἴ με σαώσεις, *say, whether you will save me*. Σκέψαι, εἰ ὁ νόμος κάλλιον ἔχει, *consider whether the law is any better*. When an uncertain future, yet to be decided, is referred to, ἐάν is employed with the Subj. mode; as σκέψαι, ἐὰν τόδε σοι ἀρέσκῃ, *consider whether this may please you*.

NOTE. Μή (*num, ne*) is employed here, as well as in direct questions; by Homer in the Subj. only; by the Attics, in the Indic. or Subj., as the case may require.

(8) Double indirect questions are marked, for the most part, by particles like those of direct ones; but not always.

E. g. by ἤ ... ἤ, πότερον ... ἤ, εἰ ... ἤ, εἴτε ... εἴτε.

(9) MODES *in interrogative sentences in general*. The use of these does not differ from the use in sentences not interrogative.

E. g. *The Indicative*, where matter of fact is expressed; as πῶς νῦν βλέπει, '*how he seeth now*, we know not,' John 9: 21. Acts 20: 18. 1 Thess. 1: 9. John 10: 6. 3: 8. 7: 27, al. Either the Pres., or the Praeter (pro re natâ), is here employed.

The Subjunctive, where that which may or can take place is designated; e. g. 'The Son of man hath not ποῦ τὴν κεφαλὴν κλίνῃ,' Matt. 8: 20. Rom. 8: 26. Matt. 6: 25. 10: 19. Mark 6: 36. 13: 11. Heb. 8: 2.

The Optative, after a *Praeterite*, and when mere opinion is indicated; as Luke 22: 23, τὸ τίς ἄρα εἴη ἐξ αὐτῶν. 1: 29. 3: 15. 8: 9. 15: 26. Acts 25: 20, al.

§ 176. SYNTAX: DIRECT AND INDIRECT QUOTATIONS. 273

§ 176. *Answers to questions.*

These are various, and receive many shades from various particles.

(a) The emphatic word is repeated, for the *affirmative;* and with οὐ, for the negative; e. g. ὁρᾶς τοῦτο; Ans. ὁρῶ—οὐκ ὁρῶ. (b) Affirm. φημί, φήμ' ἐγώ, ἔγωγε, εἶπας; Neg. οὐ φημί, οὐκ ἔγωγε, οὔ. (c) By γέ, which joins the answer intimately with the question, and makes it intensive. (d) With γάρ inserted, which is still stronger than γε, for γάρ=γὲ ἄρα. (e) By ναί, νὴ τὸν Δία, πάνυ, κάρτα, and the like. So τοί, μέντοι, οὖν, which strengthen an affirmation. (f) Μενοῦν, both in affirmative and negative answers, strengthens them. Other adverbs are occasionally employed; but they make no special difficulty.

§ 177. *Direct and indirect clause, or Oratio recta et obliqua.*

(1) The words of another person, or of one's own self, *which are cited*, give rise to these forms of speech. It is called *direct*, when the words or purpose of another are simply stated; *indirect*, when the same are made dependent on something which the narrator himself says.

E. g. 'He says: *Peace is made;*' (direct). 'He says, *that peace is made;*' (indirect).

(2) The Greek language has power to express clauses of this nature in various ways, with equal propriety.

E. g. ἔλεγε τοὺς πολεμίους ἀποφυγεῖν, *he said that the enemy had fled*, where the Inf. with its preceding Acc. is used. Again; ἔλεγε ὅτι οἱ πολέμιοι ἀπέφυγον or ἀποφύγοιεν, (the same idea), where the oratio obliqua is employed. Once more; ἔλεγε τοὺς πολεμίους ἀποφυγόντας, lit. *he announced the enemy who had fled*, is the same sentiment in a different costume, viz. the noun having a participle indicative of state or condition. It is only with the *second* method, that we are here concerned.

(3) *Oratio obliqua* of course merely cites the *opinion* or *view* of others, and does not assert facts as believed by the speaker himself. Hence the *Optative* mode (designating *opinion*) is the appropriate one for this form of sentences; but there are frequent departures from this.

NOTE 1. The Optative here must be preceded by a *historic* tense in the main clause; e. g. ἔλεξέ, σε, εἰ τοῦτο λέγοις, ἁμαρτήσεσθαι, 'he said: *In case you should affirm this, you would err.*' So, 'When dying *he said:* Whatever good Cyrus πεποιήκοι may have done to the Persians, etc.,' Herod. III. 75.

NOTE 2. In case the main clause refers to the *present* time of the speaker, then the *Indic.* is employed; e. g. λέγει, ὅτι ἄνθρωπος θνητός ἐστιν—λέγω, ὅτι αὐτός, ἐὰν τοῦτο λέξῃ, ἁμαρτιάνει. Here ἐὰν τοῦτο λέξῃ does not depend on the *oratio obliqua*, but is merely a reference to the words of the original speaker. The *oratio obliqua* itself cannot employ the *Subj.* mode, because this *oratio* relates things that are *past*, while the Subj. refers to something which may yet be realized.

NOTE 3. The Opt. in such a connection as that named above, may, and often does, take ἄν after the conjunctions which introduce the oblique clauses.

NOTE 4. No instance of the Opt. with the *oratio obliqua* occurs in the N. Test.; partly because this form of speech itself is rare in these writings, and partly because the Opt. had already gone, in a great measure, into desuetude. The Indic. is employed instead of it; the sequel will show why it may be so employed.

(4) More frequently, however, is the *Indic.* mode employed in the *oratio obliqua*; particularly where the narrator means to convey the idea, that what he cites is true or really matter of fact.

E. g. ἐβουλεύοντο, ὡς βασιλέα δικαιότατα στήσονται, *they concluded, that they should very properly appoint for themselves a king*, Herod. iii. 84. 'The people thought it proper to elect thirty, οἳ τοὺς νόμους συγγράψουσι, καθ᾽ οὓς πολιτεύσουσι, *who should prescribe laws, according to which they should regulate their conduct*,' Xen. Hist. Gr. ıı. 3. 2. (Our own language cannot imitate the Greek here). 'He ordered [them] to dwell in his own country, ὅκου βούλονται, *wherever they would*, (the Greek has the Indic. Pres.). So in indirect questions; as οἳ ἐβουλεύοντο, εἴτε᾽ κατακαύσουσι, *they consulted whether they should burn*, (Indıc. Fut.). In all these and the like cases, it is plain, that the speaker transfers himself into the place of those who consult, speak, purpose, etc., and utters the language that is appropriate to their state, i. e. he makes *objective* representation. Comp. in the N. Test., Luke 8 : 47. Matt. 18 : 25. Mark 5 : 29. 9 : 9. Acts 10 : 17. 22 : 24. A mixed construction, consisting partly of *direct* and *oblique* speech may be found in Matt. 1 : 10. Luke 18 : 9. Acts 12 : 18. The like may be found in the Classics, in all the above respects; see Winer, § 42. 5. Kühner, § 846.

(5) Sometimes the Subjunctive is employed in *oratio obliqua*, viz., where something is announced, the completion of which was still expected when the things related in the main clause took place.

E. g. 'The Athenians bound themselves by oath to use the laws [of Solon] ten years, τοὺς ἄν σφι θῆται, *whatever* [laws] *he might ordain for them;* Herod. i. 29. Comp. Acts 23 : 21.

NOTE. When different modes are employed in the same *oratio obliqua*, they preserve their appropriate meanings, in accordance with what has been said above.

GENERAL REMARK. The Greek often employs the Inf. mode with the Acc. in the room of various by-clauses. E. g. μετὰ δὲ, ὡς ἐλθεῖν τοὺς ἀγγέλους ἐς τὸ Ἄργος, *and afterwards, when the messengers came to Argos.* So ὡς δὲ τυχεῖν τὸν βασιλέα ἀνοίξαντα τὸ οἴκημα, *and when the king happened to open the house.*

The exchange, moreover, of *direct* and *indirect* speech is very frequent, which gives rise to variety and animation in discourse.

PARTICLES.

§ 178. *Nature and division of Particles.*

(1) *Particles* is the generic and indefinite name of the indeclinable parts of speech, viz. *Prepositions, Adverbs, Conjunctions,* and *Interjections.*

The name (μόρια, *parts, divisions*) seems to have been given in reference to the functions of these words, which mark the different parts of sentences; or, possibly, in reference to the *apocopated* state of the words themselves, most of them being rather fragments than whole words.

PREPOSITIONS.

§ 179. *Nature and various uses.*

(1) The original and appropriate use of *prepositions*, strictly so called, was to designate the *space-relations* of the nouns, with which they are connected, to a verb or predicate of a sentence.

E. g. ἦλθεν ἐκ τῆς πόλεως—ἔστη πρὸ τῶν πυλῶν—οἰκεῖ ἐπὶ τῷ ὄρει—ἔβη εἰς τὴν οἰκίαν. See § 85 for a fuller disclosure of the special meanings of original prepositions.

NOTE. Strictly considered, all prepositions were originally mere *adverbs of place* or *space*. They differ from such adverbs now, merely by the fact that they qualify *nouns* and not verbs. Hence many words still remain both *adverbs* and *prepositions*, i. e. they perform the functions of both the so-called parts of speech, as occasion demands. E. g. ἄντα, ἔξω, ἐκτός, ἀμφί, ἄνευ, δίχα, ἅμα, etc. So also ἕνεκα, δίκην, χάριν, etc.

(2) In its full extent, the word *preposition* would embrace all particles which govern *cases*; but there are only *eighteen* primitive and proper prepositions, the others being *adverbial* ones.

REMARK. The Syntax of prepositions has been already developed, §§ 108—113, in consequence of the connection which they have with the regimen of *cases*. Thither is the reader referred for a full account of them.

ADVERBS.

§ 180. *Nature and use of them.*

(1) Those indeclinable words which serve to designate relations of *place, time, way,* and *manner,* in connection with the *predicate* of a sentence, are named ADVERBS.

NOTE 1. Under the general designation of *way* and *manner*, are included the idea, (*a*) Of *modality*, i. e. *affirmation, negation, certainty, definiteness,*

§ 180. SYNTAX: ADVERBS.

uncertainty, and *conditionality*. (b) Of *frequency* or *repetition*, as αὖθις, τρίς, etc. (c) Of *intensity*, as μάλα, πάνυ, etc.

REMARK. For an account of the forms, comparison, etc., of adverbs, see § 84.

NOTE 2. In a wider extent of meaning, the word *adverb* might designate all words and phrases which perform the office above designated; e. g. γελῶν εἶπε—διὰ τάχους ἐποίησε—σπουδῇ ἔρχεται—τρίτῃ ἡμέρᾳ ἦλθον, and the like, where, it is evident, the words joined with the verbs perform the *office* of adverbs. But in a technical sense, *adverb* is limited to the *indeclinable* parts of speech.

(2) The Greek possesses a peculiar power of converting adverbs into *adjectives*, and employing them in a very significant manner. E. g.

(a) Adjectives may be made from *adverbs of place*; e. g. ἀγχιαλλήλων ἔπιπτον, *they fell near each other*, which may be expressed by ἀγχιστῖνοι ἔπιπτον. So with πρῶτος, ὕστατος, μέσος, θυραῖος, θαλάσσιος, ὑπερπόντιος, etc.

(b) From adverbs of time; as σημερινός, ὄψιος, νύχιος, δευτεραῖος, τριταῖος, etc. So εὗδον παννύχιοι, *they slept through the whole night*, lit. *they slept allnighters*. See Acts 28: 13.

(c) From adverbs of way and manner; as ὀξύς, ταχύς, βραδύς, συχνός, πολύς, μόνος, etc. E. g., with some variation of meaning, πρῶτος ἔγραψε, *he first of all persons wrote;* while πρῶτον ἔγραψε (adverb) means, *he wrote before* he did something else. See John 8: 7. Acts 12: 10.

(3) ADVERBS OF PLACE. These may be employed, and often are, in their local sense; but the *cases* of nouns, and nouns also with prepositions, often supply their place.

NOTE. The same is the case in regard to adverbs of *time*. In addition to nouns with their cases and prepositions, *participles* are frequently employed in expressions of this nature. In respect to adverbs of *way and manner*, the same is also true.

(4) The *modal* adverbs extend not simply to the verb with which they are connected, but to the whole thought or clause in which they stand.

E. g. Of affirmation, as ναί; of denial, as οὔ, μή; of certainty or assurance, as ἦ, μήν, πάντως, etc.; of uncertainty or doubt, as ἄν, πού, ἴσως, etc.

(5) The N. Test. exhibits nothing very peculiar as to the manner or frequency of using adverbs.

NOTE 1. Perhaps adverbs in -ως are rather more frequent than in the Classics. The *neuter* adjective is very frequent here as an adverb; and so it is also in the the Classics. But nouns with prepositions which are used *adverbially*, are unusually frequent here.

NOTE 2. Such expressions as ἐπιθυμίᾳ ἐπεθύμησα, *I have strongly desired*, (the like in John 3: 29. Acts 4: 17. 5: 28. 23: 14, saepe al.) are even more frequent in the older Attic writers than in the N. Testament.

§ 181. Syntax: Negative Particles.

REMARK. When *abverbial* particles are associated with any of the oblique cases of nouns, we may say that *they govern them*, in a sense in which this expression is usually employed. Hermann proposes (De Emend. Gr. Gramm. p. 161), that they should then be called *prepositions*, in such instances. Recent grammarians choose to name them *adverbial prepositions*. This is a description, at once, of their origin and their office.

N B The student who wishes to see a full account of all the important adverbial particles, is referred to Kuhner, § 690 seq., where he will find an orderly development of a superior character. It is to be hoped, that our Greek lexicons will undergo a more thorough modification in regard to this class of words; for such a process they greatly need, and it would be now easy to accomplish it Only a few of the most important of these particles can be particularly brought to view in the present work, for brevity forbids more.

§ 181. *Nature and use of the particles οὐ and μή.*

(1) There is a difference between these particles as to usage, while they both possess a *negative* power. Οὐ denies *positively* and *immediately* in respect to what is contained in the sentence or clause where it stands; μή *has a reference to something which lies without the sentence or clause*, i. e. to some condition, desire, command, wish, event, etc., as connected with the thing denied.

NOTE. Hermann and others make οὐ an *objective* denial, μή a *subjective* one. But this has recently been questioned, particularly by Hartung, Buttmann, Anton, and Kuhner; and it seems, indeed, to be an impracticable, if not an unintelligible, distinction; for how, on this ground, could οὐ be joined with the Opt. mode, (as it often is), which is *subjective* in its very nature?

(2) Οὐ simply denies any thing regarded in itself as *actual* or *certain*, or regarded as a *definite* supposed or imaginary case, considered as independent of other and extraneous considerations.

Hence with the Indic. every where, in the first of these cases; and with the Opt. (the *supposition*-mode) in the second; e. g. οὐ βαίνει—οὐκ ἂν γίγνοιτο ταῦτα, these things [in our view] *cannot well take place*. Also, with the Subj. when it=Fut. Indic.; as 'I have never seen such men, οὐδὲ ἴδωμαι, *nor shall I ever see* [such];' Homer.

(3) Μή stands as a *negative* in sentences of such a nature as *necessarily connect themselves with something extraneous*.

E. g. (a) With sentences of *command*, expressed by the *Imper*. or *Subjunctive*; as Imper. μὴ γράφε, or Subjunc. (=Imper) μὴ γράψῃς. But here the Indic. would be οὐ γράφεις, even in the question, οὐ γράφεις τὴν ἐπιστολήν; In the two former cases, *I desire, will, wish*, etc., is implied; in the latter (Indic.) *positivity* is the character of the expression. See Matt. 6: 19. 7: 1. John 5: 14. Luke 6: 29. Matt. 10: 34. 6: 13. The Indicative has οὐ in the Future of prohibition, e. g. Matt 5: 21. 19: 18. Acts 23: 5. Matt. 6: 5. The Imper. 3d pers. takes μή, as well as the second; e. g. Rom. 6: 12. 14: 16. James 1: 7, etc.

(b) In sentences expressing *wish*, whether Indic. or Optative ; as μή τοῦτο γένοιτο! μὴ ὄφελες λίσσεσθαι!

(c) In the Subj. *deliberative* or *hortative* ; as μὴ γράφωμεν ; *shall we write ?* Ans. *no* ; μὴ φῶμεν, *let us not say*. John 19 : 24. 1 John 3 : 18. Rom. 14 : 13. (Οὐ, used here, would merely render negative the single word with which it connects itself.)

(d) Μή is also used occasionally in *oaths, adjurations*, etc., where some conditionality may be implied.

(e) IN BY-CLAUSES, for the most part, the use of οὐ and μή is like that which has been stated above as to absolute sentences. Yet when a reference is made to something without the clause, μή is of course employed, e. g. in *causal* clauses. IN RELATIVE CLAUSES, μή is the most usual where there is an intimate connection with the main clause. But where this is not the case, οὐ is used, as ἀνήρ, ὃν οὐκ εἶδες. So in Matt. 10 : 26. Luke 8 : 17. 12 : 2. So where merely a *single* word of the by-clause is made a negative, e. g. οἵ... οὐ δύνατοι ἦσαν ζῆν, 'who... *were unable* to live.' So, when a part of a negative clause must be made *emphatic*, οὐ is employed. In the *final conditional* clauses, which are of course *dependent*, i. e. such clauses as begin with ἵνα, ὡς, εἰ, ἐάν, ὁτάν, etc.., μή is of course usually employed. But εἰ may take οὐ after it, when matter of *fact* is stated by the *Indicative*. So ὥστε with the *Indic*. takes οὐ. Indirect questions, being *dependent*, take μή ; excepting that οὐ is used when it merely qualifies a single word, or is demanded by peculiar emphasis in a part of a clause.

In clauses beginning with εἰ (if), οὐ is employed when *emphasis* is intended ; μή, when it is not ; see Winer, § 59. 5. d.

(f) Μή of course may be expected with the *Inf*. mode, as being *dependent* ; but sometimes after verbs of *speaking* or *narrating*, οὐ is employed, because the speech becomes virtually *direct*, and the relation is *objective*, i. e. not such as depends on the views of the speaker, but such as simply describes things or objects ; e. g. φησι, δεῖν οὐδὲν προσφέρειν=ὅτι οὐδὲν δεῖ, etc. When οὐ merely renders negative a *single* word, it may be used here, as well as in the case just described above. Inf. with μή ; Matt. 2 : 12. 5 : 34. Luke 2 : 26. 20 : 7. Acts 4 : 18. 5 : 28. Rom. 2 : 22. 13 : 3, al. saepe.

(g) Μή is used with Participles, when they represent an idea which may be *conditionally* expressed ; e. g. ὁ μὴ πιστεύων=*si quis non credat* ; διδασκέ με ὡς μὴ εἰδότα μηδέν=*teach me as if I knew nothing* ; 'He presented τὰ μὴ ὄντα, ὡς οὐκ ὄντα=*things in case they might not exist, as actually not existing*.' See Matt. 12 : 30. 14 : 3. 13 : 19. John 15 : 2. 12 : 48. Rom. 10 : 20. Luke 3 : 11. 6 : 49. John 10 : 1. After participles expressive of *thinking* or *saying*, οὐ expresses an independent and absolute negative, μή a subjective one, i. e. one of opinion. Οὐ before participles expresses matter of *fact* ; μή of *assumption* or *supposition*. Phil. 3 : 3. 1 Pet. 2 : 10. Gal. 4 : 8. Heb. 11 : 35. Acts 7 : 5.

(4) *Some peculiarities of* μή *and* οὐκ. These are, that after verbs expressive of *fear, solicitude, uncertainty, doubt, mistrust, denial, hindrance, forbidding*, etc., μή is employed before an Inf. with the same sense, for substance, as the Inf. would have without μή ; e. g. κωλύω σε μὴ ταῦτα ποιεῖν, lit. *I keep you back lest you should do so*, while one might also say : κολύω σε ταῦτα ποιεῖν, i. e. *I prevent your doing so*. So even before a finite verb ; as δέδοικα μὴ ἀποθάνῃ=I am afraid he will die, lit. *lest he may die*.

§ 182. SYNTAX: NEGATIVE PARTICLES. 279

So after verbs of *doubting* or *denying*, followed by ὅτι, the negative οὐ is repeated to give more effect; e. g. εἰ ἀπιστέω, ὅτι δ' οὐκ ἔστιν ἐπιστήμη, *if I doubt, whether there is any knowledge*. Such cases of *negative* particles after verbs of doubt, denial, etc., are not uncommon in other languages; e. g. in the French, Italian, etc. This idiom is unlike the English.

(5) IN INTERROGATIVE CLAUSES, after οὐ, an *affirmative* answer is expected; after μή, a *negative* one.

E. g. οὐ τῷ σῷ ὀνόματι προεφητεύσαμεν; *have we not prophesied in thy name?* Matt. 7 : 22. Ans. *yes*, i. e. according to the expectation of the interrogator. James 2: 6. Matt. 13 : 27. Luke 12: 6, al. saepe. Yet sometimes οὐ stands in interrogatives, where the expected answer is *No*; but in such cases οὐ merely qualifies the *verb*, and gives it an opposite sense; e. g. Acts 13 : 10, οὐ παύσῃ διαστρέφων τὰς ὁδοὺς κυρίου; *will thou not cease perverting the ways*, etc.? where οὐ παύσῃ=*perges*; and to this last meaning the answer is, *yes*. So in Luke 17 : 18, οὐχ εὑρέθησαν ὑποστρέψαντες; where a *negative* answer seems necessary. But here the question appears to lie in the mind of the interrogator, as one that *ought* to be answered in the affirmative, i. e. one that there was strong reason for supposing should be so answered, unless something strange had taken place; (which was indeed the fact).

Μή in a question is the reverse of οὐ. E. g. μὴ λίθον ἀποδώσει ὀντῷ; Matt. 7: 9. Ans. *No*. Rom. 9: 20. 11: 1. 1 Cor. 8: 8. Matt. 7:16. Mark 4: 21, al. saepe. Yet here too, as in the case of οὐ above, some apparent exceptions occur; e. g. John 4: 33, μή τις ἤνεγκεν αὐτῷ φαγεῖν, where an *affirmative* answer seems to be rather the one expected; but the real fact is, that the matter stands as doubtful in the minds of the inquirers, while their hopes are probably on the side of the negative. So in John 8: 22, μήτι ἀποκτενεῖ ἑαυτόν; The Jews in reality *doubt* here whether Jesus will kill himself, and express themselves as hoping that a *negative* answer may be given. Matt. 12: 23, 'Can (μήτι) this be the Son of David?' showing that the interrogators cannot after all but think, or at least hope, the answer must be *negative*. Matt. 26: 22 exhibits the same attitude of mind; and so Luke 3: 15, al. See in Kühner § 834. 4. Anm. 1, where he has stated it as a principle, that when an affirmative answer must in reality follow μή or ἆρα μή, it is against the expectations or wishes of the inquirer. Comp. Winer, § 61. 3.

NOTE. Both οὐ and μή may have their appropriate force in the same sentence; e. g. 'Can (μήτι) the blind lead the blind?' [Ans. No]. 'Will not (οὐχί) both fall into the ditch?' [Ans. Yes].

§ 182. *Repetition of negatives.*

(1) *Of* οὐ—οὐ, *or of* μή—μή, *etc.* In sentences consisting of different members in the like condition, the Greek accumulates negatives in a wonderful manner; e. g. σμικρὰ φύσις οὐδὲν μέγα οὐδέποτε οὐδένα οὔτε ἰδιώτην οὔτε πόλιν δρᾷ, *small talents never accomplish any thing great, nor serve any one, neither private person, nor city*; Plat. Repub. VI. p. 495. So οὐ δύναται οὔτ' εὖ λέγειν οὔτ' εὖ ποιεῖν. The same with μή. In such sen-

tences, i. e. so uniform in their connection and construction, the οὐ or the μή which belongs to the first member, must belong to all.

(2) *Apparent repetition in* οὐ μή. This junction of particles occurs before the Subj., or before the Indic. Future employed in a kindred way. It is now agreed among grammarians, that the phrase is generally elliptical, inasmuch as some verb significant of *fear, dread, solicitude,* etc., is always implied, where it is not expressed, and μή is to be understood here in its *original* sense of *ne? num?* Thus, οὐ μὴ γένηται τοῦτο, [I fear] *not lest this should happen,*=it surely will not happen; so οὐ μὴ λαλήσεις, [I have no apprehensions] *that you will speak,*=certainly you will not speak, etc. See in Matt. 5: 18, 20, 26. 10: 23. 18: 3. Luke 6: 37. 12: 59. John 8: 51. 10: 28, al. saep. Indic. Future Luke 18: 9. John 8: 12. 18: 38, al. saep. N. B. The distinction between the Aor. Subj. and Indic. Fut., which Hermann makes (ad Soph. Oed. Col. 853), is not applicable to the N. Test.; for the Ind. Fut. seems often to take the place of the Subj., and *vice versâ.* See Winer, § 60. 3. For further illustration of οὐ μή, see § 148. 4 above.

(3) *Apparent repetition in* μὴ οὐκ. Here lies at the basis the same idiom as in the preceding case, and the same Modes are employed; but the meaning is altered. E. g. δέδοικα μη οὐκ ἀποθάνῃ, *I fear lest he may* NOT *die;* (δέδοικα μὴ ἀποθάνῃ means, *I fear that he may die*). So ἀπιστεῖς μὴ οὐκ ἐπιστήμη ᾖ ἡ ἀρετή; *Dost thou doubt, whether virtue may not be knowledge?* Plat. Meno, p. 89.

NOTE 1. Sometimes μὴ μή is employed, instead of μὴ οὐκ.

NOTE 2. A peculiarity of idiom here is, that after phrases with a *negative* sense, μὴ οὐκ is employed; e. g. after κωλύω, δεινόν, ἀδύνατος, οὐχ οἷος, and the like; as οὐδέν κωλύει, μὴ οὐκ ἀληθὲς εἶναι τοῦτο, lit. *nothing hinders that this should not be true,*=nothing lies in the way of this truth. The same idiom extends to *participles,* and to the Inf. mode also, when following phrases which imply a *negative* sense. But in some of the cases, the usage is not uniform; for we find οὐ δύναμαι μὴ ποιεῖν, *I cannot but act;* see Acts 4: 20. 1 Cor. 12: 15.

NOTE 3. Hermann's assertion (ad Viger. p. 797), that μὴ οὐκ is *weaker* than μή, and inclines to the *dubitative,* is fully refuted by Kuhner, § 718. 3. Anm. 5. Μὴ οὐκ is plainly more energic.

REMARK. It would appear plain, then, from this account of οὐ μή and μὴ οὐκ, that in neither case is either particle *superfluous* or unmeaning in the Greek. The ground of this peculiar idiom, also, seems very plain when viewed in the light in which it has now been placed.

§ 183. *Continued or repeated negative clauses, etc.*

(1) Regularly and usually, where both clauses are of the like construction, the *negatives* are thus arranged, viz. οὐ—οὐδέ; μή —μηδέ; viz. when the clauses are to be *disjunctively* interpreted.

The meaning is, that each negative clause denotes a distinct and independent idea, (for δέ denotes *disjunction*); e. g. οὐ σπείρουσιν, οὐδὲ θερίζουσιν, οὐδὲ συνάγουσι, etc. Matt. 6: 26. Here each clause denotes an entire action by itself. So Matt. 7: 6, μὴ δῶτε τὸ ἅγιον τοῖς κυσί, μηδὲ βάλητε

§ 183. SYNTAX: NEGATIVE PARTICLES.   281

τοὺς μαργαρίτας, etc., each being a distinct action. See a mass of examples in Winer, § 59. 6.

NOTE 1. Sometimes οὐδέ is found in the *first* of two such clauses; but in such a case this οὐδέ may join that clause to some preceding negative one, and thus it stands in a predicament different from what it appears to do; e. g. in Gal. 1: 12, οὐδὲ . . . παρέλαβον, etc. But sometimes οὐδέ, in the first clause, means simply *but* . . . *not*; and this too exempts it from the general rule. See Kuhner, § 744. 2. 5. Where neither of these cases exist, οὐδέ—οὐδέ is to be suspected of being spurious.

NOTE 2. Οὐδέ sometimes stands alone and is simply *adversative*; sometimes = καὶ οὐ; and sometimes it is the opposite of καί adverbial, and means *not at all, also not*, etc. In such cases, of course the general rule does *not* apply which requires οὐ to precede. See Kuhner, § 744. 1. *a.* and Anm. 2, also No. 5. ibid.

(2) When *parts of one whole* are to be particularized, and each *negatived*, the usual negatives are οὔτε—οὔτε or μήτε—μήτε.

E. g. Matt. 11: 18, 'John came μήτε ἐσθίων, μήτε πίνων.' Matt. 6: 20, ὅπου οὔτε σὴς οὔτε βρῶσις ἀφανίζει. Acts 23: 12. Matt. 22: 30. John 5: 37, al. saepe. In the first example here, John's *self-denial* is particularized by naming parts of his demeanor; in the second, the destruction of treasures by various agents is alluded to. More plainly does the principle appear in such a case as the following; Luke 9: 3, 'Take nothing for your journey, μήτε ῥάβδον, μήτε πήραν, μήτε ἄρτον, μήτε ἀργύριον'—each of these is a *part* of a general provision for a journey, and all are linked together by one common head.

NOTE 1. But sometimes merely οὐ—οὔτε, and μή—μήτε, are said to be met with in the like sense; e. g. Matt. 12: 32. James 5: 12. 1 Tim. 1: 7. Matt. 5: 34. It is obvious, however, that as τε—τε is the usual custom of the language, so its corresponding *negatives* (οὔτε—οὔτε) mostly follow the same ratio. Indeed, the cases above cited will hardly prove the junction of οὐ—οὔτε or μή—μήτε, when strictly considered, although Winer seems to cite them for this purpose; for the οὐ and the μή of these passages merely negative the preceding verb, and belong not to a *coordinate* clause. Kuhner assigns οὐ—οὔτε rather to poetry than prose, § 743. 2. But if οὐ means *neither* (and so it may sometimes mean), then οὔτε may follow it; as in Rev. 9: 21. John 1: 25.

NOTE 2. After οὐδέ..μηδέ, may follow οὔτε..μήτε, nor is this unfrequent; but in this case the latter particles stand before subordinate and partitive clauses, not before those which are *coordinate* with the οὐδέ and μηδέ clauses; e. g. μηδ᾽ ἕπεσθαι μηδὲ πείθεσθαι μήτε στρατηγῷ μήτε ἄλλῳ ἄρχοντι, *he should neither follow nor obey either military leader or any other ruler;* here the two last clauses (with μήτε) are partitives under a generic μηδενί which precedes in the text, Xen. Mem. II. 2. 11 So μήτε—μήτε may come after μηδέ, in the like sense as above, and then μηδέ be again resumed in a following coordinate clause; see examples in Kühner, § 744. 3.

§ 184. Peculiarities of negative clauses.

There are several *peculiarities* (rather than anomalies) attached to the use of negative particles in connected clauses.

(1) Instead of the regular οὐ—οὐδέ, μή—μηδέ, we find also οὐδέ—οὐδέ, οὐδέ—οὔτε, τε—μηδέ, οὐδέ—τε or καί; also οὐδέ alone, as a mere adversative, *but not*; and οὐδέ adverbial, (as the opposite of καί *even*, etc.), so that οὐδέ then means *not indeed, not at all*, etc. So in many cases is the usage as to μή and μηδέ, in their various relations, etc., as connected with different clauses. Most of these varieties have been explained above; and the rest are easily understood.

(2) Besides the regular οὔτε—οὔτε and μήτε—μήτε, there are οὐ—οὔτε, οὐδέ—οὔτε, οὔτε—οὐ (asyndic construction), οὔτε—οὐδέ (like τε—δέ, where the latter δέ marks antithesis, emphasis, etc.), οὔτε—τε, οὔτε—δέ, (the two last, where a *positive* sentence or clause follows a negative one, and of these two, οὔτε—δέ is used where positive *antithesis* is made by the clause in which δέ stands.) The like of μήτε. Explanations of the rest are given above.

(3) It should be noted, that a *negative* clause with οὐ is frequently followed by a clause with ἀλλά; e. g. οὐκ ἐψεύσω ἀνθρώποις, ἀλλὰ θεῷ, *thou hast not lied to men, but to God*, Acts 5 : 4. Here the οὐκ in the first clause may be taken as absolute denial, (which in itself it is); but in many cases, the meaning may, from mere rhetorical exigency, be regarded as a softened and comparative negative; e. g. οὐκ ὑμεῖς ἐστε λαλοῦντες, ἀλλὰ τὸ πνεῦμα, Matt. 10 : 20, i. e. *it is not so much you who speak* [on such an occasion], *as it is the Spirit*, etc. So Mark 9 : 37. 1 Cor. 15 : 10. John 12 : 44, al. In many cases, however, the negative is absolute.

(4) Sometimes two negatives in a leading clause destroy the force of each other; e. g. Acts 4 : 20, οὐ δυνάμεθα ἡμεῖς ... μὴ λαλεῖν, i. e. *we cannot ... not speak* = we must speak. So in 1 Cor. 12 : 15 οὐ ... οὐκ ἔστιν, *it is not ... not of the body*, i. e. it is of the body. Comp. Matt. 25 : 9.

But sometimes two negatives merely accumulate the force of the negation; e. g. χωρὶς ἐμοῦ οὐ δύνασθε ποιεῖν οὐδέν, *without me ye are not able to do any thing at all.* 2 Cor. 11 : 8. 1 Cor. 8 : 2. Mark 1 : 44. 5 : 37. 15 : 4. Luke 4 : 2. 8 : 43. 20 : 40. John 6 : 63. 9 : 33. Acts 8 : 39. Rom. 13 : 8, al. saepe. This is the more frequent usage; and it is obvious that such cases must be judged of by the sense which is required. The accumulation of negatives in the way just mentioned, is peculiar at times; e. g. Luke 23 : 53, οὗ οὐκ ἦν οὐδέπω οὐδεὶς κείμενος, *where no one was ever laid.* So in Ael. Anim. 11. 31, ὡς οὐδεπώποτε οὐδένα οὐδὲν ἀδικήσας; also in Plat. Parmen. p. 166 ... τῶν μὴ ὄντων οὐδενὶ οὐδαμῇ οὐδαμῶς οὐδεμίαν κοινωνίαν ἔχει.

§ 185. Nature and use of Conjunctions.

(1) *Conjunctions* are particles which express the relation of two or more clauses or sentences to each other, so as to bind them in one general unity.

§ 185. SYNTAX: CONJUNCTIONS. 283

E. g. In the original simplicity of language, it seems to have been the usage to express each sentence, or clause virtually constituting a sentence, by itself as complete; like 'Socrates was wise; Plato was wise;' or, 'Socrates was wise; Socrates was good;' and so of other like things. Instead of this, *conjunctions* enable us now to unite and amalgamate these separate declarations, and make one sentence of them, more energetic and equally plain; e. g. 'Socrates was wise and good; Socrates and Plato were wise.' In this way most sentences become *composite* or *compound*, having several subjects, or predicates, or objects, united together by conjunctions.

(2) Clauses or sentences connected, and standing in the same predicament, i. e. not being actually dependent on each other, are called COORDINATE; but clauses expressive of *cause, consequence*, etc., which are dependent on other clauses, are named-SUBORDINATE.

(3) Coordinate clauses may be *copulative* or *adversative*.

Those which are *copulative* merely arrange and join together se veral subjects, predicates, or objects, which serve to amplify and extend the idea to be conveyed by the sentence, each annexed portion (annexed by a *conjunction*) designating some additional idea. Thus *Socrates and Plato were wise and learned*, contains no less than four distinct sentences arranged and compressed together, viz. Socrates was wise, Socrates was learned; and so of Plato. In the compound sentence, *and Plato* is put on by the copulative; *and learned* is also annexed in the same way; and by virtue of the plural verb, *wise and learned* apply equally to Socrates and to Plato. Such is the power of *conjunctions* in giving energy to language, and in making brevity of expression feasible.

Adversative clauses, on the other hand, either limit, modify, deny, or assert the reverse of, what is contained in the leading clause; e. g. 'He is brave, but prudent;' 'He is not liberal, but illiberal.'

(4) COPULATIVE CLAUSES connect together such things as are in the like predicament, or such as are added for the sake of *intensity, enlargement, explanation*, etc. This is effected principally by τέ and καί.

(1) In older classic Greek τέ is the most general connective of copulative clauses. The most common usage is, to employ it in each of two or more connected clauses; e. g. πατὴρ ἀνδρῶν τε θεῶν τε, which we may translate: *The father of both men and gods*, or *the father as well of men as gods*, or *as of men so of gods*. Τέ thus employed shows a *mutual* relation; e. g. joined with ἀνδρῶν it indicates that this word has a *coordinate* to follow, and joined with θεῶν it indicates that it has a *preordinate*. Τέ is so general in its usage, i. e. it extends to clauses of such various character, that the coordinate clauses are sometimes *antithetic* even, so that τέ—τέ in this case almost synonomizes with ἤ—ἤ (the disjunctives); and so we find in fact τέ—ἤ, ἤ—τέ. In like manner, it almost invades at times the province of μέν—δέ; for it sometimes stands in clauses the first of which is conces-

sive, and the second *antithetic*, so that we find in many cases τέ—δέ, and also μέν—τέ.

NOTE 1. Τέ is not unfrequently found *alone*, in all the cases where (which is more usual) it is employed as *double*. Then, of course, only a *loose* annexion of the word (with which it is joined) is indicated, and no reference is made to a *preordinate*. Often the word is of *secondary* importance with which τέ in this case is coupled.

NOTE 2. In the N. Test., the use of τέ is comparatively rare. Matthew uses it but *twice*; John but *once*; Mark, not at all. Paul and Luke occasionally employ it.

NOTE 3. Τέ is an *enclitic*, and of course cannot stand at the *beginning* of a sentence or clause.

(2) Καί is more energic in its meaning than τέ.

All its meanings, however, as a conjunction, may be reduced to *and*; as an *adverb*, it signifies *etiam, also, even*, etc., i. e. it is an intensive. Its energic meaning is seen plainly in such cases as the following; ἄνθρωποι καὶ ἀγαθοὶ καὶ κακοί, καὶ πένητες καὶ πλούσιοι, where the antithetic word is placed in full light; (a Greek would not say: καὶ κακοὶ καὶ πονηροί, there being no antithesis here, but κακοί τε πονηροί τε).

The usual junctions are καί—καί, which are in mutual relation, like τε—τε. But τέ—καί is very common where the clause with καί is of course the more energic. Τέ—καί differs from τέ—τέ, in that the latter expresses more the internal *mutual* relation, while τε—καί indicates *intensity* in the latter clause as well as *adjunction*; e. g. πολλά τε καὶ καλὰ ἔργα ἀπεδείξατο. Often it is used in *antithetic* clauses; e. g. ἀγαθά τε καὶ κακά; and thus it is sometimes nearly equivalent to ἤ—ἤ.

NOTE 1. Καί (like τέ) is often found *alone*; and then it gives intensity to the meaning of the clause and to the junction also. The like when καί is employed in a *question*; for the question then stands intimately connected with what has been before said. E. g. ὁ Σωκράτης καὶ ὁ Πλάτων σοφοὶ ἦσαν, where S. and P. are as it were conjoined in one generic idea. So with the Imper.; καί μοι δὸς τὴν χεῖρα! See Mark 10: 26. Luke 3: 14. 10: 29, al.

NOTE 2. So widely extended is the *adjunctive* nature of καί, that it may connect *adversative* clauses, and even *disjunctive* ones; e. g. Eurip. Herc. Fur. 508, 'Ye saw me ... about to do renowned deeds, καί μ' ἀφίλεθ' ἡ τύχη, *but* fortune took me away.' So Matt. 6: 26. 12: 5. John 1: 10. 6: 70. 7: 19. 9: 30. 17: 25. Such being the case, καί is nearly the same as ἤ (or) in such clauses as ἅ τε δεῖ φίλια καὶ πολέμια νομίζειν, *which one must regard as friendly or unfriendly*; Plato.

NOTE 3. In the N. Test. (and Sept.) the power of καί is still more extended than in classic Greek. Often is it employed as a mere *continuative* of discourse, where classic writers would employ δέ, ἀλλά, τότε, etc. As specimens, see Matt. 14: 14, 22, 34. 15: 21, 29. Mark 1: 21, 29, 40. 2: 1, 13. Luke 8: 1, 22, 26. 9: 10, 18. John 7: 1. 9: 1. 10: 40. It is less frequent in John's Gospel, but is almost exclusively the continuative particle of the Apocalypse; e. g. in Rev. 2: 8, 12, 18. 3: 1, 7, 14. 5: 1. 6: 1. 7: 1. 8: 1. 9: 1. 10: 1. 11: 1. 12: 1, 18. 14: 1. 15: 1. 16: 1. 17: 1. 18: 1. 19:

§ 185. SYNTAX: CONJUNCTIONS. 285

11. 20: 1, 7, 11. 21: 1. 22: 1, 6. Almost all the *great* as well as small transitions are in this book marked by καί. This very extensive power of καί is doubtless the effect of Hebraism, i. e. of carrying over the power of the Heb. ו conversive, etc., into Greek usage. The almost boundless latitude of ו in Hebrew, is too well known to Heb. scholars to need illustration.

REMARK. The student need not hesitate, therefore, sometimes to render καί *but, or. moreover, and yet*, etc.; but let him remember, that this liberty is due to *the nature of the sentiment* which is connected with καί, and not to the varying significaton of the particle itself Connecting as it does clauses of all hues, either synonymous or adversative, either parts of the same generic sentence or parts of the same discourse (καὶ continuative), the actual relations that exist may be properly expressed in a translation, although καί in and by itself does not really and properly designate them.

(3) Καί as an *adverb* is an *intensive* = *even, also, too*, etc.; e. g. Rom. 8: 23, καὶ ἡμεῖς αὐτοί, *even we ourselves*, Matt. 10: 30, καὶ αἱ τρίχες, *even the very hairs*. So Luke 8: 18. 1 Cor. 2: 10. Mark 9: 13. Al. saepe; and so in the classics.

And in this sense it often takes other particles with it; e. g. καὶ δέ, ἀλλὰ καί, γὰρ καί, ἐὰν δὲ καί, εἰ καί, εἴ γε καί, ἢ καί, etc.

NOTE 1. In all the cases of adverbial use, there is *an implied reference to something which precedes;* so that καί never entirely dispenses with its *conjunctive* power, even when it is an intensive.

NOTE 2. More intensity still is expressed by such formulas as οὐ μόνον —ἀλλὰ καί. So οὐχ ὅτι—ἀλλὰ καί, [i. e. οὐκ [ἐρῶ] ὅτι—ἀλλὰ καί etc.]; οὐχ ὅπως—ἀλλὰ καί, etc.

NOTE 3. Καί is often *omitted* either in the protasis or apodosis; but generally with a special purpose; e. g. καὶ ὁ Σωκράτης ταῦτα ἔλεξεν, ὥσπερ καὶ οἱ ἄλλοι. Here Socrates and others are joined so as to place them in the same predicament: but if καί had been omitted in the *first* clause, the writer would have meant to distinguish Socrates without necessarily connecting him with the *others*, for he would have left out καί as a sign of *conjunction;* if καί had been omitted in the *last* clause, then the first clause is still more emphatic, inasmuch as the *junction* is made as weak as possible.

GENERAL REMARK " Τέ adjungit, καί conjungit" Τέ, in the older classics, is a more general and looser connective, καί, in the N. Test. is almost exclusive, however, in its predominance, and forms junctions of all sorts. from the loosest ones of particular words, up to the most important ones of whole paragraphs or chapters It is stronger, broader, more variegated, and more significant, than τέ, as used in the N Testament; and indeed it is so even in the classics

(5) ADVERSATIVE ARRANGEMENT. This is marked principally by δέ and ἀλλά, with the aid of some other particles, which usually precede them and serve to give emphasis to the adversative or disjunctive clause, by more distinctly marking the clause which precedes as a *concessive* and *relative* one, from which the clause with δέ or ἀλλά stands *disjoined* as to sense, although *conjoined* as to position.

(1) Δέ is by far the most extensively employed particle that marks *ad-*

versative relation. It has a double power, viz. *it marks disjunction in sense, and conjunction in arrangement.*

(*a*) The most frequent use of δέ is in clauses which succeed other clauses marked by μέν. This last particle (=אָכֵן, for μέν is the weaker form of μήν) means *truly, indeed,* etc.; and in a leading clause it marks *concession, allowing, granting,* etc.; so that δέ with its clause forms an exception, limitation, or even (in some cases) a virtual denial of what is contained in the μέν clause; e. g. εὐωπὸς μέν, ἀνδρεῖος δὲ ἀνήρ, *the man is comely, but brave.*

NOTE 1. All degrees and kinds of *antithesis* or *distinction* are marked by δέ; and, consequently, of *concession* by μέν. The nature of a sentence must decide how much. Often we cannot translate μέν at all, as it stands in Greek merely as *the index of a concessive clause.* Sometimes we may translate it, *on the one hand, on one part, first, in one respect,* etc., and then of course we must translate δέ so as to designate a correspondent part. Thus ἐνταῦθα μέν—ἐκεῖ δέ; ὁτὲ μέν—ὁτὲ δέ; πρῶτον μέν—ἔπειτα δέ; ὁ μέν—ὁ δέ; τὰ μέν—τὰ δέ. But let it be noted, that the two parts do not always so exactly correspond, as in the examples above. Thus we have οἱ μέν—ἄλλοι δέ; οἱ μέν—καὶ οἱ. etc.; and sometimes a noun even in the second member, as τὸ μὲν μέγιστον κακῶν ... δικαιοσύνη δὲ μέγιστον ἀγαθόν.

NOTE 2. Repetition of the same word, or of an equivalent one; a series of different predicates connected with the same subject; mere external connection of things or incidents; and even *contrast* of two things; may all be connected by μέν—δέ. E. g. εἷλε μὲν τὴν Ἐπίδαυρον, εἷλε δὲ αὐτὸν Προκλέα—Γένος μὲν εἰμι ... Σκύρου, πλέω δέ, εἰς οἶκον, αὐδῶμι δὲ παῖς Ἀχιλλέως—Ἦν μὲν σιωπή, φθέγμα δὲ ἐξαίφνης θοίνξε, *there was silence, and then a voice suddenly called out.* So τὴν μὲν ἐγώ ... πέμψω, ἐγὼ δὲ κ' ἄγω Βρισηΐδα, *whom I ... will send, but I will carry off Briseis,* Il. *a.* 182.

NOTE 3. *Μέν—δέ* often qualify the *whole* clause in which they stand. Sometimes one of the clauses has a *participle* and the other a verb. Sometimes either or both of these particles are successively repeated, and then the other follows, once or more repeated. Instead of δέ in the apodosis, an equivalent word, e. g. ἀλλά, αὖ, ἀτάρ, μέντοι, etc., may be used; and even τέ, καί, or ἠδέ, sometimes appear in the apodosis.

(*b*) Both μέν and δέ may be employed *alone*. (1) *Μέν*; for any word in the apodosis, expressive in itself of *antithesis*, may dispense with δέ, as πρῶτον μέν—ἔπειτα. So the δέ clause is often merely *implied*; e. g. 'The report ἐμοὶ μὲν οὐ πιθανός, *was in my opinion improbable,* [but to others it might be probable].

(2) *Δέ*; which is in a multitude of cases employed without any preceding μέν. It may be so, when no particular reference is intended to be made in the first clause, by the speaker, to an antithetic one; or when he does not wish to prepare the hearer for such an antithetic clause; or when the antithesis is very weak; or when the preceding clause (with μέν) is merely implied. In fact, in all the clauses of such a nature as those in which μέν is usually the harbinger of δέ, the μέν may be, and sometimes is, *omitted*. When it is so, the design is to indicate, that the antithesis is intended to be less strongly marked.

§ 186. Syntax: Conjunctions. 287

This *separate* δέ, moreover, may be successively repeated, even where μέν is wholly omitted.

In case of a formal *protasis* and *apodosis*, δέ is often employed in the latter, without a corresponding μέν in the former, (but sometimes with one); and here δέ may have either an *antithetic* sense or a *conjunctive* one, according to the nature of the clauses.

(c) *Δέ continuative* is every where to be found in the N. Test., and is frequent in the classics. In this sense, and of course as standing alone, it connects *clauses, sentences*, or *paragraphs*, so that it marks *transition* in the thought and *diversity* in the action or representation. Here it sometimes =καί, although the two words in themselves are so widely diverse. But both are occasionally *continuatives* of all sorts of sentences and paragraphs; yet δέ commonly denotes more *diversity* than καί. Even *subordinate* and *causal* clauses may be joined to others by δέ; and so questions and answers may take this particle, where transition and continuation are both denoted.

Remark. In such cases as οὐδέ, μηδέ, and sometimes καὶ δέ, δέ is an adverb =*not too, not even*, etc.

(6) Besides δέ — αὖ, αὖθις, αὖτε, αὐτάρ, ἀτάρ, καίτοι, ὅμως, εἶτα, ἔπειτα, with various shades of meaning but all in an *adversative* sense, are sometimes employed in clauses of an adversative nature.

(7) The most emphatic of the *adversative* particles is ἀλλά; which, as the nature of the case may demand, indicates the *contrary* of the preceding clause, or else some limitation and modification of it.

E. g. οὐκ οἱ πλούσιοι εὐδαίμονές εἰσιν, ἀλλ' οἱ ἀγαθοί. So ἐκεῖθεν, ἀλλ' οὐκ ἐνθένδε. Modification; αὐτὸς μὲν ἐγὼ μενέω . . . ἀλλ' ἕταιρον πέμπω, *I shall stay here . . . but I will send a friend there*, etc.

§ 186. *Disjunctive clauses.*

(1) By these are meant, such clauses as express *alternatives*; so that, one of them being true, the other of course must be considered as *negatived*.

The particles employed in these are ἤ—ἤ, εἴτε—εἴτε, ἐάντε—ἐάντε. The first are the predominant ones; e. g. γέρας ἢ Αἴαντος ἢ Ὀδυσῆος, *the reward either of Ajax or of Ulysses*. Often (as in μέν—δέ) one of these particles is omitted.

Note. More often has ἤ (single) the sense of a comparative—*than*; and it then naturally stands after words which designate a *discrepancy*, such as ἄλλος, ἀλλοῖος, ἐναντίος, ἴδιος, διαφέρω, etc.; and of course here all words having a *comparative* meaning. Very frequently ἄλλος, μᾶλλον, etc., are omitted, when the sense demands them to be *mentally* supplied. On the other hand, ἤ itself is often omitted after many comparatives, e. g. πλέον, πλέω, ἔλαττον, etc.; and often before the Gen. case.

§ 187. Subordinate Clauses; (see §_185. 2).

(1) These, so far as our present purpose is concerned, may be named *causal* sentences or clauses; inasmuch as they designate either a *ground* or a *consequence* of something which precedes.

These differ essentially from *coordinate* clauses, inasmuch as they are all *dependent*, and cannot (like coordinate clauses), be taken as complete sentences by themselves. The *ground* or *causal* particle is γάρ; the *consequence* particles are οὖν, ἄρα, τοίνυν, τοιγαροῦν.

(2) The ground particle γάρ is either *argumentative* and *explicative*, or *suppletive* and *conclusive*.

This results from the γέ and ἄρα which unite in forming γάρ; for γέ indicates either *grounding* or *completion*, and ἄρα either *explanation* or *consequence*. Sometimes γάρ conveys principally the meaning of ground or reason (γάρ argumentative); at other times that of *explanation* (γάρ explicative); e. g. καλὴ ἡ καταγωγή· ἥ τε γὰρ πλάτανος αὕτη μάλ᾽ ἀμφιλαφής τε καὶ ὑψηλή. In the way of *explanation*; Matt. 1: 18, 'Now the birth of Jesus Christ was in this manner, μνηστευθείσης γάρ, etc., *namely* [as we should say] *his mother being espoused*, etc.' This usage is not frequent.

NOTE 1. Very often the clause is to be mentally supplied, to which γάρ refers in its *causal* sense; e. g. in Matt. 2: 2. 27: 23. Mark 8: 38. 12: 23. John 4: 44. Rom. 8: 18. Luke 7: 8, al. saepe. See Lex. γάρ.

NOTE 2. Γάρ as *suppletive* and *conclusive* is used mostly in exclamations, optative clauses, commands, and interrogations. In these it is often a kind of intensive, and may be expressed in our language by *then, truly, indeed*, etc., not because these words in themselves convey the real meaning of γάρ by itself, but because the clause as a whole conveys an idea which will authorize such a translation into our idiom. In most of these cases, a mental supposition of something *implied* easily suggests itself, and usually this will account for the use of γάρ.

N. B The other causal particles are less difficult, and must be left to the lexicon But especially the reader is referred to Kühner, § 755 seq , for the best illustration of them.

§ 188. *The Asyndic Construction*.

(1) By this is meant, such constructions as omit the particles of annexation or conjunction, which are usually employed.

(2) To constitute this, the clauses must stand in the same relation, both in a logical and grammatical sense.

NOTE. This does *not* imply, that all the clauses are of equal *weight* or *importance*. The object is brevity, energy, compression of thought; and where the perspicuity is not seriously injured by the asyndic construction, it is often a great beauty.

§ 189. Syntax: Ellipsis.   289

(3) In particular; apposition, epexegetical clauses, the repetition of the same or the like thought in the same or in nearly equivalent words, the commencement of a new paragraph or chapter, antitheses (specially when in pairs), a great number of separate subjects or predicates—all these, and other causes, frequently occasion the asyndic construction.

In poetry, energetic or impassioned passages, rapidity of action, crowded thought, etc., often occasion such asyndic constructions.
See as illustrations, in Heb. 11 : 37. 1 Tim. 4 : 13. Rom. 2 : 19, 20. 1 : 29 seq. 1 Cor. 3 : 2. 13 : 4—8. James 5 : 6. In the way of *antithesis*, 1 Cor. 15 : 43, 44. James 1 : 19. Eph. 2 : 8. John 2 : 10. 4 : 22. Epexegesis; Col. 1 : 14. 2 Cor. 7 : 6. 2 Pet. 2 : 18. Cases where ground or reason is subjoined; Rev. 22 : 10. John 19 : 12. 1 Cor. 7 : 15. Rev. 16 : 6. The like is every where to be found in the Classics.

ELLIPSIS.

§ 189. *Nature and kinds of Ellipsis.*

(1) Ellipsis consists in the omission of a word, which, although it is not spoken, is necessarily implied in order to make out the sense.

Note 1. Ellipsis may respect the *subject*, the *predicate*, or the *copula* of a sentence, according to the usual mode of treating this matter. But as the *predicate* is in its own nature generally an undefined thing, we can hardly suppose (the case of *Aposiopesis* excepted) that a speaker or writer would leave this to be arbitrarily supplied. Properly, then, ellipsis respects the *subject* or the *copula* of a sentence.

Note 2. Recent grammarians do not reckon as ellipsis, those cases in which the word to be supplied is already mentioned or suggested in the preceding context; e. g. εἴτε θλιβόμεθα, ὑπὲρ τῆς ὑμῶν σωτηρίας, where θλιβόμεθα is mentally repeated before the last clause, 2 Cor. 1 : 6. 1 John 2 : 19. Mark 14 : 29. 2 Tim. 1 : 5. 1 Cor. 11 : 1. Rom. 9 : 32, al. saepe. For shades of difference in the mode of supplying the ellipsis, see 1 Cor. 7 : 19. Eph. 4 : 29. Mark 15 : 8. 2 Cor. 3 : 13. John 1 : 8. Heb. 10 : 6, 8. Rom. 5 : 3, 11. 8 : 23. 9 : 10.

(2) The copula εἰμί (and also γίγνομαι) is more usually omitted. It is rarely inserted in simple propositions, except for the sake of emphasis, because it is spontaneously supplied.

E. g. μακάριος ἀνήρ, ὅς κ. τ. λ., James 1 : 12 ; τί σοι ὄνομα ; Mark 5 : 9. Heb. 5 : 13. Luke 4 : 36, al. saepe. So in the plural (εἰσί), Heb. 5 : 12.—2nd pers. sing. (εἶ), Rev. 15 : 4 ; Imper. (ἔστω), Rom. 12 : 9, al. Even in cases where εἰμί means *is=exists*, it is sometimes omitted; e. g. Rom. 11 : 11. 1 Cor. 15 : 21, al.

Note 1. When other verbs besides those which assert *existence*, are to be supplied, the context, in nearly every case, will lead the reader at once to the supply of the proper verb; e. g. Rom. 5 : 18, where διῆλθε

37

§ 189. SYNTAX: ELLIPSIS.

from v. 12 is to be supplied, of which the εἰς gives notice; comp. εἰς πάντας in v. 12. Phil. 2: 3, μηδὲν κατὰ κ. τ. λ, where ποιοῦντες is spontaneously supplied. Gal. 5: 13, μόνον μὴ κ. τ. λ, where κατέχητε is implied; and of course the *subject* (as well as the copula) is left out here. But this is spontaneously supplied by the mind, in referring back to the preceding ἐκλήθητε. So Matt. 26: 5, μὴ ἐν τῇ ἑορτῇ, sc. μὴ [τοῦτο γενέσθω]; Mark 14: 2, id. Τοῦτο δέ, viz. τοῦτο δὲ [λέγω]; comp. Gal. 3: 17. 1 Thess. 4: 15, where the verb is supplied; or the verb φημί may be supplied; as in 1 Cor. 7: 29. 15: 50. In Matt. 5: 38, ὀφθαλμὸν ἀντὶ ὀφθαλμοῦ, κ. τ. λ, one must look for the verb [δώσεις] in the original connection, Ex. 21: 24.

(3) The *subject* of a sentence is omitted, only where from the nature of the case it is spontaneously suggested, or may be easily gathered from the context.

E. g. βροντᾷ it thunders, i. e. ὁ Ζεὺς βροντᾷ; ἀναγνώσεται, let [the scribe] read. So in the N. Test.; φησί, μαρτυρεῖ, λέγει, etc., in respect to O. Test. quotations; where the meaning is, *The Lord saith*, or *The Scripture saith*.

So where the subject is easily supplied from the context; as συνῆλθον καὶ τῶν μαθητῶν, *there came together* [τινές certain] *of the disciples*. So ἡ αὔριον, ἡ σήμερον, ἡ ἑξῆς, where ἡμέρα is readily supplied; εἰς εὐθεῖαν [ὁδόν], Luke 3: 5. So ἡ δεξιὰ [χείρ], ἡ ξηρὰ [γῆ], ψυχρὸν [ὕδωρ], Matt. 10: 42; τὸ γλυκὺ [ὕδωρ], James 3: 11; τῇ ἐχομένῃ –τῇ ἐπιούσῃ –[ἡμέρᾳ]; ἐν λευκοῖς [ἱματίοις], John 20: 22. 5: 2, προβατικὴ [πύλη], etc. etc.

NOTE 1. Sometimes the case absolute is used in an impersonal way, when ἀνθρώπων or τινών may be understood; e. g. Luke 8: 20, ἀπηγγέλη αὐτῷ, λεγόντων, *it was told him*, [some] *saying*, ὅτι κ. τ. λ.

(4) Although the *predicate* cannot be wholly omitted by ellipsis, yet a part of it may be, when this part is obviously suggested by the context.

E. g. δαρήσεται πόλλας, *he shall suffer many* [πληγάς stripes], Luke 12: 47. 2 Cor. 11: 24. But all such cases we may call *breviloquence*, rather than ellipsis. So: 'Give to all their dues, τῷ τὸν φόρον, i. e. τῷ ὀφείλετε τ. φ. etc.

NOTE 1. Before μή or μήπως, used in the way of breviloquence, ὁρᾶτε or δέδοικα (*I fear*) may be supplied by the mind; often so in the classics. E. g. 'If God spared not the natural branches, μήπως οὐδὲ σοῦ φείσεται, [I fear] *he will not spare thee*,' Rom. 11: 21.

(5) Sometimes both *subject* and *predicate* are omitted; but merely because the context readily supplies them.

E. g. in Gal. 5: 13, μόνον μὴ τὴν ἐλευθερίαν etc., i. e. μὴ [κατέχητε] τὴν ἐλ. etc. Matt. 26: 5. 2 Cor. 9: 6. Gal. 3: 17. 1 Thess. 4: 15.

REMARK The unbounded license of the older grammarians, in extending ellipsis to all parts of the Greek Test, such as is developed in Bos's book on ellipsis, and other works of the like kind,* is now, by general agreement among gramma-

---

* Of this book and of Weiske on Pleonasms, Hermann says. Singulari profecto casû accidit, ut L Bosii liber *de Ellipsi* maximam partem sit *pleonasmus;* Weiskii *de Pleonasmo, ellipsis.*

§ 190. Syntax: Aposiopesis, etc. 291

rians, quite abjured. Adjectives and participles which stand in the place of nouns, are now regarded as nouns, without the feeling that any ellipsis exists Such modes of expression are considered merely as *breviloquence* So the neuters of adjectives and participles are taken as nouns, when they are employed as such So in in respect to the use of the *cases*; they are now regarded as expressing relations of themselves, and not needing prepositions to govern them ; for these only render their meaning more explicit So in respect to cases governed by verbs; the old theory was, e g. that εἶναί τινος required to be considered by the mind, as being equivalent to εἶναι υἱός τινος, but now the Gen itself is regarded as indicating the same relation as υἱός in such a case would express. So too in 'Ιωσὴφ τοῦ 'Ἡλὶ or Μαὶϑ Ματταϑίου (Luke 3 26), υἱός need not be regarded as necessary, because the Gen. of itself indicates *origin*. In a multitude of the like cases, we may consider the modes of expression simply as being *breviloquent*, not as elliptical All languages employ a multitude of breviloquent expressions ; which, in general, are, by reason of usage or by the aid of context, as intelligible as the more ample expressions

Specially were the older grammarians prone, almost every where, to introduce prepositions before the Gen and Dat cases which follow verbs, e. g. ἀντί after verbs of buying and selling, ἀπό after those of feeling, restraining, etc ; διά before the Gen of time; εἰς before the Inf of object or design; διά after verbs of abounding; ἐν before the Dat of time, place, instrument, etc ; παρά after verbs of hearing; ἕνεκα after verbs of displeasure, anger, or before the Inf with τοῦ; ἐπί after verbs of ruling, etc ; κατά before the Acc. of manner, in respect to, etc ; περί after verbs of remembering, forgetting, etc ; in all which cases the most enlightened grammarians of the present day speak no longer of *ellipsis*

So also in respect to *Conjunctions*, e g they supplied ἵνα before the Subjunctive, in cases like τί θέλετε ποιήσω ἡμῖν ; which is easily solved by simple interpunction, e g τί, θέλετε, ποιήσω ὑμῖν , *what (according to your wish) shall I do for you ?*

One need not deny, that in many cases the sense would in some respects be more explicit, had the writer supplied such words as those that have been mentioned. But if *breviloquence* is to be excluded from language, the greatest and most effectual means of vivacity and energy of style must be withheld.

APOSIOPESIS.
§ 190. *Nature and Use of it.*

(1) Aposiopesis (ἀποσιώπησις) consists in the suppression of a part of a sentence, on account of the feelings of the writer, or for the sake of brevity, energy, etc.

E. g. in Luke 19: 42. 13: 9. Acts 23: 9. So after εἰ δὲ μή, εἰ δὲ μήγε, a part of a sentence, or even a whole one, is often omitted ; e. g. 6: 1. 9: 17. Mark 2: 21, 22. Luke 10: 6. 13: 9. Rev. 2: 5, al. Cases of this nature can be judged of only by the connection and the meaning demanded by the passage.

BREVILOQUENCE.
§ 191. *Nature and Use.*

(1) In a multitude of cases, the repetition of a word or words obviously suggested by the context is omitted. Formerly this was put to the account of *ellipsis*; it is now reckoned as *breviloquence*.

NOTE 1. The exact metes and bounds of ellipsis and breviloquence can hardly be defined. They run into each other in a certain class of cases. In general, however, the omission of words, where the supply of them is most plain and obvious, and there can be no room for mistake by an intelligent reader, is called *breviloquence*.

E. g. οὐ σὺ τὴν ῥίζαν βαστάζεις, ἀλλὰ ἡ ῥίζα σέ, i. e. ἡ ῥίζα [βαστάζει] σε, Rom. 11 : 18 ; καὶ τίς ἐστι . . . . ἵνα πιστεύσω εἰς αὐτόν ; John 9 : 36. 15 : 25. 13 : 18. Mark 14 : 49. Phil. 3 : 13, 14, ἐγώ ἐμαυτὸν οὐ λογίζομαι, ἕν δὲ κ. τ. λ, i. e. ἕν δὲ [λογίζομαι] ; Luke 23 : 5.

NOTE 2. Under the head of *breviloquence* or *brachylogy* (βραχυλογία) may be classed the so-called *constructio praegnans* ; e. g. σώσει εἰς τὴν βασιλείαν, *he will save* [and bring me] *into his kingdom*, 2 Tim. 4 : 18. Acts 23 : 11, 24. 1 Pet. 3 : 20. 2 Tim. 2 : 26. Luke 4 : 38. Gal. 5 : 4. 2 Cor. 10 : 5. Mark 7 : 4.

ZEUGMA.

§ 192. *Nature and Use.*

(1) Where a verb is connected with two nouns, and has such a sense that it does not fit them both, but we must supply another verb in order to make an appropriate sense, this is called *Zeugma*.

E. g. ἀνεῴχθη δὲ τὸ στόμα αὐτοῦ . . . καὶ ἡ γλῶσσα αὐτοῦ, i. e. ἡ γλῶσσα αὐτοῦ [ἐλύθη], Luke 1 : 64 ; γάλα ὑμᾶς ἐπότισα, οὐ βρῶμα, *I have given you milk to drink, and* [have fed you] *not with meat*, 1 Cor. 3 : 2. 1 Tim. 4 : 3. This is frequent in the classics.

PLEONASM.

§ 193. *Nature and Use.*

(1) Pleonasm means the addition of one or more words in order to designate what is already designated by other words.

(2) Of this there exists a considerable number of examples in the N. Testament.

E. g. ἀπὸ μακρόθεν, ἀπὸ ἄνωθεν, ἔπειτα μετὰ τοῦτο, πάλιν δεύτερον, πάλιν ἐκ δευτέρου, προδραμών ἔμπροσθεν, ἐκβάλλειν ἔξω, πάλιν ἀνακάμπτειν, πάλιν ἀνακαινίζειν, ὀπίσω ἀκολουθεῖν, ὡς Γόμοῤῥα ὡμοιώθημεν, τὰ ὁμοιώματα . . . ὅμοια, etc., most of which occur also in the classics. So οὐκ after ἀρνούμενος, μή after ἀντιλέγω. So ἐκτός εἰ μή instead of εἰ μή ; πρὸ προσώπου (לִפְנֵי) for πρό, etc. In all, or nearly all, of these and the like cases, *intensity* of expression is designed by the writers. The words are not *unmeaning*.

(3) Different from pleonasm, properly so-named, is particularity and circumstantiality in designation.

E. g. γράψαντες διὰ χειρός · κατήγγειλε διὰ στόματος · ἐπάρας τοὺς ὀφθαλμοὺς ἐθεάσατο · ἀνοίξας τὸ στόμα αὐτοῦ εἶπεν · καὶ ἐγένετο (וַיְהִי) ὅτε συνετέλεσεν, etc. A great variety of such expressions occurs in the N. Testament ; most of which, however, add more or less of colouring to the picture.

(4) Repetition of the same words is not properly *pleonasm*,

but is designed for the sake of energy in expression, or to show deep feeling.

E. g. κύριε, κύριε! Ἀλλὰ ἀπελούσασθε, ἀλλὰ ἡγιάσθητε, ἀλλ' ἐδικαιώθετε. 1 Cor. 6: 11. Col. 1: 28. John 1: 11. 19: 10. Mark 12: 30.

Note 1. The like is the effect of synonymes; e. g. ἄνδρες Γαλιλαῖοι, like the classic ἄνδρες Ἀθηναῖοι, etc.

Note 2. A similar effect is produced by repeating a sentiment both in the affirmative and negative form; e. g. ὡμολόγησε, καὶ οὐκ ἠρνήσατο, John 1: 20. 1: 3. Eph. 5: 15. 1 John 2: 27. Acts 18: 9.

Remark. The verbs ἄρχομαι, δοκέω, θέλω, τολμάω, ἐπιχειρέω, καλέομαι, and εὑρίσκω, which even later commentators and recent lexicographers sometimes represent as *pleonastic*, all give some *colouring* to the mode of representation, and are not to be ranked under pleonasms.

In like manner the ὡς with participles has often been considered as *pleonastic;* which is beyond all question a mistake. The N. Test. has often been accused of abounding in *pleonastic* expressions; and hence the skill of its authors in writing Greek has not unfrequently been attacked. But the Greek classics afford specimens in abundance of the same or the like kind. E. g. μάχην μάχεισθαι, πόλεμον πολεμεῖν, φεύγων φυγῇ, φύσει πεφυκώς, φεύγων ἔφυγε, γονῇ γεννοῖος, μεγέθει μέγας, οἰόθεν οἶος, ὡς ἀληθῶς τῷ ὄντι, εὐθὺς παραχρῆμα, πάλιν αὖθις, τάχα ἴσως, ἀεὶ συνεχῶς, ἔπειτα μετὰ ταῦτα, παντάπασι καὶ πάντως, ἔφη λέγων, ἔλεγε φάς, ἦ δ' ὃς λέγων. So with a positive and negative form; οὐχ ἥκιστα, ἀλλὰ μάλιστα, μέγιστον δὲ καὶ οὐχ ἥκιστα, λέξω ... καὶ οὐκ ἀποκρύψομαι. The demonstrative is used for recapitulation or emphasis, as in the N. Testament; e. g. αἱ οἰκίαι... αὗται ὑπῆρχον ἔρυμα, Thuc. IV. 69. Τὰ πρόσφορα ὑμῖν... ἐκεῖνα κτᾶσθε, Cyrop. VI. 1. 17. Τὰς Κυκλάδας νήσους... ταύτας... ἐτόλμησαν, Isoc. Panath. p. 241. Ἐμοὶ μὲν... συνετιά μοι δοκεῖς λέγειν, Eurip. Phoen. 507. See Kühner, § 858.

PARENTHESIS.

§ 194. *Nature and Use.*

(1) Parenthesis means a word or phrase inserted in the midst of a sentence, which is thus interrupted or suspended; after which the sentence is resumed and completed.

Note 1. All clauses with *relatives*, added for the sake of explanation, etc., might come under this definition, taken in an *enlarged* sense. But these are *not* here meant; although many editors of the N. Testament, and critics, have not unfrequently treated them as parentheses.

Note 2. The same might be said of clauses in *apposition;* which, however, accurate philologists do not now reckon among parentheses.

(2) Real parenthesis is either, (*a*) Where the words of one individual are recited, and those of another are inserted in the midst of them.

E. g. 'That ye may know that the Son of man hath power on earth to forgive sins, (τότε λέγει τῷ παραλυτκῷ·) Ἐγερθεὶς ἆρον κ. τ. λ, Matt. 9: 6; Ῥαββὶ, (ὃ λέγεται ἑρμηνευόμενον, διδάσκαλε), ποῦ μένεις; John 1: 39. 4: 9. 9: 7. Mark 3: 30. 7: 26. 15: 42. Matt. 1: 22, 23. Luke 23: 51. John 1: 14. 6: 23. 11: 2. 19: 23, 31, al. saepe. In respect to *time;* Luke 9: 28.

(b) Where the sentence is suspended for the introduction of matter not directly necessary to its full enunciation.

E. g. Rom. 4: 11, εἰς τὸ λογισθῆναι ... δικαιοσύνην, interrupts the course of thought; and so, more or less, in Rom. 7: 1. 1 Cor. 7: 11. 2 Cor. 8: 3. 11: 21, 23. 12: 2. Col. 4: 10. Heb. 10: 7, al. saepe, especially in the writings of Paul.

REMARK Of course the limits of parenthesis will often be defined by the subjective views of the reader as to meaning and connection. Hence the great variety in regard to the usage of these grammatical signs; so that scarcely any two editors or interpreters agree in all cases. It is oftentimes, however, not very material, in regard to the sense of the author, whether parenthesis be inserted or omitted, for whether the sign of parenthesis is inserted or omitted, it cannot materially vary the sense. Hence the subject cannot be of *essential* consequence; but still, it is connected with *perspicuity* of representation.

ANACOLUTHON.

§ 195. *Nature and frequency.*

(1) By *anacoluthon* (ἀνακόλυθον) is meant, a sentence which, being interrupted by some inserted circumstance, is resumed not with a regularly continued construction, but with one differing from that with which it was begun.

NOTE 1. In writings full of thought and argument, where the author is more intent on his matter than on his manner, *anacoluthon* most frequently occurs. Paul exhibits it most frequently of all the N. Test. writers, in his epistles, although it occurs elsewhere.

E. g. Mark 9: 20, καὶ ἰδὼν [ὁ παῖς] αὐτὸν, εὐθέως τὸ πνεῦμα ἐσπάραξεν, where the regularly continued construction would be: εὐθέως ὑπὸ τοῦ πνεύματος ἐσπαράσσετο (passive). Acts 23: 30, μηνυθείσης δέ μοι ἐπιβουλῆς [τῆς] εἰς τὸν ἄνδρα μέλλειν ἔσεσθαι, which would regularly be, μελλούσης ἔσεσθαι.

Sometimes the construction begun and intermitted, is entirely dropped, and another one commenced *de novo;* as John 6: 22—24, ὁ ὄχλος ... ἰδὼν ... (v. 24) ὅτε οὖν εἶδον, after a long parentheses of two verses. Gal. 2: 6, ἀπὸ δὲ τῶν δοκούντων εἶναί τι ... ἐμοὶ γὰρ οἱ δοκοῦντες οὐδὲν προσανέθεντο, where the first construction required the sentence to be completed with a *passive* verb, but the construction is changed and an *active* verb is therefore employed. Rom. 2: 17—21, where the sentence is begun with εἰ δὲ σὺ κ. τ. λ, and then resumed in v. 21, by ὁ οὖν διδάσκων without the εἰ. Anacolutha may be found in Rom. 5: 12 seq. 9: 23, 24. 2 Pet. 2: 4 seq. 1 John 1: 1 seq. Acts 10: 36, al.

(2) *Anacolutha* are frequent, when the construction is continued by means of a *participle,* which often appears in a case different from that which would naturally be expected.

§ 196. SYNTAX: VARIED CONSTRUCTIONS. 295

E. g. παρακαλῶ ὑμᾶς ... ἀνεχόμενοι ... σπουδάζοντες, Eph. 4: 1, 2, both participles in the Nom. plural, instead of being (as we should naturally expect) in the Acc. as agreeing with ὑμᾶς. Col. 3: 16, ἐνοικείτω ἐν ὑμῖν ... διδάσκοντες καὶ νουθετοῦντες, Participles in the Nom. instead of the Dat. plural. So 2 Cor. 9: 10, 11. Acts 15: 22. Col. 2: 2. And so not unfrequently in the classics. By recommencing (as it were) a sentence with the Nom. of the Part., the meaning of it is made more emphatic and conspicuous. See § 172, where various anomalies are presented.

(3) Another species of *anacoluthon* is when, after the sentence is begun with a particle, the construction passes over into a *finite verb*, where we should naturally expect the participial construction to be continued.

E. g. Col. 1: 26, τὸ μυστήριον τὸ ἀποκεκρυμμένον ... νυνὶ δὲ ἐφανερώθη, instead of νυνὶ δὲ φανερωθέν. Eph. 1: 20, ἐγείρας αὐτὸν ... καὶ ἐκάθισεν. 2 John v. 2. Heb. 8: 10.

(4) Sometimes the Nom. or Acc. at the head of a sentence, has a verb after it which is not congruous with it.

E. g. ταῦτα ἃ θεωρεῖτέ, ἐλεύσονται ἡμέραι ἐν αἷς οὐκ ἀφεθήσεται λίθος ἐπὶ λίθῳ. Here I should construe thus: 'In regard to these things which ye see, etc.' See also 2 Cor. 12: 17. Rom. 8: 3.

(5) A kind of anacoluthon is it, when μέν is employed without a corresponding δέ.

In most cases where this is done, there is an ellipsis or aposiopesis as to the *apodosis* in which δέ would stand. The lexicons (under μέν, δέ) will give a considerable number of examples, and the requisite explanations. Μέν usually requires a δέ either expressed or implied; but a considerable number of cases exist, where no δέ is expressed. Like to this is the case of γάρ, which always implies a relation to some preceding thought, and a *sequency* after such thought; but oftentimes the particular thought to which γάρ is consequent, is not expressed, but only implied. It should be noted, however, in regard to μέν, that ἔπειτα, καί, τέ, ἀλλά, αὐτάρ, μέντοι, μήν, εἶτα, (see Passow on δέ), sometimes take the *apodotic* place of δέ; and often the apodosis is altogether omitted, in which case the sentence is a real *anacoluthon*. Winer, § 64. II. 2. e.

VARIED CONSTRUCTIONS (*Oratio Variata*).

§ 196. *Nature, extent, and object.*

(1) By *Oratio Variata* is meant a departure from a construction already exhibited by one member of a sentence, in another and corresponding member that might take the same construction as the first.

(2) This happens often, even among the best writers; and in general the object of it is, to attain more perspicuity or emphasis

by the new construction, than would be effected by retaining the one already exhibited.

E. g. Rom. 12: 1, 2, παρακαλῶ ὑμᾶς ... παραστῆσαι· καὶ μὴ συσχηματίζεσθε ... μεταμορφοῦσθε, where the two latter verbs stand in the Imper. instead of being put in the Inf. with παραστῆσαι, as they might have been, and as they regularly would be. But the *varied construction*, by adopting the Imper., throws more emphasis into the sentence. So Mark 12: 38, τῶν θελόντων ἐν στολαῖς περιπατεῖν, καὶ ἀσπασμοὺς ἐν ταῖς ἀγοραῖς, where the same construction would have required ἀσπάζεσθαι instead of ἀσπασμούς. Phil. 2: 22, ὅτι, ὡς πατρὶ τέκνον, σὺν ἐμοὶ ἐδούλευσεν εἰς τὸ εὐαγγέλιον, where sameness of construction would have demanded ἐμοί only, instead of σὺν ἐμοί. So Eph. 5: 27. Col. 1: 6. John 5: 44. Eph. 5: 33. 1 Cor. 14: 5. 2 Cor. 6: 9. Phil. 1: 23 seq. Rom. 12: 14 seq. Such constructions are frequent in the classics. Winer, p. 450.

NOTE 1. In Rev. 14: 14. 7: 9, εἶδον καὶ ἰδού take both Nom. and Acc. after them, i. e. the Nom. in respect to ἰδού, and the Acc. in respect to εἶδον.

(2) A species of *varied construction* is frequent in the N. Test., which consists in a change from the *direct* to the *oblique* method of style (oratio directa et obliqua), in the same sentence.

E. g. Luke 5: 14, 'He commanded him μηδενὶ εἰπεῖν (Inf.), ἀλλὰ ἀπελθὼν δεῖξον,' κ. τ. λ, where it is changed to a *direct* style, and the Imper. of direct address is used. Acts 23: 32, 'He dismissed the young man, commanding him to tell no one ὅτι ταῦτα ἐνεφάνισας πρός με, where the last clause according to the *indirect* style of the first part of the sentence, would be πρὸς αὐτόν. See Mark 11: 32.

(3) Another species of *oratio variata*, is the translation from the singular to the plural, and *vice versá*.

E. g. Rom. 12: 16, 20. 1 Cor. 4: 6 seq. Gal. 4: 7. 6: 1. Luke 5: 4 seq.

REMARK. All these kinds of varied construction are found in the Greek classics. In this respect the N. Test. has nothing very peculiar; except that the Apocalypse abounds, most of all, in style of this kind.

POSITION OF WORDS AND SENTENCES.

§ 197. *Nature and design.*

(1) The Greek, by the aid of its various endings of cases, etc., may depart from the most easy and natural arrangement of words without any special prejudice to perspicuity. The variety, in this respect, depends very much on the mode of thinking peculiar to the several writers.

NOTE 1. The most natural order is to arrange the adjective near to its noun; the adverb to its verb or adjective; the Gen. to the noun, etc, which governs it; prepositions to the nouns which they govern; antithetic words opposite to each other, etc. But departure from this, for the sake of emphasis, rhetorical effect, euphony, and other reasons, is frequent in all good writers.

§ 198. Syntax: Trajection of Words. 297

Note 2. It is natural, that the historical style should adopt the obvious order of words most frequently; and that the animated, argumentative, oratorical, and poetical, on the other hand, should most frequently depart from it. Paul uses more freedom, in this respect, than any of the writers of the N. Testament.

(2) Position often has speciality of meaning attached to it.

E. g. The adjective is designed to be emphatic, when it is placed before a noun, and does not stand included between an article and its noun; so φόβος μέγας, ἔργον ἀγαθόν, etc., would be the usual order of the Greek, but μέγας φόβος, ἀγαθόν ἔργον would render the adjective emphatic. To this remark, however, an exception must be made of such adjectives as ἄλλος, εἷς, ἴδιος, and some others of the like tenor. But οὗτος ὁ ἄνθρωπος is plainly different in the shade of meaning from ἄνθρωπος οὗτος, the first being equivalent, or nearly so, to *this is a man*, the second to *this man*.

Note. This whole subject, rich in information as to the characteristics of respective writers, has, as yet, been but very imperfectly investigated and explained.

TRAJECTION OF WORDS.

§ 198. *Nature and design.*

(1) Adverbs, other particles, and sometimes other words are, for the sake of euphony, or other reasons, separated from the words to which they are most nearly related.

E. g. Rom. 5:6, ἔτι Χριστός ὄντων ἡμῶν ἀσθενῶν, where ἔτι belongs to ὄντων. 1 Cor. 14:7, ὅμως τὰ ἄψυχα φωνὴν διδόντα, where ὅμως naturally would come before φωνήν. Gal. 3:15, ἕως ἀνθρώπου κεκυρωμένην διαθήκην οὐδεὶς ἀθετεῖ, where ὅμως belongs to οὐδεὶς κ. τ. λ. See John 12:1. 11:18. 21. 8.

Note. Trajection of a *negative* particle is not unfrequent, even in the Greek classics. In Acts 7:48, οὐκ is separated by several words from κατοικεῖ which it qualifies, so μή in Heb. 11:3, from γεγονέναι.

POSITION OF CERTAIN PARTICLES.

§ 199. *Various usages in respect to these.*

(1) Δέ, μέν, οὖν, γάρ, γέ, (μενοῦνγε), cannot *begin* a sentence. Δέ and γάρ may have the second, third, or even fourth place, according to the nature of the sentence in which they stand. Ἄρα (in the classics) cannot begin a clause; in the N. Test., however, it not unfrequently does this.

E. g. ἄρα in Gal. 2:17, 21. 5:11, al.; and so ἄρ᾽ οὖν, Rom. 5:18. 7:3. Eph. 2:19, al. Likewise μενοῦνγε in Luke 11:28. 9:20. 10:18, al.

38

PARONOMASIA.

§ 200. *Nature and use.*

(1) In general this consists of words being ranged together, of similar sound but differing in sense. It is a favourite figure of rhetoric in the best writers of the O. Test., e. g. Isaiah, and is not unfrequent in the N. Testament.

E. g. λιμοὶ καὶ λοιμοί, Luke 21: 11; ζωὴν καὶ πνοήν, Acts 17: 25; ἔμαθεν ἀφ᾽ ὧν ἔπαθε, Heb. 5: 8; θόνου, φόνου .... ἀσυνέτους, ἀσυνθέτους, Rom. 1: 29, 31; πνευματικοῖς πνευματικά, 1 Cor. 2: 13; αὐτοὶ ἐν ἑαυτοῖς ἑαυτούς, 2 Cor. 10: 12; πείθεσθαι ... ἡ πεισμονή, Gal. 5: 7, 8, which last word seems to have been coined for the sake of the paronomasia.

NOTE 1. Not unlike to this, but approaching nearer to what we sometimes call *playing upon words*, are the examples in various places; e. g. παρακοή and ὑπακοή in Rom. 5: 19; κατατομή and περιτομή, Phil. 3: 2, 3; ἀπορούμενοι and ἐξαπορούμενοι, 2 Cor. 4: 8; ἐργαζομένους and περιεργαζομένους, 2 Thess. 3: 11; ἐκδύσασθαι, and ἐπενδύσασθαι, 2 Cor. 5: 4; γινώσκεις ὃ ἀναγινώσκεις; Acts 8: 30. Comp. Gal. 4: 17. 1 Cor. 3: 17. 6: 2. 11: 29, 31. 2 Cor. 5: 21. 10: 3.

NOTE 2. All these usages abound even in the best Greek classics; see Elsner, Diss. II., *Paulus et Jesaias inter se comparati*, p. 24. (1821. 4). See also Winer, p. 431. But let the student beware, how he makes the mere ὁμοιοτέλευτον of the Greek verbs into paronomasia, e. g. such endings as are in ἐλιθάσθησαν, ἐπρίσθησαν, etc.

EXPLANATION

OF TECHNICAL WORDS IN GRAMMAR, RHETORIC, AND EXEGESIS, DESIGNED
TO AID THE STUDENT IN THE PERUSAL OF COMMENTARIES.

Aenigma, an obscure allegory; sometimes, a dark saying, a mystery.
Allegory, lit, where one thing is said and another meant; e. g. God is a rock. It includes *parable*, and *fable*.
Anacoluthon, where one part of a sentence does not accord, in its mode of structure, with another; § 195.
Anadiplosis, where a word at the end of one clause, is repeated at the beginning of the next; see Ps. 121: 1, 2.
Anaphora, where the same word is repeated in the beginning of several successive clauses; see Deut. 28: 3—6.
Anastrophe, the transfer of a preposition to a place *behind* (instead of *before*) the noun which it governs, so that the place of the accent on the prep. is changed; see p. 26. Note 5.
Antanaclasis, when the same word is repeated in a different sense; e. g. Let the *dead* bury their *dead*.
Anthropopathy, where what belongs to *man* is, in the way of similitude, ascribed to *God*; e. g. when *eyes, hands, feet, anger, revenge,* etc., are ascribed to God.
Antiphrasis, where the same word has opposite significations; e. g. בָּרֵךְ, to *bless* and to *curse*.
Aphaeresis, the removal of one or more letters at the *beginning* of a word; e. g. ἡ for φῆ or ἔφη.
Apocope, the cutting off of one or more letters at the *end* of a word; e. g. πάρ' for παρά.
Aposiopesis, the suppression of a part of a sentence; see § 190.
Apostrophe, (in rhetoric), where the speech is changed as to its direction. Called also προσφώνησις.
Apposition, the joining of one noun, or its equivalent, to another, for the sake of explanation or amplification; e. g. Κῦρος, ὁ βασιλεύς.
Attraction, the changing of the normal form or case of a pronoun or noun, because of the influence of some preceding noun or pronoun upon it; e. g. ἐπὶ πᾶσιν οἷς ἤκουσαν, (οἷς instead of ἅ).
Asyndeton, i. e. without a conjunction; see § 188.

Catachresis, lit. an excessive use of a word. It means, to employ it in a sense extended beyond, or out of its normal use; e. g. O foolish Galatians, who hath *bewitched* you?

Diaeresis, the separation of vowels; e. g. ὄϊς, *o–is*

Ellipsis, see § 189.
Enallage, the exchange of one tense, mode, number, person, or gender, for another.
Epanalepsis, where the same word is repeated at the beginning and end of a sentence: Ecc. 1: 2.
Epanodos, repetition of the same word in the beginning and middle, or middle and end, of a sentence; Ezek. 7: 6, 7.
Epanorthosis, a correction or limitation of what is said.
Epenthesis, the insertion of a letter in the middle of a word; e. g. πτόλεμος for πόλεμος.
Epistrophe, where the same word is repeated at the end of several clauses or sentences; 2 Cor. 11: 22.
Epizeuxis, the junction of words repeated ; e. g. *deep, deep*.

Fable, an allegory, where impossible actions are ascribed to the agents introduced, or where the agents are non-entities; e. g. the fable of Jotham; the fables of Aesop.

Gnome, a proverbial saying, a short general maxim or sentiment.

Heteroclites, see § 29. 3.
Hypallage, the transposition of words in such a way, that what is predicated of one thing belongs to another; Matt. 8: 3, ἐκαθαρίσθη ἡ λέπρα.
Hyperbaton, when one or more words are placed out of their natural order ; e. g. ἐν ἄλλοτε ἄλλῳ, for ἄλλοτε ἐν ἄλλῳ.
Hyperbole, an excessive catechresis, where a word or phrase is used which signifies much more, if literally taken, than the writer means; e. g. Thy seed shall be as *the stars of heaven*, and as *the sands of the sea shore*, for multitude.

Irony, properly *dissimulation*. It denotes the use of a word in a sense opposite to its natural meaning.

Meiligma (μείλιγμα), a softening down of an expression by some apology parenthetically inserted, e. g. Heb. 7: 9, ὡς ἔπος εἰπεῖν.
Merismus (μερισμός), when the whole is signified by specifying parts of the same ; Is. 24: 1, 2.
Metaphor, when a word bears a tropical sense, which is like to, but still different from, its literal meaning; e. g. God is our *sun*.
Metaplasm, see § 29. 4.
Metathesis, the transposition of letters from one part of a word to a different one ; e. g. κραδία for καρδία.
Metonymy, where a part is named instead of the whole, or cause for effect, etc. ; and *vice versâ*.

Oratio variata, a milder species of anacoluthon, where a construction once begun is discontinued, and a different one adopted ; e. g. παρακαλῶ παραστῆσαι ... καὶ μὴ συσχηματίζεσθε, κ. τ. λ. § 196.
Oxymoron, (lit. *acute folly*), is where contrary things are so joined, that they are absurd when literally taken, and very significant when fully understood ; e. g. he robbed the *naked* of their *garments*.

EXPLANATION OF TECHNICAL WORDS. 301

Parable, (lit. *comparison*), is applied to a fictitious narration, where the actors are merely symbols significant of realities of another kind. In a limited sense, it means only such fictitious narrations as exhibit things possible or probable.

Paroemia, proverbs, common and sententious sayings.

Paragoge, the adding of a letter or syllable to the end of a word; e. g. ἐνί for ἐν.

Paronomasia, see § 200.

Pleonasm, see § 193.

Prolepsis, anticipation of any word, by referring to it as already spoken.

Prosopopoeia, when personality or its attributes are ascribed to any thing which is not a person; e. g. Let the floods clap their *hands!*

Prosphonesis, see Apostrophe.

Prosthesis, adding a letter at the beginning of a word; e. g. σμικρός for μικρός.

Symploce, (συπλοκή), a repetition of the same word or phrase at the beginning and end of several sentences; Ps. 136. 1—3.

Synaloephe, the union of two syllables in one; either by *Crasis*, p. 26. n. 5. *a*, or by *Elision*, ib. *b*.

Synaeresis, the contraction of vowels.

Syncope, taking away one or more letters from the *middle* of a word; e. g. πατρός for πατέρος.

Synchysis, a ὕστερον πρότερον, where the order of words is inverted; 1 Cor. 9 : 10. Phil. v. 5.

Synecdoche, where a whole is taken for a part, and *vice versá*; e. g. *Jerusalem*, for Judea or the Jews; *all the world*, for many individuals.

Synizesis or *Synecphonesis*, when the vowels of two words are written out in full, but a contraction is made in reading them; e. g. χάλκεον δέ οἱ ἦτορ, (where -κεον is read -κουν).

Tmesis, when a verb, compounded with a preposition, is written separately from the preposition; e. g. ἀπ᾿ ὧν ἔδοντο, for ἀπέδοντο οὖν.

Zeugma, see § 192.

GREEK INDEX.

ὀγήγερκα, 81. 1.
ἀηδών, 56. n. 2.
αἰδοῖ, 49. n. 2. 3.
ἀκήκοα, 81. 1. n.
ἀλαλά -ᾶς, 42. b.
ἀλήλιφα, 81. 1. n.
ἀλλά, 285. 5.
ἀμφί, § 113.
ἄν, with Fut. Indic. 225. n. 1.—with Opt. § 140. —῎Αν before *all* the modes, § 142.—Alone, 233. Rem. I. — Position of, ib. Rem. II. —Repetition of, ib. Remark III. — In Praet. Ind. 238. n. 2. — With Opt. 238. 2.—With Part. 233. *f*.—With Ind. rel. 243. 2.—With Subj. ib. 3. and n. 2. — Combines with particles, 244. n. 3.—In hypoth. clauses, 249. 1. n. 1. 2, and n. 2; also 2. n. 1. 2.—With Opt. 250. 3.—ib. n. 3. —With Imp. Ind. 250. *b*. and ib. 4. —With Subj. 253. 2. 2.
ἀνά § 111.
ἀνήρ, 56. n. 3.
ἀντί, § 109.
ἀνείλατο, 92. Rem.
ἀνέωχα, -ξα, 80. n. 4.
ἀπεκατασιάθη, 80. n. 4.
ἀπό, § 109.
αὐτός, 197. 4.
αὑτός, § 42.
αὑτοῦ, 198. 5. n. 2.
ἄχρι, 31 top.

βέβληκα, 106. 5.
βορρᾶς, 42. *a*.
βούλει, 131. *b*.
βοῦς for βόϝς, 23. n. 4.

γάρ, 288. 2.
γίγνομαι, 131. 2.

γλυκίων, 63. 4.
γυνή, 56. 2.—49. *b*.

δέ, use of, 285. 5. 1seq.—continuative, 287, *c*.
δέδμηκα, 131. 1. *b*.
δέδορα, 90. 7. *b*.
δέπας, 52. n. 4.
διά, § 112.

ε—augment, 79. 2.
ἐάγην, 80. n. 2.
ἑάλωκα, 80. n. 2.
ἐάν, with Ind. 250. n. 3.
ἑαυτοῦ, § 44.
ἔγνων, 127. 1.
ἔγνωκαν, 90. n. 3.
ἐδιηκόνουν, 82. n. 2.
ἐδολιοῦσαν, 91. 8.
ἔδραθον, 131. 2.
ἔδωκα, 120. 11. n.
ἔθηκα, 120. 11. n.
εἰ for ἐάν, 250. n. 3.
εἴδαμεν, 92. Rem.
εἶκα, 120. 10. n. 1.
εἰκών, 51. n. 2.—§ 28.
εἴληφα, 81. *c*.
εἴλοχα for εἴλογα, 33. R. 5.
εἰμί and εἶμι, 27. Rem. II.—128. 2.
εἴρηκα, 81. *c*.
εἴρηκαν, 90. n. 3.
εἰς (ἐς), § 111.—186. n. 2.
εἰς, 195. 1.
εὔχοσαν, 91. 8.
ἐκ (ἐξ), § 109.
ἐκρίνοσαν, 91. 8.
ἐλήλυθα, 81. 1. n.
ἐμήμεκα, 81. 1.
ἐν § 110.—186. n. 2.
ἐξείλατο, 92. Rem.
ἐξεπέσατε, 92. Rem.

Greek Index.

ἐξήλθετε, 92. Rem.
ἔοικα, 80. n. 3.
ἔολπα, 80. n. 3.
ἔοργα, 80. n. 3.
ἐπί, § 113.
ἐπεί, 245. b.
ἔπεσαν, 92. Rem.
ἔπεσον, 131. 1.
ἔπραθον, 131. 2.—35.
ἐρήρεικα, 81. 1. n.
ἔρις, 48. 4. n. 1.
ἐς, see εἰς.
ἐτράπην, 131. 2.
εὗραν, 92. Rem.
εἱράμενος, 92. Rem.
ἐφάγαμεν, 92. Rem.
ἐφάγοσαν, 91. 8.
ἔφυγαν, 92. Rem.
ἔχεα, 91. 10. n. 1.
ἑώρακαν, 90. n. 3.

ζάω, ζῇς etc. irreg. § 76. 4.

η for ε augment, 79. 3. n. 1.
ἠβουλήθην, 79. n. 1.
ἤγαγον, 81. 2.
ἠγρόμην, 131. 1.
ἠδυνάμην, 79. n. 1.
ἧκα, 120. 11. n.
ἦλθον, 131. 1.
ἤνεγκα, 91. 10. n. 1.
ἤνεγκον, 81. 2.
ἠνείχεσθε, 80. n. 4.
ἠνειχόμην, 82. n. 2.
ἠνώχλουν, 82. n. 2.
ἤραρον, 81. 2.
ἠχοῖ, 51. Par.—52. n. 3.

θεέ, 44. n. 3.
-θητι for -θηθι, 32. n. 2.
θνήσκω, 131. 2.
θυγάτηρ, 56. n. 3.

ἵημι, 128. I.
Ἰησοῦς, 56. 1.
ἵνα, before sub. clause, § 147.

καί, nature and use, 284. 2.—Diff. meanings, 284. n. 1.—3.—Adverb 285. 3.—Often omitted, 285. n. 3,

κατά, § 112.
κατακαυχᾶσαι, 106. 5.
κατεάγωσι, 80. n. 4.
κατειλήφθη, 81 c.
κατελίποσαν, 91. 8.
καυχᾶσαι, 106. 5.
κεῖμαι, 129. 5.
κεῖσθαι, 129. 5.
κείμενος, 129. 5.
κέκληκα, 131. 1. b.
κέκλοφα, 90. n. 2.
κέκμηκα, 131. 1. b.
κέωμαι, 129. 5.
κλείς, 48. 4. n. 1.
κραδίη for καρδία, 35. 2.

λέλοιπα, 90. 7. c.
λεώς, 46. n. 1. 3.

μέν, 286. n. 1—3.
μή—μηδέ, § 183. 1.
μή—μήτε, 281. 2.—other substitutes, § 184.

νοῦς, 45. n. 2.—60. n. 1.

ξύν, § 110.

ὁ, ὅδε, demonstr. § 41.—199. 2.
ὀδυνᾶσαι, 106. 5.
ὄδωδα, 81. 1.
οἶδα, 90. 7. c.—130. 6.
οἴει, 106. 5.
οἶνος for Ϝοῖνος, 23. n. 4.
ὅπως, before sub. clause, 240. 5. — § 147.
ὄρνις, 48. 4. n. 1.
ὀρώρυχα, 81. 1.
ὅτε, 245. a.
ὅς, relative, § 40.
ὅτι, omitted, 237. n. 1. — in clauses, § 146.—in quotations, 238. Rem. I.
οὐ, in οὐ μή, 241. 4.—277. 2.—279. 5.
—οὐ repeated, § 182.— οὐ—οὐδέ, § 183. 1.— οὔτε—οὔτε, 281. 2.— substitutes for these, § 184.
οὐδείς, § 126.
οὗτος, 199. 2.
οὕτω, 30. 6. 1.
οὕτως, § 159.

ὄψει, 106. 5.

παρά, § 113.
παρέξει, 106. 5.
παρελάβοσαν, 91. 8.
παρελθύτω, 92. Rem.
πεπαιδεύαται, 107. 2.
πεπείθαται, 107. 2.
πέπομφα, 90. n. 2.
περί, § 113.
πίπτω, 131. 1. e. g.
πλοῦς, 45. n. 1.
πόλις, 53. n. 1.
πολύς, 61. 1.
πότε and ποτέ, 27. Rem. II.
ποῦς, 48. 4. n. 1.
πρίν, 245. c.
πρὶν ἤ, ib.
πρό, § 109.
πρός, § 113.

ῥόδον for Ϝρόδον, 23. n. 4.

σ, aspirate, 23. n. 5.—When it falls away, ib. — Final ς inserted or omitted, 30. 1.—Form when final in the middle of words, 31. 2.
σέλας, 52. n. 4.
σχέσθαι, pass. 83. 2. n.
σίν, § 110.

τέ, nature and use, 283. 4.
τέθεικα, 120. 10. n. 1.
τέθνηκα for τέθανκα, 131. II. 2.
τετάχαται, 107. 2.
τέτεμον, 131. 1.
τέτμηκα, 131. 1. b.
τετρίφαται, 107. 2.
τέτροφα, 90. n. 2.
τίς, τί, § 125.
τις and τίς, § 43. 1. 3.
τοὔργον for τὸ ἔργον, 26. n. 5.
τοῦτο, peculiar use, 199. 4.

ὑγιής, 60. n. 2.—52. n. 2.
ὑπέρ, § 112.
ὑπό, § 113.

φημί, 129. III.

χάρις, 48. 4. n.
χελιδών, 56. n. 2.
χρῆν for ἔχρην, 79. n. 2.
χρυσοῦς, 45. n. 1.

ὡς (to), § 111.— Before sub. clause, 237. 1.— § 147.—240. 5.— § 159.
—In parenthesis, 253. 4.—With Part., 265. 3.
ὥστε, 159. 1. 159.—With Inf, § 159. 3.
—With Infin. of design, 257. n. 1.

INDEX OF SUBJECTS.

[The numbers employed are used in the following manner; viz, when § stands before any number, the *Section* designated is meant; in other cases, the first number denotes the *page*, and the accompanying subsequent number a subdivision (not a *section*) on that page. Before the designation of *Notes* a small *n*. is placed. In some few cases, there is more than one *subdivision* on a page, which will correspond to the numbering; but a single glance of the eye will enable any one to decide which is meant.]

Accents, nature and design, 24.--kinds, 24. 3 —Names of words in respect to accents, 24. 3.—Use of the *grave*, 25. n. 1.—Of circumflex, 25. n. 2. —Place of accents, 25. 4,5.—Quantity disregarded in placing them, 26. n. 2.—Circumflex on ultimate, 26. n. 3.— Varied by change of words, 26. n. 4 seq. n. 5.—Importance of, 27. Rem. II.-When written in N. Test., 27. Rem. III.--Various usage, 27. Rem. IV. — Accentuation of composite words, 142.—Of Dec. I., 44. n. 3.—Of Dec. II. 45. n. 1. 46. n. 3.—Of Dec. III. 49. n. 4.— Of Dec. II. contracts, 54. n. 5.— Of syncopates, 56. n. 3. — Of adjectives, 59. *b*. 60. n. 1.—Of Pronouns, 65, n. 1.—Of τίς, § 43. n. 1.—Of Verbs, § 77.—Of Participles, 117. 7.—Verbs in μι, § 79. 4. 6 —Of εἰμί, 129. 3.—Of φημί, 129. 4.—Of Prepositions, 134. 2. n. —Of compos. words, 142.

Accusative case, after Verbs, § 103.— what it marks, 172. 1.—Space relations of, 173. A. — Causal relations of, 173. B.—As designating *results*, 173.5.—also object wrought upon or affected, 174. 6. — After verbs of motion, 175.7.—designates time passed through or how long, 175. 8.—also measure and weight, 175. 9.—Acc. of special limitation, 175. 10.—*Two Accusatives*, § 104.

—They express objects affected indirectly, 176. 2.—Acc. with the pass. voice, § 105. — Used as an adverb, § 84. *d*. 3.--Acc. absolute, 189. 4.—Exchanged for other cases before the Inf. 258. n. 1.

Adjectives, terminations and flections, § 30. — Par. of three endings, 58. —Contracts with three, ib. — Accentuation, 59. n. 1. *b*. — Peculiar accent in contract forms, 59. n. 4. —With two endings, § 32. Par. 60. —With one ending, § 33.—Anomalous, § 34.—Compared with Participles, 61.—Degrees of comparison, 62. — Anomalies in comparison, 63. Declension of comparatives, 64.—*Concord*, 191. 1 seq.— Repetition, 191. 3.—Adj. for nouns, 192. 5.—Place supplied by Gen. case, 192. 6 seq.—Fem. for neuter, 193. 8.—Periphrases for adj. 193. 9. —Used adverbially, 193.10.--Comp. and Superl., § 118.

Adverbs, numeral, 65. 5. — Nature, classes, use, 132.—Formation, ib. 3. —Cases of adverbs, 132. *c*.—Comparison of, 133. 4.—Syntax, § 180. —Converted into adjectives, 276. 2. —Of place, ib. 3.—Of mode, ib. 4.

Alphabet, 19. Sound of the letters, 20. —Time of introduction, 20.-Comp. with the Hebrew, 21. — Ancient letters dropped, 21.

Anacoluthon, § 195.

Anastrophe, 26. n. 5. c. 134. 2. n.
Anomalies in declension, § 29. As to case-ending, 1.—As to ground form, b. 2.—Defective, 57.5
Aorist, nature and use, 72. 6—Seldom two forms of the same verb, 75. 10.—Syntax, 220. 5.
Aorist I., formation, 91. 10.—94. 7.—95. 3.—Syntax of, 220. 5.—In derived modes, 222. 6.
Aorist II., used in but few verbs, 74. 7.—Not used in pass., when found elsewhere, 74. 9.—Formation, 91. 11.—94. 8.—95. 4.—96. 4.—Marks same time as Aor. I. 222. b.
Apodosis omits ἄν. 232. Note.—With Perf. and Pluperf., marks *past* time, 232. Note—In hypothetical sentences, 248. 5.—Relation to protasis, § 157.—Omitted in hypoth. clauses, 251. n. 4.
Apposition of nouns, § 116.—Extent, 190. 2.—For substance made by Gen., 190. 3.—Case of it changed by attraction, 190. 4.
Aposiopesis, § 190.
Apostrophe, when employed, 29. 3.—Object, 30. n. 3.
Article, forms of, 42.—Nature and uses, § 89.—Before leading nouns, 144. 2.—Omission before same, ib. b.—Omission before abstract nouns, 145. n. 5.—before material substances, 145. n. 6.—before a word indef. but limited by adjuncts, 145. 3. — Before well-known objects, 146. 4. a. — objects mentioned, ib. b.—Before subject and predicate, 147. 5.—Before nouns in apposition, 147. 6.—Omitted after verbs *to be, to call*, 148. 7.—Usage before nouns of diff. gender, 148. 8.—Of the same case and gender, 148. 9.—General view of it, 149. Gen. Rem. — With adjectives, § 90. — Omitted before adj. *predicates*, 149. 2.—With adjectives when used as nouns, 150. 3.—Same with participles, § 91.—Before Part. used as verbs, 151. 2.—Before Part. qualifying nouns, 152. b.—Before adjunct clauses to nouns, § 92.—Before Gen. adjunct, 153. 2.—Special usages before pronominal words, § 93. — Before adverbs, 155. 6. — Before the Inf. mode, 155. 7.—Before words quoted, 155. 8.—Article as pronoun, § 94.
Asyndic construction, § 188.
Asyndeton, § 188.
Attic Future, 89. 5.
Attraction, changes the case of nouns in apposition, 190. 4.—Of rel. pronouns, 201. 2.—Of nouns also, 201. 3.—Of the subject of Infin. 259. Remark.
Augment, 79.--Syllabic, 79. 3.--When omitted, ib. n. 2.—Temporal, 79. 4.—Par. of vowel-changes made by it, ib.—Anomalous cases, ib. n. 1. — Variable usage, 80. n. 2. — Temporal augment excluded, 80. b. — General principle of all augments, 80. Gen. Rem.—In compound verbs, § 57.

Breathings, smooth and rough, 23.—When employed and how written, 23.—Ancient ones now dropped, 23. n. 4. 5.
Breviloquence, 291.

Cardinals, 195. 1 seq.
Cases, number of, 40. 3.—Nature, meaning and object, § 96. 1 seq.—Absolute, § 115.—Abs. in Participles, § 171.—Gen. ib. 2.—Dat. ib. 3.—Acc. ib. 4.—Nom. ib. 5.—
Circumflex accent, 24. 3.—How formed, 25. n. 2.
Citations of others' language, § 177.—Direct and indirect, ib. 1—3.—Modes, ib. 3—5.
Comparative degree, § 118.—Expressed by positive, 193. 2.—Followed by παρά and ὑπέρ, 193. 3.—Object with which compared implied, 194. 4.
Comparison, of adjectives, § 36.—Of Adverbs, 133. 4.

Composite Words, formation in various ways, § 87.—Loose and close composition, 140. 1 seq.—Accentuation of them, 142.
Concord, of adjuncts with nouns not always observed, 157. n. 2.—Of verb and subject, § 128.—Anomalies, 205. 2.
Conditionality, marked by ἄν, § 142.—
Conjunctions, nature and use, § 185. —Kinds, 283.
Consonants, number and classification, 21.—Changes by euphony, § 10.—To avoid concurrence of too many, 34. R. 17.—Doubling and transposition, § 11.
Constructio pregnans, of εἰς and ἐν, 186. n. 2.
Constructio ad sensum, 205. 2. *b.*—
Contract nouns, of Dec. III. § 25.— *First form*, 51. 1.—Parad. ib.—Peculiar modes of contraction, 52. n. 2. and n. 4.—Fem. nouns here anomalous, 52. n. 3.—*Second form*, § 26.—Endings and parad. 52. 1 seq. —Various ways of contraction, 53. n. 1 seq. Peculiar accentuation, 54. n. 5.—*Third form*, endings, parad. § 27.—Peculiarities of some nouns here, 54. n. 1. seq.— *Syncopated* nouns of Dec. III. § 28.—Peculiarities of some nouns § 29.—Contract adjectives, 59. n. 4.
Coronis, nature, and use, 30. 4.
Correlatives, § 47.
Crasis, 26. n. 5. *a.*—30. n. 3.

Dative, ending of sing. 41. 2.—After verbs, § 106.—Object and use, 177. 1.—Distinction between Gen. and Dat. 177. n. 2.—Dat. of locality, 178. A.—Of time, 178. 4.—Of circumstances, 178. 5.–The Dat. proper of *direction*, 178. B.—*Causal* 179, 8.—Verbs placed before it, 179, *a.* seq.—Of possession, 180. 9.—In respect or regard to, 180. 10.—Instrumental, 181. C.—Of ground or reason, 181. 12.—Of means or instrument, 181. 13.—Of way and manner, 182. 14.—Measure, price, worth, 182. 15.—Of material, 182. 16 —Other constructions instead of Dat. 182. *a.*—Dat. preceded by Acc. with same verb, 182. *b.*—Dat. after adj., adverbs and nouns, § 107.—Absolute, 189. 3.
Declensions, what, 40. 1.—number of, ib. How distinguished, 40. 4.— General principles of, § 19.— Originally but one, 40. 2, and 41. n. 1.—Dec. I. 42—endings, 42. 1. —principles of, 42. 2.—Contracts of, 43. *e.* Paradigms, 43.—Remarks, ib.—Accentuation of, 44. n. 3. —Dec. II. 44.—Endings and forms, 44.—Original forms, ib. n. 1, 2.—Oxytone neuters, 45. n. 4.— Contracts of Dec. II. 45.—Anomalies of same, ib. n. 1. — Attic forms of. 45 seq.—Anomalous accentuation of these, 46. n. 1—4.— Dec. III. characteristics, § 24.— Formation of Nom. 47. 2 seq.—of the other cases, 48. 4 seq.—Accentuation, 49. n. 4.—Paradigms, 50. Declining with a vowel not contractible, 50. n. 1.—Anomalous forms, 51. n. 2.
Demonstratives, article as such, § 41. 1.—Pronoun, ib. 2, 3.
Deponent verbs, § 61.
Derivate words, § 86 —Original roots, ib. 1 seq.— Derivate verbs, 135. 4 seq.—Derivate nouns, 136. 6 seq. —Different classes of them, 137. *c.* —Derivate adjectives, 138. 7 seq.
Dialects, forms of in verbs, 106. 7. 121. 7.
Diastole, Hypodiastole, 29. 2.
Digamma, name and office, 23. n.4.— When it falls away, 23. n. 4.
Diphthongs, proper and improper, 22. —Pronunciation, 22.—Manner of writing them, 22.
Disjunctive clauses, § 186.

Elision, 26. n. 5. *b.*
Ellipsis, of subject, 204. 3.—Of predicate, 204. 4.—Of copula, 204. 5.

308   INDEX OF SUBJECTS.

—Nature of, § 189. — Of copula, ib. 2.—Of subject, ib. 3.—Of predicate, ib. 4.
Enclitics, when accented, 24. 2.— Pronouns enclitic, 65. n. 1, also 67. n. 1.— εἰμί enclitic, 129. 3.—Also φημί, 129. 4.

Future, nature and use, 73. 7.—Excluded from Subj. and Imper. 73. 3.—Fut. midd. for Fut. active, 84. 5. n.—Attic, 89. 5. — Fut. Indic. used to indicate certainty, 225. 2. —Used for the Imper., 229. 4.— Fut. Indic. with ἄν, 231. a.
Future I., formation, 89. 4.—92. 2.— 95. 2.—Future Attic, 89. 5.—Syntax, 222. 7.
Future II., when not used in act. or midd. voice, 74. 5.--Formation, 92. 12.—92. 2.—96. 2.—Like Fut. I. as to meaning, 223. N. B.

Gender, kinds and modes of designating it, § 16. — Neuter gender applied to *persons*, 158. 3. — Fem. for neuter, 193. 8.—Neuter adverbially, 193. 10.
Genitive, ending of the plural, 41. 1. —Original form, 41. g. — Nature and uses, § 98.—Opposite to the Acc. in meaning, 162. 2. — Gen. after other nouns, with varieties of meaning, § 99.—attributive in such instances, 164. Gen. Rem.— *Genitive after Verbs*, § 100.—nature and meaning of, 164. 2.—compared to the English idiom, 165. 3. — Gen. of space, 165. I.—of time, 166. II. —Gen. of *causal* relation, 166. III. — of origin, 166. 9. — of possession, 166. b.—of that which comprises, or Gen. *partitive*, 167. 10. —of material, 168. 11.—of ground or reason, 168. 12.—of mutual relation, 169. 12.—After verbs which may also govern other cases, 170. Gen. Rem. 1 seq.— After partitives, adjectives, participles, 171. —After compar. degree, 171. 3.—

After participials, 172. 4. — After adverbs, § 102.—Absolute, § 115. 3.

Hebraism, as to pronouns, § 126.—As to Part., § 173.
Heteroclites, 56. 3.
Hypothetical sentences, 247. 4 seq. Peculiarities of, § 158.

Imperfect, nature and use, 71. 4.—Only in the Indic., 73. 2.—Formation, 91. 8.—94. 5.—Conveys a conditional and negative sense, 225. 3. —Syntax of, 217. 2.
Imperative, nature of, 229.1.–of permission, 229. 2.—When = Fut. 229. 3.—Place supplied by Fut. 229. 4. Diff. use of Pres. and Aor., 230. 5. Peculiar sense of Imper. Perf. 230. n. 3.—Syntax, § 141.—With μή, 230. 6.
Impersonal verbs, § 174.
Indeclinable nouns, 57. 6.
Indicative 70. 2.—Independent, §138. —With ἄν, 231. a. b.—In subord. clauses, with and without ἄν, 237. 1, seq.—With μή, 241. 2.— In relative clauses, with and without ἄν, 243. 1. 2.—Adverb. clauses, 245. 2. —§ 156. 2. n.—In hypoth. clauses, 249. 1.2.–Ind. Imp. with ἄν, 250. b. In clauses of way and manner, § 159. 2.—Of comparison, 253. 2. 1.—In oratio obliqua, 274. 4.
Infinitive, nature, 70. 6. § 161.—Old forms, 77. 2.—Inf. verbs in μι, 119. 8.—With ἄν, 233. e.—With ὡς, § 159. 4. —Distinguished from Part., 254. n. 1.— Without the Article, § 162.—Subject of a sentence, 255. 2.— *Object* of same, 255. 3.—Place supplied by other modes with particles, 255. n. 2.— What verbs it follows, 256. 5. 1 seq. —Inf. complement, 256. 4.—Inf. explanatory, 256. 5. 260. 3. — Of design, with ὥστε, 257. n. 1.— With the article, 257. Rem. § 165. —Inf. for Imper., § 163.—With cases after it, § 164.—With the

INDEX OF SUBJECTS. 309

same subject as the principal verb, 258. 1.—With a diff. subject, 258. 2.—Subject and object of a sentence, § 165.—Inf. with τοῦ before it, 260. 3.—Inf. with τῷ, 261. 4.—With prep. requires the Article, 261. 4. Gen. Rem.—Tenses of, § 166.
Interjections, 134.
Interpunction, origin, object, etc., 28. 1 seq.
Interrogative, sentences, § 175.—Direct, 271.—Indirect, 272.-Answers to interrog. § 176.—To interrog. with οὐ, and μή, 279. 5.

Koppa, 21. n. 4.

Labials 21, 2.
Letters, Sound of, 20.—division, 21.— Double letters, 21. 1.— Original number, 20. n. 2.—compared with Hebrew, 21. n. 3.
Linguals, 21. 2.
Liquids, 21. 2. *b.*—Verbs with § 66.
Liquid Verbs, how augmented, 87. *d.* Formation of tenses, 96.—Synopsis of various kinds, 110.—Synop. of Perf. pass., 111.

Metaplasm, 57. 4.
Metathesis, in verbs, 131. 2.
Middle Voice, used intransitively, 212. Rem. III.—figuratively, 212. Rem. IV.—Peculiar tenses of, § 132.— Meaning of, § 131.
Modes, kinds, 70.—distinctions and general principles, § 137.—In independent sentences, 225.—Modes of dependent sentences, § 145.— Exceptions, 236. 3.—In relative clauses, § 151.— In hypothetical sentences, 248. 6 seq.
Mode-Vowel, 76. n. 3. 2.—Parad. of same with explanations, 77.
Mutes, classification, 22, also 31.— Changes when they come together, 31 seq.—Before a rough breathing, 33. R. 5.—Changes before σ, 33. R. 6.—Before μ, 33. R. 7 seq.—Peculiar changes in the third class of, 33. R. 10.—Changes before ν, 34. R. 11 seq.

Negative clauses, repeated, § 183.— Destroy the force of each other, 282. 4.
Nominative case, the subject of a sentence, 160. 1.—Used absolutely, 160. 2.—for the Voc. ib. 3.—After a *copula*, ib. 4. and n. 1.—Irregular use of it in apposition, 161. 5.—Absolute, § 115.
Nouns, number and gender, § 95.— Plural with the sense of the sing., 156. 2.—Plural with generic sense, 157. *c.*—Attracted by the case of a relative, 201. 3. Formations, 136. II. seq.
Number in Greek, § 17.—In verbs § 58.—Plural as sing. 206. *c. d.* § 95. 2.—Variations of, 207. 5. *a.*
Numerals, Paradigm, 64.—Use of, § 119.

Optative, nature, 70. 4. 224. 2 seq.— Opt. of verbs in—μι, 119. 7.—Peculiar forms in Contracts, § 76. 1. —Distinguished from Subj., 224. 3.—Peculiar in verbs in μι, 120. 4. — Independent, 228. — Opt. of wish, desire, 228. 3.—Of moderate command, 228. n. 3.—With ἄν, 228. 4.—In moderate commands, 229. 5. — With πῶς ἄν, 229. 6.— With ἄν, 233. *d.* — In subord. clause, 239. 3. — After primary tenses, 239. *b.*—With ἄν in such clauses, 240. 4.—With μή, 241. 3. —In relative clauses, § 152.—In adverb. clauses, 246. 4.—§156. n. —Clauses of way and manner, § 159. 3 —Comparison, § 160. 2. 3. —In oratio obliqua, 273. 3.
Oratio Variata § 196.
Ordinals, 64.-Used adverbially, 195.3

Palatals, 21. 2.
Paragogic, Nun 30. 5.—Parag. of pronouns, § 48.

Parenthesis, independent, 253. 4. — § 194.
Paronomasia, § 200.
Particles, nature and kinds, § 178.
Participles, compared with Adjectives, 61.—Root-ending, 78 after Par.—Of Verbs in μι, 120. 9.— Participial adverbs, 132. *b*.—Part. with ἄν, 233. *f.*—Nature and construction, § 167. — Distinguished from adjectives, ib. n. 1. 2.—Concord, 262. 2.—Concord with subject, 262. 3. *a*.—With object, ib. *b*.—Excluded by some verbs, 262. 4.—Distinguished from Inf., 262. n. 1.—From a finite verb, 263. 1. —Objects answered by the Part. § 168. — Sometimes it expresses *subordinate* action, ib. n. 2.—Designates *adverbial* relations, § 169. — Of time, ib. 3.—Causal and conditional, ib. 4.—Of way and manner, 265. 5.—Special uses of, § 170.—Part. with ὡς, 265. 3.— With verbs of existence, 265. 4.— Part. absolute, § 171.—In all the oblique cases, ib. 2—5.—Anomalies of Part. § 172.—With Gen. absolute instead of other cases, 268. 2. *a*.—*c*.—With Acc. instead of other cases, 268. 3.-With Nom. instead of other cases, 267. 1.— Use of tenses in Part., § 173.
Passive Voice, use of, § 133.—With Acc. after it, 259. 3.
Paulo-post Future, nature and use, 73. 8.—In the pass. only, 74. 6. —Syntax, 223. 8.
Perfect, nature and use, 71. 5.—Not usual out of Indic , 74. 4.—Parad. of Perf. passive, 105.—Perf. pass. of pure verbs, with σ, 111. 5.
Perf. I. Formation, 90. 6. 93. 3. 95. 1. 97. 6.—Syntax, 219. 3.
Perf. II., used in but few verbs, 74. 8. —Formation, 90. 7. 97. 7.—Syntax, 219. 3.
Person, endings in Verbs, 78.—Number of, § 58. Variation of, 207. 6 seq.-Conforms to antecedent,§150.

Pleonasm, § 193.
Pluperfect, nature and use, 72. 6.— Only in the Indic., 73. 2.—Formation, 91. 9—94. 6—95. 2.—Syntax, 219. 4.
Position of words and sentences, § 197.—Of particles, §'199.
Predicate, must be a verb, or its equivalent, 204. 4.—Ellipsis of, 201. 5. —Gender of, 206. *b*.
Prepositions, § 85. § 179.—Primitive, 134.—Classification,134.3.—Cases governed by them, § 108.—Origin in space relations, § 96. 7. § 108. 1. —Retain the same meaning every where, 184. 2.—Mark dimension relations, 184. 3.—Also time and causality, 184. 4.—Before Gen. or Dat. or Acc. only, 185. — Before Gen. and Acc., § 112. — Before Gen., Dat., and Acc., 186.—Prep. εἰς and ἐν with constructio pregnans, 186. n. 2. — Repetition of, 187. n. 4.—Adverbial use, 187. n. 5. —Compounded with verbs, § 114. —Syntax, § 179.
Present tense, nature and use, 71. 3. —Formation, 88. 3—92. 1—95. 1. Syntax, 216. 1.
Proclitics, 26. n. 5. *d*, and § 7. 2. note.
Pronouns, personal, 65.—Relative,66. Demonstr.66.—Defin. 67. — Indef. and Interrog., 67. — Reflex., 68. — Recipro., 68 — Correllative, 69. — Paragogic, 69. — Laws of gender and number, § 120.—Use of personal pron., § 121. — Possessive, § 122.—Dat. case for possessives, 198. 3.—Demonstrative, § 123. — Often omitted, 199. 3. 243. 3. — Relative, § 124. 242. Rem. I. — Differ often in gender and number from antecedent, 200. 1. *a* seq. — Interrog. § 125.—Indef. 202. 3.
Protasis, often omitted in sentences with Imperfect tense, 226. n. 3.— Omitted before apodosis with ἄν, 231. n. 2.—Of hypoth. sentences, 247. 4.—Relat. to apodosis, § 157.— Omitt. in hypoth. clauses, 251. n. 3.

INDEX OF SUBJECTS.   311

Reduplication, what and when, 80. 1.
— Exceptions, ib. 2. — ἑι in the room of it, 81. *c.* — Attic Redup. § 56.—Common in Aor. II., 81. 2.
Relative Sentences, § 149.
Roots of Verbs, simple and augmented, § 62.—Pure and impure, 86. 2, 3.—Augmented in diff. ways by consonants, 86. 4 seq.—By vowels, 87. 5.—Par. of same, 88.

Sampi, 21. n. 4.
Semi-vowels, 21. 2. *b.*—No other consonant can *end* a word, 22. n. 2.
Sentences, simple, § 127.—Composite, § 143 —Principal and subordinate 234. 3 seq. — Essential parts of, 235. 6. — Classes of subordinate sentences, § 144.—Relative, § 149. —Adverbial, § 153.—Of place, § 154 —Of time, § 155.—Hypothetical, 247. 4.—Adverbial, way and manner, § 159.
Stigma, 21. n. 4.
Subject of a sentence, § 127. 2.—Disagrees with the predicate, 206. 3. — Copula verb may conform to subj. or predicate, 207. 4.—Anomalies of various kinds, 207. *a* seq. — Several subjects to the same verb, 207. 6 seq.
Subjunctive, nature, 70. 3. 224. 3. — Peculiar form of in verbs in -μι, 119. 6.—Distinguished from Opt. 224. 3.—Independent, when, 227. —Hortatory, 227. 2.—Deliberative, 227. 3. — With ἄν, 232. *c.* — With ἄν joined to other particles, ib. — Aor. Subj. marks the *future*, 232. *c* and n. 1.—In sub. clauses, 239. 3.—Subj. after historic tenses, 239. *a.*—With ἄν in sub. clauses, 240. 4.—With μή, 241. 3.—In relative clauses, 243. 3.—In adver. clauses, 246. 3. — In hypothetical clauses, 249. 2.—In comparison, § 160. 2. —In oratio obliqua, 274. 5.
Subordinate clauses, § 187.
Subscript Iota, 30. 6.
Superlative degree, 194. 6 seq.—How made by the positive,194. 7.—Heb. superlative, 195. 8.
Syllabication, § 14.
Syncope, in verbs, 131.
Synizesis, 30. n. 3.

Trajection of words, § 198.
Tenses, nature, 71. 1. and § 135. — Division, 71. 2. — Limited use of, 73. 1 seq. — Classification, 75. 1. — Par. of endings, 76. — Leading characteristics of forms, 76. n. 1. —Tense-endings, 76. n. 3.-Tense-character, ib.1.—Personal endings in the tenses, 77. 3.—Par. of same, 78.—Formation of, § 63.—Formation of, like to verbs in μι, § 80.— Relations of, to time, §135.—Relative and absolute, 214. 3 seq.— Primary, 216. 6.—Distinctive Use, § 136.—Pres. ib.—Imperf. 217. 2. —Perfect, 219. 3.—Pluperf. 219.4. —Aorist,220. 5.—Aor. exchanged with various tenses, 220, 1, 2, seq. — Aor. for action often repeated, 221. *c.* — for Future, 221. *d.* — in derived Modes, 222. 6. — Future, 222. 7.—Paulo-post Fut. 223. 8.— Tropical use of the tenses, 223. Gen. Rem. — Peculiar use of historic tenses, 240. 6.—Tenses with Inf. § 166.—With the Part. § 173.
Varied Construction, § 196.
Verbal adjectives, forms and power, § 82.

Verbs, Nature and Kinds, 69.—Pure and impure, § 67. Mute Verbs, 98. 3.—Synopsis, 99.—Paradigm, 100. —Illustration of forms, etc., in mute Verbs, 105 seq.—Synoptical Par. of various Verba muta, 107 seq. —Accentuation, 116.—Exceptions to its general rules, 116. 4. seq.— Accent of Compound Verbs, 117. 6.—Anomalous verbs in the N. Test., 130. 7.—Verbs with several subjects, 207. 6 seq.—Distinctions in kinds of, § 129.—Have their basis in space relations, 208. 2.—

Transitive and intrans., 208. 4 seq.
—Causative and permissive, 212. note. Reflexive, 212. Rem. I.
Verbs compound, with preposition, § 114.—Repeat the prep. after them, 188. 3.—Verb does not always accord in regimen with its prep., 188. 2.—Trans. and Intrans. § 129. 3.
Verbs Contract, what class contract, § 73.—Contractions, how made 112. 3.—Technical rules for them, 112. n. 1 seq.—Synopsis, § 113.— Paradigms, 114. seq—Notes on them, 116.
Verbs Liquid, § 66.
Verbs deponent § 134.
Verbs in -μι. Distinctive traits, 117. 1 seq.—Limited number of tenses, 117. 1. c.—Classes, 118. 2.—First class, from contract-roots, 118. 3. —Second, with ννυ or νυ inserted, 118. 4.—Prolongation of root-vowel, 118. 5.—Subj. mode peculiar, 119. 6.—Formation of pass. and midd. voices, 120. 10. — What tenses are regular, 120. 11. — Notes and explanations, etc., of peculiar forms, § 79.—Par. 122

—Anomalous forms in -μι, § 81.
—Other peculiar ones, 129. III.
Verbs Pure, peculiarities, 111.—Formation of, derived tenses, 111. 2.
—Exceptions to general rule, 111.
3.—Peculiar Perfect pass. 112. 4.
—Synopsis, 113.
Vocative, general form, 41. 3.—Of Dec. III. 49. n. 2.—Of Part., like the Nom. 61. 3.—With or without ὦ 161. 6.
Voices, 82. 1.—Act., ib. 2.—Pass., 83. 3.—Midd., ib. 4.— In what cases they adopt the same forms, § 60.— Tenses of one voice with the meaning of another, 84. 3—5.— Distinctions of diff. voices, § 130. Middle voice, § 131. Passive, § 133.
Vowels, number, 21. — Quality and kinds, 22.—Exchanges of, § 12.— Changes of quantity, 35. 2.—Elision, 36. 2, and § 8. 3, 4. — Contraction proper, 36. I.—Improper, 36. II. Rules for the same, 36. II, 1 seq.

Zeugma, § 192.

END.

www.ingramcontent.com/pod-product-compliance
Lightning Source LLC
Chambersburg PA
CBHW050431240426
43661CB00055B/2347